This multivolume *History* marks a new beginning in the study of American literature. It embodies the work of a generation of Americanists who have redrawn the boundaries of the field and redefined the terms of its development. The extraordinary growth of the field has called for and here receives a more expansive, more flexible scholarly format. Previous histories of American literature have been either totalizing, offering the magisterial sweep of a single vision, or encyclopedic, composed of a multitude of terse accounts that come to seem just as totalizing and preclude the development of authorial voice. Here, in contrast, American literary history unfolds through a polyphony of large-scale narratives. Persuasive by demonstration rather than assertion, each narrative is ample enough in scope and detail to allow for the elaboration of distinctive views (premises, arguments, and analyses); each is authoritative in its own right; and yet each is related to the others through common themes and concerns.

The authors were selected for the excellence of their scholarship and for the significance of the critical communities informing their work. Together, they demonstrate the achievements of Americanist literary criticism over the past three decades. Their contributions to these volumes speak to continuities as well as disruptions between generations and give voice to the wide range of materials now subsumed under the heading of American literature and culture.

This volume, concerned with works written between 1940 and the present, brings together two altogether different sets of materials and narrative forms: the aesthetic and the institutional. Robert von Hallberg traces the course of American poetry since World War II through close readings and aesthetic evaluations, portraying American poetic production as a *cultural* achievement – a process of aesthetic development connecting directly to developments in the society at large. Beginning with the legacy of the Great Modernists, von Hallberg progresses through the changing avant-garde of the Beats and the Black Mountain poets to the poststructuralist Language Poets of New York and San Francisco. Offering a history of intellectual movements and debates of the same period, Evan Carton and Gerald Graff describe a parallel development, the growing profession of literary criticism, from the earliest roots of the New Criticism to the rise of deconstruction and poststructuralism, the emergence of feminist and minority critiques and the spread of cultural and New Historicist studies. Common threads link the two narratives: the academicization of poetry, the bridging of art and politics, the expansion of what we consider "literary." Discarding the traditional synoptic overview of major figures, the authors settle in favor of a history recounted from within unfolding processes – a history of interstices and relations, equal to the task of considering the contexts of art, power, and criticism in which it is set.

THE CAMBRIDGE HISTORY
OF AMERICAN LITERATURE

Volume 8

1940–1995

THE CAMBRIDGE HISTORY OF AMERICAN LITERATURE

Volume 8

Poetry and Criticism

1940–1995

General Editor

SACVAN BERCOVITCH
Harvard University

CAMBRIDGE
UNIVERSITY PRESS

Published by the Press Syndicate of the University of Cambridge
The Pitt Building, Trumpington Street, Cambridge CB2 1RP
40 West 20th Street, New York, NY 10011-4211 USA
10 Stamford Road, Oakleigh, Melbourne 3166, Australia

© Cambridge University Press 1996

First published 1996

Printed in the United States of America

Library of Congress Cataloging-in-Publication has been applied for.

A catalog record for this book is available from the British Library

ISBN 0-521-49733-7 hardback

CONTENTS

ACKNOWLEDGMENTS

FROM THE GENERAL EDITOR

My special thanks to Eytan Bercovitch, Susan Mizruchi, and Cyrus Patell. I would also like to acknowledge gratefully the assistance of Mary Anne Boelcskevy, who compiled the index; Christine Edwards, who helped with proofreading; and Kate Philips, who helped prepare the bibliography. Finally, my thanks to a Times-Mirror Foundation Fellowship at the Huntington Library, which gave me the time and resources for completing the editorial work in this volume.

Sacvan Bercovitch

POETRY, POLITICS, AND INTELLECTUALS

Parts of this book were written while I was on leave with support from the John Simon Guggenheim and the Alexander von Humboldt foundations and well situated, thanks to Berndt Ostendorf and Hans Gabler, at the Amerika Institut of the University of Munich. I am grateful as well to the many master's students at the University of Chicago, whom I then temporarily left behind, for many discussions of recent American poetry over the last decade; the classes tend to run together into a single conversation that, happily, is ongoing. A few friends have read parts of this book and advised me to make more changes than I could, though I am pleased to have an opportunity to thank Jessica Burstein, Ralph Johnson, Keith Tuma, Alan Golding, Marjorie Perloff, and Alan Shapiro. My thanks are due as well to Stephanie Hawkins who wrote the biographical notes, and to David Grubbs for his research on my behalf. To Saki Bercovitch I am very grateful for his original invitation to write this history, and then later for generous-spirited collaboration.

Robert von Hallberg

CRITICISM SINCE 1940

We have worked over all materials collaboratively, rather than dividing them into separately authored chapters. At times we have inscribed our own dialogues and debates into the text.

A Guggenheim Fellowship, along with funding from the University of Texas at Austin Research Institute, enabled Evan Carton to spend part of a year's research leave on this project in its early stages. Gerald Graff profited at its later stages from a fellowship at the Center for Advanced Study in the Behavioral Sciences at Stanford. We are grateful to these institutions for their support. For skilled research assistance we also thank University of Texas graduate students Janet E. Hayes and Kathleen M. Kane and Northwestern graduate student William Savage. In constructing and revising our central chapter on "The Canon, the Academy, and Gender," we benefited greatly from the advice and criticisms of feminist colleagues Ann Cvetkovich, Jane Marcus, Lillian Robinson and graduate students Mary Anne Boelcskevy and Kathleen M. Kane. We also wish to thank Sacvan Bercovitch for his guidance and patience throughout this long collaborative effort.

Evan Carton
Gerald Graff

INTRODUCTION

THIS MULTIVOLUME *History* marks a new beginning in the study of American literature. The first *Cambridge History of American Literature* (1917) helped introduce a new bracnh of English writing. *The Literary History of the United States,* assembled thirty years later under the aegis of Robert E. Spiller, helped establish a new field of academic study. This *History* embodies the work of a generation of Americanists who have redrawn the boundaries of the field. Trained in the 1960s and early 1970s, representing the broad spectrum of both new and established directions in all branches of American writing, these scholars and critics have shaped, and continue to shape, what has become a major area of modern literary scholarship.

Over the past three decades, Americanist literary criticism has expanded from a border province into a center of humanist studies. The vitality of the field is reflected in the rising interest in American literature nationally and globally, in the scope of scholarly activity, and in the polemical intensity of debate. Significantly, American texts have come to provide a major focus for inter- and cross-disciplinary investigation. Gender studies, ethnic studies, and popular-culture studies, among others, have penetrated to all corners of the profession, but perhaps their single largest base is American literature. The same is true with regard to controversies over multiculturalism and canon formation: the issues are transhistorical and transcultural, but the debates themselves have often turned on American books.

However we situate ourselves in these debates, it seems clear that the activity they have generated has provided a source of intellectual revitalization and new research, involving a massive recovery of neglected and undervalued bodies of writing. We know far more than ever about what some have termed (in the plural) "American literatures," a term grounded in the persistence in the United States of different traditions, different kinds of aesthetics, even different notions of the literary.

These developments have enlarged the meanings as well as the materials of American literature. For this generation of critics and scholars, American literary history is no longer the history of a certain, agreed-upon group of American masterworks. Nor is it any longer based upon a certain, agreed-upon historical perspective on American writing. The quests for certainty and agreement continue, as they should, but they proceed now within a climate of critical decentralization – of controversy, sectarianism, and, at best, dialogue among different schools of explanation.

This scene of conflict signals a shift in structures of academic authority. The practice of all literary history hitherto, from its inception in the eighteenth century, has depended upon an established consensus about the essence or nature of its subject. Today the invocation of consensus sounds rather like an appeal for compromise, or like nostalgia. The study of American literary history now defines itself in the plural, as a multivocal, multifaceted scholarly, critical, and pedagogic enterprise. Authority in this context is a function of disparate but connected bodies of knowledge. We might call it the authority of difference. It resides in part in the energies of heterogeneity: a variety of contending constituencies, bodies of materials, and sets of authorities. In part the authority of difference lies in the critic's capacity to connect: to turn the particularity of his or her approach into a form of challenge and engagement, so that it actually gains substance and depth in relation to other, sometimes complementary, sometimes conflicting modes of explanation.

This new *Cambridge History of American Literature* claims authority on both counts, contentious and collaborative. In a sense, this makes it representative of the specialized, processual, marketplace culture it describes. Our *History* is fundamentally pluralist: a federated histories of American literatures. But it is worth noting that in large measure this representative quality is adversarial. Our *History* is an expression of ongoing debates within the profession about cultural patterns and values. Some of these narratives may be termed celebratory, insofar as they uncover correlations between social and aesthetic achievement. Others are explicitly oppositional, sometimes to the point of turning literary analysis into a critique of liberal pluralism. Oppositionalism, however, stands in a complex relation here to advocacy. Indeed it may be said to mark the *History*'s most traditional aspect. The high moral stance that oppositional criticism assumes – literary analysis as the occasion for resistance and alternative vision – is grounded in the very definition of art we have inherited from the Romantic era. The earlier, genteel view of literature upheld the universality of ideals embodied in great books. By implication, therefore, as in the declared autonomy of art, and often by direct assault upon social norms and practices, especially those of Western capitalism, it fostered a broad ethical–aesthetic antinomianism – a celebration of literature (in Matthew Arnold's words) as the criticism of life. By midcentury that criticism had issued, on the one hand, in the New Critics' assault on industrial society, and, on the other hand, in the neo-Marxist theories of praxis.

The relation here between oppositional and nonoppositional approaches makes for a problematic perspective on nationality. It is a problem that invites many sorts of resolution, including a post-national (or post-American) perspective. Some of these prospective revisions are implicit in these volumes, perhaps as shadows or images of literary histories to come. But by and large "America" here designates the United States, or the territories that were to become part of the United States. Although several of our authors adopt a comparatist trans-Atlantic or pan-American framework, and although several of them discuss works in other languages, mainly their concerns center upon writing in English in this country – "American literature" as it has been (and still is) commonly understood in its national implications. This restriction marks a deliberate choice on our part. To some extent, no doubt, it reflects limitations of time, space, training, and available materials; but it must be added that our contributors have made the most of their limitations. They have taken advantage of time, space, training, and newly available materials to turn nationality itself into a *question* of *literary* history. Precisely because of their focus on English-language literatures in the United States, the term "America" for them is neither a narrative *donnee* – an assumed or inevitable or natural premise – nor an objective background (*the* national history). Quite the contrary: it is the contested site of many sorts of literary–historical inquiry. What had presented itself as a neutral territory, hospitable to all authorized parties, turns out upon examination to be, and to have always been, a volatile combat-zone.

"America" in these volumes is a historical entity, the United States of America. It is also a declaration of community, a people constituted and sustained by verbal fiat, a set of universal principles, a strategy of social cohesion, a summons to social protest, a prophecy, a dream, an aesthetic ideal, a trope of the modern ("progress," "opportunity," "the new"), a semiotics of inclusion ("melting pot," "patchwork quilt," "nation of nations"), and a semiotics of exclusion, closing out not only the Old World but all other countries of the Americas, north and south, as well as large groups within the United States. A nationality so conceived is a rhetorical battleground. "America" in these volumes is a shifting, many-sided focal point for exploring the historicity of the text and the textuality of history.

Not coincidentally, these are the two most vexed issues today in literary studies. At no time in literary studies has theorizing about history been more acute and pervasive. It is hardly too much to say that what joins all the special interests in the field, all factions in our current dissensus, is an overriding interest in history: as the ground and texture of ideas, metaphors, and myths; as the substance of the texts we read and the spirit in which we interpret them. Even if we acknowledge that great books, a few configurations of language raised to an extraordinary pitch of intensity, have transcended their time and place (and even if we believe that their enduring power offers a recurrent source of opposition), it is evident upon reflection that concepts of aesthetic transcendence are themselves timebound. Like other claims to the absolute, from the hermeneutics of faith to scientific objectivity, aesthetic claims about high art are shaped by history. We grasp their particular forms of beyondness (the aesthetics of divine inspiration, the aesthetics of ambiguity, subversion, and indeterminacy) through an identifiably historical consciousness.

The same recognition of contingency extends to the writing of history. Some histories are truer than others; a few histories are invested for a time with the grandeur of being "definitive" and "comprehensive"; but all are narratives conditioned by their historical moments. So are these. Our intention here is to make limitations a source of open-endedness. All previous histories of American literature have been either totalizing or encyclopedic. They have offered either the magisterial sweep of a single vision or a multitude of terse accounts that come to seem just as totalizing, if only because the genre of the brief, expert synthesis precludes the development of authorial voice. Here, in contrast, American literary history unfolds through a polyphony of large-scale narratives. Because the number of contributors is limited, each of them has the scope to elaborate distinctive views (premises, arguments, analyses); each of their narratives, therefore, is persuasive by demonstration, rather than by assertion; and each is related to the others (in spite of difference) through themes and concerns, anxieties and aspirations, that are common to *this* generation of Americanists.

The authors were selected first for the excellence of their scholarship and then for the significance of the critical communities informing their work. Together, they demonstrate the achievements of Americanist literary criticism over the past three decades. Their contributions to these volumes show links as well as gaps between generations. They give voice to the extraordinary range of materials now subsumed under the heading of American literature. They express the distinctive sorts of excitement and commitment that have led to the remarkable expansion of the field. And they reflect the diversity of interests that constitutes literary studies in our time as well as the ethnographic diversity that has come to characterize our universities, faculty and students alike, since World War II, and especially since the 1960s.

The same qualities inform this *History*'s organizational principles. Its flexibility of structure is meant to accommodate the varieties of American literary history. Some major writers appear in more than one volume, because they belong to more than one age. Some texts are discussed in several narratives within a volume, because they are important to different realms of cultural experience. Sometimes the story of a certain movement is retold from different perspectives, because the story requires a plural focus: as pertaining, for example, to the margins as well as to the mainstream, or as being equally the culmination of one era and the beginning of another. Such overlap was not planned, but it was encouraged from the start, and the resulting diversity of perspectives corresponds to the sheer plenitude of literary and historical materials. It also makes for a richer, more intricate account of particulars (writers, texts, movements) than that available in any previous history of American literature.

❧

Every volume in this *History* displays these strengths in its own way. This volume is perhaps especially notable for the parallels between two altogether different sets of materials and narrative forms. The first is aesthetic: the course of American poetry since World War II, which Robert von Hallberg explores, appropriately, through close readings and detailed evaluation. The second is institutional: the growth during this period of the profession of literary criticism, which Evan Carton and Gerald Graff describe through analyses of intellectual movements and debates. It would seem to make for a familiar set of dichotomies: creative and critical, aesthetic and cognitive, bohemia and academia. Instead, the narrative in each case builds on the interactions between both sets of terms. Von Hallberg's account of the poetry is the story of a *cultural* achievement, a process of aesthetic development which connects directly to developments in the society at large, and one of whose strong themes is the academicization of poetry. That is also a main theme for Carton and Graff, and they, too, tell of a singular cultural achievement, bridging art and politics (in the broad sense of that term). Indeed, they show how American literary criticism since 1940 has steadily, if turbulently, enlarged the scope of the "literary" to include the entire spectrum of cultural concerns, from philosophy to mass culture. And in both cases, the authors tell their stories by way of an inside narrative: an account from within unfolding processes, rather than a synoptic overview of established major figures.

Their choice of approach is not necessarily a function of the contemporaneity of their materials. In fact, histories of the present have tended self-consciously towards monumentalization: an Olympian overview designed to counterbalance the immediacy of judgments by separating the masterpieces from the passing spectacle. Such judgments are implicit in this volume as well, and here, too, there are major figures and central works, but their importance emerges from historical narrative. Biographical data on these figures are documented separately – in appendices which (among other things) provide authoritative bibliographical guides. But the narrative focus is on cultural moments and events, so that the reader's view is simultaneously processual and contextual: poetry in the making, decade by decade, sometimes year by year, as the poets experienced it; critics at work, from one controversy to the next, one set of issues to another, as the profession expanded and changed.

Von Hallberg's inside narrative is a testament of faith in poetry as a discourse. His premise is that the health of a literary culture is established by the level of excellence attained by many poets – the forty influential ones rather than the classic three. And from this perspective he demonstrates the "truly exceptional" achievement of contemporary American poetry as a whole, a social–political–aesthetic organism sustained by a diversity of poems that continue to live in the writing of successive generations of young poets. His demonstration comes by virtually every historical venue: journals, networks, and enclaves; the relation between poetry and other arts (from abstract expressionism to the jazz of Charlie Parker and Miles Davis); the growing involvement of poets in civic and academic institutions (and the consequences for poetry of this professionalization of literary life); the effect upon poetry of political events (from regional economics to international war); and a variety of intellectual communities and social movements: the shift during the forties and fifties from public protest to radical (eventually radically self-doubting) subjectivity; the anxieties of belatedness through the sixties and seventies that followed in the wake of the Great Modernists; the changing face of the avant-garde from the Beats and the Black Mountain Poets to the poststructuralist Language Poets of New York and San Francisco.

This variegated cultural history is conveyed, strikingly, through a narrative of and *by* the poetry itself. Von Hallberg writes as though the New Criticism had been absorbed, not transcended. His organizing categories (politics, avant- and rear-guardism, formality, sincerity, etc.) are those that divide the living poets of the United States; his selection from poets in every camp is guided by considerations of aesthetic (not doctrinaire) value; and quotations from the poetry are ample enough to allow readers to evaluate for themselves. The result is a remarkable blend of tradition and innovation: poetic analysis as cultural history; cultural history as aesthetic criticism.

The work by Carton and Graff might be described in similar terms, with literary criticism substituted for poetry. The conjunction itself is no surprise, since poets in the past have so often shaped the course of criticism. But that conjunction was a form of symbiosis: criticism nourished by poetry, the critic as the keeper of the sacred flame. What distinguishes our period, as the bulk of Carton and Graff's work is meant to suggest, is the rise of a new institutional reality, a vast secular scholasticism grounded in the conceptual elasticity of "literature," as extending (in Emerson's words) beyond "the courtly muses" to include the entire range of human concerns: that which has been negligently trodden underfoot, "the literature of the poor, the familiar, and the low," "the philosophy of the street," "the meaning of household life."

This shift towards a democratic aesthetics has issued in an equally significant shift in the profession of letters. The key to the hermeneutic transition from theology to literature was the Romantic substitution of poet for priest. The current transformations in literary academia have been labelled the substitution of critic for poet. As Carton and Graff tell the story, it is somewhat different: a transition from the well-made poem, the old "verbal icon," to the cultural "text," the verbal configuration whose "depth" consists not so much in hierarchies of meaning as it does in the multiple layers of experience it reaches down to, the range of common problems it raises, and the vistas of ordinary life it brings into focus. To paraphrase Whitman: the divine literatus departs, the democratic poet arrives, accompanied by professors of literature and culture.

Or perhaps the other way around: the professors arrive accompanied by the poet. For the fact is that this transition, like the one before it, has been deeply conflictual. One merit of Carton and Graff's narrative is that they address these conflicts, rather than evading or trivializing them. Another merit is that they present the issues on all sides sympathetically. In effect, they revise familiar dichotomies between creator and critic in terms that allow for variable reciprocities between the two. It is fitting that the transformation of the literary profession should be charted so comprehensively for the first time alongside an equally comprehensive account of the vitality of contemporary poetry.

It is fitting, too, in view of earlier transformations, that the story which Carton and Graff tell – the dramatic changes they record in pedagogy and scholarship – should so often take the form of continuities. They open with a skirmish in our current "culture wars," and proceed to show how it characterizes (rather than threatens) the modern discipline of literary study. That is, they seek to understand our past by contextualizing our present. From the start, it turns out, the academicization of criticism was a source of anxiety. Throughout the process of academicization some groups of critics denounced the "jargon" of other groups. Consistently, the denunciations have been directed against the encroachments of the vulgar, the not-yet-dead (or not dead enough), and the merely popular – the menacing small-c "cultural" infiltrating the walled-in sanctuaries of Culture. And consistently, in Carton and Graff's account, this immemorial struggle between "high" and "low" opens out to engage the novel challenges embedded in a democratic aesthetics:

disciplinary interchange versus disciplinary autonomy, fluid versus fixed categories, negotiation versus separate spheres, layers versus levels of meaning.

Chronologically, the narrative moves from the critical–scholarly battles of
the forties to the nineties debates within and about literary and cultural
studies. Along the way Carton and Graff trace the New Critics' problematiza-
tion of textual meanings; the influx of theory during the fifties and sixties; and,
during the seventies and eighties, following the Civil Rights Movement, the
Women's Movement, and the Anti-war Movement, the influx into the literary
academy of women, minorities, and social activists. The narrative plot-
structure, however, is conceptual: synchronic, self-reflexive, and issue-
oriented. One section includes a comparison between this *History* and others
that preceded it. The chapter headings name the major sites on the critical map
of our time: deconstruction, new historicism, feminism, postcolonialism, and
so on. In Carton and Graff's account, these formidable structures (and the
reaction against them) provide the setting for a cumulative series of dialogues,
so that similar issues are reassessed as it were in a variety of critical languages.

There is a strong integrative thrust to these dialogues, connecting critical
movements and critical moments, and subjecting each mode of discourse to
critiques that are inscribed in the others. This is complemented by a strong
particularist emphasis. Because Carton and Graff self-consciously enter into
the debates, they are self-consciously judicial and balanced in their analyses.
They are at once participants, advocates, and explicators, clarifying the
intricacies of deconstruction, evaluating the uses of relativism, and contextualizing the theoretical and often absolutist conjunctions of art, power, and
criticism (conservative and radical) within institutional practices.

Considered together, these two narratives offer an extraordinary bi-polar
view of their subject. They illuminate the dual meanings of *literary,* as poetic
language and as literary study. They convey the visionary and institutional
meanings of *American,* as these are manifest (1) in a history of literary criticism set in the context of the making of an American literature; and (2) in a
history of American literature-in-the-making set over against (complementary to, parallel with) a history of the criticism that established what it is we
mean by American literature. Finally, these histories are exemplary for the
methods they deploy. The writing of history is always, for any period, a
mediation between stories we tell and truths we seek, between what it seems
like to us and what it's like (or was like) for them, out there. These inside
narratives by Carton, Graff, and von Hallberg are models of how to make the
process work as a history of the present. Each of their narratives, in its own
way, testifies to the advantages of learning from American literary history as
process – not as memorial or as essence or as telos, but as a project in the
making – open to making again, to making over, and to making anew.

POETRY, POLITICS, AND INTELLECTUALS

Robert von Hallberg

INTRODUCTION

A HISTORY of American poetry since 1945 is uncomfortably like a history of the present. To what sense of the present should such a history conform? I imagine that this book will be read by those with more curiosity than knowledge of its subject – a general reader, as we say, meaning students. A student may well try to find a path that passes between professors and poets, and so have I. Professors read poetry in order to discern patterns of significance that persist from year to year, poet to poet, and from one field of inquiry to another. For them, the important poems are the representative ones, those that allow one to draw out general claims about continuity and so on. But poets read for poems, looking for gold wherever it may be found. Pound said that the history of art is the history of masterpieces, not mediocrity.

Continuity is not exactly the concern of poets; discontinuity is. A poet rather fears writing a poem that has already been written. As Eliot said, poets learn the literary tradition in order to know what is already alive, what has already been achieved. Poets read literary criticism and history in order to find out what does not need to be done again. Poems that have achieved their effects perfectly – those are the ones that young poets shouldn't try to repeat. And the readers of contemporary poetry? They too read looking for the gold. They want to know what's been done perfectly so that they can enjoy those poems. I imagine my readers to be looking for pleasure, driven by passion, and ambition too.

Professors, when they write about the formation of literary canons, tend to think, not surprisingly, that professional literary historians determine which poems count for literary history. But the more traditional way of understanding literary history is as the record of the poems that have continued to live in the writing of young poets.

I have tried to read with two goals. The test of one reading is the coherence of the narrative in terms of the themes that connect intellectual disciplines. Now political and social theory and history provide the terms for bringing literature together with other fields of inquiry, whereas in the late 1940s and the 1950s theology would have been a plausible neighbor field for literary history, and in the 1960s it would have been psychology. In order to read as a poet might, one must to a large degree guess about what aspects of the art of poetry will come to matter most to poets in the future. But one can safely rest one's case on only those poems that seem most accomplished of their kind. The poems that matter for poets are not the representative but the exceptional ones. The test for this kind of reading is of course time. But I have drawn together the poems discussed below in order that my readers can see for themselves whether the poems I take as determining the literary history of the last fifty years are in themselves compelling. Although I have a number of historical propositions to advance here, the first and most important of my claims is that poetry since 1945 has been very distinguished, that this has been a particularly rich period in American poetry, despite the sad fact that poetry has lost currency in the literary culture. The poems I have selected constitute the evidence for this claim. I have held my commentary very close to the poems so that a reader can read this history in poems. I intend for this study to be part anthology as well as commentary. Only an anthology can support the claim I am most concerned to make convincingly.

In general I have limited myself here to the writing that seems to me truly exceptional; poems that can only be called representative of some number of other poems are overlooked almost entirely in the pages that follow. And for that matter, I have not attempted to sketch out the careers of most of the poets I discuss; nor do I trace the development of all the various movements and affiliations of poets in the last fifty years. In place of the representative text, I have tried to construct contexts for exceptional poems by analyzing the state of literary opinion evidenced by several literary journals. I have taken journals to stand for the grounds of collaboration among writers; although magazines may only poorly express the surprising poet, they do adequately express the area of agreement for numbers of poets. For so brief a history, I have had to make choices that leave many important, significant, representative, yes, interesting poems and poets out of account. Instead, I hope to have made a fresh selection of exemplary poems. None of my readers will be familiar with all the poems I discuss; few will be familiar with many of them. Where this selection departs from current literary opinion, it may seem merely eccentric or even erratic, though my hope is that it will rather justify my enthusiasm about the high quality of poetry of this period.

The distinction I am describing between two different ways of reading poetry is not merely methodological. In the last fifty years the relations between these two types of readers have changed quite dramatically. One of the major themes of this book is the consequences for poetry of the professionalization of the literary life of America. There is surely a greater gulf between my two sorts of readers now than existed in 1945, but the problem is more complicated than this suggests, as I mean to suggest in Chapter 1.

I

❦

THE PLACE OF POETRY IN THE
CULTURE, 1945–1950

I N 1945 poetry occupied an altogether different position in the literary
culture than it does now, a half-century later. In the winter of that year a
critic in *Partisan Review* could plausibly claim: "no one will deny that the
discussion of poetry is one of the highest proofs of civilization that a society
can give." Delmore Schwartz then named America's most famous living
poet, T. S. Eliot, a culture hero, "who brings new arts and skills to mankind." Poetry, painting, and jazz seemed to be the healthy arts; drama and
fiction were ailing. (Literary criticism was thriving, but no one thought then
to call it an art form.) Randall Jarrell, reviewing new books by Elizabeth
Bishop, William Carlos Williams, and others, said that America had better
poetry than it deserved, "how queer it is that *our* age should have poets like
these."

Young poets like Jarrell, Robert Lowell, and John Berryman, who moved
in the literary circles of New York, enjoyed a special status within this
culture. Their poems and reviews were published regularly in the most
prestigious journals and, quite interestingly, the ideological differences between, say, *Partisan Review* and *Sewanee Review,* or the *Kenyon Review* did not
matter for poets. Distinguished poet–critics Allen Tate and John Crowe
Ransom edited two of these journals. The editors of the *Partisan* gave these
young poets extraordinary latitude to range around in their critical reviews,
though serious political differences might have separated Lowell, a conscientious objector, never a Marxist or an anti-Stalinist, from the explicitly engaged editors of this journal. Although certain essayists could appear in only
one of these reviews, one cannot tell just from reading whether a particular
poem or review of poetry was published in one or the other of them. "The
successful poet," Clement Greenberg said in 1948, "still dominates the
literary and academic scene, even if he is not read by as many people as the
novelist is." Poetry was a kind of crown that even a journal like *Partisan,*
committed to an anti-Stalinist, democratic socialist position, wanted to wear
without consideration of ideological consistency.

The literary culture that treasured poetry was in no way disaffected or
aestheticist. In the years during and just after the war, American writers

understood that they might affect the course of political events. One of the attractions of liberalism, as Granville Hicks said, was that at this point in the ideological spectrum intellectuals could genuinely communicate with "nonintellectuals," as he put it. Arthur M. Schlesinger Jr., claimed that in fact liberals had allowed themselves to indulge in too great a sympathy for the Soviets; the "clarity, logic, and rigorous insistence on facts" that constitute what is meant by critical judgment were just what liberal intellectuals ought to work harder at employing, in order to maintain their proper roles within the political discussion about postwar reconstruction. The possibility of political participation was attractive to intellectuals, and some of them policed others to meet the necessary conditions for participation.

The world that confronted intellectuals in 1945 was much different from any that my generation has known. That autumn George Orwell wrote from London to the readers of *Partisan Review*:

Western Europe is mostly on the verge of starvation. Throughout eastern Europe there is a "revolution from above," imposed by the Russians, which probably benefits the poorer peasants but kills in advance any possibility of democratic Socialism. Between the two zones there is an impenetrable barrier which runs slap across economic frontiers. Germany, already devastated to an extent that people in this country can't imagine, is to be plundered more efficiently than after Versailles, and some twelve million of its population are to be evicted from their homes. Everywhere there is indescribable confusion, mix-up of populations, destruction of dwelling-houses, bridges and railway tracks, flooding of coal mines, shortage of every kind of necessity, and lack of transport to distribute even such goods as exist. In the Far East hundreds of thousands of people, if the reports are truthful, have been blown to fragments by atomic bombs, and the Russians are getting ready to bite another chunk off the carcass of China. In India, Palestine, Persia, Egypt and other countries, troubles that the average person in England has not even heard of are just about to boil over.

We now suffer some of the consequences of the troubles Orwell described and can understand that intellectuals after the war felt a need to speculate boldly about how the political, social, and economic institutions of the West might be reorganized. The map of Europe in 1945 was hazier than it had been in modern memory. Where would the boundaries of Germany, Poland, Czechoslovakia, Hungary, and Yugoslavia be drawn, and how would they be enforced? Writers, responding to the moment, spoke to these issues. In 1945, even before the war ended, intellectuals were discussing the ways in which the postwar world should be structured.

What interested them above all was foreign policy. T. S. Eliot wrote as "man of letters" that "At the end of this war, the idea of peace is more likely to be associated with the idea of *efficiency* – that is, with whatever can be *planned*," as a matter of deliberate policy. On the left, in the pages of *Partisan,* a strong interest in the formation of a federation of European states would develop in the late 1940s. In 1947 Orwell spoke for many readers when he said that "a socialist United States of Europe seems to me the only worthwhile political objective today." Among liberal centrists, the plans for the formation of the United Nations were developing directly out of the Allied war effort. The first U.N. declaration, signed January 1, 1942, set forth the Allied war objectives. In the summer of 1944 the Dunbarton Oaks conference expanded the range of the participants, and the San Francisco conference of the following spring led to the signing of the charter in June 1945. (The poet Charles Olson worked for the representation of Polish interests in the U.N. in 1946, because Poland had as yet no stable government.) On the right, too, there was hope that the absorption of smaller nations by the superpowers would eliminate some of the causes of war. Wyndham Lewis wrote in the *Sewanee*:

We should, of course, instead of this [one country, one vote plan], be insisting upon small states merging themselves into larger units, not the perpetuation of insignificant polities, the accidental creations of a world very different from ours. To go into a conference insisting that Russia and Santo Domingo possess the same voting power, as we did at San Francisco – so that two Santo Domingos outvote the Soviet Union – is as dangerous as it is silly.

In a literal sense, much of the earth's surface was up for grabs in 1945. Some of the poets, like Olson and Bishop, who came to intellectual maturity in time to see the maps change with the morning news, continued long after this period to write poems about the claims of geography rather than of nation–states.

There was a sense then too that postwar American society would have to look much different than it did in the 1930s. Old problems and new ones would need to be resolved. For instance, after the integration of the armed services, racist laws would be harder to uphold. The southern writer Donald Davidson published a controversial essay in the *Sewanee* in 1945 in defense of states' rights to legislate against interracial marriage and to impose poll taxes; he also opposed federal antilynching laws. It had become clear that the federal government would emerge from the war much stronger and more comprehensive than it had been just four years earlier. In 1945 Jarrell published a poem, "The State," in the *Sewanee* spoken by one whose mother had been killed and whose sister drafted by the State; the speaker broke down, though, when his cat was inducted into the New Dealish Army Corps of Conservation and Supply. The federal government was expected to wield new influence especially in higher education. From the beginning of the war soldiers began to appear on campuses, and after the War they would come in great numbers. An extensive literature on the education proper to a modern

democracy developed. Eliot argued for an internationalizing elitist education, based upon the study of Latin, Greek, and pure science; Sidney Hook
and John Dewey proposed an education based upon knowledge of how a
modern society functions. Marshall McLuhan thought that English studies
might take over the synthesizing role that classical studies had formerly
played in European education.

These pedagogical controversies were recognized as having a direct bearing
on the life of letters. As institutions of higher education expanded after the
war, poets and critics would have increased opportunities for employment –
these were naturally welcome. At the same time, the literary culture would
become professionalized in short order. John Crowe Ransom had argued in
1937 the no longer controversial point that literary criticism belonged in the
universities. It can hardly be said to exist elsewhere now. Ransom used the
Kenyon Review to demonstrate the potential strengths of an academic literary
criticism. The *Sewanee Review* in 1945 ran an article, "The Present State of
American Literary Scholarship," proudly recounting the achievements of the
preceding four years of "the systematic study of our literature." The editors of
Partisan, however, were skeptical of the growing literary professoriate. William Barrett, then an editor of *Partisan Review* and professor of philosophy at
Columbia, wrote in 1946:

Being determines thought, and you cannot live in the midst of an English faculty
(with the peculiar qualities of professional American scholars) without becoming
infected, especially under the urgency of academic advancement, with the point of
view of your colleagues, who for their part have stakes in preserving their own form
of bureaucratic specialization expressed by PMLA. Much of the critical writing by
the academic avant-garde in recent years has tended to differ from the PMLA
contributions of their colleagues, not so much in fundamental interest or temper, as
in mere choices of subject – Eliot and the late Yeats instead of, say, Shelley and
Browning.

The evidence marshalled to support this view appeared in *Partisan* in
occasional reviews of scholarly works that were too polite or generally uncritical of literature. Early in 1947 the editors took the occasion of some remarks
by Mark Schorer (then a young English professor at Berkeley) and Harry
Levin (assistant professor of comparative literature at Harvard) to say that
"the self-indulgent obscurantism of the new brand of literary academician" is
shown in the professors' unwillingness to commit themselves politically and
their unease with writers who do commit themselves. Academic literary
critics were said to be indifferent to literature in general, but especially so to
modern literature, mistrustful of distinguished prose style, and priggish
about poets, and clerical.

Behind this already familiar split between critics and scholars were two historical developments, which had been discussed forthrightly a few years earlier. The first was the betrayal of the Soviet revolution by Stalin, and the second was the prospect of the already burgeoning American state and public economy. When Barrett used the word "bureaucratic" to characterize the Modern Language Association's systematic study of literature, he was invoking a particular context of significance that has now been lost. This word recurs throughout social and literary criticism of the late 1930s and the 1940s. When Jarrell wanted to criticize the verse of Josephine Miles (another Berkeley assistant professor) as too complacent, he said, quite awkwardly, that she "is sadly bureaucratized." This was a term that carried so much feeling in the mid- and late 1940s that even artful writers went out of their way to employ it. In 1937 Kenneth Burke spoke of the "bureaucratization of the imaginative" as an historical process inevitable to revolutions:

An imaginative possibility (usually at the start Utopian) is bureaucratized when it is embodied in the realities of a social texture, in all the complexity of language and habits, in the property relationships, the methods of government, production and distribution, and in the development of rituals that re-enforce the same emphasis.

The bureaucratized utopia uppermost in Burke's mind, and in the minds of his contemporaries, was obviously Stalinist Russia. Marshall McLuhan spoke of the prophecies of Marx having been brought to a "bureaucratic parody" by 1946.

James Burnham, from 1948 to 1952 an advisor to *Partisan,* published a very influential book in 1941 entitled *The Managerial Revolution.* His claim was that communism, fascism, and capitalism were all developing toward a state and economy dominated by the managers of production. The first major step in this direction was the Russian Revolution. Stalin's regime, he asserted, followed naturally and inevitably upon Lenin's. When Burnham described the condition of Russia in 1940, the year the book was written, his passion showed through the prose:

Russia speaks in the name of freedom, and sets up the most extreme totalitarian dictatorship ever known in history. Russia calls for peace, and takes over nations and peoples by armed force. In the name of fighting fascism Russia makes an alliance with the world's leading fascist. Proclaiming a fight against power and privilege, Russia at home drives a great gulf between a stratum of the immensely powerful, the vastly privileged, and the great masses of the people. The only country "with no material foundation for imperialism," in theory, shows itself, in practice, brutally and – for a while at least – successfully imperialistic. The "fatherland of the world's oppressed" sends tens of thousands to death by the firing squad, puts millions, literally millions, into exile, the concentration camp, and the forced labor battalions, and closes its doors to the refugees from other lands. The one country "genuinely against war" performs the act that starts the second world war.

This litany of disillusionment suggests that he meant to speak especially to other intellectuals who felt similarly betrayed by the Stalinist state, and in 1940 they were legion. The new ruling class of managers might be called bureaucrats, he conceded: the distinction is immaterial for the most part. These capable, confident, cynical young managers would establish the basis for a new international ideology, not yet well formulated, of discipline rather than individualism, security rather than initiative. Their revolution was already well underway in 1940 and, according to Burnham, the real basis of the regimes of Stalin, Hitler, and even, in an attenuated but still unmistakable form, of Roosevelt's New Deal. Bureaucracies proved themselves, for Burnham's contemporaries, especially durable in the 1930s and through the war. The most grotesque example of the dependence of the right and the left likewise on extraordinary bureaucratic organization was the fact, reported in *Partisan,* that the S.S. exploited the organizational skills of communist prisoners in the concentration camps: "Prisoner–bureaucrats were better fed, better housed, and better clothed than the plebeians; they were armed with clubs and whips, and were themselves rarely beaten."

There was a rosier view of this phenomenon, which was also common in the postwar years. Lewis and Hicks seemed to share with each other, with Burnham, and the other editors of *Partisan* the belief that the managers or bureaucrats of the world were the genuinely powerful. Intellectuals of various political allegiances, like Lewis and Hicks, looked forward to the beneficial possibilities of exploiting powerful bureaucracies, but this prospect had particularly persuasive appeal for liberals who, never having been Marxists, were not disillusioned by the development of Soviet bureaucracy. The sociologist David Bazelon reviewed a study of the British civil service for *Partisan* in 1945 and concluded with incredulity that the idea of bureaucracies being democratically representative could be taken seriously. Yet Arthur M. Schlesinger, Jr., arguing exactly this two years later in the same journal, wrote: "the politician-manager-intellectual type – the New Dealer – is intelligent and decisive . . . and can get society to move just fast enough to escape breaking up under the weight of its own contradictions." Although, by Burnham's analysis, the Soviet state was furthest along in the process of bureaucratization, American culture was seen to have, in its tradition of technological ingenuity, a special claim on the future of the bureaucratic state. And professors were considered the bureaucrats of the intellectual sphere. In an interview with Burnham, André Malraux said, "With us the representative of culture is the artist. With you it is more likely to be the professor."

Several writers felt, as Lionel Trilling did, that the universities provided a good intellectual environment for literary critics, though a less advantageous one for poets, novelists, and dramatists. Yet by 1948 there was much agreement with R. P. Blackmur that the universities would inevitably become the center of the literary culture: "The economic, political, and cultural drifts of our society are towards the institutionalization of all the professions; their special freedoms will lie *only* in their own work, which to those with the American experience seems too little." The editors of *Partisan* circulated a questionnaire in 1948 asking what effects could be seen in literature of the academicization of writing. On the one hand, Ransom had already argued in 1947 that Shakespeare's Latinate diction reflected an effort to exploit the delicate academic resources of the English language; no more legitimating precedent for academic poetry could be imagined. On the other hand stood William Carlos Williams' diction ("from the mouths of Polish mothers") as the recognized alternative to academic poetry. The choice for poets should have been easy. By 1948 a period style in poetry had developed out of Auden's example, and this was often spoken of as the academic style, appropriate for minor poets. In Berryman's words, the poetry scene was "good for union members but bad for artists."

The reviews and essays on poetry that appeared between 1945 and 1948 often seemed to tell young poets: "Dare to be minor!" As a critic, Eliot had resuscitated the distinction between major and minor poetry for his generation and the next. Ransom referred to himself as a minor poet. One critic after another, writing about Ransom or John Peale Bishop, seemed to praise highly the idea of a minor poetry operating within well accepted conventions. Yet Eliot, as John Guillory has shown, was crafty about this term. The term minor seems often to have kept alive, though only secretly, the dream of a major poetry. For the generation of Lowell, Berryman, and Jarrell, Dylan Thomas's career was a stunning spectacle of a poet who openly refused to be minor. He was spoken of as another Shakespeare, or as a fake, but not as a minor or academic poet. Those who wrote in support of minor poetry often meant less to renounce the higher ambitions of the art than to provide for a taste too skeptical to accept bombast and overassurance.

Exactly because some poets were close to the center of literary prestige, and because too that center esteemed poets, as Greenberg said, a generation grew up with intense ambitions for themselves. Lowell was well known for measuring poetic reputations constantly. He and Berryman and Jarrell were often obsessed with their places in literary history, as John Hollander said of Lowell. In 1948 Berryman became furious at Ransom for reversing the order of two poems in the *Kenyon Review*. W. S. Merwin and Bruce Berlind tried to calm him, but he replied, "You people are amateurs . . . I'm a professional. In a year's time I'll be a national figure." One sees other sorts of career planning too in Olson, Robert Duncan, Allen Ginsberg, and Sylvia Plath.

For poets born in the 'teens and later, poetry was a profession, like many others, in which one attempted to succeed.

The ambitiousness of some of these poets, such as Lowell, Berryman, Jarrell, and Plath, moved into a single channel, whose political significance has been obscured. *Partisan* fostered a literature that stressed the neurotic anxiety of exceptional sensibilities within grotesque political situations: Kafka was the model, though few *Partisan* critics read German. In the 1940s *Partisan* context Kafka stood for the best that modernism in literature had produced, partly because formalist criteria were irrelevant to his work. Hannah Arendt pointed out in 1944 that he "engaged in no technical experiments whatsoever." This taste was championed under the banner of Freud's influence on modern literature, but it was just as surely understood as a fit reaction to Stalinism, which made practical political hopes very difficult to maintain for American intellectuals on the left, as William Arrowsmith wrote in a sharp demurral to *Partisan's* anxiety canon. Lowell, though he himself was not ideologically committed to *Partisan's* political positions, was just the poet to live up to *Partisan's* literary tastes. His daughter's first words, he once said, should have been "Partisan Review." After Lowell, Berryman, Jarrell, and Plath would follow too this same deadly path to renown.

In the second poem in *Lord Weary's Castle* Lowell says:

> The world out-Herods Herod; and the year,
> The nineteen-hundred forty-fifth of grace,
> Lumbers with losses up the clinkered hill
> Of our purgation. . . .

Lowell was always a poet of strong lines, so why would he so lugubriously spell out the date in the manner of a revival preacher? His strain here expresses the well-founded and uneasy sense that 1945 was an epoch-making year: the wars in Europe and Asia brought to conclusion; the publicizing of what had transpired in the concentration camps; and the detonation of the first atomic bombs. Because the historical moment was so dramatically represented, intellectuals felt their contemporaneity keenly. As Harold Rosenberg remarked in 1948, "The area which intellectuals have most recently staked out for themselves as belonging to culture *par excellence* is the common *historical* experience." Despite the talk of anxiety and despair, there was great hope in the late 1940s for a new art to fit the historical moment. "The great art style of any period," Clement Greenberg said, "is that which relates itself to the true insights of its time." Many poets wanted to be the "poet of the age," though this is a dangerous dream, as every poet knows. Who envies Longfellow, or, in Coleridge's words, the "immortal Southey"? Jarrell, reviewing Lowell's first book in the *Partisan,* said, "His world is our world – political, economic and murderous – cruelly insisted upon, with all our green and pale hopes gone, their places taken by a blind and bloody Heaven." Lowell sought success in these terms, and he achieved just that. The most famous essay on his work, by Irvin Ehrenpreis, was entitled "The Age of Lowell."

Lowell took an adversarial role at just the moment when American culture was at its utmost strength and unity, fighting a popular war. His poems give no sense of a just war; nor do they represent fascism as a dangerous foe or a powerful ideology. The book that made Lowell's reputation in 1946 is about the dead, the dying, and the mad – and they are the victors. The real defeats in *Lord Weary's Castle* are above all the refusal of Christ in history, but also the failure of the British settlers to make a really fresh nonmercantile start in the New World. These of course were not the failures that interested *Partisan:* Lowell's ideas about history were comfortably irrelevant to the political commitments of the anti-Stalinist left. From an ideological perspective, he was a crank. In 1945 Jarrell said, "A few years ago he would have supported neither Franco nor the Loyalists; one sees him sending a couple of clippers full of converted minute-men to wipe out the whole bunch – human, and hence deserving." He could be fondly appreciated without danger, because his rhetoric suited so well the *Partisan* sense of how literature ought to speak to history. When Congress approved Lowell's appointment as Poetry Consultant to the Librarian of Congress in 1947, the point was officially made that on the high ground of Christianity American poets had the right to dissent, though Pound, who held the low ground of political ideology, remained incarcerated in a Washington insane asylum; Lowell himself had been in prison for resisting induction only four years earlier.

Lowell took his critique of America as a mercantile state back to the seventeenth-century roots of the country. He sees the country as continuously rapacious; "Our North Atlantic Fleet" is only a recent incarnation of Melville's whalers. But this critique of capitalism is both abstract and anachronistic. "Our mighty merchants" are almost allegorical ("Mammon's unbridled industry") or theatrical props around which strong emotions can be expressed. There is an odd discrepancy between Lowell's attitudes and their ostensible occasions. In 1946 the age of the great merchants was well past; the great wealth of America was already concentrated in large public corporations. Politically, Lowell's critique was more bookish than astute. His real point was one of style.

Lowell's style is the opposite of the urbane, fluent, even facile style of Auden. Lowell screwed his style so hard with neologisms, Anglicisms ("munching"), arcane terms of whaling ("swingle," "gaff") and willful, lyrical twists of common usage ("guns unlimber / And lumber down the narrow gabled street") that he was instantly seen to reject the civility of the period style so attractive to poets like John Ciardi, Karl Shapiro and others. Lowell's wit was leaden ("the Nether Land of Holland"), where the academic taste was for lightness. The incivility of his style is registered not just in his phrasing, but more generally too in his expression of coarse bigotry toward east European immigrants in "Christmas in Black Rock":

> . . . drunken Polish night-shifts walk
> Over the causeway and their juke-box booms
> *Hosannah in excelsis Domino.*

Under the pressure of what must be spoken of as Lowell's vision, these ordinary defense workers are transformed to infernal beasts: ". . . Poland has unleashed its dogs / To bay the moon upon the Black Rock shore." Lowell's representation of contemporary America as hellish goes well beyond any standards of fair and solid judgment; everything about his treatment of his nation is overdone. The book displays a wide range of historical subject matter, but a narrow channel of willful, intense feeling. "Colloquy in Black Rock" is a deliberate chanting on of hysteria: "My heart, beat faster, faster." Lowell's intelligence is not the sort that one would trust with difficult political choices. Distinctions dissolve before this poet's eye: "All discussions // End in the mud-flat detritus of death." The strength of these poems is in their excessiveness, their wild unreasonableness.

This kind of poetry did not enjoy prestige very long after 1950. But the *Partisan* aesthetic, which rested on anti-Stalinist ideology, would have another life altogether, when in 1959 Lowell published *Life Studies* and initiated a turn toward what has been called confessional poetry. The poetry of Lowell, Berryman, and Sylvia Plath was based very much on the *Partisan* sense of the private, extreme sensibility caught in a public nightmare. Their lives too played out the literary politics of reputation-making. Auden was reported to have quipped that Berryman's suicide note said: "Your move, Cal."

2

❦

POLITICS

U NTIL ABOUT 1965, the term "political" referred to the activities of
the state: the conduct of foreign policy, the exercise of police authority, the control of borders, the use of the ballot, and so on. These
were the matters that American intellectuals thought of as political, and
most Americans still hold to this sense of the term. Poets such as Robert
Lowell, Allen Ginsberg, and Robert Bly have spoken to these issues, often
powerfully. But what comes under this statal sense of the political varies in
detail from country to country and year to year, because the nature of a state
is unstable – the areas in which state authority is exercised and the differences between one state and another are great. For instance, the Soviet state
governed enough of life that the notion of privacy was political there, though
it was the ostensible essence of what liberal Americans, before the advent of
identity politics, considered unpolitical. *Partisan Review* told how Anna
Akhmatova's silence about all things political from 1923–39 was itself an act
of political defiance – and the grounds for punishment in Stalinist Russia.
And the history of recent American political poetry, its strengths and weaknesses, is inseparable from the unusual status that the term privacy acquired
just after World War II.

This period begins dramatically with the arrest of Ezra Pound in Rapallo
on May 3, 1945. He was brought to an American military prison near Pisa,
where he wrote his most personal and elegiac poetry, *The Pisan Cantos* (1948),
and later to St. Elizabeths in Washington. His career is the most spectacular
instance in American literary history of the problematic relationship of poetry
to politics. His name gave focus to the difficulty of bringing modernist art
together with democratic politics. While Pound sat in a Washington asylum,
various intellectuals took positions on the question of a poet's proper role in a
republic. In the spring of 1945 Blackmur asked, "can contemporary artists in
any probable society permit themselves the pride, or the waste, as the case
may be, of the total role of the artist?" He was urging that writers affiliate
themselves with the American university system, then about to begin a
period of sudden growth. Tate answered that the eccentric position of the
artist is the fit sign of his or her "*real* if insecure relation to our society." In

the same issue of the *Sewanee Review* Eliot argued that the man of letters should keep a vigilant watch on politicians and economists, "for the purpose of criticizing and warning, when the decisions and actions of politicians and economists are likely to have cultural consequences." He may well have had in mind his friend Pound, who was then under a treason indictment for doing just that.

Pound represented one case history of the engagement of rightist poets, and Louis Aragon, as Harry Levin said, was the complementary leftist case. Aragon, who during the war wrote Arthurian parables and other tradition-ally symbolic poems, was translated by Malcolm Cowley and published in the *Sewanee Review* along with commentary in 1945. As part of the Resis-tance, he had maintained the purity of poetry; the collaborators were the engaged poets. The idea of engagement included, as Blackmur suggested, some compromise with the powers that be. There was great interest in America then in *la littérature engagée;* one could easily imagine then the argument for a liberal or leftist poetry of political engagement. Yet Sartre, whose *Qu'est-ce que la littérature?* was serialized in the *Partisan Review* in 1948, said that poetry could not be part of *la littérature engagée* because "Poets are men who refuse to *utilize* language." Valéry had been quoted two years earlier in the *Sewanee Review* to the effect that poetry is unaffected by political events. Sartre and Valéry spoke for what would soon be demon-strated to be the dominant view of literary intellectuals at the time. In February 1949 the Bollingen Foundation gave its first Award in Poetry to Pound for his first collection of autobiographical poems, *The Pisan Cantos.* Those intellectuals who respected the granting of the award to Pound under-stood it as an affirmation of the separability of poetry and politics. Dwight Macdonald said that the award meant that "clear distinctions should be maintained between the various spheres [of poetry and politics], so that the value of an artist's work or a scientist's researches is not confused with the value of their politics." This represented a major shift in literary opinion for New York intellectuals. Clement Greenberg argued that "The American artist has to embrace and content himself, almost, with isolation, if he is to give the most of honesty, seriousness, and ambition to his work." In the *Partisan Review* in 1948 Leslie Fiedler claimed that Frost's *A Masque of Mercy* was damaged by the poet's refusal to remain a private writer. In a grim, black-bordered ad for the *Pisan Cantos* in the *Partisan Review,* Pound's pub-lisher pleaded for an objective hearing for Pound, whose poems should be enjoyed "for their beauties as poetry." The Bollingen Award was intended and understood as proof that Pound got just the objective, which is to say nonpolitical, reading that his publisher advocated.

Intellectuals often spoke of the opposition between poetry and politics, but at other times this was understood through overlapping terms: art and life, isolation and engagement, individual and collective, private and public. Pressure from literary critics, who were exhausted by ideological debates, pushed poets toward the first term in each of these dichotomies; but the causes of this pressure included an ideological motive. As the editors of *Partisan* doubtlessly knew, the major controversy among poets in the Soviet Union from 1943 to 1954 was the role of individualism in poetry. The American esteem for the privacy of the poet was the ideological mirror image of the Stalinist Writers' Union. The results of this Cold War prestige for lyric poetry have been mixed and widespread. The most attractive consequence has been that since 1945 American poets have produced a small but serious body of poetry that is political without being sharply satiric. The poets I have in mind write from a sense of their own involvement in the acts of empire. These poets are not trying to blink away the worst facts of American political might; their poems describe torture and extermination. But neither do these poets indulge fantasies about the possibility of altering the course of empire in the near future. They express their own complicity, not their superiority to the agents of the state. Theirs are mixed feelings, which are what citizens of this empire often have good cause to feel. The stress on the privacy of poetry has actually helped some poets to write self-critical political poetry. It is an important political point that all citizens, and especially members of the intelligentsia, bear some measure of responsibility for the actions of the state in a republic. The empire is within, at least to the extent that its direct and indirect benefits are enjoyed, and it may be judged the way we judge ourselves, with close scrutiny but also with a healthy desire at some level to accept and affirm.

One commonly reads now that American poetry is predominantly lyrical, personal, introspective, that American poets have little interest in politics – in short, that poets have followed the anti-Stalinist critical injunctions of the late 1940s. "When I read . . . accounts of the American destruction of Cambodia . . . ," Terence Des Pres wrote in 1980,

I think, my God, how can I *go back* to the next poem in our magazines, the next volume of poetry praised for its sturdy solipsism. I am heartened by the women's movement, poetry by Rich and Piercy, for example . . . But then it occurs to me that among the few poets in America worth caring about, at least three, Brodsky, Walcott, Simic, are not native to our tradition and speak partly from another world.

From this point of view, the trouble is that political poets are always "over there" somewhere, writing about the political lives of other countries or of other social groups. This is a convenient and widely held perspective in American letters. The *New York Review of Books* and the *New Republic* devote few pages to poetry, and many of these few concentrate on poetry from elsewhere. Joseph Brodsky and Derek Walcott, for instance, appear regularly in these journals. How convenient to have a Russian emigré and a Caribbean black as the political poets to honor in New York and Washington: one from the old world, one from the new. How much more unsettling it would be to bring Thomas McGrath, Edward Dorn, Turner Cassity, and Baraka into the pages of these journals. The effort of intellectual journals and literary critics to appear cosmopolitan in their literary tastes is left over from the years just after the War, when American cultural imperialism was unashamed.

Over the last two decades the area of political controversy among American intellectuals has gradually become less the state's activities than the relation between the sexes, and more generally the concept of sexuality itself, which in 1945 was regarded as supremely private. The personal, as Rich says, is now the political, and the distinction between private and public poetry is no longer so sharp as it was in 1945. Family life has been for at least twenty years a subject with some political significance for the culture. Beginning with *Life Studies* in 1959, which begat a great many poems about parents, the constitution of gender roles has been examined.

Here I want to consider as political the part of experience that can be changed by consensus or external authority. The possibility of change itself, not the state, is after all the source of political passion. Political poems concern situations that might be otherwise. Causes and consequences, choices – these are the concerns especially of political poets. If this sounds rationalistic, one should remember that political writing addresses the possibility of deliberate action.

Distinguished political poetry, as I see it, challenges the political opinions of its audience; it does not merely extend the blunt discourse that is routine in political controversy. The best political poetry draws lines differently than the newspapers do, and this is exactly the challenge to its audience. Political poets can make categorical thinking difficult. Poets who are satisfied with rousing simplifications or confirmations of their audience's views sell short the possibilities of their art.

Challenges to categorical thinking can be concretely measured in contemporary poetry, if one bears in mind that the audience for poetry is largely in humanities divisions of universities, and that these readers (reasonably well studied by sociologists) are predominantly left of center. So long as conventional left-of-center views are dressed out in verse, this audience is neither challenged nor criticized. I certainly do not mean to outlaw left views from poetry, but no poet deserves special attention for calling to the notice of American liberals the facts that, say, numerous minorities, women, and workers are regularly oppressed.

There is really only one problem with recent political poetry in America: poets, like many Americans, often do not take politics seriously enough in political terms. They write about the possibility of change in civic life, but their poems are – quite rightly – of no interest to politicians, statesmen, and political administrators. Poets, like Robert Bly, do not begin from a belief in political processes or agents as inherently interesting. In a country where the divorce rate is over 50%, the difficulty of reaching agreement or resolving conflict between two people who care for each other is well known. How one might reconcile differences and forge liveable arrangements between great numbers of people who care little or not at all for each other is an immense imaginative problem, but it does not engage many poets.

Many poets often attribute mean motives and low intelligence to their political adversaries, as though virtue or cleverness could make a great difference. Most political poems, however offensive they would be to those who do not read them, are sympathetic to those who do. One often remembers Pindar as a poet who merely praised the powerful, but Anne Burnett has recently shown that he founded the genre of the praise poem in such a way that, through mythological allusions, his songs often had a subtle, critical underside. Marvell's Horatian Ode is the most famous example in English of how a praise poem can express measured admiration and independent political analysis. Many sermons for the converted can be found in anthologies of recent verse. Rarely do poets see that they are no authorities on the motives or intelligence of their enemies; nor do they usually see political problems as difficult to solve, or as ethically problematic.

Humility and Curiosity might be the expected patron saints of poets who do propose that great numbers of people live differently, but they are hard to find in the poetry of, say, Allen Ginsberg, Robert Bly, Galway Kinnell, Robert Duncan, or Denise Levertov. According to the dominant literary thinking of the late 1940s, poets ought to rise above partisanship; this is why politics is a dangerous subject. Although many recent poets have abandoned this view, I think it ought not to be abandoned entirely. If political poets began by thinking that, as poets if not as citizens, they owed their adversaries as well as their allies unusually deep understanding, the political poetry they could produce might make greater difference than it does.

But there are several good reasons why most poets have not taken politics more seriously. First in importance is the fact that American political discourse, if not American political life itself, is hard to take in earnest. Second is probably the 1940s view that poets should not deal in politics at all: when they do write about political subjects, poets often feel and act like renegades. Third, political poetry is known to American readers chiefly as satire, and English satire deals not in depth of understanding but in sharpness of invective.

These three causes have made it hard for American poets to produce distinguished political poems, yet a fair number of poems that deserve to be taken seriously as political writing have appeared since 1945. Most of these express some degree of complicitousness with their adversaries. I have singled out these poems for special attention, largely because since World War II American intellectuals, from whom the audience for poetry is self-selected, have participated in the operation of the state to an unprecedented degree. Poets should realize that intellectuals as a group are not altogether separable from the state itself.

❦

The focus of critics and poets on private, personal subjects may seem to be merely a literary expression of postwar liberalism, but it went well beyond avowed liberalism. Thomas McGrath joined the CPUSA in the 1930s and maintained his membership through the trials and purges, the War, until 1957 or later. Unlike many of his contemporaries, he was no repentent-Marxist-turned-liberal. He held tenaciously to an extreme left position, and paid for it with lost jobs. Yet when he undertook a long poem, in autumn of 1954, he structured it as an autobiography with flashes forward and back to the late 1920s, the 1930s, and the war years. He deliberately took up the populist line in American poetry, from Whitman to Vachel Lindsay and Carl Sandburg, and among McGrath's contemporaries Allen Ginsberg. "One's self I sing." And thereby America too. This poetic tradition – nationalist, but more lyric than narrative or dramatic – reinforced the postwar liberal emphasis on the individual sensibility.

McGrath, like Whitman, is an exuberant poet, ready always to celebrate anything ("O impeccable faubourgs / Where, in the morning, you fought bedbugs, for your shoes!"), but with a broad and redeeming sense of humor. Also like Whitman and the populist poets, much of his full-throated writing is just awful: verbose, trite, inflated. His worst characteristic is appalling coarseness, chiefly in connection with women and sexuality: "O great kingdom of Fuck! And myself: plenipotentiary!," "The great Vulvar Shift and the Gemination of Cunt," and "rehearsed equals from the whoring cunts in the wild world of the yard." He imagines himself a great devoté of women, but in a barroom manner that prevents him from writing interestingly or intelligently about the women in his life. Yet this coarseness is intriguing, because it is a reaction, ultimately political, against the pain he first felt when he encountered what he takes as male sexuality.

McGrath's writing, like Yeats's and Roethke's, is organized in a now old-fashioned way around symbols and recurrent phrases. On the cover of *Letter to an Imaginary Friend, Parts I & II* (1970) an idyllic passage from the typescript of the poem is reproduced. This concerns Jenny, a North Dakota farmgirl, McGrath's first sexual partner: "lying beside my darling girl, my hand on the bush of her belly / The whole enormous day collected within my palm . . . / Around us the birds were singing their psalms," and so on. The writing is undistinguished, which makes its appearance on the cover all the more emphatic. The passage seems simply willed and hastily sketched in (like many passages in the poem) as a contrast with the immediately following scene about Jenny ("Or another Jenny . . ." – poor Jenny is the archetypal victim of English literature, from *The Beggars' Opera* to "Hugh Selwyn Mauberley") being gang banged by the farmhands in the hayloft. The thematics of the poem require the idyllic passage for a contrast between gentle, innocent sexuality and "the violent / World of men" – to which supposedly Jenny introduced him. But he had had an earlier introduction when his uncle, a farm boss, had assaulted his father's friend and employee, Cal, a Wobbly who dared to speak for the striking farmworkers. When his uncle punches Cal, the young McGrath hears "the meaty thumpings." Years later, when he is living in Santa Monica, he sees how brutally sexuality is exploited for profit, and the thumping goes across three pages. Cal's Wobbly world is one of male workers banding together out of the need to barter and the pleasure of song and "tall talk" – "the circle of hungry equals" – not out of a predatory instinct.

Yet the "cantrip [i.e. magic] circle" has its ominous side too, and McGrath is candid enough to admit the contradiction: "that circle where solidarity and the obscene / Lie down like the lamb and the lion." The men in the hayloft circle around poor Jenny for the gang bang, just as they circle to spit and talk tall elsewhere in the poem. Male solidarity is not all song and barter, it is violence and brutal coarseness too. When Cal, a Colt-packing anarchistic wanderer, is beaten by McGrath's uncle, the male society extends to him no immediate assistance or sympathy: "They had left Cal there / In the bloody dust that day . . ." [my ellipsis]. The tough guys leave him to the shame of having been beaten by a tougher guy. "But they wouldn't work after that." Political solidarity does not replace the individualistic macho code of the west, whereby men fight one on one and gather together to sing, boast, spit, and gang bang farmgirls. McGrath adopts with bravado – guilty, I think – the style of this solidarity, even though it sometimes repels him. The solidarity rests on sentimentality for the western Wobblies and a disciplined acceptance of male brutality. His coarse language is a recurrent reminder that he has made this choice, and that solidarity is costly. Brutality, however, seems to derive from a human need that is neither foreign nor altogether repulsive. Jenny was not an unwilling victim: "She wanted it so." She wanted

> To enter.
> To burn
Alive . . .
To live on other frequencies, at more intolerable
   depths . . .
To rip up the tent of solitude, to step out of the skin,
To find among the damned the lost commune and to found
   there,
Among the lost, the round song and the psalm of the living
   world.

The gang bang is an extreme expression for her — and for the men? — of a need for solidarity; that is the tragedy of the really down poor.

> I stood deadstill in the barndoor dirt
> (Hearing the overhead thump and thinking of sweating
> quarters
> Of dying meat upstairs
> those souls
> consumed and consuming)

Male solidarity is the measure of all else in Parts 1 and 2 of the poem: When it was lost to profiteering during World War II, so was the future. The extension of consumer credit after the War provided enough affluence that the Revolution was lost. "Once it was: *All of us or no one!*" McGrath says, "Now it's *I'll get mine!*" The Depression had left Americans so hungry for affluence that when it arrived all else was forgotten. "Still, hard to blame them."

Part of the pathos of the poem is the loss of "what / Was: the Possible; that is: the future that never arrived . . ." But another part derives from Mc-Grath's recognition that a Marxist program cannot succeed in America exactly because affluence disarms political extremes. The American dream of a quick, solitary ascent to prosperity was wildly unrealistic after the War, but the Revolution was decaying just as fast as that dream. "Perhaps the commune must fail in the filth of the American night," he concedes, " — Fail for a time . . ." And in the meantime? In the postwar years, among the claims that ideology had been superseded, the dream of change seemed, like history itself, frozen in stone. "But all time," he claims, in rebuttal of "Burnt Norton," "is redeemed by the single man — / Who remembers and resurrects. / And I remember." His sense that radical socio–political change is unlikely in America is expressed toward the opening of Book II, which was finished in 1968. Poetry is put forward there as some alternative arena: "The beginning is right here: / ON THIS PAGE."

McGrath set out in 1954 with full awareness that he would not live to see a new American beginning. "Hoping toward laughter and indifference," not revolutionary social change, he says in the fourth line of the poem. His poem is frankly elegiac from the outset; the political struggle had been lost before 1954, which is why the poem includes so little statement of political policy. What the poem affirms is seen through nostalgia: "The gist of it was, it was a bad world and we were the boys to change it. / And it *was* a bad world; and we might have." When a revolutionary recommends the cause as well meant, it is thoroughly lost: "What was real was the generosity, expectant hope, / The open and true desire to create the good." The turning point of the poem comes at the end of Book I, with the attainment of indifference to political failure, but without the compromise of human solidarity. Thereafter, for McGrath, as for Ginsberg a couple of years later, "All changed; the world turned holy; and nothing changed: / There being nothing to change or needing change; and everything / Still to change and be changed . . ." McGrath turned to the icons of the Hopi, Ginsberg to Buddhism. For a North Dakota Irish-American Catholic and a New Jersey Jew, these are remote fields of reference, and that is the point: the American socio-political future was firmly set in the mid-1950s. No more accessible terms of transcendence offered themselves to American poets.

McGrath is a genuinely gifted lyric poet who writes movingly about landscape, his son, old friends, and boyhood experiences, though many adult experiences, such as marriage, divorce, the death of friends and family, and serious conversation, are not within his range. Most of the people named in the poem, including his mother, are not described in sufficient detail to be spoken of as characters. The feelings and thoughts of other people have rather little existence in this lyric autobiography. McGrath too often refers to people, feelings, and objects, which seem not really to engage his imagination, if fresh detail is a fair test of engagement. He seems more interested in some general point. For instance, he berates his teachers at Moorhead State College at length for not knowing how to teach, and he claims to have learned to teach, though without saying a word about what actually constitutes teaching. And he refers to his mother praying over his brother's bones, though his brother is not named nor his death in any way described. The relationship between particularity and generality is especially important in political poetry, because therein lies the basis of a poet's authority: which particular experiences, whether the poet's or not, can be made to stand plausibly for a class of social experience? McGrath wants to create a leftist American legend, based on the assumption that he has had the "essential experience of his time." At conveying a sense of the experience of farm workers and War workers in the west, he succeeds nicely. However, the criticism to which this political poem is most vulnerable, as he seems once to realize, is that his own experiences were anachronistic, that, growing up on a North Dakota farm, he had no access to the experiences that were to remake American society in mid century. The representations of his family life glow with sentimentality, partly because that whole way of life is gone forever, but partly too because McGrath simply tends to ascribe generalizing qualities to particular people and experiences.

His best quality is paradoxically humaneness, and this one has no reason to expect from so politically committed a writer. In Part 3, section III, 2, he gives an account of his own early Catholicism, but in the context of his mature thoughts on the erection of cathedrals ("Man will do anything to be saved but save himself . . .", the donation of stained-glass windows by bourgeois parishioners who want to be remembered ("Mr. & Mrs. P. J. Porkchop and all the rest / Of the local banditti and bankers, the owners of God"). Inside the church, though, irony dissolves:

> And yet it is sin I can smell
> Around me now as the confessional rises again in its shaft:
> The smell of hellfire and brimstone: spice and herb to that
>   incense
> Of sanctity and sweat: the stink of beasts' and angels'
>   couplings . . .

Easy enough to satirize the Porkchops, but this version of a child's guilt is wholly convincing and sympathetically done. On the commonplace that the young have nothing to confess, McGrath writes a wonderfully comic story of his effort to overpower his confessor with a list of offenses: " 'I am guilty of chrestomathy, Father.' " But this Irish-American parish priest more than holds his own and a sense of proportion in the end: three Our Fathers and three Hail Marys. The shift of McGrath's tone from satire to childish wonder, and then to rollicking clowning – this flexibility of attitude is winning and follows from a sense that life is more various and funny than ideological perspectives – anticlericalism, for example – admit readily. Self-examination, social criticism, and good-natured joking about the folly of all – that is the essential mix of the poem. He calls his clowning "japery" in the poem, invoking a medieval, Chaucerian sense of the value of comedy, and it accounts for the punning, consonance, and cursing. He constantly indulges a coarse, barroom bravado – "Holy Mother of Christ what a pisscutter Spring!" – and his taste for the cheapest of lyrical effects, such as paired terms of consonance – "gleamed and gloomed"; "the wars and the whores and the wares and the ways" – puts little bells all over the poem. *Letter to an Imaginary Friend,* by far his greatest achievement, is only intermittently successful on the verbal level, though the imaginative achievement of the whole is considerable (which is not as damning as it sounds: it is exactly true of Blake, one of McGrath's masters, as well).

❦

Adrienne Rich is the most popular political poet writing in America; her books are routinely reprinted. Poetry with explicitly political subject matter generally enjoys unusual popularity, despite what is commonly said about American poets ignoring politics. Carolyn Forché's 1981 book about El Salvador, *The Country Between Us,* was widely reviewed and discussed on radio, and Denise Levertov's poems about the need for nuclear disarmament also sell well. Gary Snyder, who in the 1950s and 1960s was spoken of as an avant-gardist, has said that poets who cannot sell 3,000 copies or so of their books (a poetry collection commonly sells 2,000) ought to reconsider their efforts. Rich, Levertov, Snyder, and others have found audiences for free verse that is very close to the ideological discourse one reads in politically committed journals. For poets now to take political positions in their verse certainly does not risk a loss of audience or critical attention – quite the contrary. Rich now writes explicitly as a lesbian feminist poet. One thinks of *The Will to Change* (1971) as her first directly political collection of poems, and of *Diving into the Wreck* (1973) as her first feminist book, but this is a misleading way of conceiving of not just her career but of the development of feminist political poetry.

In the 1950s Rich wrote, as she herself has said, under the influence of Auden and the canons of taste that prevailed in the mainstream literary quarterlies. Yet even then her art was moving in a feminist direction. The feminism that she ultimately developed has some of its roots in the postwar liberalism of literary intellectuals. Liberals of the 1940s and 1950s often thought that Americans could *think* their way out of political and social problems. Because academics had entered the government in unprecedented numbers in the 1950s, and because the college and university system was greatly expanded then, there was a great deal of stress on the role of mind and intellect in preventing social conflict and political catastrophe. This outspoken insistence on intelligence in the 1950s was partly the self-promotion of a professional group.

The excellence of particular poems was said in the 1950s to rest on such intellectual qualities as complexity, irony, and rich structural patterns. Several influential literary critics, such as Northrop Frye, claimed further that the intellectual qualities of poetry could be of use in training the minds of students, and various poetry anthologies, especially Brooks and Warren's *Understanding Poetry,* found a large audience in American colleges in the 1950s. It was nevertheless common then to hear that the intellectual beauty of poetry and of art generally was poorly appreciated by the American culture at large. There was a common but strong sense that art and life, beauty and utility, were separated in the culture, however much mind might be said to be shaping the foreign and domestic policy of the nation.

In 1958 Rich wrote that

> Beauty is always wasted: if
> not Mignon's song sung to the deaf,
> at all events to the unmoved.

This poem is spoken by a man who attends the wedding of a beautiful woman he admired greatly. In the second part of the poem he looks back at her after nine years. Now a mother, she is bringing in the frozen laundry from a clothesline during a windy winter. "I see all of your intelligence," he says, "flung into that unwearied stance." She has resisted the erosion of nine years of marriage. In the last lines, he wishes her husband well,

> who chafed your beauty into use
> and lives forever in a house
> lit by the friction of your mind.
> You stagger in against the wind.

This is not one of Rich's best poems; the last line shows her propensity for tritely grand figures, and other passages (stanzas 1–2) show the then common academic irony with Elizabethan diction. Yet the poem illustrates how her ideal of feminine strength rested on the notion that beauty is an intellectual thing, and that intellect has a role to play even in a domestic household. She conceived of woman only partly in the terms commonly offered to women (housekeeping and fidelity), but more interestingly in the terms offered to college-educated men who wished to take their places in the professionalized society of the 1950s. Intellect resists bourgeois routine, and it grows richer, developing persistence, in its own struggle against the pressures of dailiness. This woman grows wise rather than resentful from her husband's chafing against her; and unlike Mignon she survives.

The strongest poem in *Snapshots of a Daughter-in-Law* (1963) is the title sequence which examines the oppression of women in light of the English and American literary tradition. In the penultimate section she takes up Johnson's notorious remark about women preachers:

> *Not that it is done well, but*
> *that it is done at all?* Yes, think
> of the odds! or shrug them off forever.
> This luxury of the precocious child,
> Time's precious chronic invalid, –
> would we, darlings, resign it if we could?

> Our blight has been our sinecure:
> mere talent was enough for us —
> glitter in fragments and rough drafts.

This sort of writing could be admired by New Critical standards, and it deserves some notice still. Here Rich is tough on herself and on women who too easily accept or reject the culture's ready polarization of male and female qualities. The profit and loss of the gender system can be more finely reckoned. How costly it would finally be, she shows, to dispense with the privileges that even a rude remark like Johnson's conveys to exceptional women. The "new woman" Rich envisages would be too intellectual to be condescended to in postwar America: "Her mind full to the wind," Rich says, "I see her plunge / breasted and glancing through the currents. . . ." Again, that taste for heroics spoils the last section of the sequence, but her willingness to examine her own interests critically gives this poem a special place in the development of political poetry since World War II.

Snapshots for a Daughter-in-Law ends with a poem, "The Roofwalker," dedicated to Denise Levertov, in which Rich sees herself being drawn by some force toward a public poetry that goes against the contemplative inclinations of the literary culture with which she grew up. The poem draws to a close with these lines:

> A life I didn't choose
> chose me: even
> my tools are the wrong ones
> for what I have to do.
> I'm naked, ignorant,
> a naked man fleeing
> across the roofs
> who could with a shade of difference
> be sitting in the lamplight
> against the cream wallpaper
> reading — not with indifference —
> about a naked man
> fleeing across the roofs.

Rich would sound this note often in the following decades, and it would spoil much of her writing. Her proclivity toward heroics developed directly into self-aggrandizement: as though she were struggling, despite odds, against her personal inclination and her craft itself, to become the public writer the world needs. (This was a common theme in 1960s poetry; one finds it in LeRoi Jones's *The Dead Lecturer* and in Levertov's *To Stay Alive*.) The cute inversion of the situation at the end is calculated to appeal to the paradox mongering and the reflexivity for which literary academics are notorious;

Rich wanted to indicate that her heart lay more in reading than in rooftop striding. What drew Rich in 1961 toward a kind of art she mistrusted was the Civil Rights movement. Had it been feminism, the roofwalker would not have been represented, even when the poet speaks of being naked, as a man. Rich's feminism – and she was surely not alone in this regard – was postponed by the Civil Rights movement and later by the war in Vietnam.

The irony that was appreciated in the 1950s had a particularly corrosive effect on the authority of liberal poets. As Rich came to see that her writing would become more political, she saw too that the literary techniques she had mastered would render little service to her:

> To live illusionless, in the abandoned mine-
>   shaft of doubt, and still
> mime illusions for others? A puzzle
>   for the maker who has thought
> once too often too coldly.

The ironic tone she had learned from Auden and others seemed to her in 1960 a measure of bad faith in political poetry. Instead, she wanted to speak plainly of whatever she could take as the truth, but what could that be for an educated writer in 1960?

> Since I was more than a child
>   trying on a thousand faces
> I have wanted one thing: to know
>   simply as I know my name
> at any given moment, where I stand.

From the years just after the war, when Olson lamented the uncertainty of liberals, this hunger for conviction had been an enduring curse on intellectuals. Communists and Fascists knew their own minds, Olson said, but New Dealers like himself were unsure. Unlike Olson, many postwar intellectuals had fought in Europe or the Pacific. Soldiers fighting Fascism had little reason to be plagued by uncertainty: the war was popular and the lines were clearly drawn. The years after the war lacked the clarity of battle for those intellectuals attracted to the political center. The Winter 1946 issue of *Partisan Review* included these lines about soldiers generally: "Admire them, sang the cricket in the twilight, / Say that they knew their purpose when they died."

In poetry this appetite for certainty came to be satisfied much later by a turn toward very personal, autobiographical subject matter that is usually dated by the publication of Ginsberg's *Howl* (1956) or Lowell's *Life Studies* (1959). The realm of public, political discourse was regarded by literary intellectuals of the 1950s as one of half truths and pale approximations;

private experiences were taken as the source of greater intensity. About one's family experiences, for example, one had a right to strong feelings. Rich's "Face to Face" (1965) shows that this desire for intense, private poetry has distinct roots in American literature. The last line derives from a poem by Emily Dickinson ("My Life had stood – a Loaded Gun") that Rich had quoted a decade earlier. In 1945 F. O. Matthiessen had entitled an essay on Dickinson "The Problem of the Private Poet." The lonely poet of intense conviction that Rich begins by disowning is just the one she has constantly turned back to in her career. The lure of personal convictions and even Calvinist New England privacy were a constant source of fascination for liberals, like Olson, Lowell, and Arthur Miller, who felt drawn toward the public discourse of the late 1950s and 1960s. Rich's poem shows how seductive and American that private life can be, and how too this is the dangerous seductiveness of authority – "a hand / longed-for and dreaded."

Since 1968 Rich's poetry has been anything but private. "*The moment when a feeling enters the body,*" she wrote in 1969, "is political. This touch is political." However progressive this idea has been in politics (particularly in the women's and the gay rights movements), there is reason to doubt its value to poetry. Since 1968 Rich has written as one whose private self has been regularly subordinated to her sense of the political–ideological work to be done. By 1971 she had come to demand for her persona the range of a Whitman: "It is strange," she wrote, "to be so many women . . ." – and a short catalogue of wives and mothers follows. In "From the Prison House" (1971), she claimed to have developed a visionary eye, the trouble with which is that it sees only what fits her ideological allegiances, though she claims that its vision is clear:

> This eye
> is not for weeping
> its vision
> must be unblurred
> though tears are on my face
>
> its intent is clarity
> it must forget
> nothing.

The first thing to say of such a conclusion is that it is hopelessly corny and self-satisfied. Beyond this is a still more serious failing. Rich sees "detail not on TV," as she puts it, "the clubs and rifle-butts / rising and falling," and

> the fingers of the policewoman
> searching the cunt of the young prostitute
> . . .

> the roaches dropping into the pan
> where they cook the pork
> in the House of D[etention].

When northern urban police attacked antiwar demonstrators in the late 1960s and early 1970s, they became stock enemies for liberal and left intellectuals. The details cited in this poem are powerfully revolting, but they are in no way the tough details for a poet on the left. These were the sights that, after all, confirmed one's conviction that the police were villainous, that fair-minded people were up against unfair odds, and so on. Rich's adversaries are not taken seriously in intellectual or ethical terms. The policeman who takes the report of a rape victim is indistinguishable from the rapist, or from other men on the block. The bad guys are true to their type, and the choices offered in her poems are always reassuringly easy.

One speaks, Sartre notwithstanding, of political poets like Rich as engaged, but poems of retirement are traditionally political too. Political poetry is about alternatives, even when they are only implied. A large part of the significance of Gary Snyder's poetry is in the selection of his subjects. His poems seldom employ metaphor – the bringing together of different subjects; instead he strenuously selects just that which he wishes to attend to, and one knows always how much and exactly what has been excluded. The political significance of his writing is often in what has been left out. Just as Rich dramatizes her own engagement, Gary Snyder dramatizes his retirement. He wrote a poem about a visit by then Governor of California Jerry Brown to Snyder's home in the Sierra foothills. Brown lounged and recovered from a trip to the abstract "east," then with Snyder he shot arrows at a bale of hay. The title draws out the point: "He Shot Arrows, But Not at Birds Perching." The poem concerns what the Governor did not do, his choices and restraint. This is a version of an ancient Chinese poem by Lun yü. Snyder moves the verse through counterpointed lines of free verse structured in phrases of stress and of slightly irregular iambic pentameter (ll. 2, 4, 7–9, 12) toward a final line of anapestic trimeter: "Striking deep in straw bales by the barn." The prosodic structure of the poem seems intended to render musically both a sense of ceremony and a struggle to discover local principles of order and harmony. In the late 1970s Snyder was enthusiastic about Brown and his administration, and thought of him as the only interesting candidate for President in 1979, when quite another former Governor of California was on his way to the office.

Snyder has revived the ancient genre of the praise poem on chiefs of state. In the late 1970s he agreed to serve on the California Arts Council: "I thought it was a really excellent opportunity to stand inside the fence for a while instead of being on the outside throwing rocks as I had always done before." His is a frank form of complicity with the government, though he had long ago realized, after working on an oil freighter, that "everybody's involved in it. . . . Making a living is to connect yourself with the economy."

Robert Lowell also wrote praise poems, several for former presidents and one for a presidential candidate in the 1968 election, but that Snyder has attempted this genre is more surprising, because from the start of his career he has rigorously pursued alternatives to the 1950s liberal consensus in politics and to the New York literary circles that lent support to that consensus. In 1954 he sent poems to the *Partisan Review, Kenyon Review,* and *Hudson Review,* as Rich must have too, but none was accepted. What might a young poet accomplish by beginning elsewhere and ignoring the cultural activities of New York? And would so different a beginning have political significance for poetry? Snyder's career provides one set of answers; Olson's and Duncan's provide others. *Partisan Review* and the other mainstream reviews of the late 1940s and 1950s regularly published Letters from Paris, London, Berlin, Munich, Spain, and Rome, but no Letters from Seoul, Tokyo, or Kyoto. Literary intellectuals were not particularly interested in Asia, though American troops were stationed in the Pacific as well as the Atlantic and the Mediterranean. And America would fight its next two wars in the Far East. Literary intellectuals sought the prestige of European culture, in the postwar years, not a grasp of the political future. The literary reviews were centered on the American effort to take over political and cultural responsibility for Europe. Snyder's move to Kyoto to study Zen Buddhism in 1956, like Olson's trip to the Yucatan in 1949, was the counterpart to the flight of many, mostly east coast, poets to European capitals.

What kind of critique of American political life might come from this alternative view of the world? On the face of it, Synder was employing a well known modernist strategy: Picasso turned to African and Pacific art in the first years of this century. Modernist artists implicitly rejected the national and academic traditions of European art when they turned to exotic and primitive models, and for Snyder the attack on American nationalism is especially important. He sees his work as directly counter to the notion of the nation—state. He does not want to locate his writing in that part of life that pertains to the state at all; he wants above all a lot of distance between his own life and that of his countrymen. A poem about the birth of his son Kai in 1968 ends:

> Masa, Kai,
> And Non, our friend
> In the green garden light reflected in
> Not leaving the house.

> From dawn til late at night
>   making a new world of ourselves
>   around this new life.

The new world begins in the garden, with family and friends, not in the streets.

Despite his claims for isolation, Snyder comes out of the West Coast political tradition of anarchism, which he knew through Kenneth Rexroth; and several of his poems recall fondly the experiences of workers in the 1930s. Liberals in the late 1940s considered anarchism a morally attractive but impractical alternative to consensus politics. Snyder's political sensibility seems to derive from his father's experience of the breakdown of the American economy; this is one reason why he can imagine (and hope for) the collapse of this economy and state again.

The advantages and obligations of the state begin with people working, because, for Snyder, as for other intellectuals such as Daniel Bell who experienced the 1930s, the economy is at base labor. In "The Late Snow & Lumber Strike of the Summer of Fifty-Four," he brings together the theme of retirement and the politics of capitalism. Loggers in the Pacific Northwest often work only six months of the year, because logging trucks cannot negotiate the roads in winter. The irony of the poem is that these strikers have undramatically "all gone fishing," because they are accustomed to leisure. Their strike itself is like a late snow. One expects a poet to write about the suffering of the striking workers, about their desire for work and the means to support their families, and about the brutality of the bosses. But this poem ends with regret that Snyder must return to the warm-weather lowlands:

> I must turn and go back:
>   caught on a snowpeak
>   between heaven and earth
> And stand in lines in Seattle.
> Looking for work.

Snyder cannot wholeheartedly wish for more work, but there is nothing sublime about collecting unemployment compensation. He is an unenthusiastic participant in the welfare state.

In another early poem, "Makings," he recalls with unabashed nostalgia, in a loose iambic tetrameter, the good old days of the 1930s:

> I watched my father's friends
> Roll cigarettes, when I was young
> Leaning against our black tarpaper shack.
> The wheatstraw grimy in their hands
> Talking of cars and tools and jobs
> Everybody out of work.

That handsome, manly world was lost in the war, which brought prosperity. "It seems," Snyder says, "like since the thirties / I'm the only one stayed poor." For the workers of his own generation, Snyder feels ambivalence. "Americans," he says, "are splendid while working – attentive, cooperative, with dignity and sureness – but the same ones seen later at home or bar are sloppy, bored and silly." He returns in several poems throughout his career to the attractions and difficulties of talking and drinking with working-class people: the issue is how to engage their political views. "Dillingham, Alaska, the Willow Tree Bar" (1983) is a touching poem about the self-destructive drinking and brawling that are common in "the working bars of the world." An almost Christian sense of labor as a curse burdens the workers, who are

> Drinking it down,
>
> the pain
> of the work
> of wrecking the world.

Snyder was born in 1930, and had some impression of the Depression. He came to maturity in the years when the American economy began its shift from primary production to service, and the Pacific, where labor is cheaper, became the center of production. Snyder's poems are critical of this development in certain obvious ways. He celebrates the pleasure of direct manual labor, even when it is in the service of logging companies. With this subject goes a concentration on the pleasures of intense sensual experience of other kinds, because the alienation of labor reaches into all aspects of life. In "After Work" he describes the life that properly ought to follow the right sort of labor: pungent as garlic, hot as a stove, sharp as an axe, and so on. The senses are tuned less to the finer frequencies than to the loud, clear ones. Many of Snyder's contemporaries, such as Richard Wilbur, Charles Olson, George Oppen, and Robert Creeley, wrote often about the need to know the world directly: the epistemological theme – what one can know with certainty – dominated American poetry from 1945 to 1965. The first decade of this period was also the time when intellectuals were especially concerned with theology; these poems were part of an effort to locate some basis of belief after the supposed end of ideological thinking.

Snyder claims that there is no way to avoid vagueness and alienation within the dominant but ghostly economy of postwar America. But his sense of how one knows the world is rudimentary, concerned with sharp contrasts rather than fine shadings, and it is predatory and excessively virile as well, unless one imagines that women are charmed by cold hands under their shirts. Snyder places women in the period following labor, and this, however accurate for the logging industry, is more generally anachronistic. Women were crucial to the domestic war effort in America, and after the war they continued to enter the work force in unprecedented numbers. Snyder's poems present a nostalgic dream of manly labor, and this was attractive to postwar male intellectuals. Daniel Bell wrote in 1956 of the ways in which the quality of labor after the war had been paradoxically impaired by the introduction of psychologists into the workplace working. What he speaks of as the "tyranny of psychology" began with the introduction of a nurse into a Philadelphia textile mill in 1925. She was a "sympathetic ear," and "the workers began to pour out their troubles," with the result that production rose. Bell attributes the rise of counseling in the workplace "largely" to the presence of women in the work force. The unattractive consequence has been that "the problems of work are projected outward and swathed in psychological batting." The terminology of nursing here suggests that Bell thought that the entry of women into the postwar work force had reduced male workers to the passivity of patients. Bell's language speaks for a generation's worry that a feminizing influence on labor would make the direct conflict between labor and management that might lead to improved working conditions less likely. Snyder's poems evoke an economy in which one need not address such issues. The poems are often striking, as "After Work" surely is, but how closely, and how pertinently, is one instructed?

Snyder's limits as a political poet follow partly from his concentration on short, anecdotal poems. From him, as from Williams or the Imagists, one cannot expect ideas to be elaborated, qualified, turned this way and that, as they can be by discursive poets like Robert Pinsky, A. R. Ammons, Edward Dorn, and Charles Olson; ideas are treated most successfully by Snyder when they remain implicit. Snyder aims at rendering his beliefs poignant and his experiences sometimes stunning. The political corollary to this poetic method is that change begins with a moment of personal recognition, as when a thief "Suddenly stopped those long black legs / Covered his ears with his hands / And listened to the humming of his mind." The long processes whereby various individuals join together in a common cause or negotiate resolutions, these and many other political acts cannot be rendered by this method. Snyder has chosen a particular range of possibilities to explore, in poetry and politics, and he has succeeded well within that range.

Since 1974 he has aspired to the poet's role as teacher. In a touching short poem from *Axe Handles* (1983), the poet Lew Welch, who shot himself in 1971, comes back from the dead to tell Snyder: "teach the children about the cycles. / The life cycles. All other cycles. / That's what it's all about, and it's all forgot." As Snyder has become increasingly sure of his own authority, his poems have grown less compelling for skeptical readers. They were better before he knew so much. The pressure in his best writing derives from what is left out, suppressed, or just passing overhead, like a test bomber. In the wisdom poems he is too content with the truths he has to tell. But in a little poem like "Looking at Pictures to Be Put Away" (1968) he is able to write about mixed feelings: on one hand, the charm of his own desire for an unconstrained pastoral life and, on the other, the superficiality of that life: "What will we remember / Bodies thick with food and lovers / After twenty years." The girl in the photo is forgotten, not because of the West's exploitation of fossil fuel (about which so many poems go on), but because he has just known too many girls not well enough. The poet too knows wastefulness and spoliation, and not just in others. He has moved "In and out of forests, cities, families / like a fish," as he says in a related poem, without any lasting sense of the lives he has touched. In these poems one hears convincing testimony of the ways in which the infectious greed of an imperial culture reaches into the private lives of even its critics.

Snyder's achievement as a political poet, though limited, is considerable. He has written a number of poems that make severe retirement from urban or even modern society seem the result not of petulance but of austere sanity. He celebrates the plain, homely attractions of family life and friendship without the ill temper of his master Robinson Jeffers. This is to say that his political position seems the result of his loves, not of his hates. There is also a quality of mature responsibility in his writing, which one does not find in the work of many of his contemporaries: he never presents his life as a symptom of a social or cultural malady, and this is exactly what Ginsberg attempts in the first line of *Howl*.

Snyder's practical political proposals, however, are stunningly authoritarian. This is an obvious danger for a poet who is accustomed to writing about politics from a great remove from the center. In *Turtle Island* (1974) he suggests that politicians begin work on "the only real solution," which itself is an unpolitical phrase in a democracy:

Demand immediate participation by all countries in programs to legalize abortion, encourage vasectomy and sterilization (provided by free clinics) – free insertion of intrauterine loops – try to correct traditional cultural attitudes that tend to force women into child-bearing – remove income tax deductions for more than two children above a specified income level, and scale it so that lower income families are forced to be careful too – or pay families to limit their number.

This program for social action, appended to a book of poems, is an odd mix of strenuous legislative measures and advocacy of bargains on birth control paraphernalia. There is little evidence that Snyder has thought long about the difficulties of encouraging other nations to exercise particular forms of social control or of balancing respect for the rights of others with concern for the environment. After using terms like "demand" and "force" here, he goes on to say, as though growing squeamish about his own zealotry: "Great care should be taken that no one is ever tricked or forced into sterilization." Tax penalties against parents of three or more children (Snyder has two) and paychecks for those submitting to sterilization constitute neither force nor trickery, as he naively sees it.

In the same collection he begins a poem, "Tomorrow's Song," in his wisdom mode:

> The USA slowly lost its mandate
> in the middle and later twentieth century
> it never gave the mountains and rivers
>   trees and animals,
>   a vote.
> all the people turned away from it
>   myths die; even continents are impermanent
>
>   Turtle Island returned.

Until the mid-twentieth century, Snyder apparently believes, America had a mandate from the people of the world. About the particular failure of the American government to extend the franchise to animals and the inanimate, he is utterly in earnest. The court should appoint someone to represent trees, animals, and so on in the U.S. Congress; this is "very simple," he says, without any sense of the political difficulties entailed by the idea of representation, of speaking for others who are profoundly different. Shamans spoke for wild animals and plants, and despite the absence of shamans in American culture, Snyder believes that the court could find adequate representatives for the mute plants and animals. He sees himself as a "spokesman in the society of the enemy," and imagines the trees and birds as his supporters. This idea has led to charming poems, such as "We Make Our Vows with All Beings," but to unconsidered political statements too. Why this court-appointed legislator would do better than the presidentially appointed minister of the interior is not explained, nor is the constitutional problem of having the judicial branch of government appoint members of the legislative branch. These are the proposals of a poet who is impatient with political problems, which is why he can speak of them as simple, though he has acknowledged that the result of his own experience in political administration in California was the recognition that political action is "very complicated." Poets in their poems, Snyder believes, are not answerable to contemporary social institutions, but to the eternity of the present; they are healers.

The healing truths for the future are evidently simpler than the political deliberations of citizens in the present.

❦

Allen Ginsberg wrote *Howl* one year after he met Snyder in 1954. This poem has enjoyed an immediate and, so far, lasting success like no other American poem: there are over 300,000 copies in print. Unlike most other poets of this time, both Ginsberg and Snyder have drawn comfort from their sales; their popularity has led them to feel confident that they genuinely speak for an important part of the culture. Ginsberg, like Lowell in "Inauguration Day: January 1953," sees the whole of American culture as deadly wrong, dominated by Moloch. But just what had gone wrong in 1955? Moloch is capitalism, industrialization, aggression, and reason, as Paul Breslin notes. Ginsberg was twenty-nine years old when he wrote *Howl*. He begins with the assertion that he has seen "the best minds of my generation destroyed by madness." To speak of "minds," rather than persons, is a way of locating the failure directly within the favorite terms of intellectuals in the 1950s. He speaks a few lines later of these young people as having "passed through universities . . . hallucinating . . . among the scholars of war." Ginsberg refers to those who, like himself, were disenchanted with the liberal dreams of a vigorous intellectual culture based in the universities. Universities are instead seen here in terms of their complicity in the formulation of military and political policy. The poem presents the underside of the 1950s liberal consensus.

Ginsberg's indictment of America seems comprehensive. All the American details he cites, with Whitman's expansiveness, symbolize the vast corruption of the country's culture. The atomic bomb ("the sirens of Los Alamos") and the proliferation of mass media (*Time* magazine and television) have raised the stakes of political failure. The all-or-nothing rhetoric of the poem derives from these two facts: 1) nuclear weapons meant that war could quickly become apocalyptical; and 2) television and the mass press had rendered American culture monolithic. Yet there is a sense in *Howl* and certainly in "America" in which the condemnation of the country is less than total. Ginsberg is frankly sentimental about the Wobblies and the New York Communist Party of the 1930s. In the not so distant past, pockets of political opposition existed in America, but after the War the New York intellectuals turned dramatically against the idea of organized practical political opposition. Even *Partisan Review* supported the liberal consensus of the 1950s. In "America" one sees plainly what is less strong but also present in *Howl*: Ginsberg's desire to embrace his nation – to "hug and kiss the United States under our bedsheets." As social criticism, *Howl* has a soft edge, and in "America" Ginsberg's effort to present himself as personally charming demonstrates that the social critique of the poem derives from a plausibly human, not ideological, perspective. The poem is nowhere so satiric as *The Waste Land, MacFlecknoe,* or *The Dunciad.* Ginsberg writes with humor and affection for the country, and that tone – his mix of outrage and affection, seriousness and playfulness – is just what makes the poems I have mentioned rise above the level of the cultural document.

Robert Bly's "The Teeth Mother Naked at Last" (1970) is a later effort at the culture–poem that Lowell and Ginsberg had written in the 1950s. Bly's poem is a powerful expression of a severely critical and comprehensive view of American culture. The evenness of his tone owes something to Ginsberg. Bly manages to convey a sense that American foreign policy is grossly iniquitous and yet inevitable. The cruelty of American soldiers is equated with the natural cycle of destruction and creation:

> *The Marine battalion enters.*
> This happens when the seasons change.
> This happens when the leaves begin to drop from the trees
>   too early.

Bly moves well beyond predictable outrage. "Do not be angry at the President," he says, after representing very wittily the way Presidents Johnson and Nixon routinely lied in press conferences. The very funny lies that Bly has the President tell are just the ones that, in a serious sense, go to the roots of the culture. The President answers the questions – when did the Appalachian mountain range rise? what is the population of Chicago? what is the weight of the adult eagle? the total area of the Everglades? what is the capital of Wyoming? – that are asked of schoolchildren by their teachers and parents. The President's ridiculous lies suggest that American foreign policy is being conducted by bad boys, but the further suggestion is that the intellectual development of the nation is being severely impaired. Like the bomber pilot dying in the first section of the poem, the President wants to die, and this is why he lies. "The ministers lie, the professors lie, the television reporters lie, the priests lie": a whole nation has gone bad. Bly claims, in the leaden moments of the poem, that American wealth leads naturally to a death wish: "This is what it's like to have a gross national product." Although Bly names officers of the American government in some of his poems, there is no suggestion that American foreign policy could be different if the personnel were changed.

Bly's analysis of the Vietnam War is not political really; it is first ethical (the President is a liar) and then, more importantly, psychological. The bomber pilot, whose hand Bly holds "has an empty place inside him, / created one night when his parents came home drunk." One is reminded not only of Whitman in Washington in 1863, but of Ginsberg's reference as well to "Children screaming under the stairways! Boys sobbing in armies! Old men weeping in the parks!" The corruption of the dominant male culture of America begins in the family, as these poets see it, and continues from the cradle to the grave. Politics change from moment to moment, but psychology persists.

The tone Bly achieves follows from the surrealism of his method.

> Helicopters flutter overhead. The death-
> bee is coming. Super Sabres
> like knots of neurotic energy sweep
> around and return.

Here the equanimity of the long opening lines of the poem is disturbed and the verse is forcefully enjambed, as though under some new pressure. But the next line changes the tone dramatically:

> This is Hamilton's triumph.
> This is the triumph of a centralized bank.

Bly sees the war from an Olympian distance, though he claims to be as close as Whitman was to the dying. Whatever connection can be drawn between Hamilton's fiscal policy and the bombers in Vietnam needs to be carefully explained. Without discursive explanation, the movement from one line to the next invokes some transcendent understanding on the poet's part, and as well his unwillingness to analyze the immediate political causes of American military actions in Southeast Asia. Here too one can sense a poet's impatience with politics. When Bly purports to analyze and explain, his poem becomes surrealistic:

> It's because the aluminum window-shade business is doing so
> well in the United States
> that we spread fire over entire villages.

This is a parody of an explanation, and yet the jokes of this poem are meant seriously too. Bly's claim is that Americans are estranged by their own affluence from the concrete consequences of their actions. Window shades, on some level, do keep out the fire of bombs. Both Ginsberg and Bly suggest that psychology determines political history, that the family romance is at the base of American politics, and that the American social status quo is mad.

❦

For poets fifteen or twenty years younger than Bly and Ginsberg, it became necessary to reclaim some of the emotional and technical range that these older poets had successfully kept out of most American poetry until the mid-1970s. In the work of Pinsky and C. K. Williams one can see this effort at recovery bringing not just meter but also coherent narrative back into the mainstream of American poetry. Writing to his daughter in his *Explanation of America* (1979), Robert Pinsky says:

> Someday, the War in Southeast Asia, somewhere –
> Perhaps for you and people younger than you –
> Will be the kind of history and pain
> Saguntum is for me; but never tamed
> Or "history" for me, I think.

His poem has at its center a shadow that he sometimes calls an American love of death, but it is cast largely by the American experience of Vietnam. This is the shadow that Bly in "The Teeth Mother" imagines as going out across the plains, with the President's lies, "into the prairie grass, like mile-long caravans of Conestoga wagons crossing the Platte." W. S. Merwin imagines it sticking to the landscape as a sign of destruction. In poetry generally, it is the shadow of American foreign policy in the 1960s. Pinsky's problem as a poet is to come out from under the shadow, to have access to a wide range of American subject matter and style in the mid-1970s. *An Explanation* is an effort to rehabilitate certain attitudes and ways of treating American subjects that had fallen out of poetry in the extreme political and cultural climate of the 1960s.

This poem is written in blank verse, whereas the most famous poets of the 1960s – Lowell, Rich, Merwin, Levertov and Kinnell – explicitly broke with the conventions of metrical verse: Free verse was a convention of the 1960s that carried ideological as well as artistic justification. Kinnell and others spoke of metrical verse as authoritarian. In returning to the central metrical norm of English poetry, Pinsky conspicuously rejected the restriction of formal possibilities that came with the renewed attention to poetry in the 1960s. More generally, his style is insistently reasonable. Here are the opening lines of the poem:

> As though explaining the idea of dancing
> Or the idea of some other thing
> Which everyone has known a little about
> Since they were children, which children learn themselves
> With no explaining, but which children like
> Sometimes to hear the explanations of,
> I want to tell you something about our country,
> Or my idea of it: explaining it
> If not to you, to my idea of you.

Pinsky reclaimed the resources of discursive prose as well as those of metrical English verse. The poet who wrote this first sentence has no complaint about the constraints of prose syntax: this is a very long, grammatically complex sentence that depends upon rules of subordination in English. A poet who pushes English syntax toward an almost German length and elaborateness of clauses is letting his readers know that he dissents from the procedures of modernist verse set in London by Pound and T. E. Hulme in 1911, and that he declines to have his poetry confined to the revelation of stunning or puzzling fragments.

Pinsky uses the poem the way one does an essay, to think through and explain something abstract, here, the nature of his country. He clearly means to speak in a careful, measured, and even hesitant manner; one who writes this way does not ask readers for the special license of a poet. Several consequences follow from Pinsky's subtitle to his *Explanation of America: A Poem to my Daughter.* The style of address displays the parental virtues: humaneness, consideration, circumspection, easy affection, concern, and consistency, and these were irrelevant to Bly's "The Teeth-Mother." A poet in the late 1960s could not possibly orient a style on the parental virtues. Edward Dorn's "The Problem of the Poem for my Daughter, Left Unsolved" (1965) is a case in point.

Those who expect poets to imagine a radically different world in the future or the past, and to oppose utterly the one we know together in the present, must be disappointed by the fact that this poem on America is addressed to a young daughter. Pinsky is interested in continuity from one generation to the next and presupposes that her world will resemble his. She, with her own "Essay on Kids," is obviously her father's daughter; his most distinguished longish poem before this book was entitled "An Essay on Psychiatrists." She will surely recognize her father's world in her own. "Children are dangerous hostages to fortune," he says, "They bind us to the future." Pinsky imagines his nation getting over the experience of the Vietnam War, even if he and his contemporaries will always bear its marks: "As if we were a family, and some members / Had done an awful thing on a road at night, / And all of us had grown white hair, or tails . . ." As a parent, he hopes for a future worthy of his daughter, but this is not so grand as what is meant when one speaks of the optimism of Americans. The American religion of the country's own founding, manifest destiny for this chosen people, is the brutal form of American hope. "New Hope is born again," he says,

> And though it demand an Aztec vivisection
> Everything lost must be made whole again.

This poem examines a sort of hope that is reasonable for an American in the 1980s. "Living inside a prison, / Within its many other prisons, what / Should one aspire to be?" This is the central question of the poem. Unlike

Bly, Pinsky loves the "plural-headed Empire" that is in any case "Beyond my outrage or my admiration." His America is a dream conglomerate sufficiently diverse that no one "ever will mediate / Among the conquering, crazed immigrants." This ethnic conglomerate, described wonderfully in "III. Local Politics" (ll. 58–85), is no more than the individualistic consumer society that many other writers despise. Pinsky claims that this society's manifold achievements as well as its schlock and crimes provide sufficient reason for him to show humility when speaking of its nature or worth. The country is beyond any one explanation or judgment that he might come up with, though he does explore several of the most common explanations of the nation, trying to locate their truth as much as their weaknesses.

Pinsky's modesty or distrust of the severe judgments of the 1960s brings him to a statement of the belief that the country becomes mellower with age (and atrocity).

> Because all things have their explanations,
> True or false, all can come to seem domestic.
> The brick mills of New England on their rivers
> Are *brooding, classic;* the Iron Horse is quaint,
> Steel oildrums, musical; and the ugly suburban
> "Villas" of London, Victorian Levittowns,
> Have come to be civilized and urbane.

Things get better by themselves, from this view, which is a good thing, because political action is limited to the vote. Pinsky wants to speak for the acceptance of the limits of the prison of empire. "Denial of limit has been the pride, or failing, / Well-known to be shared by all this country's regions, / Races, and classes." He urges his daughter to be fond of its craziness and modestly satisfied with its limits.

The clear danger to this position is complacency. Pinsky translates a Horatian epistle on the advantages of life on the Sabine Farm, the attractions of the peaceful countryside within close proximity to Rome. The issue for Horace is the choice between a life of retirement and one of engagement in the activities of the imperial metropolis. Pinsky says that

> It would be too complacent to build a nest
> Between one's fatalism and one's pleasures –
> With death at one side, a sweet farm at the other,
> Keeping the thorns of government away. . . .

In the end he chooses for himself, he says, "to struggle actively to save / The Republic," but for his daughter, "something like a nest or farm; / So that the cycle of different aspirations / Threads through posterity." The poem begins with the family life of suburban Boston (a play staged by his daughter's Brownie group), with his own life, that is. When he speaks of a nest or farm, that is a way of speaking of an affluent, sweet suburb outside a major American city. The life of struggle to maintain the American republic is not represented in the book. There is no American Brutus here: that aspiration is left only in words and a figure from Rome. His aspiration for his daughter is not so different from his own comfortable life. The strength of this poem is partly in Pinsky's daring to take what, among literary intellectuals, is an extreme position: that contemporary America is something to be more treasured than condemned. His poem reasserts the right of his generation and of his daughter's to take pleasure in the lives they actually live, rather than dreaming or pretending to dream of some alternative.

C. K. Williams's "From My Window" (1983) is part of a trend in recent poetry to restore narrative to verse. Williams is a story teller, which means that formally he is somewhat retrograde. He is out to restore the narrative conventions that were unsettled by the modernists of the 1920s. If Pinsky's poem approximates the form and style of a discursive essay, Williams's is like a short story. The narrative is clear, straightforward, and the language is loose and unselfconscious like some serviceable medium for prose fiction. There are even places where the writing seems slack, as though he least of all wanted to be taken as a skillful verse writer: the story is the thing.

Stories have a specific significance for recent political poetry. The Vietnam War, as everyone knows, was the most photographed and the first televised war. The narrative mode is saturated with guilt, because complicity as well as horror is what one felt watching the Vietnam War on the nightly news. Charles Simic, for example, called attention to "the way in which the world's daily tragedies are brought to us every morning and evening. It's really the raw data of history given to us so soon after the event and in such detail that makes each one of us a voyeur, a Peeping Tom of the death chamber."

Walter Benjamin said that the introduction of mechanized warfare in the First World War ended storytelling. Soldiers came back from the Front silent after seeing their own insignificance in battle. Williams's poem draws out the guilt in the idea of telling stories about other people, especially about those whose lives were maimed by battle. The guilt is based not just on the sense of having seen something one should not have seen; the further issue is that one could do nothing after having seen horrible killings on TV. One's own courage was destroyed by one's sense of helplessness. The war and the idea of political agency both seemed to be trivialized by the nightly presentation of the day's actions. Howard Nemerov's recent poem, "On An Occasion of National Mourning," satirizes the nation's ability to broadcast emotion and thereby falsify grief.

> It is admittedly difficult for a whole
> Nation to mourn and be seen to do so, but
> It can be done, the silvery platitudes
> Were waiting in their silos for just such
> An emergent occasion. . . .

The telling of stories, like the raising and lowering of flags, only helps the country to get used to atrocity, and to proceed further in the same direction. The Vietnam War called into question the distance of the citizens of the metropolis from the outer edge of the empire, and this distance is what allows for narrative. The returning soldier tells his tale.

Williams's poem is structured in a conventional fashion: it begins with spring and ends with a memory of winter. The vet and his buddy weave an erratic path toward Williams's building, and the poet recalls the buddy's asymmetrical figure eight path last winter. This symbolic structure itself, beyond the narrative of the poem, raises questions about survival and re-newal, and about memory. The symbolic framing of the story sets the vet under the sign of eternity, of the returning seasons and the figure eight. Like the crocuses, he comes out in the spring and gives the world another try, but the wintry conclusion shows how easily and naturally his presence is erased from the metropolitan scene.

What I am referring to as the guilt of the narrative mode is not just the guilt of a left-liberal poet seeing the consequences of a war he opposed; that in itself is not surprising or especially creditable. Williams draws attention to the way that looking at others muddies clarity on both sides. The word "contriving" (l. 14) suggests that the scene that takes place under his window is somehow staged for him. The buddy seems to have known all along that he was being watched. There is a hint of duplicity on the part of the buddy, as though he wanted sympathy of some kind, or just craved attention. The city puts everything in the form of a spectacle; the urban life is all selfconsciousness. Perhaps the point is only that Williams himself is too jaundiced by spectacle to overlook the possibility that even this scene has been contrived for him. Nothing can be taken for granted as simply itself.

The remark "I wonder if they're lovers" nicely gets at the way the 1980s sensibility collides with these casualties of the 1960s. Are they gay? We can understand that now, though that was not the issue of the 1960s. And that aspect of American culture is irrelevant to them of course. How prurient too to ask the question, even of oneself. Prurience is exactly the issue of the poem and of telling stories: this is what the art of poetry and the sensibility of the 1980s have to offer by way of understanding. Williams is just as much a voyeur as the real estate agents across the street. He tries to assert his superiority to the middle-American real estate agents ("they're not, at least, thank god, laughing," l. 19), but in the end there is no difference between bourgeois and poetic voyeurs. This is what I mean about complicity and complication being part of the best political poems.

The buddy pacing in the snow is an insistent reminder of the human suffering in the year and in the state. In a few hours or even minutes of snow, his tracks disappear, and the city goes on as though he never were. The joggers and surveyors return in the spring, as though the War and its casualties never were, or were manageable with Legion halls and "benefits." The Vietnam War survives into the mid 1980s as one more spectacle to be watched from a distance, and misunderstood.

❦

The recovery of traditional poetic techniques that one sees in the work of Pinsky and Williams rests on a mature sense of the limits of resistance in America, not just on some inevitable cyclic reaction. The last two poets under consideration suggest that these limits are not peculiar to America but endemic to empires. Alan Dugan's "The Decimation Before Phraäta" (1983) is a variation of an ancient Greek poem about the Roman imperial troops. The legionnaires shouted to their officers, "Please decimate us!" And the officers obliged. Every tenth soldier was slain by his own sword, because the troops had broken "some 'rule' " or other. This was how the imperial army effectively maintained extraordinary discipline. The barbarian resistance at Phraäta was overcome, but the Romans did not claim the city, and instead marched away, as though the military objective had been insignificant all along. "That empire is incomprehensible," the barbarian speaker says, "but we are in it. / They came back for Phraäta and now we are the light horse / auxiliary of the XIth Legion (Augustan) of the Empire / and have no home."

The military advantages of an imperial force are great, even against the guerrilla tactics of the barbarians. The empire befuddled its adversaries by seeming not to care about expansion, by decimating its own troops. It appeared to be driven by some mysterious abstract idea beyond self-interest. The enemies of the empire, and the troops themselves, are psychologically as well as militarily overpowered. Most important of all, the empire is ubiquitous: "we and our horses are with them on the flanks / because there's nowhere else to go and nothing else / for us barbarians to do or be: it's a world empire." Those last, pathetic words of the poem speak to the experience of Americans who see no way of avoiding or undermining the inescapable, all encompassing order of the American social economy. Poets, critics, and professors, as surely as soldiers, are part of this empire.

Anthony Hecht wrote a similar poem in 1967, "Behold the Lilies of the Field," about the Roman emperor Valerian, taken captive by a barbarian king. Valerian was tortured and humiliated before his troops, who were made to watch. Yet he resisted by not surrendering his dignity. Suddenly the torture stopped, and his wounds were dressed. He recovered and was well treated until, just as suddenly, he was slowly flayed alive before a public gathering. The speaker of the poem was one of Valerian's subordinates, but he is also a patient telling his psychoanalyst the story of his mother's loss of honesty. Hecht stresses the timelessness implied by Dugan's imitation of a Greek poem about the Roman empire (and Dugan's version deliberately recalls Herodotus's account of the Persian troops): for these poets, imperialism rises well above historical details and ideas of nationality. Whether Persian, Greek, Roman, or American, imperialism is brutal, apparently irrational, and relentless in the imposition of authority. The political ideologies of particular empires matter not at all, these are abstract political poems. The speaker of Hecht's poem is emasculated by his mother's lies, and by Valerian's example. Valerian was the last political figure to maintain his integrity; he is now a stuffed doll. "And with him passed away the honor of Rome. // In the end, I was ransomed. Mother paid for me." His mother lies by maintaining one way of speaking to her friends and another for speaking to her family; she saves the truth for her private life. That distinction makes her, in the eyes of her son, a whore, but it is this dishonor that permits her son to survive.

The idea of the public role of the poet is an antique memory for Hecht and Dugan. The time has passed when a poet could resist the force of the empire. As an adversary to the state, he is now a quaint doll in the wind. Political motives are not especially relevant; the structure of imperialism itself, whether Roman or American, eliminates the possibility of opposition. Even moral outrage is beside the point; there is no external position that an adversary can occupy. The empire takes everyone in.

The trick is that Dugan's barbarians never had a climactic moment when they were forcibly inducted, nor when they capitulated. They were rather slyly absorbed into the Roman legions. The experience of capitulation is a blank around which these poems move, not evasively but analytically. For American intellectuals in the late 1960s and the 1970s, the question whether to resist an imperial culture had some point, but so too did the question whether, like Dugan's barbarians or Hecht's Romans (the party lines nicely cross at this level of analysis), even the adversarial intellectuals do not wind up in the army too. Aren't we all collaborators? The empire has absorbed its opponents: they too are part of the spectacle of liberal order. In 1968 one read that the *Partisan Review,* America's most respected adversarial journal, was subsidized by the Congress for Cultural Freedom, which was funded by the CIA. Some poets surely knew, as they traveled from campus to campus reading poems against the Vietnam War, that this too was a kind of soldier's job. The greater army has its paid adversaries whose dogged protests validate the empire's claim not just to tolerance, but also to pluralistic comprehensiveness.

❧

My thesis here is that the critical context in which politics and poetry were discussed in the late 1940s emphasized a poet's obligation to the private experiences out of which poetry can come. Poets seem to have absorbed this notion, even though in the following three decades they certainly did not restrict themselves to private subjects. Instead they produced varieties of political poetry that bring, however variously, political subjects around to the edge of what can be called personal experiences. One consequence has been a psychologizing of politics. But another has been a focus on complicity, for that is where politics becomes painfully personal. Several of the poets I have discussed tend to feel personally answerable for the political actions of the nation. This aspect of recent poetry derives from the honesty of these poets, but also ultimately from the postwar stress on the private quality of poetry. This high esteem for privacy had a damaging effect on the poetry of Rich and Levertov, who dramatized the public demands brought by the times on the private poet. The claim that the American poet after 1945 should be a private figure led in several directions, one of which was toward a particular kind of measured analysis of a citizen's complicity in an imperial republic.

3

❦

REAR GUARDS

EAR GUARD – who covets that designation? In the last fifty years only too many artists have claimed to be avant-garde. It would be easy enough for a poet to speak of meter as an aspect of technique that does or does not work for him or her, some of the time or always – Lowell sometimes explained his choices this way. But the adoption of metrical form in the years just after the war was more commonly taken as a sign of affiliation, and the predictable consequence was a War of the Anthologies in the 1950s. Certainly since 1960 free verse, the technical sign of experimentalist poets, has dominated verse writing. Yet a deeper truth about the postwar era is that it has been predominantly reactionary against the avant-garde experiments of the generation born in the 1880s. The reaction really began when Eliot and Pound returned briefly to quatrains in 1919; it continued in the work of Hart Crane, John Crowe Ransom, Allen Tate, and Yvor Winters in the late 1920s and the 1930s. Auden's emigration to New York in 1939 reinforced this reaction, as he gained influence on young American poets through the 1950s. Immediately after the war, many poets did want to be known as rear guard. There was then an urgent desire among young poets to set the modernist generation off to the side, as though American poetry had never crossed with the international avant-garde, as though it were still English poetry. Three considerations made the idea of a rear guard attractive. First, to intellectuals generally and to journalists, the political record of the modernists was a dubious heritage in 1945. Second, more than just politically, poets like Pound and Eliot were difficult to assimilate to the intellectual milieu represented by the large-circulation magazines – *The New Republic,* for instance. The abstruse references in the *Cantos* and the *Waste Land,* and the foreboding doom in these poems did not suit the enthusiastic, social-sciencey intellectual atmosphere being constructed after the War. Third, to poets more particularly, the prospect of working gradually out from under the shadows of Pound, Eliot, Williams, and Stevens was altogether daunting: the generation born in the 1880s had rightly come to seem giants by 1945. How could one *develop* modernist techniques beyond the *Cantos* and *The Waste Land?* Free verse, collage, associative procedures – this technology was not just tried out by the modernists, but mastered. The late poems of Pound, Eliot, and Williams – the *Pisan Cantos* (1948), *Four Quartets* (1936–43), and *Paterson* (1946–58) – actually restore important features of premodernist verse: a coherent lyrical persona, discursiveness, and narrative respectively. Marianne Moore has been especially beloved by rear guard poets, exactly because she makes it easy for younger poets to seem to accommodate modernism, as though it were charming eccentricity.

The free-verse modernism of Pound, Eliot, and Williams was understood among poets as the exact opposite of what, with some unfairness, was called academic verse. The term "academic" indicated broad institutional favor: poems published in the quarterlies, several of which were based in universities, but in *The New Yorker* as well. Awards, publication, and notice in wide-circulation journals went to metrical poetry from 1945 until near the end of the 1950s. Later Allen Ginsberg would dismiss one of these poets, Mona Van Duyn, as an author of magazine verse, but in the fifteen years following World War II the more loaded derogatory epithet was "academic," because of course it indicated conformity, conventionality, and timidity, but also because it suggested where the energy and authority of the literary culture were located: in universities. The avant-gardists were well aware of the burgeoning wealth and authority of American universities; they came from the most prestigious of these institutions: Olson, Creeley, Ashbery, O'Hara, and Bly from Harvard; Ginsberg from Columbia; Robert Duncan and Gary Snyder from Berkeley. The term academic verse revealed a love-hate relationship between poets and social authority in the postwar years. The poets who in the 1950s used "academic" as a term of derision showed in the 1970s that they aspired at least as warmly as their adversaries to recognition from the university-based literary culture that was taking shape in the 1950s.

More than anyone else, Richard Wilbur has been known as a 1950s poet. When he collected four previous volumes together for his *Poems* in 1963, he arranged them in reverse chronological order: he was plainly uncomfortable about being understood only in terms of his early success. His newest work, he presented first, understandably, to stress his departures from the poems of the previous decade. Wilbur had won prizes and admiring reviews in the 1950s; his poems appeared regularly in *The New Yorker.* His reputation had been made in the mainstream literary journals of the time. The later Wilbur, however, never really emerged. His career has not developed markedly, and he has published less and less of his own poetry since 1963. There was something static or, worse, self-satisfied about 1950s metrical verse, as though stylistic development were inherently unattractive. Lowell sensed this as early as 1959 and pursued a new direction with *Life Studies.* Merrill seems to have come to a similar conclusion much later with the *Book of Ephraim* (1976). Other poets like Anthony Hecht, John Hollander, Richard Howard, and even Elizabeth Bishop kept faith with styles they established for the tastes of the journals of the 1950s. James Dickey put the matter cruelly, when he pretended to allay his own doubts about Wilbur's lack of development, "if someone is already the most charming and amiable man in the world there's no need for him to try to be something or somebody else." Wilbur is still admired, but really as the best poet of the 1950s.

A number of features of 1950s verse are epitomized in his style. His poems are deliberately ornate, obviously rich in consonance and assonance, superficially indebted to Hopkins. His language is insistently figurative. Everything is seen in terms of something else – "this mad *instead*," he calls it in a self-critical moment. To emblems, similes, and pretty phrases, he is devoted – to just those types of figurative language that make no claim to spontaneity or sudden revelation. His poems constantly offer the charm of wit, but rarely the force of conviction. Throughout poems in the academic style of the 1950s is a mild Anglophilia: words like "blow" for "bloom" show how poets like Wilbur were looking over their shoulders for European admiration, which in terms of literary, though not political, history was anachronistic. The conventions of 1950s subject matter – paintings, social types, animals, foreign sights – are all in evidence in Wilbur's work. Above all is the convention that the subject of a poem need not be in any sense great; the death of a toad will do nicely. Fifties poets characteristically claimed no intense feelings for their subjects. This was art, not life. The standard critical reaction against this verse is that it is superficial, aloof about social and political problems, and, in a damning word, complacent. But Wilbur is not so aloof as he seems, and surely not politically complacent.

In the background of his poems is a sense, almost always vague, of the horror of political history. This is clearest in the poems that derive explicitly from his experiences as an infantryman in Europe during World War II. "Mined Country" (1946) is a nature poem about the postwar European landscape that had been planted with explosive charges. Wilbur claims that the traditional associations with landscape have become merely quaint: "Some scheme's gone awry. // Danger is sunk in the pastures, the woods are sly, / Ingenuity's covered with flowers!" The experience neither of traps nor of explosives was new at this time, which leaves some doubt about the significance Wilbur attributes to a mined landscape. The poem concludes with a mix of moods that suggests he has dealt only indirectly with his subject:

> Sunshiny field grass, the woods floor, are so mixed up
> With earliest trusts, you have to pick back
> Far past all you have learned, to go
> Disinherit the dumb child,

> Tell him to trust things alike and never to stop
> Emptying things, but not let them lack
> Love in some manner restored; to be
> Sure the whole world's wild.

First, a phrase like "Sunshiny field grass" indicates that Wilbur is not concerned here to capture any particular landscape, that the general idea of a pastoral landscape is the issue. Second, the imperative to restore love for the landscape is mysteriously abstract: why should love be restored? Wilbur seems at a loss to say more about this restoration: "in some manner" will have to do. Third, what warrants the apocalyptic assertion of the last clause? Soldiers are already sweeping this landscape with mine detectors to remove the traces of the war (ll. 9–12). The feeling that military technology has radically altered traditional human understanding is not well justified by the poem, which seems rather driven by a force greater than what Wilbur is willing to discuss. The new technology of the war had nothing to do with mines. The points of strain in this poem suggest that Wilbur wanted to express feelings generated by nuclear war, but that he could broach this hot subject only indirectly.

"Potato," the poem printed alongside "Mined Country" from 1946 to 1963, is written in the same accentual pentameter, and expresses a skeptical attitude toward aspiration in a world gone wild. This poem concerns the value of homely persistence, the potato that nourishes simple people in times of hardship. The flowers that this plant produces are "second-rate," but beautiful to the hungry, who were legion in Europe in 1946. When writing in this 1950s emblematic mode Wilbur felt free to employ more exact descriptive language than that in "Mined Country":

> Cut open raw, it looses a cool clean stench,
> Mineral acid seeping from pores of prest meal;
> It is like breaching a strangely refreshing tomb:
>
> Therein the taste of first stones, the hands of dead slaves,
> Waters men drank in the earliest frightful woods,
> Flint chips, and peat, and the cinders of buried camps.

Here the consequences of political history (slavery, fright, warfare) are displaced onto similes and left just a little distant from the topic Wilbur professes to discuss. The conventional distinction between tenor and vehicle keeps the political aspect of his subject in view only on an angle. His strategy is to stay small, oblique, to persist by shunning greatness; like potatoes or those who eat them, he seems to mean only to survive. Aspiration is constantly mistrusted in these poems, as though grandeur were inherently duplicitous. This attitude is pointedly political as well as literary. In a talk for the Voice of America, Wilbur referred to an account by the Soviet Minister of Culture of how the Party inspires Soviet poets. Wilbur's point was the standard liberal democratic one: "I should not care to limit my poetic thought to politics and economics, which are not, after all, the whole of reality; I should not like to be forbidden that honesty that comes of the admission of doubts, contradictions, and reservations." The alternatives are a totalitarian approach to political poetry, brought into the talk as an instance of a principled account of the connection between poetry and ideas, and a liberal inclination to leave political subjects alone, at least some of the time, and to be skeptical of the "synoptic intellectual structures" that ambitious poets build.

This mistrust is directed at modernists of the previous generation like Pound and Yeats who had eyes for totalitarianism, not for second-rate flowers. Wilbur's contemporaries needed no reminder that their early careers lay in the shadow of greatness. The poem opening Wilbur's second collection, *Ceremony* (1950), is called simply "Then" (1948) – before the fall:

> Of lineage now, and loss
> These latter singers tell,
> Of a year when birds now still
> Were all one choiring call
> Till the unreturning leaves
> Imperishably fell.

Although the poem is couched in the terms of legend, this is nonetheless a particularly gloomy note on which to begin a book when most Americans, in and out of the universities, could see distinct gains of the present as measured against the immediate past: peace where there had been world war; prosperity where there had been depression; husbands, wives, and children together where they had recently been separated; and growing consensus where there had been ideological and class strife. But for poets in 1948 the "ample season" of song could be only a memory. Wilbur's poetry, like that of many of his contemporaries, is academic in the sense that it insists upon a special history and special interests of its own, distinct from, and indeed opposed to, those of the nation at large.

He imagines an art that answers the pressure of politics and economics not at all by adopting some political allegiance or other, as Pound did, but rather by claiming an otherness for art. In "Driftwood (1948) he reflects on the fate of some pieces of driftwood cast up on the shore in ways that suggest the specific political and economic pressure Wilbur meant to resist. Once they were green wood, "knowing / Their own nature only, and that / bringing to leaf," before they were taken for use – in the building of cities and the waging of war (ll. 9–12):

> . . . on the great generality of waters
> Floated their singleness,
> And in all that deep subsumption they were
> Never dissolved . . . (ll. 17–20).

In postwar American society the notion of an individual seemed endangered by the spread of prosperity and the promotion of uniform desires for consumer items. The signs of ideological, class, ethnic, and professional differences were becoming obscured by consensus politics, mass media, and consumer credit. People were identified less by character than by profession, by social utility. In this milieu the mere idea of distinctness acquired the panache of resistance. Individualism, an old but steady mainstay of capitalist ideology, gathered adversarial significance for Wilbur and many of his contemporaries. In the last two stanzas the political significance of the poem is made explicit:

> In a time of continual dry abdications
> And of damp complicities,
> They are fit to be taken for signs, these emblems
> Royally sane,
>
> Which have ridden to homeless wreck, and long revolved
> In the lathe of all the seas,
> But have saved in spite of it all their dense
> Ingenerate grain.

The liberal politics of 1948 were characterized by abdications and complicities, the dissolution of individual responsibility, which left the notion of exiled royalty an apt figure for rising above a base political milieu. But the figure of the individual lyric poet can serve the same function. Wilbur's poems on sparrows, toads, and driftwood express stubborn unwillingness to engage the large, public themes of one kind of major poetry – Robert Lowell's, for instance. Better the eccentricity of Dickinson, Hopkins, or Marianne Moore than the overreaching of Pound. Wilbur's resistance to his time is sometimes expressed as a taste for ceremony; in all his poems the display of craft proposes an implicit alternative to the junk economy and the bad art it fosters. Clarity and exactness instantiate alternatives to abdications and complicities. Wilbur's narrow range of subject matter is meant to facilitate clear, sharp perception, which is rare in imperial America. But clarity cuts both ways here. It is a painful self-discipline for a poet devoted to figurative language: "To a praiseful eye / Should it not be enough of fresh and strange / that trees grow green, and moles can course in clay, / And sparrows sweep the ceiling of our day?" It should be unnecessary to dress sparrows, moles, and trees in fanciful array. Yet at least once Wilbur realizes that his attraction to the "poignancy of all things clear" is less a devotion to plainness than an unwillingness to deal with the fluid, obscure world he actually inhabits. "Clearness," he wrote in 1950, is chimerical.

> This was the town of my mind's exacted vision
> Where truths fell from the bells like a jackpot of dimes,
> And the people's voices, carrying over the water,
> Sang in the ear as clear and sweet as birds.
>
> But this was Thule of the mind's worst vanity;
> Nor could I tell the burden of those clear chimes;
> And the fog fell, and the stainless voices faded;
> I had not understood their lovely words.

"The Mind-Reader" seems to me the fulfillment of Wilbur's work. This poem is inescapably about sympathetic perception, and imagining specificity. The speaker, like Wilbur, is a master of evocative description (ll. 4–10, e.g.). One great strength of the poem is the marvelous mixing of discursive language with detailed description, types and particulars.

> Some things are truly lost. Think of a sun-hat
> Laid for the moment on a parapet
> While three young women – one, perhaps, in mourning –
> Talk in the crenellate shade. A slight wind plucks
> And budges it; it scuffs to the edge and cartwheels
> Into a giant view of some description:
> Haggard escarpments, if you like, plunge down
> Through mica shimmer to a moss of pines
> Amidst which, here or there, a half-seen river
> Lobs up a blink of light. The sun-hat falls,
> With what free flirts and stoops you can imagine,
> Down through that reeling vista or another,
> Unseen by any, even by you or me.
> It is as when a pipe-wrench, catapulted
> From the jounced back of a pick-up truck, dives headlong
> Into a bushy culvert; or a book
> Whose reader is asleep, garbling the story,
> Glides from beneath a steamer chair and yields
> Its flurried pages to the printless sea.

The Mind-Reader speaks as though specifics were easy, as though their glistening particularity could always be found, or invented. The power of these lines derives partly from the apparently casual weave of syntax over this blank-verse paragraph. But more striking still is the presentation of an imagination racked but in no way incapacitated by paradoxes. The references to generic scenes – "a giant view of some description," "that reeling vista or another" – suggest that the speaker is not truly engaged, as Wilbur always has been, by specificity. Those offhand phrases "if you like" and "you can imagine" imply that details are for the tastes of other people, not for him. Yet the truth is rather that specifics draw out his imagination with extraordinary effectiveness. That one young woman, "perhaps in mourning," is an imagined particular, whose life opens onto another untold story as soon as she appears in words. Hers would be, if he told it, a story of loss, confirming the deeper sense of the opening sentence, that not only sun-hats and wrenches but people too are lost to us. What makes the speaker so engaging as a character is his imaginative range, his fluency and his penetration. The range is right there in the diction: "the crenellate shade" and "Haggard escarpments" are phrases that live only in literary English, while "plucks" and "scuffs" and "lobs," like many other active verbs here, come easily to an American tongue (they are ballpark words). Sun-hats and pipe-wrenches, steamers and pick-up trucks are all part of the Mind-Reader's timeless imagination.

His style is a worldly approximation of omniscience: not that like God he knows everything, but that he is acquainted with books and people, the past and the present, the seen and the unseen, the remembered and the forgotten. The poem actually expresses that surplus of feeling, intuition, and knowledge that does not fit neatly into a secular rationality. What access have we to religious experience? The poetry of the Mind-Reader is Wilbur's reply. The Mind-Reader's words evoke Druids (ll. 39–41), Satanic worship (l. 71), astrology (ll. 72–3), Persian priests (l. 74), and the Delphic oracle (l. 87). His religious sensibility is jaded by knowledge and experience. Like a poet, he makes a living by thinking and speaking sympathetically (ll. 91–2). When this fails him, he fakes plausibilities so that others can experience an inexplicable community (ll. 119–20). His art rests on the belief that what we understand as profundity is the work of memory.

> What can be wiped from memory? Not the least
> Meanness, obscenity, humiliation,
> Terror which made you clench your eyes, or pulse
> Of happiness which quickened your despair. (ll. 60–3)

To be able to recall what others have forgotten brings only disillusion and weariness. The one further step he can imagine is a Christian God, "some huge attention . . . / Which suffers us and is inviolate." Only from that perspective can a "deflected sweetness" be heard in the rancor of the world (ll. 131–5). Without that step of faith that he cannot take, one has wine and the desire for oblivion.

This is a tremendously artful poem, but it is without vanity because its art is not worn proudly. The speaker wants to give up his art, which is 90% sympathy and 10% fraud, but 100% unimproving because of the smallness of people's desires. The charm of the character is that he is so self-aware. He knows the disappointments of an inquiring mind, and he accepts them, without pathos. He acknowledges how bogus his own art is, and yet maintains faith that everything is remembered. He is so capable of describing lost or imagined things – no difference for him – and yet dismissive of his art, without ambition to match his skill. The inexactness of our knowledge, the way that hypotheticals dominate our thinking, and yet the inextinguishable sense that maybe our experience is somehow systematic, coherent – these are some of the thematic contours of the poem, and they provide the sense that it is about not only the art of poetry but also the situation of the reluctantly secular modern intellectual.

❧

Whereas Olson and Ashbery gladly associated their work with that of John Cage, and other avant-gardists affiliated themselves with painting, music, or philosophy, most metrical poets of the 1950s and later have avoided large intellectual currents beyond poetry itself. Partly this is the result of Auden's and others' experience of Marxism in the 1930s. The savvy thing in the late 1940s and the 1950s was not to stake one's art on social, political, or intellectual schemes. Yet the work of poets like Merrill, Hecht, and Cassity does indeed open onto a broad intellectual range. Merrill, Hecht, Bowers, and others have deliberately resisted that attraction and produced poems that make no claim to an intellectual milieu. However, the allusiveness of this poetry does in fact gesture warmly toward, if not a set of ideas, a social institution, the modern university, where the books alluded to are taught to students. The great exception to this observation is Merrill's *The Changing Light at Sandover*, which does indeed try to bring verse and science together. Merrill is one of the few poets who have felt the force of Milosz's claim that poets need to write about science.

There were several motives behind the turn to metrical verse in the late 1940s and 1950s. One of these, however, has special meaning in terms of American political and economic history. One group of young poets drawn to metrical composition in the 1950s had a special interest in demonstrating facility, the ability to compose easily, fluently in metre. This was never the intention of Lowell, say, nor the effect of his early style. But poets such as James Merrill, Anthony Hecht, and John Hollander have attempted from the 1950s to the present to display their artfulness in terms of facility. As a result the border between light and serious verse has grown shadowy. Indeed the question of seriousness is of crucial importance to the recent work of the most celebrated of these poets, Merrill's *Changing Light at Sandover*. The genuine fluency of these poets, especially of Hecht and Merrill, has often meant that even their best poems seem padded.

But the question of facility has a particular significance in terms of the efforts of American poets to achieve international recognition. Auden, who was long recognized as being extraordinarily adroit at metrical composition, came to America in 1939 and became a particularly influential figure for young poets. He edited the Yale Younger Poets series, which published the first volumes of Hollander, Ashbery, Merwin, and others. Auden's career was a model to young poets: the genuinely talented poet can compose verse about anything whatsoever. Indeed, metered verse is easier than prose, and so forth. Free-verse poets are often mocked for a naive esteem for authenticity in art, but young poets following in Auden's mould sought authentication for themselves as "gifted" writers by demonstrating facility in metrical composition. Furthermore, their writing was understood to stand as evidence of the artfulness of American culture generally at a time when its cultural credentials were under scrutiny in Europe among intellectuals who felt the weight of the postwar American military and economic presence. (American culture remains indistinguishable from vulgarity for many Europeans.) In poetry as in painting, poets centered in New York in the 1950s were demonstrating the viability of the American push, as Olson called it. Meter was the outward sign of that ambition.

The antithesis of the fluent metrical style of Merrill, Hecht, Hollander, and Howard is the terse style of Winters, Cunningham, Bowers, and Cassity. As a young man in New Mexico and California, Winters wrote free-verse poems under the influence of Native-American models, the French *symbolistes,* and W. C. Williams. But in the late 1920s he renounced free verse, partly because of the decline he saw in his friend Hart Crane, and programatically fashioned a tight, insistently traditional, fiercely regular metrical style. In the last chapter of *Primitivism and Decadence* (1937) Winters develops an unusual but influential view of poetic convention. He claimed that the stylistic conventions of the past carry with them conventions of feeling. A poet in the twentieth century could invoke certain traditional attitudes and feelings by exercising the stylistic conventions of the appropriate style. This view was quite contrary to Eliot's widely adopted view that poets need to create a context for the feelings they wish to evoke. Winters held that poets and their readers may more economically agree that certain feelings correspond to particular stylistic devices. In the 1930s Winters wrote masterfully in the mode he developed: "Slow Pacific Sea Swell" and "A View of Pasadena from the Hills" are acknowledged masterpieces. After 1945 he wrote rather little verse, but his students at Stanford University took his poems as models and pushed this style in directions that broadened the range of metrical poetry from then until now.

For many years Cunningham was regarded as the one truly excellent

Wintersian poet. Although Cunningham is an excellent poet, this view was rather damaging, because he is so anomalous. Robert Pinsky has said that Cunningham wrote as though he lived in the sixteenth century. Cunningham's style invokes the ideas and values of sixteenth and seventeenth century England by means of his style. One of his great resources is the disparity between the antiquity of his style and the contemporaneity of his subject matter, as in "To What Strangers, What Welcome 6."

"The Aged Lover Discourses in the Flat Style" is a perfectly regular, strict Petrarchan sonnet.

> There are, perhaps, whom passion gives a grace,
> Who fuse and part as dancers on the stage,
> But that is not for me, not at my age,
> Not with my bony shoulders and fat face.

Cunningham's mastery lies in the play of the voice against the meter, and of course in the play of this old cynic's sentiments against the courtly discourse of Petrarchan lovers. Although the third and fourth lines scan perfectly as iambic pentameter, no ear hears them that way without a counterbeat. The last two feet of the third line register as trochees, and the counterpoint nicely catches the press of a dissenting personality. The presence of a governing intelligence, Cunningham's, is there in the meter and syntax. Where one might write: "yes, those," Cunningham has "perhaps." The pronoun itself is quietly elided, with only a hedging "perhaps" in its place. The dancer-lovers are more ghostly than a hypothesis. The fourth line gets the living flesh altogether convincingly, again against the meter. The self-deprecation there is just right to establish good humor alongside skepticism. His doubts are intellectual without any trace of sourness. His brief is for exact fairness, against the lure of the swoon. And this is expressed throughout by explicit statement and the implications of details of what he calls the flat style. For this lover, all can be divided equally, so that even caesurae fall, however awkwardly, in the middle of the third foot of lines 6, 12, and 13, leaving just five syllables on each side. Half a line for you, and half for me. For all the forceful regularity of Cunningham's poems, their formal properties are cleverly and finely expressive. The prosody, seeming repeatedly to stumble, gives its own teasing version of the aged lover's romantic avowals. This is what an equitable romance sounds like:

> To be so busy with their own desires
> Their loves may be as busy with their own,
> And not in union. (ll. 10–12)

Edgar Bowers, Charles Gullans, and others writing metrical poems with Winters' principles in mind were gloomy in comparison with Cunningham,

who for all the constraint of his style showed sufficient range in his poems to
be fully human.

In 1973 Edgar Bowers collected his poems in *Living Together,* and the
poignance of the last poem there is a measure of his success:

An Elegy: December, 1970

Almost four years, and, though I merely guess
What happened, I can feel the minutes' rush
Settle like snow upon the breathless bed –
And we who loved you, elsewhere, ignorant.
From my deck, in the sun, I watch boys ride
Complexities of wind and wet and wave:
Pale shadows, poised a moment on the light's
Archaic and divine indifference.

The poem is personal, intimate, even though no one – only a moment – is
named, but that is a small part of its appeal. More powerful is the collision of
an especially meaningful moment, such as the death of a loved one, and one's
merely normal ignorance of what is really happening to one moment by
moment. Still more striking is the way this collision is refused drama: the
surfers do not crash into the elements, they ride them out, for a short while.
They are boys. The sunlight that falls on Bowers on his California sundeck,
on the surfers, is the same that fell in Greece 2,500 years ago, as anyone
comparing the landscapes can appreciate. That warm California sun cares not
at all for the snowflakes falling in the east. Somehow, the poem suggests, life
is not more tragic but more stately for this indifference.

Bowers packs these eight lines with such gravity partly by means of the
dense blank verse, but still more by that of the diction, which rises surprisingly in line six to a level of analytical abstraction that is constantly Bowers's goal. The voice that lovingly stretches out "Complexities of wind and
wet and wave" is just the one that wants allegory always to emerge from
description. Bowers, even more than Cunningham, seemed especially in the
1950s to need abstraction, personification, and allegory, and in this he was
typical of his generation. Within his poems generally, a certain code is used
to express what is a deep disappointment with the life of the flesh. He seems
to speak with self-reproach of his own love life as "inconstant and perverse"
in "Clairvoyant." Mind and passion are the kernel terms of this code. And
for the minds of most people these poems show no particular respect; "The
mind of most of us," he has Haydn write to Constanze Mozart, "is trivial; /
The heart is moved too quickly and too much." Passion corrupts the mind.
Mozart was the rare exception in producing an art that brought thought and
the senses together in a dialectic: "the perfect note, emotional / And mental,
each the other one's reproach." The traditional emblem of accord between

mind and flesh is the Virgin Mary, "body took the image of the mind," who offers the unworldly counsel of chastity. Within this traditional mind-body dichotomy, Bowers can only pine for "the certain meaning in the end, // Which will abide when such as we are lost." The allegorical style that dominated his first two books, *The Form of Loss* (1956) and *The Astronomers* (1965), expresses the quest for "The perfect order trusted to the dead," who are beyond sexuality. Until the 1973 publication of #2 of the "New Poems," one could not have known with certainty that the 1950s allegorical mode for Bowers was a way of writing about homosexuality. The most successful of his allegorical poems is "In the Last Circle," a sonnet about someone described only abstractly who has become hatred and contempt. That this poem of disgust should be the realization of his allegorical mode indicates just how inhuman this style was for Bowers.

In 1990 he published a surprising new book of poems, *For Louis Pasteur,* in which many of his stylistic habits were reversed. If he yearned for abstraction before, now he relished concrete detail, even where it didn't lead to some dominating precept. Prosodically and otherwise, his earlier work was severely austere – the mastery of pruning. In the new book, though, the blank verse bears along many extra syllables. The first poem in the book, "Richard," ends with two lines of hexameter: The extra syllables eventually declare a new norm. Bowers has opened his poetry to the plenty of other people's lives.

> The space between his parents and his bed
> Seems a thick dull plastic, the San Diego
> Newspaper and the flowers they brought grey wax. (ll. 1–3)

With the prosodic irregularity of the second line (unimaginable in his earlier work) comes a kind of impressionistic imagery that is striking and new to his writing. Bowers has not exactly turned on his earlier style, as Lowell did in 1959; rather, he has broadened it dramatically.

> By their inaudible cries of helpless love
> Bewildered and annoyed, intent upon
> The cancer in his lung, he looks instead
> On time's cold hardening surface for the child
> Complicit with his fate. . . . (ll. 4–8)

The compactness of his earlier writing is here too: every adjective draws a sharp line, seriously modifying the sense of the statement, depicting with exactitude the feelings of these three characters. And the old abstractions are there too: love, time, fate, and (later) mortality. One difference is that this poem is rich in imagery that produces a plausible psychological perspective. Richard dreams of the camaraderie of sailors (ll. 8–20), the sanitary brightness of male society. That, not a family's bond, is life itself. Bowers's earlier efforts to produce someone else's perspective – "From J. Haydn to Constanze Mozart (1791)" and "From William Tyndale to John Frith" – are mere exercises in comparison with the poignance here. "Richard" and its more touching but less analytical sister poem, "Mary," are poems of sympathy, the exact counterparts to Bowers' successful poem of contempt, "In the Last Circle."

❦

But feelings of contempt, distaste, and disapproval do comprise an important part of the emotional range of the poets who learned their craft from Winters. Turner Cassity is the one poet of this group who has brought together the abstract standards of judgment that make these poets, when least successful, sound moralistic with the satirist's attachment to minute particulars. The result is a poetry that is indeed chilly and unforgiving.

The Strange Case of Dr. Jekyll and Dr. Jekyll

I drink no potion. To the Double life
I bring no goatish hint of the exotic,
Have no weight of guilt to offer; have,
For now, no chilling drive of the fanatic.

My fleshpots – give them credit for perception –
Know me as the slummer that I am,
As I know them for applied corruption.
What we are, to what we are we come,

And only too prepared to settle for it.
Commerce comforts, in these middle years,
Once one has learned the young do not abhor it.
Curious that hard cash and that sneers

Win out where youth and eagerness did not,
But wholeness in that age is antiseptic.
It is what one had instead of Hyde.
It also is the reason, not now cryptic,

That today I buy and do not plead.
Part capital, my cautious potion-sippers,
Wholly venture. There the surgeon's blade –
It cuts both ways – succeeds to Jack the Ripper's.

But one of the virtues of such a poem is the sharp analysis of human behavior. Jekyll presents himself frankly as a pederast who buys sexual favors – far from any term of endearment. Cassity has written that the lyrical emphasis of English and American poets has for two centuries narrowed the range of poetry dramatically; he has celebrated, of all poets, Kipling as a more attractive model than Yeats. This antilyricism – which oddly links Cassity with the Language Poets at one end of the spectrum and with the New Formalists at the other – leads to tough presentations of character, such as that of Dr. Jekyll, who goes a long way to avoid any hint of charisma. He artfully shuns the attractions of decadence in the first quatrain, and condescends unattractively to his prey. In the middle of the poem, though, this brittle character begins to crack, when he indirectly concedes that to imagine being abhored by his willing prey has troubled his composure in the past (l. 11). And looking back he recalls the rejection he suffered when, naively, he courted with eagerness instead of sneers and cash. Lines 11–17 do indeed produce pathos and draw on the resources of lyric, because one learns in the poem to measure Jekyll's ostensible coldness against the hardness (l. 13) and staginess (l. 14) of youth that everyone can remember. Yes, this surgeon's blade has cut both ways.

Cassity clearly enjoys being outrageous. His work shows the romance of reaction, or dissent. But he is not merely outrageous; his willful poems usually violate received ideas – as in "I the Swineherd," when he lists love along with greed as the swinish demons he has pursued through his life. But in the last quatrain of this short poem he states his reasons. Evidence and reasons govern his poetry, not just attitudes.

> The need
> Grows weaker, and who lived to wait,
> To guard, to hope to discipline
> Soon learns. He learns his trust was bait.
> It vanished, his vocation's gone.

The vocation of swineherd is gone for two reasons. One, the need for love and sexual gratification weakens with age; and, two, one learns with age that the belief that one can manage one's desires is false. The poem's grim truth is that one wastes one's life in the disgusting pursuit of love and sex. One can complain that this strong poem is harsh and inhumane, but one must concede that Cassity states his reasons for being cynical, and that they are considerable.

❦

Although there is no necessary connection between formal prosody and notions of political authority or control, analogies between the orders of syllables and of citizens have seduced poets since at least as early as Milton's note on the verse of *Paradise Lost.* Prosodic categories bear whatever meaning poets or readers decide to ascribe to them, and at times these ascriptions are explicitly political. In the 1960s, for example, iambic pentameter was commonly associated with authoritarian politics, though this careless equation must now be embarrassing to poets like Bly, Levertov, and Kinnell. Possibly in the next century poets will be free to use traditional prosodic tools without worrying about how analogically minded readers may construe this part of the craft of verse. Richard Wilbur recently remarked that political–prosodic analogies have little force now, yet actually the analogies have been revived and are being effectively enforced in ways that can only constrain the stylistic options of poets. In the early 1980s a group of young poets, enthusiastic about the resources of traditional prosody, began to link formal prosody with conservative political ideology. These were the New Formalists: in particular Robert Richman, Brad Leithauser, Timothy Steele, Dana Gioia, Herbert Morris, and Elizabeth Spires have been associated with this effort.

In September 1982 Hilton Kramer launched *The New Criterion* with an Arnoldian complaint that, as a direct consequence of the intellectual ascendancy of the Left since the 1960s, criticism degenerated into ideology or publicity. A disinterested criticism employing a "criterion of truth" was what his journal would try to provide. Joseph Epstein, who has become a regular contributor to the journal, followed the inaugural editorial with a piece that softened the tone of resentment:

> In its intellectual life, ours has been preponderantly a political age. By age I mean roughly the past twenty-five years or so; by political age I do not mean to imply that no interesting literary work has been done in that time, only that the chief issues, questions, and preoccupations have been political, not literary. Communism, the Cold War, the Third World, the kind of society America is or ought to be, these are among the subjects that have used up so much of the intellectual oxygen of the past quarter-century. Nothing in literature has been able to hold a candle to them.

Kramer has suggested consistently since 1982 that the political affiliations of academic critics, not political events themselves, have politicized the criticism of the arts to an unnecessary and unhealthy degree. Epstein rather thinks – and he is surely not alone in this – that, through no fault of its own, literature looks small next to the newspaper. But Epstein does believe that only a poetry capable of commanding the mnemonic resources of metrical verse could recover much of poetry's earlier readership and authority.

A number of the New Formalists have deliberately affiliated themselves with the neo-conservative political position of *The New Criterion,* and these writers have done more to politicize the criticism of poetry, especially of poetic style, than have any writers since the early 1970s. Only very rarely do the poems in the journal relate thematically to neo-conservatism; the political significance of the poetry is intended by the editors to lie almost exclusively in formal properties. Certainly not all poets writing in meter are underwriting the ideology of Norman Podhoretz, Hilton Kramer, and Joseph Epstein. The recent invigoration of metrical verse goes back at least as far as

Robert Pinsky's *An Explanation of America* (1979) and includes many poets whose political allegiances do not suit those of Hilton Kramer. Even those who publish poems in Kramer's journal do not all mean to lend authority to his political position. I asked Alan Shapiro if he thought about this affiliation when he published poems in the journal. "I thought," he said, "about the $75 the journal pays." (Later he disavowed the affiliation in a *Critical Inquiry* essay.) Nonetheless the poems in a politically committed journal do lend credence to that political commitment. Eliot once said that ideologies that produce great art earn credibility by virtue of that art. Especially among contemporaries, a political position that seems to be held by a number of artists often seems to represent that which is creative in our historical situation. The editors of *The New Criterion,* to their credit, attempt to cover the activities of contemporary poets, novelists, painters, sculptors, dramatists, and musicians. No journal of the Left or the Center has made a similar commitment. This commitment, though, stands as evidence of the ability of neo-conservatism to encompass the arts today. To the degree that a school of poetry can be identified with the neo-conservative ideology of *The New Criterion,* the artistic achievements of that school come to count for the fertility of the ideas and values espoused by neo-conservatives. The editors of *The New Criterion* understand this dimension of cultural politics perfectly. Samuel Lipman, the publisher and music critic of the journal, concludes an essay on the CBS takeover of the Steinway & Sons firm:

For the first one hundred twenty or so years of its existence, the Steinway piano was indubitable proof that a great artistic tool, itself rising to a kind of art, could be made under the conditions of American capitalist democracy. As long as there are people who are willing to make money by working hard to produce something, even artistic needs can be satisfied.

If pianos can be made to underwrite the authority of the economic and political status quo, poems surely can. Even writers whose implicit or explicit political commitments conflict with those of the editors of *The New Criterion* ultimately lend authority to neo-conservatism when they appear in the journal, because they count as (in fact, much needed) evidence of the tolerance and wide-ranging vision of this tendentious journal.

Robert Richman, from 1982 until 1984 the business manager of *The New Criterion* and thereafter its poetry editor, has expressly argued that the New Formalists comprise "the most important group to have emerged in the last fifteen years." His publicity for metrical verse includes the claim that recent poets have confederated with one another in response to the feeling that the last decade or so comprises a special period: the 1980s were a "period of cultural transition," presumably from free to metrical verse, and from a Left-to a Right-affiliated literary culture. He conveys the sense that recent poets have crossed a historical juncture:

> It looks, in fact, as if American poetry in the Eighties has found its way back to the kind of high style and high seriousness that characterized its finest achievements thirty and forty years ago.

The Arnoldian phrase here implicitly places Richman's view of the poetry of his time in line with the broader Arnoldian remarks of Kramer and Epstein. Richman is explicit about wanting to resurrect the literary milieu of the 1950s when Eliot, Auden, and the New Critics presided over the discussion of poetry in the quarterlies – and poetry, rather than literary theory, was the common currency of literary discourse.

The desire to recover an illustrious past is an important and attractive part of the New Formalist position. Hecht, Merrill, and Wilbur "had the good fortune," Leithauser has written, "to begin their careers during the Forties and Fifties, when an orthodoxy of formal verse obtained." In his first contribution to *The New Criterion,* however, Richman claimed extravagantly that Edward Thomas was the most significant poet in English poetry between 1910 and the early 1920s – in the time, that is, when Hardy's *Poems 1912–1913* and Yeats's *Responsibilities* (1914) were written, to say nothing of the work of the Americans Eliot, Pound, Stevens, Williams, and Moore. The particular literary history Richman elaborates was strangely eccentric, though now others have adopted it. His admiration of Thomas is based on two features of this wonderful poet's work: 1) that Thomas, like (and before) Frost, sought a style that imitated speech in syntax and idiom; 2) that Thomas was untouched by the modernist propensity toward irony after World War I. The second issue is what motivates this eccentric historical argument: Richman means that Thomas is outside what he calls the "sentimentality of 'opposition.' " Thomas, that is, like other Georgians, was a patriotic Briton, whereas Richman's contemporaries are kept from expressing approval of their own nation by a too little considered (hence sentimental) commitment to opposing the national consensus. When Richman says that Thomas is part of "the tradition of 'disinterested' lyrics," he directly invokes not only Arnold but, more pointedly, Kramer's use of Arnold's term in the inaugural editorial of the journal. Kramer's claim was "that capitalism, for all its many flaws, has proved to be the greatest safeguard of democratic institutions and the best guarantee of intellectual and artistic freedom . . . that the modern world has given us." This is a view that the corrosive irony of modernist writing does not uphold; getting beyond irony enables this sort of patriotic affirmation. Of course one wants to agree with Stanislaw Baranczak and Milosz that the prospect of "poetry as a possible source of hope" is central to the office of the art, but complacency is no sound basis for hope. Poets are praised in *The New Criterion* for modesty and restraint, as though not to express vehemence were itself a sign of greatness. Bishop's art is magnificent, in Bruce Bawer's judgment, because "it knows its place, which is [sic] not out to shake things up but, with the utmost care and delicacy, to discern and depict things as they are, if only for a moment in time."

Part of what Richman, along with other critics of very different tastes, including Turner Cassity and Marjorie Perloff, denigrates is the "extremes of subjectivity and introspection" in poetry since 1959 especially. According to the literary history constructed by various critics in the journal, Edward Thomas and Robert Frost are the poets of the modernist era whose work still lives, because they 1) reconciled metrical forms and spoken idioms, 2) presented modest expectations of what poetry might achieve, 3) wrote about subjects other than themselves, and 4) did not denounce the political and cultural status quo. Eliot is inexplicably understood to be on the side of metricality, though he wrote mostly free verse. Williams is rather the ultimate "father of this rebellion against formal verse." Although Lowell, Berryman, and Plath are seldom named, "confessionalism" is frequently cited as the literary sign of the corrupt culture of the 1960s, against which the New Formalists propose indirectness of statement, which is meant to tease the reader coyly. Allen Ginsberg is the poet whose work shows best the failures of subjective and of oppositional poetry, though Bly too is understood to offer only "the same old solipsism." Bruce Bawer argues that Ginsberg is mindlessly "just *against, against, against,* and holds him personally responsible for making drug use fashionable among the educated young. "It was in the Sixties," Hilton Kramer argues (as Trilling had), "that modernism first established its authority as a mainstream culture." Richman praises Gioia for exerting "an especial effort to end things on an optimistic note." One antidote to subjectivity is the public, historical, plain-style verse of writers like James Fenton, but Richman believes that this path, despite the authority of Auden's precedent, leads to a selling short of the poet's job of looking beyond the certainties and known quantities of political discourse – to journalism instead of poetry.

There is a facile cynicism expressed frequently by publicists for the New Formalism, and this has impeded a refined account of the advantages of metrical verse. Bruce Bawer begins an essay on Guy Davenport, an experimental writer of Rightist affiliations – an exception, that is, as Bawer sees it – with this observation:

> It's hard, these days, not to be suspicious of experimental writing. So much of it seems to be produced by ego-happy no-talents whose main reasons for writing in an unorthodox manner are that (a) they are incapable of writing in the usual way, and (b) they know that it is a great deal easier to attract attention in some critical quarters by being different than by being good.

It is not difficult to show that much of the writing designated by large categories like "experimental writing" or the "New Formalists" is undistinguished. A critical assessment of experimental or formalist poetry must engage only some fraction of the writing of the very best poets of these groups. Bawer and Richman, however, like Joseph Epstein and Hilton Kramer, let sarcasm do the work of argument; they present themselves as intelligent men who have grown impatient with the crowd of fools surrounding them, and more generally with "these days." The National Endowment for the Arts, or any academic conference – these are the sorts of foes against which the *New Criterion* tilts its weapons. Genuine exchange is ruled out in advance by this sort of polemic: positions are not modified in the face of an adversary's argument, but are merely repeated. Sarcasm is blunt, and literary criticism excels insofar as it identifies closely discriminations among different kinds of writing. Manifestos are of course not expected to be anything other than blunt, but even the longer essays on behalf of poets who are admired by this group are disappointing as criticism. Brad Leithauser, for instance, praises the work of L. E. Sissman in terms that are unworthy of serious consideration:

His virtues are surely formidable: an enviably tenacious memory, a huge . . . vocabulary, a profound sympathy for the hapless and the victimized, a wizardry with wordplay, and a powerful, affecting nostalgia that manages to avoid turning sentimental and soft-edged through an almost astonishing conversancy with the hard world of things – the automobiles, the furniture, the paint. . . .

If Richman, Bawer, and Leithauser were engaged in debate with admirers of an antithetical sort of writing, they would have to refine their evaluative principles well beyond huge vocabulary, tenacious memory, conversancy with consumer items, and wizardry at wordplay. There are serious ways to praise poets for their diction, for their command of the past, for their sensitivity to the feel of the present, and for verbal artistry, but they entail complications that Leithauser seems not to have considered.

Leithauser and Timothy Steele are the two most distinguished poets who publish their work often in *The New Criterion*. Leithauser's first book, *Hundreds of Fireflies,* appeared in 1982 and instantly won him wide recognition. Many of the poems had already appeared in large-circulation magazines such as *The New Yorker, The New Republic,* and *The Atlantic Monthly.* Before his second book, *Cats of the Temple* (1986), appeared, he had received fellowships from the Ingram Merrill, the Guggenheim, and, most munificent of all, the MacArthur foundations. Timothy Steele published his first book, *Uncertainties and Rest,* in 1979 and his second, *Sapphics Against Anger,* which won three different awards, in 1986. Steele's impressive prose polemic against free

verse, *Missing Measures,* appeared in 1990. Of these two poets, Leithauser has
received far more acclaim, though Steele seems to me the stronger poet.

Leithauser is a very modest poet: he sticks largely to description, to nature
poetry. "The Return to a Cabin" goes beyond the prettier poems about insects
and animals for which he is now well known. Like Wilbur, one of his masters,
Leithauser constantly insists on the importance of the apparently slight:
moths, potatoes, shadows, and reflections. His work is the fulfillment of the
New Formalist rehabilitation of the Georgians, about whose taste for little-
ness Eliot joked. "One need only consider the Georgians," according to
Leithauser, "to see that an era's orthodox poetry may be durably lithe and
lively." Like Wilbur too, Leithauser draws a firm but complicated connection
between the fragile beauty of small things and the brutal violence that threatens urban Americans constantly. The last nine lines of "The Return to a
Cabin" are about the natural and routine suppression of fear. Solitude and
nightfall in the country catch and maybe tear "like a burr / in the chest."
Delicacy is always measured against its contrary, violence, and this is quite
unlike Leithauser's Georgian predecessors. In the title poem of his second
collection he admiringly describes tigers painted on a gold-leaf screen by a
Japanese artist who had never seen a tiger. The syntax, as is characteristic of
Leithauser, winds across line breaks and stanza ends as though, like webs,
they barely existed. Leithauser, like Marianne Moore, has a cool, light attitude toward prosodic form, as if its rules merely sustained a game one played
with the left hand, while the poet's real dexterity is devoted to fine description. He is an oddly exquisite formalist in that he treads like a city jogger
trying not to step on a crack; the requirements of iambic verse are met and
skirted in line after line. The music that results is seldom eloquent in the
sense of inspiring confidence. The many feminine endings and substitutions
express more than freedom within form: this is a poet whose music plays
against the prosodic format of English verse at the same time that it meets the
demands of formal verse. The resistance to the meter is a kind of vanity, a
refusal to be assimilated to formal verse without constant protest. "*A poem
should undergo just as much prosodic suffering,*" he has written, "*as does not actually
kill it.*" The vanity here is that prosodic counterpoint and variation are not
justified in terms of sense, but rather just in themselves, that is as display.
Musically the poems evade expectations and refuse the collaborative pact
between reader and writer that he especially treasures in formal verse, but
without a claim that refusal is principled.

Violence is one of the great subjects of formal verse, because metrical
regularity heightens the perception of destruction. The New Formalists deliberately work to reassert control over this particular subject. Fine, artful
description is intended to suspend the violence of life. "*All bloodshed is
forbidden / here. . . . / That's the hidden / message of these grounds*" repre-

sented on the Japanese screen. And this is quite like the poem, "The Steeple Jack," opening Moore's *Collected Poems:* "It could not be dangerous to be living in a town like this." Art is a preserve for Leithauser, where fine things are given time and space to display an alternative to destruction, and where dangerous things – tigers, deaths – are held in place.

There is a sonnet in his first book, "Old Hat," that seems to express misgivings about his stylistic range. This is an elegy written in the stanza of love poetry:

> It was like you, so considerate a man,
> to have your papers in order, to leave
> your belongings neat; while compelled to grieve,
> we were spared the hard, niggling tasks that can
> clutter and spoil grief.

By the time the word "neat" arrives, one is ready to reconsider just how earnest is the author's appreciation of this "considerate" man: These are not the terms of humane praise. But the words "clutter and spoil" make clear that the poet truly does treasure tidiness even where it may seem inappropriate. He aestheticizes death and grieving, so that he can remain unflappable. That is what this style is all about – maintaining composure in the face of . . . well, anything. Here a cap left on a hook as though the bereaved would go for yet another walk is what undermines that composure:

> What we want is to store such things outside
> The slow, spiraling loss of love and pain
> that turns you, day by day, into a stranger.

The strong formal close to the poem, the straightforward use of apt figures and the eloquence they can impart, is uncharacteristic of Leithauser and seems to come from a self-critical countercurrent in his work. This is a plainer, less decorative way of writing than is usual for him. My sense is that what turns the bereaved to a stranger is not just time but the tidy sensibility of Leithauser's poetry. Neither pain nor love gets through that neat manner.

Steele's ten-line poem "Wait," in heroic couplets, gives a good sense of the differences between his and Leithauser's approach to meter.

> Six beds in a square room: you give your name
> And sleep for days. Then the comeback – the shame,
> The Thorazine, and long walks in the sun
> As thought retreats from the oblivion
> It took on trust. And through it all, you sense
> Only your ruin and fatigue as dense
> As sleep. What happened? They won't answer you,
> But just solicit your submission to
> The judgment they'll "in due time" formulate.
> And till then? Get some rest. Be patient. Wait.

In a strict sense this poem is perfectly regular: exactly one hundred syllables that can be fit into an iambic grid. But the sound of the poem is altogether surprising, because the phrases pull against the meter in response to the sense of particular lines. The first six syllables, for instance, scan (abstractly, of course) as iambic: "Six BEDS in A square ROOM." But any reading voice would read the first two and last two syllables as more spondaic than iambic: "SIX BEDS in a SQUARE ROOM," which leave this opening clause with a boxed-off sound structure that tells the body in some sense how enclosure feels. That done, the rhythm and the meter come together for six lulled iambic syllables, only to part again in the second line: "THEN the COMEback –" with two feet that stunningly reverse the iambics of the previous six syllables. Obviously these trochaic syllables express in sound the surprise and the push of an effort at physical and psychological recovery. And the sense in which the last six syllables of the third line – "and long WALKS in the SUN" – lope toward a dactyllic rhythm that just as obviously suits the sense of walking. If all that one could find in the rhythms of poetry were imitative of the sense of its statements, the pleasure to be had from listening carefully would be pat and predictable. The ear, like the mind, wants all kinds of variety. In the first three lines here the caesurae, as I have suggested, divide the sound into units of four and six syllables. But with the seventh line that pattern is broken, when one pause comes after two syllables and then another in the middle of the third iambic foot. The three caesurae of the last line (all mid foot) produce three sets of three syllables and the final lonely syllable reiterating the title. One might construe this last caesura as somehow imitative of the sense of the poem, but the variousness of the pauses in the poem as a whole conveys a rhythm that often suits (and thereby emphasizes or dramatizes) the sense but sometimes just pleases as variety does. The appeal of variety itself is what Leithauser avows and displays, and that is one of Steele's resources too. But Steele gives a greater sense of seriousness to his poetry by using the sound structure to give appropriate bodily shape to the sense of his statements. Here in "Wait," the sounds that are not merely iambic seem in most, though not all, cases to be determined by Steele's commitment to finding the most expressive sounds he can for the statements he makes about a friend who has suffered from schizophrenia (the condition treated by Thorazine). I stress the poem's subject matter because exactly that is what gets stressed by the expressive rhythms of this short poem. Steele's skill as a versifier is plain to the ear, but the poem presses that skill into the service more of expression than of display – insofar as these two aspects of any art can be distinguished.

The subject of psychosis – exactly the passive suffering that Yeats, after Arnold, thought improper to poetry – has a particular bearing on the controversy about meter, because Lowell at the height of his fame in 1959 abandoned meter in order to write concretely and convincingly about his own psychotic episodes. This is the subject that famously defied meter. Unlike Lowell, Steele takes up the subject in the second, not the first person; Steele accepts the distanced perspective of an observer. Although the beds are numbered and the prescription named, the language here is impressively abstract. "Thought," "oblivion," and "trust" are engaged at their most generalized level, well beyond any particular thought or act of trust. "Shame," "ruins," and "fatigue" are somewhat less general, though still abstract, because they are attributed directly to the friend. Steele's poem can manage the weight of such abstractness (which in other poems by disciples of Winters – Steele studied with Cunningham – seems overly grave) because the experience of degradation is so evident here that what concreteness the poem offers is altogether enough.

The New Formalists have sought deliberately to reinvigorate narrative verse, but with only modest success. There is nothing inherently reactionary about metrical poetry, as I have said, but there is a special danger of apparent complacency in certain kinds of metrical composition. Vickram Seth is the one New Formalist who has enjoyed real popularity, and his verse novel, *The Golden Gate* (1986), illustrates my point. Bruce Bawer, in his review of Seth's book for *The New Criterion,* said quite rightly that "Seth . . . never takes anything too seriously, himself least of all; on the contrary, he pokes playful fun at nearly everything available – his poem, his hero, even the conventions of verse to which he is scrupulously conforming." The humor that is everywhere conveyed by Seth's jaunty prosodic form is altogether indulgent, smiling. What the poem advocates is liberality, flexibility, tolerance, capaciousness; these values are put over by the display of prosodic dexterity as much as by narrative.

The poet whose work has best illustrated the possibilities of story–poems, if not narrative verse, is Alan Shapiro, who has explicitly disavowed affiliation with the New Formalists. Shapiro's first book, *After the Digging* (1981), comprised of two sets of monologues by fictional characters, one who suffered a famine in Ireland and the other the persecution of dissenters in 17th century New England. Starvation, emigration, and witchhunts were his first subjects. He has understood that the stories that interest Americans now concern extreme adversity or cruelty. The great advantage of his work is that he scrutinizes these subjects so carefully that the grosser dimensions of his material slip from view as one considers the whys and wherefores behind extreme suffering. His work is a serious mix of sensationalism and subtlety.

The subtlety derives from his dissatisfaction with the apparent significance of stories of extreme suffering. The title poem of his third book, *Happy Hour*

(1987), is written from the perspective of the husband of an alcoholic who becomes aggressively uninhibited as she drinks. "My little prig, don't you want / to fuck me?" It would be easy enough to tell how alcoholics destroy their marriages and prey on their partners. In this poem, though, Shapiro focuses instead on the sober husband's cultivation of victimhood, greedy for the security that comes to one who knows he endures too much. Shapiro's objective, though, is not just to show that victims seek their tortures, but further to assert the bedrock of human nature that makes one want punishment. He reaches this level of generalization by means of humor above all: "All he can do is smile back / as though she's made a harmless / good-natured joke, and struggle / not to look around to see / who's heard, who's watching." That grim smile through the teeth is actually sort of funny, because one can so easily imagine one's way into the self-consciousness Shapiro depicts: the man is not endearing, but he is familiar, as his imagination of his wife's words is too ("and never could"). With that phrase Shapiro moves into the man's mind just as the man seems to move into his wife's mind. Those turns of argument are known to everyone, and for that reason, pleasing.

The humor I am highlighting is more powerful in "Extra," which begins wonderfully:

> The heart disease was worth it,
> like a gorgeous blouse, expensive
> but his favorite color,
> like the last word on the subject
> they've been arguing for twenty years.

The first line is hilarious, and like the others deeply wicked. "Extra," like "Happy Hour," assesses the costly pleasure of management. The wife's perspective here is insidious in details one can appreciate only on rereading. The adversative in the third line registers the husband's not the wife's thinking. For her, the beauty of the blouse is that it is expensive *and* his favorite color: he won't be able to rest comfortably in either his stinginess or the confirmation of his own taste. The blouse and the heart disease have the appeal of something extra, fulfillment beyond the normal exchange of daily injury. The professional sense of the word "extra" – someone, at the bottom of the acting profession and its payscale, whose appearance is filmed but whose speech is not recorded – focuses the sense in which the wife can make herself felt by her dull husband only through physical action, the heart attack, the self-inflicted exhaustion of her grocery shopping; what she says counts for very little with her husband, or with the poet who tells her story for her. Both husband and wife are extras in the sense that their East-Coast lives as American Jews do not fit the formulaic banality of the Americans in the west whose remarks like "It's been a long time since El / Paso" carry the authority of closure. Theirs are not the ways of bikinis and check-out stands. No, they are comfortable torturing each other inventively and living enviously outside what they imagine as "the rich / stunning heart" of life: Beverly Hills, say. Grim, yes, but their lives are funny, imaginative, and intense, which is way beyond the rutabagas of the postethnic, mass culture of Southern California. The imagination is in fact much richer, which is to say needier, than the imagined worlds of mass culture. What the poet in some sense affirms against the flat, secular tele-culture is the acuteness of the outsider: the wife constructs her own world, even her bleak marriage, unnecessarily cruelly, masochistically, but attentively. The power of the poem is borrowed from her. It is her imagination that ostensibly provides the most striking figures in the poem: the California apartment "was a Jerusalem of tastefulness, / making their old life back east / a shabby makeshift exile"; and "she could feel / . . . the yellow bruise on her hip / from the angiogram begin to ache / so much that she imagined it was / flashing to the check out girl . . . that she was old and sick." The difference in tone between these two passages marks a change of authorial viewpoint from amused irony to poignant sympathy, and this is the progress of the poem. But the difference between the kinds of figures in the two passages – traditional allusiveness and surrealistic subjectivity – indicates the complex range of this character's imagination. The achievement of Shapiro's poetry is the traditional one of extending understanding and sympathy beyond their normal bounds. In narrative poems such as "Extra" and "The Lesson" (1989), in which he conveys the pathetic boyishness of a child molester, the extension of sympathy is wide, plainly challenging, and in a sense obvious. In short lyrics, such as "The Host," he extends his understanding of the intricacies of his own motivation, which is penetrating and often painful.

❦

Poets have turned to meter for a number of different reasons since 1945. But most of the metrical poets have deliberately refused to exploit the most accessible ideas of contemporaneity. Against the sense that the war brought a historical rupture, these poets have displayed the possibilities of traditional, conventional poetic form and thereby insisted on continuity in literary history. This resistance to widespread claims about the special character of contemporary culture was not a resistance to contemporaneity itself, as Cassity's work makes perfectly clear. These poets take special pleasure (and give special pleasure) in engaging very contemporary subject matter with the traditional structures of poetry. This bifocal method is actually a refusal to surrender all judgment to exigency. Meters keep alive in poetry the idea of a standard or measure that survives historical change. They suggest another time and place from which the present can be scrutinized, judged, or simply ordered. They dramatize endurance. For poets of very different temperaments and commitments, the idea of a poetry from another time and place has been enormously attractive for a long time. Steele's "Golden Age" sounds like a translation of some Roman poem.

> Even in fortunate times,
> The nectar is spiked with woe.
> Gods are incorrigibly
> Capricious, and the needy
> Beg in Ninevah or sleep
> In paper-gusting plazas
> Of the New World's shopping malls.
>
> Meantime, the tyrant battens
> On conquest, while advisers,
> Angling for preferment, seek
> Expedient paths. Heartbroken,
> The faithful advocate looks
> Back on cities of the plain
> And trudges into exile.
>
> And if any era thrives,
> It's only because, somewhere,
> In a plane tree's shade, friends sketch
> The dust with theorems and proofs,
> Or because, instinctively,
> A man puts his arm around
> The shoulder of grief and walks
> It (for an hour or an age)
> Through all its tears and telling.

Here is the romance of reaction – literary, political, and intellectual. Metrical form and traditional diction ("cities of the plain") express the idea of the "faithful advocate" who speaks with the authority of enduring principles. This is of course a self-serving view of adversity and minority, which is why one can accurately speak of these poets exploiting reaction romantically.

4

꩜

AVANT-GARDES

CRITICS SPEAK OF avant-gardes, artists rarely do. Just who counts as avant- and who as rear guard is sternly contested by critics – and rightly so. The term avant-garde, which is widely abused in the promotion of everything from pullovers to poets, expresses a critic's dream of social and cultural opposition, of a progressive alternative culture, and a consumer's lust for novelty. By my count, four literary avant-garde scenes since 1945 have mattered to poetry: Black Mountain College (1950–56); Greenwich Village (1950–63); the Black Arts Movement (1962–70); and the Language poets of New York and San Francisco (1979–89). The definition I employ has four elements: 1) avant-gardists are motivated by a will to produce the dominant art of the future, not just by a desire to receive recognition of their own talent; 2) to this end, they form a public confederation of artists in different media, 3) who oppose the established conventions of a contemporary art community. Finally 4) an avant-garde has an explicit view of the relation between art and society.

The literary avant-garde of 1950–56 followed avant-garde movements in painting and in jazz, which by 1950 had already taken on their own shapes. The abstract expressionist painters of the mid- and late 1940s (Pollock, Rothko, deKooning, Hofmann, Kline, Motherwell and others) were recognized by poets as having produced an avant-garde painting, and the bebop jazz musicians of the same period (Charlie Parker, Thelonius Monk, Kenny Clarke, and Dizzy Gillespie) were even more often acknowledged by poets as forerunners. Poets in North Carolina, New York, and San Francisco, in that order, pushed the art of poetry in directions that had been indicated by work in these other arts. The literary avant-garde of the 1950s was a deliberate and late creation of admirers of painting and jazz.

What held avant-garde efforts in poetry, painting, and music together was the concept of performance, which entailed a radically nontraditional view of the literary text itself. From a historian's viewpoint, a performative aesthetic might well have come from the Italian Futurists, but in the 1950s they were seldom discussed. However, Artaud's Futurist hope for a "metaphysics drawn from a new use of gesture and voice" did get serious attention from

M. C. Richards and others at Black Mountain College and from Kenneth Rexroth in San Francisco. Yet the most famous statement of a performance aesthetic was Harold Rosenberg's 1952 essay on the action painters: "At a certain moment the canvas began to appear to one American painter after another as an arena in which to act – rather than as a space in which to reproduce, redesign, analyze or 'express' an object, actual or imagined. What was to go on the canvas was not a picture but an event." The canvas as an objet d'art was gone, and in its place stood the record of an artist's engagement with the materials of the art. "In this aesthetic," Duncan argued in connection with the painters and the poems of Olson, "conception cannot be abstracted from doing." A European contributor to *Origin* in 1955 wrote that "The surface of the painting is the arena of the action. . . . Painting, conceived thus as the friction of rhythmic figures upon the dedicated place, participates in the vivid world of theatre and dance." This notion of performance, which had been news in painting and jazz in the mid- and late 1940s, had crossed from Greenwich Village and Harlem and come back by the mid-1950s; it was a common term in discussions of poetry.

The field of the poem, according to Duncan and Olson, is analogous to the scene of Merce Cunningham's dance and the music of John Cage, fellow collaborators at Black Mountain College. This particular nexus of the arts was understood by poets as an alternative not just to the formalist aesthetics of the New Criticism, but just as surely to the emotional neo-Romanticism of Dylan Thomas, who from 1950 to 1953 enjoyed enormous popularity in America as a performer of his own verse. The French painter and poet René Laubies complained in *Origin* that "Certain abstracts today want to free themselves of all emotion. Conceived frigidly in some 'laboratory', they work endless variations on the triangle & circle. Such dryness will never be a *painting*." But what Olson wanted was in fact a very dry poetry derived not from the sympathetic emotions commonly addressed in love lyrics and elegies, but from the poet's thought and intellectual engagement, traditionally expressed in georgics and epistles, which surely have their own emotional range too, though it is more austere than that of neo-Romanticism.

In New York in the mid-1940s, but uptown from Greenwich Village, first in Harlem and then in 52nd Street, Parker, Monk, Gillespie, Clarke, Christian and others pushed improvisational techniques so far that the distinction between performer and composer, which had racial significance (since black performing artists had long been acknowledged, but not black composers), lost its edge. The beboppers produced a music that was less obviously melodic, which is to say that the grounds of collaboration between individual performers became harder to locate, calling into question the idea of musical collectivity that had brought financial success to the white dance bands of the 1930s and 1940s. In the mid-1940s jazz entered a period of intense individualism; the technical virtuosity of solo performers was everything. And this concentration on technique had obvious political significance, because very few white players could vie with the black musicians. The black musical avant-garde was aimed directly against the popular swing audiences that had made wealthy and famous the white imitators of Fletcher Henderson, Duke Ellington, and Count Basie. The beboppers hit their target: the poet Weldon Kees wrote in *Partisan Review* that bebop was "uniformly thin, at once dilapidated and overblown and exhibiting a poverty of thematic development and a richness of affectation, not only, apparently, intentional, but enormously self-satisfied." This critique of performance-oriented arts as affectation would later be routinely leveled against poets like Olson and Duncan.

Bebop is often discussed, with some justice, as the expression of powerful emotions deriving from racism and poverty. Some of Parker's work fits this characterization, but he delighted in just the contrary sort of music too: he lightened the emotive burden of romantic ballads by focusing his attention and that of his listeners on the formal pleasures of artistic invention and elaboration. His version of Gershwin's "Embraceable You" makes light of the romantically expressive dimensions of swing jazz. Familiar ballad melodies were ironically revised by beboppers so that they could be voiced only by a scat singer; Sinatra's romantic version of "These Foolish Things," for instance, is a joke after one has heard Monk's version. The distance from the human voice was a measure of their effort to eliminate the rhetorical appeal to romantic emotions. Parker's was largely an art of subtraction, of taking away from ballads their melancholy resonance and giving them instead the appeal of sweetly made art. In "Klaktovedsestene" one hears him dropping out the inessentials of the melody until only its skeleton remains, on which he reconstructs another music.

Olson was once asked about the poetic of the Black Mountain poets. "Boy, there was no poetic," he said. "It was Charlie Parker. Literally, it was Charlie Parker. He was the Bob Dylan of the Fifties." Creeley remembers that between 1946 and 1950 he himself did little else besides listening to bebop records. In the Preface to *All that Is Lovely in Men* (1955) he claimed that his own prosody was closer to Parker and Miles Davis than to any poet he could name. The austerity and lightening of Parker's music must have appealed to both Olson and Creeley. They were as appalled by Dylan Thomas's neo-Romantic popular appeal as were Philip Larkin, Donald Davie, Kingsley Amis, and other British poets. The postwar success of Robert Lowell showed that the expression of intensely felt emotions was what intellectual audiences, such as that of *Partisan Review*, wanted from poets too. Against this, Olson wrote in his 1950 manifesto "Projective Verse" that the goal was to eliminate the interference of the lyrical ego. The hopes of the 1950s American avant-garde were invested, after the example of bebop, in a technical revolution, in a new music, and this is curious because none of these avant-gardists was the equal in terms of technique of Lowell, Bishop, Merrill, or Wilbur. There was no parallel, that is, to the technical virtuosity of black jazz musicians, though literary polemics suggest how attractive the bebop approach to technique was. The technical orientation of the modernists' polemics and the bebop insistence on technique and not theme as the point of change assured that the Black Mountain poets would hold questions of technique foremost, and with often comical results, in their own polemics. The years 1950–6 did not produce innovations in verse writing at all comparable to those of the years between Pound's *Cathay* (1915) and Eliot's *Waste Land* (1922).

The bebop critique of the romantic appeal of ballads had a direct parallel in poetry. From Olson and Creeley to Ashbery and O'Hara and right up to the Language writers of the 1970s and 1980s, poets of the avant-garde have sustained a critique of the lyrical dimension of poetry. Olson and Creeley developed an intellectualist approach to poetry that circumvented the lyrical mode; Ashbery and O'Hara, like Monk, constantly joke about the kitschy emotional materials that they all exploit. Bruce Andrews, Charles Bernstein, and Ron Silliman have taken the lyric mode of the 1970s seriously but have written powerful critiques of the predictability of this recognizable rhetoric.

Other forces fueled the literary avant-garde of the 1950s, and its story cannot be understood only in terms of the efforts to imitate painters and jazz musicians. But the question of avant-garde originality has a special point in the postwar period. In 1909 the Italian Futurists were truly original. All avant-gardes thereafter have been haunted by the contradiction involved in the idea of a continuity or tradition of the avant-garde. In the postwar period, the avant-gardists of the 'teens and 'twenties were venerated as forgers of just such a tradition. Williams and Pound were most often revered in these terms, but a good deal of the editorial effort of the avant-garde magazines of the 1950s *Origin* and the *Black Mountain Review* was devoted to the uncovering of much more of this tradition. The aspiration toward a traditional avant-garde art (the sons of Ezra and Bill) involved another contradiction. The avant-garde of the 1950s was often insistently scholarly at the same time that it claimed to oppose the burgeoning academic literary culture of the time. The growth of universities in the 1950s was so great that the outsiders as well as the insiders were charmed by dreams of empire. The academy sometimes seemed an attractive alternative to the 1950s political context. Olson spoke of the need to show that the American push was not all coca-cola, but that some of it was scholarly research.

∻

Williams wrote in 1953: "We live in a new world, pregnant with tremendous possibility for enlightenment but sometimes, being old, I despair of it." This mix of feeling was characteristic of the early 1950s. Avant-gardes typically set themselves in utter opposition to the cultural status quo, and at the same time express burning enthusiasm for the possibility of fresh creation. Poets like Robert Creeley, Cid Corman, and Theodore Enslin strenuously held the familiar position that great art must convey a sense of its immediate context. The second issue of *Origin* closed with a quotation from a letter by Creeley: "I just don't understand that woman's logic [she isn't even named]: (listen) 'Until you realize that GREAT poets are never significantly contemporary . . .' THAT'S SHIT . . . THEY ARE THE LIVING FACT: DAMN YOU." The issue was obviously aesthetic: What aspirations to greatness might a contemporary poet sustain? But it was implicitly political too: What have been the consequences for poetry of the extension of the franchise in western politics and the spread of mass culture in the middle of the twentieth century?

Poets did not want to be confined to the cultural arena of middle-America during the McCarthy years. "I can live a twentieth century life," Enslin wrote, "without necessarily thinking of it in terms of TV or Joe McCarthy." The Black Mountain poets agreed with academic cultural critics that the sense of the present offered by the mass culture was paltry. In the universities irony and chagrin were conventional in discussing the relationship between the literary past and present. These were years when the degressive view of history that Eliot and Yeats had adopted dominated the academic literary culture. Among avant-gardists, however, this crippling view was resisted. In 1954 Lysander Kemp argued in the *Black Mountain Review* that Eliot had misrepresented the issue by unfairly contrasting the literary past with the historical present. By definition, the present actuality looks low when set next to artistic representations of the past; this is just a paraphrase of the traditional dichotomy of art and life, and not a statement about history at all. Most of an issue of *Origin* was devoted in 1953 to a translation of Artaud's *The Theatre and Its Double* in which the Futurist diatribe against masterpieces was revived:

We must have done with this idea of masterpieces reserved to a self styled elite and not understood by the masses. . . . Masterpieces of the past are good for the past: they are not good for us. We have the right to say what has been said and even what has not been said in a way which belongs to us, which is immediate, direct, corresponds to present ways of feeling, and everybody will understand.

Artaud's emphasis upon contemporaneity as a matter more of form than of subject matter suited the avant-gardists of the 1950s nicely. Williams often spoke as though the chief problem of a poet were to find a prosody "suitable to our time." Following Olson, he claimed that traditional metrical schemes were Euclidean: "nothing in our lives, at bottom, is ordered according to that measure; our social concepts, our schools, our very religious ideas, certainly our understanding of mathematics are greatly altered." For Williams, as for Artaud, the artist's problem is to find a form appropriate to the dominant features of the Zeitgeist. Artaud had said in 1938 that "agitation and unrest [are] characteristic of our epoch." In 1951 Creeley wrote that "poetry is, now, more able than prose, or more able to make itself an extension of the present context, this life, etc., . . . [and this has] first to do with the fact of its ability, (1) to compress, and (2) to project supposition, as fact." The contemporary situation that faced Creeley was large and uncertain; compression and hypothetical statements were the proper means for engaging it. Social strife was not the issue, as it had been in the late 1930s in Europe; rather the enormous growth of the state and the "changing immediacy," as Corman said, referring to the architectural, economic and political restructuring of America, were the features of the social reality that seemed to undermine the fixities of traditional poetic statement.

The characteristic gesture of avant-gardes is dismissal of the past – the burning of the library dreamt of in *Paterson* – in the name of urgent contemporaneity. The Holocaust offered the avant-garde a special sanction for this eradicating gesture, but that privilege was exercised rather cautiously. In 1949 Caresse Crosby, who two decades earlier had been Ezra Pound's publisher, printed a folder of five short poems by Olson and several drawings by Corrado Cagli, an Italian artist who had ridden into the death camps with Allied troops at the end of the Second World War. Cagli's sketches of that spectacle led Olson in 1947 to write "La Préface," which he placed first not only in the 1949 booklet, *Y & X*, but also four years later in his first book of poems, *In Cold Hell, In Thicket*. He meant this poem to dramatize the opening of his late-starting literary career. But his references to Odysseus, Osiris, Dante, and the Tarot make it plain that he was not starting from scratch: this was the debut of a self-declared second-generation avant-gardist. The allusions to Eliot's *Waste Land* and Pound's *Cantos* are gestures of deference, but also claims to authority. In late 1919 Pound and Eliot took a walking tour in the south of France. After they parted, Eliot went on to see the cave drawings at Dordogne – it was Picasso who went to Altamira. Eliot then returned to London to write "Tradition and the Individual Talent," claiming the importance of the best of western art from Magdalenian drawing to Yeats for young poets starting out from St. Louis or London. Three decades later something similar seemed right to Olson. He too wanted the broad canvas that the examples of Pound and Eliot occupied, though many of his contemporaries, like Richard Wilbur, had prudently drawn back from the bird's-eye view of modernism that landed in a cage in Pisa in 1945.

Buchenwald was a kind of Altamira for Olson's generation. After the death camps there was no good reason for poets to think and write within national boundaries. The Holocaust made one lesson of modernism inescapable: the world, like art, here and there, then and now, is one. Every postwar citizen is responsible for accepting or imagining a synthesis. Tarot, electronic circuitry, Blake, Southwell, Dante are equally relevant. After Buchenwald, distinctions between East and West, heterodox and orthodox no longer held for this enthusiast. Olson presents himself and Cagli, meeting in New York in May, 1940 without a common language, scraping signs in the earth, as new cavemen. The war had not so much made a clean sweep of the past – though in a sense it had done that – as it had provided a clear justification for the literary methods of the avant-gardists of the 'teens and 'twenties.

The postwar avant-garde was unlike any other in insisting on the value of distinct literary and artistic traditions. Seen narrowly, the poetic tradition was comprised of the examples of Pound, Williams, Stevens, Crane, and Whitman, in descending order of importance, all of whom – but above all Williams – were often discussed piously, and almost never anxiously. Duncan and Paul Blackburn frequently wrote poems about subjects (Artemis and Peire Vidal, for example) that derived directly from Pound. Corman and Rexroth did what they could by publishing translations of Artaud, who presented himself as a descendent of Marinetti, to establish a link to the continental avant-garde, but the Black Mountain writers, "La Préface" notwithstanding, were not particularly international. Many of Creeley's short poems are deliberate imitations of sixteenth and seventeenth century English lyrics, and Duncan's archaic diction alone was a way of flaunting the influence of the early Yeats and of English Romantic poetry, especially of Shelley. "I was, after all," Duncan has said, "to be a poet of many derivations." Whereas the continental avant-gardes had audaciously routed their predecessors, the American avant-gardists were priestly in their devotion to their American models, as though the continuation of a school of poetry had all along been the ambition of these writers.

As one would expect, the Black Mountain writers were severely critical of the burgeoning academic establishment of the 1950s. When Cid Corman was launching *Origin* in 1950 he was offered financial assistance from Brandeis University. Olson, who had given up on what had looked like a brilliant academic career in 1939, urged Corman to refuse the offer. This hostility toward the universities had several targets. First, and most generally, Olson claimed that the specialization of the modern university was itself compromising: "KNOWLEDGE either goes for the CENTER or it's inevitably a State Whore – which American and Western education generally is, has been, since its beginning." The modern historical scholar is represented in a short story opening the fifth issue of the *Black Mountain Review* as being forced "to produce, not educe. He has to win the next war in a hurry, or make a profit for a corporation, or conquer a disease, or do some god-damn thing or other in the service of his country." These avant-gardists, sitting in a tiny, financially imperilled alternative college in the hills of North Carolina – "the quintessential retired place," Olson said – were simply opposed to the technological, professionalized university of the postwar era. But under threat of losing the College, Olson proposed to the faculty of Black Mountain College that "a magazine might prove a more active advertisement for the nature and form of the College's program than the kind of announcements they had been depending upon." *The Little Review* and the *Nouvelle Revue Française* were the models Olson proposed of journals centered on a nucleus of writers. But there were academic models too for this literary advertisement: the contributors's notes look much like those of conventional academic journals, listing academic affiliation and recent publications: "A critical symposium on CHARLES OLSON'S work will appear sometime this coming year, as well as the second book of his long poem, *The Maximus Poems*. ROBERT HELLMAN is now teaching at Iowa and working on a novel." And Creeley deliberately departed from the model of *Origin* in including an "active, ranging critical section." The first half of the first issue was devoted to poems, stories, and reproductions of paintings and drawings, and the remaining half consisted of reviews and critical essays.

The Black Mountain writers complained that academics gave the touch of death to their subjects. "Try never to think of any field as a subject in a school curriculum," Bertram Lippman warned, "That's one of the slow horrors of our civilization." The surest proof of this view was what had become of the literary culture in the era of the professional university. Literary scholars, Olson said, "know nothing in not knowing how to . . . pass over to us the energy implicit in any high work of the past. . . ." "Literature," Martin Seymour-Smith said in 1954, "is an industry." What literary scholars produced under the rubric of criticism was an industrial product, and so too was most of the poetry published in the quarterlies favored by literary academics.

Nonetheless, as the format of the *Black Mountain Review* suggests, the avant-gardists were not altogether contemptful of the quarterlies and their poets. In 1938 Artaud had said: "The library at Alexandria can be burnt down," but he was ultimately an avant-gardist of another place and time. The Black Mountain writers were cagey and prudent about their academic rivals. The entire fifth issue of *Origin* was devoted to an interpretative essay on Stevens that would have been more at home in one of the academically affiliated quarterlies. In 1954 Corman published a long letter to John Crowe Ransom by Wade Donahoe, a regular contributor to *Origin*, that begins by praising Ransom and the *Kenyon Review*:

> You manage somehow to get successfully written poems – and even represent the range of new poetry well, with some lack of the Pound and Williams factions which perhaps produce poems too incomplete in themselves for the purposes of your review. Perhaps, also, there is some lack of continuing attention to modern French literature in your review.

Such fawning must have embarrassed Corman, Olson, and especially Duncan, whom Ransom refused to publish after Duncan publicly avowed homosexuality; yet Donahoe went on to articulate a critique of the typical Poem About Culture that Ransom published, and with the substance of the critique they would surely have agreed. One of his examples is an "excellent poem by Anthony Hecht" that "presents a progression of references to cultural objects, without, so it feels to me, much of a spiritual occasion. He doesn't connect with reality, doesn't mean what he says, doesn't believe it, except very distantly, slackly, and without sufficient action on the terms he encounters to warrant a reader's entering the world the poem makes." What the Black Mountain avant-gardists decried in established poetry was a lack of earnestness.

Poems published in the prestigious quarterlies seemed vain and predictably cool. This poetry, Louis Dudek wrote, "is a subject for self-display or self-analysis; at best, an ironic picture of the 'intellectual' in a hostile environment." The antidote Dudek called for was "words that teach," "conviction," "a guide to action," and a " 'criticism of life.' " The Arnoldian tag shows how conservatively the Black Mountain group imagined the function of poetry. Both Olson and Duncan idealized the life of learning. "It is appropriate," Duncan wrote, "that the concept of learning which becomes a Splendour – that is abstracted from all distinguishings – a luminosity – should be pictured above a concept of love between reader and writer, who know nothing of each other, a love which takes place in an imagined world, in a 'communication,' a rush of waters." Duncan wrote pedantic notes to his poems, and Olson tried to bully his readers with massive documentation of his scholarship. Theirs were profoundly academic sensibilities.

Compared to Richard Wilbur, James Merrill, W. S. Merwin, Lowell, and Berryman – the best of the poets favored in the quarterlies – Olson was crude. The tone of "La Préface" is extremely earnest; the young poets winning the awards and publishing in the literary quarterlies of the late 1940s and early 1950s sounded witty and urbane. Here instead was a poet with no apparent concern for the established taste of his time. The archaisms of the fourth and fifth lines are audacious and wooden. Olson's willful earnestness often left him sounding artless, ponderous, and easy to parody. But this was the natural consequence of the avant-garde critique of the poets who were then called academic. Disgusted by the wittiness of the poets influenced by Auden, the avant-gardists attempted to renovate the idea of didactic poetry.

Although Eliot once spoke of poetry as a "superior amusement," the painters, sculptors, musicians, dancers, and writers of the 'teens and 'twenties generally took art very seriously. The poet who began with the claim that 1910, the year of his birth, marked a new era was trying to bring that seriousness to a later generation of writers: "We are the new born . . . " But the generation born in the 1920s came to maturity with the belief that avant-garde ambitions ended in an insane asylum in the nation's capital. For Pound, as for Olson, the poet, like Kung, is a teacher. "Literature," Pound said, "is the art of getting meaning into words." In terms of technique, this meant, as Olson, in "I, Mencius, Pupil of the Master," said, that "no line must sleep, / that as the line goes so goes / the Nation!" However flawed "La Préface" is by Olson's pontificating tone, each line does carry the sense of the poem forward. Unlike Wilbur, Bishop, Lowell, and Merrill – all better craftsmen than Olson – he gives himself no room for the play of similes, metaphors, or epithets that commonly count as signs of poetic skill. Olson, Duncan, and later Dorn knew they were following Pound in turning away from verbal wit toward what Creeley called "the PLAY of a mind, that shows whether a mind is there at all." Pound's fascism effectively discredited avant-gardism in American poetry, though not for Olson and his colleagues at Black Mountain College.

The didactic poetic that emerged from the Black Mountain writers had two often contradictory aspects. On the one hand, poets agreed with Zukofsky (who was quoting Wittgenstein) that all adequate literature "must communicate a new sense with old words" – the exact reverse of the Popian formula. The example of Parker radically revising such worn melodies as "Cherokee" and "Embraceable You" made this point musically; to the bebop aesthetic, innovation was a matter of style, not theme. Edward Dahlberg, Olson's predecessor at the College, wrote of the poet as sage, but Olson claimed that wisdom was never anything so stable as a "new sense," but rather the expression of an engaged person in the moment of engagement. Wisdom for Olson was tied less to ideas than to acts and even performance.

Olson's poems mix rhetorical directness with an enigmatic generality. Many of his best poems, like "La Préface," are oratorical, Whitmanesque. It is American, to speak with a clear objective in view. The opening of "The Kingfishers" – "What does not change / is the will to change" – is a regular thesis statement no academic could miss. The directness of this approach to poetry must have seemed refreshing when the poem first appeared in 1950, for then the prevailing literary taste was tuned to the delicate obliqueness of Wilbur, Merrill and other young poets who were influenced by Stevens and Marianne Moore, as well as Auden. Although Olson took up the didactic office from Pound, whom he calls his "next of kin" in "The Kingfishers," the opening of the "The Kingfishers" alludes to Stevens's *Notes toward a Supreme Fiction*, and when Olson refers in "In Cold Hell" to "the necessary goddess," he must have meant to invoke Stevens's necessary angel. Stevens and Olson wrote poems given over more to thinking than feeling. Neither had a great deal to say of particular experiences or powerful emotions. The second line of the poem: "He woke, fully clothed, in his bed." Who is he? He is named Fernand, but he could as well be Crispin or Canon Aspirin – a cipher. There are other unidentified "he"s and "she"s throughout Olson's poetry – and even in this poem. Their identity matters less than what they say and what can be done with what they say. At the end of the poem one of them (actually Pound, in *Guide to Kulchur*) asserts: "I commit myself, and, / given my freedom, I'd be a cad / if I didn't." "Which is most true," Olson says: the truth or falsehood of a statement establishes its authority, not its source. Unlike Pound, Olson obscured most of his source, because his ideas, like those of Stevens, were more general than specific.

> To be in different states without a change
> is not a possibility
>
> We can be precise. The factors are
> in the animal and/or the machine the factors are
> communication and/or control, both involve
> the message. And what is the message? The message is
> a discrete or continuous sequence of measurable events
>   distributed in time
> is the birth of air, is
> the birth of water, is
> a state between
> birth and the beginning of
> another fetid nest
> is change.

These lines from "The Kingfishers" read like a radical condensation of several paragraphs of an essay. Olson wanted a truncated ratiocination in his poems, without whimsicality, facetiousness, or anything sufficiently artful to be called precious. The differences between Olson and Stevens, Creeley's two masters in the early 1950s, were many and great, but they both conceived of poems as tools for putting together and taking apart general ideas about what constitutes the life of the mind.

"The Kingfishers," "In Cold Hell, in Thicket," and "The Praises," like most of Olson's best work, are poems of knowing: they explain, even proselytize. But "The Kingfishers" is also a piece of guess work, and this is the contradictory and plainly performative aspect of Black Mountain didacticism: conjecturing, taking chances about what some monument, document, or story means. The E on the Delphic stone is a puzzle. "I thought of the E on the stone . . . I hunt among stones," Olson says, defining himself by these choices. "The Ring Of," "The Lordly and Isolate Satyrs," and "A Newly Discovered Homeric Hymn" seem antithetical to "The Kingfishers," "In Cold Hell," and "The Praises," because these imitations of traditional, anonymous poems explicitly deal with limits to knowledge. They are poems of deference. "Limits / are what any of us / are inside of," Maximus says. Here tradition provides clues; ingenuity and the record, literary or generic (in the case of "The Lordly"), set limits.

"The Ring Of" demonstrates a fresh way of speaking about the flight of love and beauty without pathos, with just curiosity, trying to figure out why love goes where it does. The one-time editor of *Poetry*, Daryl Hine, has translated the Homeric Hymn to Aphrodite in a way that makes Olson's characteristic motives clear. This passage from Hine's version shows what it meant to ignore the examples of Pound:

> . . . the Hours with their golden tiaras
> Welcomed her graciously, wrapping ambrosial garments about her
> Crowning her heavenly head with a beautiful, handsomely
>   fashioned
> Garland of gold; through the lobes of her ears, which were
>   pierced, they depended
> Flowers of copper alloy and of valuable gold, and around her
> Delicate neck and upon her silvery bosom.

Hine reproduces the spectacle of Aphrodite dripping gold, copper, silver, and "ambrosial garments." His verse is driven by a baroque desire to ornament; he takes time to mention that gold is valuable, and that Greek earrings required pierced ears, because he defers, as Olson does not, to the literal ancient text. Olson fairly skips over the carrying to the gods of this weighted-down Aphrodite in order to get to her response, and how it may be interpreted. The meaning, not the sight, is the issue. His Aphrodite may not look good enough to eat, as Hine's does, but Olson does make a point of saying that she was not made by patient labor, which may bear on why love is fleeting.

❦

Since Marinetti gave speeches to industrial workers in Milan, the avant-garde has been politically engaged, tendentious, whether on the right or the left.

In the 1950s, however, avant-gardists deliberately avoided explicitly political statements. The Black Mountain poets were in a sense drop-outs. Olson himself had left a career in Washington as political administrator to pursue research on Mayan glyphs and later to preside as rector of Black Mountain College. The Black Mountain poets were provocatively asocial, whereas poets like Pound and Eliot had become prolific social critics in the 1930s and 1940s. "The habit," Olson wrote of Pound, "to look to society to make it / new. / bah." "If I want sociology, economics, uplift, or metaphysics," Irving Layton wrote to Corman, ". . . I know my way around a library as well as the next man." Social critique had been degraded by modernist poets to right-wing propaganda, or by university professors to professional discourse. Although Olson's course at Black Mountain College "History: Present" included the televised McCarthy hearings, references to American politics and society were few in the pages of the avant-garde journals. Casual ironic remarks about McCarthy or Hiroshima pepper the pages of *Origin* and the *Black Mountain Review*, and the threat of nuclear war is constantly in the background but never analyzed. The socio–political scene was so dismal that they just left it alone. The Black Mountain writers successfully fabricated a sustaining intellectual and literary milieu less as a specific critique of American society of the 1950s than as a gesture of dismissal.

The engagement of the writers of the 1930s metamorphosed in the 1950s into a fight against science or general social forces, and this seemed to Creeley merely sentimental. A hard-boiled attitude was more attractive. The avant-garde prayer was not to fall for any political prospect: "O lord of my poverty / defend me from doing evil / Guard me from illusions of virtue in a high place." "In the present," Maximus says, "go / nor right nor left; / nor stay / in the middle." The left and the right were debased by the war, and the center by the fabrication of a pax Americana. According to Paul Blackburn, "To sing the democratic man today / or the marxist man, for that, / is no proposition. / So I sing goats." To the German poet Gottfried Benn, writing in *Origin*, the perversion of politics could seem new only to the naive – that is, to Americans: "Perverted when? Today? After ten years? . . . (a century?)" American poets felt that special disappointment that comes to those who expect from political events something well beyond politics as usual.

This suppression of political allegiance is a sign of a powerful longing for political effect among avant-gardists, but it was a longing that would not come to any fulfilling affiliation; the white avant-gardes of the 1950s remained beyond practical politics. Olson especially tended to allude to the political significance of this or that, as though a political interpretation of culture were some bottom line: "There are reasons, political reasons that . . ." But what followed from remarks like these was never altogether clear. "Polis" in his usage was a utopian term, and its contrary, "pejorocracy," was even blunter than Pound's usura. Actual politics seemed beyond the reach of these writers partly because political events were themselves operatic, more histrionic than literature; the rhetorical devices of literature could do nothing to heighten this subject. American politics of the 1950s was populated by characters so stock as to seem parodic, or so venial as to be less than real. "The choice," Louis Dudek wrote, "is not between a McCarthy and a Marx, or the Church and TV. One might try to be honest and straight-thinking, in the Greek way, for example, outside the log-jam of inherited stupidities." Polis. That was the brave hope of the Black Mountain writers: to withdraw so far from the political center that one's political independence and acuteness would be uncompromised by a debased milieu. And Olson urged them to take heart from the example of Mao's 1949 success; withdrawal can be strategic.

In "The Desert Music," published in *Origin* in 1952, Williams wrote these undistinguished but revealing lines:

> But what's THAT?
> the music! the
> *music*! as when Casals struck
> and held a deep cello tone across Franco's
> lying chatter! and I am speechless.

That figure of art holding its power aloof from political mendacity goes a long way toward explaining the political attitude of the avant-garde of the 1950s. The lack of topicality in their writing is striking, because one expects avant-gardists to be interventionist, after the examples of the Futurists, the Berlin Dadaists, and the Surrealists, but also because in the 1960s several of them – Robert Duncan, Denise Levertov, and Edward Dorn – would show that they were in fact engaged by political issues. The New Critics in their academic phase are often chastised for having insisted on the autonomy of art, against the call for an art engagé. However, the Black Mountain poets saw good political reasons for insisting on the distance between art and politics – for staying "out in the cold," as Olson put it. A poet "makes himself of USE to society" by registering in language, not in political acts, "his own resistance." Exactly because poets, unlike architects, dramatists, and composers, do not require capital for their art, they are able, as Williams told Creeley, to "escape the perversions which flourish elsewhere."

"We live in the heyday of the liar," Dahlberg wrote. "There is . . . not . . . one who sighs for candor who is not Iago. The only way to return to wisdom, to Plato, Aristotle, Solon, Erasmus, Linnaeus is to expunge from the lexicon the words honest, genius, art, and beauty." This reaction against the abuses of ideology was so powerful that throughout the 1950s and 1960s one poet after another wrote about this stripping away of the intellectual vocabulary. This impulse was expressed positively as a desire to penetrate to some undeniable immediacy, to what Derrida speaks of as the illusion of presence. The attraction of ostensibly certain knowledge is, as Richard Rorty says, that it removes the heavy burden of making political choices. From the question, What must be done? poets felt driven back to the logically prior question, What can be known?

The lure of an epistemological closure attracted Wilbur, Oppen, and other poets from diverse camps, but it had particular importance for the Black Mountain performative poetic, because a poem spoken by a human voice, especially that of the composer, was regarded with a special piety. At just the moment when literature in America was becoming the responsibility almost exclusively of teachers and professors, training young people for a service economy, these poets spoke out for poetry unmediated by social institutions, unobscured by false ideas about it. Like their predecessors the Objectivists, they held to philosophical nominalism, though one motivated less by philo-sophical argument than by a reaction to the professionalization of intellectual life and to the ideological strife of the late 1930s and the war years. Dahlberg's phrase "the heyday of the liar" refers to the disappointment felt by intellectuals in 1939, when the Soviets seemed to betray the Popular Front, and later when American liberal ideologues attempted to formulate terms – wholly uncon-vincing, Olson thought – for the motivation of western democracies.

Young writers after 1945 commonly felt that ideas, along with ideologies, had been drained of meaning by the war. In 1954 Thomas F. Williams pub-lished a short story called "Pictures" in *Origin*. The narrator – protagonist says that he suffers from having in his head a "cold memory that photographed a series of hard, moodless pictures, and this memory that I could not control shifted whimsically from one detached scene to another." Then he realizes the cause of his nominalistic limitations:

When I first went overseas my mind was controlled by a single strong belief. I was very young then, and in the intensity of my ignorance, I could not keep this big belief from pushing out most of the smaller beliefs. It was the kind of belief that soaks and overflows the brain, so whatever was not pushed out was flooded with the main belief.

Then, with the necessity for seeing a little more clearly or differently came small doubts in large swarms to perforate the fullness that the belief gave me. Finally, the belief was drained away and what caused the real trouble was that most of the small beliefs were drained away with it.

During the war, this sailor loses confidence in the ideology with which he grew up, because he is compelled to see more clearly than he was accustomed to doing. He is left with only clear but meaningless pictures. "It's not pleasant," Creeley says, "doubting your own knowing, since that seems all you have. If you lose that, or take it as somehow wrong, the whole thing goes to pieces." Ideological agnosticism was the experience of Creeley's generation, but it was seldom discussed in political terms. It was common instead to invoke, as William Bronk did, the abstract, apparently nonpolitical meditative mode of Stevens for this subject.

> How good to know.
> So good if we could part with circumstance
> because we know what something finally is,
> and go, go somewhere, follow to the end,
> for facts would never turn upon themselves
> or vanish in the middle of the air,
> but lead from known to known, and hold the whole
> burden of the world without a loss, without
> this fragmentation, this weak chaos.

The wish to move above circumstances to principles is unfulfilled, and Bronk, like many of his contemporaries, felt stranded with only fragments of his sensual experience where he would have had instead some systematic and certain knowledge. The ideological agnosticism that resulted was different from the enthusiastic liberal claim of Daniel Bell and Arthur M. Schlesinger, Jr. that America had moved beyond ideologies, but the possibility of an alternative political allegiance was effectively frustrated by this malaise.

Many of Bronk's and Creeley's contemporaries resolved their agnosticism by affirming knowledge derived from the senses. The example of the Imagists took on fresh significance in the early 1950s. Herbert Read said in response to Dahlberg's remark about the heyday of the liar:

But truth, too, is a word to expunge from the lexicon, for it is in the name of truth that the biggest crimes are now committed. That is why I think it is better to insist on the image, on the icon, on the vision that has not yet been smeared with unctuous morality.

The poet's job, he claimed, is to cleanse the eyes of the tribe and thereby its dialect. A clean language would be altogether without terms for metaphysical understanding and value, which would mean that they would remain always implicit and out of critical scrutiny. "The big words?" Irving Layton asked, "I'd rather find lips / Shaping themselves in the rough wood." The master of this poetry of the eyes was neither Stevens nor Pound, but Louis Zukofsky, who as a fellow-traveler of the CPUSA had gone through the ideological wars of the 1930s and managed, unlike George Oppen, to continue writing by narrowing his subject matter toward his own sense experience and his relationship with his wife and son.

❦

Robert Duncan's *The Opening of the Field* (1960), Olson's *In Cold Hell, In Thicket* (1953), *The Maximus Poems* (1960), and Robert Creeley's *For Love* (1963) are the four major achievements of the Black Mountain group, which all emerged from the collaboration of these writers with colleagues and students at the College or with others through the two journals *Origin* and *Black Mountain Review* from 1950–7. Once Donald Allen's anthology, *The New American Poetry* (1960), was published, the poetic avant-garde of the 1950s began to receive a kind of national attention that did not help their writing. Olson's work declined dramatically, but even Creeley and Duncan, who did not settle into the role of guru, never again produced books so stunning as those of the 1950s. After 1960 this avant-garde became obsessed with the story of itself. In retrospect Duncan is the one hardest to see as a typical character in that story.

He has said that poetry properly evokes awe with excited language. He was alone among his collaborators in writing poems that are visionary, dream oriented, and lush in a late-nineteenth-century sense. "This Place Rumord to Have Been Sodom," for example, begins in a thoughtful, modest, and hesitating fashion: "might have been" is the first line, completing the syntax initiated in the title. By the end of the first strophe he has talked himself out of a pensive tourist mode and into a biblical voice. The mock-sestina format allows him, altogether decorously, to work himself up to a tone of excitement, as he repeats the closing line of the first strophe:

> It was measured by the Lord and found wanting,
> destroyed by the angels that inhabit longing.
> Surely this is Great Sodom where such cries
> as if men were birds flying up from the swamp
> ring in our ears, where such fears that were once
> desires walk, almost spectacular,
> stalking the desolate circles, red-eyed.

Duncan once praised Olson's craft as far superior to his own, which is preposterous. Duncan is the only poet of his generation who has clearly succeeded in writing an incantatory verse that evokes Pound's visionary Cantos (Canto XVII, for example) without embarrassment. He is no master of formal verse, though a number of his poems, such as "This Place Rumord to Have Been Sodom," are free-verse approximations (and therefore vague) of the architectonic possibilities of conventional metrical forms, as if Duncan wished for the resources of Merrill, Wilbur, or Lowell. Duncan's ear was tuned instead to the possibilities of rich, emphatic free-verse rhythms. In these lines ghosts of iambs and anapests alternate irregularly until the strophe closes with a quasi-spondee. The music is not subtle, but it is effective in evoking "that state of perhaps real trance," as Yeats said, of perception and meditation. In this musical atmosphere he is able to suggest calmly that angels are destroyers, that desires become fears, that longing is a curse.

This music expresses the pathos of desire. The mystery is that the Sodomites gathered together in spirit, that they indulged extremes of desire out of spiritual hunger Duncan associates first with Judaism and then with Christianity, and that the hand of the Lord "named at last Love" destroyed them, though their images survive. Desire leads tragically to excess and even to violation, longing for the calm of fulfillment. "Men fuck men by audacity," he wrote in an early poem, "Yet here the heart bounds / as if only here, / here it might rest." The hand of the Lord likewise moves mysteriously, destroying those "found wanting" while holding them also "blessed." Love and destruction, observance and violation are entwined in ways that Duncan, without explaining, evokes with the sad music and intertwined images of the poem. "This Place Rumord to Have Been Sodom" is a characteristic Duncan poem, well beyond the range of either Olson or Creeley, who with discursive rather than imagistic diction push constantly toward what can be understood intellectually.

Politically, this is an audacious poem in that Duncan associates the historical Sodomites with contemporary Zionists. When he says that "The devout have laid out gardens in the desert," he invokes a standard self-representation of the modern state of Israel. Those he refers to as "The devout" (l. 17), "the faithful" (l. 21), and "these new friends" (l. 27) are at once homosexuals and contemporary Israelis. Gays and Zionists are here entrapped by the pathos of desire just as firmly as the historical Sodomites were. Duncan's feeling toward these new friends are ambivalent. On the one hand, they seem degenerated from men who once lusted; the new friends instead are listless (l. 24). On the other hand, he has referred to himself elsewhere as a Sodomite in the straight-forward sense of male homosexual, and the language of the last strophe is given over entirely to the pathos of the damned. The aspirations of the damned, their "images and loves," survive in the image of the crucified God. Duncan's refusal here to see the nation-building political desires of contemporary Israelis as distinct in kind from the extreme desires of male homosexuals fits well with the integrationist argument that he courageously made in "The Homosexual in Society" in *Politics* in 1944; the homosexual artist who narrows his concerns to "the *camp*, a tone and a vocabulary that is loaded with contempt for the human," surrenders a range of subject and feeling that a great artist needs. "The Zionists of homosexuality," he wrote in 1944, "have laid claim to a Palestine of their own, asserting in their miseries their nationality." The vision of this poem, as Thom Gunn says, "is larger than one of mere sexuality, though including it."

The most impressive poem in Duncan's 1960 volume is surely "A Poem Beginning with a Line from Pindar," and perhaps this is the single best poem to come out of the Black Mountain group during the 1950s. The line that starts the poem – *The light foot hears you and the brightness begins* – is a mish mash of Pindar's words that makes no plausible sense in English. Reading Pindar late at night, Duncan reports, his

mind lost the hold of Pindar's sense and was faced with certain puns, so that the words *light, foot, hears, you, brightness, begins* moved in a world beyond my reading, these were no longer words alone but also powers in a theogony, having resonances in Hesiodic and Orphic cosmogonies where the foot that moves in the dance of the poem appears as the pulse of measures in first things."

Duncan has said that it is important for him to attend "responsibly" to his errors, because just there he may be able to get beyond his own ambition to master his materials. There the poem may begin to tell him more than he knows. And it does. Human feet do not hear anything (though they may be said to obey a lyre – *höeren* and *horchen* catch the pun for a German translator), but presumably a god treads with a fuller sensitivity to the presence of mortals: "god-step at the margins of thought, / quick adulterous tread at the heart." Error is a violation of normalcy, or human orders, as are gods, and adultery too. These are some of the first thoughts generated by a misreading of Pindar, before the sight of Goya's "Cupid and Psyche" (which he once saw at a museum in Barcelona) returns to him,

like a wave, carrying the vision . . . the living vision, Cupid and Psyche, were there; then, the power of a third master, not a master of poetry or of picture but of story telling, the power of Lucius Apuleius was there too. . . . I stood in the very presence of the story of Cupid and Psyche – but, in the power of those first Words – Light, Foot, Hears, You, Brightness, Begins – He was the primal Eros, and she, the First Soul.

Duncan's description of the painting is erotic in a Preraphaelite manner, with tingling fingertips and nipples, throughout the poem's first section, except that he ranges easily from fascination with seductive descriptive language to difficult, close abstract phrases that define the meaning of the scene: "the deprivations of desiring sight" (l. 15) and "a sorrow previous to their impatience" (l. 20). This latter is the analytical, discursive manner of writing that Olson and Creeley developed against the grain of the 1950s.

The magical evocation of the first soul and primal eros gives way, in the second section, to consideration of subsequent souls. "In time," Duncan says, "we see a tragedy, a loss of beauty / the glittering youth / of the god retains [remains?] – but from this threshold / it is age / that is beautiful." Pindar, Goya, and Apuleius display the charm of the antique and remote. Their art does not fit the postwar American affluence and banality, and exactly that is its power: it errs in the sense of wandering away from contemporary American normalcy. In 1951 and 1952 W. C. Williams suffered strokes which left his handwriting impaired and his spelling erratic. Duncan plays with Williams's misspellings until he had [blood]clot/clod/[hydrogen]cloud invading the poet's brain, as a clot had recently moved into then President Eisenhower's brain. American presidents from Eisenhower back to Johnson, the successor to Whitman's Lincoln, are described as "idiots fumbling at the bride's door": for their errors Duncan shows no curiosity or compassion. Pindar is the source of a genre of political poetry that has disappeared from western democracies: the praise poem. American history is represented as "great scars of wrong" across which Duncan reaches "toward the song of kindred men" – Williams, Whitman, Lincoln, and in section three Ezra Pound at Pisa. Duncan, unlike Olson and Creeley, was a direct descendent of the modernist political notion that the State itself was an evil. He stood on the other side of liberal politics and regarded the politics of his own time from such a distance that his distinctions could only be wholesale. Olson was an advocate of the expansion of the modern state along the lines of the New Deal, but Duncan regarded FDR, Olson's hero, as the originator of the "Permanent War Economy." "I saw the State and the [Second World] War," he said, "as diseases, eternal enemies of man's universal humanity and of the individual volition." Like Pound, Wyndham Lewis, and the writers gathered around *The Egoist* in the years before the First World War, Duncan's opposition to the interventionist politics of liberalism bordered on libertarian anarchism. In section 2 Lincoln is the only admirable American president, and he is represented elegiacly. The following section presents another elegiac hero, Ezra Pound incarcerated for treason in Pisa. The extraordinary thing here is that Duncan condemns FDR along with Harding, as though they were somehow birds of the same feather, and then writes elegiacly about a notorious apologist for Italian fascism. The political jumble here does not trouble the poet, because he is moving on some higher plane where such differences matter little.

By the mid-1960s, after the Black Mountain poets had been nationally publicized by major presses, Dorn, Levertov, and Duncan, had begun to write explicitly political poems. Duncan's *Bending the Bow* (1968) includes a number of important poems against American activities in Vietnam. The infernal visions of Dante, Blake, and Pound were his models in "The Fire," "Up Rising," "The Multiversity," "Earth's Winter Song," and "Moira's Cathedral," all of which express a strong satisfaction with the rebirth of mythology and the fulfillment of poetry's lyrical and satiric offices. Jones, Rich, and others wrote about how their art resisted the political pressures of the moment, but not Duncan. "Earth's Winter Song" is a lyric celebration of the idealism of young demonstrators against the Vietnam War. "Up Rising,"

"The Fire," and "The Multiversity" are bitter denunciations of American politicians – Lyndon Johnson, Adlai Stevenson, Barry Goldwater, Richard Nixon, Eisenhower – but without any complicating sense of the good gone bad, or of the strains between foreign and domestic policy. Instead the poems vigorously exercise the rhetoric of Duncan's infernal masters, with the consequence that the differences (apparent and actual) between Stevenson and Eisenhower, Johnson and Goldwater, are simply ignored. In the mid-1960s, American politics moved beyond the banal into the truly vicious, and in that subject poetry had a traditional stake. There was no longer reason for the former avant-gardists to hold themselves away from politics. As political commentary Duncan's poems are not to be taken seriously, though as texts for performance they were formidable evocations of "the true history hidden in history," the "intent within intent." Their intellectual limitations derive from the fact that they grotesquely simplify the motivation of persons in authority in order to realize a mythic pattern. Duncan imagines "eager biologists" "dreaming of bodies of mothers and fathers and children and hated rivals swollen with new plagues, measles grown enormous, influenzas perfected." Where demonic drives have produced chemical weapons research, the job for right-thinking people might be simple and clear: punish scientists and forbid research. However moving these poems are, they are intellectually trivial, because they reduce issues that have elsewhere been shown to be complex to the simple dichotomies of traditional Christian myth: angelic protesters (in "Earth's Winter Song") and satanic statesmen.

It is clear enough why Duncan lampoons Lyndon Johnson, Adlai Stevenson, and others, but his animus against Clark Kerr, President of the University of California, is less obvious. He speaks of Kerr, a successful liberal educational administrator who advocated enormous growth for public higher education, as a Blakean Nobodaddy, "reduced in spirit," and equates him rightly with Stevenson, another liberal intellectual. Kerr's vision of the modern multiversity was just what Olson spoke of in 1951 as education becoming a State Whore. Duncan's animus against Kerr suggests that the avant-garde had been speaking indirectly to institutionalized intellectuals all along. Olson and Creeley had studied at Harvard, Duncan at Berkeley. These poets first came in contact with a literary culture in the best American universities. In the 1950s they tried to select for their journals and for students at Black Mountain College the most worthwhile work being done by American scholars. In a very early poem, Duncan wrote about the University of California: "The reaches of the campus, lawn and grove, / all the leafy stillness seemd / leafy stillness of our mind. / This is my paradise, I said." But in the 1960s they felt that these institutions had been betrayed by their custodians. The professors killed the dream of the didactic avant-garde.

The special pleasure of Duncan's poems comes from their direct solicitation of faith in intense feelings that do not derive from relationships with other people. When he succeeds, Duncan evokes the powerful feeling that various apparently discontinuous areas of experience and knowledge are actually connected, that, to put it baldly, life has secret meaning. This meaning is in a way asocial, because the strong feelings he evokes are those of a romantic individual outside of social relationships.

ॐ

The connections between the New York artistic scene and the predominantly literary milieu of the College in the 1950s were firm. Several of the New York painters taught at Black Mountain College, especially during summer sessions (Robert Motherwell in 1945; Willem and Elaine de Kooning in 1948; Franz Kline and Jack Tworkov in 1952) and others, like John Chamberlain, Kenneth Noland, and Robert Rauschenberg, were students there. Dan Rice referred to the Cedar Tavern, the gathering place of painters in Greenwich Village, as "Black Mountain away from Black Mountain." However, the poets more properly associated with the New York painters, Frank O'Hara, John Ashbery, James Schuyler, Kenneth Koch, and Barbara Guest, were quite a separate group from the Black Mountain writers. Although Duncan, Olson, and Creeley expressed admiration for the Abstract Expressionists, for some reason the poets and painters at the College did not collaborate closely. The New York poets, however, moved in the same social circles with painters in the 1950s, and collaborated easily with the painters, as Marjorie Perloff has shown. "We shared that whole painting scene," Kenneth Koch has said.

Nonetheless the result of this collaboration was not a New York literary avant-garde. The poets came to the painting scene rather late. In 1952 Harold Rosenberg decried the scandal that American writers had not discovered the Action Painters, and twenty years later Dore Ashton made a special point of saying that the Abstract Expressionists of the 1940s did not enjoy the encouragement or understanding of contemporary poets. The enthusiasm of the New York poets in the 1950s was mostly for the so-called second generation – Larry Rivers, Helen Frankenthaler, Grace Hartigan, Robert Rauschenberg and others – who were not making a radical break with the art institutions of their time, but rather were trying to clear professional space for their own careers in the shadow of the immediately preceding generation. The New York painters and poets collaborated well within the recently established commercial art institutions of the city. The connection between poets and painters was deliberately exploited by the Tibor de Nagy gallery, which published in 1952 and 1953, respectively, the first poems of O'Hara and Ashbery in order to promote the painters whose works were sold through the gallery as avant-garde. Similarly, the art criticism of O'Hara, written mostly in the late 1950s and early 1960s, was not adversarial. He promoted the careers of painters who after 1955 were already reasonably well recognized and prosperous. As curator for the Museum of Modern Art, his job was to establish careers and popularize painting not, like an avant-gardist, to undermine established art institutions. Neither the poets nor the painters of this group sought much more than a shift in taste to accommodate a fresh range of style. Moreover, they had nothing to say about the relationship between art and society.

The painters of the second generation were conciliatory insofar as they restored to painting a figurative dimension that had been under attack in European painting since about 1910. They were playful and witty too, where the first generation had been earnest. "Abstract Expressionism is not [fun]," O'Hara said, it is rather "the art of serious men." The lightness of the second generation is especially clear in connection with the adopted philosophy of the Abstract Expressionists – existentialism, with which Rivers, O'Hara, Ashbery, and Koch showed no sympathy. Rivers referred to the first generation's existentialism as "*ich-schmerz.*" The younger painters and the New York poets too were out to reclaim the gentler tones of art. Schuyler commended Helen Frankenthaler's special courage "in going against the think-tough and paint-tough grain of New York School abstract painting." The New York poets and the second-generation painters were deliberately anti-intellectual, insofar as *Partisan Review* in the late 1940s and early 1950s constituted the life of the mind. Rivers and Rauschenberg showed instead a special taste for the tritest materials of American culture. "What could be dopier," Rivers said to O'Hara, "than a painting dedicated to a national cliché – Washington Crossing the Delaware." "I have found my 'subject,' " Grace Hartigan said in 1956, "it concerns that which is vulgar and vital in American modern life." Rivers and others were in express reaction against the pieties of the Abstract Expressionists: "Embarrassment with seriousness. . . . Perhaps accident, innocence and of course fun and the various reliefs experienced in the presence of absurdity. It is these things I think which account for much more in my choosing portions of Mass Culture than the obvious everyday humanistic or politically responsible overtones."

The spirit of spoof coupled with a touching willingness to consider anything, however vulgarly American, worthy of art are essential to O'Hara's poetry ("oh Lana Turner we love you get up"), and responsible too for much of the pleasure as well as difficulty of Ashbery's poems. Ashbery's "Instruction Manual" (1956) to an imagined tour of Guadalajara is a pastiche of clichés, and banal phrasing is pervasive in his poems, as all his critics have remarked. Ashbery is difficult partly because of the ambivalence of his own feelings: he has said that his intention is not to satirize the banality, but rather to exploit the language that most commonly expresses our feelings. In the same spirit, Schuyler praises the painter Alex Katz's courage to risk banality. Ashbery is radical in his effort to imitate the actual movement of a mind that is only fitfully meditative, easily distracted, often acutely perceptive, but obtuse as well.

This mimetic impulse of the New York poets was sharply at odds with the work of the Black Mountain poets, though it drew support from the theoretical writing of another Black Mountain figure, John Cage, who gave a famous lecture on "Something" at the Club in 1949. Cage collaborated with Cunningham, Olson, and others at Black Mountain, but he never published in the journals associated with the College, probably because they were dominated by an unsympathetic literary program. Olson is oddly taciturn about Cage, though he wrote a fine poem, "Merce of Egypt," about Cunningham. Olson seems to have felt that some of the recitals organized by Cage and Cunningham were insufficiently serious – "trivial" was evidently his word.

Cage's aesthetic, like O'Hara's and Rivers's, is anti-intellectual: "The mind may give up its desire to improve on creation and function as a faithful receiver of experience." An artist is properly humble in the face of experience, but oddly passive too: "We are made perfect," Cage said in 1949, "by what happens to us rather than by what we do." With this, Olson and his collaborators could not possibly have agreed. Nor will the notion of passivity take one very far in explaining Ashbery's or O'Hara's poems. What they admire is better spoken of as receptivity and generosity in place of the critical, earnest, and exclusive attitude of the *Partisan Review* intellectuals and the Abstract Expressionists. Cage, O'Hara, and Ashbery conceive of the artist's job as not quite reflecting an environment so much as incorporating in music or poetry the sounds, subjects, and distractions deriving from those experiences that are constantly accessible to everyone, regardless of social class or political allegiance.

In retrospect it is clear that Ashbery's first book, *Some Trees* (1956), illustrated ways of writing that would continue to engage experimental poets for three decades. The title itself establishes a casual attitude toward his subject and his art: not the trees of New York, or Paris, just *some* trees. The title poem, first published in 1949, gets off to a fittingly banal start:

> These are amazing: each
> Joining a neighbor, as though speech
> Were a still performance.
> Arranging by chance

> To meet as far this morning
> From the world as agreeing
> With it, you and I
> Are suddenly what the trees try
> To tell us we are:

Ashbery talks his way through the vagueness and incoherence of ordinary experience. The paradox of the second and third lines is left unexplained; the fourth line simply introduces another. Rather than explain, he spins out an incoherent analogy in lines four through nine. He seems only to initiate a syntax he cannot master, as people commonly do when they think they can explain more than they truly can. But after this erratic beginning, he introduces a clear, exact discursive passage to stand at the center of the poem: "That their merely being there / Means something; that soon / We may touch, love, explain." This landscape's message is altogether empirical, agnostic, and social. Like Cage, Ashbery takes heart from the presence of such common things as some trees: "And glad not to have invented / Such comeliness, we are surrounded: / A silence already filled with noises. . . ." Success here is measured by the prospect of loving and comprehensible contact with another, but also by the ability to shape language as it had been shaped by poets in the seventeenth century:

> Our days put on such reticence
> These accents seem their own defense.

That a poem beginning with such undistinguished language should end so elegantly is an indication of the range of writing that Ashbery produces. O'Hara simulated casual speech, but Ashbery's language is too wide ranging to offer the straight-forward pleasures and consolations of coherent psychological representation. One aspect of Ashbery's poetry ambitiously refuses to present a "self" in language. On the other hand, his one collection that comes closest to offering such pleasure, *Self-Portrait in a Convex Mirror* (1975), is the book by which he is best known.

Ashbery's poems have seemed obscure even to audiences trained by the modernists to cope with difficulties of interpretation. Ashbery cultivates a different kind of disjunctiveness in his writing. Pound spoke of the ideogrammic method as a means of establishing centripetal force in poems of juxtaposition. Eliot referred to the mythical method of Joyce. Both ultimately aimed at a central consciousness for even their most difficult poems. In *Some Trees* and *The Tennis Court Oath* (1962) the idea of a central consciousness seemed almost irrelevant. "He" (1953) is a joke about how syntactic structures predicate actions by which some psyche is supposedly known. In the title poem of *Rivers and Mountains* (1966) Ashbery writes with characteristic particularity about a landscape as though it were the site of some narrative, but so specific are the references that the nonexistent context is the real subject of the poem. The poem is a demonstration of the limits of narrative language: without a context even specific statements – such as those of the last six lines, which seem to evoke the sensational events of a coup – about events are wholly obscure. In *The Tennis Court Oath* Ashbery turned away from psychological models toward what he later called (and renounced as) "automatic poetry." But after 1962 Ashbery deliberately attempted to "keep meaningfulness up to the pace of randomness," as he put it. On the one hand, he systematically estranges his language so that no central consciousness holds the lines together in one overall significant structure. The words of his poems seem to construct not one context, but rather several. Ashbery does not disclaim referentiality, but the pull of his words toward some referent or signified is made at once strange and forceful by the absence of a single context to render that pull plausible or natural. On the other hand, poems like "Clepsydra," "The Skaters," "Soonest Mended," *Three Poems*, and "Self-Portrait" are at the same time lures into reverie; in order to construct a continuous sense one attempts to follow a very elliptical mind moving intimately from reflection to reflection.

The first of Ashbery's discursive successes was "Clepsydra" (1966), in which the pronouns can be followed no more closely than they can in reverie. "You," "it," and "he" are loose and absorbent, as the poem shifts directions every few lines. With this poem Ashbery, like Olson in 1950, showed that discursive verse could be pushed well beyond the example of Auden's "Horae Canonicae." Eliot's *Four Quartets* (1936–43) had rehabilitated discursiveness, as though the modernist presentational mode had been inadequate to the religious–philosophical subject of Eliot's last poems, and Auden's poems of the 1940s seemed to confirm the lesson. The connection between Eliot's and Ashbery's poems is particularly significant. Eliot's musical title indicates that he too was after an especially protean meditative mode. Ashbery has said that music, more than painting, is the sister art to which he feels closest:

What interests me in music is the ideas in it, and these are, of course, ideas that cannot be put into words, as so many great ideas that occur to us can't be. And it is this way of presenting an argument rather than the exact terms of the argument that attracts me.

For Ashbery's longer, more ambitious poems, paraphrase is less adequate than it generally is to the task of interpretation, though these poems seem insistently committed to an overall meaning. A reader's task is to attend rather to the movement of the words themselves, and to imagine the contexts they may evoke. The paraphraseable passages in these poems —

> Each moment
> Of utterance is the true one; likewise none are [sic] true,
> Only is the bounding from air to air . . .

— are sufficiently memorable that critics quote them repeatedly, but the poems are comprised of these moments of self-reflexive lucidity no more than of such unsettlingly obscure lines as:

> A recurring whiteness like
> The face of stone pleasure, urging forward as
> Nostrils what only meant dust.

The descent from understanding to befuddlement is just what Ashbery is after, for only that approaches "some kind of rational beauty within the limits of possibility, that would not offend everyday experience, even of the coarsest or most monotonous kind." Life is every day surprising, according to Ashbery, only rational categories insulate one from the surprise.

"Clepsydra" begins oddly with a truncated question: "Hasn't the sky?" The special power of this poem, and of Ashbery's other discursive successes, is that it is, first, a metaphysical inquiry into the nature of one's perception of the sky, the surrounding physical element, in the absence not only of a presiding God but as well of an anxiety about that absence. There is a sense that the physical world has moved closer to us. But, second, the poem introduces (ll. 57–70) an overlapping theme: a failed love by which one measures time and change; and, third (ll. 130–40), the structure of a self. The poem begins very abstractly with a comprehensive theme and then narrows down until all three themes are present in the one most personal theme. After the second and then the third themes are introduced, one cannot be certain at any one point just which is uppermost in the poet's mind. The richness of the poem is admittedly hazy, but it brings into verse an understanding of the world that otherwise was not there. American poetry would be poorer without it.

❦

The New York avant-garde came under attack in the early 1960s from the Black Arts Movement, when it became clear that careers were to be the fruit of the 1950s avant-garde. LeRoi Jones (Amiri Baraka) achieved great notoriety in the late 1960s as an avant-garde poet and playwright turned political activist. His career set an influential pattern for other writers of his generation, most plainly for Adrienne Rich. This black poet, playwright, and essayist saw in the civil rights movement of the early 1960s, well before white artists did, what sort of political challenges to the status quo were practical; and likewise he earlier felt the urgency of reconciling a literary life with the demands of a politically turbulent time. The pattern Jones/Baraka enacted begins in a romantic fashion: he explicitly focused his writing on the relationship between his personal sensibility and his authorial persona. This kind of reflexive writing takes a poet's career – or the development of a sensibility in language – as a central subject matter. To the extent that this is an especially individualistic approach to art, it was easy for those raised on the post-1945 *Partisan Review* view of the poet to feel the pathos of Jones's position.

In his first book of poems, *Preface to a Twenty Volume Suicide Note* (1961), Jones constructs a lyrical persona of "soft feelings" who is in tension with the tenor of his times. In "The New Sheriff," a poem first published in the avant-garde *Evergreen Review*, Jones sets out the claim of multiple selves:

> There is something
> in me so cruel, so
> silent. It hesitates
> to sit on the grass
> with the young white
> virgins
> of my time.

He presented himself as, in part only, a terrible menace – a "blood- / letter" – to the white world. This stagey terribleness is set out as something that does not come altogether easily to the author of charming lyrical poems on comic strip characters. He claims to have "Inside [him] / the soft white meat / of the feelings." But this new sheriff is deliberately going to offend the tolerant urban liberals he could count on reaching through the *Evergreen Review*. Where they might like to speak of the "animal grace" of black men, he says, "not that, but / a rude stink of color / huger, more vast, than / this city suffocating." The echo of Milton aptly invokes Promethean heroics, especially the impending transformation of an angel into his diabolical antithesis.

Jones, to his credit, was always disinclined to play to what his readers would readily approve. He turned on them and the liberal ideology they avowed. Within a few years, white liberals would become accustomed to the aggressiveness of black writers and activists, but in 1961 Jones was writing poems he knew would violate the tastes of his predominantly white readers:

> Inside
> your flat white stomach
> I move my tongue.

Within one year Jones developed his art into utter opposition to the New York avant-garde. "The Politics of Rich Painters" appeared in July 1962 in his own little magazine, *Floating Bear*; that is, just two years after Donald Allen's anthology had presented a broad poetic avant-garde group, including Jones, to a national reading public.

> Just their fingers' prints
> staining the cold glass, is sufficient
> for commerce, and a proper ruling on
> humanity. You know the pity
> of democracy, that we must sit here
> and listen to how he made his money.
> Tho the catalogue of his possible ignorance
> roars and extends through the room
> like fire. "Love," become the pass,
> the word taken intimately to combat
> all the uses of language. So that learning
> itself falls into disrepute.

Jones had been an enthusiastic participant in avant-garde groups in Greenwich Village, and he had associated with the Black Mountain poets too. In his *Autobiography* he tells of his one-time admiration for the Abstract Expressionist painters with whom he met regularly at the old Cedar Tavern. "Franz Kline's style, not only his painting but his personal idiosyncrasies, we set out to emulate." But by 1962 Jones had come to see that ideologically the New York avant-garde was indefensibly vapid: the values its members could articulate came down to the most abused term of all; all arguments end in the affirmation of an undefined, unexamined love. The existence of an artistic avant-garde is also exploited by the dominant culture to provide an affirmation of itself: "a proper ruling on / humanity." An avant-garde like this is supposed to make everyone look good, and it makes money too. There had been a forum at the Village Vanguard with Jones, Archie Shepp, and Larry Rivers talking about art and social change. When Shepp spoke of revolution, Rivers withdrew from the discussion. Jones turned to him and said, "Hey you're all over in these galleries, turning out work for these rich faggots, you part of the dying shit just like them!" Jones says in his *Autobiography* that the effect of this aggressive remark was to undermine the supposed "intellectual and emotional connection between us." By 1962 the collaboration of writers, musicians, and painters in New York seemed to him a mere commercial fiction – certainly no basis for an oppositional movement. The comforting notion that people of good conscience could agree easily with each other, despite racial differences, was just another sham, like "Love."

Like his friends Olson, Creeley, and Ed Dorn (to whom *The Dead Lecturer* was dedicated), Jones had no taste for the poetry appreciated by the academic culture of 1962 – for Auden, Wilbur, Merrill, Hollander, and (at that time) Rich and Merwin, say – but in "The Politics of Rich Painters" he speaks from an intellectualist, even academic point of view. The last sentence of the strophe above is uttered without irony. Jones abhors the vagueness of ideology based on some "love," partly because language and learning can provide exact and definite knowledge. The language of the poem is at times coarse and offensive to an academic sensibility – "mother's iron tit" and "those faggot handmaidens of the french whore" – and the tone is close to rant. Yet the movement of the lines imitates the development of a paragraph in an expository essay, just the way Olson's verse of the early 1950s did, and it is from an idealized intellectualist point of view that Jones, like Olson and Dorn, writes. The values he upholds against the New York avant-garde derive from his experience (and Olson's) of the skeptical, critical discourse of American academic culture at its best. He certainly does not mean to speak from the viewpoint of those in the academy who are entrusted with the literary culture – "So much *taste* / so little understanding" – but rather from that of those in departments of, say, history, economics, and sociology. The final argument of the poem is that the literary culture that matters most – André Malraux, Senghor, James Baldwin, Yeats, and Pound are the canonical figures here – answers to that range of experience addressed by social scientists with more than vapid talk of love.

❧

The prospect of a literary avant-garde outside the academic institutions that dominate literary culture disappeared with the expansion of universities in the 1960s. The Language poets of the late 1970s and 1980s, who organized a "proactive, oppositional literature" against what Charles Bernstein called "the smugness of social and literary conventionality" expressed in "official verse culture," were a test case. In 1984, immediately after $L=A=N-=G=U=A=G=E$ magazine ceased just four years of publication, Southern Illinois University Press issued a 300 page anthology of pieces from the magazine, and here are some revealing sentences:

A language centered writing not only codes its own flow but also encodes its own codicities. (Steve McCaffery)

Texts (tests) like these will do the *denaturalizing*; they problematize reality. (Bruce Andrews)

References are not foregrounded. The body of work is not organized around the referential axis. Therefore, is not genitally organized? No 'discharge' of a specific substantive kind leaves the polymorphous play of linguistic units. (Bruce Andrews)

The enigma, cued only to itself, faces nothing. However, it is not bracketed. (Alan Davies)

Words are known by the company they keep in the world at large, not just within a single text, as Language poets suggest. One of these poets, Peter Schjeldahl, wrote that "From the stand point of being a poet, what is interesting about poetry today is that it is the occupation most completely without professional status in our society." This romantic view of the poet as outsider is wholly anachronistic, for poets now, whether rear or avant-gardist, all contribute to the legitimacy of the social structure that directly supports literary institutions, only some poets do so more or less under protest. The sentences from Alan Davies, Bruce Andrews, and Steve Mc-Caffery show that the poetic theories of these poets derive directly from recent academic literary theorists – Derrida, Kristeva, Barthes, Jameson – whose prestige and influence have been established by professional literary conferences and Ph.D. seminars. "Once, just once," Eliot Weinberger has written, "someone should write a defense of 'language' poetry without employing the words trope, paratactic, temporality, historiography, semantic, semiologic, reification, dehistoricization, teleological, dialectical, syllogism, figuration, rhetoric of equivalence, homology, strategy."

When young poets lean on the words that comprise the poetic diction of their contemporaries, they do so rather deliberately: often unaware that these words have become mere counters, but completely aware that they help to establish a writer's own authority within contemporary conventional opinion. With the buzz words of critical theory – "inscribes" is one of Silliman's favorites, and "always, already" – the Language poets deliberately court the authority of the most prestigious sector of current academic literary opinion. "Literary workers," Bernstein has argued, "have as their natural allies literary, political and cultural theorists and commentators." The Language poets have joined the attack on the ideas of a coherent or transcendent self, of narrative, and of reference. Olson took aim at Eliot and Lowell in the 1950s; thirty years later Ron Silliman argues against the long haggard Wellek and Warren. The antiacademic polemics of these poets are directed only at those critics who, despite the influence of Derrida, understand texts as coherent expressions of the thought of their authors. The Language poets themselves were not academics until the late 1980s, which means that their ambitious affiliation with academic theory was all the more notable. That academic literary theory should have yielded a new group of poets as a byproduct is a sign that an explicitly oppositional literary movement must situate itself squarely within the academic scene. Academic literary culture, far from resisting this Marxist literary avant-garde, has eagerly embraced it as a subgroup of professorial encampments. The radical change that avant-gardes seek by opposing art institutions is impossible within an academic context, because academic institutions cope with challenges in a liberal fashion by expanding and pluralistically incorporating adversaries. To the academic sensibility, the Language poets comprise one more trend in a poetry scene characterized by diversity.

Eliot once spoke of the "aesthetic sanction" as the historical fact that the ability of any system of thought to issue in major literary creation is on the face of it a kind of proof of the seriousness of that system. His examples were Lucretius and Dante. "Any way or view of life," he wrote, "which gives rise to great art is for us more plausible than one which gives rise to inferior art or none." The other side of this proposition is that literary theories that are ignored or contradicted by literary artists may well subside into the steady drone of academic literary history. Jameson has revived the term postmodernism in order to construct a comprehensive account of the poetry, fiction, music, film, video, and literary theory of the last quarter century. If the most significant artistic creation in all of these fields can be plausibly connected to professional academic literary theory, literary theory can no longer be dismissed as a parochial concern of professionals. Yet if Jameson is wrong on this score, he will effectively give force to the claim that academic literary theory has produced only a discourse for professors writing for favor in each other's eyes; that is, that criticism has become independent of literature itself. The issue faces a test that literary critics understand: does the discourse of contemporary literary theory provide a compelling account of the most important questions for literary artists in our time? Does the late 1960s break in the history of literary criticism that one associates with the importation of the Marxism of the Frankfurt School, of structuralism and deconstruction correspond to a plausible account of periodization in the history of poetry, fiction, film, video, and music? More pointedly, the question is whether academic Marxism offers a cogent account of American culture of the last twenty-five years.

Jameson answers these questions affirmatively, and the Language poets count as part of his evidence. No comparable rapport between American poets and professors has been achieved since the writing of Robert Lowell in the late 1940s and early 1950s gave renewed credibility to the theories of the New Critics. Language writing was presented in the late 1970s and early 1980s as an alternative to academic writing, whereas it aspired to the rhetorical authority of academic literary discourse. Since then, a number of Language writers – Barrett Watten, Bob Perelman, Jed Rasula, for example – have moved through Ph.D. programs and begun academic careers in English departments, and others, like Bernstein and Susan Howe, have taken chairs without doing Ph.D. training. The intention of Language writing to address professional academic literary opinion is clearer now than it was in the early 1980s. One sees now too that the results of this group's critical writing have been a genuine refreshment and focusing of professional literary debate about modern writing, and not only modern writing. Susan Howe has written brilliantly on nineteenth century writers in a recent book published by Wesleyan University Press. Bernstein's essays, most recently published by Harvard University Press, are engaged in critical dialogue with academic theorists such as Jameson. And the influence of Language writing can be seen now – with Lawrence Venuti's *The Translator's Invisibility* (1995) – even in the area of translation theory, which is surprising because the Language poets, as Weinberger has noted, have done so little to promote poetry in translation. What mattered in the late 1940s was that so obviously *good* a poet as Lowell wrote from an understanding of poetry that derived from the New Critics, especially from Ransom and Tate. But are the Language Poets as accomplished somehow as the author of *Lord Weary's Castle?*

Jameson identifies two literary characteristics of postmodern art. The first is pastiche, the playful, not satiric quotation or imitation of historical styles that is familiar to readers of Eliot, Pound, Stevens, and Joyce, as well as O'Hara and Ashbery. The second Jameson speaks of as a schizophrenic use of language, the way in which many recent styles tend not to construct a coherent self at the center of the text. The instances to cite are many: from Ashbery who presents himself as symptomatic to James McMichael who in *Four Good Things* (1980) expressly analyzes the contemporary relevance of a schizophrenic sensibility.

Jameson quotes Bob Perelman's poem "China" as an example of postmodern poetry, and the case deserves close attention.

> We live on the third world from the sun. Number three. Nobody
> tells us what to do.
> The people who taught us to count were being very kind.
> It's always time to leave.
> If it rains, you either have your umbrella or you don't.
> The wind blows your hat off.
> The sun rises also.
> I'd rather the stars didn't describe us to each other; I'd
> rather we do it for ourselves.
> Run in front of your shadow.
> A sister who points to the sky at least once a decade is a
> good sister.
> The landscape is motorized.
> The train takes you where it goes.
> Bridges among water.
> Folks straggling along vast stretches of concrete, heading
> into the plane.
> Don't forget what your hat and shoes will look like when you
> are nowhere to be found.
> Even the words floating in air make blue shadows.

If it tastes good we eat it.
The leaves are falling. Point things out.
Pick up the right things.
Hey guess what? What? *I've learned how to talk.* Great.
The person whose head was incomplete burst into tears.
As it fell, what could the doll do? Nothing.
Go to sleep.
You look great in shorts. And the flag looks great too.
Everyone enjoyed the explosions.
Time to wake up.
But better get used to dreams.

This is how Jameson argues for the significance of this text:

. . . it does not seem quite right to say that these sentences are free-floating material signifiers whose signifieds have evaporated. There does seem to be some global meaning here. Indeed, insofar as this is in some curious and secret way a political poem, it does seem to capture some of the excitement of the immense and unfinished social experiment of the new China, unparalleled in world history: the unexpected emergence, between the two superpowers, of "number three;" the freshness of a whole new object-world produced by human beings in some new control over their own collective destiny; the signal event, above all, of a collectivity which has become a new "subject of history" and which, after the long subjection of feudalism and imperialism, speaks in its own voice, for itself, for the first time ("Hey guess what? . . . I've learned how to talk."). Yet such meaning floats over the text or behind it. One cannot, I think, read this text according to any of the older New-Critical categories and find the complex inner relationships and texture which characterized the older "concrete universal" of classical modernisms such as Wallace Steven's.

Jameson has good reason to say that his interpretation "floats over the text or behind it." This political interpretation of the poem, which presumes that Perelman formulated certain statements about the People's Republic, exploits conventional notions of reference and significance that defy the program of the Language poets and of Jameson's postmodernism. Jameson goes on after another paragraph to admit to his problem in an amusing way. "But now the secret of this poem," he says, "must be disclosed."

It is a little like Photo-realism, which looked like a return to representation after the anti-representational abstractions of Abstract Expressionism, until people began to realize that these paintings are not exactly realistic either, since what they represent is not the outside world but rather only a photograph of the outside world or, in other words, the latter's image. False realisms, they are really art about other art, images of other images. In the present case, the represented object is not really China after all: what happened was that Perelman came across a book of photographs in a stationery store in Chinatown, a book whose captions and characters obviously remained dead letters (or should one say material signifiers?) to him. The sentences of the poem are *his* captions to those pictures. Their referents are other images, another text, and the "unity" of the poem is not *in* the text at all but outside it in the bound unity of an absent book.

Jameson wanted a paean to the People's Republic, but got instead a list of slight jokes. The poem does not permit ordinary reference or coherent intentions on the level of practical politics at all. Politics is displaced to the level of theory, where Jameson is chastened by this example of, as they say, "intertextuality." Once he has revealed the joke, he can say no more about the poem. For this avant-garde, poetry does lead to political action ("It is class war," according to Silliman), but only through the frustration and disruption of linguistic expectations – exactly here is this avant-garde plainly academic. The Language poets propose a strictly formalist approach to politics that rests upon a blunt equation of verbal and political order ("language control=thought control=reality control," according to Bernstein). The examples of Pound, Ginsberg, Snyder, Bly, Rich, Levertov, and one might add Baraka to the list – all poets whose insistently referential poems address the political issues of fellow citizens – Bernstein counts as evidence of a discouraging "confusion of realms": even the great comedies and tragedies "have never changed anything." As Jed Rasula has said, "a poem is simply not a politically efficacious form." The disappointment expressed here is exactly that of the academy: after all the issue-oriented political engagement of the 1960s, the political center shifted far to the right. The civil rights and antiwar movements of the 1960s achieved specific victories, to which poets contributed; yet the limits of such political action seem great in light of the conservative shift throughout American society of the 1970s, 1980s, and alas the 1990s. Bernstein's hope (and Silliman's and Rasula's too) is that the destruction of socially established patterns of usage in poetry will prefigure large scale social change.

Jameson took the title of Perelman's poem to refer to a political and geographical fact, rather than to a book of photos. The Language poets argue that referentiality is a consequence of capitalism, which has suppressed the gestural, or performative, aspect of language in order to exploit the descriptive, narrative, and expository dimensions of language. Since Stein, they claim, poets have increasingly insisted that meaning derives from signifiers themselves, not from character, plot, or argument. Words, not poets, produce poems. The proper means of interpreting a poem, therefore, is less the reconstruction of the intention of the author than the sorting out of permissable associations with the words of the text. Jameson was on the approved track. There are two notorious problems with this sort of interpretive procedure. The first is that one's associations with particular words are determined largely by one's social position and political commitment. The more a text relies upon associations, the less likely it is to move beyond the ideological horizon of its contemporaries. The second problem is that each reader's association with one word or another will be idiosyncratic, insofar as ideology neglects this word. Silliman accepts the consequences of this problem and asserts that each reader will produce a different poem from the same text. What used to be treasured as dramatic tension within the ostensible intention of the poem is now meant to exist between competing interpretations of a poem. The Language poets regard this aspect of their reception as attractively democratic: these poems, as Jackson Mac Low says, "allow each reader or hearer to be visionary himself"; they resist what Silliman often calls the "tyranny of the signified." To just the extent that one relies upon a reader's associations with one word or another, one accepts a correspondingly wide range of inexactness in communication.

Jameson is finally unsure how to assess postmodernism. Are postmodern writers, such as the Language poets, oppositional or complacent? At the end of the essay that discusses the Language poets, he cannot answer this question. Four years later, in 1986, he said that

postmodernism *really expresses* multinational capitalism, there is some cognitive content to it. It is articulating something that is going on. If the subject is lost in it, and if in social life the psychic subject has been decentered by late capitalism, then this art faithfully and authentically registers that. That's its moment of truth.

Postmodernism, then, displays the symptoms of an ailment; it offers no understanding beyond the symptoms, let alone a cure, or even words of consolation.

The acuteness of symptoms can be fascinating, though they have no bearing on a particular poem's worth. The postmodern text is, in Jameson's term, "disposable," less something to be reconsidered than a sign of the condition of multinational capitalism. In postmodern art one experiences "a process done in very expert and inventive ways; and when you leave it, it's over." Jameson requires so little of postmodern art because he so deplores the capitalist empire that underwrites its moment of truth. At the end of Rilke's poem on the archaic torso that he saw in the Louvre, one is left with art's tougher challenge to take life more seriously: "Du mußt dein Leben ändern" (You must change your life).

Jameson's interpretation of Perelman's poem is blocked by the story of the poem's composition, and yet becomes the poem's authoritative interpretation. According to this insistent technicism, the poem is all instrument without any final cause, and only the poet knows how the instrument operates. Despite the talk of "perceiver-centered" humility, the Language poets press their wills upon their texts no less firmly than Lowell did in 1946, only the verbal traces of that press are less apparent. Silliman speaks of poets *using* overdetermination to produce some effect or other, but overdetermination is a concept designed to identify the places where a poet is insufficiently in charge to employ an economy of means. The Language poets' stories about the arbitrary circumstances in which their poems were composed are intended partly to debunk sappy claims about poetic creativity and genius. Yet these poets effectively present themselves as a guild with a large group of members and a body of secret technical knowledge, though they are willing to display their secrets upon demand. "Get a friend or two friends," Bernadette Mayer and her colleagues suggest, "to write *for* you, pretending they *are* you." This is witty and a legitimate critique of the romanticization of poetic personality, but these recipes for poems rest on an expressly utopian dream of delicious results, of large-scale social change instructed in part by a new kind of poetry.

The surprise is that this ambitious, professionally aware avant-garde milieu actually encouraged at least two extraordinary experimental writers. Susan Howe has produced books drawn from historical documents that remind one of the strength of Olson's precedent. She would never construct a central persona like Olson's Maximus; instead her pages contain lines and phrases that won't just come together in a unifying form, speech, or episode. Lines perhaps pair with one or two others, then characteristically move off by themselves.

> Summary of fleeting summary
> Pseudonym cast across empty
>
> Peak proud heart
>
> Majestic caparisoned cloud cumuli
> East sweeps hewn flank
>
> Scion on a ledge of Constitution
> Wedged sequences of system
>
> Causeway of faint famed city
> Human ferocity
>
> dim mirror Naught formula
> archaic hallucinatory laughter
>
> Kneel to intellect in our work
> Chaos cast cold intellect back

These lines, alone on a page in a sequence, "Articulation of Sound Forms in Time," about a military expedition in Connecticut in 1676, push off toward different contexts of plausible utterance. Lines four and five, for example, invoke familiar romantic figures for draping landscape with significance, but the third line is austere, self-rebuking, and, as a phrase, powerfully sensual too. Clearly Howe put these fifty-five words together, but they have apparently come in smaller units from her reading. The third and the last line give convincing testimony of the ability of a phrase or clause regardless of its informational burden (which here is reduced nearly to zero) to command one's imagination. The last line – is it an imperative or a simple past construction? – was typed out by one who loves the force of the English language and knows that "peak proud heart" is a suitable reproach to intellectuals; these, the most sensual of the lines here, hang together in a thematic structure pertaining to intellectual overreaching. One feels her ferocity, often in lines that were collected rather than written by Howe, even though she resists lures to the pathos and self-display that damages Rich's poems.

> Loving Friends and Kindred: –
> When I look back
> So short in charity and good works
> We are a small remnant
> of signal escapes wonderful in themselves
> We march from our camp a little
> and come home
> Lost the beaten track and so
> River section dark all this time
> We must not worry
> how few we are and fall from each other
> More than language can express
> Hope for the artist in America & etc
> This is my birthday
> These are the old home trees

This passage from "Articulation of Sounds" coheres more easily, as a letter by a participant in the expedition. A combination of pathos and utopian aspiration is now and then admissible in the voice of a character found in the archive, but no stable basis for perspective in the sequence (as in Bidart).

Howe's excavation of the documents of seventeenth- and nineteenth-century New England follows very obviously the example of her teacher Olson, though she reaches an intensity of expression that is beyond his range. In the last half-century, beginning with the Black Mountain poets and continuing with the Language poets, the notion of an avant-garde has been deliberately constructed as a tradition, a story of continuity rather than rupture. Olson proselytized on behalf of the poets who taught him most, Pound and Williams. Howe, Bernstein, and many other of these writers have reconstructed the modernist canon to emphasize the importance not only of these masters but also of Gertrude Stein, Laura Riding, and Louis Zukofsky. They have supplemented – and thereby challenged – the academic histories of modernist writing. Avant-gardism in American writing has become traditional, even scholarly in its attention to modernist predecessors.

The sense of poetry as an access to transcendent or religious knowledge is actually preserved in this only apparently secular and non-Romantic avant-garde. Palmer and Howe, like Duncan before them, bring into their poems a richness of language that evokes coherence beyond that of grammars, though the evidence of order is always manifest in the sound or structure of language. Here is the third of Michael Palmer's "Six Hermetic Songs," dedicated to Robert Duncan:

> The body in fog and the tongue
> bracketed in its form
>
> The words as if silvered – coated
> and swallowed, cradled and erased
>
> The marks whereby the body
> was said to be a world
>
> The walled rehearsals
> The curve of abandon,
>
> twinned and masked
> The calls and careless fashionings,
>
> digits thrown like dice
> I don't think about that anymore
>
> Send me my dictionary
> Write how you are

What he claims not to think about is a paradisal state in which language was not evidence of a former significance but rather fulfillment itself. Like Duncan, Palmer imagines a body of language and a world's body as one. The various methods of access to these bodies have been tried and exhausted. The poem rests in the patient discipline of philology and the steadiness of companionship.

*

The four avant-gardes I have discussed all drew on one aspect or another of a performative aesthetic, which is commonly said to be the defining characteristic of art in our time. For Olson in the 1950s, as for his follower Jerome Rothenberg in the 1970s, performance is a means of claiming special authority; performance has become a synonym for presence, for that which is not open to debate. The attraction of performative poetics has everything to do with what it is not. In the 1950s poets, like intellectuals generally, were in retreat from ideas, not just ideologies. Olson, more than any of his contemporaries, was a poet of ideas, and yet he was altogether unsure how to defend his political ideas in particular. His advocacy of a performative poetic was one way of getting around this difficulty and others. Then as now, no one coveted responsibility for drawing a line between ideas and ideologies. How much easier it would be if one could say, as Olson did, that what counts is the moment of utterance. One can understand the further appeal of performance poetics, when one considers that an oral poetic seems inherently oppositional when written information is the chief national commodity. Ronald Reagan, a professional performer whose chief political asset was the imitation of charisma, was the most popular American president since FDR, Olson's hero. Olson's Maximus, like Duncan's persona and Jones' too, enacts the romance of authority in a culture where authority is so diffuse that its icons evoke nostalgia. In the 1980s, however, the idea of performance narrowed dramatically: for the Language poets the performative dimension of poetry resides in the language itself, one step further removed from ideas – though at least one step closer to the academy. The academic literary culture has held a distinct attraction for avant-gardists since 1945, though at the same time the universities supplied the villains that avant-garde polemics require.

5

❦

AUTHENTICITY

IN THE 1960s certain notions of authenticity gathered very great cultural prestige, and not only in the United States. Theodore W. Adorno's critique of Heideggerian existentialism, *The Jargon of Authenticity* (1964), claims that German intellectuals produced a jargon based on the premise that moments of present experience are full of special significance and deserve greater esteem than thought or critical analysis. The criterion of authenticity inevitably produces dreams of origins unsullied by historical experience; the Adamic theme in American letters is all about authenticity. Adorno's book is a useful reminder, though, that this traditional American theme gained surprising currency in Central and Western Europe in the 1960s. Several aspects of American and continental thought came together in what was then recognized as a sensibility for the moment.

Although this sensibility was rapidly and effectively exploited by the mass media, its hold was strongest on the intellectual class. One thinks of the 1960s as the decade of the young; but the times belonged more specifically to those young people whose lives were oriented to the universities. The prestige of notions of authenticity derived from intellectual culture. This is an interesting point, because many of the images then taken to express authenticity did not come from intellectual life. The hunger for authenticity often seemed to express envy of the lives of other classes. Admittedly the many representations of innocent heterosexual love making, in violation of the strictures of legally certifying institutions, were not far from the lives of university students. But acts of individual violence, another emblem of authenticity, were actually very rare among such people, as was manual labor, and carried similar authority. The motivation of intellectuals in quest of authenticity began in ideas of alternatives, not in particular material circumstances or even in typical experiences. Authenticity was an idea.

Allen Ginsberg was interviewed by the poet Tom Clark in 1965, and he told a story of his realization in 1948 in the Columbia University bookstore "that everybody knew. Everybody knew completely everything." Clark asked if he still believed that: "I'm more sure of it now. Sure. All you have to do is try and make somebody. You realize that they knew all along you were trying to make them. But until that moment you never break through to communication on the subject." The breakthrough Ginsberg describes is to knowledge, and the validation of the knowledge is sexual. Sex and ideas. What stood in the way of liberation? Only a childish fear of rejection, and the Cold War. "The whole cold war," Ginsberg claimed, was a matter of ideas, "the imposition of a vast mental barrier on everybody." On May Day in 1965 he was elected King of the May by Czech students in Prague; then he was deported by the government.

Poetry itself – not just American poetry – took on a generic authority because of its traditional claim to authenticity, enhanced by its dissociation from the cynical duplicity of the mass media. The government's misrepresentations of the Vietnam War, in newspapers and television reports, were the nadir of this notorious duplicity. "The President lies," Bly wrote wittily, "about the composition of the amniotic fluid, he insists that Luther was never a German, and insists that only the Protestants sold indulgences." Poetry stood against all that, as though art had to be on the left – a widespread sentimentality that seemed plausible in the mid- and late 1960s. This was the closest American poetry has ever come to paralleling the function of poetry in the totalitarian Warsaw Pact nations – in the German Democratic Republic, for instance, where writers could represent themselves without embarrassment as the conscience of the nation.

The audience for poetry in America expanded greatly during these years. The detractors of metrical verse in the 1950s and 1960s spoke of academic verse, the implication being that its audience could come only from the universities. The encouragement of free verse entailed hope of a new audience for poets. And when free verse became the established mode, larger audiences than poetry had had before – or has had since – did appear. The size of poetry book printings enlarged, new poetry journals were founded, and established ones like *Poetry* increased their readership dramatically. In particular, the many poets who in the late 1950s and early 1960s had shown impatience with the constraints of artifice – Allen Ginsberg, Gary Snyder, Robert Bly, Sylvia Plath, W. S. Merwin, and Adrienne Rich – experienced great popularity. Much free verse of this period and later was intended for readers who otherwise did not read a great deal of poetry. Such poems were meant to be direct where metrical, "academic" poems were circumspect, hedged with ironies, veiled with allusions. Arguments for plainness in poetry, though often salutary, bring the danger of overstressing forcefulness. Emily Dickinson spoke of poems making the hair on the back of her neck stand up: this is a better test of rhetorical force than of authenticity in poetry. In the 1960s many American poets began to focus their efforts on forceful expression rather than on fine distinctions; the temper of the times seemed to encourage this simplifying priority.

Free verse is merely a technical or prosodic category, but for ideological reasons it has come to signify much more than the absence of traditional metrical norms. By the mid-1960s free verse had become the dominant mode of American poetry, and that dominance is holding through the century's end. Free verse commands the great center of American poetry. In MFA programs and in poetry journals young poets learn the writing of free verse. There is indeed great diversity, not just one style, among free-verse poets. But there are nonetheless features of contemporary free verse that are conventional, and these rest upon certain beliefs about the potentiality of the present moment. The new readers of poetry got very much what they wanted: assurance that indeed the quality of life in America was improving quickly. Not just materially, though that was certainly the case. The qualitative improvement that poetry and other arts expressed was just a new access for educated people to a basis for hope. One thinks of the bomb as a pall over the spirit of America, and of the Vietnam War as a later cloud, and there is evidence in poetry of this sort of gloom. But in the 1960s many college-educated Americans felt that the polity was facing contradictions – first racism, and then imperialism – that had been clouding its future. The poetry that suited this audience included a good measure of reportage; names and places familiar from newspapers and television appeared in poems by Robert Lowell, Robert Bly, and Allen Ginsberg. Beyond this topicality was a conformity of style that survived much longer than the protest poems. Many poets agreed that the best style was an invisible one, restrained and pensive, not exuberant, close to speech, apparently far from libraries. Behind this style is an optimistic sense that quite different sorts of people can understand profound experiences in terms of the scene of contemporary experience or of family life that is more or less familiar to everyone.

The currency of such stylistic features can be dated to the publication of Lowell's *Life Studies* in 1959, which shifted the dominant taste of the next three decades away from poetic artifice toward the claims of the natural and authentic. Lowell's break with the conventions of the 1950s seemed spectacular. The New Critics, who dominated the academic reception of poetry, held by the Eliotic norm of impersonality. John Crowe Ransom said in 1938 that "Anonymity . . . is a condition of poetry." Lowell, who had apprenticed himself to Ransom and Tate, has explained how his reading on the same platforms with Allen Ginsberg led him to depart from his meters extemporaneously by adding extrametrical syllables to approximate the casualness of spoken language. When Tate read poems from the manuscript of *Life Studies* he became worried for Lowell's reputation: "*all* the poems about your family . . . are definitely *bad*. I do not think you ought to publish them." On the evidence of the poems, he was convinced that Lowell was heading toward a psychotic episode. The 1960s style that Lowell founded was explicitly democratic in intention. This was a poetry for everyone, which meant that the literary devices that encourage collaboration between writer and reader were in a sense forbidden. Irony died in 1959. And for many poets, meter did too, which meant that for still more readers it would never live. The trend toward a speech-based poetic certainly did not begin in 1959, though it reached fulfillment thereafter. From the Preface to *Lyrical Ballads* until well into the 1980s, it has been hard to believe in an alternative to the language spoken by men. "Every revolution in poetry is apt to be," T. S. Eliot said in 1942, "and sometimes to announce itself to be, a return to common speech." A return: common speech is the point to which one repeatedly returns, exactly because it was the point of all setting forth. But Marjorie Perloff has pointed out that American speech has been so effectively debased by the meretricious talk shows that many important writers have refused to base their work on any model of speech.

The influence of confessional poetry has been enormous. Many poets who were not confessional writers have nonetheless exploited conventions of style and subject matter that were reinvigorated by confessional poetry. Confessional poets were radically skeptical in terms of belief. Their writing presumes that depth in poetry is not to be had by recourse to philosophical concepts or religious doctrines, or even by the representation of extraordinary moments of vision. For subject matter, Lowell, Berryman, Roethke, Plath, and Snodgrass turned to autobiography, or what was meant to pass for autobiography. Their approach to poetry implied that the deepest things one can know derive from one's own past. In particular, these poets were fully absorbed in their relations to their parents. Their own character, it seems, was constituted by the events of their familial past, by their parents' sins of omission and commission.

Scores of American poets since 1959 have turned to their own families for subject matter, as though that still were the most reliable source of deep feelings and significance, but also authority, for no one else can know better what happened before the hearth. It is easy to understand how an argument for free verse becomes one for directness of expression, but it is less easy to understand why poems about family experiences also seemed especially forceful and direct. Beginning in the 1960s and continuing until now, poems about fathers, mothers, sisters, and brothers became just as topically conventional as 1950s poems about paintings or foreign cities. The turn to family subjects in the early 1960s – *Life Studies* was the first book to register this turn – was part of the shift away from the modernists as models. Which of the American modernists offers wisdom about family relations? Neither Eliot nor Stevens, nor Moore, nor Williams. The question of filial piety interested Pound as it had Virgil and Apollinaire for what it said about literary forefathers. Actual family bonds are rather troublesome when they become absolute (Canto 13), as he seemed to think they were for Viennese Jews; the Freudian focus on the family romance elicited his ugliest misogynistic antisemitism.

> and Tsievitz
> has explained to me the warmth of affections,
> the intramural, the almost intravaginal warmth of
> hebrew affections, in the family, and nearly everything else. . . .

The other modernist poets avoided the subject.

ॐ

Lowell enjoyed two great successes in his career: *Lord Weary's Castle* (1946) and *Life Studies* (1959). That was enough: the differences between these two books, especially those of style, stand for epochal shifts of taste and sensibility in the intellectual culture generally. Insistent metricality in 1946, relaxed meters, free verse, and even prose in 1959; rotund religiosity in 1946, urbane secular autobiography in 1959. Just after the war Lowell wrote as an apocalyptic visionary who had no hope in significant historical change. But the author of *Life Studies* had lost the conviction that the historical world was irredeemably damned. Quite the contrary, although the important poem "Inauguration Day: January 1953" keeps faith with the earlier poems, the volume opens with "Beyond the Alps," in which the suggestion is made that some progressive changes seem to come of their own accord, even under the guise of decline. *Life Studies* is rightly taken as a landmark of literary change, but this book does express complacency with its milieu, and this is worth noticing exactly because it does not fit the common sense of this book's place in literary history. The shift from metered to free verse as the dominant period style, from the symbolic to the metonymic mode, and from cultural to personal subject matter, really raised a larger issue about the function of poetry – namely, about its adversarial role. Lowell surely understood this.

The poems in Part 1 of *Life Studies* effectively ease the shift from earlier Lowell to later; two of them are dated 1950 and 1953, and a third is set in the immediate postwar setting of Munich. The late 1950s is not left to stand on its own. And yet the most complacent aspect of *Life Studies* is its infatuation with the late 1950s, and one sees this even in its first poem. These lines are from the first strophe of "Beyond the Alps":

> Much against my will
> I left the City of God where it belongs.

> There the skirt-mad Mussolini unfurled
> the eagle of Caesar. He was one of us
> only, pure prose. I envy the conspicuous
> waste of our grandparents on their grand tours –
> long-haired Victorian sages accepted the universe,
> while breezing on their trust funds through the world.

On the face of it, this passage is an indictment of Victorian complacency. Those sages did not acknowledge the extent to which affluence permitted them to hold the large view. The advantage Lowell claims for his own generation is that postwar intellectuals acknowledge their complicity with the 1950s prosperity. One hears that acknowledgment just below the level of statement, where he tantalizingly suggests that he was compelled to leave Rome, and that the City of God belongs in Italy, where all the men are skirt-mad. Paris, or even Boston, would be another story; historical difference can be had just by changing cities, which is what Lowell is doing in this poem. The point is, though, not to take too literally the implicit and facile cosmopolitanism here, but rather to feel the charm of Lowell's composure. That charm, however winning, is complacent, and Lowell knew it.

Marjorie Perloff has described Lowell's shift from the symbolic mode of *Lord Weary's Castle* to the narrative or realistic mode of *Life Studies*. That development in Lowell and in many of his contemporaries is understood as progressive. The question is how much of the political and social status quo has Lowell accepted in making this shift. The complacency shows not only in the details about the pope shaving with a 1950s electric shaver (though that is a point Lowell wanted to make) or keeping a canary (a popular 1950s pet), but rather in the poet's belief that explanation can be found on this mundane level. Coming to earth, as Lowell describes it, seems to entail an accommodation to Italian fascism that troubled him. Caesar and the City of God, like the Parthenon, stand for a level of cultural coherence that can be only an object of study for an American in 1950. Mussolini and Pius XII mediate between the transcendent claims of dogma and the purr of an electric razor. They are audaciously equivalent figures in the poem. A secular liberal, as the poet of *Life Studies* was becoming, sees both in terms of their effects on crowds. To the secular doubters, who could not believe or even understand the dogma of Mary's assumption, Lowell replies that the authority of Mussolini and the Pope survive. In fact, at just that point in the poem, Lowell reverts to the emphatically iambic style of *Lord Weary's Castle*: "the costumed Switzers sloped their pikes to push, / O Pius, through the monstrous human crush."

In the last strophe Lowell seems to celebrate his own arrival at a Paris train station. I put it this way in order to make obvious what has been excluded from the poem. Where is the soot, noise, and odor of trains? How far beyond the Alps has Lowell come? When he arrives in Paris he is looking backward, saying bravely that "There were no tickets for that altitude / once held by Hellas." But he imagines himself as Odysseus looking back at Polyphemus in derision. Lowell's own verse – like Homer's – is indeed a ticket for that altitude. The force and obscurity of the last two lines of the poem –

> Now Paris, our black classic, breaking up
> like killer kings on an Etruscan cup.

– should make it obvious that the poet has not yet come to peaceful terms with the 1950s secularism that he avows. It is at just that point in the poem where he must regard Italian fascism and Roman Catholicism as methods of crowd control that the new style falters, and his voice echoes that of 1946.

The advantage of urbanity is its composure in the face of what unsettles a provincial sensibility. An urbane sensibility is able to accept and live or work amicably with a wider range of experience than a provincial sensibility might. Certainly Lowell has expanded the range of his subject matter in the free-verse style of *Life Studies*, and others after him have done the same. But there is a well-known sense in which the urbane willingness to accommodate others rests upon a very cutting sense of discrimination: nothing unsettles the urbane style, but everything has its place. Lowell's shift to the metonymic style of *Life Studies* indeed opened up his own poetry and that of the 1960s and 1970s generally, but Lowell was honest in exposing the underside of this style. He placed at the emotional center of his book the limits of the urbane sensibility. He confronts these limits on the intimate terrain of his own gender identity, because his urbanity discriminated severely against his father.

"Commander Lowell" opens:

> There were no undesirables or girls in my set,
> when I was a boy at Mattapoisett –

The wit of the poem is aimed directly against Lowell's own young sensibility and the milieu from which it derived. (And these lines preserve the iambic tetrameter couplets in which the poem was originally composed, before it was revised into free-verse couplets.) Lowell presents himself frankly as a one-time snob, or rather a social climber:

> Having a naval officer
> for my Father was nothing to shout
> about to the summer colony at "Matt."
> He wasn't at all "serious" . . .

In the terms of the poem, a navel is something that the real movers and shakers of the world scratch, not something to *be*. The boy Lowell understood his own acceptance by the Mattapoisett set to necessitate the exclusion of his father, at least from the formation of his own sensibility. He was embarrassed by both parents, but his relation to his father is the real focus of *Life Studies*. The mature Lowell's guilt about his insensitivity to his father derived, as he saw it, from a too ready willingness to conform to the norms of his peers. Moreover, he wrongly understood his father to be likewise a captive of this sort of conformity.

> Smiling on all,
> Father was once successful enough to be lost
> in the mob of ruling-class Bostonians.

The terms "mob" and "ruling-class" are commonly understood as contraries. Lowell's phrasing is designed to conceal this distinction, though, just as the apparent equanimity and composure of the Mattapoisett set is meant to conceal the discriminations that are predictably, but tacitly, enforced.

Lowell's work of the 1940s appealed to an important part of the intellectual community – that part centered on *Partisan Review* – in terms of his unwillingness to accommodate recent historical events, and this feature of *Lord Weary's Castle* actually spoke to issues such as anti-Stalinism and the debate about the professionalization of American society, as suggested in Chapter 1, though these are not actually Lowell's themes. When he remade his poetic style in the mid-1950s certain broad features of the *Partisan* aesthetic survived, but not this essential feature of resistance to recent historical events. The shift from meter to free verse entailed for Lowell an accommodation first to his own character, then to his father, but also to the dominant culture of the "tranquilized *Fifties*." The signs are there in the poems that this aspect of the generous free-verse style – its gesture of accommodation to contemporary culture – was troubling to Lowell. In the shift to free verse he relinquished the role of the outsider. One question *Life Studies* raises is the extent to which the dominant free-verse style of the 1960s and 1970s expresses a measure of accommodation to the contemporary scene, though we often speak of this poetry as *resisting* the dominant culture.

❦

The 1960s were years of dramatic social discontent, and yet also paradoxically of complacency too. The generous presumption that everyone's experience was terrifically valuable, that every experience was worthy of record, corresponds to the Wordsworthian belief that illumination and transport could be had anywhere – these were commonly held notions. No poet was so tempted as Robert Hass by the benefits of accommodation to contemporary American culture.

Hass's first book of poems, *Field Guide* (1973), which appeared in the Yale

Younger Poets series, selected by Stanley Kunitz, was unusually well received, and it has been reprinted and kept available since then. Hass took six
years before publishing another book, *Praise*, in order to attain a different
kind of writing. The poem most appreciated in this book, "Meditation at
Lagunitas," shows Hass's characteristic strengths:

> All the new thinking is about loss.
> In this it resembles all the old thinking.
> The idea, for example, that each particular erases
> the luminous clarity of a general idea. That the clown-
> faced woodpecker probing the dead sculpted trunk
> of that black birch is, by his presence,
> some tragic falling off from a first world
> of undivided light. Or the other notion that,
> because there is in this world no one thing
> to which the bramble of *blackberry* corresponds,
> a word is elegy to what it signifies.
> We talked about it late last night and in the voice
> of my friend, there was a thin wire of grief, a tone
> almost querulous. After a while I understood that,
> talking this way, everything dissolves: *justice*,
> *pine, hair, woman, you* and *I*.

When the poem was first published, the word "poetry" stood where "thinking" now does in the first two lines. By 1979 it was clear that the critique of
ideas of transcendence (ll. 3–6) and of reference (ll. 6–9) was more powerful
among literary theorists than among poets. The revision pitched the poem
directly at the professional academic audience, and this is now not surprisingly his most famous poem, though not his very best. The witty irony of the
second line is characteristic of Hass, who often admirably lightens the tone of
his poems with some joke or anecdote; the irony sets a bond of knowing
sophistication between reader and writer. The success of the poem derives
largely from Hass's ability to move easily among various levels of diction.
The clearest transit is from the discursive mode of the opening two lines to
the descriptive one of lines four to six. But there are other levels too, such as
that of the blackberry bramble (l. 10), which is not quite description, though
it passes for the *idea* of concreteness for a while. The word blackberry here
refers not to one berry, but to a collection of berries in a bramble, and to no
particular bramble even, but to one's idea of *the* bramble of blackberry. This
is not really concreteness, as Hass knows. Moreover, the ratio between black-
berries and ideas recalls Falstaff's lines: "If reasons were as plentiful as black-
berries, I would give no man a reason upon compulsion, I" (I Henry IV, II,
iv, 264ff.). The word that stands for concreteness is, then, in no straight
sense referential to any particular thing; it is rather a nexus of ideas and texts.

This is important, because the belief of poets in referentiality is often dismissed by theorists as naive and archaic. Hass is cagily sophisticated here, though he does speak on behalf of the physical and spiritual pleasures that are undermined by critiques of referentiality (ll. 14–16). He makes his case by recalling the concrete experience of making love to a particular woman:

> There was a woman
> I made love to and I remembered how, holding
> her small shoulders in my hands sometimes,
> I felt a violent wonder at her presence
> like a thirst for salt, for my childhood river
> with its island willows, silly music from the pleasure boat,
> muddy places where we caught the little orange-silver fish
> called *pumpkinseed*. It hardly had to do with her.
> Longing, as we say, because desire is full
> of endless distances. I must have been the same to her.
> But I remember so much, the way her hands dismantled bread,
> the thing her father said that hurt her, what
> she dreamed. There are moments when the body is as numinous
> as words, days that are the good flesh continuing.
> Such tenderness, those afternoons and evenings,
> saying *blackberry, blackberry, blackberry*.

Hass asserts his "violent wonder at her presence," though presence is exactly what Derrida has taught readers of literary theory most to suspect. The figure Hass invokes to characterize her presence is anything but fulfilling: thirst itself is a desire based upon absence of the most immediate human need; a thirst for salt is a thirst for thirst, which at least doubles the sense of absence attributed to this presence. This woman, no longer present in his life, has dissolved into a nexus of memories. The most specific of the memories themselves complicate the straight sense of referentiality. Those fish are named after a plant, which confuses two elementary categories of analysis. What he remembers about her are her manner of movement, her words, her dreams, not things but the movement of spirit around things. His affirmation is not of stony things themselves, but of the life of people with words and texts that surrounds objects. The numinosity of words and the good flesh continuing are no more concrete than the texts from which they derive; John, I:i in this case. But the life is there. And the perfect word to end the poem is Falstaff's refusal to give just reasons.

"Against Botticelli" is not addressed, as "Meditation" is, to an academic audience, though it expresses a painfully knowledgeable literary perspective. The poem begins with the sophisticated, ironic perspective that is charming in "Meditation":

> In the life we lead together every paradise is lost.
> Nothing could be easier: summer gathers new leaves
> to casual darkness. So few things we need to know.
> And the old wisdoms shudder in us and grow slack.
> Like renunciation. Like the melancholy beauty
> of giving it all up. Like walking steadfast
> in the rhythms, winter light and summer dark.
> And the time for cutting furrows and the dance.
> Mad seed. Death waits it out. It waits us out,
> the sleek incandescent saints, earthly and prayerful.

The iambic, ironic fluency of the opening line quickly dissolves in self-criticism, and the short blasts of sentence fragments succeed the voice of assurance. The easy meditative mode resurfaces repeatedly in the poem, as when Hass casually lets "it all" stand for "life" (l. 6). The power of this poem derives from Hass's unwillingness to write with consistent self-assurance; he is unsettled, and the poem is in turn unsettling. Here he pushes beyond the free-verse mode of the late 1960s and the 1970s. Melancholy was a staple of this mode; it served in place of profundity. Hass identifies this tone as the heritage of modernism, what the work of Stevens (the last three lines of "Sunday Morning" are here in lines 2–3), of Eliot (lines 6–8 recall "Little Gidding"; and lines 13–14, *The Waste Land*), and of Pound (lines 14–15 marvelously evoke "The Seafarer" and Canto II) left to a young poet: the sense that the world was not good enough. (He looks back at Romantic poetry – Keats in line 3 – coolly, with modernist cynicism.) His disgust with the preening of the melancholic type is clear in his depiction of "us" as vain saints. The word "steadfast" metamorphoses into "shamefast." Resting in shame is a credit to no one. To a literally postmodernist generation, what form will desire assume? Deliberate excess and violation determine the postmodernist form of desire. This derives, I think, from the sense of lateness and limitation that poets of Hass's generation knew personally, but which everyone in America in the late 1970s knew too. How much is possible? How much has already been done? The achievement of the generation of the 1880s was so great that poets born about the turn of the century (Zukofsky, Rexroth, Oppen, Winters, Tate, Rukeyser, and Bogan) could receive little attention. This second generation of modernists, Hass said, "wrote in an odd obscurity. The glamour of the first generation of modern poets seems to have passed directly from them to their explainers." Hass's generation (born in the late 1930s and the early 1940s) had to launch a more violent offensive in order to get out from under the shadow of the modernist achievement.

In an essay on Lowell, Hass wrote revealingly about the connection between desire and violence that this poem explores:

The fact is that there is an element of cruelty in human sexuality, though that isn't the reason for the Puritan distrust of sex. The Puritans distrusted sexuality because the sexual act dissolved human will for a moment, because – for a moment – men fell into the roots of their mammal nature. You can't have an orgasm and be a soldier of Christ. . . . And the Puritan solution, hidden but real in the history of imagination whether in Rome or the Enlightenment, was to turn sex into an instrument of will, of the conscious cruelty which flowered in the writings of Sade.

Venus has both things: "mammal warmth and the inhuman element." There is no escaping the violence; the only issue is how it will manifest itself. Hass begins the discussion of sex and violence in the essay on Lowell by saying, "I'm not sure how to talk about it." The poem delivers no firm statement of the relation of sex to violence; instead there is excess, an unmanageable surplus of feeling and sense, throughout the poem. The clearest instance is the line: ". . . irised: otters in the tide lash, in the kelp-drench." The motivation for this line is not, as it seems to be, a view of the painting: there are no otters in Botticelli's painting. The line is generated more by richness of sound, and the memory of similar lines in Pound's *Cantos*. Hass is writing over his own head, trying to explain a relationship he does not fully understand. The poem's power comes largely from that sense of slightly missed connections, of a lingering obscurity in the subject itself.

When Hass says, "We are not in any painting," he seems to suggest that all we escape is representation. We are too late for Botticelli, Bosch, or Goya. Our brutality is too frank for art. The second section of the poem opens with the knowing, ironically amused tone of the first lines of the poem; then, however, Hass tells a story of "a man and the pale woman / he fucks in the ass underneath the stars." The diction becomes abruptly brutal and prosaic, because that is appropriate to our artlessness. But this story is a representation: specifically, an allusion to Bertolucci's film *Last Tango in Paris* (1973). Hass evokes the romance of crossing boundaries and claims metaphysical depth for the man ("He is learning about gratitude . . .") in a way that is ultimately objectionable. For him, this has been exploratory sex, and Hass can speak with some specificity about gratitude and pleasure in regard to the man's feelings; but Hass's account of the woman's experience is cursory and conventional: "The woman thinks what she is feeling is like the dark / and utterly complete." The poem is limited here to the man's perspective; the woman is merely satisfied. Moreover, she is satisfied in conventional terms, however unconventional the sexual act may be. Innumerable films of the late 1960s represented moments of heterosexual lovemaking under a waterfall, on a beach, or in a pool, as completely fulfilling for both parties, despite the social or political divisions of the world that in other scenes beset the lovers. The conventional sense is that heterosexuality is authentic, distinct from the mess of professional, political, and economic relations that set characters in motion. "The woman's white hands opening, opening" might easily come from such a film; a filmmaker's gloss might well be: "The woman thinks what she is feeling is like the dark / and utterly complete." This poem is about pursuing desire beyond satisfaction and achievement, going against beauty, love and perfection. Its pieces are not lined up in a row, as those of "Meditation" are; they are jagged, unsettled, with gaps between them – until the poem succumbs to a naive estimation of the redemptive powers of heterosexuality. The sex of this poem is predatory and confused, well beyond Hass's ability to explain, as he has acknowledged. To represent any sexual act as "longing brought perfectly to closing" is to reproduce the culture's claims about sex being the basis of authenticity.

Several poems in *Human Wishes* (1989), among them the very best of the book, engage the critical perspective on Hass's work that I have been suggesting. The strongest poem in the book, "Berkeley Eclogue," is unlike anything Hass has ever written. It is a 167 line free-verse interior dialogue between the poet who wrote *Field Guide* and *Praise* and the person who knows that the poems of those books leave out too much difficulty, too much life.

> Sunlight on the streets in afternoon
> and shadows on the faces in the open-air cafes.
> *What for?* Wrong question. You knock
> without knowing that you knocked. The door
> opens on a century of clouds and centuries
> of centuries of clouds. The bird sings
> among the toyons in the spring's diligence
> of rain. *And then what? Hand on your heart.*
> *Would you die for spring? What would you die for?*
> *Anything?*
> Anything. It may be I can't find it.
> And they can, the spooners of whipped cream
> and expresso at the sunny tables, the women
> with their children in the stores. *You want to sing?*
> Tra-la. Empty and he wants to sing. (ll. 1–14)

The italicized voice is harshly skeptical of Hass's poetic ambition – to sing, to celebrate. This interrogator accuses Hass of a self-serving sincerity, hand on heart. Hass's admission is that he is willing to die for anything, to stand for anything definite in a century of clouds. A bird's song among trees that can be named might do. The lyric aspiration derives from emptiness, hopelessness, which once Hass faces, he must then dissociate yet another persona from himself, "he." Hass's attraction to the lives of affluent, educated Californians, the frequenters of cafés here and in "Museum," comes out of the apprehension that they may be justifiably complacent: they may have found what he misses.

To identify with that milieu entails the great advantage of enabling one to take credit for the bounty of the world: "Every day was a present / he pretended that he brought" (ll. 28–9). Maybe it is nothing more than this pretense of being good – sensitive to other people, to the moths and apples that serve to justify the descriptive poet's language of adequacy – that makes an ethically-based liberal politics seem the apt corollary: *"Injustice / in tropical climates is appalling, and it does do you credit to think so"* (ll. 40–2). This is withering self-criticism; none of Hass's critics could be less sympathetic.

What emerges from this painful dialogue is a glimpse of the subjects he has neglected. At the exact center of this poem is a glimpse of a father beating his son. Hass says, "The father / . . . was wailing on the boy / with fists," as a boy would say "wailing," as for a boy there is only the one father and the one boy (ll. 82–4). Although he cannot say "I," Hass must be the boy, who sees a passerby avert his look, as only the boy or the father would see (l. 85). And his father apparently battered his wife as well (ll. 88–93), though she tried unsuccessfully to conceal that abuse from her son. And the mother, alcoholic, beat her daughter (ll. 74–6). The second section of the poem is explicitly about growing up, which is understood to mean falling in love. Hass grows up by rescuing "Some old man," though the old man dies anyway. Growing up means killing the father and saving him too. Then one can love a woman.

The sunny cafés now look rather different. So too do the many references to Hass's own children. His poems are written in praise of domestic life, dailiness. His son Luke walking with "his arms full of school drawings he hoped not to drop in the mud," his daughter Kristin answering "Mommy, Daddy, Leif" to the question "Who are you?": this is all charm. "Berkeley Eclogue," though, now shows how deliberately that representation of domesticity has kept strife at bay. His best known poems are something like the masks he describes as made around the mouths: "The mouths formed cries. / They were the parts that weren't there – implied / by what surrounded them. They were a cunning / emptiness" (ll. 54–7). The poems about the good life with wife and children in sunny California were generated out of the nightmare of a battered child of alcoholic parents. "Not that again" might have been the implicit slogan of Hass's poems. All that he would not let his family become was present in the earlier poems as a "cunning emptiness." A safer version of this problem of exclusion is presented in the sketch "Museum," where Hass admires a young couple sitting with their infant in a Berkeley café reading the *New York Times*. Do these two adults, with "this equitable arrangement" of sharing the child and the sections of the paper, complacently miss the human significance of the Kathe Kollwitz exhibit? Do those who might share the straightforward sense of Hass's last words here ("everything seems possible") understand the economic constraints impressed upon most people in the world or the political constraints enforced against dissenters in Latin America? These are the questions raised more or less directly by Hass in the book, but they are easy in that they encourage a not costly and self-satisfying vigilance on behalf of oppressed others. More costly is the notion that one's most intimate hopes, expressed in the poems one writes or the family one makes are austere by excluding any hint of the suffering that families regularly bring on themselves. Hass is admitting that he may have produced an art of caricature.

In the close attention to details of landscape in the poems of his first book and in the representation of sensibilities and experiences that in his second book *Praise* (1979) seem especially Californian ("The Feast" is a good example), his poems have come to express the best of lyric poetry in the west. This is even truer of *Human Wishes*, which celebrates "the abundance / the world gives, the more-than-you-bargained-for / surprise of it" that many Californians easily feel. Since the mid-1970s he has lived in Berkeley, where he eventually replaced Robert Pinsky as professor of English at the University of California. *Human Wishes* shows him experimenting with prose poems, resisting the formalist trend that his friend Pinsky has steadily strengthened. Hass has always written in free verse and believed that the reaction against rhyme and meter that began in English in the mid-nineteenth century and has dominated poetry of the twentieth century had some special psycho–historical validity and has still a vital connection to the life of the body. But he has seen too that the free verse of his contemporaries – based on just these self-serving preconceptions – has led to a facile cultivation of personality in poetry. His work has successfully maintained the best of lyricism in American poetry without succumbing to what Pinsky called "our hard-ons of self-concern." When critics like Perloff, Jerome McGann, Charles Bernstein, and Ron Silliman want to deride American poets for their devotion to the conventions of lyricism, they assiduously avoid Hass, because he is the hard case. Lowell's sense that the free-verse mode was implicitly complacent about the present became much clearer two decades later in Hass's poetry. "Berkeley Eclogue" shows Hass facing this problem more directly than Lowell or any of his successors has.

ě

Frank Bidart came to literary maturity during the 1960s, and *Life Studies*, as he has said, was a "great model" for him. Bidart studied with Lowell at Harvard in 1966, and they became close friends in 1967. In 1969 they collaborated closely on the revision of Lowell's *Notebook*. One sees in Bidart's poems, especially in *Golden State* (1973), the importance of autobiographical

material, and his poems are so scored on the page as to register quite exactly
the sound of the voice speaking the poems. But Bidart is a poet of many
voices, none of them simply his own. The typographical scoring of the poems
shows him trying to get weight and deliberateness, gravity, into his words,
often one by one; his is certainly not a style that simply imitates speech.
Also, despite the subject matter of his work, there is no construction of a
poet's sensibility behind these poems, as there is behind Lowell's or even
Creeley's, to name another poet intent on registering the gravity of his
words. Bidart does not present himself as a personality. The voices in Bidart's
poems are intended, as he says, to "make life show itself," and it does
especially when the voices of the dead speak, in his recent poems, because
they help one to recognize life's seriousness and the weight single experiences, thoughts, or feelings can come to bear in retrospect. These poems
show that the elegiac impulse was there all along not only in the subjects of
his poems, but in the voices themselves, in their appearance on the page, in
capitals, in italics, surrounded by white.

Despite his collaboration with Bidart, Lowell could never respond sympathetically to Bidart's poems. He could not really *hear* the poems, he told
Bidart, and this makes sense. Lowell was a poet of mighty lines, and Bidart
has refused not only the support of metrical grids but even that of a stable
line or rhythm. He has stripped away all scaffolding that might get in the
way of a radical commitment to telling the unadorned truth about his
subjects. His focus is on individual words, and his typography has increasingly stressed this commitment to the resources of single words. The stress
registered by upper case and italic type reveals more about the psychology of
the speakers than about free-verse prosody.

The truth that these weighty words try to attain is not quite that of the
confessional poets. Bidart's earliest poems, which he dates to 1965, are
obviously confessional in their effort to explore the dark corners of his relationship to his father, mother, and the family household, and with this
subject goes the presumption that his character is the result of historical
circumstances. I use the word character intentionally; it suggests the idea of a
moral nature that has some independence of historical circumstances. One
wants to be able to count on a person of character to remain constant even in
the face of adverse circumstances; indeed inauspicious circumstances provide
the defining tests of character itself. This sort of essentialist thinking about
identity is at odds with the confessional poet's historical conception of identity. Bidart's work traces the limits of these two efforts to articulate truth.

In "To the Dead," the poem he placed first in his collected poems, Bidart's
effort to reach an authentic substratum of experience is clear without being
naive.

What I hope (when I hope) is that we'll
see each other again, –

  . . . and again reach the VEIN

in which we loved each other . . .
It existed. *It existed.*

There is a NIGHT within the NIGHT, –

  . . . for, like the detectives (the Ritz Brothers)
in *The Gorilla,*

once we'd been battered by the gorilla

we searched the walls, the intricately carved
impenetrable panelling

for a button, lever, latch

that unlocks a secret door that
reveals at last the secret chambers,

CORRIDORS within WALLS,

(the disenthralling, necessary, dreamed structure
beneath the structure we see,)

that is the HOUSE within the HOUSE . . .
[ellipses in original].

Bidart's insistence in line five is characteristic; the typographical scoring of
rhetorical stress by upper-case and italics where none is normally used similarly expresses resistance against surface appearance. His poems are often
concerned with the very moment of definition, when one can say that something exists. Existence itself here offers a powerful consolation. In the current
intellectual environment it is no longer easy to claim that some feelings and
experiences are more authentic than others. The counter claim – that no vein
of authenticity exists – is made repeatedly visible by the rhetorical turns on
certain phrases of definition and assertion, as in line five. The romance of a
secret chamber has particular appeal in Bidart's work, partly because his
glimpses of the substratum occur in inauspicious circumstances. Even a late-
night television screening of an old Ritz Brothers comedy may provide a
means of accurately explaining the nature of the authentic substratum.
Bidart masterfully shows how the apparent banality of ordinary life is not at
all ordinary. His claim is that the secret chamber is "necessary" and
"dreamed" – to which one might easily assent – but also "disenthralling": so
far from conceding that the imagination enthralls minds, he argues that the
ordinary appearance of the world is enthralling; penetration to a dreamed
substratum is what brings one out of the spell. The poems are a working out

of a skeptical desire for a deeper awareness, not a presumption of that awareness: "Is this wisdom, or self-pity?" he asks, without resolving the choice. One wants to believe in the wisdom so as not to lose one's dead loved ones, so as not to lose one's own time to superficiality. Bidart's work shows the critical sense in which confessional poetry continues to matter for very strong poets long after it was fresh and surprising as a mode of writing. Bidart continues the mode, but with complicating signs of strain.

After repeated exposure of the government's conspicuous mendacity in the late 1960s, taciturnity gained fresh authority. In 1967 Louise Glück said, "I sensed that . . . some vision – of language, of human relations – had played itself out." It was then that asceticism took over American poetry, when W. S. Merwin's *Lice* appeared. His diction severely narrowed the range of the language: simple, concrete words took on new power when he refused the syntactic structures that elaborate complexity. He repeated the same words over and over, as though writing in a code: silence, dark, snow, stone, eating, and so on. The result was a poetic diction for the 1970s that Robert Pinsky satirized brilliantly. Although this style emerged in a culture enthralled by authenticity, an ascetic ideal then seemed to writers a counter measure to vulgar notions of the amplitude of immediate experience. Merwin's code was like a screen mediating expression of contemporary experience, an explicit reminder of the poverty of immediate experience.

> once more I remember that the beginning
>
> Is broken
>
> No wonder the addresses are torn
>
> To which I make my way eating the silence of animals
> Offering snow to the darkness
>
> Today belongs to few and tomorrow to no one.

There is no point of presence in this idiom: origins are remembered repeatedly, while the planet's flora and fauna are systematically and recklessly ravaged. The present is vacuous, and the future implausible.

This ascetic style dominated American poetry for more than a decade; it produced a wealth of magazine verse, but also some genuine accomplishments among a small set of writers. Louise Glück in particular understood very well how to turn the taciturn manner to powerful and rich effect. She admired in George Oppen "not a mind incapable of response but a mind wary of premature response; a mind, that is, not hungering after sensation." Hers is an anorexic strength through denial. She denies herself the comforts of the scenic mode, in which a poet paves a reader's entry with the appearance of a concrete scene. Frost's companionable "you come too" in the poem that opens his collections is just what she refuses. She once expressed her admiration for Sylvia Plath, because "Plath invests almost nothing in circumstance." In this sense, Plath was quite unlike the confessional poets with whom she is most commonly associated. These are just the terms Glück has elsewhere used to speak of her own writing: "My work has always been strongly marked by a disregard for the circumstantial, except insofar as it could be transformed into paradigm." Her first poems were published in the mid-1960s in the large circulation magazines that had earlier been Plath's targets: *Nation, Mademoiselle, The Atlantic Monthly, The New Yorker.* They were both ambitious in conventional terms, and they both sacrificed tonal range for a concentration of force.

The taciturn style of life is unsurprisingly gendered male. Glück's father "showed / contempt for emotion. / They're the emotional ones, / my sister and my mother." "I was born," she says,

into an environment in which the right of any family member to complete the sentence of another was assumed. Like most of the people in that family, I had a strong desire to speak, but that desire was regularly frustrated: my sentences were, in being cut off, radically changed – transformed, not paraphrased. . . . I had, early on, a very strong sense that there was no point to speech if speech did not precisely articulate perception. To my mother, speech was the socially acceptable form of murmur: its function was to fill a room with ongoing, consoling human sound. And to my father, it was performance and disguise. My response was silence.

She seems then to take up asceticism as a third option, emulating neither parent.

> that's what you want, that's the object: in the end,
> the one who has nothing wins.

But in the poems the ascetic silence is not a third position; it's the father's. In "Birthday" she tells the story of her mother's admirer who arranged for a dozen roses to be delivered to her mother annually, even for a decade after his own death. "All that time," Glück says, "I thought / the dead could minister to the living."

> I didn't realize
> this was the anomaly; that for the most part
> ——the dead were like my father.

Silent and unreachable. Her mother tries to show her deceased husband that

> she understands,
> that she accepts his silence.
> He hates deception: she doesn't want him making
> signs of affection when he can't feel.

To express but what we feel, and to feel very little: this was the family ethos that Glück inherited. This is not life's normal duplicity. To cultivate this species of authenticity is to play dead.

The sense that connection with other people, particularly loved ones, is injurious comes directly from Plath ("Tulips"). "Daddy" and "Lady Lazarus" shape the impulse to hatred into art. These are the sources of Plath's intensity. The poems gathered posthumously in *Ariel* (1965) had a lasting impact on literary taste. The controversy they originally produced centered on the role of extremist perspectives in poetry, but eventually it became clearer that the crucial issue was rather gender. Plath's novel *The Bell Jar* originally appeared under a pseudonym in January 1963, not quite three weeks before she killed herself on February 11. This book about a middle class young WASP woman who, despite her many advantages, tries repeatedly to take her own life had no American publisher until 1971; its mass paperback edition is now in its sixth American printing. It took a long time for readers and critics to appreciate the importance of gender in Plath, and among confessional poets generally. Lowell confesses to a failure to sympathize adequately with his father. Plath, though, reveals a severity in her feelings about her father that makes questions of fairness or sympathy entirely moot. "Daddy, I have had to kill you," she states plainly. Hers is a stunningly performative poetic:

> There's a stake in your fat black heart
> And the villagers never liked you.
> They are dancing and stamping on you.
> They always *knew* it was you.
> Daddy, daddy, you bastard, I'm through.

Here in the last strophe of "Daddy" literal biographical truth is obviously irrelevant. The construction of a voice – nasty, proud, murderous – is what matters. The second and fourth lines here recover the meanness of an angry child, and the insistent rhymes running through the poems she composed in a rush just months before her suicide repeatedly evoke the source of strong feeling in childhood. After two decades in which American and English poets concentrated their efforts on complications of tone, carefully measured ironies, Plath breaks through to the art of the fantastically overdone.

Glück brings a more worldly sensibility to this bitch voice in American poetry. She finds irony in her repeated failures to rise above the enclosures of identity.

> It is not the moon, I tell you.
> It is these flowers
> lighting the yard.

I hate them.
I hate them as I hate sex,
the man's mouth
sealing my mouth, the man's
paralyzing body –

and the cry that always escapes,
the low, humiliating
premise of union –

That cry is mocking in the common sense, because it shows that human nature, even biology, leaves one always ready to be suckered by some still greater hope. The simple conclusion is that gender difference is the biological fact to which one must always return – this is familiar enough, and to just that extent uninteresting. Glück had made the point thuddingly at the end of "Grandmother" (1980) that a man's love is like a hand over a woman's mouth. But in "Mock Orange" she develops not this familiar thesis about stable but conflicting male and female identities but rather the sense that each person is comprised of multiple personae – "the old selves, the tired antagonisms" – that are ultimate divisions.

One's sense of Glück's worldliness comes partly from her mordant humor, which surprises by lightening the tone of this severe verse, and partly too from her persistent intellectuality. "The true, in poetry," she has written, "is felt as insight. It is very rare, but beside it other poems seem merely intelligent comment." She represents the humiliation of sexuality as a logical failure. The premise is mistaken; "We were made fools of." There is fierceness here, as in Plath, but there is no way of attributing her ferocity to excessive emotionality: she is an insistently analytical writer who regards emotionality as a trap that gets us in our unwary moments of transport. Lovers are manipulable by their desires; one can be played, like an instrument, especially after one has revealed, in intimate moments, vulnerabilities ("Marathon"). The vein of strong feeling that is constant in her work is generated by asceticism, a cutting off of the ordinary sources of feeling: sexuality, friendship ("The Triumph of Achilles"), parental affection.

Elms

All day I tried to distinguish
need from desire. Now, in the dark,
I feel only bitter sadness for us,
the builders, the planers of wood,
because I have been looking
steadily at these elms
and seen the process that creates
the writhing, stationary tree
is torment, and have understood
it will make no forms but twisted forms.

That Glück's is a conservative and intellectual poetry should be clear to any reader of this poem. The predicates, from first to last, are intellectual. She looks at the trees in order to distinguish need from desire and to understand the forms that desire can take. Torment and twisting are inevitable, because the world is not made for desire; the human climate is set against fulfillment. Asceticism is itself rationalistic insofar as it aims not only at self-discipline but further at a representation of a way of life. The refusal of the body's appetites, as Geoffrey Harpham says, is what renders a life "eminently imitable." Ascetics refuse to fall victim to appetite and choose instead to teach by example. Glück's stripped-down art ("we worship clarity") derives from her wish to "leave behind / exact records." Stylistic asceticism is audible everywhere. The lines are shaped, as most of the lines by most of her contemporaries are too, above all by rhetorical and grammatical considerations, not by any notion of musicality. When line breaks do not simply coincide with clause and phrase boundaries, they underline rhetorical emphases governed straightforwardly by the semantic significance of the sentences. This means that there can be no counterpoint in her verse, no pull away from an expected metric or even rhythm. "Metrical variation," she wrote, "provides a subtext. It does what we now rely on tone to do." Prosodically, hers is a one-dimensional art; the poet goes it alone, with just the sense of her statements and her control of irony to render the sounds of her words memorable, compelling, and exact.

It's a short step, looking back, from "Elms" (1985) to the religious verse of *The Wild Iris* (1992), though *Ararat* (1990) intervened, and *Wild Iris* was not what one expected. Her earlier religious poems, most obviously "Lamentations" (1980), were more cosmological than human or earthly; they were "seen from the air." *The Wild Iris*, which won the Pulitzer Prize, is a collection of religious poems seen explicitly from the earth. The Vespers series is addressed directly to a Christian God by a smart, bitter Protestant believer:

> You thought we didn't know. But we knew once,
> children know these things. Don't turn away now – we
>   inhabited
> a lie to appease you.

This is an argument very much with God the Father, a duplicitous trickster whose promise of consolation is utterly empty. The drama of these poems is partly in Glück's analytical turns, but just as much in her shifts of tone. The second line, for instance, loses the initial disapproval for a moment in affirming the knowledge of children and then sets out a sharply reproving imperative, showing God as a guilty and ashamed malefactor. The austerity of Merwin and later Glück and others is, on the one hand, a refusal of the easy resort to authenticity that more romantic poets took in the 1960s and later.

But austerity expresses another variety of authenticity: Glück strips down, as she imagines her father to have done, in order to stay true. These barbed prayers to an unkind and petty God record her unwillingness to take any consolation for granted. It is not surprising then that she invests childhood and the garden with the fullness of life that is everywhere else witnessed only by traces marking absence. "I remember," this poem continues,

> sunlight of early spring, embankments
> netted with dark vinca. I remember
> lying in a field, touching my brother's body.
> Don't turn away now; we denied
> memory to console you.

What she has lost is a bond of shared pleasure with her brother, which stands for innocent but forbidden sexuality, and more generally for the direct pleasure of the earth. Gardening is an elegiac discipline for remembering and honoring losses. These poems remind one of the rationalizing of seventeenth-century Protestant religious poetry, but Glück comes back repeatedly not to God's greatness but to his meanness. He envies any bond because it postpones the solitude in which his followers find their way to Him. *Cui bono?* she asks – not a new question, but an audacious one here.

> Who else
> would so envy the bond we had then
> as to tell us it was not earth
> but heaven we were losing?

Poems variously achieve forcefulness and directness; Bidart's resources are mostly stylistic, though with poems on anorexia, murder, necrophilia, and amputation, he too has exploited the resources of hot topics. Writers since 1945 have witnessed spectacles of violent social change and new technologies of force. Poets might have felt that the resources of compact metrical verse that J. V. Cunningham and Turner Cassity exploit were fitting to the objective of a forceful, direct sort of verse, but most poets, like most Americans, have thought of force in personal and physical terms: the body, not the polity, is our measure of directness and force. Just the reverse of the epigrammatic style has been taken as the norm for direct expression: talk, relaxed and casual speech, despite its looseness and redundance, is the basis of the discourse most poets since 1959 have thought of as especially direct. This infatuation with force and directness can be seen all over recent poetry, but Sharon Olds has done best with this invisible style.

Hers is obviously a poetry of the body; Helen Vendler has called it pornographic. But eroticism is only one aspect of a poetry or culture of physicality. Elegy is the genre that copes with the hazards of physicality. Olds' most recent book, *The Father* (1992), is a sequence of short poems about her dead father, removed from her in life by his gender and inarticulateness, and now removed by death. Not surprisingly, the poems concentrate intensely on his physical presence in order to get from him in verse what could not be had in life. These are the opening lines of "The Glass," which indicate how strenuously Olds pursues the direct presentation of human physicality in verse:

> I think of it with wonder now,
> the glass of mucus that stood on the table
> in front of my father all weekend. The tumor
> is growing fast in his throat these days,
> and as it grows it sends out pus
> like the sun sending out flares, those pouring
> tongues. So my father has to gargle, cough,
> spit a mouthful of thick stuff
> into the glass every ten minutes or so,
> scraping the rim up his lower lip
> to get the last bit off his skin, then he
> sets the glass down on the table and it
> sits there, like a glass of beer foam,
> shiny and faintly golden, he gargles and
> coughs and reaches for it again
> and gets the heavy sputum out,
> full of bubbles and moving around like yeast –
> he is like a god producing food from his own mouth.

Olds exhibits the physical facts of disease and death forthrightly; my own discomfort, after many readings, remains intense. She engineers my response by invoking so many terms to suggest the imbibing of this glass of phlegm. But she will not settle for my disgust; in the end she insists instead on the transformative power of this appalling image.

> . . . I would
> empty it and it would fill again
> and shimmer there on the table until
> the room seemed to turn around it
> in an orderly way, a model of the solar system
> turning around the sun,
> my father and the old earth that used to
> lie at the center of the universe, now
> turning with the rest of us
> around his death, bright glass of
> spit on the table, these last mouthfuls.

I cannot see this glass as a sun drawing us all around it, because the thought of drinking the phlegm is too disgusting. I have invested heavily, at Olds's instigation, in the physicality of her poems: there is no leaving *physis* behind for this *nous*. The invisible style ends by leaving the force in the subject matter.

There is a sense in which, although I have taken Lowell as the originator of confessional poetry, one has to acknowledge the roots of this mode as far back as the origins of lyric. Sappho is at the basis of poetry's claim to intimacy. "No other lyric poet since the world began," Lawrence Lipking remarks, "has ever drawn such praise. She is our *perfect* poet." Her intensity comes from the position of the abandoned lover. This Sapphic intensity is connected directly to the notion of poetry as the genre of the body. Sappho's most famous poem, the Second Ode, called simply "the best," is her report on the state of her own body when she sees her lover marry another. That's the site of the lyric's beginning: the drama of the body's processes, the woman abandoned.

From this nexus Susan Hahn has produced two books, *Incontinence* (1993) and *Confession* (1997), that develop the resources of confessional poetry toward the performative. The abandoned woman has obvious access to pathos: she is hurting, and someone in particular has made her hurt. Hahn (or her persona "Susan Hahn"), like Plath and Glück, turns the abandoned woman into a scary bitch. "Hahn," married, aging, takes a lover in *Incontinence*; he does not fully return her love, and then he sees other women. She telephones him repeatedly and hangs up. She calls one of the other women too and stays silent on the line.

Jealousy

She sings *Hello* with a hold
on the *lo* as if it were part of a lullaby
and children were happily napping
around her, so safe in

her voice, while I smother
my breath and hope for anger
when I say nothing back –
lips bitten to cracked.
No matter how many times
I call her sweet mood

won't change as my spine twists
and discs lurch out of place.
Over and over I split

my nails as I punch
her number and she is there, lenient
mother against my sunken silence.

Good mother; twisted witch. Hahn presents a complex account of the abandoned woman's agency. The woman is angry at the lover who has left her, malicious and sneaky in her harassment of him, and unreflective about her own betrayal of her husband. She is a witch who wants to drug her lover. But love makes her do it. As she prepares for her suicide, she writes:

Love

> has leveled my body,
> broken the fine bones
> of the soul – it will not float up.

And her body made her love in the first place. Nature made her red, "ragged in the moon-held spasms, swollen / in the messy crimson of grief over the death / of a friend or what I've seen on TV." The moon, menses, blood of her friends. Suffering is inflicted on her, and she forgives herself for her own aggression: "the phone – the only weapon this victim / has for not feeling so alone." If this self-pity were all she knew, the book would be a small thing. But the witch twists herself. The book is loaded with self-loathing, far more compelling than mere loneliness.

Mania

> Sometimes I talk too much
> at a shrill pitch and the bitch
> part of me carries off
> my conversation in directions
> I'd never travel with more peaceful
> lips. But when my brain swells
> and pushes on the small bones
> of my face, what spills out
> seems so rich. I think
> everyone loves me so much.
> Until, alone with the bloated
> moon, I hear the rattle
> of my voice and its twist –
> the gnarled path it takes running
> after any catch, grabbing
> first place in a race
> it does not want to enter,
> accepting the trophy with a curtsy practiced
> for royalty. Hater of both halves
> of myself – raving
> slave, desperate dictator.

Nothing is disavowed here, neither the self-pity nor the absolving biological determinism, but there is a level of self-awareness that rises far above these vices. Her vanity is left nakedly exposed (ll. 8–10), plump and comical.

Then comes the cruel twisting again, driven by her own dual nature, there from the beginning, once some parent's sweetie, now her own bitch.

❧

The cult of authenticity obviously has political dimensions, though they do not necessarily converge on any single practical political position. Philip Levine counts himself not surprisingly an anarchist – "I don't believe in the validity of governments, laws, charters, all that hides us from our essential oneness" – though he has taught for many years at a state university. *What Work Is* (1991) won the National Book Award at a moment when Americans were especially aware of the problems of unemployment. But Levine's work is not timely in that sociological sense, partly because his poems characteristically recall the working-class culture of Detroit that he knew as a young man, in the 1940s and 1950s. This was an industrial culture, when working meant living with the grime of large machines. His usual theme is the way working people, even poor people, manage to create something remarkable out of the routine waste of industrial city life.

> Out of burlap sacks, out of bearing butter
> Out of black bean and wet slate bread,
> Out of the acids of rage, the candor of tar,
> Out of creosote, gasoline, drive shafts, wooden dollies,
> They Lion grow.

Black people especially – the dialect of the fifth line is meant to be Black English – have emerged from industrial wastelands to become examples of gladiatorial strength (The Detroit Lions football team is the particular reference). "From 'Bow Down' come 'Rise Up' " – their oppression led eventually and inevitably to their great strength. Another lion here is that of the 1967 riot – or in Levine's terms "insurrection" – in Detroit. "Bearing butter," he says, referring to the heavy grease used to lubricate wheel bearings. But the language bears its own sense that even this thick black goop is nutritious and even tasty somehow, like butter, to be eaten perhaps with wet slate bread. Politically the poem affiliates its white author with the Black Power movement of the late 1960s and early 1970s. Just as "the earth is eating trees, fence posts, / Gutted cars," so the Lion is feeding on the pigs: "From the sweet glues of the trotters, / Come the sweet kinks of the fist." Pigs and fists were contrary emblems for millions of Americans in 1967. Levine locates himself easily in this allegory: "From all my white sins forgiven, they feed." The logic of the poem is altogether traditional, and it runs through Levine's work generally. The regenerative gist is there in his poems in a sometimes surprising form: "the true and earthy prayer / of salami," it is called in

"Salami," where terror, guilt, and "the need to die" that seizes Levine in a nightmare are overcome by the sight of his sleeping son, by a parent's hope, and the realization that cultures produce value out of what might seem worthless – dried cat heart, for instance. Put this baldly Levine sounds merely faithful, but the poem is constructed around a memory of a song with a refrain – here, the ridiculous word "salami." A faintly clowing tone puts this poem over, whereas Bly, Merwin, and others of Levine's generation succumb to portentousness.

One of the hazards of looking for authenticity is that some people, one thinks, have it, and some don't; but life is not so simple. "Coming Close," even in its title, is an important poem that works just this distinction, and regrettably does not get any further; regrettably because like Levine's best work, this poem has real force. "Take this quiet woman," it begins, as though she demonstrated a point,

> she has been
> standing before a polishing wheel
> for over three hours, and she lacks
> twenty minutes before she can take
> a lunch break. Is she a woman?

The shift from lines three to four is especially important: one might reasonably expect the fourth line to begin with "polish." That is certainly true: this polisher of brass tubes in the end has more brass than polish. But the fourth line rather gets right at the heart of working experience: the management of time. She is a prisoner of time, as wage slaves are. His question is to what extent industrial labor has deprived her of sexual or gender identity; the implication at the outset – utterly misleading – is that she is less a woman than she might otherwise be. The biologist's account of her body that immediately follows is irrelevant: "You must come closer / to find out, you must hang your tie / and jacket in one of the lockers / in favor of a black smock." Levine's counsel is that one must, as Dorn says, dance the dance, or remain an outsider. The sentimentality of the poem, and of many others less distinguished, is that certain forms of language and of sexuality are either authentic or false. The physical labor of carrying dull brass tubes to her to be polished – "feeding her" at the figurative, but also literal level – supposedly brings one closer to this woman. This is a poor measure of authenticity: carrying heavy tubes to her, or – figuratively – putting something into her, nutrition or the like. The first thirty-three lines of the poem are rhetorically affecting, but intellectual kitsch. An industrial accident or power outage might cause her to ask,

> "Why?" Not the old *why*
> of *why must I spend five nights a week?*

> Just, "Why?" even if by some magic
> you knew, you wouldn't dare speak
> for fear of her laughter, which now
> you have anyway as she places the five
> tapering fingers of her filthy hand
> on the arm of your white shirt to mark
> you for your own, now and forever.

That last line captures the pontifical quality of Eliot's *Four Quartets*. He is marked as a sympathizer, a low form of reptilian life. The smudge on the sleeve stands for knowledge: she knows the difference between them, and now he knows that she knows. The unequal distribution of income in America is not so bad in itself, Levine once said, but having to look at those differences in broad daylight is indeed infuriating.

The poem "Every Blessed Day" sets out, on the other hand, the condition of males in contemporary industrial culture. The young man going to work, as Levine once did, at Chevy Gear & Axle #3 exemplifies a form of alienation that is represented as particularly male:

> If he feels the elusive calm
> his father spoke of and searched
> for all his short life, there's
> no way of telling, for now he's
> laughing among them, older men
> and kids. He's saying, "Damn,
> we've got it made." He's
> lighting up or chewing with
> the others, thousands of miles
> from their forgotten homes, each
> and every one his father's son.

The physical details of his surroundings he knows perfectly well, but "Where he's going or who he is / he doesn't ask himself, he / doesn't know and doesn't know / it matters." His father lived for suspended moments of calm – for interruptions of his life. But the son probably feels no such thing. He lives instead for moments of male solidarity and the illusion that having a job is "having it made." Levine's critique of male industrial culture is that it promotes a lack of self-consciousness, a complacent indifference to alternatives. The strength of the poem is in the move beyond authenticity toward the realization that knowledge counts more than action, that even the imagination rests upon understanding.

❦

During the 1960s many free-verse poets set poems in the typographical format of stanzaic verse while suppressing the musical resources of the En-

glish language. John Hollander observed that this period-style was characterized by a line of "25 or 30 em . . . and a strong use of line-ending as a
syntactical marker." Readers who regard music as essential to poetry may feel
the disappointment of one holding a counterfeit note, though no fraud is
intended. Rita Dove's poems suggest that the flatness of much of the free
verse of the 1960s and 1970s was due less to inadvertence or ineptitude,
though these are always the cause of much poor verse, than to a deliberate
refusal of lyricism. Lyricism came to stand in the 1960s for the mainstream
and philistine sense of poetry as consolatory. Many poets resisted the conventional expectations of their audiences in this period, but African American
poets confronted particularly loaded expectations about lyricism. The intention of antilyrical writers has been to locate some new basis for a sense of
authority. In 1903, before modern jazz and urban blues, W. E. B. Du Bois
said that music is "the singular spiritual heritage of the nation and the
greatest gift of the Negro people." The music produced by black people in
North America is, as Pound said of the John Adams–Thomas Jefferson
correspondence, "a national shrine and monument," properly praised by
black and white poets. Despite the familiar racist claims that black people
lack cultural achievement, the music keeps on moving the world. But the
sensuality of music is turned to racist use when African American music is
treated as the expression of the body, not the mind. And poets not surprisingly have been reluctant to fortify those stereotypes.

Black Arts poets of the mid-1960s claimed for African American poetry a
special relationship to the music – principally blues and jazz – and speech of
black Americans. Stephen Henderson traces one feature after another of
African American poetry to authenticating patterns of black language use.
This was part of the separatist black aesthetic of LeRoi Jones, Larry Neal, and
many others in the late 1960s. Dove's poems occasionally draw on just these
linguistic resources, as in "Genie's Prayer under the Kitchen Sink" and more
subtly in "Summit Beach, 1921," but these are rare occasions. When a
convincing spoken voice is central to one of her poems the subject matter is
usually explicitly black. For instance, here is a poem from her first book,
"Nigger Song: An Odyssey":

> We six pile in, the engine churning ink:
> We ride into the night.
> Past factories, past graveyards
> And the broken eyes of windows, we ride
> Into the gray-green nigger night.
>
> We sweep past excavation sites; the pits
> Of gravel gleam like mounds of ice.
> Weeds clutch at the wheels;

We laugh and swerve away, veering
Into the black entrails of the earth,
The green smoke sizzling on our tongues . . .

In the nigger night, thick with the smell of cabbages,
Nothing can catch us.
Laughter spills like gin from glasses,
And "yeah" we whisper, "yeah"
We croon, "yeah."

This is kitsch, which is the point of the poem: that the world loves nigger song. The proud iambic rhythm, easy alliteration, and pleasing metamorphic figures render the very notion of a lyric style complicitous with an ideology that will have its black culture sensual and affirmative. But in the failed iambics of the third line one hears the desire for another style, a flat one that will not transform factories and cemeteries into jewels, and this is the dominant style of her recent work. The concluding poem of *Grace Notes* (1989), "Old Folk's Home, Jerusalem," dramatizes the politics of her stylistic choices.

Evening, the bees fled, the honeysuckle
in its golden dotage, all the sickrooms ajar.
Law of the Innocents: What doesn't end, sloshes over . . .
even here, where destiny girds the cucumber.

So you wrote a few poems. The horned
thumbnail hooked into an ear doesn't care.
The gray underwear wadded over a belt says So what.

The night air is minimalist,
a needlepoint with raw moon as signature.
In this desert the question's not
Can you see? but *How far off?*
Valley settlements put on their lights
like armor; there's finch chit and my sandal's
inconsequential crunch.

Everyone waiting here was once in love.

The arrangement on the page of these fifteen lines of free verse alludes to the most renowned form of love poetry, the sonnet. English sonnets begin with a musical unit of four lines, whereas this poem has a typographical unit of four lines at the outset followed by another such unit of only three lines: one line short of another quatrain, one short too of the *volte* or turn of the Italian sonnet after eight lines. The next typographical unit – of seven lines – is one line too long for the Italian sestet that completes the traditional sonnet, though it completes the sum of fourteen lines for the English and Italian sonnets. The fifteenth line is prosodically superfluous (though to an

English eye it is one line short of the necessary concluding couplet), but it does more than just slosh over the sonnet form. The last line places the theme of age under the eyes of love, whereas for fourteen lines those of Mars have led the way. Just as important is the flattening achieved by this line, which defies one's will to hear more iambics, after the preceding line of regular iambic trimeter.

The tug of war between this free verse and the ghosts of greater and lesser sonnets invoked by typography is a contest between lines for the eye and poems for the voice. The latter are brought close enough to be refused. Throughout Dove's work one sees rather how much she has invested in the pleasures that poems can give to the mind's eye. Horned thumbnail and gray underwear: this is what Pound called phanopoeia. *Can you see?* is the question she implicitly asks her readers. One hears the song of finches, the "chit," and the crunch of gravel underfoot. But these sounds are there only to be transformed: "finch chit" is unavoidably "bird shit"; and the Anglo-Saxon "crunch" of gravel is rendered latinate: inconsequential, the mind says to the ear. The mind at pun or etymology is what she means to address, though seldom without some hint of what has been sacrificed: black lyricism. The refusal of lyricism here is set in the context of political survival. The lights of an Israeli settlement are armor against threats of attack, fears of annihilation. "So what?" is the greeting for a book of poems in an old folk's home in Jerusalem. Sonnets, lyrics of any musical sort, say so little to the aged surrounded by enemies. "Everyone waiting here was once in love," and they are dying in the desert anyway. Dove's embarrassment at the resources of lyricism can stand for the sense of many writers who felt that political extremity, in Israel or Los Angeles, made conventional poetry seem far from necessary. These were some of the poets drawn to some variety of stylistic asceticism.

☙

Elizabeth Alexander's first book, *The Venus Hottentot* (1990), includes some memorable poems celebrating the achievements of African American composers and musicians, particularly Duke Ellington and John Coltrane. (The affirmative dimension of African American writing is very strong, and unparalleled among white American poets. Few white poets love their culture.) But three poems that appear one right after the other in the last section of the book sound a different note. The first and best, "Letter: Blues," invokes music in the title itself; yet the point is rather that her blues are set to English prosody: heroic couplets gathered into quatrains. The form, requiring a rhyme every ten syllables, displays plainly the poet's ability to improvise within a form. The poem is written to a distant lover, asking him to wait for her, but only in the last three words. The prosodic form provides an exercise in distraction, a way of keeping the mind a little off the pain of separation and uncertainty. The pleasure of the poem depends on the recurring threat of loss to disrupt the equanimity encouraged by the call for rhymes. Consider the fourth line of the fourth quatrain:

> The women that we love! Their slit-eyed ways
> Of telling us to mind, pop-eyed dismays.
> We need these folks, each one of them. We do.
> The insides of my wrists still ache with you.

Her reverence can't get her through all four lines of the quatrain: she runs out of words in the third line. And the fourth line lets the suppressed subject – the absent lover – squarely into the poem. Only there – in the poem's heart – is it clear how well the English heroic couplet served this woman with the blues. It's a moderately demanding musical form that helps writers express obliquely the thoughts and feelings that generate poems. The poem is about what barely gets into it, what the prosody holds at bay with all those rhymes.

Derek Walcott, Alexander's teacher, wrote "The Glory Trumpeter" in the main line of English poetry, unrhymed iambic pentameter, blank verse – the musical measure of Shakespeare, Milton, and Wordsworth, among many others. This might seem odd, because it is a poem about a black trumpeter, written by a black Caribbean poet, for whom the music Eddie makes is dirgelike and reproachful. There is an unsettling ambiguity about the music and about Eddie: his eyes are derisive and avuncular at once; he plays both secular and sacred music, blues and spirituals out of "the same fury of indifference." The funereal black men of the third strophe hear the music as the expression of "patient bitterness or bitter siege." How one hears the music depends on what one knows (l. 23). In the last strophe, Walcott sits as one of a "young crowd" and the music comes across a gulf of generations:

> In lonely exaltation blaming me
> For all whom race and exile have defeated,
> For my own uncle in America,
> That living there I never could look up.

The music is full of accusation: Walcott has not maintained the bonds of family and community assiduously enough. The exaltation of the music is intensely painful for this poet, because it rises above so many dead people, whose claims on the present, and on this poet, have been too hard to honor.

Walcott has written in Caribbean idioms, but his strongest poems are in the metropolitan styles of his contemporaries Robert Lowell and Elizabeth Bishop. He aspires not to a style in service to the culture of a subject people, but rather to one that combines, as his friends Lowell and Bishop did, the dream of candor and the pride of art. In "Nearing Forty" he remembers a friend whose life embodied a "style past metaphor," and admires the commitment to "set your lines to work / with sadder joy but steadier elation." But against this ethos stands the thirty-two line iambic pentameter sentence, elaborately rhymed, displaying no alternative to metropolitan forms but a virtuosity trying to pass as "the bleak modesty of middle age." Walcott is not at all a modest poet. His ambition is to maintain fidelity to the Caribbean within the art of the metropolis.

Kamau Brathwaite is also Caribbean, but closer to the British than to the American metropolis. In "Stone" he goes a long way toward bringing into verse not just the music of a black speech, though that is definitely achieved, but that too of an experience of dissolution. The music accompanies the death by bleeding of a victim of stoning, a well-known Jamaican performance poet, Mikey Smith; it is compelling and altogether seductive. Yet Brathwaite's rendering of the "nation language" of a Jamaican poet holds some obvious questions at bay: Who killed Mikey? And why? Furthermore, what was done about the murder of Mikey? At the end one has danced this death in syllables. "i am the stone that kills me," are the last words. Like Mikey we take this violence into our own bodies, find homes for it, and accept the end toward which this music moves. The music establishes a basis for feelings of complicity. Mikey says that he is the instrument of his own destruction. In order to follow the poem at all one needs to move into Mikey's state of mind and seem to die with him. Whatever he did, for a moment his readers do too. The music, beautiful and violent, washes away the distance upon which analytical questions about agency and causation rest. Brathwaite has closed the distance to a music with all the authenticity of black speech, but the speaker is dead.

The poem in Alexander's *Venus Hottentot* just after "Letter: Blues," "Boston Year," comes out of a hard year in a notoriously racist city; it opens with the violence of whites against this black poet and goes on to recall some bright spots in a grey year of estrangement from loved ones. The next poem, "Kevin of the N.E. Crew," gets at the connections between authentic speech and violence.

> From the bus I see graffiti:
> "Kevin of the N.E. Crew."
> These walls cave walls hieroglyphics –
> Who am I sit next to you?
>
> Turn your head, boy. Look at me, boy.
> Dark day, sweet smell, smoke smell blue.
> Split-lip black boy brain smell sweet boy,
> Look my way, boy. Look at you.

Nine boys smoking angel weed
Saw a lady that they knew,
Dragged the lady in the alley,
What they do –

Don't look for an explanation
(Broken glass and foot-long pole)
"Baby Love," "Snot-Rag," "Lunchbox," "Crissie" –
Cave walls heart walls silent hole

Who tongue bled imagination?
who is know, boy? Who are you?
Hey girl. You girl. Look my way girl.
Look at me girl look at you.

Made them. Claim them. These nine black boys.
Bus stops. Off. Stops. Passing through.
Smoke   glass   cave   walls
        weed   fence   pole   split
Kevin.

The three poems by Alexander that I have mentioned come together near the opening of the fourth section of her book *The Venus Hottentot*. The preceding section includes poems in celebration of African American artists: Albert Murray, Duke Ellington, Paul Robeson, James Van Der Zee, Romare Bearden, John Coltrane. Kevin of the N.E. Crew is a different kind of brother. The African American artists of the book's third section are the builders; Kevin is a breaker. The poem is about looking at the breakers. Alexander sees the gang graffiti and is reminded of the prehistoric cave drawings in southern France and Spain. Kevin, a cave man, comes into the book at some cost to the poet: she looks at the nine young men and addresses them in their idiom: "Who am I sit next to you?" She has to give up the distance of an observer in order to get the music of this urban American black speech. She moves in so close she smells the Kevin she's made, sees the scar on his lip, and smells even the thoughts in his head. She is taken by him, in a figurative sense raped by the nine young men. The poem dramatizes a writer's ambivalence and apprehension about immersion in black culture. A year in the white world is gruesome, but immersion in an urban black world is not only empowering, it's hazardous. This is a sympathetic but also scared view of the authentic speech romanticized by Baraka, Larry Neal, and others in the 1960s.

❧

Robert Hayden's deservedly famous poem "Those Sunday Mornings" is printed on the page facing another great but less well-known poem, "The

Whipping." Both poems draw on childhood memories. He gets to painful memories in "The Whipping" by way of identification with a young neighbor boy being beaten perhaps by his grandmother.

> The old woman across the way
>   is whipping the boy again
> and shouting to the neighborhood
>   her goodness and his wrongs.
>
> Wildly he crashes through elephant ears,
>   pleads in dusty zinnias,
> while she in spite of crippling fat
>   pursues and corners him.
>
> She strikes and strikes the shrilly circling
>   boy till the stick breaks
> in her hand. His tears are rainy weather
>   to woundlike memories:
>
> My head gripped in bony vise
>   of knees, the writhing struggle
> to wrench free, the blows, the fear
>   worse than blows that hateful
>
> Words could bring, the face that I
>   no longer knew or loved. . . .
> Well, it is over now, it is over,
>   and the boy sobs in his room,
>
> And the woman leans muttering against
>   a tree, exhausted, purged –
> avenged in part for lifelong hidings
>   she has had to bear.

African American poets have been engaged quite powerfully for over thirty years with the problems of violence. This poem, unlike Alexander's "Kevin of the N.E. Crew" or Brathwaite's "Stone," does not pursue the romance of immersion. Hayden is caught, nonetheless, in the fourth stanza with his head held in the knees of an adult while he is beaten. This is the woundlike memory that flowers from the stormy weather he observes. The music of this poem is conventional, alternating iambic tetrameter and trimeter. Not surprisingly the poem is analytical in just the ways that Alexander and Brathwaite cannot be. Music is an art that demands immersion. Even the music of another's speech draws one into another life, if only imaginatively. It's all about sympathy: when you hear the music you feel the blows. Alexander and Brathwaite make the music idiosyncratic, and the immersion is therefore in another distinctive person. Hayden's music is traditional, and the immersion is less individual than communal; his revery takes him to what he shares with this neighbor victim, not to the victim's distinctive personhood. Hayden places his own hateful words as a boy before the blows of the disciplining adult: those words brought on the beating he is recalling. His first extension of sympathy is to the boy, but his second is to the punishing adult. She has led a life of repression that these beatings resist. The beatings help her. Hayden, Alexander, Brathwaite, and other African American poets have dealt honestly with the problem of violence. There is no effort here to suggest that violence is someone else's problem.

❦

None of the poets discussed here invented their issues; they all worked with the notions of authenticity available in the intellectual culture of the 1960s. In 1965 J. Hillis Miller argued very effectively for a view of twentieth-century poetry that led to a "new immediacy" of objects and people; younger writers, he claimed, turned especially to Williams, for the sense of a "presence, something shared by all things in the fact that they are." A few years later, in 1969–70, Lionel Trilling delivered the Norton lectures at Harvard with the title *Sincerity and Authenticity*. The poets exploited what power they could in these notions, remade their art to appeal to the widespread hunger for the real then, and managed nonetheless to examine illusions of presence and authenticity too. Even Bidart, who has a deep sense of the need for notions of authenticity, struggles against the counter argument. And Susan Hahn slips through any simple notion of authenticity by staging her own funeral, as Pound had done in 1920. The best of the free-verse poets kept in clear view the dangers of the 1960s romanticism that held out this or that experience – sex or violence, hiking or farming – as somehow more real than thinking and talking about the complications of our self-representations. The utopian hope of finding an authentic speech or code, which Merwin, Rich, Baraka, and others at one time credited, never commanded the sustained belief of the best poets; that project is now, like bell bottoms, a reminder only of a different era. But the rhetorical appeal of various forms of relatively authoritative utterance is still a resource for various sorts of free-verse poets who feel some sort of sympathy with the projects of the 1960s.

6

❦

TRANSLATION

THE MOST HIGHLY ESTEEMED POET among American intellectuals is probably the Irishman Seamus Heaney; the most widely honored is surely the Lithuanian Czeslaw Milosz. I mean not only that American readers have a special attraction to foreign poets, but also that the recent history of American poetry can exclude neither the writing of foreign-born American residents nor the efforts of American-born poets to rewrite the poetry of other languages. In "The Day Lady Died" (1959), Frank O'Hara casually records picking up "an ugly NEW WORLD WRITING to see what the poets / in Ghana are doing these days." American poetry since 1945 has been cosmopolitan in an obvious imperial sense: it has absorbed much more than American poetry ever has before. "The simile of an exhausted, Hellenic Europe surrendering its fate," George Steiner remarked in 1964, "to an imperial, Augustan America gained a certain currency. There was, until circa 1959 a touch of Rome about American power, and a shade of Greece about the nervous, worn brilliance of European artistic and intellectual life."

I am purposely making a wide circuit around the topic of translation, because my real subject is the interaction of American literary culture with other literatures, not just what is usually called translation. Our half-century has been especially greedy, especially curious about the world's art, as well as its other resources. Clearly, we have a poetry of global ambitions partly because our economy is global and our political interests extensive. It is much too simple, though, to say only that one causes the other. Poets, professors, and plumbers often begin their days with a newspaper, or relax in the evening with the television news. We wear shirts made in Asia for American or European designers. The kitchens and restaurants that feed us produce facsimiles of international cuisine, daily, everywhere, for various classes of Americans. None of us escapes the constant awareness that we live well beyond our national boundaries. Of course, American poets wonder what poets in Ghana are up to.

What happens when foreign poems are naturalized, as the expression goes, into American products? What kind of poems do Americans want to naturalize, and why? What about the poets who are themselves naturalized? What difference does it make to them that they have been naturalized into American literary citizens?

Translation is ostensibly one of the humbler functions of the poet, but it also presents a path to the highest aspirations of poetry. Allen Grossman, whose poems are often in a high style, speaks of poetry as "a demonized activity . . . it is not . . . the speech of a mortal or merely singular person. Poetry in *my* view has its power because it is the speech not of an individual but of another who is more than and different from the individual." Skeptical, agnostic audiences do not easily give credence to demonized activity, but translations are different: one can believe that someone in another country or at another time was entitled to speak vatically. The very label of translation provides a hedged access to a kind of poetry that, as agnostics, we otherwise deny ourselves.

"Carrying over" is what the word means, and from one's awareness of displacement come questions about poetic authority. With what authority do poets speak? Does poetic language have an origin different from that of ordinary language? These questions bear on all poems, but more obviously on translations. When Pound presented himself to the London literary world in August 1908, he was an American poet with a book of poems just printed at his own expense in Venice. Six months earlier he had been an assistant professor of French and Spanish at Wabash College in Crawfordsville, Indiana – but that was no basis for poetic authority. In London he was to be a picturesque mover between the medieval and the modern, England and the continent, America and Europe. He repeatedly insisted that his authority was borrowed from other poems, even when he was not publishing translations. The early poems were written to sound like translations; he never gave up the garb of archaic poetic authority. His archaic diction and awkward syntax were exotic, from a remote origin, sanctified – that was the idea.

Translation is all about sources, which is where one goes when the branches get shallow. Translated poetry can be exactly right when one hungers for intensity and authenticity, though authenticity is just what translations can never supply; some surplus evades the compromises of a translator. Translators are intermediaries not visionaries, however motivated they are by that quest for the real thing that moves their readers. In 1955 Ben Belitt translated Lorca's influential essay on the *duende*, the spirit of "the roots that probe through the mire that we all know of, and do not understand, but which furnishes us with whatever is sustaining in art." The appeal of a poetry that penetrated to this subterranean basis of the art was very great in 1955, when Auden was editing the Yale Younger Poets series and Wilbur was an acknowledged master of the light touch. "No one, I think," said Lorca, "is amused by the dances or the bulls of Spain."

　　　　　　　　　　　　　ॐ

Max Hayward has said that translations can powerfully influence a culture only after a period of isolation. But since 1945 Americans have rather become connoisseurs of world poetry. Earlier Anglo-American modernist poetry was driven, at the outset, by contact with late nineteenth-century French poetry, then by fresh excitement about archaic poetry; Anglo-American modernist writing was unlike that of the continental avant-gardes precisely in its openness to tradition. The proliferation of translations by both sides in the Cold War was intended to establish legitimacy in a pluralist world order. Americans do not expect to be powerfully affected by translations; at this stage of saturation, all we want is seasoning for our own pot.

American poets have shown great confidence in the strength of American writing; they have approached the task of translation with special boldness, and willingness to try new things. Consider Frank Bidart's wonderful little version of Catullus:

> I hate *and* love. Ignorant fish, who even
> wants the fly while writhing.

The first four words come directly from the Latin, but the remainder is Bidart's invention. Bidart's friend Lowell translated Pasternak, though he knew no Russian. Pound's Propertius stood behind Bidart, legitimating invention. Louis Zukofsky, who began his poetic career in the early 1930s as a protegé of Pound, completed an audacious translation of Catullus in 1969.

> O th'hate I move love. Quarry it fact I am, for that's so
> re queries.
> Nescience, say th'fiery scent I owe whets crookeder.

Pound had reminded poets of the responsibility to translate poems into poems, to assure that a new poem in English is the result of their labors. Bidart has taken the point. Zukofsky, though, is not bound by the simple rule of making coherent English sense of his Latin original; he does not try to bring Catullus into a plausible English. His words are inconceivable as natural utterance; they often bear a negligible semantic relation to the literal sense of Catullus's poem. Nonetheless his too is a close translation.

> Odi et amo. quare id faciam, fortasse requiris.
> nescio, sed fieri sentio et excrucior.

Zukofsky has found English words that approximate the sound of Catullus's words, and he has followed the sequence of the syntax exactly. Zukofsky's fidelity to sound rather than sense is extremist among contemporary translators of canonical verse. Clarence Brown commented on the translation that he and Merwin did of Osip Mandelstam in 1973: "It need scarcely be said, I suppose, that we never considered the folly of trying to convey to the ear of our English readers the sounds of the Russian." Pound taught American poets that they might attempt, as Merwin did, to translate from languages more or less unknown to them, if they had a crib, as he had Fenollosa's manuscript translations for the production of *Cathay* (1915), or a knowledgeable collaborator. Robert Bly, Denise Levertov, Clayton Eshleman, Jerome Rothenberg, Robert Pinsky, Robert Hass, and many of their contemporaries translated as part of a team, where other, learned members bore responsibility for the literal sense of the original language. But in imitating the situation in which one overhears an unknown foreign language, Zukofsky was way out on limb, even among his adventurous contemporaries, as Clarence Brown's remark shows. The opening poems of his Catullus show some effort to approximate the literal sense of the Latin, but the project soon moves away from any fidelity to the paraphrasable sense. His strictness lies all in the phonetic relations between Latin and English. Where a sonic equivalency produces serendipitous contact between the literal sense of the poem in two languages, Zukofsky seems to feel his project justified. These magical moments motivate the poet consistently: wonderful, that the meaning of utterances can be carried from one language to another on waves of sound over the heads of those who think they know Latin or English.

The boldness of Zukofsky's translation expresses something important about the period: first, the secure sense that American poets are entitled to make whatever they can of the history of poetry; second, the belief, particularly among avant-garde poets, that language bears meaning that cannot be explained historically (i.e. by philological methods); and, third, that the differences between Rome and America, the archaic and the contemporary, are not to be overcome by claims about continuity of ideas or meaning. A chasm stands between Catullus and Zukofsky, and Zukofsky wanted it to be visible, in Lawrence Venuti's terms. In 1977 Ronald Johnson, one of Zukofsky's readers, published *Radios*, based on Milton's *Paradise Lost*. Here is a passage:

> What if the breath
> Awaked, should
>   plunge us in the flames; or from above
>   if all
>   were opened,

One day upon our heads;

Each on his rock transfixed,

all things at one view?

then, live

at the spear

in time.

By excision, Johnson translated Milton's English blank verse into American free verse. He perforated an 1892 edition of Milton in order to let the figure of his versions stand exposed, as the title *Radios* is a reduction of *Paradise Lost*.

> *What if the breath* that kindl'd those grim fires
> *Awak'd should* blow them into sevenfold rage
> And *plunge us in the flames? or from above*
> Should intermitted vengeance arm again
> His red right hand to plague us? what *if all*
> Her stores *were op'n'd*, and this Firmament
> Of Hell should spout her Cataracts of Fire,
> Impendent horrors, threat'ning hideous fall
> *One day upon our heads;* while we perhaps
> Designing or exhorting glorious war,
> Caught in fiery Tempest shall be hurl'd
> *Each on his rock transfixt,* the sport and prey
> Under yon boiling Ocean, wrapt in Chains;
> There to converse with everlasting groans,
> Unrespited, unpitied, unrepriev'd,
> Ages of hopeless end; this would be worse.
> War therefore, open or conceal'd, alike
> My voice dissuages; for what can force or guile
> With him, or who deceive his mind, whose eye
> Views *all things at one view?* he from Heav'n's highth
> All these our motions vain, sees and derides;
> Not more Almighty to resist our might
> Than wise to frustrate all our plots and wiles.
> Shall we *then live* thus vile, the race of Heav'n
> Thus trampl'd, thus expell'd to suffer here
> Chains and these Torments? better these than worse
> By my advice; since fate inevitable
> Subdues us, and Omnipotent Decree,
> The Victor's will. To suffer, as to do,
> Our strength is equal, nor the Law unjust
> That so ordains: this was at first resolv'd,
> If we were wise, against so great a foe
> Contending, and so doubtful what might fall.

> I laugh, when those who *at the Spear* are bold
> And vent'rous, if that fail them, shrink and fear
> What yet they know must follow, to endure
> Exile, or ignominy, or bonds, or pain,
> The sentence of thir Conqueror: This is now
> Our doom; which if we can sustain and bear,
> Our Supreme Foe *in time* may much remit
> His anger, and perhaps thus far remov'd
> Not mind us not offending, satisfi'd
> With what is punisht; whence these raging fires
> Will slak'n, if his breath stir not thir flames.

Johnson has abstracted Belial's speech to the council in Hell (II, 170–214). His poem, like Milton's, advocates the acceptance of limits, particularly those imposed by mortality. What Belial describes as God's possible ire seems in *Radios* rather a reflection on the pain that would follow a full awareness of "all things." Belial's argumentation is pruned back into an expression of awe at the prospect of divine knowledge. Restraint is not at all what the free-verse mode warrants. Johnson transforms a counsel of prudence into *carpe diem*: "live / at the spear / in time."

Eric Cheyfitz has argued that "translation was, and still is, the central act of European colonization and imperialism in the Americas." Among literary scholars, there is now a widespread suspicion of translation on political grounds. The editors of a new series on translation studies with Routledge define translation as "manipulation, undertaken in the service of power." After kindly saying that one translates what one has fallen in love with, Richard Wilbur then adds that one wants to "claim it for one's own tongue." The very terms for discussing translation, its motives and consequences, are saturated with the ideology of expansion and conquest. "One conquered when one translated," Nietzsche said. But the other view of translation – as benign, not predatory – has its adherents too.

"It will do you no harm, Latin," [a lyric poet] says, "if I take this lyric of Catullus and try to bestow it as a gift on my own language, which suddenly seems to me impoverished without it; you will still have Catullus when I am through, quite undamaged, and something new, not otherwise possible, will have come into existence."

There was a good measure of naive optimism about translation in the mid- and late 1960s. Vincent McHugh and C. H. Kwock said that literature "embodies the one common language down under all the others: the universal language of human feeling. It's our one chance for all men to get in touch with each other. Straightforward access to a universal language, to peace, harmony, and so on? Probablement pas.

Translation brings poets up against the fact of citizenship. Facing pages of

French, Spanish, or German, Bly, Hecht, and Hass are plainly American poets, though in the streets of Paris, Madrid, or Berlin they may feel the less obvious fact of being citizens of the world, or of the republic of poets too. The German fiction writer Hans Erich Nossack, who brought Joyce Cary and Sherwood Anderson into German, recalled feeling at one time that it was "more important to translate a foreign book than to write one myself." "There is, for each individual writer," he said,

> something that seems to exist that could only be called a feeling of national solidarity with other members of the literary community, a feeling of citizenship in literature as a supranational and antinational and, one might add, ahistorical community. In certain moments this feeling of solidarity intensifies – most often as a defense against the recurring historical tendency to be dominated and controlled by one single ideology. It then becomes more important for the individual writer to advocate literature as a whole than to offer his own individual contribution to literature.

One dreams of a republic of poets and tries even to live responsive to its laws, but translators know that passports are never put altogether aside. Paradoxically, translation enhances the national culture of the translator, while also producing a supranational sense of artistic culture. Dante Gabriel Rossetti said that the "only true motive for putting poetry into a fresh language must be to endow a fresh nation, as far as possible, with one more possession of beauty." "Each nation is imprisoned by its language," Octavio Paz has remarked, but thanks "to translation, we become aware that our neighbors do not speak and think as we do." The history and theory of translation is laden with the imperial ambitions of the Romans, the French, Germans, or British, but also with Englightenment cosmopolitanism. Dryden speaks of it as "an art so very useful to an enquiring people, and for the improvement and spreading of knowledge, which is none of the worst preservatives against slavery." "Translation," as Nossack says, "represents a means of exchanging news between one human being and another, a kind of underground radio station used by partisans of humanity throughout the world to send news of their endangered existence." Poetry maintains the large view, Paz claims, because "No trend, no style has ever been national, not even the so-called artistic nationalism." Any account of the consequences of translation has to hold on to the doubleness – conqueror, cosmopolite – of the project.

❦

The years since 1945 have been rich in verse translations of canonical texts that are regularly taught to college students. Richmond Lattimore's *Iliad* (1951), Lattimore and David Grene's *Complete Greek Tragedies* (1959), Robert Fitzgerald's *Odyssey* (1961), and Allen Mandelbaum's *Aeneid* (1971) are still standard American textbooks. In 1964 Guy Davenport said that "Something like a second classical renaissance seems to be happening, or about to happen. Archeology has been partly responsible; the return of modern art to immemorial forms has been more responsible than we imagine. . . . Every age has to translate for itself, of course, but our age has the double undertaking of reaching with our particular interest and assurance toward the original text, and of fumigating the furtive and hot-house predilections of the foregoing age." Davenport was reworking modernist doctrine fifty years later, which is revealing. There was a conscious sense of continuity between modernist aesthetics and the academic program of translation undertaken after World War II. Reuben Brower said in 1964 that "the most natural thing is to discover the ancients through the moderns." During just the years when literary critics find a flowering of postmodern literature, the literary culture was institutionalizing the programs of Pound, above all, but of Eliot and Joyce as well. Now at the century's end, this activity continues. Robert Pinsky has just produced an ambitious, brilliant new translation of Dante's *Inferno* (1994), with consonantal rather than vowel rhymed terza rima, and David Ferry has published a wonderful blank-verse version of *Gilgamesh* (1992). Another sense of translation is operating now: the musicality of the English is exactly the issue; for these translators of canonical texts, there can be no letting the original music lie mute or unacknowledged in the English. This much is progress.

The optimism about translation in the 1960s derived from the collaboration between modernist literary doctrine and professional academic scholarship and criticism, which was the achievement of John Crowe Ransom, his *Kenyon Review*, and the New Criticism generally. "My impression," Robert Fitzgerald said in 1964, "is that the present generation of scholars is far more awake to literary questions than the one under which I grew up." The literary map of the early-1960s seemed just primary colors; readers were invited to think that the choice was between the literary classicists and the Beats: Allen Ginsberg's dismissal of the prosodic forms of Greek poets was used to close the 1964 symposium in *Arion* on "The Classics and the Man of Letters."

The book trade has supported canonical translations, because the expansion of access to higher education in America, especially from the war through the 1960s, provided a captive audience for translations that had academic approval. George Steiner remarked in 1966:

The sentiment that Homer and Juvenal are part of the status of civilized consciousness remains genuine. It has found an influential economic and technological ally in the activities of the American university campus and in the hunger of the paperback. To keep the machines fed, paperback publishers have raided the past and the foreign. . . . American academic and commercial editors have directly commissioned much of the best of recent verse translation.

Lattimore and his editors at the University of Chicago Press knew in the late-1940s that this market could support large-scale translation projects. He found a warm welcome when he approached the press with the first book of the *Iliad*. Similarly David Grene, proposing in 1947 to translate thirty-three Greek tragedies, was given enthusiastic support. "There is, as you know," Grene wrote the editor,

a steadily growing public for translations of Greek classics and particularly of the dramas. It is also almost the best kind of public, as far as diligent and intelligent reading is concerned – that composed of students in Humanities courses, general literature courses and drama courses.

The poet Hayden Carruth, who later became Grene's editor, said that the editors of the press "believe very firmly that these translations will be by far the best ever published in the English language and that they will, when they are completely published, be a valuable property both for the Press and for the translators." In 1953 Jason Epstein, then of Doubleday, tried to arrange a mass paperback reprint of the Greek tragedies –

Not only will we sell the book [Lattimore's *Oresteia*] in thousands of trade and newsstand outlets, but we will promote it with great vigor, and by the time you are ready to publish your two-volume basic edition, the name Lattimore will, I guarantee, be a household word.

After a lot of internal discussion, Chicago declined the offer, because the director of the press was persuaded that the notion of a mass market was an illusion; the real market was that for textbooks, and he did not want the Doubleday mass paperback edition to undercut his press's command of that market. Academic publishers knew that their world had begun to change after 1945, but the new order of the publishing market was not understood until the mid-1950s. (In 1960, one year after Chicago published a four-volume edition of *The Complete Greek Tragedies,* the Modern Library did bring out a compact edition for a larger audience.)

These academically oriented translations were represented as contemporary poems, but surprisingly little effort went into determining how they might be genuinely poetic. In the introduction to his *Iliad*, Lattimore says that he has brought Homer into "plain English" or "the language of contemporary prose." His statements about the prosody of his translation correspond to this sense of plain diction. The "free-running lines of six beat verse . . . [permit] the reader to recapture, better than could be done through prose, blank verse, or conventional English forms, the speed and flexibility of the Homeric lines." At one point Grene cautioned Lattimore that his six-beat line might become monotonous over the long haul, and the press editor advised

Lattimore to take this issue seriously. But the press, understandably, had so little sense of the music of Lattimore's poem that the project's first editor spoke of the translation in 1949, after he had seen many samples of the text, as "written in rhythmic prose." Lattimore and Grene themselves also dealt loosely with prosodic matters in the tragedies. "The general assumption," Lattimore wrote in 1950, "is a negative one: that they [the translated plays] will not be in formal *rhymed* stanzas, heroic couplets, etc. . . . Perhaps David [Grene] would even question my principle about prose. But, subject to his protest, I should say, set as verse." Speaking of Grene's versions of the Greek tragedies, D. S. Carne-Ross said, "Nothing here intervenes between you and the Greek: no flourish of style, for there is no style; no persuasion of rhythm, for there is no rhythm." This bland product is the result of "deference to a mistaken doctrine of literalness." For some reason, it seemed valuable to academic translators and their publishers to present their work as contemporary poetry, though they were content to leave the distinction between poetry and prose unexamined.

The classicists were intent on showing that the translations done for classroom use were actually evidence of the vitality of America's contemporary literary culture. Americans were said to possess a sense of the importance of aesthetic matters. Europeans were divided by political issues and ideologies, but Americans, partly because of their distance from Europe, were said to be freer and more high-minded than European readers. Carne-Ross claimed that Americans successfully translate Greek exactly because they maintain the nineteenth-century myth of Greece produced by German translators. According to Carne-Ross, Americans are more open to classics of European literature than contemporary Europeans are, because they see Dostoevsky, Nietzsche, and Kierkegaard as world authors, obviously relevant to American concerns, whereas Europeans see them as Russian, German, and Danish writers. Europeans make literature somehow smaller because of their historical awareness.

The effort to encourage translations derived from ambivalence about the present. Kenneth Rexroth remarked, "translation saves you from your contemporaries." The classics in translation seemed to promise an alternative to the professionalized culture that came inevitably and lamentably after the war, as I explained in Chapter One. Northrop Frye said that "The Greek and Latin civilizations formed the basis of a humanist education for so long because they were complete civilizations: they could be studied as laboratory specimens of culture, with a detachment impossible in studying one's own. Hence it was possible for a Classical education to breed a liberal attitude; an education based on the contemporary can develop only a managerial one."

William Duffy and Robert Bly started a new journal in 1958: *The Fifties,* that later became *The Sixties* and *The Seventies*, under Bly's sole editorship. The first issue began with "Ten Pages of Modern European Poems," and Bly identified himself militantly with the need to translate Latin American and European poetry into English for the benefit of American poetry. He became enormously influential as both advocate and translator. Imagery, as he saw it, is the essence of poetry, the source of its power and depth; many diversely positioned writers and critics of the 1960s agreed that images were the essential matter to be translated. Nabokov, no natural ally of Bly, said in 1969 that "a poet's imagery is a sacred, unassailable thing." "The metaphorical act," Jack Ludwig stated, "the transforming gesture, should come from the language of the present grasping the delicate and historical toughness of the past. The translator must courageously, perhaps dangerously, choose his metaphorical equivalents for words, sounds, dramatic confrontations." For Ludwig, Bly, and many others, the target was the language of the exact present moment. The obvious implication is that that elusive moment is like no other, here or elsewhere. American poets were therefore justified in feeling urgency and license in their translations. The focus on the image was like a search for the coin that happens to fit the slot – Canadian quarter, German five-pfennig piece.

Jerome Rothenberg said that discussion of the image followed from the logically prior notion of poetry's distinction from ordinary language. Many poets and readers too turned to foreign poetry, under Bly's influence, in search of stunning images. By 1960, however, a few poets had begun to respond critically to this development. Creeley wrote to Rothenberg:

I think translation, dealt with too loosely, has not been able to surmount the problem of logopoeia, and this has made an accumulation of loosely structured poems exciting mainly for their "content," their reference as "pictures" of states of feeling etc. I'd hate to see that generalizing manner become dominant, no matter the great relief of having such information about what's being written in other countries etc.

Creeley was right to worry about the generalizing manner of translated poetry becoming dominant: the influence of Merwin and of translated Latin American and East European poetry produced a period style in the late 1960s. Rothenberg answered that poetry is translatable at the level of the image and that the effort to talk across national and linguistic boundaries was imperative. This was the basis of his advocacy of what was called Deep Image poetics in the early 1960s and associated with the little magazine *Trobar*. "The editors of TROBAR [George Economou, Joan and Robert Kelly] believe that American poetry must re-establish contact with the perennial strength of the deep im-

age." Deep image poetry, according to Robert Kelly, was designed to bring all
the force of other poetries into contemporary American: "The American language of today provides the only reliable linguistic patterns for the poet of
images. Verbal expression of the image demands an urgency and directness
that only the spoken language of poet and reader can supply, the language of
here and now. The language of the image must come across vividly and
urgently, without cuteness or distraction." There was an expansionist dimension to Rothenberg's polemics, though how politically aware he was then is
unclear. He has said that he finds an "ALL-AMERICAN poetry" "too small."
"Translation is simply one of the key devices," he said in 1975, "for that greater
incorporation that it seems to me most of us are moving towards. . . . always
towards the expansion of poetry and opening up of the domain." Language
about translation may inevitably sound imperialistic; nonetheless, the aspirations of poets in these years of American expansion naturally followed the
examples set by the economy, military, and State Department. It is easy to be
critical of this, but it is important to hold in view the well-meaning impulses
at play here. Rothenberg and Dennis Tedlock founded *Alcheringa* in 1970 in
order "to encourage poets to participate actively in the translation of tribal/oral
poetry." This project rested on a view of translation as benign, not predatory.
They wanted to encourage as well "a knowledgeable, loving respect among
them [young Native Americans and others] for the world's tribal past &
present."

This sharp emphasis on contemporaneity was explicit, acknowledged, and
altogether different from our fin de siècle. Rothenberg convened a symposium
on ethnopoetics at the University of Wisconsin, Milwaukee, in April 1975 and
began with a quotation of Robert Duncan: "The drama of our time is the
coming of all men into one fate, the dream of everyone, everywhere."
Rothenberg and other poets, particularly avant-gardists, of the 1960s and
1970s had a vision of global culture, a poetry "of a fundamental human
nature." The present was the universal moment. Rothenberg argued for "total
translation" that was thought to mean bringing the new piece to exist "totally
in the present without necessity of recourse to the past." Critics of the Deep
Image poetic, such as Denise Levertov, claimed that there was a naive sense of
impersonality in these poems "that seems to arise from the poets sharing a
conception of what is poem-stuff and what is not – a literary conception akin
to what was once believed about 'poetic diction.' " Rothenberg acknowledged
in 1975 that it

was easy to come to believe that there was a particular series of resonant words that
represented the deep situation, whereas other words didn't. In short there were words
with power & words without power & there was a danger that one might move into a
limited poetic vocabulary (a new set of image conventions as culturally controlled as

the old) without ever exploring the full range of language that might also lead to the deep image. . . . There was a code & sometimes it was really a kind of old romantic code that we were engaged in.

With this romantic diction comes too a vatic sense of the poet that Rothenberg accepted too easily. The idea of a code was reasonable because he was presuming a universal, Jungian language of images underlying the particular languages out of which American poets might translate. By 1975 dozens of books of Merwinesque code-poems had revealed the limits of this sort of poetic.

Shortly before the founding of *Alcheringa* in 1973 Rothenberg began to move away from an image-oriented method of translation toward, instead, an insistently aural one – "total translation." "My intention was," he said, "to account for all vocal sounds in the original but – as a more 'interesting' way of handling the minimal structures & allowing a very clear, very pointed emergence of perceptions – to translate the poems *onto the page*, as with 'concrete' or other types of minimal poetry." He had learned from Navaho and Senecan texts that nonsense syllables might be important to the text and performance; the linguist Dell Hymes had informed him that meaningless sounds in Kwakiutl songs might be keys to the songs' structure. Rothenberg described his method in working with some Navaho songs:

I translated first for meaning & phrasing in English, adding small words to my text where the original had meaningless syllables; then distorted, first the small words so that they approximated to "mere" sound, then within the meaningful segment of each line toward more or less the density of the original; e.g. . . . "all are & now some are there & mine" became "all ahrenow some 're there & mine."

Rothenberg was moving in the direction shown him by Zukofsky's Catullus: following sound at the expense even of sense. The objective is a radical contemporaneity: the moment of Navaho performance might sound like the moment of Rothenberg's performance.

What was emerging was the premise that the body is the basis of language, that sounds made by a speaking body in one locale may be likened to similar sounds made by a speaking body in a distant locale or time – regardless of the syntactic and semantic systems often confined within the boundaries of political regimes. The aspiration toward a universal humanity is inherent in Deep Image poetics and in the tribal ethnopoetics of *Alcheringa*. Rothenberg and Quasha had no problem in 1973 referring to "our total human experience on this continent," as though the divisions of political history, ethnicity, class, and landscape were superable by translation. The archaic has that possibility of standing for the permanent. Rothenberg refers to "Upper Paleolithic Notations" which "bring us back to something universal maybe: the last truly intercontinental culture until our own." Politically, in the late 1960s and 1970s, this was a liberal, not radical, approach to poetry. Rothenberg felt awkward in 1972 presenting Amerindian poems in a context where identity politics had segregated ethnic communities from one another. "The idea of translation has always been," he wrote in 1972,

> that such boundary crossing is not only possible but desirable. By its very nature, translation asserts or at least implies a concept of psychic & biological unity, weird as such assertion may seem in a time of growing disintegration. Each poem, being made present & translated, flies in the face of divisive ideology.

This was an unpopular view of the divisions of racism in these years, and it remains sharply inconsistent with identity politics at the end of the century.

The interaction of these different political and literary assessments of contemporaneity is best seen, I think, in the work of Jay Wright, who, exploring the ethnopoetics of Rothenberg and others associated with *Alcheringa*, published a book-length poem, *The Double Invention of Komo* (1980), that draws together strands of Bambara and Dogon cosmologies in a narrative of initiation. This poem seems superficially to be enacting the will to have a replenished religious poetry, as though Wright were responding to Hart Crane's injunction: "Lie to us, dance us back the tribal morn!" Editors have repeatedly asked Wright to append explicatory notes to his work, exactly because he does not establish a clear mediating ground between a secular audience and a subject matter that is religious. In this sense he seems close to poets like Duncan and Grossman who exert without argument the prerogatives of religious or shamanistic poetry. *Komo* is dedicated, however, to the memory of the anthropologist Marcel Griaule, whose work, along with that of other anthropologists, is acknowledged in the poem's Afterword. Although Wright tries to recreate in English a sense of Bambaran and Dogon rituals, this poet is content to write with secular distance ultimately from the religions of Africa. "A poem is not ritual," Wright has said, "The poetry's goal, early and late, has always been to bring a critical and creative version to bear on an enlarged realm of experience. . . . "

The enlargement that Wright manages is based on a liberal attitude toward racial politics. In *Komo* he speaks of undertaking a return to African roots out of a sense of his own hybridity. "I elevate the trinity of races in my blood."

> I take this road again
> to articulate my discontent
> with what is given.
>
> I have learned
> that there is a blessing
> in my body's disrupted blood.

"We black African Americans have been much too ready," he has argued, "to allow other people to divest us of our other selves. No black African American can have escaped grounding in other cultures. You can have escaped critical confrontation with and assimilation of them. . . . What is necessary is to think carefully about what you possess, and I contend that we all possess more than we know and are willing to acknowledge." Wright begins not with a fiction about any essential Africanness, but with the knowledge that his identity has no one essence:

> the seed of my being
> does not exist,
> except in the act
> of taking notice.
> . . . . .
> You see I have the faculty
> of being absent.
> . . . . .
> Father – I call you –
> spirit of the apprehension
> of absence, the precedent
>   refusal.

One of the most lucid passages of *Komo* concerns the son's recollections and reconstructions of his absent father, though the patriarchal Christian God is also part of the passage. The speaker seems to have lost his father to the fast life. At the level of American narrative, the father stands for separation, loss, excision: he left the family. Wright's sense of identity derives from this sense of loss, absence. The process of history is one of reconstitution, through inquiry, attention, and compassion. Wright has no interest in a prelapsarian moment of African blackness; the job of maturation is one of reconstruction. And the politics of this are deliberately liberal, not radical. "We have a picture of a world," Wright has said, "in which all relations are ordered but in which the significance of any event is its ability to lead to reconciliation and self-realization, call it integration." Integration is the yardstick for measuring the significance of all acts.

Clearly Wright means more than racial integration here, but he means that too. Integration is a metaphysical process he sees everywhere:

> There is always the going forth
> and the returning;
> there is always the act,
> the slow fusion of being.
> All things,
> by the strength of being joined,
> will continue;

the sin is to turn away;
ignorance is inattention
to the voice, which feeds you.

How far have we come toward integration? Very far, is the answer given by this poetry – for three reasons. First, the basis of ritual generally is "separation, transition and incorporation." Boys become men by passing through such a process; culture teaches what must follow separation. Second, African Americans enact this process in bold terms. "You must note the central position of transition in this process. . . . That test is a paradigm of Afro-American experience, a consciousness of risk, separation, self-alienation and, ultimately, reconciliation." Third, this process of integration involves conscious decisions that are hard to acknowledge publicly. But privately, often secretly, cultures are always crossing: three cross in Wright. He discriminates African Americans from black African Americans, because many African Americans are not seen as black. The issue is not whether cultures will integrate, but whether individuals will attend to the ways their cultures and their bodies have already integrated differences that can be understood. The Dogon and Bambaran myths and religious practices that Wright translates into African American poetry provide a deep sanction for a political program that in an American context is hard to advocate full-throatedly, though in fact the lives of many American intellectuals are in fact dedicated to racial integration. The authority of a translated culture here (more than a text) gains a hearing for a cause with more adherents than advocates – integrationist politics.

Milosz is one of three Nobel poet laureates living in the United States, none of whom was born in America or to American parents. They have all adopted this self-denigrating literary culture – not only because it regards them highly. "We do not look to our [American] poets," Sven Birkerts has admitted, "even the best of them, for clues about how to live in the face of Fear. . . . When the spirit feels the clutch of that fear, the hand reaches for Milosz, Mandelstam, Celan, Montale, Akhmatova, Zbigniew Herbert, Heaney, Brodsky. . . ." The poet Bruce Murphy has responded:

Literary journals, the popular press, and publishers have made household names of a handful of Eastern European writers: Czeslaw Milosz, Joseph Brodsky, Zbigniew Herbert. One is regaled with chestnuts about ordinary people in the Eastern bloc who care about "the Word," manuscripts passed from hand to hand, even poems preserved orally. Inevitably, the questions are revived: Where are the great American poets? Has American poetry been reduced to private confessions and personal trivia?

Why is it that our poetry lacks that public, political relevance? The answer to such questions is often that we do not have the weight of History on our backs, the state oppression under which, as Milosz says, "poetry is no longer alienated," no longer "a foreigner in society," and can become more important than bread.

Milosz has come to stand for this alternative poetry. His work, much of it compellingly presented to American readers by his translators (now American Poet Laureate) Robert Hass and Robert Pinsky, makes the best case for the view that American poetry is thin by comparison to what is available in translation.

Milosz's presentation of himself as an exile has been enormously effective. He regards himself as no less Lithuanian because he lives in Berkeley, California, and frankly asserts that his merit as a writer derives from his Eastern European identity, his personal experience of the history of the twentieth century. But his secondary claim to authority is contradictory because it derives from his estrangement from the very culture that shaped his sensibility. Writers often say that exile awakens memories of the lost home and strengthens feelings for lost loved ones and landscapes; exiled writers are commonly patriots. But that is not Milosz's point, however much it bears on his own career. He more interestingly suggests that becoming American was possible exactly because displacement is essential here: American "inhabitants have always suffered from homelessness and uprootedness, later called alienation (for who besides the Indians was not an alien?)." Easy assimilation is a consoling byproduct of a situation that Milosz generally represents as quite destructive. As a young man, he planned to become neither a poet nor a professor but a naturalist. The working-life he wanted would have demanded his immersion in the landscape and life quite local to Lithuania. After the war, however, when he became cultural attaché to the Polish embassy in Paris, he knew that he had chosen an intellectual life that depended both on his distance from his home country and, paradoxically, on his reluctance to accept exile and surrender his passport. Living in Paris he was permitted to "publish impudent articles and poems whose every word was an insult to the Method [of Soviet Marxism]." If he had lived in Warsaw or Vilno he would have enjoyed less latitude. He was tolerated in Paris because the risk that he would defect "was not great. Almost more than anyone else, I felt tied to my country. I was a poet; I could write only in my native tongue; and only in Poland was there a public – made up chiefly of young people – with which I could communicate." The postwar Polish regime, like the one in East Germany, knew that most writers would isolate themselves from their audiences only very reluctantly. "The abyss for me," he wrote, "was exile, the worst of all misfortunes, for it meant sterility and inaction."

Milosz has made an advantage of his adversity, and in ways that illuminate the literary taste of our era. There is another specifically literary benefit that comes to exiles in the American literary context. Exiles feel stripped of cultural baggage: first of all, of native language, but much else falls by the wayside too. Theirs are borrowed clothes, whether their Polish poems are translated into English, as Milosz's are, or they actually compose poems in English, as Joseph Brodsky has done. Yet as anyone knows who has lived with a foreign language, it can be simpler to say some things in a borrowed language. When Pound wished to express tender feelings or fond beliefs in the *Cantos*, he spoke French, Italian, or even Latin: "le paradis n'est pas artificiel"; "tell Caro, te amo"; "amo ergo sum." The catastrophic experience of Eastern Europe, which is what brought Milosz and many other exiles to America, led him, as he says, to treasure simplicity. Eastern European exiles have greater access to basic, central issues of human experience, he claims, than their American-born colleagues do. "I am familiar with the events of the past years," Milosz wrote in 1953, "not from the dry notes of historians; they are as vivid for me as the faces and eyes of people one knows well."

The sanction he wants here is conventional in American letters: I was there and saw the Real Thing. We've always wanted to hear from just these people. His translator, Robert Hass, remembers ironically how he thought of Milosz in the late 1960s: "a man who had witnessed the operations of the great beast and told terrible truths. . . ." Robert Pinsky, who has also translated Milosz, has articulated the widely held general view that certain "parts of the world that have experienced totalitarian regimes are fertile ground for this kind of direct approach [to ideas and beliefs], while our own good fortune in not having experienced war on our terrain for over a hundred years, nor having experienced a totalitarian regime or a police state, makes us less capable of such writing." Milosz's particular experience was, first, the expansion of the Third Reich. The Nazi era was "a test for every writer. The real tragedy of events pushed imaginary tragedies into the shade. Whichever of us failed to find an expression for collective despair or hope was ashamed. Only elementary feelings remained: fear, pain at the loss of dear ones, hatred of the oppressor, sympathy with the tormented." Certain literary conventions became particularly attractive in this context: subject matter took on a particular importance; true poetry needed to concern itself with first and last things. "Probably only those things are worth while which can preserve their validity in the eyes of a man threatened with instant death." Farewell, Chaucer, Pope, and Byron. In stylistic terms the pressure for simplicity, an unadorned diction, and straightforward prose syntax felt fitting and friendly after 1945. A not altogether articulate, let alone fluent, manner seemed most credible: "It is sometimes better to stammer from an excess of emotion," according to Milosz, "than to speak in well-turned phrases. The inner voice that stops us when we might say too much is wise." Short, spare, severe poems were suited to the experiences Milosz discusses. "From time to time," he said, "we are thrown into situations that distill, as it were, our somewhat indefinite feelings; they cleanse from them everything superfluous and reduce them to a few basic lines."

The Nazi invasion of Poland in September 1939 was just that cleansing, distilling catalyst, with the consequence that certain ordinary objects gained new cachet for writers and some sorts of discourse lost all credibility: "That long-dreaded fulfillment had freed us from the self-reassuring lies, illusions, subterfuges; the opaque had become transparent; only a village well, the roof of a hut, or a plow were real, not the speeches of statesmen recalled now with ferocious irony. The land was singularly naked, as it can only be for people without a state, torn from the safety of their habits." Milosz was surprisingly close to Williams in this one regard: "I would like to trust my five senses, to encounter naked reality nakedly, but between me and what I see and touch there is a pane of glass – my conception of nature. . . ." The young poets like Creeley and Olson who turned to Williams in the postwar years were responding not just to polemics about meter but more importantly to international disgust at what ideas and ideology had made of the world. They all saw history as *maya*, or what Milosz characterizes as a labyrinthine cocoon of mental constructs from which he would like to escape altogether, though he acknowledges, as Williams never did, that "We are unable to live nakedly." But the audience for Milosz's writing was in the *Partisan Review*, not in the *Black Mountain Review*. The cult of naked experience had a political significance in New York: it meant opposition to utopian ideology. In literary terms this cult attached itself to the translation of central European writing and undergirded a plain, even flat style – anonymous, joyless.

It is always commonplace for journalists to celebrate poets for their extraordinary lives and experiences, whereas poet–critics remind readers that poets deserve celebrity only for their writing. In the case of Milosz, however, even poet–critics take the journalist's tack; the poems are presented as documents of a special life more than as artifacts. Seamus Heaney has expressed his admiration of Milosz's short poem "Incantation" in a way that illuminates the issue greatly.

It counted for much that this poem was written by somebody who had resisted the Nazi occupation of Poland and had broken from the ranks of the People's Republic after the war and paid for the principle and pain of all that with a lifetime of exile and self-scrutiny. The poem, in fact, is a bonus accruing to a life lived in the aftermath of right and hurtful decisions, and it elicits the admiration of English-speaking readers partly because of this extra-literary consideration. It is therefore typical of work by many other poets, particularly in the Soviet republics and the Warsaw Pact countries, whose poetry not only witnesses the poet's refusal to lose his or her cultural memory but also testifies thereby to the continuing efficacy of poetry itself as a necessary and fundamental human act.

The celebration of Eastern European poetry has produced an embarrassing martyrology, as Heaney goes on to suggest, but it has reminded American readers nonetheless of the resources and authority of poetry. If American readers treat poetry as marginal, translation has demonstrated that the art itself is not to blame. It may be that, as Heaney says, poetic "greatness is shifting away from [the English language]." Or, one might say, with Joseph Epstein and many others, that American poets have not answered to the responsibilities of their art. One problem with the appreciative response to translated poetry has been the challenge that American poets, if they wish for an audience, produce a similar product.

There are many reasons to object to the biographical approach to Eastern European poetry, but it is exactly the approach that Milosz himself has more or less requested. "By fusing individual and historical elements in my poetry," he wrote in his autobiography, "I had made an alloy that one seldom encounters in the West." He has done more than simply write about the Nazi invasion of the East and the experience of the Holocaust; he has established in his poems a personal angle on these momentous events. His poetry is deliberately presented as a witness to history, and his readers and collaborators have been satisfied to take him at his word.

It has to be admitted that Milosz's dwelling on the idea of history – and this idea has been a fixed feature of American poetry since long before his work received attention – often produces a kind of ponderous melancholy.

> – For history
> Is no more comprehensible. Our species
> Is not ruled by any reasonable law.
> The boundaries of its nature are unknown.
> It is not the same as I, you, a single human.

But there is no reason to judge poets by their weaknesses; the job is rather to account for the strengths, and Milosz's are great.

If by history one means narratives or explanations about how the significant events of the past have shaped the present, it is clear that readers, journalists, and critics surely do not want that in poetry; otherwise Charles Olson might be a popular poet. Rather, history is commonly meant to signify not the explanations of the past but the force of the past itself, and what is alleged is that certain poets have felt that force and retain the memory of it, that they somehow embody that force. This is important, because history as a body of discourse is regarded as a source of knowledge, though the critics who complain about the absence of history in American poetry do not look to poets for knowledge. They look instead for feeling, and expect a memory of the past, like an echo chamber, to amplify that feeling's significance. The feelings that, in Milosz, arise in response to history-as-force are interestingly not those that seem appropriate to a sense of history-as-knowledge. Knowledge of history is usually complicated, not simple; thoroughly mediated, not direct and straightforwardly present; impersonal and unsympathetic. Is this what the poetry of Milosz presents?

A Confession

My Lord, I loved strawberry jam
And the dark sweetness of a woman's body.
Also well-chilled vodka, herring in olive oil,
Scents, of cinnamon, of cloves.
So what kind of prophet am I? Why should the spirit
Have visited such a man? Many others
Were justly called, and trustworthy.
Who would have trusted me? For they saw
How I empty glasses, throw myself on food,
And glance greedily at the waitress's neck.
Flawed and aware of it. Deriding greatness,
Able to recognize greatness wherever it is,
And yet not quite, only in part, clairvoyant,
I knew what was left for smaller men like me:
A feast of brief hopes, a rally of the proud,
A tournament of Hunchbacks, literature.

Berkeley, 1985

This wonderful short poem, translated with Hass, seems to me a long way from historical knowledge, and not because history is not mentioned in the poem. The poem's pleasures are charismatic and come from the shapely revelation of character, not from any specificity of local life. Milosz's verse consistently invokes imagery, as here, in a generic fashion, often even in his best poems (as in "In Music"), sentimentally remembering the *Dorfleben* of Eastern Europe; in other poems, like "Bypassing Rue Descartes," using cities as settings for historical parables. The vodka, herring, and cinnamon here stand, credibly, effectively, for the urbane pleasures of the body, in Eastern Europe. The confession is of apparent veniality, and how clever to begin with strawberry jam. The strength of the poem is in its assured reticence: he knows himself and is comfortable to leave much only partly said. For example, the pleasures of the body seem innocent, yet the confession is real, because the disturbing issue is what he would do for food, drink, or women, what trust he would betray. That he has so betrayed trust is tacitly acknowledged in the sequence of questions – is that venial? Is pride? He won't question whether the spirit has truly visited him; that much is presumed. "Desiring greatness . . . ," his ability to see it in others comes from that – ambition, striving, envy. His corruption, like his greatness, is presented in relation to that of others – the tournament of hunchbacks is right here: yes, he names his avarice bitingly (ll. 9–10), but what matters to him is not only the fact of his corruptibility but also that they, the justly chosen, saw it. The last line is stunning and harsh as a characterization of the literary life, yet, after this speech, plausible, maybe only just.

Milosz presents himself generally not simply as one who happened to be present at certain historical events; he has argued explicitly that the twentieth century deserves to be defined not in terms of scientific or technological achievement, or philosophical development, but rather in terms of the elevation of history to a new status. "In modern times," he wrote, "the great metaphysical operation has been the attempt to invest history with meaning." History, he said in 1953, "has taken the place of God in this century." On the one hand, this elevation of history was the work of Marxists attempting to rationalize brutal oppression: sacrifices had to be made in the pursuit of revolution; the future justified them. This is Stalinist logic, which Milosz deplored. On the other hand, though, he agreed that the Stalinist priests of the New Faith understood their moment: the sanction of history is the highest authority a modern writer can invoke. No wonder that Milosz seeks just this.

In historiographical terms, however, Milosz is a strict constructionist. History shows that people are capable of anything and everything. He rejects the revelationist or scientific (read: Stalinist) notion that history is "governed by unshakable and *already known* laws," though this is the basis of the Marxist claim for the authority of historical proof. On the contrary, his claim to having witnessed momentous events expressed the sense that only one who has seen what was unimaginable in fact occur can understand the transience of governments and institutions. As a boy during World War I Milosz and his family lived in a covered wagon: history is entirely fluid, life is "ceaseless wandering." His condescension to western, particularly American writers derives from the belief that those who have not witnessed the destruction of their homes and the dissolution of their governments cannot know what life has to offer. "The man of the East cannot take Americans seriously," Milosz wrote bluntly, in a book addressed to an American audience, "because they have never undergone the experiences that teach men how relative their judgments and thinking habits are." With no sense of history, they naively think their institutions and environment immutable.

Milosz's view of American culture is a European commonplace. The naiveté, however, is rather with the Europeans who, like Milosz, believe that

America is without its history. This is quite a different belief from the claim that Americans naively ignore their own history. Only once in his prose does Milosz notice similarity between European and American history: when reflecting on the courage of the Donner party, he is reminded of the fortitude of the prisoners of the concentration camps. Why does this man of two lives, one as European, one as Californian, so seldom find similarity between European culture and that of North America? It is particularly revealing and disappointing too that the one time he identifies such a similarity the two historical events are themselves lurid. Europeans like to conceive of American history in extremist terms: slavery, racism, and war are the topics of historical experience that recur in European discussions of American history. Milosz might well have some acquaintance with American social, economic, or diplomatic history, say; cannibalism and genocide are the lurid hot spots of history. The danger here is that history be conceived as operatic.

This is not to say that Milosz is in fact dismissive of American culture generally. He has repeatedly referred to the intellectual and cultural achievement and promise of America: "it is clearly becoming the most poetic and artistic country in the world." The future looks so bright to him because of the American investment in research and higher education. He argued strenuously in his 1983 Norton lectures at Harvard that poets of our time have not adequately responded to the challenges brought by the expansion of scientific knowledge. What he sees in America's future is not only the cultural effects of its prosperity; his argument runs much deeper. There is a brutality about the American experience that has taught him strength and humility. The American experience does, in his view, reinforce the Cold War vision of a future "beyond ideology." Here he has come to see not only the folly of utopian ideologies, such as Marxism, but more generally the limits of intellectual control of the future. Europeans often express horror at the complacency of Americans before the banality of life here. He understands the American experience as essentially "corrosive": beliefs, values, and hopes drop away in the course of American life. Life in the American empire, as in the Roman, seems to breed toughness: "America pushes you to the wall and compels a kind of stoic virtue: to do your best and at the same time to preserve a certain detachment that derives from an awareness of the ignorance, childishness, and incompleteness of all people, oneself included." America is, as Milosz said, "the unintentional precursor of modern life," because communities all over the world must come to terms with estrangement from their immediate past; hierarchies everywhere have collapsed, and Americans are ahead insofar as they survived the collapse long ago.

❦

In the first half of this century, young poets had to reckon the costs to them of staying in America, as Williams, Stevens, and Moore did. Pound and Eliot, who had decided early to move to London, the literary metropolis, seemed more obviously to be making literary history. In the second half of the century, the tables turned. British poets had to attend closely to what happened in America, unless they wished to join Larkin in his militant Little Englandism. Since World War II many poets from all over the world have come to live, as poets, in America. American literature has always proceeded in the shadow of English literature. British and American poets, unlike, say, Polish and American poets, cannot escape the sense of a standing literary rivalry between the two nations. One can measure the rise of the American literary empire after World War II, by listing the poets who have come to New York, Boston, or California. One can assess the significance of American poetry, in part, by attending to what British poets, like Donald Davie and Thom Gunn, have made of the work of their American contemporaries.

Like Milosz, Donald Davie too lived for many years (1969–78) in the San Francisco Bay area; then later in Nashville, Tennessee (1978–88). But unlike Milosz, Davie has had only a very small audience here. One learns less about the taste of American readers from him than about the international influence of American modernism in the last half-century. Davie is one of the most acute commentators on American modernist poetry, especially that of Ezra Pound. His intellectual life has been entwined with Pound's literary achievement, a decades-long worrying over the ethical and political significance of modernism in the liberal democratic postwar era; Davie has written repeatedly of what Pound's career ought to mean to English-language poets. Marjorie Perloff has written that Pound's legacy as a poet has been indisputable in four areas:

(1) the drive toward precision, particularity, immediacy – *le mot juste*; (2) the "break-[ing of] the pentameter" in favor of the "musical" free verse line; . . . (3) the use of translation as the invention of a desired other[;] . . . and . . . [4] the new conception of the poem as "the tale of the tribe" that no longer privileges lyric over narrative . . . , that can incorporate the contemporary and the archaic, economics and myth, the everyday and the elevated.

She develops this succinct account of Pound's influence by emphasizing the last area, which she rightly argues has become especially important among recent American writers. Perloff's Pound is obviously the chef d'ecole of modernism, though she knows of course that his work is not seamlessly modernist. Davie is an insistently British poet, and Pound's importance for him fits this modernist pattern only partly. One need only recall Davie's fine iambic trimeter poem, "Ezra Pound in Pisa" (1969), to see that the drive toward precision for Davie's generation of British poets was often reconciled beautifully to accentual–syllabic metrics. Metricality has consistently helped Davie, and Larkin, and Thom Gunn, say, to achieve the lapidarian quality that is conspicuous in passages of the *Cantos* that Perloff and Michael André Bernstein examine in detail – the mixing of discourses – and incidentally sympathetic to the anti-modernist doctrines of his poet–critic predecessor at Stanford, Yvor Winters.

Pound clearly showed Davie, at an early stage of his career, that poetry is deeply translatable, and that poets learn a great deal from reading and writing translations. Poets like Bly and Lowell turn to translation in order to place their own work, to fortify their own strengths. Pound spoke quite differently of translation in the eugenicist idioms and figures of the late-nineteenth and early-twentieth century: one literature might be "crossed" with another to provide readers of one nation or race (the terms were synony-mous for Pound and many other intellectuals then) access to ways of think-ing, feeling, and speaking that were otherwise inconceivable. According to this view, the foreign element ("the desired other," in Perloff's phrase) that enters through translation is a supplement to the traditions of the target language. Davie has gone to Russian and American poets when he felt impatience with his own achievements and those of his compatriots. Hass has said that he turned to the translation of Milosz with a similar dissatisfaction with what was possible in American poetry in the late 1960s and early 1970s. The modernists Pound and Yeats turned to personae for voices of difference. Pound and Davie, in their self-recriminatory moments, put aside personae to speak with their own voices against themselves.

Pound enters Davie's poems less as a translated supplement than as an alternative to the British literary traditions that allow Davie to write. Pound's example has rebuked Davie, and to great effect. There are surely moments when Davie uses Poundian language or figures to supplement his own, but much more important is the fact that Pound's work has made Davie feel an intellectual imperative to criticize himself – and has shown him too the literary resources of self-reproach. Davie's very best poem, "In the Stop-ping Train" (1977), is a critique of the intellectual life generally, but more particularly an indictment of the emotional life of a particular British poet. One wants to say, "of Davie himself," but Davie's relationship to the subject of "In the Stopping Train" is vexed. Pound's example helped him gain access to a range of feeling and expression that he might not have had, if he had accepted the constraints of autobiographical accuracy. The recriminatory mode of Pound's work is there in literary examples, independent of Pound's or Davie's particular historical lives.

Pound the rebuker is easy to locate. At the outset of "Hugh Selwyn

Mauberley" (1920), the poem Davie the critic has returned to repeatedly, Pound speaks of how Mauberley was not good enough: "Wrong from the start – // No, hardly, but seeing he had been born / In a half-savage country, out of date . . ." The notorious difficulty of the poem is in the dissociation of Pound the author and Mauberley the subject of the sequence. Is the poem thoroughly recriminating of the early Pound? Well, no, not thoroughly. Just exactly how far Pound's self-recriminations went is not entirely clear, as the interrupted syntax suggests. A quarter-century later, in the *Pisan Cantos* (1948), Pound would again strike a note of self-recrimination.

> J'ai eu pitié des autres
> probablement pas assez, and at moments that suited my own
> convenience (Canto 76)
>
> I have been hard as youth sixty years (Canto 80)

These are attractive and uncharacteristic moments in Pound's writing. If one believes that these famous passages express a thorough self-incrimination, one finds other passages in the Pisans to confirm that the poet has remorse in his heart: "Absouldre, que tous nous vueil absouldre" (Canto 74). Pound does expose a sense of his own limitations and failures, but there is abundant evidence in the Pisans that he could not finally settle in remorse. However much we want him to renounce fascism along with anti-Semitism, his regrets did not go that far. Pound's drawing of limits to his self-reproach is very much to the point.

Davie and others have spoken with good reason of the *Pisan Cantos* as prefiguring the confessional poetry of the late 1950s and early 1960s. Pound clearly broke through the constraints of the modernist impersonality to manage autobiographical subject matter poignantly. But the relevant sense of confession goes beyond mere autobiography: the more telling point is this turning of the poet against himself. One confesses, that is, not merely to having a personal life, but more particularly to human failures and corruptions. This is Davie's distinction between the Wordsworthian sort of confessing to virtue – that is, to having a rich private life – and the Baudelairian or Byronic confessing to vice. Lowell confessed to having overlooked his father's kindness. Davie has been an astringent critic of the autobiographical poetry we loosely call confessional, but "In the Stopping Train" plainly exploits the promise of autobiographical revelation. Only a few poets feel a need to turn against themselves, to turn even against the poetic principles that have guided them for decades. Pound did it in 1920 and again in 1948, and Davie did it in 1977. We speak easily about the ambitiousness of poets who build on their earlier work by moving into larger genres, attempting long poems, and so on. But there is another kind of ambitiousness that makes one wish to break with one's own achievements, to toss them to the ground and walk away.

Between the third and fourth quatrains of "In the Stopping Train" – when Davie says, "words like 'laurel' won't help. // He abhors his fellows . . ." – a crucial thematic gap is crossed. On one side is the poet's unfamiliarity with the referents of his own words: he cannot identify the flowers he names. On the other is his hatred of other people. No bridge between these two themes is named, exactly because the poet cannot confidently explain how the one entails the other, though this is what he feels. One implication is that no explanation of this correspondence is entirely adequate to the fact.

> He never needed to see,
> not with his art to help him.
> He never needed to use his
> nose, except for language.
>
> Torment him with his hatreds,
> torment him with his false
> loves. Torment him with time
> that has disclosed their falsehood.

Time is "the exquisite torment" because it robs one not only of the ability to feel strongly but also of hope, which is the problem of the stopping train. The stops are not the problem; the problem is rather "the last / start, the little one; yes, / the one that doesn't last." A start that doesn't last is a hope that isn't sustained. Davie has now and then resorted to the commonplace that hope is more accessible to Americans than to Europeans. To Thom Gunn, he says, "Hope springs not eternal nor everywhere."

> For these our friends [here in America], however,
> It springs, it springs. Have we a share in it?
>   . . . What are we doing here?
> What am I doing . . . ?

Quite similarly, at the close of "Recollection of George Oppen in a letter to an English friend," he says,

> Not a bit
> of help to me was George, or George's writing;
> though he achieved his startling poignancies,
> I distrusted them, distrust them still.
> But hope, such hope he had, such politics
> always of hope! Hope is a strenuous business;
> I hope the roar of it enlivens your
> west-country dell, as a whisper of it mine.

The self-recriminations of "In the Stopping Train" come just when hope runs out. But Davie has spoken of hope as having been only a whisper in his dell anyway, something that he was all along only translating, like some foreign element, into his life and work. In the two poems quoted, a lack of hope is something these fellow Brits supposedly share. Nonetheless he has reproached himself in earnest for ". . . the squeamish / mistaken resolve never to sound like Whitman." Repeatedly he represents his native temperament as essentially angry. "Oh I was a bombardier," he has said of himself in "Devil on Ice," another great poem of self-recrimination, "For anyone's Angry Brigade." One is meant to take him at his word when he says, "I am opinionated and embittered, / Inconsiderate, gruff, low spirited, / Pleased and displeased at once, huffy and raw." There is pathos in this when it comes late in life, too late to hope for change, when self-recognition is all that one can aspire to.

Hope, a sense of sustainable starts possible always, is just what he wants from American poetry.

> Time and again he gave battle,
> furious, mostly effective;
> nobody counts the wear
> and tear of rebuttal.
>
> Time and again he rose
> to the flagrantly offered occasion;
> nobody's hanged for a slow
> murder by provocation.
>
> Time and again he applauded
> the stand he had taken; how much
> it mattered, or to what
> assize, is not recorded.
>
> Time and again he hardened
> his heart and his perceptions;
> nobody knows just how
> truths turn into deceptions.

Debate itself is coarsening, and controversy over time is petrifying.

The strength of the poem is not only in its bite. The further point is that Davie, like Pound before him, is not altogether sure how far to go with his self-incrimination. The poem won't reduce to any one criticism, and the poet here is not just Davie, plain and simple. After describing the way that the life of words has numbed him, he reproaches his words with not sitting still:

> "Dulled words, keep still!
> Be the inadequate, cloddish
> despair of me!" No good:

> they danced, as the smiling land
> fled past the pane, the pun's
> galvanized *tarantelle*.

Neither words nor England itself is to blame for his petrifaction; he is. Likewise, after criticizing himself for not being adequately open to love, he satirizes "That sort of foolish beard / . . . took / some weird girl off to a weird / commune, clutching at youth." The weak note here, quite near the end of the poem, is the mistaken suggestion that these are the alternatives: angry self-refrigeration or running off to a commune. The hedges that remain, as in his equivocation about his own hopelessness, make it clear that self-rebukes do not just come naturally to this writer. He is struggling to come to terms with his self-judgments, and to get them just right.

The most painful passage of the poem comes when Davie acknowledges that his wife and daughter might not have told him how egotistical he has been less out of love or pity for him than out of blank despair. One asks then what he could have hoped to achieve in poetry that he sacrificed his family so thoughtlessly. The answer seems to come in the next poem in the collection, "His Themes," where Davie's tone becomes openly derisive. Here the poet's inflated sense of his own importance is openly derided. He thinks that he is bard, seer, and legislator, like the romantics, that he tells the tale of the tribe, like the modernists. But this sort of grand ambition, the poet claims, is only spilt religion, and this conclusion is necessarily more forceful for a Christian like Davie than it can be now for his agnostic readers.

There has been a critical doubling-back in Davie's poetry since its beginning. That is one of the virtues of a distinctively intellectual poetry, and American readers have appreciated this since at least the New Critics. "Hearing Russian Spoken" (1957) is one of Davie's early achievements in this line. But one could not have foreseen how severe this doubling-back would become in Davie's later work. "In the Stopping Train" came as a surprise to his readers. He took this unforeseen step partly because he remembered how an American poet had done something similar as early as 1920, but more comprehensively in 1945 in Pisa.

Robert Duncan was a Poundian poet in that, like his master, he too wanted the sense of religious authority in his work. Both poets saw that literary texts confirm the permanences in experience. The recriminatory mode, however, is atheistic and secular in the sense that it refuses the authority that comes from resonance, from repeated experience. A good deal of Davie's poetry since 1980 has been explicitly religious, but Davie has made no use of the religious dimension of Pound. His Pound is a writer of sharp judgment rather than a poet of transcendence. That is to say, the feature of Pound's work that has led Davie to his own best work is one that derives not from Pound's modernism. Modernist writing, partly at Pound's instigation, dispensed with the discursive apparatus that makes judgment persuasive. "Probably," for example, is a word that is crucial to the discursive elaboration of judgment. Pound knew that this word had no place in his work, so he displaced it into French: "probablement pas assez." Davie, when quoting this famous passage as an epigraph to his own poem "Brantome," simply misquoted and deleted it: "J'ai eu pitié des autres. / Pas assez." He takes away Pound's hedge, knowing what such words hope to achieve. The Pound he remembers is more frankly self-rebuking than Pound actually was. "Probablement" is not interesting, but the severity of "pas assez" is rather different. That sharp cutting against one's own grain fascinated Davie, and it is fascinating too in Bidart's "Confessional" and Hass's "Berkeley Eclogue," which looks back bitterly on all that had been excluded – alcoholism and child beating – from his own earlier poems. With a derisive internal dialogue reminiscent of "In the Stopping Train" and "His Themes," Hass has shifted away from the complacencies of his California eclogues – and so this way of writing has migrated back into the center of American poetry with great effect.

❧

Thom Gunn came to California in 1954 on a fellowship to study poetry with Yvor Winters at Stanford. He has lived in San Francisco for four decades. His second book, *The Sense of Movement* (1957), showed fascination for mass cultural representations of American life: his poems on motorcycle hoods in the early 1950s drew on the films of Marlon Brando and James Dean. That cultural product exported efficiently. Gunn has continued to write in metrical and stanzaic verse, even during the 1960s when many American poets renounced traditional verse; in this sense he has remained audibly English, though he also writes free verse. The surprising thing is that in the late 1960s, when American youth culture again became prominent in his writing, he held to his meters. Poems like "Moly" and "Rites of Passage" translate the subjects of American youth culture together with archaic Greek myth into what then seemed British stanzas. Many readers responded to the contrast between the order of the verse and the representations of drug-induced disorientation: this reading puts the poems in tension as form versus chaos. Yet one can also sense how the concentration of force that is achieved by the heroic couplets of "Moly," for instance, suits the intensity of intergenerational warfare.

Gunn's work constantly presents the choices among alternatives in poetry as choices about life as well, but his poems show that commonplace notions about the restraints of metrical form have very little power in explaining the risks that poets take. His fascination with sexual adventure and drug experimentation is often expressed in terms that suggest as well national differences between Britons and Americans. "The Differences" Gunn takes as his title in 1992 are national as well as personal.

> Reciting Adrienne Rich on Cole and Haight,
> Your blond hair bouncing like a corner boy's,
> You walked with sturdy almost swaggering gait,
> The short man's, looking upward with such poise,
> Such bold yet friendly curiosity
> I was convinced that clear defiant blue
> Would have abashed a storm-trooper. To me
> Conscience and Courage stood fleshed out in you.
>
> So when you gnawed my armpits, I gnawed yours
> And I learned to associate you with that smell
> As if your exuberance sprang from your pores.
> I tried to lose my self . . . I did the opposite,
> I turned into the boy with iron teeth
> Who planned to eat the whole world bit by bit,
> My love not flesh but in the mind beneath.
>
> *Love takes its shape within that part of me*
> (A poet says) *where memories reside.*
> *And just as light marks out the boundary*
> *Of some glass outline men can see inside,*
> *So love is formed by a dark ray's invasion*
> *From Mars, its dwelling in the mind to make.*
> *Is a created thing, and has sensation,*
> *A soul, and strength of will.*
>
> It is opaque.

His lover is all-American: hearty, brash, unintimidated, moral, innocent – and fond of a different kind of poetry. Gunn is only too willing to be instructed. But he comes up against his limits just when he meant to leave them behind. The eight-line alternately rhymed stanzas of iambic pentameter hit a glitch just at the expected point of identification. The ellipsis in the twelfth line is for rhyme, on the lover's smell, that never came; the line ends not with a matched sound (or odor), but with "opposite." Instead of surrendering his self, he rediscovers the force of a subterranean fantasy. The boy with iron teeth is a mechanical monster, not a naïf to stare down storm-troopers. In the third stanza Gunn lets Guido Cavalcanti's *Donna mi Prega* speak for him about the source of love. Cavalcanti is known to modern poetry through Pound, who translated this poem several times, most famously as Canto 36, though Gunn does not quote Pound's translations. George Dekker has argued that the point of Pound's Canto is that Cavalcanti had a language for analyzing the nature of love, but that Pound's translation must be obscure because English has no such language. Pound deliberately presented his translation as obscure in order to demonstrate the cultural decline from the thirteenth century to the twentieth. Gunn's poem is a dialogue with Pound about the opacity of love, about its power to draw men into their childhood nightmares just when they think they will be free.

Freedom is the key issue when British poets consider American poetry, free verse, above all. In the second decade of the century American poets, Pound and H.D. in particular, helped formulate an Anglo-American version of the European avant-garde drawing a great deal of press attention then. Imagism has had an abiding effect on American poetry. One of its tenets – to compose in the sequence of the musical phrase – was intended to elicit a new music in verse, something endemic to no national tradition but inherent in a particular statement. The very short poems of Pound in particular were meant to seem spontaneous aperçues:

> The apparition of these faces in a crowd;
> petals on a wet, black bough.

The actual genesis of these lines shows that they were anything but spontaneous, but still they were meant to seem so. "Free verse," Gunn has said, "invites a different style of experience, improvisation." Duncan was the recent master of improvisation, in Gunn's view. We have had a cult of spontaneity in American poetry since the publication of *Howl* (1956), and it was not much earlier that American jazz showed how a new music might come from improvisation rather than scored arrangement. When Gunn published a poem called "Improvisation" (1992) about street life in San Francisco, its connections to the policies of American poets were clear.

> I said our lives are improvisation and it sounded
> un-rigid, liberal, in short a good idea.
> But that kind of thing is hard to keep up:
> guilty lest I gave to the good-looking only
> I decided to hand him a quarter
> whenever I saw him – what an ugly young man:
> wide face, round cracked lips, big forehead
> striped with greasy hairs. One day he said
> "You always come through" and I do, I did,
> except that time he was having a tantrum   10
> hitting a woman, everyone moving away,
> I pretending not to see, ashamed.

Mostly
he perches on the ungiving sidewalk, shits
behind bushes in the park, seldom weeps,
sleeps bandaged against the cold, curled
on himself like a wild creature,
his agility of mind wholly employed
with scrounging for cigarettes, drugs, drink
or the price of Ding Dongs, with dodging knife-fights,
with ducking cops and lunatics, his existence   20
paved with specifics like an Imagist epic,
the only discourse printed on shreds of newspaper,
not one of which carries the word improvisation.

The first three lines are casually formulated, humane in acknowledging the difficulty of holding to an improvisatory ethic consistently, as to a law. The fourth line admits with good humor that even his altruism can be a disguise for erotic desire. The apparently easy resolution of this problem is the commitment to give him quarters consistently. The paradox is of course that he is demonstrating his own predictability by consistently giving alms to an ugly man. The shame he expresses in line twelve is complicated: shamed to look away, to pretend not to see the woman in need of help; shamed too to be involved as benefactor to this malefactor; and perhaps shamed too not to intervene directly and spontaneously in the life of this man whom he intended to help, or even befriend, as the ugly man suggests in line nine. He withdraws into superficiality, which is what was behind the resolution to give alms at the outset (ll. 4–5).

The second paragraph lists the physical properties of the ugly man's life – the sidewalk, the shit, the bandages, the cupcakes, the drugs. His life is entirely superficial, "like an Imagist epic." This is the ethos of modernist poetry, and no honorific like "improvisation" helps to prettify it. Yet there is a problem in trying to renounce the original proposition – "our lives are improvisation." It is easy to say that when one is free to invent laws now and then to suit particular circumstances (l. 5). On the one hand, a life of improvisation is repulsive, as the first paragraph suggests. Yet the invention of laws to remedy some excess or other is full of paradoxical difficulties. There is no escape from improvisation in the invention of laws, and the improvisation of excuses (l. 12) does not help to evade the laws of humanity. And poetically, the poem is unimaginable, with its telling details, without the precedent of the modernist poetic that is shamed by this narrative.

What does this say about British and American poetry? In the eyes of the British poets who have most engaged American poetry, the test of the vigor and authority of American poetry is not a professional matter. Issues of craft are not the main thing, it appears. On the contrary, Davie and Gunn see the claims of American poets as bearing quite directly on the lives of poets and citizens. Davie seems to test Poundian practice against his personal life, as Gunn does too. Gunn tests Imagist poetics on the streets of San Francisco, among just those citizens whose lives seem to be calling into question the dominant society's claim to control itself effectively and democratically.

❧

Much of what I have discussed here is not translation in the narrow and common sense of the word, but all of it is a carrying over, sometimes of a poem, sometimes of a career, sometimes of a nontextual cultural practice. In all these transactions, questions about the source of authority arise. When foreign poets look at American poetry, they often seek the authority of genuineness, as Gunn and Davie have done. The mere pursuit of the genuine in some foreign place or text is usually sentimental, as the American taste for Milosz and other Eastern European poets usually is; but critical examination of any claim to genuineness is indeed valuable, and that is what one has in Milosz's, Gunn's, and Davie's poems. We should not hastily speak about the imperialism of translations, I think, because so often they stir admirable curiosity, and self-skepticism; and poets writing translations are often seeking to experience differences that may change their work or life, not just consolidate their authority. Although there are certainly translations, attractive and compelling ones, that borrow authority from other times and places, there are still others that question the authority of our contemporary cultural practices, or of the poet's own writing, most obviously in Davie's "In the Stopping Train." Translation provides an opportunity for contemplating limits and boundaries. Lawrence Venuti argues cogently for the need to mark those boundaries linguistically. None of the poets cited here has tried to obscure or slide over the differences between one poetry or culture and another. American poetry of this half-century has been extraordinarily rich in this art of the provisional, where texts themselves are obviously divided within themselves. Boldness and audacity have indeed been abundant in recent translations, but not self-satisfaction.

CONCLUSION:
THE PLACE OF POETS, 1995

IMAGINE A TIME when a young poet looks to the critical essays published in journals with eagerness, excitement even. Critics would then genuinely influence the poems being written. Young poets would learn their craft from the models also dominating the academic curriculum, and college students would not be mystified by the poems of their near contemporaries – to say nothing of how their instructors would approach contemporary poetry. Critics would then lead the audience for poetry, and poets would be in an indirect relationship with their readers. This would be the sort of culture in which questions of whether literature counts for anything at all might seem implausible. It would also, of course, be one in which literary conventions, period styles, in short, orthodoxies would be easy to establish. Once orthodoxies were in place, one might well have good reason to expect the formation of an avant-garde to move against those conventions, for without established conventions, there can be no avant-garde. In fact, the young poet was Robert Lowell, the time was 1937, and the critics were Allen Tate, T. S. Eliot, R. P. Blackmur, and Yvor Winters. This was the first flowering of the New Criticism. "The world was being made anew," Lowell thought.

Nothing, it seemed, had ever really been read. Old writings, once either neglected or simplified and bowdlerized into triteness, were now for the first time seen as they were. New Writing that met the new challenges was everywhere painfully wrestling itself into being. Poetry was still unpopular, but it seemed as though Arnold's "immense future" for literature and particularly poetry was being realized.

That was a different literary world from the one poets know now. The universities were then an exciting place for poets; there was a good deal of hope for a literary culture that would welcome the contributions of the arts and of the academic disciplines.

The critics Lowell recalled were all poet–critics. Along with Ezra Pound and John Crowe Ransom, they were the writers who for about twenty-five years explained what modernism had meant. They are all long gone, and their places have not been filled. Indeed their places have been lost, because the current literary culture has a radically different order from that of the prewar years. The greatest change has been the professionalization of literary studies as institutions of higher education have proliferated. In 1937 the Modern Language Association had 4,200 members and a budget of $23,000; there were 31,864 members in 1994 and the expenses for the fiscal year ending in August 1994 were $8.5 million. The professionalization of poetry has occurred mostly since 1960, when there were fewer than a dozen graduate creative writing programs; there are 230 now. In 1941, the distinguished Anglo-Saxonist and bibliographer A. G. Kennedy, then chairman of the Stanford English Department, told Yvor Winters that poetry and scholarship do not mix, and that Winters' publications had disgraced the department. Winters took this disagreement seriously and tried unsuccessfully to find another job. Two decades later he would talk at the weekly Stanford department lunches of Airedales and fruit trees. Once one of his colleagues said, "Yvor, you always talk about gardening and dogs, and never about literature." "That's because none of you knows anything about literature," he is said to have replied. The animosity between poets and academicians is felt on both sides of the divide, and it is nothing new, though it intensified in the 1980s and 1990s.

The first half of the twentieth century produced extraordinary American poet–critics: T. S. Eliot, Ezra Pound, Marianne Moore, John Crowe Ransom, Allen Tate, Winters, and others. From 1945 until about 1960, poets had behind them this generation that had distinguished itself with critical prose as well as poetry. Coleridge and Arnold, as these critics knew, had established antithetical models for critics. Coleridge saw criticism and indeed poetry too as aligned with the permanence of philosophy. "No man was ever yet a great poet," he claimed, "without being at the same time a profound philosopher." In the *Biographia* he aspired to "an honest and enlightened adherence to a code of intelligible principles previously announced, and faithfully referred to in support of every judgment on men and events." Arnold, on the contrary, was an improviser, who valued "a free play of the mind." He wrote for particular occasions and invoked principles and terms as he needed in order to get the job at hand under some control. He was in fact satisfied to wield very little control over his terms. Remember that he gives no definition of his evaluative criterion "high seriousness," and prefers merely to exemplify the quality in a series of quotations. The history of poet–critics is a dialogue between these two manners of proceeding: by reference to a systematic philosophy or a fixed perspective, and by repeated adjustment of perspective to the exigencies of the moment. Most of the poet–critics of this century have been improvisers, though a few, responding to particular opportunities or emergencies, tried to construct systematic positions; Pound is the best example. In the 1930s he tried to explain everything in terms of economics and was reluctant to correspond with anyone who would not grant the primacy of economic analysis. This veering toward method certainly damaged Pound's writing and credibility, and Eliot's criticism too suffers neglect today partly because of his attempts in the same period to generalize about the nature of society. Not that we reproach them for trying to generalize. Arnold said that Wordsworth didn't know enough, that he hadn't read enough, which is something like what is said of Pound and Eliot as social critics: they thought they knew much more than they actually did. The failure of modernist social criticism to address a liberal democratic future did not at all discredit the specifically literary authority of poet–critics. From the mid-1930s until the late 1950s, American poet–critics maintained great literary credibility.

The currency poets have lost is among general readers in the academic culture; they maintained an audience in the larger public. As poetry lost its general currency, poet–critics became commentators on a special, reduced sector of the literary culture. Their writing has evolved into a separate, alternative literary discourse with special, not much coveted responsibility for poetry. Since 1945 the differences between the writing of poet–critics and that of academic critics and theorists have become extreme. Here are the opening sentences of an essay by Robert Hass:

> I told a friend I was going to try to write something about prosody and he said, "Oh great." The two-beat phrase is a very American form of terminal irony. A guy in a bar in Charlottesville turned to me once and said, loudly but confidentially, "Ahmo find me a woman and fuck her twenty ways to Sunday." That's also a characteristic rhythm: ahmo FIND ME a WOman / and FUCK her TWENty WAYS till SUNday. Three beats and then a more emphatic four. A woman down the bar doubled the two-beat put-down. She said, "Good luck, asshole." Rhythms and rhythmic play make texture in our lives but they are hard to talk about and besides people don't like them to be talked about.

Among students of poetry, prosody is wrongly spoken of as especially dry and pedantic. Hass begins with this sort of anecdote because he knows that the scholarly discussion of prosody is just what he wants to avoid, and his readers should know this at the outset. He begins outside of academia, at a bar near one of the most distinguished English departments, where he then worked. Vulgarity seems to be his point too. The power of rhythm in language can be coarse, brutal even; it does not depend upon literary history. Literary history depends upon organisms. And criticism does not depend on universities. To a poet–critic, instances do not need always to be representative of a larger class, so long as they are telling in themselves. Hass's criticism often proceeds by anecdote. He would rather be thought of as a narrator than an explainer. By beginning with this particular anecdote, he implies a measure of hostility against those conventions of academic criticism that lead to what we speak of as powerful explanations, for as literary art most academic criticism might be called many things before one got around to the word powerful.

When we speak of powerful explanations, we usually mean to refer to a compelling logic linking a series of propositions. Critics who have elaborated systems to support practical criticism enjoy a special prestige among many literary scholars, especially younger ones – for one generation, Kenneth Burke, Northrop Frye, and Harold Bloom; for the next, Raymond Williams, Fredric Jameson, and Julia Kristeva – and often the sharp distrust of most poet–critics. We speak of critical method, as though the best critics proceed according to rules of some sort. The poet–critic Karl Shapiro claimed that the "honest critic has no system and stands in no dread of contradicting himself," but Shapiro was admittedly anti-intellectual. The poet Howard Nemerov, who was in fact influenced by Burke, wrote of the objective of one of his own critical books, "Critical method. To try not to have one." We know well where this argument comes from, and where it leads, which is why it arouses our misgivings. Arnold took wicked glee in repeatedly conceding his limits to his critics:

An unpretending writer, without a philosophy based on interdependent, subordinate, and coherent principles, must not presume to indulge himself too much in generalities. He must keep close to the level ground of common fact, the only safe ground for understanding without a scientific equipment.

About twelve years later he complained that "Critics give themselves great labour to draw out what in the abstract constitutes the characters of a high quality of poetry. It is much better simply to have recourse to concrete examples." And the touchstones followed, consigning our hope of explanation to the mist of a seriousness that somehow transcends principles. Contemporary poet–critics have not taken Arnold's extreme position often. Indeed, they have used what methodicalness they could muster as a means, if not of discovery, of argument. Randall Jarrell explained this procedure in 1952:

It is true that a critical method can help us neither to read nor to judge; still, it is sometimes useful in pointing out to the reader a few gross discrete reasons for thinking a good poem good – and it is invaluable, almost indispensable, in convincing a reader that a good poem is bad, or a bad one good. (The best critic who ever lived could not *prove* that the *Iliad* is better than [Joyce Kilmer's] *Trees;* the critic can only state his belief persuasively, and hope that the reader of the poem will agree.)

Although we rarely read systematic criticism written by poet–critics, they are in fact far more direct about stating their premises than academic critics. Poet–critics often say something, for instance, about what they think poetry is or does.

The poem, new or old, should be able to help us, if only to help us by delivering the relief that something has been understood, or even seen, well. (Robert Pinsky)

There is a great difference between such a statement and a critical method, but poet–critics are forthright as well in speaking of the kind of criticism they wish to practice:

A work of art is the embodiment of an intention. To realize an intention in language is the function of the writer. To realize from language the intention of the author is the function of the reader or the critic, and his method is historical or philogical interpretation. (J. V. Cunningham)

By comparison with the explanations of method or first principles one reads in the works of academic critics, these statements are strikingly unmetaphorical and direct; there is nothing fancy here, above all no striving after novel formulation. If these critics are talking about life in general, as they often do, one can expect the same sort of directness: "Humaneness is the fine art of enjoying other people" (Kenneth Rexroth). They allow themselves the pleasure of putting grand things simply. And when defining life rather than just literature, they often do go after fresh conceptions and formulations.

It seems to me that we all live our lives in the light of primary acts of imagination, images or sets of images that get us up in the morning and move us about our days. I do not think anybody can live without one, for very long, without suffering intensely from deadness or futility . . . images are powers: It seems to me quite possible that the arsenal of nuclear weapons exists, as Armageddon has always existed, to intensify life. It is what Rilke says, that the love of death as an other is the great temptation and failure of imagination. (Robert Hass)

Literary criticism cannot tell us as much as speculation about life in general; it is a thoroughly limited affair, poet–critics tend to think. After writing at length about Whitman's merit, Jarrell wrote:

Critics have to spend half their time reiterating whatever ridiculously obvious things their age or the critics of their age have found it necessary to forget; they say despairingly, at parties, that Wordsworth is a great poet . . . There is something essentially ridiculous about critics, anyway: what is good is good without our saying so, and beneath all our majesty we know this.

Explanations of literature are at base rhetorical, aimed at the misunderstandings of a particular moment. In time the value of literary works becomes clear; the critic's job is useful only in the short run. He or she will ultimately not be needed, and should never really be believed anyway, since a critic speaks always for effect.

If someone has a good enough eye for an explanation he finally sees nothing inexplicable, and can begin every sentence with that phrase dearest to all who professionally understand: *It is no accident that* . . . We should love explanations well, but the truth is better; and often the truth is that there *is* no explanation, that so far as we know it is an accident that . . . the motto of the city of Hamburg is: *Navigare necesse est, vivere non necesse.* A critic might say to himself: for me to know *what* the work of art is, is necessary; for me to explain *why* it is what it is, is not always necessary nor always possible.

We like to think that evaluative principles especially, but interpretive ones too, should be spelled out, and that particular judgments or claims should follow logically from those principles, though we know they often don't, which is one reason for speaking of "insights." For poet–critics, criticism is an improvisatory art, unpredictable, full of inconsistencies, never better than approximate. "Criticism, in whatever fancy dress," Nemerov said, "remains an art of opinion, and though the opinion would be supported by evidence, even that relation is a questionable one."

What then counts as justification? Reading and a sense of fit between what a critic says and an experience of the test. A standard trope for poet–critics is to beg off of explanation in favor of a plea for a reading.

Nothing I can say about these poems can make you see what they are like, or what the Frost that matters most is like; if you read them you will see. (Jarrell)

We come to a point in these later books where [James] Wright's poetry is so compressed with self-reference, with recurrent meditation on these images and themes, that tracing them belongs to long reading and not the ten thumbs of criticism. (Hass)

Jarrell wrote mostly appreciative criticism; he stops himself with a reminder of the impossibility of adequate explanation. But Hass halts because it would be just tedious to go on with the sort of patient explanation that scholar–critics often produce. Both writers agree, though, that a critic ought not to push too hard; one should defer to the act of reading, and it is rhetorically important not to be tardy with that deferral. Scholar–critics all too often press for conviction on the page.

When Jarrell in 1952 said that critics are rightly methodical only in order to be persuasive, he had a broad sense of the rhetoric of criticism; persuasion "covers everything from a sneer to statistics." "Vary a little, vary a little!" he said. Range is the issue: how rich are the stylistic resources of contemporary scholar–critics? Though they are their own overseers, they sometimes seem to mine only a single vein of lead. Their chief concern often is the establishment of their own authority and the maintenance of consistency and seriousness. When B. H. Haggin, the music critic, admitted he had changed his mind about some of Stravinsky's work, Jarrell remarked: "This sort of admission of error, of change, makes us trust a critic as nothing else but omniscience could." You might say that it is relatively easy to admit to short sightedness, once one has made the appropriate adjustment of vision. Yet the poet–critics sometimes just make a point of saying that they haven't quite mastered their subjects. "I don't entirely understand it [Marianne Moore's "Armour's Undermining Modesty"]," Jarrell wrote, "but what I understand I love, and what I don't understand I love almost better." And when Hass gets to the topic of sexual violence in Lowell's poems, he says simply, "I'm not sure how to talk about it." These are not critics in danger of taking themselves or their work too seriously. Cunningham gathered his own essays together in one volume in 1976, and this is the sentence that introduces over thirty years of literary criticism: "There is less to be said about literature than has been said, and this book adds a little more." He would not have said the same about his poetry, or that of others, but criticism is a minor art.

My interest is in the reception of poet–critics. The examples of Pound and Eliot, even more than of Coleridge and Arnold, set the terms for poet–critics after World War II. Younger poet–critics were quite reluctant to produce social analysis: Pound had publicly disgraced himself, and Eliot too was embarrassed by *After Strange Gods* (1934). It took two decades to bring poet–critics back into the public arena with social criticism. In 1960 LeRoi Jones began writing social essays, which were collected in the volume *Home* (1966), which by 1970 had been reprinted seven times. Jones, very much with Pound's example in mind, attacked the liberalism of white American intellectuals at just the moment when liberal intellectuals were in power (1961). In 1962 he began his attack on racial integration and nonviolence, at just the moment when these objectives were gaining wider support in the black and white communities. Jones understood that his displacement from the mainstream, as an African American and as a poet, gave him an opportunity to write truly critical social essays; he must have known too that he would make many enemies.

The example of these essays and a very unpopular war helped white poet–critics like Adrienne Rich and others to begin to write social criticism in the mid- and late 1960s. The critical prose of the poets who were finding their bearings between 1945 and 1970 is timid by comparison with that of Pound, Eliot, and Williams. The essays of Richard Wilbur, Robert Lowell, even Berryman and Jarrell, or W. D. Snodgrass, James Merrill, and Anthony Hecht are in a lesser league than those of the modernist generation. The later generation was savvy enough to understand that, after Pound and Eliot, it was better for their careers not to write prose, certainly not to write wide-ranging critical prose. Charles Olson was the notable exception: he refused to be quieted by the embarrassments of the modernists. He was nearly alone among his contemporaries in recognizing that a poet–critic properly writes about more or less everything at once – poems, history, philosophy, geology. But this wilfully modernist generation had to invent an alternative public for critical prose, and the tradition of the modernist poet–critics went underground to the 1950s avant-garde. The mainstream literary public wanted nothing from these writers until nearly 1965.

❦

Since 1975 two poet–critics, Rich and Bly, have reached very large publics with quite wide-ranging critical prose; they broke the pattern of their contemporaries. Their reception shows what general readers of this last quarter-century want from poet–critics. Both writers wisely refrained from publishing a collection of literary critical essays until they had first published books of expository prose on identity politics. *Of Woman Born* (1976) was Rich's first prose book, and *Iron John* (1990) was Bly's. They used the genre of a poet's social criticism to redirect their careers. Rich's essays, in the three prose volumes following *Of Woman Born*, were in many cases written in response to invitations from colleges and universities for lectures and commencement addresses, or from scholarly associations for talks at conventions, particularly of feminist scholars; she writes as well for *Ms.* magazine and other nonacademic publications, but she has found her public largely among academic groups. Her essays draw on scholarship in various fields and are addressed to those who look to such sources for validated information. Bly has aimed his prose rather differently. *Iron John* is addressed to a popular audience whose contact with academic culture is slight. The essays in *American Poetry: Wildness and Domesticity* (1990) were published largely in the journals Bly himself published and refused to send to university libraries (because of Defense Department contracts with universities during the Vietnam era). At the back of the paperback edition of *Iron John* is an ad from Random House offering audiocassettes of Bly reading an abridged version of the book. And his appearance on Bill Moyers' show made him a public television star. Although Bly too cites scholarly publications now and then, he is largely dismissive of academic culture, as Rich is not. Rich's notion of a large public owes something to the traditional one of the academic popularizer, one who can sum up scholarly work in a field and relate it to other fields. Bly is rather an anti-academic who tries harder than Rich does to reach working people directly.

The surprising thing is that Rich and Bly have reached large publics by addressing directly the special interests of particular groups. And other poet–critics like Gary Snyder and Wendell Berry have done similarly. What is wanted is that poets address the special interests of feminists, masculinists, ecologists, and so on, but with the authority that derives from a genre of writing that, while few people wish to read it, is widely recognized as deriving from first and last things. The ambitiousness and audacity of these poet—critics reinstates the larger offices of the poet—critic, but what do we make of their profiting from the public's appetite for sages? If there must be sages, let them try harder than Rich and Bly do to unsettle the programmatic perspectives of special interest groups.

❧

Rich's poems convincingly exhibit an acute sense of the desires and soft spots of more than one generation of readers. She is tempted to play to those tastes, and the result is often, as she seems to know, sentimentality. (I interpret her constant disavowals of sentimentality in her prose as a sign of self-awareness in this regard.) Certainly the large printings of her prose books are evidence that she meets the needs of a large public for poets. I find three salient features of her critical prose that reveal her public's taste. These saliences bear not only on prose: they suggest what readers want generally from poets, maybe even from poetry itself.

First, her most recent critical volume, *What Is Found There* (1993), is cast in a personal form, a journal. The obvious implication is that this writing follows particularly closely the life of the poet. An implication that is made more quietly, also by formal means, is that her life represents other lives. For example, like many poet—critics, she quotes long sections of the verse and prose of other writers without offering any particular commentary. This procedure suggests not only that quotation is sufficient, but that what she has to say is well said by other writers whom she admires, that there is a common identity of those writers with particular political and social concerns. A still further implication surfaces repeatedly: that the lives of these writers constitutes not only literary history, but social history as well; that these writers *are* the oppressed people of history. "I wrote and signed my words as an individual," she says in the Foreword to *Blood, Bread and Poetry*, "but they were part of a collective ferment."

There is more to this than the obvious rhetorical excess. In a passage dated Labor Day, 1992 Rich praises the alternative celebrations of the 500th anniversary of the voyage of Columbus:

An enormous grass-roots countermovement has risen in resistance to these official celebrations. . . . The primary voices [of this countermovement] are those of the political, artistic, and intellectual movements of American Indians, Mesoamericans, mestizos, and mestizas, Chicana/os, Mexicana/os, Puerto Riquenos, Puerto Riquenas, movements building since the 1960s, through all the years when the Left was being pronounced defunct. . . . It's a movement of peoples who, despite wars of extermination, enslavements, the theft of their lands, children, and cultures, have never ceased to recognize poetry as a form of power.

The point here is familiar; she speaks as one commonly does about how identity is inherited and coherent. But this way of speaking entails contradictions for Rich. She implies that the actual participants in these counter demonstrations are survivors of wars of extermination, enslavement, and so on, whereas she really means that the ancestors of these participants suffered egregious oppression. (Whatever the level of racism now, Rich refers in the last sentence quoted to historical depredations.) This is a common rhetorical excess, but it disguises an important issue. The participants in the counter movement might well represent themselves as different from their ancestors in terms of having experienced cultural hybridity; they may well claim to have benefited from some of the institutions – courts, schools, universities – that are the sites of the state celebrations. Their identities, that is – and the issues they engage – are much more complex than this sentimental rhetoric can manage. Although Rich says that "she herself has a complex identity," her rhetoric leads her to some of the commonest misconstructions of her topic. At the close of an essay entitled "North American Tunnel Vision," for instance, she says that Native Americans "have somehow retained identity and memory, and still assert the original values which connected their people to this land," that African Americans have "synthesized an old/new culture," and that Jews "have survived." People of the earth, magpies, and survivors – these views of the history of ethnic identities in the United States are patronizing and vulgar; they reveal no complications of the representations of identity one finds in mass media.

Second, Rich offers her readers the consoling notion that social and literary progress are one and the same. Liberational social movements on behalf of women, gays, and oppressed ethnic groups have turned out, in her view, to have dramatically, unproblematically enriched literary history.

I see the life of North American poetry at the end of the century as a pulsing, racing convergence of tributaries – regional, ethnic, racial, social, sexual – that, rising from lost or long-blocked springs, intersect and infuse each other while reaching back to the strengths of their origins. (A metaphor, perhaps, for a future society of which poetry, in its present suspect social condition, is the precursor.)

She admits to wanting "to feel the pull of the future." For her, the responsible poet is the responsive one who is "most aware of the great questions of her, of his, own time . . . the deep messages of crisis, hope, despair, vision, the anonymous voices, that pulse through a human community as signs of imbalance, sickness, regeneration pulse through a human body." Rich has a romantic understanding of the appeal of contemporaneity. She sees little complication in the timeliness of the literary expression she admires. Tennyson listened attentively to just those anonymous voices telling him of the great questions of his time; "[*In Memoriam*] is rather the cry," he said, "of the whole human race than mine." Baudelaire listened to his own outsider's voice and wrote *Les Fleurs du Mal*. Baudelaire was fined for the publication of his poems; Tennyson was made poet laureate. Can Rich really prefer *In Memoriam*?

Third, she constructs an abject nationalism that flatters her readers with the notion that *they* are the body politic, that nationality indeed provides a significant structure to cultural as well as political life. It is easy to agree with her, to believe that of course we are Americans – or, more liberally, North Americans – before we are anything else. She repeatedly expresses the desire to concur with Virginia Woolf's statement in *Three Guineas* that "as a woman I have no country. . . . As a woman my country is the whole world"; but the claims of her American identity, she admits, are just too powerful. References to national identity in her work are legion, but the more interesting point is that the national identity she constructs is so morose.

October 1990. Time to say that in this tenuous, still unbirthed democracy, my country, low-grade depressiveness is pandemic and is reversing into violence at an accelerating rate. . . . When we try to think about this, if we're not too tired to think, we're driven to name old scores within the body politic: racism, homophobia, addiction, male and female socialization. You are tired of these lists; I am too.

Her conception of American identity is comprised of contradictory elements: 1) she speaks warmly of its potential, not yet fully emerged; and 2) she characterizes this common identity as fatigued. We are very young, not yet even born, really, but already too tired to think. These contradictory elements are reconciled by the familiar notion (artfully expressed in William Carlos Williams's *In the American Grain* [1925]) that the experience of the North American continent did indeed offer fresh potential to Europeans 500 years ago; but the Europeans chose repeatedly to deny that freshness in favor of racist imperialism. Because Rich asserts that Europeans in North America have been one people, she can plausibly claim that "the national psyche" or "the body politic" bears scars of the racist wars against its colonized peoples. Other nations, she concedes, have also been founded on conquest and racism, but America is different because it wrongly alleges itself to be exceptional – a product of enlightenment, not racism, cruelty, greed, and extermination.

Rich has in mind a psychoanalytic sense of identity: a "national fantasy" of innocence actually produces illness. The vitality of the body politic is maintained by those instruments – particularly poetry – that can reach the repressed energies of the national psyche: "poetry . . . keeps the underground aquifers flowing." The political poetry she admires is exactly what she sees emerging now from this diseased national psyche:

At the worst time in this continent's history, when indeed the old, dying forces seem to have pitched us into an irreversible, irremediable disaster spin – air, water, earth, and fire horribly contaminated, the blood pulse in the embryo already marked for sickness, sewage of public verbiage choking the inlets of the mind – an abundance of revolutionary art is still emerging.

The poems of Rich herself, of June Jordan, Audre Lorde, and many others are the return of the repressed. Poems are the consolation for depressed nationalism. It is embarrassing to see intellectuals take their nationalism in this form. We sentimentalize our bonds to other citizens when we cast them in a narrative of disease. Why are intellectuals so drawn recently to pathos? Rich's references to "the depressive nation," "our national despair," to "massive national denial," and to America as "a society in depression with a fascination for violence" provide a packaging of nationalism for intellectuals. We'll buy that because it's obviously not like working-class nationalism. I'm abject, you're ok.

❦

One of the appeals of Bly's prose has always been its lucidity. He is eminently quotable exactly because he relentlessly simplifies. The simplifications are based often on straight-forward contrasts: not this, but that. Not outward, but inward poetry. Not the conscious, but the unconscious mind. Not the waking, but the dreaming mind. Putting Eliot next to de Nerval, Bly says, "The attitudes could hardly be more opposed," pleased to end his paragraph there. David Ignatow is said to make "a stark contrast with poets such as James Merrill." Bly thinks in stark contrasts and of course quotes Blake, "Without contraries is no progression." His readers remember these distinctions easily. And this sort of manipulation of contrastive categories surely makes one feel, if only briefly, that one is fast getting somewhere with the analysis, say, of literary history. Objections to this sort of rhetoric go back at least as far as Arnold himself; Bly is quite traditional as a poet–critic when he resorts to simplifying contrasts.

To his credit, though, he often pulls his readers a little beyond the contrasts. The Blake citation refers to a progression beyond contraries, a third point. Bly rarely has a clear sense of how to progress to a synthesis, but he often rejects his own instinct to go for one or the other term of a contrast. Once he sets up Wallace Stevens and Etheridge Knight as "two poles of North American poetry," for instance, he concludes by saying that

"One doesn't have to choose and make one artificial, the other natural; one complicated, the other direct; one elegant, the other piercing. Nothing is as elegant as words that remain in truth. What do we expect of poetry?" Poetry is the one area, then, where what Bly sees as rational processes don't have to be permitted to close down on the casualties of logic. He praises Donald Hall, for instance, exactly because Hall has progressed beyond the sort of contrastive thinking that comes naturally to Bly and pleases his readers: "The psychology in his early books tends to be clear – too clear, with naked oppositions of country and city, conscious and unconscious, repression and expression that take place against a mess of lies hinted at in the background. Now he brings the messy background to the foreground."

I have described Bly's attraction to contrastive analysis abstractly, because such habits of mind have considerable force above and beyond the particular subject matter that is made to conform to them. Now I want to recover some of the referentiality of Bly's prose in order to move ahead with my own analysis of Bly's habits of thinking and writing.

Bly the critic is best known among readers of contemporary poetry for his advocacy of what was retrospectively called Deep Image poetics in the early 1970s. Bly the poet has never had such success as he did then with his imagistic political poetry:

> It's a desire to take death inside,
> to feel it burning inside, pushing out velvety hairs,
> like a clothes brush in the intestines.

"The poetry we have now," he wrote as early as 1963, "is a poetry without the image." The real seriousness of poetry, as he described it, derives from the power of poetic images to express parts of the mind that are otherwise silent. Referring to his tripartite faculty psychology, he says, "Great poetry activates energy from the ancient, recent, and new brain structures by using images appropriate to that particular memory system." It is impossible to take seriously Bly's versions of the reptilian, mammalian, and "new" brain structures, but his insistence that poetry's business is with just what does not fit into conventional discursive structures is serious; the strange image is the sign, for Bly, of a poet's resistance to his contemporaries's habits of thought and association. "Couldn't we say that images," he asks, "when used by a genius, make up a kind of living face of the unknown?" Generally he means by the unknown something that derives from the unconscious mind, but he also means to esteem what he, given his intellectual habits and commitments, has not known; in other words, what other people may know better than he.

Bly was successful at arguing for an image-oriented poetry, but consider this short statement: "I like intelligence when it appears debating both sides of a question in the discursive poem, and I also like intelligence as it appears in an image." This is his "both and" mode. He is expressing his admiration for the sort of poetry associated with Robert Pinsky, a poet–critic he elsewhere treats unfairly, and also reasserting his esteem for the other thing too, the image poem. What is worth noticing in this is an element of self-criticism: Bly acknowledges the limits of his own partiality. In his critique of Whitman's expansiveness, he says, "Our task here is not to point fingers, for the fingers would simply curve and point at us – author and reader alike – but to work toward an understanding of the grandiosity that has eroded both poetry and society in the twentieth century." On the one hand he said early in his career that "Great poetry always has something of the grandiose in it." He criticized American academic poetry for its timid refusal to risk grandiosity. Yet he praised the dialogic poems of Yeats for their "restraints on grandiosity." And his criticism of the confessional poets for their escalation of hot subjects – nothing "less than a divorce or a nervous breakdown" – could justify a poem put him in the camp opposed to grandiosity. Grandiosity is not merely a matter of style or subject matter. Bly's claim is that American culture – political and economic not just literary culture – is based on infantile grandiosity, on a grotesque wish to have everything.

꙳

The poets who have successfully found really popular audiences for their critical prose have not been at the forefront of American poetry since the early 1970s. They are writers from the 1960s, and the features of their prose that I have analyzed stem largely from that era too. The straightforward analogies they perceive between poems and social structures have long since been superseded in literary criticism, as have Rich's sentimental notions of stable ethnic identity and Bly's syncretic Jungianism. What America wants from poet–critics is a spectacle of engagement, which has not been a live part of the intellectual culture for twenty years. To knowledgeable readers of contemporary poetry, Bly and Rich are picturesque; their significance is less what they say than their very presence in the newspapers or on public television. To the larger public, perhaps the same is true: they may reassure many readers that the modes of intellectual engagement that emerged in the mid-1960s survive in the 1990s – at least for poets, those sages who, even in a managed society like ours, speak with a constant awareness of death, lies, and secrets. One might say that for biting prose one goes to younger poet–critics, like Pinsky, Hass, Bernstein, and Silliman; that the social criticism of middle-aged writers is predictably conciliatory. But Eliot was 46 when he published *After Strange Gods*, 51 when the *Idea of a Christian Society* appeared, 60 when *Notes toward the Definition of Culture* appeared. Pound was 50 when he published *Jefferson and/or Mussolini*, 53 when *Guide to Kulchur* appeared; these were mad books, but they could not have reassured Pound's countrymen and -women, as Bly and Rich have done.

❦

What do Americans think of poetry itself in 1995? For the last half-century, they have actually been more inclined to think about poets than about poetry. "The successful poet," Clement Greenberg said in 1948, "still dominates the literary and academic scene, even if he is not read by as many people as the novelist is." At the outset of the Age of Lowell, the poet was the prince among artists. That sense of poetry survives now in the mass media, but not among intellectuals. The formality of poetry is commonly understood as hardly distinguishable from social formality, which is of course suspect in America. In Barbet Schroeder's film *Barfly* (1987), based on Charles Bukowski's writing, where the poet–character is graphically vulgar, he speaks with estrangement from his surroundings. Wanda tells him, "You're the damnedest barfly I've ever seen. It's the way you walk across the room. You act like some weird blueblood or royalty." And he replies, "I was not aware of that, but thank you." His formality of speech and carriage comes naturally, inevitably; he is not a bum, he reminds his friend Jim. Despite the saliva and whiskers on display, the poet has something princely and archaic about him.

In the mass media, poetry is antique, charming. Peter Weir's film *Dead Poets' Society* (1989) makes just this point. The film is set in 1959, the year confessional poetry emerged; Weir imagines the significance poetry might have had for the young people born in 1942, the college class of 1963. The reading of poetry has two settings in the film. The first is in the English classroom of John Keating, just returned from London, at an Anglophilic New England prep school. The principles of the school are marched out on banners as the film begins: Tradition, Honor, Excellence, and Discipline – and there poetry has its institutional place. Outside the institution is the "old Indians' cave" where the generation of 1942 imitates John Keating's generation by reading poems aloud: once a jivey version of Vachel Lindsay's "Congo," once a new composition declaimed to the accompaniment of a berated saxophonist (really, a clarinettist trying to make his way as a sax man), once some lines from Cowley written on the backside of a *Playboy* bunny foldout. Poetry has, then, some cachet as a source of visible alternative culture, resistance.

"We were romantics," Keating says of his generation, "dedicated to sucking the marrow out of life." The poetry he taught his students was written out of passion and love, devoted to romance and beauty. "Make your lives extraordinary," is what the dead say to the young, according to Keating. "No matter what anyone tells you," he says, "words and ideas can change the world." Keating has to be fired in the end, because his poetry was not the world that these future bankers and lawyers were to inherit, but the poetry was good for them all the same. About half of his students stand up for him literally, and their lives will be somehow influenced by him, though they will surely find their ways to the banks and courtrooms. The film affirms a nostalgic view of an art that once played a beneficial role in the lives of young men. Poetry is a tonic, good in short drafts for the young.

As the century closes, however, poets are the paupers of the intellectual world: even in the movies they have to be fired. The academic institutions that came to dominate the literary culture after 1945 have focused attention in the 1980s and 1990s on literary theory and the prose fiction of social groups that have obviously suffered political suppression. Poetry has lost much currency but not all its authority. American readers, even those in universities, still want something from poets, but what they want is prose. Poets are still thought to speak with a romantic authority, as though they tell profound truths while others make strategies. Allen Grossman's *Summa Poetica* (1990), is based explicitly on the claim that poetry derives from death. We want from poets the certainty of the dead. Truth, naked and deep, not ideology, not special pleading.

In a much discussed essay, "Who Killed Poetry?" (1988), Joseph Epstein claimed, as I have here, that poetry has lost cultural authority and prestige since the 1950s. His hypothesis is that the professionalization of poetry has done much to bring about this sorry state. His account of the professionalization of poetry is largely right: many undistinguished writers manage now to earn their living teaching in creative writing programs of colleges and universities. He sees two problems with this. The first follows from the numbers of poets involved. His epigraph from La Bruyere states that "There are certain things in which mediocrity is intolerable." The second is that the professionalization of writing means that these staff poets do not participate in the intellectual life of their institutions; they preserve a claustral professionalism in their creative writing departments. Epstein reveals, however, that he has only a shallow sense of what a vital literary culture entails. "Where did all [the] elegant, potent, lovely language [of the modernists] go," he asks, "or, more precisely, where went the power to create such language?" He cites examples of the language that poets like Philip Larkin and Elizabeth Bishop (amazingly, his examples) have not given him: "Complacencies of the peignoir"; "in the room the women come and go . . ." and so on. The potent language planted in Epstein's head is exactly what was anthologized repeatedly and discussed by commentators for college students of the 1950s. Epstein has the chestnuts of modernist poetry in his head, and he laments that the poetry of his contemporaries has not yet been so packaged for him.

Paul de Man noted that Walter Benjamin's commitment to the notion that poetry is a "sacred, ineffable language" was the archaic aspect of this notion. To Hans Robert Jauss, Benjamin's "messianic conception of poetry" is essentialist where modern critics need to be constructionist, but for many academic theorists and readers this premodern poetic remains alluring. Benjamin insisted that poetry has supreme cultural authority. This religious view of the art is as out of favor among poets as it is among critics. Robert Duncan and Allen Grossman are the rare recent poets who plainly shared this traditional view of the poet. Most of the poets in this book ask to be taken less as priests than as contemporaries, who share with their readers a world held in place not by a creed, but by a liberal democratic political order, in which poets like professors have only the status of citizens. Between the poet as priest or visionary and the poet as citizen, between Dante or Blake and Horace or Auden, lies a gulf of difference. Who among academic theorists advocates the interests of poets as citizens? That secular, mundane role for the poet is unattractive to academic critics; Bloom, de Man, and others prefer the visionaries. The easiest thing is for poets to inherit visionary authority automatically by writing in a genre itself regarded as sacred. Since the beginning of this century the best American poets have instead taken pains to explain the grounds of their writing, not to try to fit into the remains of a romantic conception of the poet. The most secular version of the citizen poet is the poet–critic, who speaks against what is not good enough, not for a vision. They compete with academic critics, not for authority so much as for currency. To understand the roles that recent poets have desired, we must understand the function of poet–critics.

✢

At the outset of this book I spoke of the need to examine not the representative poems but the exceptional ones, to read as poets, not as professors, do. I have nowhere claimed that the poems discussed here express some overall sensibility or zeitgeist. About forty poets are discussed here; in the preceding volume of this series, Frank Lentricchia has let four poets stand for modernist poetry. I doubt that the second half of this century is as entitled to its own historical rubric as the first half is, though effort to construct an overarching -ism for these years is, as Fredric Jameson says, hard to resist now. Yet this resistance matters, if one is to hold open the possibility of a literary culture that does not merely ratify the discursive interests of the professionalized academic disciplines.

Jameson has formulated the most ambitious account of the postwar era as that of postmodernism. His argument for this category is attractive partly because he is so explicit about his intention "to offer a periodizing hypothesis." His analysis of the styles of postmodernist cultural expression is explicitly subordinate to the argument that postmodernism is "vaster than the merely aesthetic or artistic." *Postmodernism* is nonetheless peppered with expressions of reasonable doubts about the validity of this periodizing hypothesis. He acknowledges the dubious attractiveness of a category that "gives intellectuals and ideologues fresh and socially useful tasks," and articulates the suspicion that postmodernism may be merely a mystification, even after he has resolved "for pragmatic reasons" (finishing the book?) to work with this category. Historical periodization is one of the basic curricular tools of academic literary historians: it leaves no blanks; all years are accounted for by periodizing. There is even a tendency for all periods to be discussed as somehow equivalent specialties within the academic discipline. Where there are glaring discrepancies between the relative worth of the art of one period and that of another, generic distinctions help to equal things out: Victorian drama is self-evidently weaker than modern drama, for instance, but the Victorian novel is so strong that the authority of the period is unimpeachable. Jameson does not argue that the nature of the historical period is to encourage cultural expression. On the contrary, he sees the development of " 'new social movements,' micropolitics and microgroups," encouraging the fission of postmodern culture to the point where contemporary poetry, for instance, is "a badge of local in-group membership." On the other hand, architecture thrives in this political and economic context because its materials are close to the essential issues of postmodernism. And academic theory seems to him uniquely well suited to its time, because it manages to produce just what academic discourse has established as the paradigms of historical movement: "schools, movements, and even avant-gardes where they are no longer supposed to exist." The effort of academics to imitate the former object of historical study does not appear problematic to Jameson. He says, without apparent misgiving, "that 'postmodern political art' might turn out to be . . . not art in any older sense, but an interminable conjecture on how it could be possible in the first place." Like W. J. T. Mitchell and many others, Jameson is at peace with the notion that ours is a golden age of academic theory in which the artists have often not managed to rise fully to the aspirations of the professors.

There should be no doubt that the economic and social structures of American experience changed markedly in the years following World War II.

Jameson is unarguably right about the importance of the globalization of production, and the structure of American political interests and alliances has been enormously extended in this era. Moreover, the claims of historians about the technological innovations of this period are irrefutable. There are strong material reasons for conceiving of the postwar years as a historical period. But exactly because one may wish to resist the notion that art is principally reflective, that it mirrors its social and political context, the utility of a periodizing hypothesis may not be great in the history of poetry. It may be, that is, that the attractiveness of poetry and perhaps of the literary culture, is that unlike architecture, which depends directly upon patronage and the formation of large capital, poetry is relatively autonomous from the economic structure of society. This is not to say that poets have no grip upon the subjects of imperialism, war, displacement, terror, and famine, only to suggest that these experiences may command a lesser part of some arts than of others. The achievement of poetry in our time may be exactly its nonconformity to the structures of the social, political, and economic experiences we recognize in other discourses. The attractiveness of this art for intellectuals might not be the charisma of major figures, the sonorous accompaniment of our efforts to work for social progress, or the confirmation of our historical hypotheses, but the construction of an art discourse, which sometimes runs parallel to other discourses but sometimes goes off on its own, exploiting just that relative autonomy from the dominant experience of the time that brings Jameson to speak of contemporary poetry as a cultish interest. Poetry is unsettled still; may it remain unsettling.

APPENDIX I
BIOGRAPHIES OF POETS

This appendix is designed to provide the fullest and most up-to-date biographical information available to students of contemporary verse. In addition to consulting scholarly analyses of the poets and their works, I have made use of information available in *Contemporary Authors* (Detroit: Gale Research Co., 1962–), *The Dictionary of Literary Biography* (Detroit, Gale Research Co., 1978–), *Great Women Writers: The Lives and Works of 135 of the World's Most Important Women Writers, from Antiquity to the Present*, ed. Frank Magill (New York: Holt, 1994), *The Norton Anthology of Modern Poetry*, 2nd edition, eds. Richard Ellman and Robert O'Clair (New York: Norton, 1988), and *Postmodern American Poetry: A Norton Anthology*, ed. Paul Hoover (New York: Norton, 1994). I have conferred with the individual poets to confirm and augment this information when at all possible.

ELIZABETH ALEXANDER (1962–)

Elizabeth Alexander was born in New York City in 1962, and attended Yale University as an undergraduate. After receiving a B.A. in 1984, she went to Boston University on a Martin Luther King Fellowship to study with the West Indian poet and playwright Derek Walcott. There she took an M.A. in 1987. Alexander completed her graduate education at the University of Pennsylvania (Ph.D., 1992), writing a doctoral dissertation entitled *Collage: An Approach to Reading African-American Women's Literature*.

While at Boston University, Alexander had poems published in *Callaloo*; her first book, *The Venus Hottentot*, appeared as part of that journal's poetry series in 1990. Alexander's work has been selected for inclusion in a number of recent anthologies, including *A New Geography of Poets* (1992), *Every Shut Eye Ain't Asleep* (1994), and *A Formal Feeling Comes: Poems in Conspicuous Form by Women* (1994). Her second book, *Narrative: Ali*, was published by Fisted Pick Press in 1994.

Alexander has taught at the University of Chicago since 1991. In recent years, she has been the recipient of *Poetry* magazine's George Kent Prize (1992), a Creative Writing Fellowship from the National Endowment for the Arts (1992), and the Illinois Arts Council Literary Award (1993).

JOHN ASHBERY (1927–)

John Ashbery was born in 1927 in Rochester, New York, and grew up near Lake Ontario. He attended Harvard as an undergraduate; after completing his B.A. in 1949, he went on to take an M.A. at Columbia. In 1955, he won a Fulbright scholarship to France, where he spent several years writing art criticism for the European edition of the *New York Herald Tribune* and working on a book on the avant-garde writer Raymond Roussel. Ashbery translated the French surrealist writers, and his poetry would come to be associated indirectly with them, and directly with the New York school of poets.

His first collection of verse, *Turandot and Other Poems*, came out as a chapbook in 1953. Three years later, *Some Trees* was selected for the Yale Series of Younger Poets Prize by W. H. Auden, a writer whom Ashbery would identify, along with Wallace Stevens and Laura Riding, as one of "the writers who most formed my language as a poet." Although Ashbery would capture some 15 grants and awards over the next two decades, many readers regarded early works, especially *The Tennis Court Oath* (1962), as needlessly obscure. He gained widespread critical recognition only in 1976, when his *Self-Portrait in a Convex Mirror* (1975) won all three of the major poetry awards for that year.

Self-Portrait in a Convex Mirror takes its title from a piece by the Renaissance painter Francesco Parmigianino. Like the painting, Ashbery's book bypasses the merely imitative to create the artist's own nonrepresentational version of the world. Critics have drawn parallels between his poetry and modern art, comparing the poet's departure from stylistic norms to the methods of the Abstract Expressionists. Indeed, Ashbery's knowledge of art is extensive; over the course of his life, he has worked as an art critic for *ARTnews*, *Art International*, *New York*, and *Newsweek*. His essays on art are collected in *Reported Sightings* (1989).

For Ashbery, as for many contemporary philosophers and literary theorists, meaning is constantly in flux. "My poetry," he comments, "imitates or reproduces the way knowledge or awareness come to me, which is by fits and starts and by indirection. I don't think poetry arranged in neat patterns would reflect that situation. My poetry is disjunct, but then so is life."

In addition to being active in the art world, Ashbery has also taught at Brooklyn College, New York University, Harvard, and Bard College. His numerous books include *Rivers and Mountains* (1966), *The Double Dream of*

Spring (1970), *Three Poems* (1972), *Houseboat Days* (1977), *As We Know* (1979), *Shadow Train* (1981), *A Wave* (1984), *April Galleons* (1987), *Flow Chart* (1991), *Hotel Lautréamont* (1992), and *And the Stars Were Shining* (1994). In 1985 he won the Bollingen Prize for the body of his work.

FRANK BIDART (1939–)

The early autobiographical poem "Golden State" captures the feel of Frank Bidart's early life and his troubled relationship with his father. Born in 1939, Bidart knew from an early age that he wanted a future very different from his father's farming life. He developed an interest in cinema, the "most accessible art form" in the Southern California town of Bakersfield; immersing himself in movie reviews and books, he hoped to become a "*serious* film director."

As an undergraduate, Bidart attended the University of California at Riverside, where he discovered literature. He was especially influenced by the criticism of Lionel Trilling and Francis Fergusson and the poetry of Eliot and Pound. The *Cantos*, in particular, opened up his idea of poetic scope: "They were tremendously liberating in the way that they say that anything can be gotten into a poem . . . if you can create a structure that is large enough or strong enough, *anything* can retain its own identity and find its place there." Bidart's poetic technique of splicing together fragments of conversations and letters owes something both to Pound's "ideogrammic method" and to cinematic montage.

After completing his B.A. in 1962, he went to Harvard, where he studied with Robert Lowell. (He would later help Lowell revise poems for publication, and this collaboration became the foundation for their friendship. Lowell also introduced him to Elizabeth Bishop, about whom Bidart has written "Elizabeth Bishop: A Memoir" [1993].) Bidart was uncertain about his academic goals, but "wrote a great deal," even as his interest in course work waned. These first poems, he has said, tried to emulate writers like Yeats, Pound, Eliot, and Ginsberg, but fell short: "they were terrible; no good at all." He wrote the first poems worth keeping in 1965, after he realized that "confronting the dilemmas, issues, 'things' with which the world had confronted me – had to be at the center of my poems if they were to have force." Two years later Bidart completed an M.A. at Harvard, but left without writing a dissertation.

In the early 1970s, Bidart met Robert Pinsky, forming one of his most "crucial artistic and personal relationships." They worked on manuscripts together, often reading and critiquing each other's verse over the phone. By this time *Golden State* (1973) had been accepted for publication; the results of their interaction first appear in Pinsky's *Sadness and Happiness* (1975) and Bidart's *The Book of the Body* (1977). Bidart brought out his third volume, *The Sacrifice*, in 1983; it was followed in 1990 by *In The Western Night*, a book that also includes a long interview designed as an introduction to his work.

Bidart currently teaches poetry at Wellesley College. His honors include a Guggenheim Fellowship and two grants from the National Endowment for the Arts, as well as the Bernard F. Conners Prize (1981) for "The War of Vaslav Nijinsky," the Lila Wallace–Reader's Digest Writers' Award (1992–4), and, most recently, the Morton Dauwen Zabel Award (1995). He is currently editing the *Collected Poems of Robert Lowell* (1996) and finishing work on *Desire*, a book of verse that is due out in 1997.

ROBERT BLY (1926–)

The son of a farmer, Robert Bly was born in Madison, Minnesota in 1926. He served in the U.S. Navy during World War II, and upon his return commenced his studies at St. Olaf's College. After a year, he moved to Harvard University. He graduated in 1950.

Bly discovered poetry during his Navy days, when he met a man who wrote verse. He was impressed, and started writing his own poetry in an attempt to dazzle a woman. Although the attempt was a flop, Bly was hooked, and "One day while studying a Yeats poem I decided to write poetry the rest of my life." He has been an amazingly prolific writer, turning out literally dozens of books since *The Lion's Tail and Eyes* and *Silence in the Snowy Fields* appeared in 1962. Among his most notable works are *The Light Around the Body* (1967), *The Teeth Mother Naked at Last* (1971), and *Sleepers Joining Hands* (1973).

In addition to composing his own poetry, Bly has translated writers such as Trakl, Neruda, Vallejo, Kabir, Transtroemer, Garcia Lorca, Machado, and Rilke. His connection with these authors goes beyond rendering their words into English: as the editor of the Fifties (later, Sixties, Seventies, Eighties, and Nineties) Press, he has been an important advocate for their work, particularly that of the Latin-American surrealists. Like these poets, Bly uses powerful imagery to explore the mystical underpinnings of modern life. He rejects what he sees as the distancing academic obsession with tradition and technique: "Unless English and American poetry can enter, really, an inward depth, through a kind of surrealism," he cautions, "it will continue to become dryer and dryer."

Bly's aversion to convention, both in literature and in society, extended into another arena in the 1980s when he began leading seminars for men that focused on the myths associated with initiation and manhood. Modern men are alienated because they have lost touch with their masculinity, he contends; in order to become strong, courageous, and whole, men need to rediscover the "Wild Man" inside themselves. The ideas behind these gatherings attracted widespread notoriety with the publication of the bestselling *Iron John: A Book about Men* (1990). Bly has also produced a number of videotapes on the subject, including *On Being a Man* (1989), *A Gathering of Men* (1990), and *Bly and Woodman on Men and Women* (1992).

Although he gives readings and workshops, Robert Bly has repeatedly declined offers of academic affiliation, preferring instead to remain "in residence" in rural Minnesota. Some of his most recent works are *The Rag and Bone Shop of the Heart: Poems for Men* (edited, 1992), *Gratitude to Old Teachers* (1993), and *Meditations on the Insatiable Soul* (1994).

EDGAR BOWERS (1924–)

Edgar Bowers was born in 1924 in Georgia, and grew up in the South. After graduating from high school in 1941, he entered the University of North Carolina at Chapel Hill, but his formal studies were cut short after two years when he was called up by the draft. Bowers studied French at Princeton in preparation for counterintelligence work overseas; assigned to the 101st Airborne division while abroad, he found himself "abandoned . . . in Berchtesgaden in summer of 1945, where I stayed until Spring 1946." When allied activity and the "de-Nazification" process wound down, he went back to college in North Carolina. He would return to Europe several years later on a Fulbright grant (1950–1), this time spending most of his time in Paris.

After finishing his B.A. in 1947, Bowers went to study with Yvor Winters at Stanford University, where he completed his Ph.D. in 1953. Two years later, *The Form of Loss* (1956) won the New Poetry Series Award from Swallow Press (Winters's publisher). Critics remarked on the poems' serious subject matter, classical forms, and tight control; some reviewers would later account for Bowers's relative neglect by contrasting this precise and cultivated poetic voice with the "confessional" tone so widespread in the 1960s and 1970s. Still, this spare style was not without significant admirers: his early work was anthologized by Ted Hughes and Thom Gunn, and his third book, *Living Together* (1973), was awarded the California Commonwealth Club Silver Medal for Poetry. More recent honors include the Harriet Monroe Poetry Prize (1989), the Bollingen Prize (1989), and the American Institute of Arts and Letters Award (1991).

During the 1950s, Bowers taught for several years first at Duke University and then at Harpur College (now the State University of New York at Binghamton). In 1958, he took a teaching position at the University of California at Santa Barbara, where he would remain until his retirement in 1991. His poems appear in *The Astronomers* (1965), *Witnesses* (1981), *Walking the Line* (1988), *13 Views of Santa Barbara* (1989), *For Louis Pasteur* (1989), and *How We Came from Paris to Blois* (1990). Bowers currently resides in San Francisco.

ALLEN TURNER CASSITY (1929–)

Son of a family in the lumber business, Allen Turner Cassity was born in 1929 in Jackson, Mississippi. He began his formal education at Millsaps College, and, after completing a B.A. in 1951, continued on to Stanford University where he studied with Yvor Winters. Cassity earned his M.A., but his education was broken off by the Korean War; in 1952, he was sent to the Caribbean, where he served in the Army for two years. When he returned, he enrolled at Columbia University and took a degree in library science (1956).

Cassity went home to Mississippi the following year to work at the Jackson Municipal Library. He stayed there only a brief time before he was engaged by the Transvaal Provincial Library, which signed him on as a member of the South African civil service. Hired by Emory University in 1962, Cassity came back to the American South to work at Woodruff Library. He remained there the rest of his working life.

Cassity's travels have informed both the backdrop and subject matter of his poetry. What he has called his "colonial pastorals" are set in "exotic" (or ironically exoticized) locations like the Caribbean and South Africa; his first book, *Watchboy, What of the Night?* (1966), is divided into sections based on such regions. America, too, appears as an exotic locale – straight out of Hollywood, as one critic has noted. Cassity's ironic take on the colonial project is spotlighted in the verse drama "Men of the Great Man." Included in *Yellow for Peril, Black for Beautiful* (1975), the play deals with the demise of Cecil Rhodes, British financier, imperialist, and loon. While his toadies manage to conceal his eccentricity from the press, it is patently obvious to his black servants.

Turner Cassity's works include *Steeplejacks in Babel* (1973), *The Book of Alna: A Narrative of the Mormon Wars* (1985), *Hurricane Lamp* (1986), *Mainstreaming: Poems of Military Life* (1988), and *Between the Chains* (1991). He has won several awards for poetry, including the Blumenthal–Leviton–Blonder Prize (1966) and the Michael Braude Award for light verse (1993).

ROBERT CREELEY (1926–)

Robert Creeley was born in 1926 in Arlington, Massachusetts. After the death of his father, he moved with his family to rural West Acton, where he spent the rest of his youth. Creeley enrolled at Harvard in 1943, but left after his freshman year to join the American Field Service; he served as an ambulance driver in India and Burma for a year before returning to school. He married in 1946, and in 1947 quit college for good, just one term before graduation.

After leaving Harvard, Creeley spent a number of years moving from place to place. He lived first on Cape Cod, then took up residence in New Hampshire, where he spent three years living on a poultry farm and listening to jazz records. During this period, he struck up a friendship with Cid Corman, who ran the radio show "This is Poetry," and began to submit poems of his own to little magazines.

Around that time, Creeley decided to start a literary journal. In the first decades of the twentieth century, little magazines had played a major part in printing and promoting the works of the literary avant-garde: *The Waste Land*, *Ulysses*, some of the *Cantos*, and countless other modernist works made their first appearance in the pages of these journals. Creeley was familiar with the writings of Pound and Williams, and in 1950 he contacted these and other poets, asking for assistance in starting a little magazine of his own. While the project was ultimately unsuccessful, it helped Corman establish *Origin*, a journal which would be instrumental in advancing his friend's poetic career.

The Creeleys continued their peregrinations in the early 1950s, moving to France and then to Majorca, Spain, where Robert founded the Divers Press. His first book, *Le Fou*, appeared in 1952, followed swiftly by *The Immoral Proposition* and *The Kind of Act Of* (1953). In 1954, Charles Olson, whom Creeley had befriended four years earlier, asked him to join the faculty of Black Mountain College. He accepted.

Moving to North Carolina, he established and edited the important *Black Mountain Review*, which served as a major outlet for the work of the Black Mountain poets. The college awarded him a B.A. in 1955. When his marriage crumbled, Creeley left the school and travelled to San Francisco where he met some of the major Beat poets. Between teaching at a boys' school in Albuquerque and on a coffee plantation in Guatemala, he took an M.A. from the University of New Mexico (1960).

Though Creeley often writes about love, as indicated by the title of the commercially successful *For Love* poems (1962), his style is compact and unornamented; he rejects traditional devices like imagery, and conventional meter and rhyme, for "form is never more than an extension of content." He takes the attempt to present "what I feel, in the world . . . for that instant" to extremes in collections such as *Words* (1967) and *Pieces* (1968), where his improvisations are, in places, reminiscent of Gertrude Stein's *Tender Buttons*. Some critics have attributed such poetic eccentricities to Creeley's experimentation with drugs.

Creeley taught at the University of New Mexico in the 1961–2 school year, and has held visiting professorships at a variety of colleges ever since. In 1966, he began his association with the State University of New York at Buffalo, where he is currently the Samuel P. Capen Professor of Poetry and the Humanities. Verse from the beginning of his career has been assembled in *The Collected Poems* (1982); later works include *Echoes* (1982), *A Calendar* (1983), *Mirrors* (1983), *Memories* (1984), *Memory Gardens* (1986), *Windows* (1990), and most recently, *Loops* (1995). He published the *Collected Essays* in 1989 and an autobiography in 1990. In 1992 he was appointed Poet Laureate of the state of New York.

JAMES VINCENT CUNNINGHAM (1911–1985)

James Vincent Cunningham was born in 1911 in Cumberland, Maryland. He grew up in Montana, and was educated at Jesuit schools; during his youth he was immersed, as he later wrote, in "the tradition of Irish Catholics along the railroads of the West." Heading farther west for college, he enrolled at Stanford University, where he became one of the chief figures in the group of writers associated with Yvor Winters. Cunningham completed a B.A. in 1934; after "wandering in the depression," he returned to Stanford to pursue his Ph.D., which he received in 1945. Cunningham's doctoral thesis, published in 1951 as *Woe or Wonder*, was one of the earliest works in a distinguished body of prose that would include the critical study *Tradition and Poetic Structure* (1960) (one of his first works to be printed by Swallow Press), as well as several essays on poetry. *The Collected Essays* came out in 1977.

As an undergraduate, Cunningham had poems accepted by *Commonweal*, *The Bookman*, *Poetry*, *Hound and Horn*, and the *New Republic*. His first book of verse, *The Helmsman*, appeared in 1942; *The Judge Is Fury* followed in 1947. Although his work was not widely read, it was praised for succinctness, precision, and wit. This style lent itself to the epigram, a form featured prominently in the collections *Trivial, Vulgar, and Exalted* (1957), *Some Salt* (1967), and, ultimately, *The Collected Poems and Epigrams* (1971). By the end of the 1950s, he was in fact celebrated primarily for his epigrams; Winters, for one, called him "the most finished master of the form in English."

Cunningham's skill as both poet and critic earned him fellowships from the Guggenheim Foundation, the National Institute of Arts and Letters, the National Endowment for the Arts, and the Academy of American Poets.

J. V. Cunningham began his teaching career as an English instructor at Stanford University. After a wartime stint as a math teacher at an Air Force base in southern California, he went on to hold positions at the University of Hawaii, the University of Chicago (where he was denied tenure), and the University of Virginia. Cunningham joined the faculty of Brandeis University in 1953, and was Professor Emeritus at that institution until his death in 1985. His final work, *Let Thy Words Be Few*, appeared posthumously one year later.

DONALD DAVIE (1922–)

Born to a Yorkshire Baptist family in 1922, Donald Davie acquired a taste for poetry at a young age. His mother, a schoolteacher before her marriage, knew many songs and poems by heart, and she passed this love of verse along to her son. The family's literary interests were not exceptional among the Baptists of Barnsley, and Davie learned to respect the intellectual traditions of the Dissenting church. During these years, he was also introduced to medieval church architecture by the art teacher of Barnsley Grammar School. Religious thought and architecture would both become important themes in his critical and creative writing.

In 1940, Davie enrolled on scholarships in St. Catharine's College at Cambridge University. There he studied literature, taking advantage of the extensive holdings of the English Faculty Library to read seventeenth-century sermons and tear through "One tome after another" of "histor[y] and critical commentar[y]." "I was never disappointed," he comments, "No book of scholarship could disappoint me then. . . . The only trouble was when to stop." His exploration of the library did stop, temporarily, when he enlisted in the Royal Navy in 1941. Sent abroad to northern Russia in 1942, Davie was stationed in Polyarno, Murmansk, and then in Archangel. Reading Kipling and Conrad peopled his mind with "Englishmen gone to the bad abroad," and he watched warily for strange transformations in this strange land. He vividly recounts his memories of this time in *These the Companions* (1982).

In 1943, Davie returned to England, and then to Cambridge, where he became devoted to the ideas of F. R. Leavis and his journal *Scrutiny*: he confesses wryly that between 1946 and 1950, "*Scrutiny* was my bible and F. R. Leavis my prophet." To this influential magazine, he submitted (unsuccessfully) a poem on Pushkin, one of the many literary results of his stay in Russia.

Davie had only picked up enough Russian abroad to barter with the villagers who came to trade balalaikas for tobacco. Back in Cambridge, he turned to Russian literature to make sense of his foreign experiences. He read works by Aleksandr Solzhenitsyn, Ivan Bunin, Mikhail Sholokhov, and Boris Pasternak; the verse of Pasternak, especially, came to have an important influence on the young poet's works. In the 1960s, Davie translated *The Poems of Dr. Zhivago* (1965), and edited *Russian Literature and Modern English Fiction* (1965) and *Pasternak: Modern Judgements* (1969); later in life, he would publish *Slavic Excursions: Essays on Russian and Polish Literature* (1990).

After taking a series of degrees at Cambridge that culminated in a Ph.D. (1951), Davie went to Trinity College, Dublin. He remained in Ireland until 1957, teaching at Trinity and at the Yeats Summer School. During these years, he brought out two important works of criticism, *Purity of Diction in English Verse* (1952) and *Articulate Energy: An Enquiry into the Syntax of English Poetry* (1955). These studies argued for conventional poetic genres and forms on ethical grounds: meter, for Davie, is "part of the heritable property of past civilization"; thus, "to dislocate syntax in poetry is to threaten the rule of law in the civilized community." He understood *Purity of Diction* in part as an attempt to explain the aims of the verse he published in the contemporaneous *Brides of Reason* (1955) and *A Winter Talent and Other Poems* (1957). Along with writers like Philip Larkin, John Wain, and Thom Gunn, Davie rejected the neoromantic verse of the previous decades in favor of "crisp, supple, and responsible" language, rational content, and conventional forms. This group of poets became known as The Movement.

In the fall of 1957, Davie went to the University of California at Santa Barbara to replace Hugh Kenner, who was on sabbatical in Europe. He met with two of his important correspondents while in California. At the invitation of the Polish scholar and critic Waclaw Lednicki, he came up to give several lectures at Berkeley; Lednicki had encouraged his Slavic interests and his adaptation of selections from the epic poem *Pan Tadeuz* (published as *The Forests of Lithuania* in 1959). Davie would visit Poland, Yugoslavia, and Hungary during the early 1960s, serving as the British Council lecturer in Budapest in 1961.

He also went to visit Yvor Winters, with whom he had corresponded since he discovered *In Defense of Reason* at Cambridge. Critics have noted similarities between the Movement poets and Winters's students, and in the late 1950s, Davie thought of "the Stanford school of poets" as "perhaps the most interesting feature of the poetic scene in the U.S." Despite subsequent critical differences with Winters, Davie would write an introduction for the *Collected Poems of Yvor Winters* in 1978.

In 1958, Davie returned to Cambridge University, where he taught at Gonville and Caius College. Six years later, he helped found the University of Essex, serving as a professor and later as pro–Vice–Chancellor. After teaching first at Stanford (1968–78) and then at Vanderbilt (1978–88), he retired to Devon, England. Davie has received fellowships from the Guggenheim Foundation and the American Academy of Arts and Sciences, and has been named an honorary fellow at St. Catharine's College, Cambridge, and Trinity College, Dublin. Among his important critical works are *Ezra Pound: Poet as Sculptor* (1965), *Thomas Hardy and British Poetry* (1972), *A Gathered Church: The Literature of the English Dissenting Interest, 1700–1930* (1978), and *Dissentient Voice* (1982). His collections of verse include *Essex Poems: 1963–1967* (1969), *In the Stopping Train and Other Poems* (1977), *To Scorch or Freeze* (1987), and the *Collected Poems* (1990). In 1992, Davie received the Cholmondeley Award for Poets.

RITA DOVE (1952–)

Rita Dove was born in 1952 in Akron, Ohio. She was educated at Miami University in Oxford, Ohio, where she graduated *summa cum laude* in 1973. After graduation, Dove attended the University of Tübingen on a Fulbright fellowship, then returned to the U.S., where she enrolled in the creative writing program at the University of Iowa. She completed her M.F.A. in 1977, and published the chapbook *Ten Poems* the same year.

Dove brought out a flurry of works in the early 1980s that culminated with the Pulitzer Prize–winning *Thomas and Beulah* (1986). This collection of verse is roughly based on the everyday experiences of Dove's maternal grandparents. In *Thomas and Beulah*, as in Dove's work as a whole, race is not a primary focus; as the poet explains, she writes "poems about humanity, and sometimes humanity happens to be black."

Dove taught at Arizona State University between 1981 and 1989, then moved to the University of Virginia in Charlottesville. In 1993 she was named the first black Poet Laureate of the United States, an appointment she called "significant in terms of the message it sends about the diversity of our culture and our literature." She has been affiliated with a number of literary journals, including *National Forum*, *Callaloo*, *Gettysburg Review*, and *Tri-Quarterly*. Her books include *The Only Dark Spot in the Sky* (1980), *The Yellow House on the Corner* (1980), *Mandolin* (1982), *Museum* (1983), *Fifth Sunday* (1985), *Grace Notes* (1989), and *Mother Love* (1995).

ALAN DUGAN (1923–)

Alan Dugan was born in Brooklyn in 1923, and was reared there and in Queens. He began his studies at Queens College (now the City University of

New York), but was drafted before he could finish his degree. He spent three years in the Army Air Forces. After the war, Dugan enrolled at Olivet College, then transferred to Mexico City College where, in 1949, he finally completed his B.A. Following a year of graduate study, Dugan returned to New York City and held a variety of nonacademic jobs.

Although he had received an award from *Poetry* magazine as early as 1946, Dugan's first book was not published until 1961. That year, in fact, he published two books: one was privately printed as *General Prothalamion in Populous Times*; the other, *Poems*, was selected by Dudley Fitts for the Yale Series of Younger Poets. *Poems* did not meet with unmitigated approval, but in the end, skeptical voices were drowned out by critical approbation. *Poems* ultimately secured Dugan the National Book Award, the first of two Pulitzer Prizes, and the Prix de Rome.

Perhaps the time in Italy (1962–3) gave him a taste for travel, for he spent the next years on the move. The first of two Guggenheim fellowships (1963–4) took him to Paris; after a reading tour of the U.S. and a short appointment at Connecticut College, Dugan took off again, this time for Central and South America on a grant from the Rockefeller Foundation (1966–7). Upon his return, he spent several years in residence at Sarah Lawrence College, and began his long-term association with the Fine Arts Work Center in Provincetown, Massachusetts.

Among Dugan's later honors are the Shelley Memorial Award (1982) and the Award in Literature from the American Academy and Institute of Arts and Letters (1985). His works are collected in *New and Collected Poems 1961–1983* (1983) and *Poems 6* (1989).

ROBERT DUNCAN (1919–1988)

Robert Duncan was born Edward Howard Duncan to a family in Oakland, California in 1919. His mother died in childbirth and his working-class father soon discovered he was unable to care for the baby, and gave him up for adoption. At the age of six months, Duncan was adopted by the Symmes family, and was renamed Robert Edward Symmes, the name with which he signed his early contributions to journals like *Phoenix* and *Ritual*. The couple had selected the child based on his astrological sign, and their interest in reincarnation and the occult left a lasting mark on his poetry. In Donald Allen's *The New American Poetry: 1945–1960* (1960), Duncan would comment, "There is a natural mystery in poetry. We do not understand all that we render up to understanding. . . . I study what I write as I study out any mystery. A poem . . . is an occult document, a body awaiting vivisection, analysis, X-rays."

Encouraged by an English teacher, the young man made the decision to become a poet while still a teenager. He attended the University of California at Berkeley starting in 1936, but withdrew in 1938 to go east with a lover. That year he began coediting the *Experimental Review* along with Sanders Russell; the journal published the works of writers like Lawrence Durrell, William Everson, Anaïs Nin, and Henry Miller. Duncan served briefly in the U.S. Army in 1941, but was slapped with a psychiatric discharge; three years later, he printed a pioneering essay on gay rights in the journal *Politics*. "The Homosexual in Society" (1944) called candidly for straight artists and critics to "recognize homosexuals as equals," and for gay intellectuals to stand up for their rights. Breaking new ground, Duncan discovered, is not without risk; after becoming aware of the article, John Crowe Ransom reneged on an offer to publish him in the *Kenyon Review*.

Duncan returned to Berkeley in 1948, where he studied medieval history with Ernst Kantorowicz and edited the *Berkeley Miscellany* (1948–9). By that time the poet had brought out his first book of verse. (Although *Heavenly City, Earthly City* [1947] was the first collection to appear chronologically, it only contained poems written between 1945 and 1946; *The Years as Catches*, which included verse from as early as 1939, did not appear in print until 1966.) Duncan left Berkeley in 1950, and spent some time traveling and living in Majorca, Spain. In 1956, he went to join Charles Olson at Black Mountain College; there he taught and wrote some of the poetry that would be collected in *The Opening of the Field* (1960). He remained in North Carolina only a short time, then returned to California where he served as assistant director of the Poetry Center at San Francisco State College under a Ford grant (1956–7). During these years, he received the first of several awards from *Poetry* magazine (1957, 1961, 1967).

Critical of the arms race, pollution, and exploitation, Duncan, like many American poets, was disgusted by the Vietnam War. The poems he wrote during the 1960s under Guggenheim (1963–4) and National Endowment for the Arts (1965, 1966–7) grants, such as those collected in *Bending the Bow* (1968), became increasingly political. In "Up Rising," he portrayed the U.S. president as an almost mythical figure of destruction: "Now Johnson would go up to join the great simulacra of men, / Hitler and Stalin, to work his fame / with planes roaring out from Guam over Asia, / All America become a sea of toiling men / stirrd at his will." Even a love poem like "Passage over Water" was haunted by wounds, depth-bombs, and death.

Duncan published few books in the 1970s, having declared after *Bending the Bow* that he would not bring out another major work for 15 years. The fruit of these years was *Ground Work: Before the War* (1984), a volume which won the Before Columbus Foundation American Book Award (1986), and inspired the creation of the first-ever National Poetry Award for lifetime contribution to the field (1985). In 1986, Duncan won the Fred Cody Award for Lifetime Literary Excellence.

Duncan's other significant works include *Roots and Branches* (1964), *The Truth and Life of Myth: an Essay in Essential Autobiography* (1968), *Fictive Certainties: Five Essays in Essential Autobiography* (1979), and "The H.D. Book," a long work dedicated to the modernist poet H.D. (1886–1961), and published in fragments in various literary journals. Robert Duncan died in 1988. He was the long-time companion of painter Jess Collins.

DAVID FERRY (1924–)

David Ferry was born in 1924 in Orange, New Jersey. After serving in the U.S. Army Air Forces during World War II, he completed a B.A. at Amherst College in 1948. He finished his education at Harvard, taking an M.A. in 1949, and a Ph.D. in 1955.

Ferry first gained critical attention in 1959 with *The Limits of Mortality*, an influential book on the poetry of Wordsworth; during the same time, he edited and wrote a critical introduction for an analogy entitled *The Laurel Wordsworth* (1959). His first book of verse, *On the Way to the Island*, appeared one year later. Ferry helped edit the third edition of the anthology *British Literature* (1974), but brought out no more books of his own until 1981, when he published a slim volume of poems, *A Letter, and some Photographs*, in a limited edition. These pieces were included in *Strangers: A Book of Poems* two years later.

In 1992, Ferry published *Gilgamesh: A New Rendering in English Verse*. Basing his work on several literal translations, he adapted the ancient *Gilgamesh* epic into blank verse, an adaptation which was praised for its ingenuity and imagination. The following year, he published *Dwelling Places*, a collection of verse comprised of original poems and translations. These pieces suggest, as the poet has written, "what it feels like to inhabit a world where there are no certain dwelling places . . . a world of bewildering effects whose causes are always elsewhere and unknown." Civilization's discontents, characters like the mad protagonists of "The Guest Ellen at the Supper for Street People" and "Mary in Old Age," wander through the book in a daze; even the sane are full of unanswerable questions. Yet beyond the confusion, Ferry offers a sense of hope – the possibility of reaching understanding through the knowledge that the poems reveal about the world. In the end, as he says, "the poems themselves are dwelling places."

Ferry was hired by Wellesley College as an instructor in 1952, and worked his way up to full professor in 1967. He spent the rest of his academic career there, with two exceptions – a visiting position at Brown University (1981–

2) and a Writer-in-Residence post at Northwestern University (1986). Recipient of the Pinansky Prize for Excellence in Teaching at Wellesley, he devoted many of his courses to Romantic and modern poetry. Ferry served as the Sophie Chantal Hart Professor of English from 1971 until his retirement. He currently lives in Cambridge, Massachusetts.

ALLEN GINSBERG (1926–)

Allen Ginsberg, born in 1926 in Newark, New Jersey, received his early education in nearby Paterson. His ties to this industrial city are personal and literary: one of his early poetic advisers was William Carlos Williams, who was writing *Paterson* when the poet Louis Ginsberg brought his son to meet the eminent modernist. Williams discouraged the young man's imitations of Renaissance verse, advising him instead to "Listen to the rhythm of your own voice. Proceed intuitively by ear." Given the importance of oral performance to his later work, it would seem that he paid attention.

Ginsberg enrolled at Columbia University and, though suspended in 1945 for scrawling obscene graffiti on his dorm room window, eventually completed his B.A. in 1948. Five years later, he went to San Francisco. There he renewed his acquaintance with William Burroughs, Gregory Corso, and Jack Kerouac, writers who would play prominent roles in the Beat movement.

The Beat writers sought alternatives to the artistic stagnation of a society they perceived as moribund. In contrast to the classical, polished formalism of mainstream poetry, their verse was free-flowing, exuberant, and spontaneous. Ginsberg wrote of his seminal work, *Howl*, that he wanted to "write . . . without fear, let my imagination go, open secrecy, and scribble magic lines from my real mind." Kerouac described the poem's effect at a reading at Six Gallery on "the night of the birth of the San Francisco Renaissance": "wailing his poem . . . drunk with arms outspread," Ginsberg inspired the audience to chants of " 'Go! Go! Go!' "

That was 1955. In 1956, *Howl* was printed overseas, and appeared under the City Lights imprint; the second edition of this radical work was intercepted, and obscenity charges were brought against it. After listening to a barrage of expert witnesses, the judge conceded that the work must have *some* "redeeming social importance." This trial excited public interest, and both *Howl* and Ginsberg's circle became increasingly popular. Eventually, exposure would become overexposure; the subversive movement would degenerate into a pose adopted by the more daring members of the in-crowd.

Not just black berets and a funky lingo, the Beat experience included experimentation with chemical substances. Ginsberg was not one to hang back. He admitted to writing some of his poetry under the influence; works like "Aether" explicitly record his hallucinogenic visions. Still, he grew increasingly ambivalent about the use of such "mechanical aids," and spent much of the early 1960s traveling in Asia, searching for other roads to enlightenment. "The Change," written in 1963, chronicles Ginsberg's eventual renunciation of drugs. By the end of the decade, he would regard the narcotics industry as part of a conspiracy to keep the people docile; he published a booklet – dauntingly entitled *Documents on Police Bureaucracy's Conspiracy against Human Rights of Opiate Addicts & Constitutional Rights of Medical Profession Causing Mass Break-Down of Urban Law and Order* (1970) – that implicated the U.S. government in drug trafficking.

In 1965, he received a Guggenheim Fellowship, and toured colleges across the U.S. with his long-time companion Peter Orlovsky. Ginsberg was a favorite visitor, and his charismatic readings popularized poetry as hip and socially relevant. Active in radical causes throughout his later life, he was instrumental in organizing opposition to the Vietnam War among students and poets alike.

Ginsberg's status as a cultural icon has at times threatened to overshadow his poetic achievement; he himself has spoken of his three dozen books of verse as by-products of his search for enlightenment. Despite such remarks, his works provide invaluable insight into the tensions present in post-McCarthy American culture. His earlier verse has been assembled in *Collected Poems, 1947–1980* (1984); later poems appear in *White Shroud* (1986) and *Cosmopolitan Greetings* (1994). In 1994 Ginsberg brought out *Holy Soul Jelly Roll*, a recording of poems and songs.

LOUISE GLÜCK (1943–)

Born in New York City in 1943, Louise Glück grew up in Long Island. She enrolled at Sarah Lawrence College in 1962, but dropped out after six weeks; the following year she became a non-degree student in the School of General Studies at Columbia University, where she attended poetry workshops with Léonie Adams and Stanley Kunitz. Glück left these workshops in 1968, the same year she published *Firstborn*. She was later awarded honorary degrees from Williams and Skidmore colleges.

Critics have praised Glück's poetry for its direct language and emotional intensity. She has received many honors, including a grant from the Rockefeller Foundation and multiple fellowships from the National Endowment for the Arts and the Guggenheim Foundation. Her literary prizes include the American Academy and Institute of Arts and Letters Award (1981), the National Book Critics Circle Award for *The Triumph of Achilles* (1985), the Bobbitt National Prize (1992) for *Ararat*, and the Pulitzer and William Carlos Williams prizes (1993) for *The Wild Iris*. *Proofs and Theories* (1994), a volume of essays on poetry, won the PEN/Martha Albrand Award for First Nonfiction in 1995.

Glück has been affiliated with writing programs at many different institutions, including Goddard College, Warren Wilson College, and Harvard, where she was the Phi Beta Kappa Poet in 1991. She has taught at Williams since 1984, and recently served as the Morris Gray Lecturer at Harvard and the Steloff Lecturer at Skidmore. In 1996, she will be the Fannie Hurst Professor at Brandeis. Glück's collections of verse include *The House on Marshland* (1975), *Descending Figure* (1980), *Ararat* (1990), and *The Wild Iris* (1992). She is a fellow of the American Academy of Arts and Sciences.

THOMSON GUNN (1929–)

Thomson Gunn was born in Gravesend, Kent in 1929, the son of two writers. His father was a respected London newspaperman; his mother, too, worked in journalism until her children were born. A well-read woman with socialist and feminist leanings, she encouraged her son Thom to read and write, asking him to put together a novel for her birthday when he was twelve (he complied, with a worldly little book he called "The Flirt"). From the time he was eight, Gunn spent most of his youth in the affluent London suburb of Hampstead, where Keats had once lived. Though he has described his memories of Hampstead as happy ones, his parents divorced not long after the family moved there, and his mother died when he was in his mid-teens.

Gunn, like many urban schoolchildren, was evacuated to the countryside during the London Blitz in World War II. For several terms he attended a school in Hampshire, where a sympathetic English teacher gave him a copy of Auden's anthology, *The Poet's Tongue* (1941). Thanks in part to this teacher, the young Gunn was exposed to a vast number of writers, including Marlowe, Milton, Tennyson, and Keats, "the first poet who really meant something to me." He read, wrote prose and verse, and dreamed of becoming a novelist, poet, or dramatist.

After completing school and spending his mandatory two years in the British Army, Gunn went to Paris. There he took a clerical job with the public transportation system, read Proust, and tried to write a novel. When he returned to England at the end of six months, he began to focus on verse; he would quip later that he "didn't have the staying power to be a novelist, and . . . didn't have very much sense of being able to write dialogue . . . So I got stuck with poetry." In 1950, he enrolled at Trinity College, Cambridge to study English literature.

During his first year at Cambridge, he became a pacifist and declaimed radical poetry at the meetings of the CUSC; he also had his first poem published in the antiwar number of the undergraduate journal *Cambridge Today*. Although he felt that he learned more from his peers than from his teachers, Gunn found F. R. Leavis's lectures useful: his "discriminations and enthusiasms helped teach me to write, better than any creative-writing class could have. His insistence on the realized, being the life of poetry, was exactly what I needed."

He edited the student anthology *Poetry from Cambridge* during his final year at school, and in 1954 brought out his first book, *Fighting Terms*. When this work appeared, its author was immediately identified as a member of "The Movement," a group of British poets who rejected the grand flourishes of the neoromantic bards for precise forms and diction. This group included writers such as Donald Davie, Kingsley Amis, and Philip Larkin. Gunn, who had never met most of his supposed colleagues, regarded the whole thing as an invention of the press. By the time the term gained currency through the publication of Robert Conquest's *New Lines* anthology (1956), Gunn was on the other side of the world.

While at Cambridge, Gunn had fallen in love with Mike Kitay, an American "who became the leading influence on my life, and thus on my poetry." Determined to follow Kitay back to the States, he applied for a writing fellowship at Stanford University, and after several months in Rome, went to California in 1954. There he met J. V. Cunningham and Yvor Winters; of Winters, he wrote, "It was wonderful luck for me that I should have worked with him at this particular stage of my life."

At the time that his verse was progressing towards a more traditional aesthetic, Gunn's social life was moving in another direction. He began exploring the gay bar scene in San Francisco; visiting the Black Cat for the first time, he enjoyed it so much that he returned the following night. This odd combination of strict metrical forms and countercultural topics appears in Gunn's second book, *The Sense of Movement* (1957), a volume that won the Somerset Maugham Award in 1959.

Although it resembles his first book both in style and in devotion to action, *The Sense of Movement* features completely different subject matter. "On the Move" celebrates leather-clad motorcycle gangs; other poems find their subjects in the slightly seedy worlds of cafés and street fairs. Gunn's heroes are still people with the passionate will to overcome, but this time, they stand outside of mainstream culture.

At the end of his first year at Stanford, Gunn went to join Kitay in San Antonio, where he taught for a year before resuming his studies. Back in Palo Alto, he attended Winters's workshops "less and less," finally leaving without a degree to take a position at the University of California at Berkeley in 1958. He began to experiment with free verse and syllabics during these years. *My Sad Captains* (1961) was looser and more contemplative, moving away from what some critics had seen as an attraction to fascism, and toward the natural world.

After spending a year abroad in London, Gunn returned to the euphoric San Francisco of the 1960s. He gave up his position at Berkeley and reveled in the "new territories that were being opened up in the mind" by LSD: "every experience was illuminated by the drug. . . . These were the fullest years of my life, crowded with discovery both inner and outer, and we moved between ecstasy and understanding. . . . [LSD] has been of the utmost importance to me, both as a man and as a poet." *Moly* (1971) contains several poems that deal explicitly with Gunn's positive experiences with drugs; *Jack Straw's Castle*, published five years later, explores the disenchantment of bad trips and coming back down.

The Passages of Joy (1982) was somewhat of a watershed book for Gunn. He had acknowledged his homosexuality to himself in his Cambridge days, after having "eye[d] the well-fed and good-looking G.I.s who were on every street, with an appreciation I didn't completely understand." His early poems, however, were written from a heterosexual point of view; it was not until *The Passages of Joy* that Gunn wrote explicitly about his relationships with men.

Gunn teaches at Berkeley, where he has been a senior lecturer for many years. He has won many awards and honors, including grants from the American Institute of Arts and Letters and the Rockefeller, Guggenheim, and MacArthur foundations; he has also received the PEN/Los Angeles Prize for poetry (1983), the Robert Kirsch Award (1988), the Shelley Memorial Award (1990), and the Forward Poetry Prize (1992). His prose includes *The Occasion of Poetry* (1982) and *Shelf Life* (1993). The *Collected Poems* appeared in 1993.

SUSAN HAHN (1941–)

Born in 1941, Susan Hahn grew up in the suburbs of Chicago. After an unhappy year at a women's college, she transferred to Northwestern University, where she received a B.A. in psychology (1963), and completed the requirements for an M.A. two years later. After graduation, she worked at the Woodlawn Mental Health Center, and in 1972 was licensed as a group therapist.

In the mid-1970s, Hahn enrolled in a program at the Gestalt Institute of Chicago that trained psychotherapists how to use art for therapeutic purposes. She subsequently introduced the works of Anne Sexton and Sylvia Plath to the members of her group, and encouraged them to do their own writing as a form of self-expression. Hahn took part in these exercises along with her patients. Although her writing had not originally been intended for public consumption, she eventually decided to submit some of her works to *Poetry* magazine. *Poetry* was interested.

While Hahn eventually gave up the mental health profession to pursue a career as a poet, her interest in human behavior did not diminish; she describes her verse as drawing on what she learned in college, and on memories of her work as a psychotherapist. Writers, she says, must "write about what they know best."

Her first book of poetry, *Harriet Rubin's Mother's Wooden Hand*, was published in 1991. Two years later came *Incontinence* (1993), a collection for which she received the Society of Midland Authors Award for Poetry in 1994. *Confession*, written on an Illinois Arts Council Fellowship, is forthcoming early in 1997. Susan Hahn is currently coeditor at *TriQuarterly* magazine, where she has worked since 1980.

ROBERT HASS (1941–)

Robert Hass was born in 1941 in San Francisco. He was raised and educated in California, attending St. Mary's College in Moraga as an undergraduate. After he completed his B.A. in 1963, he enrolled at Stanford University where he attended a few lectures by Yvor Winters, and associated with poets like John Matthias, James McMichael, John Peck, and Robert Pinsky. During these years, Hass received Woodrow Wilson (1963–4) and Danforth (1963–7) fellowships; he would go on to hold Guggenheim and MacArthur grants in the 1980s. Hass finished his Ph.D. at Stanford in 1971.

His first volume of poetry, *Field Guide*, was published in 1973 when Stanley Kunitz selected it for the Yale Series of Younger Poets. As Hass has explained, the book really is a sort of guide: "The whole post-war explosion in America was going on, and [*Field Guide*] was a way of holding on, a way of making things that I valued stay put. By getting to know one species of grass from another, one species of bird from another, and by knowing the names, they could stay put. I thought." The importance of the names of things remained a concern in his prize-winning collection, *Praise* (1979), which explored the relationship between names and things. By the time of *Human Wishes* (1989), Hass had begun experimenting with the way he put words together to depict an experience, and his work became less traditionally metrical and more fragmented.

Hass is not only a poet, but also a reviewer, critic, translator, editor, and teacher. He has authored the highly acclaimed *Twentieth Century Pleasures: Prose on Poetry* (1984), a critical work which garnered awards from the National Book Critics Circle and the Bay Area Book Reviewers Association.

Hass's first significant translation came out the same year: along with Pinsky, he rendered Nobel laureate Czeslaw Milosz's *The Separate Notebooks* from the Polish. More recently, Hass has worked with Milosz on books like *Unattainable Earth* (1986), *Collected Poems, 1931–1987* (1988), *Provinces* (1991), and *Facing the River* (1995). He has also edited and translated a book of Japanese poetry, *The Essential Haiku* (1994).

Robert Hass has taught at the State University of New York at Buffalo, St. Mary's, the University of Virginia, Goddard, and Columbia, and is currently a professor at the University of California at Berkeley. In 1995 he was named Poet Laureate of the United States.

ROBERT HAYDEN (1913–1980)

Robert Hayden was born in 1913 in Detroit. His family was supportive of his literary interests, but could not afford to send him to college immediately after he finished high school. He therefore pursued his studies independently for a time, reading the poets of the Harlem Renaissance, the more traditional twentieth-century American poets, and the English classics. Later he was able to enroll at Detroit City College (now Wayne State University). After receiving his B.A. in 1936, Hayden researched black history for the Federal Writers' Project in Detroit. This occupation provided him with a knowledge of history that would appear again and again in his work. His poems on slavery and the Civil War would win a Jules and Avery Hopwood Poetry Award in 1942.

In 1940 came the publication of *Heart-Shape in the Dust* and a brief stay in New York City. Returning to the midwest, Hayden enrolled at the University of Michigan, where he studied poetry with W. H. Auden. After receiving his M.A. in 1944, he taught first at Fisk University and then at the University of Michigan.

Hayden often wrote about the African American experience using traditional European poetic forms. Unlike many in the racially charged 1960s, the poet did not see these categories as mutually exclusive; he preferred to be considered a poet who happened to be black rather than a Black Poet. This attitude was controversial: while white critics applauded his lack of strident ethnocentrism, other blacks reproached him with selling out his heritage.

In 1966, Hayden won the Grand Prize for *A Ballad of Remembrance* (1962) at the Dakar (Senegal) World Festival of the Arts. His reputation grew steadily after the publication of his *Selected Poems* (1966), and in 1976 he became the first African American to be selected as Consultant in Poetry to the Library of Congress. Robert Hayden died in 1980. His *Collected Poems* came out posthumously in 1985.

ANTHONY HECHT (1923-)

Anthony Hecht was born in 1923 in New York City. After receiving his B.A. at Bard College in 1944, he spent three years in the U.S. Army, serving in both Europe and Japan. Although some of his earliest published poems deal with his wartime experiences, he has commented that "the cumulative sense of these experiences is grotesque beyond anything I could possibly write."

Upon his return to America, he took a succession of teaching positions that included a year at Kenyon College, where he studied with John Crowe Ransom from 1947 to 1948. Ransom had founded and edited the *Kenyon Review*, and this journal was the first to print some of Hecht's poems. After his time in Ohio, the young poet returned to the East Coast, where he worked informally with Allen Tate, Ransom's former student, and eventually took an M.A. at Columbia University (1950).

In 1951, Hecht won the Prix de Rome, and went to Italy to spend a year in residence at the American Academy. Three years later, he published his first collection of verse, *A Summoning of Stones*, which was characterized by formal virtuosity and what reviewers criticized as overly ornate diction. Hecht later dismissed this book as "something like an advanced apprenticework." His style underwent a radical shift between the publication of his first and second books, and critics regarded the simpler language of *The Hard Hours* (1967) as a mark of poetic maturity. This book won the Pulitzer Prize in 1968. With *Millions of Strange Shadows* (1977) and *The Venetian Vespers* (1979), Hecht returned to a more complex diction, but one that added to, rather than detracted from, his poetic technique.

Hecht has taught at the State University of Iowa, New York University, Smith College, Bard College, the University of Rochester (where he was the John H. Deane Professor of Poetry), and Harvard. He is currently Professor Emeritus at Georgetown University. Among his honors are several Guggenheim and Ford Foundation fellowships, the Brandeis University Creative Arts Award in poetry (1965), the Russell Loines Award (1968), the Miles Poetry Prize (1968), and the Bollingen Prize (1983). He has also served as Poetry Consultant to the Library of Congress. In addition to coediting *Jiggery-Pokery* (1967), an anthology of light verse, and collaborating on a translation of Aeschylus's *Seven Against Thebes* (1973), Hecht has written a book of critical essays, *Obbligati* (1986). In 1993 he published *The Hidden Law: The Poetry of W. H. Auden*.

SUSAN HOWE (1937-)

The daughter of an Irish mother and a Bostonian father, Susan Howe was born in Boston in 1937. During her childhood, the United States moved from the Great Depression to military involvement in Europe and Asia, and a consciousness of those historical events would later inform her writing. She went to Ireland in 1955 and spent a year acting and designing sets at the Gate Theater in Dublin. Returning to America, she studied painting at the Boston Museum School of Fine Arts between 1957 and 1961, and then went to New York City, where she showed pieces in a number of group exhibits. Through her painting and her increasing interest in performance art, she moved gradually into writing verse. She published her first book, *Hinge Picture*, in 1974, and from 1975 to 1980 produced a radio show on poetry in New York City.

Structurally, Howe's poetry often recalls her training in the graphic arts. Some poems treat words as an artistic medium akin to the pieces of a collage: she arranges words in patterns on the page in a manner somewhat reminiscent of the avant-garde poets Guillaume Apollinaire (1880–1918) and Filippo Marinetti (1876–1944). Other poems experiment with the sense that emerges from the irregular distribution of letters on the page; the line "He plodded away through drifts of i / ce" from the title poem of *Pythagorean Silence* (1982) contains a layering of meaning available to the reader specifically on a visual level.

The formal and syntactical fragmentation of these poems alludes to one of the central concerns of Howe's project. This project, as she explains in the prologue to *The Europe of Trusts* (1990), is to piece together and "lift from the dark side of history, voices that are anonymous, slighted – inarticulate." She devotes *The Liberties* (1980) to uncovering and giving a voice to one such figure. In *The Liberties*, Esther Johnson, known to history as Jonathan Swift's Stella, takes center stage; no longer his creature, she speaks with words of her own. Swift himself appears only as a ghost. The image of the author as ghost reappears in *A Bibliography of the King's Book: Or, Eikon Basilike* (1989), where Howe wonders about the authority of the forged *Eikon Basilike*, a collection of writings originally ascribed to Charles I.

Through a critical examination of authorial voice, and through the use of pun and wordplay, Howe calls meaning itself into question. Her mistrust of the way that language works has aligned her with the Language poets of the San Francisco Bay Area; her poems have been printed in their magazines as well as in anthologies like *The L=A=N=G=U=A=G=E Book* (1984), *In the American Tree* (1986), and *Language Poetry* (1987). Howe's own books of verse include *The Western Borders* (1976), *Secret History of the Dividing Line* (1978), *Cabbage Garden* (1979), *Defenestration of Prague* (1983), *Articulation of Sound Forms in Time* (1987), *Singularities* (1990), and *The Nonconformist's Memorial* (1993).

In addition to poetry, two critical books form an important part of Susan Howe's oeuvre – *My Emily Dickinson* (1985), and *The Birth-mark: Unsettling the Wilderness in American Literary History* (1993). She has twice been awarded the Pushcart Prize (1980, 1989), and has twice received the American Book Award from the Before Columbus Foundation, for *Pythagorean Silence* and *My Emily Dickinson*. She was recently awarded the new Roy Harvey Pearce Prize by the University of California at San Diego. Howe currently teaches at SUNY Buffalo, where she was the Butler Fellow between 1988 and 1989.

LEROI JONES (1934–)

LeRoi Jones (later, Imamu Amiri Baraka) was born in Newark, New Jersey in 1934. He attended Rutgers for a year, then moved to Howard University, where he received his B.A. in 1954. After graduation, he spent two years in the U.S. Air Force. When he returned to New York, he continued his studies at Columbia and the New School of Social Research, and associated with Beat poets like Allen Ginsberg, Frank O'Hara, and Gilbert Sorrentino. *Preface to a Twenty Volume Suicide Note*, Jones's first published collection of verse, came out in 1961.

In the same year, his award-winning essay *Cuba Libre* criticized the Beat generation for its disengagement from the realities of American culture. As he explained in *Home: Social Essays* (1966), a visit to Cuba in 1960 had opened his eyes. While abroad, he came into contact with artists whose works explicitly addressed political concerns such as poverty, hunger, and tyranny. His interaction with these people convinced him that American artists, too, needed to engage the problems of their society in order to effect change. To "drop out" as the Beat poets had done, according to Jones, was politically ineffectual; he sought an alternative form of protest against white America. In *The Dead Lecturer* (1964), he examined the alternatives: either he could remain assimilated, or he could throw in his lot with an ethnic cause. Between these positions, there was no middle ground for Jones; he had little patience with African Americans who sought compromise and integration. In 1965, following the assassination of Malcolm X, he became a black nationalist.

Jones's repertoire spanned many genres, from poetry and essays to short stories, novels, and plays. Several of his dramatic works were produced off-Broadway during 1964, including the Obie-winning *Dutchman*, as well as *The Toilet* and *The Slave*. The same year, he moved to Harlem, where he established the Black Arts Repertory Theatre. In all of his work, he began to reject European traditions in favor of artistic forms evoking authentic African standards. This quest for authenticity was perhaps most elegantly articulated in his 1963 study, *Blues People: Negro Music in White America*. The book outlines the history of African American music, describing blues as the unique heir of the interaction between African and American cultures in the South. Jones was well-respected for his writings on music, which included *Black Music* (1968) and *The Music: Reflections on Jazz and Blues* (1987).

Having taken on the problem of racial conflict in his works, Jones became not only an influential writer, but a significant cultural and political leader within the black community. His critique of white art went beyond a personal rejection of mainstream American culture: as he wrote in *Home*, the place of the black artist was to "aid in the destruction of America as he knows it." Jones's outspoken views did not go unheeded. During the riots in the summer of 1967, he was arrested for carrying a concealed weapon, and received an uncommonly severe sentence. In explanation, the judge cited lines from "Black People": "We must make our own / World . . . and we can not do this unless the white man / is dead. Let's get together and killhim, my man . . ." Jones was cleared in a later trial. After a period of intense involvement in black nationalist politics in Newark, he would ultimately reject the movement as racist in 1974, and would come, via Third World Marxism, to emphasize the issue of class over race.

Despite the discomfort of some mainstream critics with Jones's radical position, he has been a visiting professor at a wide variety of colleges, and has received numerous awards, including a Guggenheim Fellowship (1965–6), a grant from the National Endowment for the Arts (1966), a Doctorate of Humane Letters from Malcolm X College (1972), and the 1984 American Book Award for *Confirmation: An Anthology of African-American Women* (1983). In 1984, he published *The Autobiography of LeRoi Jones/Amiri Baraka*. He currently teaches at the State University of New York at Stony Brook in the Department of Africana Studies.

BRAD LEITHAUSER (1953–)

Brad Leithauser was born in 1953 in Detroit, Michigan. He was educated at Harvard University, where he took a B.A. in 1975 and a J.D. in 1980. After graduation, he spent three years as a research fellow in Kyoto, Japan, a city which would later serve as the backdrop for his novel *Equal Distance* (1985).

Leithauser's first book, *Hundreds of Fireflies* (1982), was nominated for the National Book Critics Circle award in 1982. The metrical, rhymed poetry was well received; reviewers likened his verse approvingly to that of writers like Marianne Moore, Elizabeth Bishop, and Robert Frost. His second effort four years later also received a nomination, although the critical response was not uniformly positive. While some critics applauded the work for its precision, others saw *Cats of the Temple* (1986) as overly fastidious and emotionally empty; Leithauser was also accused of leaning, rather than building, on his literary forebears. Despite a mixed reception, his writing has garnered plenty of awards, including an Amy Lowell travel scholarship (1981–2), Guggenheim (1982–3) and MacArthur Foundation (1982–7) fellowships, the Peter I. B. Lavan Younger Poets Award (1983), and a Fulbright Fellowship to Iceland (1989).

Leithauser has taught at Amherst and Mount Holyoke, and has served on the editorial board of the Book-of-the-Month Club. In addition to the poetry he published in *Between Leaps* (1987) and *Mail from Anywhere* (1990), he has produced the novels *Equal Distance, Hence* (1989), and *Seaward* (1993). *Penchants and Places*, a collection of essays, appeared in 1995.

PHILIP LEVINE (1928–)

Philip Levine was born in 1928, the son of Russian-Jewish immigrants. He grew up in Detroit, and attended Wayne (now Wayne State) University where he studied with John Berryman. After completing his A.B. (1950) and A.M. (1954), he moved to the University of Iowa, where he taught and pursued his M.F.A. (1957). The following year, he won a poetry fellowship from Stanford University, where he met and worked with Yvor Winters.

As a child, Levine learned about the Spanish Civil War (1936–9), and admired not only the revolutionaries, but also the common people who had to struggle to survive. His connection with the working class became more personal in the early 1950s, when he took a series of "stupid" industrial jobs in his hometown. This experience convinced him of the need to provide a voice for the workers: "In terms of the literature of the United States they weren't being heard. Nobody was speaking for them. . . . [so] I took this foolish vow that I would speak for them and that's what my life would be." This interest in the common people and in the Spanish anarchist movement has animated his work ever since. He has traveled extensively in Spain, and has been influenced by the Latin-American surrealists and their champion, Robert Bly.

Levine has taught at California State University at Fresno for many years. He has received grants from the National Endowment for the Arts, the National Institute of Arts and Letters, and the Guggenheim Foundation, and has won the American Book Award, the National Book Critics Circle Award, the National Book Award for Poetry, and the Bobst Award in Arts and Letters. Among his myriad works are *On the Edge* (limited edition, 1961; second edition, 1963), *Not This Pig* (1968), *They Feed They Lion* (1972), *1933* (1974), *The Names of the Lost* (1976), and *What Work Is* (1991). *The Simple Truth* (1994) recently won the Pulitzer Prize.

ROBERT TRAILL SPENCE LOWELL, JR. (1917–1977)

Robert Traill Spence Lowell, Jr., was born in 1917, the descendant of two blue-blooded Boston families. Both the Winslows and the Lowells dated back to the early days of New England, and the latter clan could claim the poet and diplomat James Russell Lowell and the imagist poet Amy Lowell among its notable members. Robert Lowell was fascinated by his heritage; it would serve as the subject of many of his works.

Lowell attended preparatory school at St. Mark's, where he met the poet Richard Eberhart, and enrolled at Harvard University in 1935. In 1937, he quarreled with his father, and left Massachusetts for Tennessee where the poet Allen Tate was living. As Lowell recollected many years later, "I think I suggested that maybe I'd stay with them. And they said, 'We really haven't any room, you'd have to pitch a tent on the lawn.' So I went to Sears Roebuck and got a tent and rigged it on their lawn. The Tates were too polite to tell me that what they'd said had been just a figure of speech. I stayed two months in my tent and ate with the Tates."

The time in Tennessee altered Lowell's academic trajectory almost immediately: he transferred to Kenyon College in order to work with Tate's former teacher, John Crowe Ransom; there he also got to know Randall Jarrell and Peter Taylor, writers with whom he would maintain lifelong friendships. After graduating *summa cum laude* in classics (1940), Lowell spent a year studying with Cleanth Brooks and Robert Penn Warren (Tate's college roommate) at Louisiana State University.

Lowell married the writer Jean Stafford in 1940, and converted from Episcopalianism to Roman Catholicism. A number of the poems in *Land of Unlikeness* (1944) and the Pulitzer Prize–winning *Lord Weary's Castle* (1946) reflected his newfound faith; by the time *The Mills of the Kavanaughs* was published in 1951, however, Lowell had left the church and the marriage. During this difficult period, he suffered his first significant bout of manic depression, an illness that would trouble him for the rest of his life. He would marry again in 1949; this marriage, to the writer Elizabeth Hardwick, would end in divorce as well.

After the publication of *The Mills of the Kavanaughs*, Lowell made a lecture tour of the West Coast, where he discovered the innovative poetry of the San Francisco Beat poets. He lived principally in Boston during the latter part of the 1950s, teaching at Boston University and Harvard. Episodes of mania and depression still plagued him, and he had difficulty writing in the mode to which he had been accustomed. Working on the piece that would become the award-winning *Life Studies* (1959), he found he had "no language or meter that would allow me to approximate what I saw or remembered. Yet in prose I had already found what I wanted, the conventional style of autobiography and reminiscence. So I wrote my autobiographical poetry in a style . . . that used images and ironic or amusing particulars. I did all kinds of tricks with meter and the avoidance of meter. . . . I didn't have to bang words into rhyme and count." Filled with colloquial language and candid personal anecdotes, the poems of *Life Studies* heralded a new poetic mode that the critics would dub "confessional poetry." This mode would become immensely popular amongst American poets beginning in the 1960s.

Lowell moved to New York in 1960. He commuted to teach at Harvard between 1963–70, and taught there intermittently for the rest of his life. The poetry he brought out during these years, published as *For the Union Dead* (1964), *Near the Ocean* (1967), and *Notebook 1967–68* (1969) reflected the political turmoil of the age. A conscientious objector who had been jailed during World War II, Lowell was deeply involved with the antiwar movement during the 1960s. He rejected President Johnson's invitation to the 1965 White House Festival of the Arts in protest against America's continued involvement in Southeast Asia, and staunchly championed Senator Eugene McCarthy's peace platform. The unrhymed sonnets of *Notebook 1967–68* (revised as *Notebook* in 1970) are based on Lowell's experiences with the peace movement and in McCarthy's presidential campaign.

Taking refuge from political and domestic troubles, Lowell moved to England in 1970, where he taught at the University of Essex and Kent University. He divorced Elizabeth Hardwick and married Caroline Blackwood in 1972. The following year he brought out three volumes of sonnets, *History*, *For Lizzie and Harriet*, and *The Dolphin*. Some of Lowell's readers, discovering that the poet had used sections of Hardwick's personal letters verbatim in *The Dolphin*, were outraged; despite the critical scandal, the book was awarded the Pulitzer Prize in 1974.

Other works by Lowell include the plays collected in *The Old Glory* (produced in 1964), and several translations – most notably the award-winning *Imitations*, which contained versions of poems by Homer, Sappho, Rilke, Mallarmé, Baudelaire, and others (1961). *Day by Day*, Lowell's final book of new poetry, appeared in 1977, shortly before his death of congestive heart failure. He received the National Book Critics Circle Award posthumously in 1978.

THOMAS MCGRATH (1916–1990)

Thomas McGrath was the grandson of Irish Catholic immigrants; enticed by visions of a golden land teeming with promise, his grandparents had come across the ocean to homestead in the American West. He was born in 1916 near Sheldon, North Dakota, and grew up on the family farm. Aware of the importance of a cooperative, unified labor force to keep the struggling farm afloat, McGrath was introduced to the tenets of the Industrial Workers of the World by some of the farmhands, and adopted a radical political philosophy at an early age. After attending the University of North Dakota (B.A., 1939) and Louisiana State University (M.A., 1940), he worked as a labor organizer in the 1940s.

He brought out his first book of poetry, *First Manifesto*, in 1940, and contributed a piece to Alan Swallow's *Three Young Poets: Thomas McGrath, William Peterson, James Franklin Lewis* two years later. During these years, McGrath spent much of his time on the move, working at a variety of jobs to finance his writing. For a brief time, he was employed as a shipyard welder in New York, where he served as the editor of a union paper. The latter experience stood him in good stead; he would later hold editorial positions with *California Quarterly* (1951–4), *Mainstream* (1955–7), and *Crazy Horse* (1960–1). During his time at the docks, McGrath was popular with the waterfront leftists. In 1949, he wrote *Longshot O'Leary's Garland of Practical Poesie* for the men "who'd come by, drink my coffee, interrupt my day's work, and instruct me how *poetry ought to be written.*"

McGrath served in the Aleutian Islands with the U.S. Army Air Forces during World War II, and in 1947 won a Rhodes Scholarship to Oxford University. Upon his return, he spent several years writing for the radical press in New York, and in 1952 went to teach at Los Angeles State College of Applied Arts and Sciences (now California State College, Los Angeles). His time there would be brief.

The 1950s were rocky years for people suspected of radical ties, let alone actual members of the Communist Party. Despite pressure from the House Committee on Un-American Activities, McGrath refused to compromise on his political convictions: "A teacher who will tack and turn with every shift of the political wind," he told the Committee, "cannot be a good teacher. I have never done this myself, nor will I ever." He lost his job in 1954. McGrath remained in Los Angeles for several more years, during which he cofounded Sequoia School, worked as a woodcarver, and began writing television and movie scripts. After leaving California for the plains of North Dakota, he started *Letter to an Imaginary Friend*, a book-length autobiographical poem widely regarded as his most important work. It was written in four sections: the first was published in 1962 (the year McGrath was included in Donald Hall's *New Poets of England and America*), the second in 1970, and the third and fourth in 1985. Other notable works of poetry include *The Movie at the End of the World* (1972) and the prize-winning volumes *Echoes Inside the Labyrinth* (1983) and *Selected Poems, 1938–88* (1988). He also published two novels, *The Gates of Ivory, the Gates of Horn* (1957) and *This Coffin Has No Handles* (1988).

McGrath returned to academia only in 1960. He taught at C. W. Post College (1960–1), North Dakota State University (1962–7), and Moorhead State University (1969–82). With the exception of the Alan Swallow Poetry Book Award for *Figures from a Double World* (1955), most of the literary prizes he received came late in his poetic career: he received the American Book Award in 1985 and the Lenore Marshall/Nation Prize in 1989. Thomas McGrath died in 1990, two months before his seventy-fourth birthday.

CZESLAW MILOSZ (1911–)

Born in 1911 in Szetejnie, Lithuania, Czeslaw Milosz spent his early childhood in Czarist Russia. His father, a civil engineer, was drafted to build roads and bridges for the Russian Army during World War I, and the rest of the family accompanied him in this "nomadic life" until 1918. After the Polish–Russian War, the borders of Eastern Europe shifted, and Wilno (now Vilnius, Lithuania), where the Miloszes settled, was incorporated into the new Polish state.

Milosz attended a Catholic school in Wilno, and then enrolled at the University of Stephan Batory, where he associated with a Leftist literary circle. This group of writers became known as the Catastrophist school for their grim visions of the future. Milosz began publishing poems and articles; for him, this "so-called poetry of social protest . . . had no connection with the living springs of art; it was journalism, which I wrote to redeem myself for not taking part in the workers' clashes with the police."

Despite his literary activities, Milosz studied law, feeling that "literature should not feed on itself but should be supported by a knowledge of society." He eventually lost interest in his legal studies, and graduated (M. Juris, 1934) mainly "on the strength of endurance and great quantities of black coffee." The diploma allowed him to apply for a state scholarship, however, and he spent a year from 1934 to 1935 studying literature in Paris.

The following year, Milosz returned to Wilno, where he became a bureaucrat at the local Polish Radio station. Bored by the paperwork and the routine, he was not entirely disappointed to be dismissed for his radical politics. After a trip to Venice in 1937, he was rehired by a sympathetic director in the Head Office of the Polish Radio, and transferred to Warsaw where he worked alongside other displaced intellectuals.

When the Nazis entered Poland in 1939, Milosz went east to Wilno, which had been occupied by the Red Army and ceded to Lithuania. After this country was engulfed by the Soviet Union, he returned to Warsaw to avoid "life imprisonment within a system that . . . might never fall": "I could not regard National Socialism as a durable phenomenon. A wolf is no doubt a dangerous animal, and should he bite, consolation is no help; yet together with the image of his fangs and claws another image rises within us: of automatic weapons, of tanks, of planes, against which the wolf is powerless. For me the Revolution and Marxism were the equivalent of this higher technology." He describes his harrowing journey through Eastern Europe in the autobiographical *Rodzinna Europa* (1959; published as *Native Realm*, 1968). In Warsaw, Milosz became active in the Polish underground, publishing his pseudonymous *Wiersze* ("Poems," 1940), a typewritten journal of anti-Nazi articles, and an anthology of poetry called *Piesn niepodlegla* ("Invincible Song," 1942).

Milosz secured a job in the diplomatic service after the war, and spent several years in America and France. Upon his return to Warsaw, he discovered that Poland had become a "Stalinist nightmare," and defected to the West in 1951. In a speech to the Congress for Cultural Freedom he proclaimed, "I have rejected the new faith because the practice of the lie is one of its principal commandments and socialist realism is nothing more than a different name for a lie." He discusses his reasons for this break with the East in *Zniewolony umysl* (*The Captive Mind*, 1953). Between 1951 and 1960, Milosz lived in Paris as a translator and free-lance writer; in 1960 he accepted a teaching position at the University of California at Berkeley, where he would remain until his retirement in 1978. He became a naturalized citizen of the United States in 1970.

Milosz writes in Polish, collaborating on translations of his work with writers like Robert Hass and Robert Pinsky. His prose includes *Zdobycie wladzy* (*The Seizure of Power*, 1955), *The History of Polish Literature* (1969), *Emperor of the Earth: Modes of Eccentric Vision* (1977), *The Witness of Poetry* (1983), and *Unattainable Earth* (1986). Among his books of verse are *The Bells in Winter* (1978), *The Separate Notebooks* (1984), *Collected Poems, 1931–1987* (1988), *Provinces* (1991), and *Facing the River* (1995). Milosz's literary abilities have been richly rewarded with honors like the Prix Littéraire Européen from the Swiss Book Guild for *The Seizure of Power* (1953), a Jurzykowski Foundation award (1968), a Guggenheim Fellowship (1976), the Neustadt International Literary Prize (1978), and the Bay Area Book Reviewers Association Poetry Prize for *The Separate Notebooks* (1986). He won the Nobel Prize for Literature in 1980.

SHARON OLDS (1942–)

Born in San Francisco in 1942, Sharon Olds began writing poetry when she was seven years old. She studied languages at Stanford University, graduating with distinction in 1964, then enrolled at Columbia, where she took a Ph.D. in English eight years later.

Olds characterizes her early work as "ten . . . twenty, thirty years of imitation. . . . trying to sound like poets I had read." In the mid-1970s, she attended an anti–Vietnam War reading in New York City, where she listened to Adrienne Rich, Galway Kinnell, Robert Bly, and Muriel Rukeyser (with whom she would take a poetry appreciation course in 1976). It was a groundbreaking experience for her: "I had been writing poems all my life, but that's when I heard poets who were writing about family, writing about birth, poets who were writing and were alive." By the time that her first book appeared in 1980, she had given up traditional forms and subjects, and was writing "my own stuff."

Olds writes about ordinary subjects – love, children, sex, cities, war, and the body – in a way, if not a tone, that has been compared to that of Sylvia Plath and Anne Sexton. Praised for its range and intensity of emotion, *Satan Says* (1980) won the San Francisco Poetry Center Award in 1981. Both the Guggenheim Foundation and the National Endowment for the Arts awarded her fellowships shortly thereafter. Olds's next book, *The Dead and the Living* (1984), was chosen by the Academy of American Poets as the Lamont Poetry Selection in 1984, and received the National Book Critics Circle Award one year later. Later works include *The Gold Cell* (1987), *The Father* (1992), and *The Wellspring* (forthcoming in 1996); English editions appeared in 1987 and 1991. Her poetry has been translated into Chinese, French, Italian, Estonian, Polish, and Russian.

One of the founders of the writing program at Goldwater Hospital in 1983, Olds has taught at the Theodore Herzl Institute, Sarah Lawrence, Columbia, the State University of New York at Purchase, and Brandeis. She is now at New York University, where she has been an associate professor in the Graduate Creative Writing Program since 1992. Olds won a Lila Wallace–Reader's Digest Writers' Award for 1993–6.

CHARLES OLSON (1910–1970)

The son of a Swedish father and an Irish-American mother, Charles Olson was born in 1910 in Worcester, Massachusetts. He attended Wesleyan University on a scholarship; after taking a B.A. in 1932, he completed his M.A. thesis on Herman Melville the following year. Olson went to Harvard in

1936, where he continued his studies in the American Civilization program, and in 1938 published an essay entitled "Lear and Moby-Dick." In 1939, Olson withdrew from Harvard. He began writing poetry the following year.

Active in liberal politics throughout the early 1940s, Olson worked for the American Civil Liberties Union, the Common Council for American Unity, the Office of War Information, and the Democratic National Committee. He abandoned this promising career in 1945 to devote himself to writing, and "started *Ishmael* . . . the afternoon I kissed off my political future." *Call Me Ishmael* (1947) was based on research he had conducted several years earlier, when he had located several of the most important volumes in Melville's library, including the novelist's edition of Shakespeare's plays. As in his more academic essay of 1938, Olson analyzed Melville's annotations and argued that Shakespeare's influence had transformed *Moby-Dick* from a pedestrian tale of the whaling business into a masterpiece. The book was completed in 1945. In 1946, Olson showed it to Ezra Pound, then confined to St. Elizabeths Hospital. Pound sent the manuscript on to T. S. Eliot for publication, but Eliot was not enthusiastic. The book finally appeared in 1947; Olson's first book of verse, *Y & X*, followed one year later.

In 1948, Olson went to North Carolina to give a series of talks at Black Mountain College. The success of these lectures eventually led to his assuming Edward Dahlberg's position as guest lecturer at the experimental school. After teaching for several years, Olson became rector in 1951 and in that capacity brought a number of younger poets to the college. This cluster of writers – including Robert Creeley, Denise Levertov, Edward Dorn, and Robert Duncan – became known as the Black Mountain poets. Despite individual stylistic differences, the Black Mountain poets were united by a belief that free verse could more accurately convey the vital power of speech than could traditional metrical forms. They were also interested in developing the poetics initiated by Williams and Pound at a time when Eliot, Yeats, and Auden still dominated established literary taste. Much of their early work was published in Cid Corman's *Origin* and in the *Black Mountain Review*.

Olson articulated his views on prosody in "Projective Verse" (1950), an essay that became the aesthetic manifesto of the Black Mountain poets. "Projective" verse (projective is a portmanteau word that contains elements of projectile, percussive, and prospective) is based on Williams's definition of the poem as a "field of energy." For Olson, the poem serves as a conduit for transferring energy from the poet to the reader. He dismisses traditional form as restrictive; the formal conventions "that logic has forced on syntax must be broken open," he writes, "as must the too set feet of the old line." Olson advocates instead what he calls "composition by field," the natural unfolding of the poem's form within the breath patterns of the individual poet.

"[R]ight form, in any given poem" is not something imposed from outside, but "the only and exclusively possible extension of content." "Who knows what a poem ought to sound like? until it's thar? And how do you get it thar except as you do – *you*, and nobody else."

In the winter of 1951, Olson left the U.S. to study Mayan hieroglyphics in Yucatan. He received a grant from the Wenner–Gren Foundation supporting his work in 1952, and the following year Creeley edited his *Mayan Letters* at the Divers Press. Olson's interest in anthropological and historical material extended into the rest of his work as well: *The Maximus Poems* juxtaposed people, places, and things in a manner that owed something to the *Cantos*, a work which the younger poet admired. The first section of *The Maximus Poems* appeared in 1953; the poems were collected in 1983, and won the *Los Angeles Times* Book Award the following year.

After Black Mountain College shut down in 1956, Olson taught at the State University of New York at Buffalo, and then briefly at the University of Connecticut. He died in 1970. His other important works include *In Cold Hell, in Thicket* (1953), *The Distances* (1960), *Human Universe & Other Essays* (ed. Donald Allen, 1965), and *Archaeologist of Morning* (1970). Published posthumously, *The Collected Poems of Charles Olson* (1987) won the American Book Award in 1988.

MICHAEL PALMER (1943–)

Michael Palmer was born in New York City in 1943, and grew up "down the block from the Gotham Book Mart." He attended Harvard University, where he studied French history and literature, and coedited the avant-garde journal *Joglars* (1964–5) with Clark Coolidge. After completing his B.A. in 1965 with a thesis on the works of Raymond Roussel, he enrolled in the comparative literature program at Harvard, where he took an M.A. in 1968. Palmer lived briefly in Europe after graduation, settling in San Francisco in 1969. His first work, *Plan of the City of O*, appeared two years later.

He counts among his early influences writers like Pound, Williams, Stevens, and Stein, as well as Louis Zukofsky (whom he discovered in 1963 when Robert Creeley sent a tape of the Objectivist poet reading part of his poetic sequence "A"). In a 1989 lecture delivered at a conference on Objectivism, Palmer recounts the history of twentieth-century poetics in terms that clarify his own aesthetic alliances: the generation of writers that followed the modernists rejected the innovations of poets like Pound and Williams as excessive, turning away from radical experimentation to the formalist conventions of Eliot, Auden, and Frost. Writers from the Black Mountain and New York schools attempted to counter this "conservative (and frequently reactionary) impulse against the major discoverers and the impetus of modernism." Palmer admits to an early interest in the Black Mountain and New York poets; like them, he rejects the formalist lineage for a poetry that "will not stand as a kind of decor in one's life, not the kind of thing for hammock and lemonade, where at the end everything is in resolution."

Concerned with the political implications of style and form, Palmer writes poetry that resists closure, and is "involved with radical discontinuities of surface and voice." As such, his works question the status quo on the rhetorical level, critiquing "the discourses of power by undermining assumptions about meaning and univocality." His interrogation of words and signification aligns him with the Language poets of San Francisco; although his work has appeared in their anthologies, he comments that the way "I inhabit language, or language inhabits me, is in a sense more traditional than the way . . . many of the so-called Language poets work. In that respect, I'm a little bit outside."

In 1982, Palmer became a contributing editor for *Sulfur*, a magazine that showcases poetry and prose by experimental contemporary writers. His work has appeared as well as in *Action Poétique*, *Acts*, *Boundary 2*, *Conjunctions*, *Imago*, *Language*, *Occident*, *Paris Review*, *Spectrum*, and many other periodicals. His publications include *Blake's Newton* (1972), *The Circular Gates* (1974), *Without Music* (1977), *Notes for Echo Lake* (1981), *First Figure* (1984), *Sun* (1988), and *At Passage* (1995). He has also translated poems for *The Selected Poetry of Vincent Huidobro* (1981) and *The Random House Book of Twentieth-Century French Poetry* (1982), as well as rendering into English Rimbaud's *Voyelles* (1980), Alain Tanner and John Berger's *Jonah Who Will Be 25 in the Year 2000* (1983), and Emmanuel Hocquard's *Theory of Tables* (1994). In 1983 he edited *Code of Signals: Recent Writings in Poetics*.

The winner of several fellowships from the National Endowment for the Arts, a Guggenheim Fellowship, and the PEN Center U.S.A. West Poetry award, Palmer has collaborated on a number of works with the Margaret Jenkins Dance Company, as well as with composers and performance artists. His radio play *Idem I–IV* was produced for the public radio station KQED in 1980. He currently teaches in the poetics program at New College in San Francisco.

ROBERT PINSKY (1940–)

Robert Pinsky was born in 1940 in the faded oceanfront town of Long Branch, New Jersey. His father's family had lived there for several generations, and Robert and his younger siblings attended the same school their father had done many years before. Uninspired by his course work, Robert did not enjoy school, and his erratic work habits did not impress his teachers; in the eighth grade, he moved into a remedial class, which left him enough free time to take up the clarinet and saxophone and eventually start a band.

He enrolled at Rutgers University in 1958, taking classes with Paul Fussell and Francis Fergusson. Fussell, who used Pound's *ABC of Reading* as a textbook, introduced his honors students to contemporary poetry – "the first poetry by living writers" that Pinsky had ever read. After completing his B.A. in 1962, he went to Stanford University "to avoid the draft and to sponge off a university for a year or two." Yvor Winters put him to work: he had talent, Winters told him, but "Anybody who has only read that much can never write a good poem, except by a very unlikely accident." Studying personally with Winters, Pinsky began working in earnest, and won a writing fellowship the following year.

He published poems in several literary journals, and got to know Jim McMichael, John Peck, and Robert Hass; along with Hass, he was active in an antiwar group that would later become a chapter of SDS. In 1965 he left for England, where he read Donald Davie for the first time, and finished his dissertation on Walter Savage Landor in "about six weeks" in a frantic burst of energy. Pinsky earned his Ph.D. in 1966; the thesis was published two years later as *Landor's Poetry*.

After spending the summer in Spain, he moved briefly to the University of Chicago, and then on to Wellesley College. There he met David Ferry and, through him, Frank Bidart. Bidart and Pinsky became good friends, reading and critiquing each other's work; Bidart also introduced him to Elizabeth Bishop and to Robert Lowell, who would write a blurb for *Sadness and Happiness* (1975), Pinsky's first book of verse. Around the time he published his second, *An Explanation of America* (1979), Pinsky moved to Berkeley and renewed his friendship with Robert Hass. Beginning in the early 1980s, they worked together with Czeslaw Milosz on translations of his verse; these poems would be published as *The Separate Notebooks* in 1984.

A poet–critic, Robert Pinsky has been interested both in creative writing and in critical analysis. In addition to his study of Landor, he has also written *The Situation of Poetry* (1976) and *Poetry and the World* (1988); later poetry includes *History of My Heart* (1984), *The Want Bone* (1990), and a verse translation of Dante's *Inferno* (1994). He currently teaches in the creative writing program at Boston University.

SYLVIA PLATH (1932–1963)

Daughter of a Polish-born intellectual who died during her childhood, Sylvia Plath was born in Boston in 1932. She was literarily precocious, publishing her first poem at the age of eight. Ambitious as well, she won a number of literary contests during college, and was elected to Phi Beta Kappa. Beneath the successful veneer, however, she was troubled: she suffered a nervous breakdown in her junior year, and attempted suicide. This experience would provide the basis for her only novel, *The Bell Jar*, first published pseudony-mously in 1963.

Plath seemed to have recovered her equilibrium the following year: she graduated *summa cum laude* from Smith College and won a Fulbright scholar-ship to Cambridge. There she met and married the English poet Ted Hughes. They came back to the U.S. together, and Plath taught English at Smith from 1957–8, before giving up teaching to devote her time to her poetry. Prior to returning to England, the couple sojourned back east, where in 1959 Plath audited a course taught by Robert Lowell.

The next year marked the publication of Plath's first book of poetry, *The Colossus*, as well as the birth of her first child. Hughes reports a shift in her method of composition around this time. Before, she had struggled with her poems, fighting laboriously for each perfect word; starting with "Tulips" (1961), she wrote "at top speed, as one might write an urgent letter." Writing was indeed a matter of urgency for Plath: on February 11, 1963, she died by her own hand. In the amazingly prolific last month of her life, she had written as many as three poems a day. Plath's *Collected Poems*, edited by Hughes, appeared in 1981. She was posthumously awarded the Pulitzer Prize for the collection one year later.

ADRIENNE RICH (1929–)

Adrienne Rich was born in 1929 in Baltimore, Maryland, and grew up in "a house full of books." Her father, Dr. Arnold Rich, encouraged her to read and write, introducing her to the books in his vast Victorian library, and supervis-ing her early attempts at poetry. For "about twenty years," she has com-mented, "I wrote for a particular man, who criticized and praised me and made me feel I was indeed 'special.' The obverse side of this, of course, was that I tried for a long time to please him, or rather, not to displease him."

Rich attended Radcliffe college, from which she graduated *cum laude* in 1951. The same year, *A Change of World* was selected for the Yale Series of Younger Poets. W. H. Auden's foreword praised the work in terms a grand-parent might reserve for a well-behaved child: the poems were "neatly and modestly dressed, speak quietly but do not mumble, respect their elders but are not cowed by them, and do not tell fibs." The description does not inspire one to read on, yet perhaps the nonthreatening nature of the poetry in this first volume was one of the qualities that recommended it to Auden. Rich, as a woman, had invaded the traditionally male realm of poetry. Her obvious respect for models such as Frost, Stevens, Yeats, and Auden himself was reassuring; if she was a good girl, all the better.

In retrospect, Rich would catch glimpses of the fragmentation she experienced, even then, as a woman (who wrote) and as a poet (who was female). She felt she must "prove that as a woman poet I could also have what was then defined as a 'full' woman's life," so she married and had three children. Her husband, Alfred Conrad, was an intellectual like her father. With a family, time to herself was rare, and she found it difficult to concentrate in the few moments she could snatch when the boys were asleep. Was the selflessness demanded of a mother irreconcilable with the needs of the artist? Years later, Rich would explore the concept of motherhood in *Of Woman Born: Motherhood as Experience and Institution* (1976).

Eight years passed between her second book, *The Diamond Cutters and Other Poems* (1955), and her third, *Snapshots of a Daughter-in-Law* (1963). The poems collected in *Snapshots* signaled the beginning of a new direction for Rich: she "was able to write, for the first time, directly about experiencing myself as a woman – Until then I had tried very hard *not* to identify myself as a female poet." The change was an incredible relief for her; not so for the critics. Some found the verse to be distastefully personal, and accused her of sacrificing aesthetic integrity for political concerns. In one respect, their comments were accurate: the poems of *Necessities of Life* (1966) and *Leaflets* (1969) made it increasingly clear that politics had become an integral part of Rich's work.

During the late 1960s, Rich became involved in radical politics while teaching at the City College of New York. Her concern with issues such as the Vietnam War, the struggles of her inner-city students and, above all, sexual politics appeared in *The Will to Change* (1971) and *Diving into the Wreck* (1973), as well as in her contemporaneous essays, collected as *On Lies, Secrets and Silence* in 1979 (later prose appeared in *Blood, Bread, and Poetry* in 1986). Beginning in 1970, she joined the Women's Liberation Movement, identifying herself first as a radical feminist, and then as a lesbian.

By *The Dream of a Common Language* (1978) and *A Wild Patience Has Taken Me This Far* (1981), Rich had given up the ideal of androgyny that had figured so prominently in the title poem of *Diving into the Wreck*. Androgyny, humanism, were loaded, worn–out words she "cannot use again." Instead, she turned away from the universal to the specific, addressing women and honoring their lives and experiences.

A popular speaker, Rich has taught at many colleges over the years, including, most recently, Stanford University. She has won numerous literary honors, including Guggenheim fellowships (1952, 1961), the National

Book Award (1974) for *Diving into the Wreck* (which she accepted on behalf of all women), the Ruth Lilly Poetry Prize (1986), a Creative Arts Medal from Brandeis University (1987), and the William Whitehead Award for lifetime achievement (1992). Her most recent volume of poetry is *Dark Fields of the Republic: Poems 1991–1995* (1995).

ALAN SHAPIRO (1952–)

Alan Shapiro was born in Boston in 1952. He was educated at Brandeis University, where he studied with J. V. Cunningham, and spent a year in Ireland on a Sacher Writing Scholarship. After receiving his B.A. in 1974, he went to Stanford University on a Stegner fellowship (1975), and served as a Jones lecturer in creative writing (1976–9).

Shapiro published his first book of verse in 1981. *After the Digging* is subdivided into two groups of poems, one set in nineteenth-century Ireland, the other in seventeenth-century America. The poet chose these radically foreign scenarios, as he has explained, in order to grasp more fully the cultural and historical conditions that produced the Irish potato famine and the Salem witch trials. Taking place in a more contemporary world, the lyric poems of *The Courtesy* (1983) deal chiefly with personal experience. Shapiro's goal, however, is not so much "autobiography or confessional self-exposure," as "distilling from personal experience some sort of understanding." He distances himself from the majority of his contemporaries both in his willingness to use traditional forms, and in his preference for a less directly personal poetry.

In addition to working at Stanford, Alan Shapiro has also taught at Northwestern University and the University of North Carolina at Greensboro. He is currently a professor at the University of North Carolina at Chapel Hill. The National Endowment for the Arts (1984) and the Guggenheim Foundation (1986) have honored him with grants, and in 1987 the Poetry Society of America presented him with the William Carlos Williams Award for *Happy Hour*. He has also received the Lila Wallace–Reader's Digest Writers' Award. Shapiro has written critical essays and reviews since the late 1970s; in 1993, he brought out the collection, *In Praise of the Impure: Poetry and the Ethical Imagination*. His most recent book of poetry is *Covenant* (1991).

GARY SNYDER (1930–)

Gary Snyder was born in 1930 in San Francisco, and was brought up in the Pacific Northwest. Attuned to environmental issues from his youth, he admired Native American cultures for their harmonious relationship with nature, and read up on their myths and lore. Snyder enjoyed spending time out-of-doors, and became adroit at mountain climbing and wilderness survival techniques.

When he could get away from his studies at Reed College, Snyder spent time on the sea and in the woods, working variously as a sailor, logger, trail maker, and forest lookout. He received a B.A. in anthropology and literature in 1951. After a stint at the University of Indiana, Snyder enrolled at the University of California at Berkeley where he studied Chinese philosophy and T'ang poetry between 1953 and 1956.

By the time he moved to the San Francisco area, Snyder was already deeply involved with Zen Buddhism, and had begun writing poetry. Generally dissatisfied with Western society, he fell in with a group of rebellious writers that would come to be known as the Beat poets, though Snyder would never be as much a part of the Beat scene as writers like Allen Ginsberg and Jack Kerouac. He won a scholarship from the First Zen Institute of America in 1956, and was on the road by the time the Beat movement captured the country's imagination.

Snyder spent most of the next twelve years studying at a Buddhist monastery in Japan and traveling around the Far East. He saw India and Indonesia, and during a stint on an oil tanker, voyaged as far as Istanbul; these journeys are catalogued in part in the prose works *Earth House Hold* (1969) and *Passage through India* (1983). While in Japan, Snyder met and married his third wife, Masa Uehara. Their son Kai is featured in many of the poems of *Regarding Wave* (1970).

Recognizing his responsibility to work for ecological awareness, Snyder returned to the States after the birth of his son, and in 1972 served as a member of the United Nations Conference on the Human Environment. Much of his later poetry has sought to promote sympathy with the natural world. Valuing "the fertility of the soil, the magic of animals, the power-vision in solitude, the terrifying initiation and re-birth, the love and ecstasy of the dance, the common work of the tribe," Snyder writes, "I try to hold both history and wilderness in mind that my poems may approach the true measure of things and stand against the unbalance and ignorance of our times."

Snyder has served as a visiting lecturer at a variety of universities and workshops, and has taught at the University of California at Davis since 1986. His books include *Riprap* (1959), *Myths and Texts* (1960), *The Back Country* (1967), the Pulitzer Prize–winning *Turtle Island* (1974), *The Real Work: Interviews and Talks* (ed. Scott McLean, 1980), *Axe Handles* (1983), and *Left Out in the Rain* (1986). He has also translated poems by Han Shan and Miyazawa Kenji; these pieces are included in *Riprap & Cold Mountain Poems*

(1965) and *A Range of Poems* (1966). The recipient of Frank O'Hara and Levinson Prizes, Snyder won the Fred Cody Memorial Award for lifetime achievement in 1989.

TIMOTHY STEELE (1948–)

Timothy Steele was born in 1948 in Burlington, Vermont. After growing up in New England, he attended Stanford University, where he received his B.A. in 1970. Although Yvor Winters had retired from Stanford four years earlier, Steele wrote his Ph.D. thesis on the history and conventions of detective novels at Brandeis under the supervision of one of Winters's most notable students. J. V. Cunningham, a formidable poet and critic in his own right, not only oversaw his dissertation, but also commented upon his poetry. The comments were, as Steele has noted, typical Cunningham – supportive and brief.

Steele returned to Stanford for two years as a Jones Lecturer in Poetry, and completed his Ph.D. (1977) at the end of that time. He was hired by the University of California at Los Angeles where he taught between 1977 and 1983. During this time, he brought out two books of poetry. The verse collected in *Uncertainties and Rest* (1979) was remarkable for its formal regularity, employing rhyme and traditional stanzaic forms. Steele's decision to write in meter was regarded as old-fashioned and, not surprisingly, the volume was largely overlooked. For the poet, however, meter is what makes the poetic experience: "My keenest pleasure in reading poetry has from the beginning been bound up with the metrical experience; and I write in meter because only by doing so can I hope to give someone else the same degree of pleasure that the poetry I most love has given me."

Steele's use of meter and rhyme aligned his work with the more traditional poetry espoused by a group of poets living in California at that time. In Southern California, this tendency was represented by writers like Charles Gullans, Thom Gunn, and Janet Lewis; Edgar Bowers, Dick Davis, John Ridland, and Alan Stephens clustered around the University of California at Santa Barbara, where Steele was a visiting lecturer in 1986.

Although Steele held a Guggenheim Fellowship from 1984 to 1985, it was not until 1986 that he secured real recognition. *Sapphics Against Anger and Other Poems* (1986) collected together most of the shorter works he had published after *Uncertainties and Rest*. With its publication, he won the Peter I. B. Lavan Younger Poets Award (1986), the Commonwealth Club of California Medal for Poetry (1986), and the Los Angeles PEN Center Literary Award for Poetry (1987).

Steele has taught at California State University at Los Angeles since 1987.

In 1990, he published *Missing Measures: Modern Poetry and the Revolt against Meter*, a critical work which argues that the "innovation" of free verse has led to poets who are "merely following, by rote and habit, a procedure of writing, and breaking up into lines, predictably mannered prose." Steele's recent books of poetry include *The Color Wheel* (1994) and the collection *Sapphics and Uncertainties: Poems 1970–1986* (1995).

DEREK WALCOTT (1930–)

Descended from both African and European ancestors, Derek Walcott was born in Castries, St. Lucia in 1930. His father Warwick was a civil servant and amateur watercolor painter; while his role in the government aligned the family with the ruling élite, their ethnic background linked them to the common people. The theme of divided cultural loyalties, prominent in Walcott's writing, appears as early as his first commercial book of verse in "A Far Cry from Africa": "Where shall I turn, divided to the vein? / I who have cursed / The drunken officer of British rule, how choose / Between this Africa and the English tongue I love?"

Warwick Walcott died in 1931. As a young man, Derek was interested in the visual arts as his father had been, and exhibited some of his work in a group show in 1950, but soon realized that his vocation was writing rather than painting. He explains his decision in the autobiographical poem *Another Life* (1973). Later in life, Walcott worked as an art critic and amateur painter; one of his still lifes appears on the cover of his *Collected Poems* (1986).

Walcott's mother, a teacher and amateur actress, was instrumental in introducing him to poetry and drama. Headmistress at a local Methodist school, she possessed an extensive library and encouraged her children to read. Derek was a bright and enthusiastic student, and became enthralled with European poetry during his classical education; at the age of fourteen, he published his first poem, a Wordsworthian piece called "1944," in the local paper. The Methodist Walcotts were a minority in a primarily Roman Catholic culture, and the Catholic Church was openly critical of the young poet's view of God. As he recalls, "The priest wrote a mechanically witty reply, in heroic couplets, accusing me of pantheism, of animism, in short, of heresy. It was a painful shock to a fourteen-year-old boy to be told that he loved what he thought were the natural manifestations of a God in a wrong way; and an equal horror to find that the metre at which he had laboured could be so facile a form of argument." Four years later, Walcott borrowed $200 from his mother to privately print his first book of verse, *25 Poems* (1948). These poems, too, were criticized by the Church, but were hailed as the work "of an accomplished poet" by the writer and critic Frank Collymore; with such a recommendation, Walcott peddled the little book successfully, and was able to pay his mother back. Of his early verse and drama, he has said, "I saw myself legitimately prolonging the mighty line of Marlowe, of Milton."

Walcott left St. Lucia in 1950, and entered the University of the West Indies in Jamaica on a scholarship from the British government. After taking his B.A. in English, French, and Latin in 1953, he taught at several different Caribbean schools. During this time, he was working on the poems that would appear in *In a Green Night* (1962) as well as on several plays, and in 1957 he was awarded a Rockefeller fellowship to study theater in the United States. He went to New York where he worked under José Quintero for several months and wrote furiously; despite his productivity, he was dissatisfied with the state of black theater in New York, and gave up the rest of his grant to return to the West Indies to create an acting troupe along his own lines. By the time he wrote *Ti-Jean and His Brothers* (produced in 1957), Walcott had begun to integrate Caribbean folk stories, language, and music into his dramatic works. He has produced some two dozen plays in his lifetime.

Walcott founded the Trinidad Theatre Workshop in 1959. He was active in theater throughout the 1960s and 1970s, writing, producing, and directing plays for his group, including the Obie-winning *Dream on Monkey Mountain* (produced 1967). During this period, he also published *The Castaway and Other Poems* (1965) and *The Gulf and Other Poems* (1969). Walcott resigned from the Workshop in the mid-1970s, and took a series of teaching positions at American universities, including New York University, Yale, and Columbia. In 1979, the year *The Star-Apple Kingdom* was published, he was appointed an honorary member of the American Academy of Arts and Letters.

Walcott's later poetic works include *Sea Grapes* (1976), *The Fortunate Traveller* (1981), *The Arkansas Testament* (1987), and *Omeros* (1990). He has been affiliated with Boston University's Creative Writing Department since the 1980s, and divides his time between the Caribbean and New England. His many awards include Rockefeller and MacArthur fellowships, the Guiness Award (1961) for *A Green Night*, the Heinemann Award from the Royal Society of Literature for *The Castaway and Other Poems* and *The Fortunate Traveller* (1966, 1981), the Cholmondeley Award for *The Gulf and Other Poems* (1969), the *Los Angeles Times* Book Prize for poetry (1986) for *Collected Poems*, and the Queen's Gold Medal for Poetry (1988). In 1992 he won the Nobel Prize for literature. Of him, the Nobel committee said, "In his literary works Walcott has laid a course for his own cultural environment, but through them he speaks to each and every one of us. In him, the West Indian culture has found its great poet."

Born in New York City in 1921, Richard Wilbur grew up in North Caldwell, New Jersey, where he developed a love of the country. He was interested in painting during his youth, and it seemed initially that he would follow in the footsteps of his artist father. There were journalists in his family too, however, and Wilbur eventually decided to pursue a career in writing. He attended Amherst College (A.B., 1942), where he penned editorials, stories, and poems for the school paper, but did not write seriously until he was stationed in Europe during World War II. "One does not use poetry for its major purposes, as a means to organize oneself and the world," he explained, "until one's world somehow gets out of hand." The ordering of chaos was a major preoccupation of his first book, *The Beautiful Changes and Other Poems* (1947).

After the war, Wilbur returned to Massachusetts, and took an A.M. at Harvard University in 1947. He was named to the Society of Fellows, and spent three years writing poetry; *Ceremony and Other Poems* (1950) came out at the end of this time. Following a four-year stint as an assistant professor at Harvard, Wilbur began his affiliation with a few of the most notable small liberal arts colleges in New England; over the next 33 years, he held professor-ships at Wellesley (1955–7) and Wesleyan (1957–77), and was Writer-in-Residence at Smith (1977–86). In 1987, he succeeded Robert Penn Warren as Poet Laureate of the United States.

Laureateships have not traditionally been awarded to the avant-garde. To England's dubious credit, the British poet laureateship was once held by no less a person than Colley Cibber – who went down in history as the king of the dunces in Pope's immortal *Dunciad*. Cibber (1671–1751), widely re-garded as one of the worst poets to have held the position, admitted that he was appointed because he was a good Whig. He was no doubt aware that John Dryden had been dismissed several decades earlier for refusing to take an oath of allegiance to the crown. While the American appointment, as an annual honor, may be less politically loaded, it rewards radical experimenta-tion just as little: Wilbur writes well-crafted metrical poems very much in the traditionalist vein.

This elegant, exquisitely regular, jewel-like verse had seemed to stand still in the 1960s, a period swirling with the suddenly popular innovations of the Beat, Black Mountain, and Confessional poets. Wilbur reacted strongly to charges that his work had not adjusted to the times, insisting that "the strength of the genie comes of his being confined in a bottle." "I don't like, I can't adjust to, simplistic political poetry, the crowd-pleasing sort of anti-Vietnam poem. I can't adjust to the kind of Black poetry that simply cusses and hollers artlessly. And most of all I can't adjust to the sort of poem, which is mechanically, prosaically 'irrational,' which is often self-pitying, which starts all its sentences with 'I', and which writes constantly out of a limply subjective world." Wilbur would hail the advent of the New Formalism in the early 1980s with glee.

Wilbur's verse collections include *Things of This World* (1956), *Walking to Sleep* (1969), *The Mind-Reader* (1976), and *New and Collected Poems* (1988), as well as the *Opposites* series for children. He is known not only for his poetry but also for his translation of French verse, particularly Voltaire's *Candide* and the plays of Moliére and Racine. He was received a plethora of honors, including two Pulitzer Prizes (1957, 1989), the National Book Award (1957), the Bollingen Prize (1963, 1971), the Shelley Memorial Award (1973), the American Academy and Institute of Arts and Letters Gold Medal for Poetry (1991), and the Edward MacDowell Medal (1992). Wilbur currently lives in New England.

CHARLES KENNETH WILLIAMS (1936–)

Charles Kenneth Williams was born in Newark, New Jersey in 1936. He began his studies at Bucknell University, and completed his B.A. at the University of Pennsylvania in 1959. Nine years after graduation, he published his first work, a long poem entitled *A Day for Anne Frank* (1968).

That year, Williams met the poet Anne Sexton at a reading at Temple University. She read over the manuscript for *Lies*, and encouraged him to submit it to her publisher, Houghton Mifflin. Like *A Day for Anne Frank*, the poems of *Lies* rely on simple, sometimes crudely physical images to suggest that it is lies that make the world go round. Williams condemns this world for destroying souls like Anne Frank, who becomes nothing more than "a clot / in the snow, / blackened, a chunk of phlegm." When Houghton Mifflin balked at the explicit language and subject matter, Sexton insisted on the quality of the work, calling the young poet a "Fellini of the word." Largely on her recommendation, the press accepted her protégé's manuscript, publishing it in 1969.

Williams sustains the anger and intensity of *Lies* (1969) in *I Am the Bitter Name* (1972), a book seething with frustrated rage at America's continued involvement in the Vietnam War. Perhaps the most effective piece in the collection is "In the Heart of the Beast." The epigraph of this poem, "May 1970: Cambodia, Kent State, Jackson State," recalls the vivid wartime images plastered on the front of the newspaper and on television. Such images recur throughout the poem, recalling the violence spawned by this seemingly endless war, both on the battlefields of Southeast Asia, and on the campuses back home. The poem is a powerful indictment of America. Several of the most overtly political poems from this volume were also included in *The Sensuous President* (1972), a collection of drawings and verse that slammed Richard Nixon. The anthology was edited by Williams under the Kafkaesque pseudonym "K." His later works include *With Ignorance* (1977), *Tar* (1983), *Flesh and Blood* (1987), and *A Dream of Mind* (1992), as well as translations of Sophocles's *Women of Trachis* (1978), and Euripedes's *Bacchae* (1990).

Williams has served as a group therapist for adolescents at the Institute of the Pennsylvania Hospital in Philadelphia, where he was instrumental in establishing a poetry workshop for the emotionally disturbed. He has also edited and ghostwritten pamphlets, essays, and speeches in the fields of psychiatry and architecture. Currently at George Mason University, Williams has taught at a variety of colleges, including Beaver College, Drexel University, Franklin and Marshall College, the Poetry Center Workshop, and Columbia University. He has received the National Book Critics Circle Award for *Flesh and Blood* (1988), the Bay Area Book Reviewers Association Award (1989), the Morton Dauwen Zabel Award (1989) and, for 1993–6, a Lila Wallace–Reader's Digest Writers' Award.

JAY WRIGHT (1935–)

Jay Wright was born in 1935 in Albuquerque, New Mexico. As an adolescent, he discovered the writers of the Harlem Renaissance that at the same time he learned "that history mattered. . . . so it became rather natural for me to associate history and literature, or to think, at least, that they treated the same matters." Anthropological, mythical, and historical subject matter became thematically important to Wright's poetry. His influences would include writers and thinkers like Dante, Robert Hayden, W. E. B. Du Bois, Benjamin Banneker, Ralph Ellison, Hart Crane, Rainer Maria Rilke, and Wole Soyinka.

Wright played semiprofessional baseball and served in the U.S. Army, then enrolled at the University of California at Berkeley. After graduating with a B.A. in 1961, he studied briefly at Union Theological Seminary in New York, and in 1962 began his graduate work at Rutgers University. He eventually took an M.A. at Rutgers, completing all the requirements for the Ph.D. except a doctoral thesis.

In the late 1960s, Wright began a tour of black southern schools for the Woodrow Wilson–National Endowment for the Arts program, and in conjunction published a chapbook entitled *Death as History* (1967). Even before the production of the booklet, his poems had been selected for anthologies such as *New Negro Poets: U.S.A.*, ed. Langston Hughes (1964) and *For Malcolm: Poems on the Life and Death of Malcolm X*, eds. Dudley Randall and Margaret Burroughs (1967). His first major book, *The Homecoming Singer*, appeared in 1971, and was praised for its treatment of historical matter and portraits of black folk life. After its publication, Wright went to Mexico and to Scotland, where he served as the Joseph Compton Creative Writing Fellow at Dundee University. He returned to the States in 1973 and settled in New Hampshire, joining the faculty of Yale University in 1975. The following year he brought out *Dimensions of History* (1976) and *Soothsayers and Omens* (1976). Later works include *The Double Invention of Komo* (1980), *Explications/Interpretations* (1984), *Elaine's Book* (1988), and *Boleros* (1991).

Wright has served as Writer-in-Residence at a number of colleges, including Tougaloo, Talladega, Texas Southern University, and the University of Kentucky. A playwright as well as a poet, he has been a Hodder Fellow at Princeton University and has written several dramatic works including *Balloons: A Comedy in One Act* (1968) and "Love's Equations" (1983). He has also held Guggenheim and MacArthur fellowships. His work has appeared in a variety of periodicals, including *American Poetry Review*, *Black World*, *Callaloo*, *Evergreen Review*, *Hambone*, *The Kenyon Review*, *Nation*, *TriQuarterly*, and *The Yale Review*, as well as the anthologies *Black Fire*, eds. LeRoi Jones and Larry Neal (1968), *The Poetry of Black America*, ed. Arnold Adoff (1972), and *Every Shut Eye Ain't Asleep*, eds. Michael Harper and Anthony Walton (1994). Currently living in New Hampshire, Wright teaches at Dartmouth College.

CRITICISM SINCE 1940

Evan Carton and Gerald Graff

INTRODUCTION

D
URING THE PAST DECADE or more, the field of literary studies
has been a notoriously embattled one. The debates within and
around it, sometimes referred to as "the canon wars" or "the culture
wars," have expressed in various ways the identity conflict not only of our
academic discipline but of the contemporary American society and culture of
which it is a part. Our account of criticism since 1940, like the other
contributions to this *Cambridge History of American Literature,* was composed
in the midst of these debates. One of the tasks we set ourselves, accordingly,
was to situate the debates historically, to provide a narrative of the developments in modern literary, language, and cultural theory that have helped
produce the current struggles, and to illustrate the relations between our
cultural, institutional, and disciplinary moment and previous moments
within the last fifty years.

This history argues that many of the contested issues in contemporary
literary studies – issues that sometimes are represented as posing an unprecedented crisis for the discipline – not only have been repeatedly debated in
different terms at earlier moments in our period but are, in fact, inseparable
from the discipline itself. Often, these issues have been expressions of a
central and longstanding tension in the discipline between the impulse to
rigorously define and circumscribe the field, laying professional claim to a
distinctive set of literary objects, interpretive procedures, and evaluative
criteria, and the competing impulse to broaden and extend the discipline's
borders. Concerned with these conflicting impulses, our account of the principal critical theories, methods, and movements of the past half century pays
particular attention to the *academicization* of criticism, its causes, consequences, and controversies. In attending to the varieties and problems of
disciplinary definition, moreover, we have also traced the course of a question
that, throughout our period, has animated many of the debates over disciplinary identity: what critical and pedagogical practices are most suitable to the
achievement and maintenance of a democratic culture?

We have also been aware, in preparing this history, that our work was part
of a larger collective project on the history of American literature. To our

section of this project fell the task of explaining the shifts of critical vision and interest – and the disciplinary reconstructions of each of the project's three key terms, "history," "American," and "literature" – that demanded a new major history of American literature. Throughout our history of criticism since 1940, then, we have noted the points of intersection and lines of influence between particular developments in critical theory and arguments over the content, character, and control of the American literary canon. And we have sought not just to chart the assumptions and vocabularies that inform the work of our co-contributors to the *Cambridge History of American Literature* but, at times, to raise questions about the grounds, the powers, and the limitations of these assumptions and vocabularies.

The circumstances and objectives outlined above have been the main shaping forces of our narrative. Given our limited space, this narrative is necessarily a selective one. A number of important theories, theorists, critics, and scholars of the past half century have either not been discussed at all or have not been given their due. In tracing the academicization of criticism, for instance, we have given short shrift to such brilliant cultural commentators as "The New York Intellectuals" of the 1940s and 1950s, whose largely nonacademic and cross-disciplinary criticism might be central to a different kind of account. Nor have we adequately recognized the many brilliant literary interpreters who throughout the period produced important new understandings of individual authors and works. Rather than presenting detailed synopses of the work of individual critics or critical schools – which are available in other histories and surveys such as Frank Lentricchia, *After the New Criticism* (1981); Terry Eagleton, *Literary Theory: An Introduction* (1983); Vincent B. Leitch, *American Literary Criticism from the Thirties to the Eighties* (1988) and *Cultural Criticism, Literary Theory, Postmodernism* (1992); Stephen Greenblatt and Giles Gunn, eds., *Redrawing the Boundaries: The Transformation of English and American Literary Studies* (1992); and Michael Groden and Martin Kreiswirth, eds., *The Johns Hopkins Guide to Literary Theory and Criticism* (1994) – we have chosen to trace influential ideas, critical paradigms, and disciplinary debates. That is, we have sought to tell a story, one sufficiently lucid and coherent to provide the general reader or student with a sense of where literary studies is and how it got there.

I

❦

POLITICS AND AMERICAN CRITICISM

IN A WIDELY DISCUSSED REPORT published in 1984, National Endowment for the Humanities Chairman William J. Bennett deplored the new politicization of literary study in academic criticism and university curricula. The report, entitled *To Reclaim a Legacy,* attacked new trends in literary criticism and theory, which Bennett claimed had dislodged the canon of great books that traditionally had been at the center of the American curriculum in favor of a fashionable mixture of media studies and minority writing. Bennett would return to this line of attack two years later, when as Secretary of Education under Ronald Reagan he complained that, throughout U.S. institutions of higher education, professors were promoting critical ideas, methods, and vocabularies that took literature away from students and the general public and turned it into the private preserve of a specialized academic coterie. In phrases that strikingly echoed the Republican campaign rhetoric of the moment, Bennett charged that such critics and criticism had sacrificed the "common culture" of Americans to the aims of "special interest groups."

In 1988, Bennett's successor at the Endowment, Lynne V. Cheney, revived Bennett's charges in *Humanities in America,* a report "to the President, the Congress, and the American People." Cheney extolled "the remarkable flowering of the humanities" in state humanities councils and public festivals – everywhere, in fact, but in the universities, where she too found the public interest being sacrificed to narrow professional specialization and partisan identity politics. In literary studies particularly, she observed, "the key questions are thought to be about gender, race, and class, and truth and beauty and excellence are regarded as irrelevant."

Not surprisingly, such statements by prominent government officials powerfully shaped the national debate over education and the humanities, which continues today. The late 1980s and early 1990s have witnessed a stream of caustic editorials against "political correctness," many of them directed at professors and critics who have embraced new scholarly methodologies and opened up the literary canon to traditionally excluded or devalued writers and genres. These polemics have appeared not only in neo-conservative organs such as *Commentary* or *The Wall Street Journal,* which might have been expected to echo the Reagan–Bush administration's call for a revival of "traditional values," but in liberal publications as well.

The New York Times, for example, endorsing Secretary Bennett's view that a "loss of nerve and faith" on the part of educational authorities had precipitated a crisis in the humanities, attacked recent revisions of the Western Civilization course at institutions such as Stanford University. According to the *Times* editorialist, these revisions, designed to give representation to a wider range of cultures and subcultures, were the latest evidence of American higher education's declining academic standards and its betrayal of the nation's cultural heritage. "In the early 1970s," said the *Times,* "often under pressure from students, many colleges reduced or abandoned requirements for basic courses in the humanities that for centuries had been considered a part of college education." This line of argument provided a standard way of excoriating the contemporary situation in literary criticism and education: Cultural and pedagogical traditions that had existed "for centuries" were being dismantled by political pressure groups, with the cooperation of pusillanimous administrators. Thus did the past and present state of literary criticism suddenly acquire urgency in a national controversy over the very future of American culture.

THE "CRISIS" IN HISTORICAL CONTEXT

That government officials and the national press should be lavishing such attention on the doings of college English teachers – even if only to deplore them – seems sufficiently unusual to be worth taking as our point of departure in this section of the *Cambridge History of American Literature,* which charts the movements and debates in literary criticism since 1940. We write this history at a moment when, to an unprecedented degree, important public consequences may follow from the view that is taken of where American literary criticism is going and where it has been. The fierce public contentions that have erupted over the teaching of the humanities are striking proof that literary criticism exists in a vastly different climate today than in 1948, the date of the last multivolume history of American literature, *The Literary History of the United States.*

Many of those who deplore this change, such as Bennett, Cheney, and, most notably, the conservative academic Allan Bloom, whose book *The Closing of the American Mind* became a surprise best-seller in 1987, have blamed it on the cultural attitudes and political constituencies that emerged from the turmoil of the 1960s. As our book goes to press, crucial debates over the proper direction of domestic and foreign policy turn on the interpretation of recent American history, particularly on the relation between the first half of our period and the second. Does the legacy of the 1960s represent the renewal and revitalization of American traditions after the deadness and conformism of the 1950s or the "closing" of the national mind under the banner of a spurious "openness"?

Whatever one's perspective on the women's movement, the militant protests of African Americans and other ethnic minorities, or the decade's counter-cultural challenges not only to U.S. government policy in Vietnam but to conventional national values, assumptions, and self-images, it is true that these developments prompted reexamination and even change both in higher education and in other arenas and institutions of American life. Yet as significant as the recent disruptions and contentions have been, in important ways they replay conflicts and debates that predated the upheavals of the 1960s and that had long informed the study of literature before the rise of feminism, multiculturalism, deconstruction, and modern politically oriented literary theory. This continuity is easily obscured by those on both sides of the contemporary debate, who have tended to fabricate a mythical past stability in order either to condemn or to glorify the present.

The assaults on the "political correctness" of the new literary scholarship and criticism have specialized in caricature and myth-making rather than accuracy and historical perspective. This is unfortunate not only because the American people have received a highly distorted picture of crucial changes in academic culture, but because many of these changes do in fact deserve thoughtful criticism. As Williams College President Francis Oakley has written, the wildly hyperbolic tenor of the attacks have made it "difficult to identify, much less admit, the irritating grain of truth that helped stimulate them, and to which the academy would do well to pay attention." There is much that is legitimately debatable in the competing visions of the humanities that circulate in and around the American academy today. But judicious and productive debate depends, at the least, upon accurate representation of these visions, their limits, and their histories.

To put it bluntly, those who pass for "traditionalists" in today's disputes tend to be poorly informed about the very past they so vociferously invoke. Is it really the case, for example, that the courses in Western Civilization, whose recent modification the *Times* laments, had "existed for centuries" before the 1970s? As we shall see, these courses were not centuries old at all but went back no further than the 1920s, and they were inspired by what were at the time often frankly acknowledged to be political and propagandistic motives after the conflagration of competing nationalisms in World

War I. Indeed, the study of English and European literature as central college subjects dates from only a few decades earlier, and it had similar roots in the politics of nationalism.

Moreover, the introduction of the now "traditional" literary curriculum in the late nineteenth century was greeted, by the traditionalists of that earlier day, with many of the same apocalyptic forecasts of doom with which conservatives in our time have responded to multicultural revision. As the historian Lawrence Levine has pointed out, the Eurocentric curriculum "whose alteration so many are lamenting today" had itself been "denounced as trivial, modern, trendy, and anti-intellectual" when it was adopted at the turn of the century "over the intense and passionate objections of those who saw in its emergence the end of culture and the decline of civilization." Nineteenth century defenders of the primacy of the ancient Greek and Latin languages in the curriculum were convinced that barbarism and chaos would follow if these classical subjects were to be displaced by the study of modern European languages, literatures, and culture.

One early opponent of innovation, President James McCosh of Princeton, wrote in 1868 that if colleges abandoned their traditional emphasis on ancient Greece and Rome, "our language and literature will run a great risk of hopelessly degenerating." Indeed, for traditional classicists like McCosh, the study of modern European culture was not intellectually rigorous and could not be made so. To accord that culture centrality in the curriculum would only allow "easy-going students" to avoid "the studies which require thought." To McCosh and others of his era, studying the history and literature of the postclassical West seemed about as absurd as studying popular culture still seems to some today.

McCosh's assumption that the study of one's own culture in one's own language could not possibly require deep thought is especially pertinent to current academic controversies. For a similar assumption is shared by those who oppose revising the literary curriculum to include previously ignored works by women and writers of color or the study of issues of class or race in literature. Although he does not use the term, McCosh in effect suggests, as Bennett, Cheney, and Bloom would argue more than a century later, that the invasion of the precincts of the classics by modern, vernacular texts represents the triumph of a corrupting "identity politics" that is incompatible with the academic traditions of disinterestedness and rigor. Such curricular revision represents, in other words, a capitulation to the easy and interested impulse to study and value one's own particular experience and culture rather than a larger "common" one.

Tracing the complex relations between identity, politics, and the principles and parameters of literature and literary study will be one of the central tasks of our history. For the moment, though, we wish only to note the implication of the antirevisionist argument, common to both McCosh and Bennett, that studying the self (or the cultural production of one's own social group) is illegitimate and anti-intellectual. Several challenges to this view may be, and have been, posed: do not our particular identities and cultures shape how we see the objects of our study whether they are themselves those objects or not? Is the "common" culture (the culture represented by Greek and Latin classics, by Shakespeare and Milton, or by Emerson and Henry James, for example) that identity politics challenges really a *common* culture or itself the expression of an earlier identity politics, not recognized by us because it is already established?

However these questions are answered, the fact that the degenerate European works McCosh feared would displace the classics have become the very classics that Bennett and Cheney now wish to protect suggests that the appeal to a unifying common culture in the name of a public good always involves a political appeal and a form of identity politics. If blame must be assigned, then, for imposing identity politics on literature, it should be directed at the nationalist politics without which the study of national literatures would never have come into existence in the first place. These politics predate even McCosh's historical moment, let alone our own.

NATIONALISM AND LITERARY STUDY

In the early romantic period, such thinkers as Johann Herder and Friedrich Schlegel in Germany and Jules Michelet in France popularized the argument that literature is above all an expression of the *national* spirit. According to this romantic literary nationalism, the quality of a nation's language and literature is the key index of the spiritual stature of its people. This doctrine of literary nationalism went hand in hand with a theory of "national character," which held that each nation had its peculiar character type – often attributed to biology and "race" – which the national literature expressed. As the Romantics scholar, David Simpson, has observed, eighteenth and nineteenth century "definitions of national character must be seen as rationalizations of the various political processes whereby the nation-states of Europe were trying either to come into being, to maintain themselves, or to extend their territories and their imagined moral superiorities. Each [state] defines itself in terms of, and usually at the expense of, the others."

Literary nationalism, then, established a mode of identity politics that has been simply taken for granted when practiced by the majority but is excoriated when practiced by minorities. As recent deconstructionists have argued, we define our identities by locating an "other" with whom we contrast ourselves. Literary nationalism enabled the modern nation both to mark itself off from competing nations and to define the common ground that bound its own people together – a necessity in a period when industrial and capitalist expansion were dissolving traditional agrarian communities. Given the fact that the citizens of a large modern nation–state no longer knew most of their fellow citizens personally, it was only an imaginary idea of national identity that could make them think of themselves as members of the same social body. In this sense, the nation was itself a kind of literary fiction or "imagined community" (in the cultural historian Benedict Anderson's term), which cohered in a shared consciousness rather than in concrete social relationships.

Literary nationalism played an important political role in the struggle of countries like Germany and France to overcome their traditional feudal divisions and achieve the unifying national consciousness necessary in order to compete for world power. So successful were these eighteenth and nineteenth century struggles for national identity and national consciousness, that today the grouping of a variety of literary works in categories such as English, German, or American literature seems obvious and natural, an innocently neutral act of classification, rather than a practice that once had explicit political stakes and still has political consequences.

This point has been insisted on by those contemporary critics who emphasize the "constructed" nature of national literary traditions. The theoretical premise of these critics is that characterizations of national cultures and literatures shape and even in a sense *produce* the objects they pretend neutrally to represent. They are actions or "performatives" in the world as much as accounts of it. In other words, the concepts of "national literature" and "national character" (or Secretary Bennett's "common culture") help to bring into being what they claim simply to describe, a point forcefully made by David Shumway in *Creating American Civilization* (1994). It is in this sense that the concept of a national literature is taken to be an "ideological" construction. This is not to say that it is necessarily false or evil or that it should be thrown out, but rather that the idea of a "common" national culture is a historical invention that emerges at certain moments and works to the advantage and disadvantage of different groups in ways that can be investigated.

The very act of calling a work an "American" classic, for instance, calls attention not to its literary characteristics but to its national ones – that is, its relation to a political entity, the United States. In some measure, then, this label refers the work's identity and value to political rather than strictly aesthetic criteria. Or it implies that the ability of the work to speak for the nation is itself an aspect of its aesthetic appeal. This is the implication of the early twentieth century critic Van Wyck Brooks, who is quoted on the dust

jacket of a popular edition of James Fenimore Cooper's classic American novel
The Deerslayer: Cooper's hero, Natty Bumppo, "was destined to remain the
symbol of a moment of civilization, the dawn of a new American soul." To
describe Cooper's Deerslayer as a symbol of an emerging "new American
soul" is to prescribe what the American character is supposed to consist of,
equating the novel's worth with its "Americanness." The dust jacket thus
tells the reader: here is what a real American *is,* a rugged individualist like
Natty Bumppo who lives by his gun, avoids the overcivilized ways of the
cities, and remains aloof from women.

Of course, such a description also conveys what a real American cannot be:
not an Indian, for instance, who may possess some noble savage qualities but
who is undergoing a regrettable but presumably inevitable process of extinc-
tion; and not a woman, against whom the individualist hero is defined. This
is not to dismiss Cooper's novel as a rationalization of sexism, racism, or
genocide, but rather to highlight the fact that works of literature are arenas
in which communities define themselves and competing values and self-
images are negotiated. It is in this sense that literature is deeply political.
Indeed, if literature and its critical interpretations and classifications were
not political in this way – as arenas and means of cultural definition – they
would never have become the scenes of angry contention that they are today.

One way of understanding this contention is to see that the nationalistic
principle, which long associated literature with the destiny of a particular
cultural group, has lately been borrowed and reapplied by subgroups. When
African Americans and women insist on studying literature in relation to race
and gender, they are in a real sense simply following the group–logic of
traditional literary nationalism. Though this logic has sometimes led to a
narrow particularism, it has also prompted new critical awareness of the
"hybridity" of cultures (in the theorist Homi Bhabha's term), according to
which the identities of cultural groups in modern societies are never monolithic but always mixed, impure, and inhabited by otherness.

The problem of hybridity to which some contemporary critical theorists
have recently turned their attention was in fact the political problem that
initially prompted the teaching of English literature, and later American
literature, in American high schools and colleges. It is no accident that the
rise of English literature as an academic subject coincided with the great
wave of European immigration from the 1880s to 1910. Educators saw
"English" as the perfect binding force for a population otherwise geographi-
cally, ethnically, and culturally dispersed. English would never have won its
battle over the classical languages for the centrality it now enjoys in the
school and college curriculum if it had not been seen as a means of imparting
a unifying set of cultural allegiances to populations otherwise prone to unruli-

ness and rebellion. After all, what better subject was there to Americanize the newly expanding immigrant populace than English literature?

That this argument was persuasive at the turn of this century, despite the fact that by then few Americans were "English" even at one remove, indicates how recently established is the claim that Americans have a respectable national literature of their own. Now that the subject is safely accredited in the college curriculum and the American struggle for nationhood has been completed, it is easy to forget the powerful nationalist politics that motivated and validated the category of "American literature." But in the aftermath of World War I, as the United States was consolidating its national identity and international prestige, Americanist literary scholarship harbored a distinctly patriotic mission. That scholarship, as conservative critic James Tuttleton has observed, "in large part intended to claim for American literature a stature comparable to [America's] position as a military and economic power in the postwar world." Indeed, few scholars of that time hesitated to argue that the curriculum should be a vehicle for American ideology, though like today's conservatives they did not use the word "ideology" and they assumed that their Americanism was underwritten by a higher disinterestedness, for the idea of America was synonymous with democracy, universality, and the freedom of all peoples.

Consider Charles Mills Gayley, a Berkeley professor who wrote a book in 1917 entitled *Shakespeare and the Founders of Liberty in America*, in which he interpreted Shakespeare's utterances as a sort of prophecy of the Great War then at its height, and demonstrated "that Shakespeare's political philosophy . . . was that of the founders of liberty in America, was that of the Declaration of Independence." Gayley initiated one of the Great Books courses which, according to the *New York Times,* had been required "for centuries" and which supposedly epitomized literature's transcendence of politics. In fact, as we have noted, these courses and their counterpart courses in Western Civilization were an invention of the World War I era and owed their inspiration to the propaganda needs of the war effort. Historians have traced the origins of "Western Civ" to a course called "War Issues," which was sponsored by the War Department and had the expressly political aim of reinforcing Americans' sense of the Western cultural heritage, threatened by the Germany of Kaiser Wilhelm and by Bolshevism.

As historian Cyrus Veeser points out, President Nicholas Murray Butler thought of Columbia University's widely imitated version of the Western Civilization course (the famous "Contemporary Civilization") as a means of discouraging both Communist and Fascist extremism. "For those college students who are enamored of the cruder and more stupid forms of radicalism," Butler wrote, "every instruction in the facts of modern civilization, and the part that time plays in building and perfecting human institutions, is of the greatest value." The "cruder and more stupid forms of radicalism" to which Butler refers were widely associated in these years with the growing communities of immigrants whose first language was not English.

Before the war, American literature had distinctly second-rate status in the eyes of most literary critics, some of whom believed the very idea was a contradiction in terms. But after the war, American literature, which had come to be identified with a strong tradition of moral idealism, seemed even better suited than English literature to the task of strengthening the bonds of citizenship in the face of enemies abroad and disorder at home. In 1919, Fred Lewis Pattee, one of the founding figures of American literature study, wrote that "more and more clearly it is seen now that the American soul, the American conception of democracy, – Americanism, should be made prominent in our school curriculums, as a guard against the rising spirit of experimental lawlessness which has followed the great war." Whether the "lawlessness" that Pattee had in mind was that of Greenwich Village bohemians or of Lower East Side immigrants, his statement suggests the frankly political and socializing function that early proponents claimed for American literature.

A TALE OF TWO LITERARY HISTORIES

We began this introduction by arguing that a profound historical amnesia underlies the claim of conservatives and others that literary and cultural traditions that had been intact for centuries have only recently been disrupted by politics and controversy. This amnesia itself is the product of an identifiable cultural moment, the post–World War II years in which a consensual American tradition and academic discipline were constructed by the exclusion of political debates. This exclusion of debate, in fact, is virtually an announced principle of the last major multivolume American literary history, *The Literary History of the United States* (1948).

Robert Spiller, senior editor of the *LHUS*, articulates the principle in a letter to one of the work's fifty-five authors. Requesting substantial revision of the contributor's chapter, Spiller states: "We have made a rule of thumb for the entire work that we should avoid the discussion of critical controversies and the mention of critics." Forty years later, in an essay entitled "The Problem of Ideology in American Literary History" (1986), Sacvan Bercovitch observed that, in its rhetoric and its design, the Spiller *History* expressed "a single-minded attempt at synthesis" and, in fact, helped consolidate "a powerful literary–historical consensus." That consensus has long since been shaken, but Spiller's expressed desire to avoid critical controversy suggests that the consensus was far from stable even in his time.

Bercovitch's essay outlines for the *Cambridge History of American Literature* an editorial policy founded on a very different set of critical values and assumptions. He suggests that a succession of new and competing theories and methods, responding to work in other disciplines (anthropology, psychology, linguistics, philosophy) and to social and political conditions in the United States, has not only frustrated the achievement of consensus in literary study but questioned its desirability. Thus, Bercovitch writes, any contemporary project in literary history must "make the best of what (for lack of a better term) may be called a period of 'dissensus,' " a task that the *Cambridge History* proposes to assume not by avoiding the problem posed by critical controversy but by "making the problem itself the cornerstone of the project."

Since our discussion spans the period between the initial drafting of *Literary History of the United States* and the production of the present volumes, we can gain a sense of the major changes in literary study during this period by briefly comparing the theoretical precepts, methodological decisions, and critical debates that inform the two projects. Such a comparison raises the question of the extent to which the controversies that Bercovitch proposed to highlight resemble the ones that Spiller proposed to avoid.

Consider, for example, the conceptions of textual meaning in the two histories. The avoidance of critical controversy that Spiller recommends in his letter implies a generally empirical or literalistic view of textual meaning. Since texts in themselves carry determinate meanings, according to this view, the diverse interpretations of different readers and critical schools can be factored out. Critical controversy, in other words, is separable from the story of literary history and, thus, can be safely excluded – especially given the presumption that nonacademic readers need have no interest in it.

If there is a unifying element in the disparate critical theories advanced since the mid-1960s, however, it is their argument that no text is ever experienced except through some interpretation of it, through the selection of appropriate organizing principles, dominant emphases, and relevant contexts that constitute textual meaning. These acts of selection themselves differ according to the various, culturally influenced forms of attention that different readers bring to literary texts. Texts also come to readers prescreened and predefined by a network of cultural institutions, practices, and constituencies, which includes publishers, advertisers, bookstore classifications, reviewers, prize committees, and school curricula. When differently situated readers and differently organized and motivated institutions or agencies produce clashing literary interpretations and judgments, as is increasingly the case today, we begin to see the conflict of interpretations as an unavoidable aspect of literary history and, indeed, of literature itself. This is another way of saying that textual meanings that appear to be simply given, uncontroversial, and obtained by direct observation are always refracted to us through some critical lens.

The increasing number of available "lenses" in a literary culture that is constituted more openly and democratically than a generation ago has made it all the more difficult to claim an unmediated or lens-free form of reading. Indeed, the notion of nontheoretical common sense comes to be seen as one lens among many. It follows that the meaning of a text is not a stable entity but something that changes as the text enters different contexts. This tendency to open up or "de-essentialize" the text usually means reading from a resistant rather than an empathetic or acquiescent relation to it. While the practice of resistant reading has sometimes led to narcissistic excesses that critics of current theory have rightly assailed, "reading against the grain" can reveal aspects of a text that a more sympathetic reading will ignore.

From this contemporary perspective, there is something questionable about Spiller's implied assumption that criticism interposes controversy from the outside. For Spiller, critics *bring* discord into American literary history, as if, given enough good will and self-restraint, it could be kept out, and as if critics and literary historians could stand outside and apart from it. In fact, *Literary History of the United States* is not altogether free of critical controversy, but it circumscribes it in two chapters, thereby suggesting in its very organization that literature and culture develop in an organic way while criticism has up to now remained ensnared in controversies. The editor's hope, however, is that current refinements in criticism are closing this gap. The contentiousness of critics (described in a chapter entitled "The Battle of the Books") is finally said to represent an immature stage that criticism is happily in the process of outgrowing now that it has become an academic discipline. Thus, the eightieth and penultimate chapter, entitled "Summary in Criticism," written by Morton D. Zabel and heavily edited by Spiller, acknowledges "a profound and fundamental division in critical forces of the thirties" but applauds the "correction" of this situation exemplified by criticism's "movement toward assimilation and synthesis" in the forties.

Critical sectarianism must be overcome, according to Spiller, because it impedes "the mere communication of intelligence" and "the discipline of realistic logic" upon which literary study depends, and because in a state of self-division criticism cannot hope to understand literature's essential unity. "Summary in Criticism" closes with a sentence that seems clearly to announce the project and program of the Spiller *History* itself and to enforce the distinction between the merely partial opinions of critics and the organic fact of American literary history:

Now, perhaps, the moment had arrived for a more difficult task than is possible to sectarians, extremists, or insurgents; namely, the undertaking of a whole view of literature which admits the possible benefits of diverse intellectual and critical disciplines but insists on keeping the central integrity of literature intact, and holds in view the unity of art with the total sum of human experience and its moral values.

By contrast, for Bercovitch and most of the contributors to the *Cambridge History*, ideological tension is not *imported* into literature by aberrant "sectarians, extremists, or insurgents." Rather, it is already present in any construction of "America," "literature," or "history," including the constructions made by literary texts. When Bercovitch remarks that the idea of America is "not an overarching synthesis, *e pluribus unum*, but a rhetorical battleground," he might equally be speaking of history or literature. In this view, there is no "central integrity of literature" or "total sum" of history to be kept "intact," partly because these things are too heterogeneous to be totalized and partly because we cannot stand above the battleground of descriptions of literature and history.

This means that "American literature" is not only a construction of critics and readers but a product of their conflicts and debates. What constitutes the American tradition, moreover, changes its shape with the evolving struggles to define it. From this standpoint, the claim that tradition is an organic whole that precedes or transcends interpretation is itself an ideological mystification perpetrated by many of the texts that are taken to be most essentially "literary" and by the criticism that elevates those texts, including the chapter in *Literary History of the United States* that imagined itself to be heralding the end of ideology and controversy in literary study.

In fact, Jonathan Arac argues in Volume 2 of our *History* that it is precisely this claim to wholeness and transcendence of conflict upon which American literary narrative is founded. Arac classifies mid-nineteenth century prose narrative under four headings – personal, local, national, and literary – and sees "literature" emerging to fulfill "a special function." In an era of social and economic flux, sectional conflict, political controversy, and great psychological stress, literary narrative presumably affords what Hawthorne famously called a "neutral territory," a place which Arac characterizes as "neither here nor there . . . with regard to the intensely debated political issues of the day," and one in which a new "internalized psychology" represents human character as an essentially stable object of private knowledge rather than a product of action in the world. For Arac, the privileged realm of the literary, whether advanced by Hawthorne's creative imagination or Zabel and Spiller's emerging disciplinary consensus, signifies "a wholeness that may be purely imaginary, a fictive compensation for the real fractures that provoke it."

Arac's phrase echoes the definition of "ideology" put forward by the French philosopher Louis Althusser, a definition that has been central not only for Marxist criticism but for other politically oriented theories and practices of the last twenty-five years. Ideology, for Althusser, is an imaginative representation whose function is to naturalize the social fractures of the dominant relations of production, reconciling individuals to these relations by enabling them to misrecognize them as private wholeness and free subjectivity. From this standpoint, ideology is everywhere (a position whose implications, ambiguities, and potential difficulties will concern us throughout our survey of the critical field). In the *Literary History of the United States*, by contrast, ideology is present only as a feature of criticism, and then as something to be outgrown. (The term does not appear in the index of that work between "Idealism" and "Ideality," on one side, and "Individualism," "Industrialism," and "Instrumentalism," on the other, and the only writings listed under the heading "Political Literature" are those composed between the 1770s and the 1790s and discussed in a chapter called "Philosopher-Statesmen of the Republic.") Clearly, the two literary histories exhibit completely different conceptions of ideology, reflecting their different understandings of the nature of literature and the function of criticism.

THE NEED FOR "THEORY" AND THE PROBLEM OF JARGON

The conviction that the meanings of literary texts are always mediated by the critical lenses through which they are viewed, and that neither literature nor criticism can stand free of ideology and controversy, has forced contemporary critics to become more reflexive about their own procedures and assumptions. This reflexivity underlies the concern with "theory" that clearly differentiates the *Cambridge History* from its predecessor. In part, the theoretical drive is an extension of the professionalizing and systematizing impulse that dates back to the beginnings of academic literary study in the 1940s. Unlike the theorizing of the 1940s and 1950s, however, the most prominent theories since the 1960s have sought not to consolidate and rationalize existing professional procedures and assumptions but to challenge or "deconstruct" them. At the least, the proliferation of new critical discourses and methodologies bespeaks a situation in which the definition of professional literary study – like the definition of our national literature – has become a contested issue.

In this light, "theory" is what results in a period of "dissensus," as Bercovitch calls it, a moment when premises, which were at one time so shared within a community that they did not have to be recognized as premises, become matters of open dispute, something that has happened today to formerly received ideas about what "literature" is and what counts as "great literature" or as proper "reading." As long as there was relative consensus about the definition of "literature," the social function of the arts, and the content of the literary canon, there was no immediate pressure to define these terms. As that consensus has weakened, essential definitions and functions have become objects of debate and thus have been "theorized." The condition of "dissensus" has forced even the most traditionalist literary critics to spell out explicitly what could once have been left unsaid, thereby revealing traditional arguments to be no less "theoretical" than any other.

For this reason, a moment such as the present one in literary studies poses a problem for the historian, who can appeal to few criteria of measurement certain to be shared by all potential audiences. To put it another way, not only is there now no neutral or commonly accepted story of the critical history of the last half century, there is no one vocabulary, metadiscourse, or metanarrative that can claim to tell the story without inscribing one or another partial and contested interpretation. Indeed, to say this much is already to side with the new theorists against older humanistic appeals to common sense. In fact, for traditional humanists our very use of words like "metadiscourse" and "metanarrative" betrays a choice of allegiance. In their view, what such language illustrates is not a valuable or necessary increase in critical self-consciousness, but a faddish new jargon that perversely replaces a still serviceable common vocabulary.

This sort of objection to recent criticism has been frequently – and in some instances appropriately – raised. For this reason, it seems necessary before proceeding to take up the question of "jargon," partly in explanation of the current jargon we will be using in writing this history, but also because the jargon of recent criticism is the most persistent stumbling block for readers who might otherwise be willing to give that criticism a fair hearing. To many, such jargon seems to have no function except to confer a spurious mantle of expert superiority on the critic, shrouding the discussion of literature in mysteries that exclude lay readers and students. Moreover, jargon seems particularly reprehensible when applied to literature, since, in modern times, it is literature that has been supposed uniquely able to resist language's technological debasement. Finally, the perversity of jargon seems compounded when critics claim to seek the transformation of society while speaking in a vocabulary that is incomprehensible to those whose lives are presumably to be transformed.

To this argument, however, theorists retort that the attack on jargon begs several questions in a way that is not as disinterested and public spirited as it sounds. In the first place, what is taken to be jargon is a relative matter, varying with the time, place, and rhetorical situation of a community's discourse. What counts as "jargon" in a community changes as usages become commonplace over time and modify the community's norms. Virtually any accepted word ending in "ize" is likely at its first appearance to have been regarded as jargon before being naturalized (*sic*) as part of the language of common sense. Many now generally accepted terms associated with new intellectual disciplines or scientific discourses were once disdained before their gradual entry into common parlance. A familiar example would be psychoanalytic terms such as "neurotic" and "paranoia," which were jargon yesterday but no longer seem so today. As we will see in Chapter 2, the New Criticism of the 1940s, which provides our discipline with much of the critical terminology that "traditionalists" now defend against the incursions of theoretical jargon, was widely assailed as technocratic theoryspeak when it was new. Contemporary Marxist critic Terry Eagleton drives the point home when he observes that "terms such as symbol, spondee, organic unity, and wonderfully tactile" obtrude no less of an "ungainly bulk between reader and text" than do "words like gender, signifier, subtext, and ideology." In other words, older critical terms have no more intrinsic intimacy with literature itself than new-fangled ones do.

A second response to the attack on jargon as pure obfuscation argues that the use of jargon is often a way of making a strategic point, calling attention, for example, to blind spots in the language of clarity and common sense. When Roland Barthes and other French critics attack "the tyranny of lucidity" and develop theories of the "opacity" of language, their purpose is not simply to glorify linguistic difficulty. Barthes in fact writes more lucidly than a good many traditionalists one could adduce. Their point is rather that certain forms of lucidity are misleading, implying as they do, in Catherine Belsey's words, "that what is being said must be true because it is obvious, clear, and familiar."

The use of jargon is often a way of saying, in effect, that clarity can be a form of rhetorical coercion by making a discourse look so simply true, reasonable, and self-evident that it disarms critical judgment. The celebrated John Wayne line, "a man's gotta do what a man's gotta do," makes the ethic of American masculinity seem indisputable by the appearance of simple tautological self-evidence. But it is hard to make such a point without using jargon such as "tautological self-evidence." In this respect, those who attack current critical jargon by simply evoking the self-evident value of clarity and common sense miss the point in self-serving ways that recent jargon attempts to unmask. Jargon, to use another example of it ourselves, can be a way of "defamiliarizing" the language of common sense, showing that what we take to be normal is from another viewpoint strange and therefore open to criticism. By making us aware of the medium of language and the possibility of describing things differently, jargon deflates the pretensions of familiar language to speak the obvious.

The political case for jargon rests on the premise that the language with which we try to criticize any society's established assumptions will tend toward jargon, if only because the established assumptions have a lot to do with determining what we hear *as* "jargon." Problems do indeed arise when the normal register of literary and social criticism is over the heads or beneath the interests of the citizenry on whose behalf criticism presumes to speak. But such problems are not necessarily solved by abandoning specialized registers and adopting supposedly normal language, at least not if what is at stake is an attempt to challenge and change what is taken to be "normal."

Behavior with regard to sexist language is one example of a case in which "normal" language patterns have to some degree been successfully changed. The nonsexist usages that many at first resisted as aberrant or simply awkward have come to seem less so. Of course, saying "he or she" rather than "he" and avoiding "mankind" as a generic do not involve the importation of unfamiliar terms such as "historicize." Yet it might be argued that if students and citizens were to learn to use "historicize" as familiarly as they learn to use "he or she," their disposition to think historically might increase – a point which illustrates how much may be politically at stake in the question of jargon. To use terms like "social formation" or "subject position" instead of "society" or "self" is to communicate, however gratingly, that societies and selves are not absolute facts of nature but the products of choices, of conditions and institutions that can be changed.

Like other specialized languages across the spectrum of contemporary occupations and preoccupations – from tax law to football to cooking to sexual enhancement – the language of criticism is an instance of what philosopher of language Hilary Putnam has termed the "linguistic division of labor" in advanced societies. For this reason, rather than attack critical or other jargon as such, we think it more profitable to strive to improve the condition of *translation* across different jargons. For us the fault of contemporary criticism lies not in its use of jargon but in its failure to translate and explain it adequately. Such translation and explanation is becoming especially urgent as this criticism comes increasingly under public attack.

We ourselves have tried to write clearly here, to avoid highly technical language whenever possible, and, when we do use it, to explain what it means and why it is necessary. Thus, while we cannot promise that our history will sound jargon-free to every ear, our movement between different registers of current criticism, from Advanced Theoryspeak to High Humanist to Layspeak, will attempt to create a dialogue between them.

THE EMERGENCE OF ACADEMIC
CRITICISM

IN A CULTURE marked by rapid change, nothing changes more frequently than the past. With the growth of jet travel, the once disruptive technology of the railroad came to seem almost quaintly endearing. Similarly, intellectual revolutions have a way of making the previous revolution seem less threatening than it seemed to those who lived through it. We look back at yesterday's shocking revolution as the good old days to which we now long to return. A case in point is the recent literary-theory revolution, which has made the critical movements of the 1940s look more innocuously "traditional" than they appeared to be when they were taking place. We can gain a perspective on the recent history of criticism, then, by considering how forms of academic criticism that may appear so conservative to us now were experienced by their contemporaries.

Such an effort is especially necessary today because the upheavals provoked by recent literary theory have changed how the history of criticism appears to us. As very different groups have reacted antagonistically to the new theories, party lines have been quietly redrawn, making unaccustomed allies of critics who once were adversaries. As our period promises or threatens to become an Age of Theory, middlebrow journalists and some disenchanted academics have discovered points of commonality not previously apparent to either group. By the same token, today's avant-garde often fails to see how earlier movements anticipated its ideas.

The period we begin to trace here is the one that saw the emergence of academic criticism. Whereas at the outset of our period the phrase "academic criticism" would have seemed a contradiction in terms, by the end of it "academic criticism" seems almost a redundancy. How things went from one state of affairs to the other is the story we turn to now.

THE ACADEMICIZATION OF CRITICISM

With today's sense of a crisis in the humanities that we discussed in Chapter 1, the recent history of American criticism is frequently plotted as a story of falling away, decline, and deterioration. Prestige, it is said, has lamentably shifted: from the public critic to the academic specialist; from the general intellectual who wrote for nonacademic readers (and who was accessible to students) to the high theorist who writes exclusively for other academic critics; from a humble respect for literature on the part of the critic to an attempt to elevate the critic's theories and methods over literature. As Bruce Robbins has pointed out in *Secular Vocations* (1993), the story of criticism since 1965 in particular tends to be a narrative of creeping academic professionalization, in which critics lose touch with the audience for literature and finally with literature itself.

Such is the alarmist tale told in recent books like Russell Jacoby's *The Last Intellectuals* (1987), Alvin Kernan's *The Death of Literature* (1990), Robert Alter's *The Pleasures of Reading in an Ideological Age* (1989), James Atlas's *The Book Wars* (1990), Roger Kimball's *Tenured Radicals* (1990), and a myriad of other recent works that deplore the eclipse of the public critic. The story has been reiterated so often that it is now taken for granted as simply the way things are: academics have narrowed the scope of literature, wrestling it away from lay readers and handing it over to theorists and other specialists. In some versions of the story, the blame is extended to modern and postmodern writers, who are said to have joined the critics in turning their backs on the common reader, with poets now writing mainly for other poets and novelists taking the death of the novel and the impotence of language as their primary subject.

We acknowledge an element of truth in the complaint. The self-enclosure of theoretical discourse is certainly a problem for any criticism that wants to change the world, even if it does only reflect the increasing self-consciousness and specialization of contemporary culture. At the same time, self-enclosure is hardly the whole story of recent trends in criticism and literature, which have often sought to broaden traditional concerns and expand their constituencies. In any case, the tendency toward "meta" discourse and reflexivity did not begin with contemporary theory (or with modern or postmodern art). In the lurid hues painted by the critics of theory, however, the academic criticism of the period that preceded it – between 1940 and 1965 – looks less troubled and contentious than it really was, as well as more comfortably accessible to the general reader.

This is the misleading impression created by Robert Alter, among others. Exaggerating the radical impact of Continental theories on Anglo-American criticism in the sixties, Alter depicts critics before that time as having been "by and large meager on conceptual matters and not much interested in the systematic aspects of literature." According to Alter, Continental Marxism, psychoanalysis, and semiotics imported a passion for system and rigor into a scene that had previously been dominated by a relaxed amateurism: "The discussion of literature," Alter writes, "would no longer be the province of the proverbial English professor with comfortable tweed jacket and pipe luxuriating in his chatty, complacent learning. Literature at last would be studied with intellectual rigor, against the background of philosophy, psychology, anthropology, and linguistics." The point being led up to is clear enough, and Alter makes it explicit a few pages later, when he describes the theoretical revolution of the seventies and eighties as a takeover of literature by a band of "new literary technocrats," a group which has no feeling for "literature itself" and is chiefly concerned about advancing the jargon of one or another "metadiscourse."

But Alter's picture of the past is colored by a need to make scapegoats of today's theorists. The first challenge to the image of the genial, pipe-smoking English professor with no interest in "the systematic aspects of literature" took place long before the arrival of the theoretical movements of the late sixties. In fact, the drive to replace the amateur critic with the systematic professional goes back to the beginnings of academic literary studies in the late nineteenth century, finally culminating in the rise of the New Criticism after World War II. Post sixties theory, in other words, has become the latest in a long line of convenient scapegoats for resentments against an academic appropriation of literature that had originated much earlier.

The view that criticism needed to be moved beyond its traditional state of armchair amateurism had been voiced as early as Coleridge, Poe, and the German romantics. The establishment of departments of language and literature in universities at the end of the nineteenth century intensified the call for a more systematic literary criticism. These stirrings culminated in 1925, when the British critic I. A. Richards published what would turn out to be a highly influential manifesto, *Principles of Literary Criticism*. In an opening chapter on "The Chaos of Critical Theories," Richards found that a survey of the "chief figures of criticism from Aristotle onwards" revealed that scandalously little progress had been made in answering "the fundamental questions which criticism is required to answer." The "results yielded by the best minds" over the centuries, according to Richards, added up to "an almost empty garner":

A few conjectures, a supply of admonitions, many acute isolated observations, some brilliant guesses, much oratory and applied poetry, inexhaustible confusion, a sufficiency of dogma, no small stock of prejudices, whimsies, and crotchets, a profusion of mysticism, a little genuine speculation, sundry stray inspirations, pregnant hints and random *apercus*; of such as these, it may be said without exaggeration, is extant critical theory composed.

In the United States, Joel E. Spingarn, a Renaissance scholar at Columbia, had made similar observations in 1917 about the state of American criticism, lamenting its "want of philosophic insight and precision." "Golden utterances there have been aplenty," Spingarn wrote, but "a disconnected body of literary theories" and "mere practical programmes" had "taken the place of a real philosophy of art." Thus the project of cleaning up the amateurish and disorderly conceptual situation of criticism was launched well before World War II. It was the postwar expansion of the university, however, that gave the project a secure institutional base and enabled a new academic criticism to emerge.

Until the 1940s, as we have noted, the very idea of "academic criticism" would have seemed self-contradictory. "Criticism," understood as the elucidation and evaluation of works of literature, was the monopoly of journalists, and whatever was journalistic had to be scorned and eschewed by serious professors. What professors of literature produced was not criticism, but objective "scholarship," in the form of meticulous, methodologically grounded, and impersonal historical and linguistic study.

Of course, the very idea of a "professor of literature" would itself have seemed anomalous only a short time earlier. Until the last quarter of the nineteenth century, there were no professors of literature in the small liberal arts colleges that comprised the system of higher education in the United States. College students primarily studied the Greek and Latin languages, for English and American literature were seen not as objects of study at all, but as adornments that a young gentleman would naturally acquire in his leisure time. The notion had not yet arisen that literary works required a laborious process of interpretation, much less a professionally trained class of interpreters; nor was there yet any idea of disciplinary specialization. The same professor often taught history, philosophy, religion, and rhetoric, and this person, who might be a clergyman with a general "society knowledge" of belles-lettres, might also teach the occasional English or American literary work.

These conditions changed very rapidly in the 1870s and 1880s when, under pressure to make higher education more effective in training an expanding populace for a wider and more technical array of occupational pursuits, the small liberal arts college gave way to the ambitious research university, patterned on those of Germany. In the new model, specialized departments and fields and specialized professors wielding scientific methodologies became the rule, with Germanic philology, a minute investigation of the history and development of language, becoming the dominant method of literary and humanistic studies. The clergyman who dabbled in the arts and the amateur man of letters were challenged by the professional philologist. Thus, a sharp rivalry emerged at the beginnings of academic literary study between the new breed of trained research scholars who shaped the image of the fledgling profession and those who carried on the generalist traditions of nineteenth century men of letters. The scholars disdained the amateurism of the men of letters, emphasized the importance of scientific methods, and preached the primacy of factual research over evaluative judgment, which they dismissed as inherently impressionistic. The men of letters replied by disparaging the scholars' pretensions to scientific rigor and the overspecialization to which they led, arguing that such methods violated the humanistic spirit of literature in favor of meaningless accumulations of arcane data.

The notorious conflict between the researcher and the teacher had its origin here, but it was part of a larger struggle for control that pitted the professional academic against the nonacademic. In the years that immediately precede our period, this political struggle invoked two competing models of professionalism – one with its base in the university and the specialized professional journal, the other in magazine journalism. The two types remained sharply distinct even though there was considerable interaction and overlap between them, as academics crossed over into journalism and men of letters took university positions when journalistic markets dried up. Although the conflict between "academic" and "nonacademic" critics is now often only between different kinds of professors, the lines of antagonism remain much the same.

THE TRIUMPH OF CRITICISM

By 1940, the old conflict between "scholars" (academics) and "critics" (journalists) had become a three-cornered battle among research scholars on the one hand and two distinct kinds of critics on the other – literary journalists who were either outsiders to the university or internal emigrés within it, and a new group of academically trained critics. Like the nonacademic journalists, the new academic critics claimed to be correcting the insular specialization of the research scholars. The journals that typified their work, such as the *Kenyon, Southern,* and *Sewanee Reviews,* related literature to general issues of culture and politics in much the same way, though with a more conservative political slant, as did prominent nonacademic journals such as *Partisan Review* and *Commentary.* Like the scholars, however, the new academic critics claimed also to be correcting the nonsystematic generality of book reviewers and literary journalists. And in contrast to both the scholars and the journalists, these new academic critics boasted a methodology which claimed to provide, for the first time in the history of criticism, an adequate account of the literary work itself in its full structural and semantic complexity. It was this ability to reconcile academic rigor with the more general humanistic concerns of nonacademic criticism that made the New Criticism so magnetic a rallying point in the postwar American university, where an unprecedented process of democratic expansion demanded a complete overhauling of past procedures.

The new academic criticism sought at once to further professionalize and further democratize literary study. It would professionalize literary study by rigorously defining its object – the literary mode of discourse – and by evolving a distinct set of interpretive procedures that would be adequate to this object and would thereby make criticism an autonomous discipline. In an essay of 1938 significantly entitled "Criticism, Inc.," John Crowe Ransom calls on literary criticism to define "its own charter of rights and function independently" so that it might cease at last "to abdicate its own self-respecting identity."

Though this claim seemed to cut the literary world off from the world of culture and society, the very "independence" of the literary universe could function as a kind of allegory of the battle of democratic individualism against Nazi and Soviet totalitarianism, something Ransom had implied in comparing the structure of poetry to that of a "democratic state." The new academic criticism would democratize literary study by teaching its interpretive procedures to undergraduates, who would learn more from direct analysis of literary texts themselves than they had been learning from the specialized teachings of the research scholars.

It was in the postwar era that "criticism" – as distinct from "scholarship" – finally became a respectable preoccupation of literary academics. Criticism achieved this respectability by laying claim to the same severe standards of objectivity in the domain of textual interpretation and evaluation that philological and historical scholars had claimed in the domain of historical research. It was only by establishing its credentials as a *science*, one that could hold its own in competition with the other scientific disciplines, that the study of the modern literatures and languages had managed to shoulder Greek and Latin aside and become an accredited department in the modern university.

According to the positivistic mentality that dominated both the university and its literature departments in the first half-century of their existence, the business of literary scholarship was to produce genuine scientific knowledge about language and literature, something which mere literary interpretation and evaluation presumably could not do. Interpretation and evaluation were too unreliably impressionistic to be worth the attention of a serious academic discipline. The business of literary scholarship was with matters that could be objectively tested and established, like the etymological roots of the English language, the probable date of a Shakespearean sonnet, or the influences of Milton that can be identified in the poetry of Pope or Dryden.

Even as they stressed objectivity, however, the research scholars often promoted an unabashed historical relativism whereby no historical period could be measured by standards other than its own. Ironically, the historical relativism of some recent theorists, which is now attacked as a radical assault on traditional standards, closely resembles this now-forgotten relativism of traditional historical scholars, who were trying to hold the line against the revisionists of their own time. Frederick Pottle, for example, argued in *The Idiom of Poetry* (1941) that since each age had its own peculiar standard of the "good" in poetry, it was fallacious to try to erect transhistorical standards of poetic value. The only sound scholarly procedure was to describe the *Zeitgeist* of the period in its own terms and then judge its literary accomplishments accordingly. Any attempt to judge those accomplishments from a universal or transcendent perspective only led to the sorts of ahistorical and anachronistic whimsicalities to which critics were so notoriously prone. Thus scientific objectivism and historical relativism went hand in hand. Indeed, being objective meant scrupulously refusing to judge past literature by some ostensibly universal, transhistorical standard, which would inevitably be merely an ephemeral current one. Scholarship and evaluative criticism did not mix.

The research scholars commanded internal prestige within the university, but it was the literary journalists and men of letters among their colleagues who determined the image of "the English professor" in the mind of the public and the undergraduate student body, which flocked into their lecture courses in large numbers. In *The Making of Middlebrow Culture*, Joan Shelley Rubin has given a good description of this class of "middlebrow" intellectuals. Such professorial men of letters (almost all were male) as William Lyon ("Billy") Phelps of Yale, Bliss Perry of Princeton and Harvard, and John Erskine of Columbia wrote for generalist periodicals like the *Atlantic*, served on the selection boards of book clubs, and became celebrities on the public lecture circuit. They were regarded by their scholarly colleagues as at best talented dilettantes, for the very qualities that made them popular teachers and public speakers caused their colleagues to dismiss them as mere entertainers, not serious professionals. Insofar as they were "critics," then, the men of letters could not be authentically scholarly "academics."

In short, though those on both sides of the divide bemoaned the fact, there seemed a fundamental incompatibility between the needs of specialization and the needs of generality and breadth, the spirit of the professional and of the amateur. As one scholar had put it as early as 1894:

On one side are the men of letters and those whom they inspire, looking a little disdainfully upon the patient plodding, the extreme circumspection, of the philologists . . . Their ideal of the literary discourse tends toward the elegant *causerie*, which is apt to be interesting but not true. . . . On the other side are the philologists, who feel that what the literary men say consists pretty largely of cunningly-phrased guess-work, superficiality and personal bias. For their part they wish their work to rest on good foundations. It is the solidity of the fabric, not its beauty, that they care for. Thus they are tempted as a class . . . to confine themselves to somewhat mechanical investigations, such as promise definite, exact, and unassailable results. They are suspicious of the larger and more subtle questions of literature; and so their ideal gravitates in the direction of the amorphous *Abhandlung* which is apt to be true but not interesting.

Variations on the complaint have continued to appear with great frequency from the turn of the century to the present day: the scholarly and the cultural functions of literary studies operate in separate compartments. With each repetition, however, the complaint tends to be made as if it were being offered for the first time, as if the division being described had only recently taken place.

It was the boast of the new academic criticism that emerged after World War II that it could heal this dissociation of sensibility, by means of a critical method that would show how the dissociation is healed in great literature, if not in life. The key argument advanced by the new academic critics was that, contrary to their scholarly detractors, acts of literary interpretation and evaluation need not be mere subjective expressions of taste. It was only the loose, unreflective practices of literary journalists and reviewers that had given criticism a bad name, reinforcing the positivist prejudice of the scholars that criticism *had* to be loose and unreflective. The new academic critics argued that a different and more systematic approach to humanistic value judgment would overcome the gulf between fact and value.

Nor were the stakes purely literary. Many intellectuals and public officials in this period saw the rehabilitation of humanistic judgments of value as an urgent priority after two world wars, in which humanistic values had been threatened by nihilistic totalitarianisms, and in the wake of confusions about value that were blamed on modern secularism and positivistic science. Two postwar developments that reflected this anxiety about the threat to values were the revival of interest in undergraduate general education (led by Presidents James Bryant Conant of Harvard and Robert Maynard Hutchins of the University of Chicago) and the neo-Thomist movement in philosophy (in which Hutchins' colleague Mortimer J. Adler was a key figure). Both were attempts to shore up the objectivity of value judgments in the face of various forms of modern relativism.

The issue of relativism is worth pausing over, since the conservative polemics of the 1980s and 1990s have enforced the belief that student relativism is a creation of the countercultural 1960s. The historian Gertrude Himmelfarb, for example, in *The Demoralization of Society: From Victorian Virtues to Modern*

Values (1995), traces the "de-moralization" of her title to the relativism of the 1960s. In fact, complaints about student relativism were already pervasive by the 1940s and 1950s – the period according to Himmelfarb in which Victorian virtues were still intact. Writing in *Harpers* in 1940, Mortimer J. Adler observed that the undergraduates whom he and President Robert Maynard Hutchins were teaching in their great books courses at the University of Chicago "react at once against" Plato, Aristotle, St. Thomas, Locke, or any other thinkers.

who write as if truth could be reached in moral matters, as if the mind could be convinced by reasoning from principles, as if there were self-evident precepts about good or bad. They tell us, emphatically and almost unanimously, that "there is no right and wrong" [and] that "moral values are private opinion" [and] that "everything is relative."

Adler added that "All such judgments our students had learned from their teachers."

In his essay "The Study of Poetry" (1880), Matthew Arnold had argued that, with the waning of organized religion, poetry with its "criticism of life" had been forced into a central role in the preservation of values and culture against the relativizing and individualistic tendencies of modern life, where "doing as one likes" had become the dominant ethos. Given poetry's new cultural responsibilities, it was crucial that literary criticism be grounded in objective judgments of value, for only poetry of the highest quality (as measured by the severest objective test) could hope to rescue culture from corrosive relativism and secularism. Thus Arnold scolded the historical scholars of his day for elevating the mere "historical estimate" of a poet over "the real estimate" (as he also scolded aesthetes for elevating "the personal estimate"). French scholars, for example, acting out of mistaken national pride, had overrated the poetry of François Villon. If culture was to survive, it was necessary that a poetic canon be established that rested on sound objective judgments transcending the vicissitudes of historical and personal prejudice.

Postwar academic critics directed a similar set of strictures at the relativism of contemporary historical scholars. In their neglect of questions of literary value and their obsession with the accumulation of factual information, the scholars, according to the critics, had contributed to the trivialization of the humanities and general decline of evaluative discourse. The project of the academic critic, then, became to unify fact and value, description and evaluation, judgment and analysis. (Murray Krieger's *The New Apologists for Poetry* [1956] provides the best detailed analysis of this complex argument.) This unity would be accomplished by demonstrating poem by poem that the terms of literary evaluation could be derived from a close analytic reading of the literary object, itself the ultimate embodiment of the organic unity of fact and value.

It was the academic and methodological character of the emergent postwar criticism that made it controversial. Ironically, this methodological emphasis opened the new academic criticism to the charge that it was just another instance of the technological spirit that it had set out to correct. In 1943, an essay in the *American Scholar* by Darrell Abel entitled "Intellectual Criticism" faulted this criticism for treating poetry "as an intellectual exercise" and denying "that its value consists in its appeal to the feelings." Abel added that the new style of criticism expressed a "contemptuous assumption that anything capable of appreciation by common men must be low." Abel's contemporary, Donald A. Stauffer, similarly protested that the new fashion of turning poems into complicated intellectual paradoxes and ironies ignored the fact that "a poet may write with simplicity and sentiment and still remain a poet."

This was the objection lodged against Cleanth Brooks's chapter on *Macbeth* in *The Well Wrought Urn* (1947), which analyzed the play as a complex working out of the paradoxical images of "the naked babe and the cloak of manliness." The scholar Oscar James Campbell complained that though Shakespeare's figures of speech are "easily grasped without the intervention of a new critic," Brooks "finds such simple employment" of these figures "merely an adumbration of [their] more subtle manifestations." For Campbell, the paradoxes Brooks found in Lady Macbeth's speeches represented an "over-ingenious reading" that "obscures and enfeebles the stark simplicity of Lady Macbeth's utterance."

Also coming under attack for its overcomplication and technicism was the jargon of the new academic criticism, which is now frequently held up as the popular norm from which recent theoretical criticism has deviated. The objections lodged a generation ago to such terms as "paradox," "tension," and "structure" anticipate those lodged today against "valorize," "problematize," "hegemony," and other theoretical buzz words. Like current theoryspeak, these terms at their first appearance were denounced for being dehumanizing, impersonal, and pseudoscientific, and for interposing mechanical methodology between the work of literature and its potential readers. A parody published in 1943 makes the point:

Dynamic analysis proves that the most successful poetry achieves its effect by producing an expectation in the reader's mind before his sensibility is fully prepared to receive the full impact of the poem. The reader makes a proto-response which conditions him to the total response toward which his fully equilibrized organs of apperception subconsciously tend. . . . The texture and structure of the poem have erupted into a major reaction. The ambiguity of equilibrium is achieved.

Terms like "structure," "ambiguity," and "equilibrium" may now sound staidly humanistic and traditional in the wake of "the decentering of the logo-centric subject," but these words once seemed to epitomize antihumanistic scientism, and to many nonacademics they still do.

Complaints of technicism in content and style became all the more frequent as the new academic interpretive methodologies gradually became detached from the cultural rationale that had initially inspired them and became a means of generating publishable "close readings" of a mechanical and predictable kind. In short, the complaint that once humane critics have become soulless "literary technocrats" is hardly new. The charge, which is today laid at the door of post 1960s theory, was already widely leveled at the new academic critics of the forties and fifties.

WHAT WAS "NEW" ABOUT THE NEW CRITICISM?

The term that became most prominently identified with the new academic criticism, of course, was and is "the New Criticism." But though "the New Criticism" is a coinage of the period itself, the term actually meant something rather different from 1940 to 1950 than it has come to mean since. (Spingarn had used the term "new criticism" in the 1920s, but it did not become common usage.) What we now take to have been *new* about the new criticism is its emphasis on the analysis of the "text itself," primarily in its literary or aesthetic aspects. The New Criticism, as we now think of it, is distinguished by its insistence on treating literature *as* literature, apart from its genetic sources (the object of scholarship) and its cultural and moral effects (the object of literary journalists).

Thus in an essay published in 1962, Cleanth Brooks defined the New Criticism as a "strenuous attempt to focus attention upon the poem rather than upon the poet or upon the reader." The New Criticism, according to Brooks, constituted an attempt to study "the poem as a structure in its own right," "to fix the boundaries and limits of poetry" by considering "the poem as an artistic document" rather than an expression of such extraliterary states of affairs as history, biography, politics, or philosophy.

The techniques Brooks described and employed himself in analyzing "the poem as a structure in its own right" had indeed been the invention of Brooks's generation. But if we go back to the immediate climate of the 1940s, we find that what was seen as most "new" about the criticism of that period was not the trait that Brooks singled out in 1962. That critics should emphasize the formal or aesthetic dimension of literature was, after all, hardly a new idea in the 1940s. Edgar Allan Poe had strongly asserted such aestheticism in the 1840s, attacking "the heresy of the didactic" in the process, and similar doctrines had been promoted by Walter Pater and A. C. Bradley in the 1890s and by Spingarn and H. L. Mencken in the 1920s. What initially struck its contemporaries about the university criticism that emerged just after the war was not that it was determinedly aesthetic and formal, but that it was recognizably academic – that for the first time professors were producing criticism not as men of letters but as professionals equipped with systematic methodologies.

The formalism that we equate with the New Criticism today was originally only one school among a more diverse group of new academic criticisms, whose commonality lay not in any tendency to focus exclusively on aesthetic concerns but in their systematic and rigorous character. Subsequently, the term "New Criticism" (spelled in upper case) would narrow until it came to denote the school described and exemplified by Brooks – critics who elevated the text itself above its sources and effects. That is, the term narrowed until it came to denote the victorious party in what had been a heterogeneous competition of schools.

To put the point another way, the recent trend toward the "interdisciplinary" study of literature represents a revival of the academic criticism of the 1940s, not the break with it that is usually supposed. Thus when Stanley Edgar Hyman used the term "new criticism" in his 1948 survey, *The Armed Vision; A Study in the Methods of Modern Literary Criticism*, it is significant that he did *not* characterize the movement as an attempt to study "the poem as a structure in its own right" or "to fix the boundaries and limits of poetry" by considering "the poem as an artistic document." Quite the contrary, Hyman associated the new trend in criticism with a tendency to cross boundaries rather than limit them, to blur rather than shore up the distinction between literary and extraliterary spheres.

Hyman defines "the new criticism" (which he also calls "modern criticism") as "*the organized use of non-literary techniques and bodies of knowledge to obtain insights into literature.*" What is new about the new criticism for Hyman is not the narrowing of critical investigation to the poem itself, but the broadening of it by incorporating such "non-literary techniques and bodies of knowledge" as history, biography, mythography, psychology, anthropology, and rhetoric. These of course were precisely the bodies of knowledge that were cultivated by the university. "The new criticism," then, originally meant academic criticism, criticism based on academic method and a body of specialized knowledge derived from other academic disciplines.

Indeed, for Hyman even the more aesthetically oriented versions of the new criticism are a type of interdisciplinary criticism. That is, for him what Brooks would subsequently call the "intrinsic" mode of criticism is in fact an "extrinsic" mode that derives its central terms not from the literary text itself, but from the field of *linguistics*. Hyman treats I. A. Richards and Kenneth Burke as new critics not because of their formalist leanings (which would soon get them classed as members of the school) but because of their use of the extraliterary disciplines of linguistics and rhetoric. At the end of the 1940s, then, two very different "new criticisms" were contending for the right to the name, one claiming novelty because it incorporated other academic disciplines, the other claiming it because it separated itself from those disciplines.

Such an account explains the otherwise puzzling fact that *The New Criticism*, the 1941 book by John Crowe Ransom that established the name, turns out to be a *critique* of this criticism, not the positive brief that it is now widely assumed to have been. Ransom does associate "the New Criticism" with the close analysis of "the structural properties of poetry," an analysis which, "in depth and precision," he says, "is beyond all earlier criticism in our language." Ransom goes on to argue, however, that this new literary analysis has been all too frequently adulterated by such extraliterary concerns as the emotions of readers and the morality of writers.

Before the war, Ransom's view of poetry had been deeply bound up with his own extraliterary concerns, specifically the agrarian social ideas developed by Ransom and his fellow members of the Southern Fugitives group at Vanderbilt University. But by 1941, it had become clear to the group that American industrialization and urbanization were irreversible and that the agrarian program had no future. Ransom looked back at his agrarian politics as a vestige of romantic sentimentalism, insufficiently tempered by critical irony, and also as a distraction from the proper concerns of the literary critic.

Like Hyman a decade later, then, Ransom identifies "the new criticism" with the systematic importation by academics of nonliterary interests into criticism. Unlike Hyman, however, Ransom has little sympathy with this project:

Briefly, the new criticism is damaged by at least two specific errors of theory, which are widespread. One is the idea of using the psychological affective vocabulary in the hope of making literary judgments in terms of the feelings, emotions, and attitudes of poems instead of in terms of their objects. The other is plain moralism, which in the new criticism would indicate that it has not emancipated itself from the old criticism. I should like to see critics unburdened of these drags.

In Ransom's central chapters, I. A. Richards, T. S. Eliot, and Yvor Winters exemplify three characteristic failures of new critics to "emancipate" themselves from the intrusion of extraliterary frames of reference: Richards (and William Empson) represent "the Psychological Critic," Eliot "the Historical Critic," and Winters "the Logical [and moral] Critic." Seeking a more purely literary criticism, Ransom ends the book by calling for "an Ontological Critic," one whose theory and method will respect the unique knowledge poetry constitutes, "which is radically and ontologically distinct." Ransom laments the fact that he has "yet to find a new critic with an ontological account of poetry," but he would not have to wait long. In fact, he was himself already developing the "ontological" mode of criticism that within a decade would monopolize the label "New Criticism."

By 1962, Cleanth Brooks could observe that he would be happy to "drop the adjective 'new' " for the kind of criticism that examines "the structure of the poem as poem," since it is with this kind of examination and no other that "literary criticism is concerned." The implication was that the "intrinsic" analysis performed by Brooks and his school just simply *was* literary criticism – no other kind of criticism could really claim to be literary. This view won the war: subsequent generations of students who have studied literature in the way favored by Brooks have been largely unaware that they were practicing a particular *kind* of criticism, much less that they were accepting a theory. To read literature New Critically was to do criticism, period. Dominant discourses have the luxury of going unnamed and therefore unchallenged.

But for Ransom in the early 1940s, as for Hyman at the end of the decade, criticism was still a battleground of conflicting theories, with the issue far from settled whether the new way of treating literature would be as a "structure in its own right" or as a locus of social, psychological, and cultural forces. That is, the question was still open whether criticism was properly a disciplinary or interdisciplinary practice, and it is possible to imagine a hypothetical history with a different outcome from the one that actually occurred – one in which the new academic criticism ended up stressing not the autonomy of literature, as a discourse independent of philosophy, history, psychology, rhetoric, and politics, but the interdependence of these fields (and perhaps the integration of these departments in the college curriculum). Traditional critics, after all, from Sidney to Johnson to Arnold, had assumed no major disjunction between literature and other areas of life.

Even as Hyman wrote, however, at the end of the 1940s, institutional pressures inside and outside the academy were working against a more inclusively cultural view of literature. Increasingly, the project of making criticism more systematic – and thus more academically respectable – came to be identified with the project of purifying literature of its nonliterary and nonaesthetic components. Brooks would argue in his 1962 essay that the popular critics – in *Time* magazine, for example, or in the great metropolitan newspapers – continue to print their literary chitchat, their gossip, and their human interest notes on the author of the latest best-seller. And often out of the other side of their mouths, they go on to talk about the novelist's politics, his moral asseverations, and his affirmation or lack of affirmation of "life." To such people, the discussion of literary *form* is bound to seem empty. [italics in original]

What is interesting here is how the methodological carelessness of the literary journalist is made part and parcel of the journalist's inability to keep the literary realm separate from the realms of politics, morality, and biography. (It is ironic, in retrospect, that the charge of confusing realms is today the one that journalists level against academics.) For Brooks, a lack of critical rigor goes hand in hand with a failure to observe the obvious differences between literature, morality, and politics.

This view failed to note the emergence of a new breed of literary journalism after the war that itself rebelled against genteel impressionism and cultivated its own kind of intellectual rigor. The critics who became associated with the *Partisan Review* and who later would be known as "New York Intellectuals" (their outlook was best summed up by Irving Howe in an essay of that title [1970]) followed the lead of Edmund Wilson in vigorously challenging the New Critical divorce of literature from society and politics.

Like the New Critics, figures such as Howe, Philip Rahv, William Phillips, Lionel Trilling, Alfred Kazin, Leslie Fiedler, Mary McCarthy, Lionel Abel, and Harold Rosenberg identified with the modernist literary revolution of Eliot, Yeats, and Lawrence and rejected the programmatic proletarian and progressive criticism of the 1930s with its simplistic conception of literary realism. As Trilling argued in *The Liberal Imagination* (1950), which featured a telling attack on the progressivist criticism of Vernon L. Parrington ("Reality in America"), the triumph of political and cultural liberalism had infused American literary culture with a shallowly optimistic vision of historical progress and a naive idealization of the working class, whose experience was presumably authentic because rooted in the brute "reality" of material necessity. American liberalism, according to Trilling (who identified himself as a liberal), needed to go to school to the complex, tragic, ironic perspectives of literary modernism, even if those perspectives were frequently entangled with reactionary social ideals. Fiedler argued along similar lines in *An End to Innocence* (1955), which elevated Hawthorne and Melville over Emerson and the realists for their deep psychological complexity and willingness to cry "No in thunder" (in Melville's characterization of Hawthorne's message) against a culture of liberal affirmation.

Unlike the New Critics, however, writers like Trilling and Fiedler saw literature and its rejection of progressive innocence as deeply enmeshed in politics and culture. (Rahv's attack in *The Myth and the Powerhouse* [1965] on the escape from politics and history into literary autonomy and "myth" is probably the most powerful counterstatement by the *Partisan Review* critics.) Indeed, the *Partisan* criticism of the 1940s and 1950s was marked by a paradoxical fusion of reactionary modernist aesthetic ideas and the politics of the anti-Stalinist left. At the same time, critics like Trilling, Howe, and Alfred Kazin defended the continued vitality of the realist tradition, as in Kazin's *On Native Grounds* (1942) and Howe's *Politics and the Novel* (1957). Despite some common aesthetic tastes, then, the lines deepened between the political and cultural view of literature advanced by the New York Intellectuals and the theories of literary autonomy defended by the New Critics.

That it was the autonomous view of literature that won out in the university, that professional "rigor" became identified with the restriction of criticism to aesthetic concerns, is probably best explained by the institutional conditions of the departmentalized university, in which literary study was required to claim its own unique subject matter in order to legitimate itself as an academic field. If departments of physics, history, and philosophy could clearly specify their object of study, then literature departments would also need to specify theirs. It would not do if the object of literary study could be confused with the objects of other disciplines. The advancement of literary studies thus appeared to depend on the isolation of the "literary" as a distinct mode of experience and communication, the terms of which would not be reducible to those of other fields.

Rene Wellek and Austin Warren's 1949 book *Theory of Literature*, which would become the most comprehensive theoretical exposition of the New Criticism, was organized around a severe distinction between the "intrinsic" study of literature, which for Wellek and Warren was a truly literary study, and the "extrinsic" study of literature, which had its legitimacy but whose very name marked it as extraliterary and therefore secondary. Although debate about the proper method and boundaries of literary study continued well beyond the publication of *Theory of Literature* (indeed, it continues to this day), what was clear beyond any doubt by the end of the 1940s was that the emergent American criticism would be academic: analytically rigorous, rationalized, and professional, and "armed" with one or another methodology of interpretation.

It was this methodologically "armed" quality, flaunted in the title of Hyman's *The Armed Vision*, that initially made the new academic criticism so unsettling to those of more traditional literary tastes. This was the aspect of Hyman's book that was noticed by reviewers and by poet–critics like Randall Jarrell, who clearly had academic criticism in mind when he complained in 1952, in what became a famous essay, "The Age of Criticism," that "critics are so much better armed than they used to be in the old days: they've got tanks and flame-throwers now, and it's harder to see past them to the work of art – in fact, magnificent creatures that they are, it's hard to *want* to see past them" [italics in original].

THE RISE OF INTERPRETATION AND THE INVENTION OF "MEANING"

It has become common today to attack poststructuralist theory for having promoted the importance of the critic and theorist over that of the creative artist. But poststructuralism is not the first academic school to be accused of elevating itself over its literary objects. The accusation was frequently leveled at academic critics in the early 1950s: "Criticism," wrote Jarrell, "which began humbly and anomalously existing for the work of art, and was in part a mere by-product of philosophy and rhetoric, has now become, for a good many people, almost what the work of art exists for."

While conceding that critics are "often useful and wonderful and a joy to have around the house," Jarrell nonetheless branded them

the bane of our age, because our age so fantastically overestimates their importance and so willingly forsakes the works they are writing about for them. . . . We are brought into the world by specialists; more and more people think of the critic as an indispensable middle man between writer and reader, and would no more read a book alone, if they could help it, than have a baby alone.

Here the reaction against academic criticism blended with a more generalized post-romantic attack on professionalism and technocratic specialization, which were felt to have deprived readers of what deconstructionists would later call the "self-present" experience of literature.

Jarrell's anxieties were well founded, for *The Armed Vision* was not a neutral survey but a manifesto directed against the *personal* style of criticism exemplified by Jarrell and most influentially at the time by Edmund Wilson. The two critics who come off worst in Hyman's book are Wilson and Yvor Winters, who in fact loathed "personal" criticism himself, but whose stress on the morality of poetry and the importance of evaluation linked him in Hyman's mind with Wilson and the nonacademic tradition. (As for Wilson, Hyman's chapter on him was so vitriolic that it was omitted from later editions of the book.) Thus the opposition between the personal and the disciplinary approach to literature became part of the deepening warfare between journalists (and poets) and academics.

Jarrell's response to this denigration of the personal exemplified a growing reaction against academic criticism. It was not just that academic critics had

ceased to be humble servants of literature or that, in collusion with modernist writers, they were aridly elevating the brain over the heart. What was
really dismaying to many about the new academic criticism was the centrality it accorded to *interpretation*, which challenged the traditional belief that in
its primary appeal great literature was basically *simple*. To make explication a
central function of criticism was seemingly to suggest that the grounds on
which readers had heretofore valued literature had been mistaken, that great
literature achieved its effects not through straightforward simplicity of sentiment but through complicated, self-reflective analysis, and that literature
therefore needed a cadre of professional explicators to unearth its meanings.
It was the notion that literature was a locus of complicated "meanings" that
aroused anxiety – and with good reason.

For the glorification of "meaning" was of a piece with the view of modernist
writers like T. S. Eliot that an increasingly complex and fragmented culture
requires a literature of corresponding difficulty. As Eliot put it, "poets in our
civilization, as it exists at present, must be *difficult*," for "our civilization
comprehends great variety and complexity," and therefore "the poet must
become more and more comprehensive, more allusive, more indirect, in order
to force, to dislocate if necessary, language into his meaning." Eliot was
highly ambivalent about the new state of hyperconsciousness. He recognized
that critical interpretation was necessitated not only by the increased difficulty of modern poetry, but by the dissolution of shared assumptions in a
democratized state of culture. In an urban, democratic culture, tacitly shared
assumptions break down and it becomes necessary for meanings which previously had been felt to go without saying to be explicitly spelled out. Eliot saw
that the very existence of criticism was a symptom that culture had become a
problem to be argued about rather than something that can be unselfconsciously inherited and experienced, as Eliot imagined Dante's poetry had been
unselfconsciously inherited and experienced by Medieval Europe.

Allan Bloom bitterly laments this loss of unselfconscious cultural inheri-
tance in *The Closing of the American Mind*. "[A]s soon as tradition has come to
be recognized as tradition, it is dead, something to which lip service is paid,"
Bloom writes. A living tradition is simply lived and therefore does not know
itself *as* tradition. Once tradition names itself as such, it has become mere
interpretation, theory, abstraction, existing at a secondary remove from living tradition and vulnerable to a myriad of disagreements and conflicts. Long
before Bloom's assault on multiculturalism, the spread of academic interpretation aroused such anxieties about the loss of order and shared meaning, even
among critics like Eliot, who were among its pioneering figures and who
provided it with its artistic objects. The very emergence of criticism – and
Eliot would say the same thing about the emergence of mass education –

presupposed the collapse of culture in the traditional sense and the advent of a condition of democratic dissensus. Eliot observed that "the necessity of criticism" arises "when the poet finds himself in an age in which there is no intellectual aristocracy" and power is in the hands of a "democratised" class. Accepting this development only with resignation, Eliot attacked "the lemon-squeezer school" of criticism for pushing the interpretive impulse to excess.

Here is one reason why it is important to recover the fact that the "new criticism" originally denoted the general movement toward academic and analytic criticism rather than a single school within that movement. What especially distinguished all the schools of academic criticism from traditional journalistic criticism and made them seem unusual and disturbing to popular taste was the emphasis they placed on the self-conscious interpretation of literary meanings, whether this interpretation was mounted from a formal, linguistic, psychological, or anthropological point of view. From the nonacademic perspective, certainly, this has always been the most striking and mysterious feature of academic criticism, not its formalist tendency but its obsession with the idea that texts possess something that undergraduates call "hidden meaning."

To put the point more provocatively, the effect of the new academic criticism was nothing less than to reinvent "literature" and reading. Literature ceased to be a discourse of simple home truths and familiar emotions and became a discourse of complex and self-reflexive meanings that demanded interpretive self-consciousness on the part of readers. We may eventually look back at this development, which was largely accomplished by 1955, as a far more dramatic turning point than any of the more spectacular upheavals of the 1970s and 1980s. Once literature had become a discourse of hidden meanings, requiring the ministrations of the methodologically armed critic, all criticism tended to look alien, academic, and overly methodological whether it was New Critical, feminist, or deconstructionist. Postwar academic critics transformed literature from an object of factual research and of casual appreciation into something that counts as having been successfully *read* only if the reader is aware of the work's deeper meanings. Literature was something not to be "just" read for pleasure, but to be reread, analyzed, taken apart and put back together. Reading itself was a scene not of reassuring and inspiring certainties to be turned to when the complexities of life became too pressing, but of *problems* to be endlessly worried and debated.

Again, this disturbing implication all but disappeared from view once interpretation became a routine, if not a routinized, activity in classrooms and academic journals, and once difficult modern and postmodern literary works became canonical and familiar. At the outset of the postwar period, however, the idea that literature was in need of interpretation was still a disturbing and controversial one. And the idea is still disturbing and confusing to many students and other lay people, who think of literature and the humanities as something to be enjoyed rather than analyzed or treated as a field of problems.

Insofar as the culture resisted this way of thinking, those who accused the New Critics of abandoning the common reader were right, though the New Critics would have reasonably replied that they were not betraying common readers so much as trying to retrain them (if not training them for the first time). Our culture still, however, tends to think of reading as an unproblematic activity, a mechanical skill that, once learned in the first grade, can henceforth be taken for granted. That explains much of the resentment against the notion that there is any need for a cadre of institutionalized interpreters, performing elaborate analytical operations on literature, rather than "just reading" it. New Critical theory and practice suggested that there were different, even clashing ways of reading, that reading itself could be a field of contention.

THE RISE OF EXPLICATION

What was and is so disturbing about interpretation? As Jarrell's satiric comments above suggest, the appeal and cultural value of literature had long been felt to lie not in its complexity of meaning – at least not in any sense of "meaning" that demanded rigorous interpretation – but in an intuitive accessibility that struck home to the receptive reader without elaborate efforts at analysis. (Those who did not get it clearly were unreceptive.) If anything, the personal and social consolation offered by literature was felt to operate more effectively the more the text made its impact simply and passionately, and the less it needed to be taken apart, analyzed, and rationalized by the critic. (These assumptions help explain the prominent role of memorization and recitation in literature teaching up to recently.) A work that demanded elaborate explication was felt to that extent to be an inferior, excessively self-conscious work, marred by the "cerebral" quality that Van Wyck Brooks and others complained of in modernist works like *The Waste Land* and *Ulysses*.

Though passages that would now qualify as explication can be found in the work of Coleridge, A. C. Bradley, and other nineteenth-century critics, the convention that criticism should closely analyze works of literature was surprisingly late in emerging. From the late nineteenth century to World War II, criticism still tended to be a discourse not about literary *works* at all, but about the qualities of *authors* and their general milieu. Here is how Henry James wrote about Hawthorne in his biography of 1875:

The cold, bright air of New England seems to blow through his pages, and these, in the opinion of many people, are the medium in which it is most agreeable to make the acquaintance of that tonic atmosphere.

And here is how Van Wyck Brooks writes of Jonathan Edwards and Edgar Allan Poe in *America's Coming-of-Age* (1915):

> The intellect of Jonathan Edwards was like the Matterhorn, steep, icy, and pinnacled. At its base were green slopes and singing valleys filled with all sorts of little tender wild-flowers – for he was the most lovable of men; but as soon as the ground began to rise in good earnest all this verdurous life came to an abrupt end: not one green or living thing could subsist in that frozen soil, on those pale heights.
> In [Poe's] pages the breath of life never stirs: crimes occur which do not reverberate in the human conscience, there is laughter which has no sound. . . . it is a silent world, cold, blasted, moon-struck, sterile, a devil's heath.
> . . . Orchids are as much a part of the vegetable kingdom as potatoes, but Poe is an orchid made out of chemicals.

This is the sort of writing that even to the journalistic eye would cease to look like genuine "criticism" in the 1940s. If any single work defined the new pattern, it was F. O. Matthiessen's massive *American Renaissance*, the first major application of New Critical explication to American literature. Whereas Van Wyck Brooks had surveyed the whole of American writing and culture in 183 pages, Matthiessen takes 656 pages to discuss five writers.

It is not surprising that Brooks, who lived long enough to witness this change, bitterly attacked the new explication as a trivializing reduction of criticism to an exercise in crossword puzzle solving by an arrogant coterie. Brooks objected in 1953 that the New Criticism "stimulates the cerebral faculties at the expense of the feelings upon which the normal growth of the writer depends," and he blamed it for having "stopped the circulation of the blood in both novels and poems." This reaction against the "cerebral" turn of criticism – which is ultimately a reaction against interpretation – would continue to resurface periodically from the 1950s through the early 1980s – in polemics like Karl Shapiro's *In Defense of Ignorance* (1960), Susan Sontag's *Against Interpretation* (1966), and Tom Wolfe's *From Bauhaus to Our House* (1981) – when it would transmogrify into the attack on "theory." Once theory had become the target, however, the New Criticism was redefined as part of the good old tradition that has been abandoned, with the very fact that it was itself once the target of this charge being forgotten.

The anti-interpretive attitude went hand in hand with a traditional belief that the social ethos of great literature was essentially *the same* as that of the respectable classes. Since the well bred reader presumably shared an unspoken moral and social consensus with the great writer, that reader was already in a sense in possession of the meaning of the work before reading it and therefore needed no intrusive interpretive critics to impart it. The hold of this anti-interpretive viewpoint helps account for the relative lateness of the emergence of the idea that the literature of our own culture needs to be *taught* in schools and colleges. Such an attitude also helps explain how James, Van Wyck Brooks, and their readers could have been content with a sentence like "The cold, bright air of New England seems to blow through his pages" as a meaningful characterization of Hawthorne's work. Such a sentence presupposes a reader who already has some familiarity with Hawthorne's work (to say nothing of New England) and who already embraces the social values presumably embodied in the work without the critic's having to spell them out. If you are used to reading Poe and sharing certain characterizations of him with friends and family, hearing Poe described as an orchid made out of chemicals can make perfect sense.

By contrast, the new idea of the critic as an analyst, interpreter, and teacher assumed an audience that did not necessarily share any particular information or social values, including the value of reading literature in the first place. It assumed that, if anything, literature had become a kind of counter discourse, in opposition to the official social consensus and its stereotyped languages. In short, the rise of interpretive criticism in the academy and its extension into the classroom was a symptom of the breakdown of a genteel consensus on the nature not only of literature but of modern society.

Here is where the threatening nature of interpretation becomes clear. If literature needs to be interpreted as well as enjoyed, if interpretation is *already* invisibly present even as literature is being read and enjoyed, then the purity and self-sufficiency of the literary experience is compromised from the start. To concede that literature requires acts of interpretation from its readers is to concede that literature is not self-interpreting, that the literary text itself does not exactly tell us how we are supposed to read it, or that a text's own self-interpretation may be disputed. That is, the need for interpretation implies a possible difference between a text's ostensible meaning and its "deeper" meaning. Even more disturbingly, it implies the inescapability of differences among readers and therefore the dissolution of a common culture.

Jacques Derrida, as we shall see in Chapter 5, reminds us that the self-division implicit in interpretation was precisely what disturbed Plato about *writing:* unlike face-to-face oral speech, Plato thought, a text cannot fully control the way it is read, cannot prevent contexts being applied to it that its author never foresaw or imagined. To concede that literature is dependent on interpretation is to concede that it lacks something and needs to be completed by readers, critics, and critical discussion. It assumes that literary traditions are created by critics, by critical selection from the sum total of literature itself, and by a process of critical struggle within and between groups of readers.

If readers are necessarily interpreters, then their acts of interpretation are bound to conflict, introducing discord and contention into a literary realm that, since the romantic period, has often been assigned the role of restoring us to the unity and wholeness that technological and commercial society presumably denies us. The conflict of interpretations – intensified by the multiplying and proliferating perspectives from which it is possible to read, and further intensified by the diversity of readers in a democratized society – threatens to intervene between the common reader and the pleasure of the text. As the clatter of critical discord echoes all about us, the common reader himself – who may be a herself – is invaded by an unwanted swarm of conflicting interpretive perspectives, casting doubt on the very idea of a single "common reader."

If the foregoing analysis is correct, then the rise of interpretive methodologies in postwar academic criticism cannot be dismissed (as many on both the left and right have dismissed them) as a self-serving enterprise that academic critics have promoted not in response to a genuine cultural demand but in order to legitimate and consolidate their institutional power. Though this motive may have played a role in academic interpretation, such interpretation has been a response to the collapse of a consensus (or the opening of debate) about the nature and cultural function of literature.

By the same token, the rise of postwar academic interpretation cannot be simply celebrated or damned as a conservative, canonizing force. It is true, as Jane Tompkins shows in *Sensational Designs*, that the academic critics of the 1940s delegitimated both the sentimental and the populist traditions of American writing in order to canonize an "American Renaissance" consisting of a small number of white male novelists and poets. It is also true, however, that postwar interpretive methodologies worked to undermine the very canonical distinctions that the critics helped construct. For there is something in the very operation of analytic methodology that tends to level status hierarchies, because such methodology can be applied to vastly different cultural objects. If analysis reveals that the same narrative structures, say, are found in certain classical myths, the nineteenth century novel, and a television sitcom, then the myth, the novel, and the sitcom begin to look more like one another than they did before.

Despite their effort to restrict concepts like complexity, paradox, and mythic vision to works of high culture, then, the postwar academic methodologies had subversive implications that their users did not intend. These implications could be seen in a linguistic analysis of a Sunkist Orange Juice advertisement by the traditional philologist Leo Spitzer. They were made explicit by Leslie Fiedler, who demonstrated in *An End to Innocence* (1955) that it was possible to "give to the testimony of a witness before a Senate committee or the letters of the Rosenbergs the same careful scrutiny we have learned to practice on the shorter poems of Donne." Long before poststructuralism arrived on the scene, then, postwar academic criticism arrived at the levelling discovery that anything can be treated as a "text."

3

❦

THE NATIONALIZING OF THE
NEW CRITICISM

THE PROJECT OF TEXTUAL INTERPRETATION that distinguished the new postwar academic criticism contained a potentially explosive contradiction. On the one hand, by challenging the anti-interpretive bias of academic scholars and literary journalists, the new academic critics exposed the breakdown of a genteel consensus about the nature and cultural function of literature. Their assertion that literature required interpretation implicitly opened literary study to conflicts that had previously been unspoken or papered over. On the other hand, the school of the new academic criticism that became the most influential – and which, accordingly, came to be labelled "the New Criticism" – emphasized the separation of literature from political and moral judgments. With its insistence that the literary text be read as "a structure in its own right," whose explication required a systematic "ontological" criticism, the New Criticism circumscribed the allowable forms of critical conflict, thereby containing the most radical implications of its own insistence on interpretation.

In several respects, however, the New Critics' radical emphasis on interpretation and their conservative exclusion of "extraliterary" arguments from the arena of professional critical debate were entirely compatible. Both tendencies enabled literary studies to establish itself as an accredited discipline in the postwar university. The New Critical theory of literature as an autonomous, self-contained form of discourse and the New Critical method of close textual analysis gave academic literary study a distinctive domain, separate from the supposedly extraliterary disciplines of sociology, psychology, history, and philosophy. And both New Critical theory and method were ideally suited to the task of teaching a vastly expanded and demographically more diverse population of college students. Lacking strong backgrounds in languages or history, such students could nonetheless elicit the "intrinsic" meanings of works of literature – especially when these works were short lyric poems of the kind that the New Critics took to exemplify literariness – by learning to apply the distinctive principles of textual interpretation. Rigorous interpretation that excluded the "extraliterary," then, fit the needs of the discipline and the student body alike.

Among the elements defined as "extraliterary" by the New Critics were the authors of literary texts, who were marginalized if not completely banished by the doctrine of the "intentional fallacy" set forth in an influential essay by W. K. Wimsatt and Monroe Beardsley (1954). Widely misunderstood then and now, this essay did not categorically dismiss the concept of author's intention but argued that the most reliable *evidence* for such intention was the work itself rather than the biography of the author (or his social milieu). Biographers, literary psychoanalysts, and historical scholars, they argued, were too often prone to substitute an account of the poet's life and beliefs for the hard work of closely reading the poem itself, which often conflicted with the poet's real-life beliefs and commitments.

The doctrine of the intentional fallacy tempered but did not discourage literary biographers, however, who incorporated the methods of the New Criticism to produce a new kind of "critical" biography. Richard Ellmann's *Yeats: The Man and the Masks* (1949) and *James Joyce* (1959) combined traditional biographical narration with thickly textured explication of *Ulysses* and other major works. Other notable critical biographies in this period include Leon Edel's three-volume work on Henry James (1953–72), which deployed a more psychoanalytic method, and Ernest Samuels' *Henry Adams* (1948–64).

New Critical strictures on extraliterary concerns in criticism would seem to present even greater difficulties to literary nationalists than to literary biographers. In the wake of the United States's postwar assumption of superpower status, many sought to celebrate American national identity by locating the "Americanness" of American literature. But, according to the prevailing New Critical view, the autonomy of a great work of literature required that it transcend its nationality, a quality extrinsic to poetic structure. The modernist generation of writers that shaped the taste of the New Critics – including figures such as Pound, Eliot, and Joyce – had been an expatriate generation that saw literature as an international rather than a national phenomenon. Strong insistence on the Americanness of American literature, then, struck the New Critics as a provincial and regressive attempt to prop up a discredited romanticism.

In *Modern Poetry and the Tradition* (1938), Cleanth Brooks had dismissed the nativist poetic school of Carl Sandburg and Edgar Lee Masters as an inferior rival of "the tradition" denoted by his title, which had been defined and exemplified by the Europeanized T. S. Eliot. The American poet who sloughed off dead conventions only "to write of American scenes, American things, and the American people," Brooks remarked, tended to become a purveyor of "self-conscious nationalism" or a "local colorist" who was "content merely with the presentation of a surface." Neither project, Brooks judged, prompted true poetic originality or enabled the would-be rebel against Victorian restrictions to make "much more than superficial changes in the organization of his poetry." Walt Whitman may have written that "the United States themselves are essentially the greatest poem," and Emerson may have celebrated the "new yet unapproachable America I have found in the West" as "a poem in our eyes . . . [which] will not wait long for metres." But for the New Critics, great poems were not created by abandoning formal conventions and making one's verse an unmediated expression of the national soul.

Ostensibly, then, postwar New Criticism and American literary nationalism did not mix. In fact, however, the New Criticism was often assimilated with surprising ease by an emergent Americanist criticism. New Critical attitudes strongly colored the work of the first generation of academic Americanists, who constructed American literature as a distinct object of study, much as an earlier generation had constructed "English." How an avowedly apolitical and asocial criticism came to celebrate American national identity will be the subject of this chapter.

NATIONAL AND DISCIPLINARY IDENTITY IN THE 1940S

Again, Spiller's *Literary History of the United States* proves illuminating. In a recent discussion of its origins and development, Kermit Vanderbilt observes that the *LHUS* was "initiated in a period of nationalistic sentiment and progressive thought that was succeeded by the heightened self-awareness and patriotic emotion that course through a nation in wartime." As the "ands" in this characterization imply, the contributors to the *LHUS* assumed that a natural connection existed between nationalistic sentiment and progressive thought, between patriotic emotion and heightened self-awareness. In hindsight, such assumed connections look more than a little ideological. For most American intellectuals of the late 1930s through the mid-1940s, however, "ideology" meant the fascism of Hitler and Mussolini and the betrayed socialist ideal exemplified by Stalin's purges and his nonaggression pact with Hitler. In relation to these totalitarian forces during the war and in its aftermath, it seems to us difficult to deny that the United States advanced progressive interests in the world. Under these circumstances, it was possible to think that belief in American democracy was not an ideology at all, but a condition that would later be described as "the end of ideology."

Subsequent events – Vietnam, chronic poverty and racial violence in liberal northern cities, Watergate, the Iran-contra scandal, U.S.-sponsored political oppression in South and Central America – would force a skeptical reexamination of this view. Indeed, at stake in current literary and cultural conflicts is often a clash between the triumphalist view that sees the last hundred years of world history as "the American century" and a critical reaction against U.S. pretensions to be a model of democracy and a neutral world arbiter.

In 1948, however, a patriotic rather than a critical self-awareness animated the study of American literature. Critics like R. P. Blackmur argued that the U.S.'s emergence as the dominant power in the postwar world required mature cultural institutions commensurate with this elevated political status. Though American literature had first come into being as a distinct academic field in the 1920s and 1930s, until the 1950s it had remained a marginal offering of English departments in American colleges. Vanderbilt reports in *American Literature and the Academy* that, of 711 colleges and universities listed in the *Educational Directory* for 1946–7, only 30 required a course in American literature for graduation and less than a quarter required it for English majors. Thus, to the editors of *Literary History of the United States* fell the unfinished task of legitimating American literature as a subject befitting America's new international prestige. That meant circumscribing American literature as a distinctive whole, isolating the works that constituted the field, identifying what was distinctively American about these works, and, finally demonstrating their parity with the established English classics.

These goals underlie the commitment to organic synthesis that is apparent in Spiller's opening "Address to the Reader," which stresses that America's "major writers" wrote literature of transcendent aesthetic value. The time is past, Spiller announces, in which historians of American literature need write either "as if they were describing transplanted English flowers and trees" or out of mere "zeal for argument and . . . eagerness to establish our originality." Rather, the historian's emphasis can justly fall on "the timeless values" contained in the works of "the Poes, the Hawthornes, and all writers who were primarily artists." America has sufficiently produced such writers. "Our national history," Spiller continues (with echoes of Emerson's "American Scholar" that were no doubt deliberate), "is already long enough to have had its periods of maturity and fruition. . . . We are not dependent upon the topical and the timely, the imitative or the unconsciously intuitive, upon the half-gods of journalism, or the sprawlings or conventions of experimental or commercialized fiction."

That historians like Spiller still needed to sound the drums for American literature, however, indicated that doubts still persisted about the field's academic legitimacy. If the professional or disciplinary status of literary criticism remained at issue during the period spanned by the composition of the *LHUS*, the standing of American literature study was even more contested and precarious. In 1940 The American Literature Group of the Modern Language Association had declined to sponsor a comprehensive history of American literature on the grounds that historical and bibliographical research on particular authors and periods was not yet sufficient. Spiller and his associates were therefore obliged to proceed with the *LHUS* as a private venture. Moreover, they did so as scholars who, given the position of American literature in the academy, were necessarily self-taught Americanists. Even F. O. Mathiessen, whose monumental *American Renaissance* (1941) more than any other single work initiated the critical recognition of American literature, had written his doctoral dissertation on the Elizabethan art of translation. Thus, a double burden fell upon Spiller's and Matthiessen's generation of American literary historians: to justify both the value of American literature and the disciplinary credentials of their critical enterprise.

This double burden inspired the new Americanists to fashion a process of mutual validation by which interpretive demonstrations of the value of the works that American literary history canonized validated the project of American literary history itself. Yet, to rigorous New Critics like Cleanth Brooks and Wellek and Warren, there was something suspect about the use of New Critical concepts to make literary history, let alone romantic literary nationalism, respectable. In an essay entitled "The Fall of Literary History," Wellek attacked the *LHUS* as a mere "omnium gatherum" of unrelated materials that only demonstrated "the impasse which literary history had reached in our time." The impasse, according to Wellek, was that the very project of "literary history" cannot be reconciled with the uniqueness and autonomy of works of literature. That was why most national literary histories were usually either not literary or not histories, Wellek claimed, but merely superficial accounts of discrete texts, movements, and authors presented in chronological order.

For literary historians, however, the old analogy between organically unified poems and organically homogeneous (as opposed to fragmented industrial) nations had never lost the charge it had carried in Carlyle, Ruskin, Arnold, and later American critics like Van Wyck Brooks. Indeed, the Southern New Critics had invoked the analogy between poetic and social organisms in their earlier agrarian period. Thus it was not surprising that the very tools that New Critics like Wellek had devised for analyzing organic literary works were used by Americanist critics of the 1950s and 1960s to demonstrate that larger organic development of American literature as a whole that Spiller and his contributors had only been able to assert.

When Spiller urged the need to see American literature's "central integrity," then, he quietly resolved the conflict between an older romantic organicism and the emergent New Criticism. Subsequent Americanist criticism would follow his lead. Evidently there was no contradiction between treating literary texts "strictly within the margins of art" and charting a coherent national tradition, both of which Spiller claimed the *LHUS* had done. Intrinsic criticism of American works could validate the credentials of American literary history, just as intrinsic criticism had validated the disciplinary credentials of the literature department.

Thus, just as Ransom a decade earlier had urged criticism to claim "its own charter of rights and function independently," so Spiller invokes a similar charter for the self-respecting, integral identity of American literature and its historical study. Approaching the *LHUS* in a manner resembling a New Critic approaching a poem, Spiller emphasizes system, eschews controversy, and adopts a characteristic tone of measured and dispassionate judgment. As the recent maturation of academic criticism had, in Spiller's view, allowed formalist critics to begin to demonstrate "the unity of art," critically informed literary historians would now give American literature a similar foundation.

Of course, both within the academy and in the general culture at midcentury, the model of dispassionate and systematic inquiry that resolves and transcends controversy was science. This image of science played an important role in the development of modern academic criticism, which defined its enterprise in ambivalent and shifting relation to scientific claims and values. During the years in which the *LHUS* was conceived and executed, the stakes of this love-hate relationship with science seemed especially high to literary intellectuals. On the one hand, Ransom and others held science responsible for the dominance of the quantitative and the abstract in modern life and the loss of quality and texture in human experience. Science neglected and devalued what Ransom called "the world's body," leaving it to be restored by literature. On the other hand, these critics themselves drew on the prestige of scientific discourse and method in defining the principles of their own discipline in an academy where science and objectivity were still the standards of all knowledge worth the name. Thus, while most of the authors of the *LHUS* tended to think of American literature – and of American democracy itself – as uniquely nonsystematic, undetermined, free, possessed of a "native suspicion of cults and dogmas" and a "very American . . . insistence on an open universe," the example of the modern sciences' "vast organized bodies of knowledge" (in Hyman's phrase) underlay their confidence that, in criticism as well, "the moment had arrived for . . . the undertaking of a whole view of literature."

THE AMERICAN CANON AS A NEW CRITICAL POEM

By the early 1960s, Spiller's hope for an organized and holistic American literary history had been realized in the work of a number of academic critics whose theorizations of "Americanness" had firmly established the field of American literature and their own credentials as "Americanists." These theorists defined and circumscribed a set of formal and thematic criteria of Americanness, much as the New Critics had defined and circumscribed the quality of "the poetic." In thus systematizing the meaning of American literature and culture, the Americanists of the 1950s and 1960s resolved the apparent incompatibility between a rigorous theory of American identity and America's presumably democratic, pluralistic, and individualistic resistance to systematic definition. The way to overcome this difficulty, it turned out, was to model the vision of Americanness on the New Critics' vision of a poem as a dialectical synthesis of opposites, a structure sustained by irony. Despite New Criticism's general mistrust of literary nationalism, moreover, Ransom himself had charted the path toward the nationalization of New Critical poetics.

Even as he stressed the "ontological" separation of poetry from society, Ransom's own metaphors at times implicitly returned poets to the role Shelley had assigned them of unacknowledged legislators of the world. In *The New Criticism,* published in 1941, as allied democracies battled the threat of a totalitarian world order, Ransom described the poem as "a democratic state." The poem, Ransom explained, was like a democratic state in that "it restrains itself faithfully from a really imperious degree of organization," allowing for and even encouraging a great deal of heterogeneity among its individual constituents – its images and details. Extending the conceit, Ransom wrote that the poem "wants its citizens to retain their personalities and enjoy their natural interests," and he distinguished on this basis between poetic and mathematical argument. The poetic argument is "weakly regulatory." It is the constituent details that have all the distinction; they "luxuriate, and display energy in unpredictable ways, going far beyond the prescription of paraphrase." The tension between cognitive "structure" and imagistic "texture" or heterogeneous detail in poetry, then, resembled the tension that American liberal democracy had resolved between regulation and freedom. To be sure, poetry for Ransom remained ultimately beyond nationality – "the poem" he analogized to a democratic state was any good poem written in any time and place. But this caveat could easily drop away if one wished to conceive the United States as a kind of New Critical poem – Whitman and Emerson had not been so wrong after all.

A similar paradoxical synthesis of formalist poetics and democratic politics is advanced in the introduction to Matthiessen's *American Renaissance.* Matthiessen's criteria for classic American literature and valuable literary criticism seem frankly political. *American Renaissance* claims and celebrates "the one common denominator" of its five exemplary mid-nineteenth century

American writers: "their devotion to the possibilities of democracy." Whatever the differences between and within the individual works of Emerson, Thoreau, Hawthorne, Melville, and Whitman, Matthiessen writes, "what emerges from the total pattern of their achievement . . . is literature for our democracy." Service to democracy was also the measure of the critic's value. Quoting the Whitman-inspired modern architect Louis Sullivan, Matthiessen suggests that

[The critic's] works must so reflect his scholarship as to prove that it has drawn him toward his people, not away from them; . . . that his scholarship has been applied for the good and the enlightenment of all the people, not for the pampering of a class. His works must prove, in short (and the burden of proof is on him), that he is a citizen, not a lackey, a true exponent of democracy.

Matthiessen's expressly political commitment, however, is uneasily coupled with a critical and literary formalism. Even as he asserts, with Sullivan, that the " 'one fundamental test' " of the critic's work is whether it advances democracy, whether he is " 'using such gifts as [he possesses] for or against the people,' " Matthiessen insists that "the critic's chief responsibility . . . is to examine an author's resources of language and of genres, in a word, to be preoccupied with form." Similarly, the devotion to democracy by which Matthiessen proposes to measure American writers is evidenced not in the direct political content of their work but in its language and form. Thus Hawthorne, a political conservative, makes it into Matthiessen's pantheon because his complex "fusions of form and content," his "variety of symbolical reference," and the characteristic "device of multiple choice" by which he creates interpretive opportunity for his reader enact the complexities and "possibilities of democracy." By contrast, the most widely read and politically effective novel written in the period that Matthiessen discusses, Harriet Beecher Stowe's *Uncle Tom's Cabin* (1852), is excluded, even though it is hard to imagine a work more devoted to democratic values or to "the good and enlightenment of all the people" rather than "the pampering of a class." Because Stowe's novel seeks not only to enact the possibilities of democracy in imagination but to promote political freedom in fact, it is relegated to the status of propaganda, according to Matthiessen's criteria for both art and democracy. (Indeed, the dismissal of *Uncle Tom's Cabin* would be a rallying point for the subsequent feminist critique of the aesthetic and political assumptions that Matthiessen and other theorists of American literature brought to the shaping of the American canon.)

In his political life, Matthiessen's socialism was genuine, active, and unquestionably progressive. Yet the vision of democracy that *American Renaissance* conveys exemplifies "the counter-Progressive consensus" that Russell Reising has traced in postwar theories of the Americanness of American literature, a consensus that emerged in the wake of the domestic and international catastrophes of the 1930s and 1940s. Drawing on the work of historian Gene Wise, Reising observes that prominent postwar historians such as Louis Hartz, Richard Hofstadter, and Daniel Boorstin shared with literary critics such as Perry Miller, Lionel Trilling, R. W. B. Lewis, and Henry Nash Smith "a model of history characterized by ambiguity, paradox, and irony" that opposed the earlier "Progressive (they would say naive) model of steady linear progress." Reising adds that these historians and critics "rejected the materialistic emphasis on economics and politics," which they felt to be an inadequate explanation of human experience, in favor of "an analysis of culture," focusing on human expression in psychology, art, and literature. To varying degrees, this shift represented an "internalization of reality."

It is no accident that many of the critics of this period came to literary criticism fresh from the disappointment of one of two kinds of reformist political agenda. The early New Critics were led by former southern agrarians, political and cultural conservatives who had in the 1930s sought to arrest America's inexorable development into an urban, secular, industrialized, and alienating mass society. Many influential early theorists of American literature were former socialists, who had been disillusioned by Stalin's betrayal of their ideals and by the rise of fascism in Europe and had settled for what historian Richard H. Pells describes as "a mixture of contentment and uneasiness with the organization and values of contemporary American society." For the postwar generation of academic critics, then, literary study was often in some degree both a refuge from their failed social programs and a way of recouping them.

Ambiguity, paradox, and irony, of course, were terms used by Brooks, Ransom, Allen Tate, and other New Critics to define the unique features of literature. They were what presumably distinguished the rich language of literature from the meanly instrumental language of science and the reductive propaganda of political discourse. Yet the New Critics also suggested that the special linguistic density that makes literature uniquely literary ultimately makes it more "real" than what usually passes for description of reality. (As Murray Krieger observed in a 1967 essay that pointed out the "existential basis" of the New Criticism, this New Critical position was influenced by contemporary European existentialist thinkers like Sartre and Martin Heidegger, who also identified literature with the deep interiority of immediate experience and saw it as an antidote to the abstraction and inauthenticity of modern technocracy.) Ransom, for example, argued that "the density or connotativeness of poetic language reflects the world's density," in contrast to "the docile and virtuous world which science pictures." Therefore, the "world of art is the actual world which does not bear restriction."

The leading historians and critics of the counter-Progressive consensus no longer believed that economic and political developments were likely to close the gap between America's ideal self-image and its social reality. Yet perhaps that was not necessary since the imaginative ideal was already "real," being deeply rooted in the culture, in Americans' inner or psychological lives. This double vision of America as an irresolvable tension, the site of a poetic quest that could neither be realized nor relinquished as a fact of American life, had particular disciplinary appeal for English professors. If, like the complex modern poem, American identity and experience were informed by ambiguity, irony, and paradox, then the explicative abilities of literary critics were crucial to the discovery of a long-sought national identity. If literature embodied the real America, then the critics' work was central to the life of the nation and criticism was not the poor relation it seemed to be to the more technical or practical occupations. Paradoxically, the disengagement and alienation of criticism and art were the keys to their cultural centrality.

MYTH AND MASCULINITY

Such arguments for American literature and criticism clearly seek to overcome the literary intellectual's sense of social marginality. And men of letters often have expressed this feeling of alienation or marginality in ways that have suggested a threatened masculinity as well. Underlying the New Critical idea of the literary text as a complex, symbolic entity was the need to establish that literature warranted the sustained attention of serious *men* who otherwise might have turned to more immediate public or commercial concerns. In order to be worthy of their commitment and analytical labors, literature would have to be shown to yield special forms of wisdom. In this way, despite (or perhaps because of) their disengagement from the sites and instruments of political power, literary critics could win cultural authority through their professional offices.

The combination of personal disengagement and professional centrality that characterized critical thinking would be read into the American writers, texts, and protagonists that Americanist critics canonized. Against the backdrop of the Cold War, with its grim images of the state suppression and mechanization of individual minds and bodies abroad, and against the conventionality and conformism of the Eisenhower years at home, the "romance tradition" in American literature, deemphasizing and sometimes demonizing collective social experience, was seen as the most uniquely American. The tragic heroism of Ahab's quest to transcend material constraints, or Huck

Finn's effort to throw off artificial social and moral conventions, was celebrated not just as the private escape it might have seemed, but as an expression of the quintessential American impulse, the recovery of intrinsic values amidst the extrinsic world of fact.

In a parallel fashion, Evan Watkins points out, "the freedoms of individual, imaginative self-realization" also motivated and justified the choice of an academic vocation itself: "these were the promises available for literary study to recruit with . . . against the attractions of money, social prestige, and practical contributions to society with which other disciplines recruited." In various ways, then, "American literature," as defined and selected by academic critics of the 1940s through the 1960s, accorded with the social and cultural circumstances of these critics – men who had chosen "individual, imaginative self-realization" over material pursuits or social involvement, who to varying degrees felt politically marginalized yet aspired to cultural centrality, and who were driven by the need to assert the masculinity and the Americanness of intellectual and imaginative activities against a materialistic society that tended to view such pursuits as feminine and foreign.

The sexual politics of academic criticism and in particular of theories of American literature will be more fully addressed in our next chapter. But a sense of beleaguered masculinity has long been a factor in the social context of American criticism and of intellectual labor in general, as literary historians such as Ann Douglas, David Leverenz, T. Walter Herbert and others have shown. In his famous 1837 address to the Harvard Phi Beta Kappa society, for instance, Emerson complained that scholars, clergymen, and other "speculative men" are "addressed as women . . . [in] a mincing and diluted speech" by the "so-called 'practical men' " who do not recognize the capacity of the American scholar for profound cultural action. During the emergent period of professional literary study, proving that such study was not effeminate was crucial to its legitimation. As Irving Babbitt sardonically observed in 1908, "the more vigorous and pushing teachers of literature feel that they must assert their manhood by philological research."

In our period, this concern was expressed by Northrop Frye, perhaps the most influential literary theorist of the 1950s and 1960s. Though Frye, a Canadian, was not especially concerned with questions of literary nationalism, his *Anatomy of Criticism* (1957) formalized the principles of myth or archetypal criticism on which many theorists of American literature drew. The academic literary critic, Frye writes,

is harassed and bedevilled by the dismal sexist symbology surrounding the humanities which he meets everywhere, even in the university itself, from freshman classes to the president's office. This symbology, or whatever one should call it, says that the sciences, especially the physical sciences, are rugged, aggressive, out in the world doing things, and so symbolically male, whereas the literatures are narcissistic, intuitive, fanciful, staying at home and making the home more beautiful but not doing anything really serious, and are therefore symbolically female. They are, however, leisure-class females, and have to be attended by a caste of ladies' maids who prepare them for public appearance and who are the teachers and critics of literature in schools and universities.

Like Irving Babbitt, Frye seems to object not to this gender hierarchy as such so much as to the placement of literature and criticism on the wrong side of it. He vigorously rejects the ladies' maid role by insisting on the first page of *Anatomy of Criticism* that the critic is not "a parasite or artist manqué."

Nor is the function of criticism to puff works of literature or even, in the conventional sense, to evaluate them. Frye's well known attack on evaluation, which he saw as lacking in objectivity and rigor and thus as insufficiently professional, reminds us that value judgment was far from central and unquestioned in the discipline of literary study before recent literary theorists began to question it. For Frye, the critic is properly a kind of scientist who conducts "an examination of literature in terms of a conceptual framework derivable from an inductive survey of the literary field." The function of criticism is to define, classify, anatomize the structural principles that inform the "order of words" which is literature. Criticism explains what literature is, as history explains what action is, as physics explains what the universe is. Frye thus shares the New Critical demand for a systematic or scientific criticism and a recognition of literature's "autonomous verbal structure." Unlike the New Critics, however, Frye does not locate such "autonomy" in individual literary objects. On the contrary, he argues that criticism can neither claim nor confer autonomy so long as it views literature as "a huge aggregate or miscellaneous pile of discrete 'works.' " Instead, criticism must constitute literature as a field, a universe, by making "the first postulate . . . of any science: the assumption of total coherence." Accordingly, Frye's "autonomous verbal structure" is not the individual poem, but Literature as a whole–and beyond that, culture, or "the total dream of man."

Frye thus reconceives literary originality as a matter of the relation of the work to the origins of literary form, the work's manifestation of the deep structure of literature itself. In deemphasizing the autonomy of the discrete work, however, Frye does not deny the liberatory energies and desires that Ransom associated with "poetic experience." For, in its purest and most original form, literature is in Frye's view – a view forged in his early work on the visionary romantic poetics of Blake and Shelley – a projection of liberatory energies and desires, an imitation of the freedom and power of gods. Literary archetypes begin, Frye writes, "with a world of myth, an abstract or purely literary world of fictional and thematic design, unaffected by canons of plausible adaptation to familiar experience. In terms of narrative, myth is the imitation of actions near or at the conceivable limits of desire." The ideal, though humanly unattainable, world of myth is "a world of total metaphor, in which everything is potentially identical with everything else, as though it were all inside a single infinite body."

Frye differentiates five modes of narrative literature (mythic, romantic, high mimetic, low mimetic, ironic), which represent various points along a descending axis from the fulfilled desire of the world of myth. In other words, a literary field extends between two poles: one represents the dream (or the ideal) of ultimate power and freedom; the other represents the nightmare (or the reality) of complete powerlessness and bondage. A simplified overview of this field places "romance" as the mediatory form between the poles of "myth" and "naturalism." Frye writes: "Myth, then, is one extreme of literary design; naturalism is the other, and in between lies the whole area of romance, using that term to mean . . . the tendency . . . to displace myth in a human direction and yet, in contrast to 'realism,' to conventionalize content in an idealized direction."

Romance is a privileged term for Frye because it epitomizes what he takes to be the essential enterprise of literature – to mediate between constraint and desire, how things are and how we would like them to be. In this sense, literature is always holding up the paradise of the "purely literary world" as a model. Even the grimmest tragedies, according to Frye, are ultimately closer to the world we desire than to the actual world, imposing as they do a tragic order and meaningfulness on life which it does not really possess. This vision of literature's structure and purpose is largely compatible with the New Critics' vision of the autonomous nature of poetry. But, in widening the concept of autonomy to include not just individual poems but poetic and imaginative vision in its totality, Frye provides another adaptation of New Critical concepts to the needs of a national myth.

Frye's archetypal criticism helped authorize the transfer of New Critical operations and theories from poetry to prose narrative, supporting the claim that what Ransom termed "poetic experience" went beyond individual poems and comprised the informing principle of American literature and literary history. American culture was seen as a struggle to realize what D. H. Lawrence called the "myth of America," an elemental confrontation with the primal forces of nature and consciousness. This myth could be traced back beyond Lawrence's provocative *Studies in Classic American Literature* (1923) through Whitman and Emerson to John Winthrop's call, before his company of Puritans had even sighted the coast of Massachusetts, for a new Jerusalem, a "city upon a hill." Despite his Canadian citizenship and disinterest in literary nationalism, then, Frye offered contemporary theoretical support for criticism of the 1950s and 1960s by Lionel Trilling, Richard Chase, R. W. B. Lewis, Charles Feidelson, and others that conceived American literature as one Big Story, at once quintessentially American and quintessentially literary.

The convergence of New Criticism and archetypal criticism in the work of these theorists of American literature is evident in their often virtually inter-changeable use of the terms "poem," "myth," "symbol," and "romance," terms usually counterposed against social reality and yet somehow explana-tory of it. Hence, Trilling claims that "the great characters of American fiction . . . tend to be mythic because of the rare fineness and abstractness of the ideas they represent" and "their very freedom from class." In much the same way, Richard Chase defines the great works of American literature as "romance," a "freer, more daring, more brilliant fiction . . . [than] the English novel," a fiction willing "to abandon moral questions or to ignore the spectacle of man in society, or to consider these things only indirectly or abstractly," yet able to find "in [its] very freedom . . . from the conditions of actuality . . . certain potential virtues of the mind, which may be suggested by such words as rapidity, irony, abstraction, profundity." R. W. B. Lewis, in *The American Adam* (1955), describes Melville's way of writing prose as "the way of a poet"; like "the best kind of poem," Melville's fiction enacts "a process of generation – in which one attitude or metaphor, subjected to intense pressure, gives symbolic birth to the next." For these critics, it is such a quest for a poetic world elsewhere, in Richard Poirier's phrase, that distinguishes American from European consciousness. Whereas the literature of Europe tends toward social realism, "Americanness" finds in romance the natural vehicle for its expression.

A commitment to the possibilities of this antirealistic process of genera-tion constitutes "the really vital common denominator" of classic American writing, argues Charles Feidelson in *Symbolism and American Literature* (1953). As Reising puts it, Feidelson's symbolist text "frees itself from the burden of the material world," or seeks to do so; in fact, "symbolism," as Feidelson sees it in American literature, is aptly characterized by Frye's definition of myth, cited above: "a world of total metaphor, in which every-thing is potentially identical with everything else, as though it were all inside a single infinite body." Leslie Fiedler writes of Chase's and his own "preoccupation with myth" or with "the archetypal symbols to which succeed-ing writers compulsively turn." And while Chase, setting forth the theory of the American romance tradition in *The American Novel and its Tradition* (1957), writes "I am not myself a 'myth critic,' " he nonetheless associates romance with the attempt to approach "a perfection" of artistic power and freedom, and he remarks: "The Romance is of loftier origin than the Novel. It approximates the poem."

So powerfully did the idea of myth discourage historical and political thinking in this period that even critics who made straightforward social points were prone to deny they were doing so. In the preface to the first edition of *Virgin Land: The American West as Symbol and Myth* (1950), the work that more than any other founded the "myth and symbol" school of American Studies, Henry Nash Smith stated that although the idealized mythic symbol of the American West had exerted "a decided influence on practical affairs," *Virgin Land* did not "mean to raise the question of whether such products of the imagination accurately reflect empirical fact. They exist on a different plane." Smith's disclaimer suited myth-critical orthodoxy but contradicted his practice in the book itself, where he actually engaged extensively in the very comparisons he disavowed between ideal myth and actual historical reality.

In a powerful chapter on "The Failure of the Agrarian Utopia," for example, Smith showed that the myth of the West as a paradise for sturdy and virtuous yeomen had taken on material expression in the Homestead Act and then been manipulated by land speculators in order to lure unsuspecting share croppers. When these farmers attempted to realize the myth in practice, they found that most of the land that had been promised to them in advertisements had previously been bought up by the railroads and speculators. Far from having refused to "raise the question" of whether the myth of the yeoman farmer "accurately reflected empirical fact," Smith's chapter had demonstrated that, in fact, the myth was a cruel hoax.

After a reviewer, Barry Marks, pointed out the contradiction, Smith revised his preface for the 1970 edition, conceding that symbols and myths do have to be seen in relation to "some process of verification," and acknowledging that *Virgin Land* is indeed concerned with such a process. It was as if the theories of the 1950s had imposed a perceptual screen that blinded Smith to the nature of his own critical practice, while the changed social climate of the 1960s had enabled him to correct this blindness.

Whether their visions of American literature revolved around the Adamic myth, the properties of symbolic language, the genre of romance, the themes of love and death (Fiedler), the machine's invasion of the garden (Leo Marx), or the stylistic pursuit of "a world elsewhere" (Richard Poirier), the major postwar Americanists all agreed that the Americanness of American literature consisted in a tension or contradiction between a mythic or ideal state of society, language, or being, and an actual or fallen state. All shared, to varying degrees, the skepticism toward the idea of steady, linear progress, toward grand narratives of political and economic development, and toward mass society and its institutions, a skepticism which, as we have suggested, also characterized the work of the most influential American historians of the period. Accordingly, the American literary canon that the Americanists popularized reflected not only the "internalization of 'reality' " characteristic of their cultural moment but also an individualization of reality. What Chase called "the originality and 'Americanness' " of American literature lay in its enactment of the individual author's or character's quest for freedom, innocence, or originality, for fullness, texture, wonder, and immediacy in experience and in language.

To sum up, then, postwar critics constructed an American literature shaped by a number of sources and circumstances. The New Critics' glorification of paradox and their celebration of "poetic experience" against "logical content" and the hegemony of "the positivist attitude" played an important role. So did the archetypal criticism that projected a New Critical vision of poetry on American literature and culture. The attitudes both of New Criticism and myth criticism fit the premises of the counter-Progressive trend in American social thought, with its emphasis on static cyclicality, irresolvable tension, and the primacy of the psychological and aesthetic realms. And this trend in turn fit the generational experience of political disillusionment shared by many leading postwar academic critics, whether they had been southern agrarians or urban socialists. Finally, there was the need of the new academic critics to solidify their professional status by exercising mastery over subtle, complex, or duplicitous texts, and to validate their ambivalent feelings of cultural alienation and claims to cultural centrality. If, as Feidelson wrote, American literature was "an adventure in discovery among the meanings of words," then critics themselves were heroes, not "ladies' maids."

Our next two chapters will take up two problems raised by the developments in academic criticism and in the theory of American literature that we have traced here. The first is the question of the canon, the academy, and gender. Frye calls myth the most "purely literary world" and he illustrates the state of fulfilled desire that defines that world as follows: "The gods enjoy beautiful women, fight one another with prodigious strength, comfort and assist man, or else watch his miseries from the height of their immortal freedom." Fiedler's mythic theory of the American novel explicitly locates both freedom and literary quality in a man's or boy's effort to escape social and sexual relations with women and with the domesticated official culture that women represent. If these are the paradigms of systematic or scientific criticism and of American literature, what share can women have in either? More generally, what are the social and political interests and consequences that such paradigms entail?

The second problem is a linguistic and philosophical one, although it too has social and political dimensions. It is the question of whether literary meaning itself is definable by a single critical method, which is to say, whether there is any single essence of "the literary" at all, much less any essence of American culture. Frye's notion of the literary and Feidelson's symbolist notion of American literature involve the striving toward "a world of total metaphor, in which everything is potentially identical with everything else." The New Critical vision of the literary that was adapted by theorists of American literature sees ambiguity and paradox as essential literary qualities; a famous essay by New Critic Cleanth Brooks in fact seeks to establish, as its title indicates, "Irony as a Principle of Structure." Literariness, in this view, consists in a self-reflexive order of words permeated by ambiguity, paradox, irony, and metaphor. Insofar as such qualities imply discrepancies between what a text says and what it means, between its manifest meaning and its latent deeper meanings, the logic of the New Critical vision ultimately leads to the destabilization of meaning itself. Though it would not become obvious until later, postwar New Critical theories and practices had opened up questions that exceeded the New Critics' intentions and arguments. These questions about the conditions of language, knowledge, and interpretation, along with the questions raised above about their social and political effects, would dominate criticism in America from the late 1960s on.

LOOKING AHEAD

Two critics whose skill in close textual analysis caused them to be frequently classed as New Critics offered powerful critiques of the New Critical theory of literary autonomy. Yvor Winters consistently challenged the New Critical distinction between the language of poetry and the language of "statement." As Winters argued, such a distinction in its radical modern form had been unknown to poets before the romantic period. It reflected a post-romantic opposition between the poetic and the practical and moral that had been elevated dogmatically into a definition of literature. In contrast, Winters argued that literature was inseparable from morality – a "morality" however that had to be distinguished from conventionality, didacticism, and propaganda. It followed for Winters, challenging T. S. Eliot's arguments on "the problem of belief," that the beliefs contained in literary works could not be dismissed as mythical, fictive, or self-ironizing structures and had to be taken seriously and evaluated accordingly. If it followed that work of Wordsworth, Poe, Emerson, Whitman, Henry Adams, Yeats, and Eliot himself was compromised by questionable doctrines, critics and readers would have to revise their judgments accordingly. Though few did, Winters provided an important alternative to the New Critical orthodoxy of the period.

A challenge that had more influence and contributed eventually to undoing that orthodoxy came from Kenneth Burke, who swam against the stream
of the general denigration of *rhetoric*. Since the poetic revolution of Yeats,
Pound, and Eliot, no idea was more agreed on than that true art must seek,
in Pound's phrase, to "wring the neck of rhetoric." For the modernist and
New Critical generation, the charged word "rhetoric" (which our culture still
pejoratively equates with debased, corrupt, and deceptive forms of language)
summed up everything that was wrong with a society given over to reductive, utilitarian, and blindly instrumental mental habits. Burke, however,
consistently argued that literature, like all language, was inevitably a form of
rhetorical persuasion, not least when it sought to disguise itself as refusing to
descend to rhetoric. Literature, contrary to the New Critics, functioned as a
form of action in the world; literary works functioned as "equipment for
living," as a set of "strategies for encompassing situations," as "symbolic
action." To see literature as a "strategy for encompassing situations" was to
see literary texts not as self-contained organisms, but as entries into a *conversation* with other utterances and texts both inside and outside literature.

For New Critical theory, strictly speaking, no literary work could be in
dialogue with any other work, much less any nonliterary text. Its meaning
was self-contained. Burke, however, in *The Philosophy of Literary Form* (1941),
points out that meaning is inherently conversational and dialogical:

Let us suppose that I ask you: "What did the man say?" And that you answer: "He
said 'yes.'" You still do not know what the man said. You would not know unless
you knew more about the situation, and about the remarks that preceded his answer.
    Critical and imaginative works are answers to questions posed by the situation in
which they arose. They are not merely answers, they are *strategic* answers, *stylized*
answers.

In these deceptively simple remarks, published at the very beginning of our
period, the key assumption of New Critical poetics are undermined: literary
and critical texts, far from being fundamentally different species of discourse
with fundamentally different worldviews, are both forms of rhetoric; far from
being autonomous entities, literary works are answers to questions posed by
situations, dependent for their comprehension on the practical contexts in
which they arise.

In *The Rhetoric of Fiction* (1961), Wayne Booth demonstrated what followed
from the application of Burkean rhetorical principles to the genre of fiction.
Taking up one by one the anti-rhetorical orthodoxies of modernism (and New
Criticism), Booth proceeded to demonstrate how questionable they are: "All
authors should be objective," "True art ignores the audience," "Tears and
laughter are, aesthetically, frauds," and, most important, true art does not

stoop to "Molding beliefs." Booth's revival of rhetoric is accompanied by a corresponding shift of critical attention from the genre of poetry to that of fiction. Whereas for the New Criticism, short lyric poems like Marvell's "To His Coy Mistress" had been paradigmatic of "literariness," the literary for the post New-Critical generation would be exemplified most characteristically by the more "impurely" temporal and social genres of narrative.

In addition to Burke (whom he would later discuss extensively in *Critical Understanding: The Powers and Limits of Pluralism* [1979]), Booth was also influenced by the Chicago School of Criticism that had frequently crossed swords with the New Critics in the 1940s and 1950s. Like the New Critics, the Chicago group (whose main figures included R. S. Crane, Elder Olson, Norman Maclean, and R. W. Keast) had reacted against the tendency of traditional historical scholarship to substitute an account of the *Zeitgeist* of a period or of an author's biography for a scrupulous analysis of the literary structure of the literary text itself. Unlike the New Critics, however, the members of the Chicago school argued that neither the meaning of the text itself nor the nature of poetry or literature as such could be determined a priori. (Crane called that kind of thinking "the high priori road.")

Following Aristotle's *Poetics*, the Chicagoans maintained that critical accounts of literary works and of literature generally needed to be based on an inductive analysis of the specific operations of literary works, not on a priori postulates such as the New Critical postulate that good poetry is always paradoxical, ironic, and antithetical to the language of scientific statement. In practice, this meant looking for the Aristotelian "final cause" of a work — as Aristotle had located the final cause of tragedy in its arousal and purging of pity and fear — and then analyzing the other components of the work in relation to that final cause. Poets, Crane argued, had aimed at a great plurality of final causes over the course of literary history, so that criticism needed itself to develop a pluralism of questions and approaches if it was to canvass the realm of poetry systematically. At the same time, Crane also suggested that there were certain characteristic forms of pleasure that were unique to literary works and could be invoked to distinguish most literary forms of discourse from other forms. This latter argument (which turns certain kinds of literary pleasure into an a priori) prevented the Chicago School from radically challenging the New Critical separation of literature and rhetoric. In *The Rhetoric of Fiction*, however, Booth begins to move toward such a radical challenge, as does fellow second-generation Chicagoan Sheldon Sachs in *Fiction and the Shape of Belief* (1964). Henceforth and with increasing intensity, American criticism tends to dismantle the New Critical opposition between the literary and the practical and to see literature as a form of rhetoric.

4

❦

THE CANON, THE ACADEMY,
AND GENDER

OUR ACCOUNT of the emergence of academic criticism in the 1940s and 1950s has emphasized the effort of the new academic critics to establish literary criticism as a discrete, systematic, even "scientific" discipline within the increasingly rationalized disciplinary structure of the postwar university. As we showed, the New Critics and myth critics, and the theorists of American literature who derived from them, all assumed the burden of this legitimating task. All argued for the autonomy, the structural literariness, of the literary works they valued. This argument entailed Cleanth Brooks' distinction between the fallen worlds of politics or morality and the redeemed world of art, and Northrop Frye's between "the world [man] sees and the world he constructs, the world he lives in and the world he wants to live in," the mere brute "environment" and the meanings by which we humanize it. To differentiate art, imagination, and desire from "the environment" was to enhance the special authority of the professional critic.

The feminist critics who in the late 1960s struggled to enter and to change the established field of literary studies also sought authority in the academy and in the larger society, as the new academic critics had done a generation earlier. But, the sources, means, terms, and goals of the quest for authority on the part of feminist critics differed sharply from those of their male predecessors. Most centrally, authority for these women was not a matter of asserting the autonomy of the individual artist or hero against an allegedly routinized mass culture; nor was it a matter of sustaining a place for the humanistic intellectual in a positivistic and materialistic society. Rather, it was an expressly collective empowerment that feminists demanded in response to the historical disempowerment of women as a class. At its outset, the primary inspiration of feminist criticism in America was the revival of the women's movement in the 1960s. Its primary goal was to analyze, combat, and overcome the situation of women summarized by Florence Howe in 1969: "In spite of a century of sporadic hue and cry about women's rights and in spite of our rhetoric about the equality of women, women remain a passive majority of second class citizens."

If much academic criticism from the late 1940s to the early 1960s was influenced by the dominant counter-Progressive strain in American social thought, feminist criticism by contrast grew out of left wing political activism: the women's liberation movement, the civil rights movement, and the Vietnam antiwar movement. If for critics of the postwar era the academy in general and literature in particular had been a means of transcending the degraded realm of politics, feminist critics saw both literature and the academy as steeped in politics, as instruments of the dominant social order rather than havens from or alternatives to it. For them, in other words, Frye's sharp antithesis between "man's" imagined and actual worlds did not hold or was not to the point: the world men constructed was the world women lived in.

Examining the academy, early feminist critics found the position of women there to reflect the general situation that Howe articulated. Women were meagerly represented in the professoriate and, where they were present, they usually occupied the lowest ranked, lowest paid, and least prestigious places. Often, women were employed chiefly as academic temporaries with little or no opportunity for job security or advancement. Even smaller than the space for women in the profession was the space for the study of women. Few, if any, works by women were included on the reading lists of courses that purported to survey the literary history of a nation, to define the masterworks of literature, or to represent the Humanities. This fact was rarely remarked upon, for great literature, presumably, had no gender; it was the embodiment of human experience, which transcended gender differences. Stereotypical or misogynistic images of women in works by men usually went unnoticed because they were presumably irrelevant to what was important, valuable, or *literary* about literary works.

Surveying this situation, feminist critics conceived their project not only as a critique of literature but as a challenge to the academy, whose reigning critical principles and methods rendered most women's works invisible and images of women aesthetically inconsequential. Analyses of sexism, according to these principles, were similarly subprofessional and outside the boundaries of the discipline. Just as anti-Vietnam War activists denied the disinterestedness of "pure" research in the physical sciences that contributed to the development of weapons technology, so early feminist literary critics insisted that the purely literary investigations claimed by their discipline served political, often destructive, ends.

THE FEMINIST CRITIQUE OF AMERICAN LITERARY HISTORY

In this chapter, we will take the early feminist critique of American literature and of its self-justifying theories as a useful point of departure for our account of feminist criticism over the past two decades. Our discussion of the course of feminist criticism here will also introduce many of the practical and theoretical issues that we will take up in subsequent chapters – issues that have shaped not just American literary history but recent literary study and critical theory in general. It should be noted at the outset, however, that our examination of the changing forms of feminist critical practice, and of the concerns and conflicts that both distinguish feminist theory and affiliate it with other theoretical positions, does not centrally address what was for first generation academic feminists the overriding purpose of feminist criticism: the creation of an intellectual and institutional space for the study of women and of gender issues. It was less important, early academic feminists held, to agree on a program for feminist criticism than it was to secure the presence of women and of feminist criticism in the academy, to build what Jane Marcus calls "a material power base."

These women did that in a variety of ways: by establishing a women's caucus of the Modern Language Association and campaigning to elect sympathetic Association officers; by lobbying, and encouraging students to lobby, for women's studies courses and programs; by founding *The Feminist Press* and feminist journals such as *Signs, Feminist Studies, Tulsa Studies in Women's Literature,* and *Women in Literature*; by helping to establish women's bookstores, many of which were called "A Room of One's Own," after Virginia Woolf's generative feminist treatise (in which she had urged women collectively to write and to recover the lost voices of their silenced foremothers); by lobbying university presses to publish multiauthored collections of essays through which feminist criticism could be defined and legitimated as a field; by soliciting foundation grants to subsidize new work and new programs; and by providing financial and other sorts of support for academic women who had been denied tenure (as several leading early feminist critics were) and who had charged their universities with sex discrimination.

As these efforts to professionalize feminist criticism in the American academy began to succeed, women readers of American literature and students of its prominent theories turned their attention to the authorized academic canon and to the critical methods, motives, and assumptions that had established and sustained it. As we have seen in earlier chapters, the question "what is American literature?" has elicited various answers over the course of this century and, more importantly, has served various professional and more broadly cultural and ideological ends. When feminist critics began to ask it, their answer, as Judith Fetterley bluntly and challengingly put it in her book *The Resisting Reader* (1977), was that "American literature is male."

This deceptively simple assertion entails a complex set of ramifications. It points out that "American" and "literature" do not function in the academy and in the culture as innocent, obvious, or natural categories. Indeed, as we have noted, the very coupling of "literature" with a national and political designation like "American" invests the judgment of literary quality or importance with claims of social representativeness. Works selected as part of the canon of American literature presumably *speak for* the entire culture in a way that others do not. But who decides that a work speaks for all Americans? Clearly, to designate a narrow range of writings – out of everything written on the American continents or in the United States, or written by residents or even U.S. citizens – as "American" and as "literature" is to favor certain social groups, ideas, and experiences and to protect them from contact or competition with others. The dominant theories and practices not only have ensured that "American literature" is overwhelmingly authored by men, Fetterley's sentence implies, but, for all critical intents and purposes, define Americanness and literariness as themselves male gendered qualities.

Indeed, to restate a point made in Chapter 3, the Americanness of American literature was often located in a theme or myth of heroic quest for the meaning of America itself. As Alan Trachtenberg has said, every prominent academic theory of American literature produced in the postwar period claimed "that the inner substance, the essential content of all significant American writing is (virtually by definition) America itself – that is, America as an idea of selfhood, or the writer himself as America." As an idea of selfhood, of personal liberation, this "America" usually referred not to the multitudes of women and men of different origins, creeds, classes, and colors, who lived or had lived in central North America, nor to the social relations and political institutions that they established. On the contrary, "America" was a state of personal transcendence achieved – or, more typically, tragically quested for – by a solitary male hero.

American literature, more specifically, was typically a story about a would be autonomous self who revolts against a corrupt or stultifyingly conventional society – a society, as Fetterley and others noted, characteristically associated with the women left behind. This paradigm had been powerfully articulated in Leslie Fiedler's study, *Love and Death in the American Novel* (1960), which accorded Americanness to works that exemplified Fiedler's mythic vision of "a nation sustained by . . . the dream of an escape from culture and a renewal of youth," works that revealed a sexually insecure and guilty American society whose "final horrors . . . [are] but intimate aspects of our own minds." Literature by women that might have been seen to articulate entirely different dreams and horrors, or literature that offered more social description than psychological self-projection, did not contain what Fiedler's thesis had defined as "the essence of American experience."

Dominant theories of American literature, feminists argued, not only effectively excluded women as writers and subjects but actively erased female subjectivity through their objectification of the female either as the social and conventional obstruction to male self-realization or as the natural field upon which such realization must be won. Thus, these theories and the texts they validated shared a design upon the woman reader – to coopt her, in Fetterley's words, "into participation in an experience from which she is explicitly excluded [and in which] she is required to identify against herself." Only by learning to be a resisting reader could a woman reclaim her subjectivity, Fetterley concluded, offering her book as a "self-defense survival manual for the woman reader" lost in the masculine wilderness of American literature.

Fetterley's language subversively appropriates the classic American frontier theme for those whom the theme had erased, implying that the real heroic struggle in American culture is the struggle of women to survive it. Similarly, Nina Baym has challenged the distinction between "significant (male) American writing" and the sentimental (female) writing that academic critics had assumed to be non-American and subliterary. In a persuasive 1981 essay, Baym characterizes the most celebrated and "representative" American fictions as "melodramas of beset manhood," arguing that it is only through the deceptive filter of dominant theories of American literature – whose authors may themselves be enacting melodramas of beset manhood – that such texts appear to express the essence of "America itself." In fact, Baym suggests that, despite the theories' nationalistic emphasis, their constructions of American literature ultimately and ironically "[arrive] at a place where Americanness has vanished into the depths of what is alleged to be the universal male psyche."

The feminist critique of "American literature" thus developed within the larger project of the women's movement to assess and alter the cultural assumptions and institutional practices that contributed to the oppression, devaluation, and silencing of women. Accordingly, the object of this critique was not so much the sexism of canonical American writers, or even the patriarchal biases of the framers of the canon, but the prevalent values and procedures of academic criticism in general – especially, its investment in professionalized, technologized and ostensibly objectified approaches to knowledge. For, the field of American literature and the discipline of academic criticism (as distinct from the older scholarship) arose simultaneously and both were structured according to many of the same principles. Indeed, one effort of early feminist criticism was to make visible the parallel structures that informed and legitimated canonical literature, textual criticism, and the discipline of literary studies, and to identify the link between these structures and patriarchy. Thus, the solitary hero of American literature who disdains and flees society may be seen as an analogue of the text itself, examined and celebrated in its aesthetic integrity by critics trained in the "intrinsic" method of Wellek and Warren, and, in turn, this autonomous work of art may be seen as a figure for the discipline, established as a distinct academic field through arbitrary differentiations and interested rationalizations. At each level, separation is valued over relationship; each entity, in fact, is constituted by severing and denying its connections to others or its place in some larger, more multiplicitous and interactive whole.

FEMINISM AND NEGATIVE HERMENEUTICS

These parallels suggest that disciplinary principles and methods are tools that produce, rather than merely probe, their objects, that they create meaning and values (in this case of literary texts) in their own image rather than simply discovering them. One radical consequence of this suggestion – a consequence that, as we have suggested in earlier chapters, would be felt throughout the discipline of literary studies from the early 1970s on – is to turn criticism's focus back upon itself and its own shaping contexts, conditions, and connections. Thus, the opening sentences of Baym's "Melodramas of Beset Manhood" declare: "This paper is about American literary criticism rather than American literature. It proceeds from the assumption that we never read literature directly or freely, but always through the perspective allowed by theories."

Feminism was not the only or the first critical challenger to the positivistic claims and framework of modern Western thought. Pragmatism, existentialism, and a range of social criticisms dating back to the early Romantics also offer contextualist and historicist counterstatements to the dominant mode of empirical rationality. But, in literary studies during our period, feminist criticism most effectively articulated the human stakes of this philosophical debate. For feminism, the issue was not just that the known and the real rested upon theoretical (and therefore unstable, nonempirical) ground; it was that the theories which produced knowledge and reality – and produced the subjects of knowledge and objects of reality, including authors, readers, and literature as well – had the effect of naturalizing and stabilizing an order of existence that excluded or alienated half of humankind.

It is worth pausing here to consider the objections of those who responded to the feminist "resisting reader" with apprehension and counter-resistance. This response cannot be dismissed as merely a self-protective sexist reaction on the part of the guardians of entrenched disciplinary power. For some critics, "feminist literary criticism" seemed simply a contradiction in terms, since such criticism focused not on the aesthetic qualities of literature but on "extrinsic" questions of gender and power relations. The fact that these questions are very much present in literature did not dissuade these critics, who argued that the real value of literature and business of literary criticism was or should be elsewhere. What others found disturbing in feminist criticism was not the focus upon gender politics in literature so much as the very idea of reading as resistance. Early feminist criticism of male-authored texts shared this idea and practice with other critical methods – such as deconstruction, psychoanalytic criticism, and Althusserian marxism – that began to gain currency in the American literary academy at about the same and that often prompted the same suspicious reaction in newly "traditional" academic critics.

These critics assumed what they took to be the common sense position that reading was an appreciation of the qualities of a literary work and that the project of literary criticism was to enhance the depth and the breadth of the reader's appreciative capacities. From this perspective, the argument that a woman reader who is taught to appreciate certain canonical works on their own terms may pay too high a personal and political price for the instruction seems to reject the literary critical project itself in favor of an ideological agenda. The feminist response, of course, is that an ideological agenda is *already* in place in a definition of the critical project that privileges certain kinds of attention to literary works and rules other kinds of attention out of bounds. While traditionalists have often deplored such responses, it is worth observing that the claim of feminists and others that resistance may be an appropriate form of critical attention extends a key precept of traditionalist critics like F. R. Leavis and Yvor Winters: if literature is a bearer of values, then literature and its pleasures can be dangerous.

To read as a mode of resistance, however, is indeed to assume a different orientation toward the literary object than is assumed in forms of critical reading that take pleasurable appreciation to be their goal. This orientation of the resisting reader has been termed negative hermeneutics, or a hermeneutics of suspicion. That is, it rejects the subordinate role for criticism of helping to illuminate and affirm a work's ostensible, intended, or self-contained meaning and seeks to expose significances – contradictions, ideological limitations, repressed possibilities – of which the work may be unaware. Negative hermeneutics thus involves relocating meaningfulness in social contexts and signifying systems larger or deeper than the work itself, a practice whose purpose is not necessarily to dismiss the intention of the author of a literary work, but to reveal the cultural codes that shape or indeed make possible that intention. A key difference between American feminism and recent European critical movements, though, is that, for feminists, the hermeneutics of suspicion did not begin as an elaborated theory of interpretation but as a practice necessary to the project of contesting the authority of the canon, the images of women in literature, and the subordination of women in the academy.

The challenge to the authority and autonomy of the text that is offered by a negative hermeneutics extends as well to the agency of the author; social and historical contexts and theories constitute human subjects just as they do literary objects. This is not to say, despite the appearance of essays and symposia that provocatively examine "the death of the author," that recent critical movements deny that authors exist and that individuals write works of literature. Rather, as we will explain at length in our discussion of deconstruction and poststructuralism in Chapter 5, these movements seek to show how the conceptual categories and expressive possibilities out of which texts are produced – and how the individuals who produce them – are socially and historically conditioned or determined. Breaking down the bourgeois model of integral, unencumbered selfhood, which has been a primary concern of poststructuralism, is another critical enterprise pioneered by feminists, for whom this model of identity was a masculinist myth born of the denial of relation and of women. Jessica Benjamin succinctly puts the feminist argument we have been summarizing in her book, *The Bonds of Love:*

From a feminist point of view, the missing piece in the analysis of Western rationality and individualism is the structure of gender domination. The psychosocial core of this unfettered individuality is the subjugation of woman by man, through which it appears that she is his possession, and therefore, that he is not dependent upon or attached to an other outside himself.

As we will shortly see, however, feminist critics have not taken a single antagonistic position on the question of autonomous selfhood or bourgeois subjectivity. In fact, this question has been hotly contested within academic feminism and has often marked a division between a more theoretical form of feminist critique, which has viewed "unfettered individuality" as a masculinist myth to be exploded, and a practical feminist critique, which has viewed the same individuality as a traditionally male privilege that must be shared.

MILLETT AND FEMINIST CRITICISM'S FIRST PHASE

Kate Millett's *Sexual Politics* (1970), the most influential of the early feminist literary studies in America, is distinctly a work of practical criticism. But, while Millett is not engaged in systematic theorizing about language and interpretation, or about reason and subjectivity, recent feminist critics such as Toril Moi understate the theoretical dimension of *Sexual Politics* by representing it as a simple, if powerful, "fist in the solar plexus of patriarchy" delivered in (the academic equivalent of) the "style. . . . of a hard-nosed street kid." Two important principles of much poststructuralist theory, the socially constructed nature of human identity and the capacity of modern society to extend domination by conditioning minds rather than punishing bodies, accord closely with Millett's insistence "that sex is a status category with political implications" and that the system of conventional gender roles and relations helps a social order that subordinates women appear natural and inevitable, even to its victims. Anticipating Benjamin's suggestion that gender domination is the psychosocial core of Western rationality and individualism, Millett argues that "sexual caste supersedes all other forms of inegalitarianism: racial, political, or economic," and that "[the division of] humanity into two groups and [the appointment of] one to rule over the other by virtue of birthright. . . . underlie and corrupt all other human relationships as well as every area of thought and experience."

The relationship between sexism and the other forms of inegalitarianism that Millett mentions here becomes a significant point of debate within later feminist criticism, as we will see. Millett's central theoretical engagement, however, is with the issue of whether the sexual division of humanity is grounded in any differences beyond those of anatomy and reproductive function. On this issue, Millett argues and cites evidence for "the overwhelmingly cultural character of gender" (which she defines as "personality structure in terms of sexual category") and points out that "whatever the 'real' differences between the sexes may be, we are not likely to know them until the sexes are treated differently, that is alike." In other words, Millett deftly suggests, in the absence of identical environmental conditions for male and female development and expression (conditions which do not yet exist in our society and have never existed in Western culture), one cannot responsibly either confirm or deny that there are any natural differences, beyond anatomical and reproductive ones, between men and women. Only after social and cultural equality has been achieved might we learn whether or not there are significant natural differences between men and women.

Sexual Politics depicts patriarchy as "a governing ideology without peer," a system of thought, representation, and institutionalized power relations designed to sustain male domination by disguising the cultural character of gender differences and presenting them, instead, as universal, biologically determined distinctions that confer superiority upon men. Millett provides a historical background to the modern literary instances of patriarchal ideology, in which she examines some nineteenth and early twentieth century challenges to patriarchy and the counterrevolutionary intellectual and political responses to them. In this account, Sigmund Freud figures as the premier reactionary patriarch, the provider of a new scientific respectability to a social order whose religious and economic rationales had been shaken: "the effect of Freud's work, that of his followers, and still more that of his popularizers, was to rationalize the individious relationship between the sexes, to ratify traditional roles, and to validate temperamental differences."

Millett's claim is that Freud saw the disorders of his female patients not "as evidence of a justified dissatisfaction with the limiting circumstances imposed on them by society, but as symptomatic of an independent and universal feminine tendency," which he named "penis envy." According to the theory of penis envy, she contends, "the definition of the female is negative": "the female's discovery of her sex is, in and of itself, a catastrophe of such vast proportions that it haunts a woman all through her life and accounts for most aspects of her temperament," especially those aspects that "[Freud] took to be the three corollaries of feminine psychology: passivity, masochism, and narcissism." Later feminist studies, beginning with Juliet Mitchell's *Psychoanalysis and Feminism* (1974), would attack Millett's reading of Freud, contending that "psychoanalysis is not a recommendation for a patriarchal society, but an analysis of one" and that "a rejection of psychoanalysis and of Freud's work is fatal for feminism." The debate about the disposition of psychoanalysis toward women, and its usefulness to feminism, continues today. Some recent psychoanalytically trained French feminists, to whom we will return, have taken this debate in new directions, but the earlier points of contestation – is Freud's theory descriptive or prescriptive? does it hold sexuality to be a social construct or a biological essence? – remain at issue.

Each of Millett's three modern literary representatives of patriarchy – D. H. Lawrence, Henry Miller, and Norman Mailer – shares Freud's fascination with sexual difference and male sexual identity. And each figures in establishing American literature as a drama of masculine struggle for autonomy, imaginative freedom, and instinctive life against social constraints and coercions embodied in femininity. Lawrence, the non-American of the group, famously pointed the way in *Studies in Classic American Literature* (1923) for the later theories of American fiction that Miller's and Mailer's novels, with their convention defying, first-person artist–heroes, would exemplify. Reading against the implied perspective of these authors, Millett finds that their understandings of masculine individualism and creativity depend upon the victimization of women and the denial of female subjectivity. Although Millett is more concerned with overt instances of sexual degradation and violence than with its subtler literary manifestations, *Sexual Politics* was undoubtedly a pioneering and inspirational work in what has come to be known as the first phase of feminist criticism – a phase characterized, as Jane Gallop observes, by critical reexaminations of male-authored canonical works that sought "to show . . . that the images of women in literature were

distorting stereotypes that contributed to women's oppression and our alienation from self."

Within a few years, however, many feminist critics had begun to find this
enterprise limiting and, in some ways, even reinforcing to the patriarchal
structure that it deplored. To focus on images of women in male-authored
works, some argued, was necessarily to examine women in their traditional
role as objects of male perception and desire rather than to assert and explore
female subjectivity. A feminist criticism synonymous with the exposure of
misogyny and of debilitating stereotypes restricts itself to viewing women
only in relation to men. From such a standpoint, moreover, patriarchy's
power of subordination seems so absolute as to preclude the possibility of
female achievement, community, and expression. It was no surprise, then,
that Millett – who wrote of patriarchy that "no other system has ever exercised such a complete control over its subjects" – failed to mention works by
women that resisted or challenged the images produced by her literary chau-
vinists, or that, as some charged, *Sexual Politics* inadequately acknowledged
its debts to earlier feminist writings by such critics as Simone de Beauvoir
and Mary Ellmann.

Published two years before Millett's book, Ellmann's *Thinking About
Women* (1968) uses the phrase "sexual politics" in connection with its critique
of the omnipresence of "sexual analogy" in Western thought and language,
the tendency to "comprehend all phenomena, however shifting, in terms of
our original and simple sexual differences; and . . . classify almost all experience by means of sexual analogy." Whereas Millett assails mysogynistic
content in literary texts and in a few modern political and intellectual movements, Ellmann seeks to expose the more subtle sexual politics embedded in
style – in a culture's prevailing habits of speaking and thinking. Her point is
that these habits are irrational, that the analogies they produce are generally
silly, and that the gender roles upon which they rely – and which they
attempt to sustain – are irrelevant and anachronistic in a society that no
longer survives by virtue of the physical strength of its men or the fecundity
of its women. Ellmann's own style is itself meant to discredit the stereotypes
that underlie sexual analogy. Her detached, logical, ironic prose (all conventionally "male" traits) uses the prejudice of a society in which "books by
women are treated as though they themselves were women" to undo that
society's own assumptions. Ellmann, then, might be described as an early
campaigner against sexual essentialism, or the tendency to identify any cultural phenomenon or human quality with one sex or the other. The effect of

this system of sexual analogy upon women, in particular upon women writers, she argues, is that "the individual is assumed into the sex and loses all but typical meaning within it. The emphasis is finally macabre, as though women wrote with their breasts instead of pens."

In the last few years, feminist critics have increasingly challenged the idea that there is a natural or essential female character. Judith Butler, for instance, in her book *Gender Trouble: Feminism and the Subversion of Identity* (1990), does not merely argue against the prejudice that certain qualities characterize all women, but insists that "the category of women as a coherent and stable subject" itself participates in "an unwitting regulation . . . of gender relations" that is "precisely contrary to feminist aims." Butler and other antiessentialist feminists suggest that, as paradoxical as it seems, "women" as an identity category "ought not to be the foundation of feminist politics," whose aims may be realized "only when the subject of 'women' is nowhere presumed." In the early 1970s, however, feminist literary critics, reacting against or seeking to complement the preoccupation of the first phase with male images of women, generally did not see it as their task to contest the category of women as a subject. On the contrary, most sought to establish and celebrate the female subjectivity that had survived, resisted, or evaded patriarchal definition, either in order to recover neglected women writers whose work might be recognized as comprising a female countertradition in literature or to elaborate an alternative to patriarchal values and social structures based on models of women's community and women's culture. Ironically, as Toril Moi observes, Mary Ellmann herself was taken by at least one contributor to this second phase of feminist criticism to epitomize a form of uniquely female subjectivity. Patricia Meyer Spacks's *The Female Imagination: A Literary and Psychological Investigation of Women's Writing* (1975) was one of the important works of this phase. (Others include Ellen Moers's *Literary Women: The Great Writers* [1976], Elaine Showalter's *A Literature of Their Own: British Women Novelists from Brontë to Lessing* [1977], Nina Baym's *Women's Fiction: A Guide to Novels by and about Women in America, 1820–1870* [1978], Nina Auerbach's *Communities of Women: An Idea in Fiction* [1978], Carolyn Heilbrun's *Toward a Recognition of Androgyny* [1973] and *Reimagining Womanhood* [1979], and Sandra Gilbert and Susan Gubar's *The Madwoman in the Attic: The Woman Writer and the Nineteenth-Century Literary Imagination* [1979].) For Spacks, Ellmann's style displays "a particularly feminine sort and function of wit" and Ellmann herself "embodies woman as quicksilver, always in brilliant, erratic motion."

In describing her own project as "explicitly antihistorical in orientation," Spacks anticipates the grounds on which the second phase of feminist criticism – sometimes known as "radical feminism" for its concern with the roots and the nature of female creativity – would itself come to be challenged from within the feminist movement. The focus on women's writing during this period and the attempt to define a distinctive female tradition, or what Showalter calls "a literature of their own," predisposed critics to posit, in Spacks's various formulations, "a special female self-awareness," "an outlook sufficiently distinct to be recognizable throughout the centuries," "the work of women writing directly as women," and a "fundamental female experience." The obvious objection that such claims – whether made by second phase American feminists or by later French feminist theorists of an "écriture feminine" – may and did elicit is that they, no less than sexist male images, essentialize and stereotype women, differing only in the positive rather than the negative value assigned to "fundamental" female traits. In other terms, this critique of radical feminism is that it gives inadequate attention to historical circumstances, to the multiple factors that affect the ways in which personal identity, gender roles, and gender relations are produced and experienced in different historical contexts. Some subsequent feminists, then, responded to such contentions as Spacks's that "female likenesses are more fundamental than female differences" by pointing out how diverse, in fact, women's identities, conditions, and experiences were and questioning whether those who argued for "fundamental" female likenesses had seriously brought factors of race, class, sexual orientation, or ethnic and religious culture into their calculations. These later critics also asked to what degree the social and historical position of the critic herself determined her definition of what counted as "female likenesses" and "female differences" and unconsciously dictated her conclusion.

Despite its susceptibility to these objections, radical feminist criticism pursued several important practical goals. To celebrate female experience and articulate a female literary countertradition or a redemptive model of female community was to help define a basis and a precedent for solidarity within the American women's movement and within academic feminism. Moreover, it was to assert that feminist criticism had a positive and independent, not simply a reactive, role in the academy, and that feminist critics possessed a distinct and neglected field of study – literature by women, and more broadly the construction of gender in literature and culture – which required representation in the literary curriculum. The institutionalization of women's studies programs in American universities and the rediscovery and republication of great quantities of overlooked or devalued writing by women are among the fruits of this phase of feminist criticism.

A price of the practical achievements of radical feminism, however, as critics like Gallop and Butler pointed out, was its tendency toward a theoretical essentialism – that is, the substitution of a feminist version (or inversion) of the patriarchal myth of natural and eternal womanhood. As we will see, this tendency is not specific to American feminist criticism of this period. In fact, the ongoing philosophical and political debate between feminist critics who take women as their "coherent and stable subject," in Butler's words, and those who reject that assumption of coherence and stability is one whose terms reappear in other attempts to identify group literary and cultural traditions. The debate recurs, for instance, over the possibility of defining other categories of group identity such as nationality, class, and ethnicity. Thus, arguments within feminism about the extent to which one can or should isolate a coherent "women's culture" or "women's experience" have been replicated in more recent discussions of the distinctiveness of black, gay, or Third World experiences and cultural identities, just as debates about female identity that began in feminist criticism of the early 1970s echoed earlier debates about the extent to which "Americanness" or "American literature" could be characterized. At the most abstract level, the problem of gender, racial, or cultural essentialism belongs to the larger theoretical controversy over the extent to which meaning is coherent and stable or indeterminate. This controversy pervades postwar criticism, and our next chapter, an account of deconstruction and poststructuralist theory, will chronicle it.

Spacks's concern in 1975, however, was not to address the political or theoretical implications of essentialism but to locate the moments and strategies of women's artistic enablement under patriarchy, in contrast to the inevitable emphasis on what was disabling among critics who analyzed patriarchal images of women. Whereas Beauvoir and Ellmann, in her view, took a woman's awareness of her female sexual identity to be irrelevant or obstructive to her self-fulfillment, Spacks insists that such awareness is crucial. Specifically, she contests the implication of these earlier critics "that women must transcend the condition of being women in order to be great artists," arguing that it is this condition and its challenges that spark the imagination and produce great women artists. Of the women writers she considers, Spacks observes that "anger provided the impetus, the subject, and the inventiveness of their work," and that, through the "patterns of suffering and compensation" that they both depicted and inhabited, they came to realize the "power implicit in art." Women writers, in other words, forge in their work a realm of "inner freedom" where "passivity [and] powerlessness . . . merge strangely into the activity and power" of artistic mastery, and where "women dominate their own experience by imagining it, giving it form, writing about it."

Such claims by Spacks and others for a fundamental female experience gave rise to charges not only of essentialism and ahistoricism, but of idealism and aestheticism. Again, we rehearse these charges here not to single out Spacks's book but to identify another important tension in feminist criticism and, indeed, in contemporary literary studies as a whole. To begin with, it might be argued that Spacks's image of a female imagination converting social suffering to artistic compensation does not much differ from the image of the American imagination established by male theorists of American literature, who celebrated an escape from social reality to a largely womanless world elsewhere of romance or personal style. But there is a deeper worry for many feminists than the questionable exclusivity of what Spacks calls "the female imagination." If imaginative activity and power compensate for passivity and powerlessness in the world, if anger is transmuted into great art, then the marginal condition of women under patriarchy is seemingly rationalized. At the very least, the implication is that woman's most profound and characteristic response to that condition is not to oppose it but to make artistic use of it.

It is not Spacks's intention, of course, to justify patriarchy or to claim that art could adequately compensate women for their sufferings. Her focus on women's imaginative use of their condition, rather than on their political resistance to it, reflects her understanding of her vocation as a literary critic. Political commitments bear on this vocation, but Spacks does not consider politics and literary criticism to be the same enterprise. Her insistence upon their distinction is nowhere more evident than in her annoyed remark about *Sexual Politics*, which had been Kate Millett's dissertation at Columbia University: "Miss Millett had it both ways: she constructed an elaborate exercise in political rhetoric, and for it she got a Ph.D. in English." While Spacks's own work "in English" is politically informed by her feminism – and while she herself centrally argues that "anger provided the impetus, the subject, and the inventiveness" of women's writing – she nonetheless wishes, as her comment on Millett indicates, to maintain a disciplinary and qualitative distinction between political rhetoric and literary study.

But *is* there a categorical difference, and, if so, on whose authority and for whose benefit? And how in particular can a practitioner of feminist criticism, which had insisted from the start that traditional literary criticism had always been a form of political rhetoric, claim this difference? The tension over the relationship between intellectual inquiry and social practice, between academic professionalism and political partisanship, that we have seen to be a central constituent of modern criticism arises here within academic feminism. If Spacks suggests that academic feminist criticism may be too political, other feminists with differently weighted allegiances would wonder whether it could be political enough.

ACADEMIC FEMINISM AND ITS DISCONTENTS

One explosion of the tension within academic feminism indicated in Spacks's comment on Millett was touched off by Annette Kolodny's essay "Dancing

Through the Minefield: Some Observations on the Theory, Practice, and Politics of a Feminist Literary Criticism." Kolodny's essay, which appeared in the journal *Feminist Studies* and won the Modern Language Association's Florence Howe Award for the best feminist essay published in 1980, briefly surveyed feminist scholarship of the previous decade and set forth three propositions that Kolodny took to be "at the theoretical core of most current feminist criticism." These propositions were: (1) that "literary history . . . is a fiction," not in the sense that any version of history is as valid as any other, but in the sense that the canon and the explanations of literary tradition which support it represent a set of choices made by people in a position to make and enforce such choices – historically, male critics whose selective canon has in certain ways reflected and naturalized men's "sense of power and significance in the world"; (2) that "insofar as we are taught to read, what we engage are not texts but paradigms" – acquired theories and conventions of literary analysis, literary value, and literary history that organize our reading experience and make prevailing critical orthodoxies appear to be natural and immutable truths; and (3) that, "since the grounds upon which we assign aesthetic value to texts are never infallible, unchangeable, or universal," we must reexamine the biases of traditional orthodoxies and forge new grounds for literary valuation and aesthetic response. To accept these propositions, Kolodny concluded, is necessarily to question "the adequacy of any interpretative paradigm to a full reading of both female and male writing" and to entertain "the possibility that different readings, even of the same text, may be differently useful, even illuminating, within different contexts of inquiry." The task for feminist critics, then, "is to initiate nothing less than a playful pluralism, responsive to the possibilities of multiple critical schools and methods, but captive of none."

For many of Kolodny's feminist colleagues, this vision of a modest, playful, pluralistic feminist criticism was, as Jane Marcus wrote, an invitation for " 'good girl' feminists [to] fold their tents and slip quietly into the establishment." The diffuse and accommodating feminism that Kolodny depicted, Marcus and others argued, authorized a dispersal rather than an expansion and intensification of feminism's oppositional agenda as it implicitly denied or abandoned meaningful points of conflict within feminist criticism itself and between feminist criticism and other more established academic criticism. Elly Bulkin, one of several respondents to "Dancing Through the Minefield" in a later issue of *Feminist Studies*, argues that Kolodny's position is not merely susceptible to cooptation by "the masculinist establishment," but that Kolodny, along with the "white heterosexual academic female critics" whom she canonizes, fosters racism, heterosexism, and classism. Kolodny "apparently does not see" that her version of feminism speaks only to and about "a specific group of women – those who are both white and heterosexual and, almost without exception, middle class in background or engaged in modes of criticism that do not challenge sufficiently the white male standards of the academy. . . . While I would argue strenuously, with Kolodny, against a single or dogmatic approach to feminist literary criticism," Bulkin adds, "I find myself unable to find anything 'playful' (or even feminist) in criticism that omits, trivializes, or distorts the lives of lesbians of all races, of nonlesbian women of color, of poor and working-class women."

Bulkin describes her critique as an effort to raise the consciousness of white academic feminists about "some of the essential differences *among* women." That these differences are so rarely recognized, let alone examined, even in a critical practice as attentive to difference as feminism, underscores, in Bulkin's view, "how each of us [who is white] is racist in a daily way." For Bulkin, then, feminist criticism must vigilantly acknowledge differences of class, race, sexual orientation, and cultural background even as it speaks of and to the experiences of women across these differences. This demand is put most directly by black lesbian feminist Barbara Smith: "feminism is the political theory and practice that struggles to free all women: women of color, working-class women, poor women, disabled women, lesbians, old women, as well as white, economically privileged heterosexual women. Anything less than this vision of total freedom is not feminism, but merely female self-aggrandizement."

But what does it mean to call for "total freedom"? Are the different interests of the groups Smith gathers together necessarily reconcilable? The condition of a poor woman of color, for example, is arguably determined far more fundamentally by her poverty or her race than by her sex per se, from which it might follow that such a woman would have common interests closer to those of poor men or of men of color than, say, to those of lesbians or disabled women as a class. It might be objected to Smith that a commitment to the articulation of total or universal liberation necessarily ignores such differences and complications and thus does not *morally* validate so much as it *practically* disables political criticism. In any event, judged by this standard, Kolodny's sense of feminist criticism as an analysis of the ways in which "the structures of primarily male power . . . have been – and continue to be – reified by our literature and by our literary criticism" is clearly inadequate. Kolodny, a literary critic working in the academy, defines her feminist project in literary and academic terms. Smith, on the other hand, insists not only that feminist criticism challenge the academy's authorized canon and traditional critical methods and values, but that it reject the disciplinary, demographic, and other institutional constraints that the academy places upon feminism's larger social commitments. Quoting Smith, Rena Grasso Patterson contends that Kolodny's narrowly *literary* concerns, as she views them, are better described as elitist than as feminist. Feminism, for Patterson, is incompatible with existing academic frameworks, especially the disciplinary framework of literary studies that most of the contributors to the first and second phases of feminist literary criticism shared with their male colleagues. The crux of her argument is that "Kolodny promotes a criticism which would confine us to contemplating and analyzing symbolic systems," an enterprise that is "removed from the concerns of real women in an oppressive society. . . . Nothing about the fiction of literary history, or paradigms, or biased aesthetic judgments supports the radical premises and commitments of activism."

GENDER STUDIES AND THE PLURALIZATION OF FEMINIST CRITICISM

The current phase of academic feminism has been described in various terms, most of which are too narrow to suggest the range of differently oriented critical practices that the field now encompasses. In general, though, current feminist criticism complicates and, in some instances, rejects or turns away from the stark binary oppositions of male/female and nonpolitical/political that informed much early feminist work. It is a more situational or historicized feminism, acknowledging differences among women and hybrid crossings between specific female traditions and subjectivities, as in black, Chicana, and lesbian feminist criticism. Feminist literary criticism of the third phase tends, too, to focus not so restrictively on writing by or about women but on constructions of gender in writing and culture generally. It is also often coalitional in its increased concern to link analyses of gender with those of class, race, and sexual orientation and in its increasing alliances with such critical theories and practices as Marxism, psychoanalysis, cultural anthropology, post-Saussurean linguistics, and deconstructive critiques of Western metaphysical philosophy. All of these feminisms implicitly or explicitly entail what Elaine Showalter, characterizing the third phase of feminist criticism, calls "a radical rethinking of the conceptual grounds of literary study."

We should caution that our use of the conventional tripartite division of feminist criticism over the past twenty-five years only roughly indicates the different directions this criticism has taken, the different periods in which one or another of these directions has predominated, and the variety of debates these differences have occasioned. In fact, analyses of men's images and treatment of women, explorations of female literary and cultural countertraditions, and "coalitional" feminist criticism have occurred throughout these years. Nor were the kinds of objections that Bulkin and Patterson raise to mainstream academic feminism unknown before the late 1970s or specific to the emergence of black feminist and lesbian feminist criticism. Most notably, Lillian Robinson argued in a series of essays published between 1971 and 1977 (and collected in 1978 under the title *Sex, Class & Culture*) for a Marxist feminist criticism centered on issues of class and race as well as gender, devoted to the analysis of mass culture as well as literary art, accessible to general readers, and oriented toward concrete social action. Robinson was an early bearer of uncomfortable but provocative news for academic feminism, or for any "engaged" literary criticism, pointing out that there was "no assurance that [it would] be productive of a vision of art or of social relations that is of the slightest use to the masses of women, or even one that acknowledges the existence and the struggle of such women," and insisting that "ideological criticism must take place in the context of a political movement that can put it to work. The revolution is simply not going to be made by literary journals."

The emergence of a black feminist criticism pressed upon academic feminism Robinson's (and Smith's, and more recently bell hooks's) demand for a critical practice attentive to issues of class and culture, as well as those of sex, and cognizant of the different experiences of gender identity peculiar to different class and ethnic origins and affiliations. Arising not only out of the women's movement but also out of the Civil Rights movement and the resurgent commitment to black cultural identity and expression that accompanied it, black feminist criticism played a key role in the reevaluation of the male/female binary and of the principles and parameters of literary study within feminist literary criticism in general. As Barbara Smith suggests in her 1977 essay, "Toward a Black Feminist Criticism," black feminists could not begin, as their white counterparts had, by critiquing stereotypical male images of women and the neglect or devaluation of female literary achievement by the keepers of a patriarchal canon. For black women were not so much objectified and trivialized by the dominant culture as they were virtually erased by it. More painfully, perhaps, they continued to be invisible even in the discourses of black male and white feminist opposition to that culture. If, for white American feminists, the relevant historical context was one in which women had been denied full human subjectivity and fair literary representation, for African American feminists, Smith points out, it was one in which black women had been "categorically denied not only literacy but the most minimal possibility of a decent human life." Moreover, as Hazel Carby observes in *Reconstructing Womanhood: The Emergence of the Afro-American Woman Novelist* (1987), the same "dominant domestic ideologies and literary conventions of womanhood" that were used to contain white women within an essentialized female sphere "excluded [the black woman] from the definition 'woman' " altogether. The title of the 1982 anthology of black feminist essays, *All the Women are White, All the Blacks are Men, But some of Us Are Brave*, captures this sense of the black woman's erasure, suggesting the challenge that black feminist criticism sought to pose to the prevailing definitions of both racial and sexual politics in America.

To some degree, black feminist criticism has assumed the same oppositional relation to academic feminism as feminist literary criticism did to the institution of modern literary study itself: each movement inherited the tools and methods of its predecessor and used them to expose its omissions and distortions. Each was committed partly to the project of its predecessor and partly to another project that originated elsewhere (in the women's movement or in the political and cultural struggle of African Americans). This is why each was accused of attacking its predecessor for inattention to issues that, it was argued, lay outside the scope of the predecessor's claims and concerns.

The tensions and self-critiques within black feminist criticism have also often replicated those we have observed within feminist literary criticism in general. Thus, while the confrontation of derogatory images in male-authored works, and, especially, the establishment of a black woman's literary tradition have been important goals, critics such as Sherley Anne Williams and Deborah E. McDowell have cautioned against a separatism that denies what McDowell calls "the countless thematic, stylistic, and imagistic parallels between black male and black female writing" and against an early impulse to "focus on how black men have treated black women in literature." The oppositional dimensions of black feminist criticism are complicated, of course, by the recognition that black men and white women, while differently privileged in relation to black women, were also victims more than they were representatives of the dominant culture.

Raising the same kind of issue, Barbara Christian has questioned whether the critical elaboration of a significant black woman's literary tradition – bolstered by the stunning contemporary array of important black women writers – does not somewhat deflect the attention of black feminists from the lesson of Alice Walker's generative essay, "In Search of Our Mothers' Gardens." The lesson is that black women "should look low" to find their creative foremothers and, by extension, as Christian sees it, that black feminist critics should concern themselves with the creativity "not only of those with a room of their own, or of those in libraries, universities, and literary Renaissances . . . [but of] those who work in kitchens and factories, nurture children and adorn homes, sweep streets or harvest crops, type in offices or manage them." Christian's argument has to do not only with what Hazel Carby calls "the pitfalls of mimicking a male-centered canonical structure of 'great black women' " rather than exploring, as the editors of *Some of Us Are Brave* proposed, "the experience of supposedly 'ordinary' Black women whose 'unexceptional' actions enabled us and the race to survive." It also assails the susceptibility of black feminist critics "to fix ourselves in boxes and categories through jargon, theory, abstraction . . . [and] our education to the very language that masked our existence." On the question of the relation of their concerns to those of poststructuralist theory, however, black feminist critics, like white feminists, remain divided. Some have made a watchword of black radical poet, Audre Lorde's remark that "the master's tools will never dismantle the master's house." Others such as McDowell, in a 1980 essay which helped initiate the trend that Christian later deplored, have found the practical character of black feminist criticism to be limiting and argued that new theoretical directions were necessary to enhance its critical "sophistication" and to keep it from being "marred by slogans, rhetoric, and idealism."

Like feminist criticism in general, then, black feminist criticism emerges as a form of identity politics that asserts the particularity of a social group or class. But, black women writers and critics have also helped to complicate, contextualize, and revise feminist identity politics by virtue of their exploration of what Mae Gwendolyn Henderson calls "the plural aspects of self that constitute the matrix of black female subjectivity," in particular the "internal dialogue" of gender identity and racial identity. Such internal dialogue is manifested in writings by black women that "enter simultaneously into familial, or *testimonial*, and *public,* or competitive discourses, . . . testimonial discourse with black men as blacks, with white women as women, and with black women as black women; . . . competitive discourse with black men as women, with white women as black, and with white men as black women." The work of Hortense Spillers also tends in this problematizing direction. Thus, literature and criticism by black feminists necessarily move (and have moved) women's studies toward a more comparative or "dialogical" cultural studies, a direction indicated by Carby's statement of her guiding theoretical principle in *Reconstructing Womanhood*: "that no language or experience is divorced from the shared context in which different groups that share a language express their differing group interests."

Lesbian feminist theory has also played an increasingly important role in shaping contemporary feminist criticism. As black feminists – and Chicana feminists, such as Gloria Anzaldua and Cherrie Moraga – have prompted something of a shift from the paradigm of women's studies to that of cultural studies in academic feminism's third phase, lesbian feminists have urged, and often exemplified, the rethinking of women's studies as gender studies. Because the lesbian is, in Kate Davy's words, "a subject defined in terms of sexual similarity – whose desire lies outside the fundamental model or underpinnings of sexual difference," she constitutes a radical challenge to the entire logic of a sex/gender system that privileges the difference between men and women. Teresa de Lauretis' phrase, "sexual indifference," suggests the basis and dimensions of this challenge. Because the woman who is defined in relation to women, who takes a woman as her affectional or sexual object, occupies the "male" position in the culture's differential model of sexual identity, she is not different but indifferent from men. She is also indifferent to men. This double "sexual indifference" constitutes both a practical and a theoretical rejection of what the influential poet and lesbian feminist poet-critic Adrienne Rich has termed "compulsory heterosexuality" and the "male right of access to women." The theoretical rejection is a rejection of the dominant system of sexual representation through which men have assumed and sustained the right to define women. This system of sexual representation, formulated in and on male terms, is charged with being at bottom a unitary rather than a binary one – a projection, one might say, of sexual indifference as sexual difference. Lesbian feminist criticism that proceeds along these lines often draws, as de Lauretis does, on the psychoanalytically oriented work of French feminists, in particular of Luce Irigaray, whose book *The Sex Which Is Not One* (1985) set out the theory of the sexual indifference that allegedly underlies all articulations of sexual difference in a male order of signification. Irigaray writes: *"the feminine occurs only within models and laws devised by male subjects*. Which implies that there are not really two sexes, but only one. A single practice and representation of the sexual."

Lesbian feminist criticism, then, not only seeks to advance the project of deconstructing the normative concept or category of the female but specifically asks, as Judith Butler puts it, "to what extent does the category of women achieve stability and coherence only in the context of the heterosexual matrix?" An implication of this question and of much lesbian feminist criticism is that heterosexism is not a particular form or expression of sexism but is its source. Accordingly, lesbian artists, writers, and critics have assaulted the "heterosexual matrix" itself, making what Butler calls "gender trouble" by playing out gender "possibilities that have been forcibly foreclosed" by it. An incisive passage from *Gender Trouble* suggests how this project may be seen as the culminating stage of feminism's original insistence that gender roles and definitions are socially produced rather than biologically given:

Taken to its logical limit, the sex/gender distinction suggests a radical discontinuity between sexed bodies and culturally constructed genders. Assuming for the moment the stability of binary sex, it does not follow that the construction of 'men' will accrue exclusively to the bodies of males or that 'women' will interpret only female bodies. Further, even if the sexes appear to be unproblematically binary in their morphology and constitution (which will become a question), there is no reason to assume that genders ought also to remain as two . . . . When the constructed status of gender is theorized as radically independent of sex, gender itself becomes a free-floating artifice, with the consequences that man and masculine might just as easily signify a female body as a male one, and woman and feminine a male body as easily as a female one.

This brief account of lesbian feminist criticism, we should acknowledge, focuses on its very recent and most theoretical phases. We have not empha-sized its interest in examining the figure of the lesbian in literature, in recovering a lesbian literary tradition, or in articulating a feminist politics unique to lesbian experience or identity. These projects, which correspond to those that black feminist criticism and, more generally, academic feminism itself initially took up, have indeed been undertaken by Bonnie Zimmerman, Lillian Faderman, Catharine Stimpson, Karla Jay, Terry Castle, and others. We have chosen to highlight the theoretical dimensions of lesbian criticism both to indicate its most distinctive contribution to feminism and to offer a specific instance of the convergence or coalition, in third phase feminism, of feminist practice and deconstructive and poststructuralist theory. For the key poststructuralist point made by Butler, Eve Kosofsky Sedgwick, Michael Warner, and other leading theorists of gay studies (or "Queer Theory," as some practitioners defiantly call it) is that sexual definitions – male, female, gay, straight – are inherently unstable, differential, and noncategorical.

FEMINISM, POSTSTRUCTURALISM, AND PSYCHOANALYSIS

As the black, Chicana, and lesbian feminist criticism of the late 1970s and early 1980s changed feminism from within, European theoretical inquiries, suffusing the American academy during the same period, spurred and facili-tated feminism's emergent third phase from without. The lesbian feminist criticism that finds gender to be a variously constructable and multiply divisible "free-floating artifice" applies continental theoretical models in which all identities and all meanings are free-floating artifices in the sense that they have no primary and stable ground. According to these models, that is, identities and meanings are not essences but effects of the signifying practices of languages, practices determined not by reference to a reality or a truth outside language but only by language's artificial conventions. Words and concepts create or shape the beings and meanings that they purportedly only name.

A more direct and sustained examination of what has been called "the linguistic turn" in recent critical theory must wait until the next chapter. But, a cursory statement of its premises here may help clarify its implications for and applications by feminism. As Catherine Belsey observes in her book

Critical Practice (1980), these premises derive in part from the work of the early-twentieth-century linguist, Ferdinand de Saussure. Saussure postulated a science of signs, known today as semiology or semiotics, based on the revolutionary idea that, as Belsey summarizes it, "language is not a nomenclature, a way of naming things which already exist, but a system of differences with no positive terms" which "precedes the existence of independent entities, making the world intelligible by differentiating between concepts." Since concepts and even objects designated by the words of different languages organize the world in different ways, it follows that language does not reflect reality so much as it constructs what we experience as the world. It follows as well that language is social and ideological rather than natural and neutrally descriptive, and that the meanings of its signs and concepts are determined not by their positive or extralinguistic content but by their relations with the other terms in the signifying system.

The implications of this insight have sometimes been exaggerated or misconstrued by Belsey and others in ways that will concern us in our subsequent chapters on "Deconstruction and Poststructuralism" and "From Textuality to Materiality." But their overstatements have served to call attention to the until recently neglected *performative* aspect of language and to its political effects in some areas. For instance, a description such as "homosexual" does in a real sense *produce* what it purports neutrally to *describe*. As Michel Foucault has shown, while people have had same-sex partners in all times and places, only in the late nineteenth century did there emerge a defined class of people called "homosexuals" who were then considered special and different. With its stress on the performative, then, the new linguistic model lends support to many of feminist and gender criticism's practical positions. It provides a theoretical underpinning for the claim that the concepts and categories of sexual identity, experience, and relations expressed by our language are not descriptions of natural and universal phenomena but conventions of and for a patriarchal signifying system. Moreover, this model generally validates the project of politically engaged literary criticism by its view of language as the shaper of human reality and by its implicit denial that literature escapes ideology or exists in some realm of aesthetic rather than social significance.

Some feminists, however, have joined Marxists such as Barbara Foley (and antitheoretical conservatives who do not embrace either feminist or Marxist politics) in their distrust of the linguistic turn in European critical theory or of the use to which American literary theorists have tended to put it. They have objected to what they see as the antimaterialism of the claim that reality is discursively produced and the radical skepticism toward any assertion of meaning or identity in the claim that there are no positive meanings but only functions of the relations between signs. Many feminist critics have wondered, too, about theories that seem to junk humanism and the notion of the autonomous subject at the very moment that women and minorities had begun to demand their full humanity and autonomous subjectivity. The Marxist feminist philosopher Nancy Fraser, for example, offers a telling critique of Foucauldian and French Derridean anti-humanism in her *Unruly Practices* (1989). Nevertheless, the current phase of feminist literary criticism has been significantly influenced by recent theories that have built upon Saussurean premises about language. For these theories support the feminist critique of traditional ideas about what is universal and natural as well as the feminist rejection of any fixed boundary between text and world. Such a rejection, which is crucial but not exclusive to feminist criticism, allows one to see literary texts as having effects in the world and to see the world itself as a text in need of interpretation.

One instance in which feminists have drawn on European discourse theory to expand or reorient feminist criticism is the current revisionary engagement with Freud and psychoanalysis. Rejecting Freudianism as a biologistic science that defines some essential psychology of women, recent feminist interpreters have tended to employ it as a critical language within which human sexuality is itself understood to be not naturally given but produced by social and signifying processes. Freud himself, Juliet Mitchell argues, provides a basis for the feminist destabilization of the patriarchal male/female binary in his insistence on "the psychological bisexuality of both sexes." It is only "society [that] demands . . . that one sex attain a preponderance of femininity, the other of masculinity"; thus, "man and woman are made in culture." Moreover, Mitchell suggests, these gendered individuals are never fixed entities in the Freudian view because, for Freud, selfhood proceeds not from the infant's experience of autonomous identity but from its identification with the image of another (the mother, for the girl child; the mother, subsequently replaced by the father, for the boy). "This identity is an imaginary construct based not in a true recognition, but on a misrecognition; the self is always like another, in other words, this self is constructed of necessity in a state of alienation: the person first sees himself in another."

The French psychoanalyst Jacques Lacan has most radically and, at least for literary critics, influentially developed this Freudian proposition in the light of post-Saussurean theories of language. In particular, Lacan's work has been central to the French feminist criticism that gained prominence in the American academy during the 1980s. In Lacanian theory, the infant attains differentiated identity upon its passage from what Lacan calls the Imaginary into the Symbolic order, terms that roughly correspond to Freud's pleasure principle and reality principle. The Symbolic order is the patriarchal order of law, culture, and, specifically, language. It is the outside power, the power of the father, with which the infant identifies when, in the Oedipal crisis, it must abandon the (Imaginary) oneness with the world that it has experienced in its symbiotic unity with the body of the mother. Lacan's revision of Freud comes in his argument that the phallus, the sign of the father's law and of the threat of castration, is not the penis itself but a *symbol* of the power found in patriarchal discourse, in language. By identifying with this power, the child is enabled to constitute itself, to say "I am." But that articulated self is a symbolic or linguistic one, achieved by the child's assumption of a particular place within the family's and the society's preestablished structure of social and sexual roles. The formation of our identities, then, depends upon alienation and repression, alienation from the realm of the body and repression of the body's desire for reunion with the world. Freud had argued that in identity formation we are torn from the mother's womb and left longing for the "oceanic feeling" of lost unity whose memory remains buried in the unconscious. Lacan takes Freud's suggestion a step further by reasoning that, consequently, we are constitutively divided beings whose identity lies in our difference from ourselves.

Psychoanalytic theory, especially Lacan's, powerfully informs the work of French feminists such as Irigaray, Hélène Cixous, and Julia Kristeva. Freud and later psychoanalysts had suggested that the superego (the repressive agent of the father and of society in the psyche) is less powerful in the girl child. They argued that female identity is more relational and interactive than male selfhood, because the ego boundaries marking the girl's separation from the mother are less absolute, and that women therefore retain in adulthood a more polymorphous sexuality than men. To Freud's argument, Lacan adds the suggestion that the female body is the very site of the antisymbolic—that is, of transgression. If the body of the mother is a realm of immediacy and fullness, it is not a part of the symbolizing social order but of what precedes that order and is usually sacrificed to its divisions and identifications. This premise is crucial to Irigaray's assertion that "woman" cannot be reduced to the man's other in the patriarchal system of signification but is, instead, precisely what is unrepresentable by that system. Upon this premise, more generally, French feminists have based their evocations and celebrations of a revolutionary *écriture feminine*, an expression or writing of the female body that perpetually subverts the patriarchal symbolic order.

This species of French feminism (there is a more pragmatic and sociopolitically rather than psychoanalytically oriented feminist criticism in France that has rarely reached the American academy) may be said to have a material emphasis in its concern with women's bodily experience. It argues, as Ann Rosalind Jones puts it, that "if women are to discover and express who they are, to bring to the surface what masculine history has repressed in them, they must begin with their sexuality." But its practice has frequently taken the form of a revisionist mythmaking, more interested in "woman" as sign or antisign than in actual women as a class. Thus, James Joyce, for Cixous, can count as a writer of *écriture feminine* insofar as his texts transgress formal and generic boundaries, while women realists like Edith Wharton and Willa Cather probably would not qualify.

This is obviously a problem. So is the notion that rational or symbolic discourse has been so contaminated by patriarchy and its assumptions as to completely exclude women from its domain. When Irigaray writes that women have no available language, that "all the statements I make are . . . either borrowed from a model that leaves my sex aside . . . or else my utterances are unintelligible according to the code in force," Denis Donoghue seems persuasive in arguing that "the charge is so omniverous that no particular man need feel intimidated by it, nor is it clear what possible course of action could redress it." Irigaray's complementary notion that female sexuality and the female body somehow comprise a realm apart from and prior to social experience or definition, moreover, is a view that renders French feminists at least as susceptible to the charge of essentialism as were second-phase Anglo-American proponents of a female literary coun-tertradition. Indeed, other feminist critics have noted that Irigaray's rhap-sodic image of the fluid and multiplicitous woman's style – which so "resists and explodes all firmly established forms, figures, ideas, concepts" that "when 'she' says something, it is already no longer identical to what she means" – is disturbingly reminiscent of the most dismissive masculinist stereotypes of female character and intellect. And, when Cixous takes *écriture feminine*, to resonate, in Toril Moi's characterization, with the music of "this nameless pre-Oedipal space filled with mother's milk and honey," the "maca-bre" sexist view that Mary Ellmann had hyperbolized ("as though women wrote with their breasts instead of pens") is almost literalized in the name of feminist subversion.

The propensity toward a new and arguably self-defeating essentialism in French feminism may be mitigated insofar as the categories of "woman" and of *écriture feminine* are emptied of any necessary restriction to one biological sex – however problematic in other ways this move may be. As just noted, Cixous has stipulated that when she discusses woman's writing it is the *writing's* sexual identity rather than the author's that concerns her. Thus, as Jonathan Culler observes of French feminist criticism, " 'woman' has come to stand for any radical force that subverts the concepts, assumptions, and structures of traditional male discourse." (Jacques Derrida had suggested as much in *Spurs* [1979].) In other words, French feminists may be understood to use "woman" and "the feminine" not as a description of a particular class of people or their qualities but as a heuristic concept from which to critique and dismantle patriarchal structures.

The most elaborated instance of this approach is the work of Julia Kristeva. Kristeva refuses to define "woman" and advances no theory of "the feminine." But, as Moi remarks, "what she does have is a theory of marginality, subversion and dissidence." A professor of linguistics and a practicing psychoanalyst, Kristeva takes up Lacan's distinction between the Imaginary and the Symbolic order, but she argues, as Freud does with respect to the pleasure principle and the reality principle, that the Imaginary is not entirely repressed with the triumph of language and patriarchal culture. Rather, the laws and structures that keep the Symbolic order orderly must constantly struggle against the heterogeneity and excess that are integral to the signifying process, much as the Freudian unconscious is to the conscious self. These disorderly elements or tendencies constitute what Kristeva calls "the semiotic." The semiotic might be described as the repressed voice of the Lacanian Imaginary, or of the primary pre-Oedipal stage, which, in Moi's phrase, exists for Kristeva "as pulsional pressure on symbolic language: as contradictions, meaninglessness, disruptions, silences and absences in the symbolic language." Certain literary practices can maximize the pressure of the semiotic on the symbolic order and, Kristeva asserts, help to make visible what and whom it represses and marginalizes. The course of any successful challenge to the patriarchal power structure, she writes, must "pass through that which is repressed in discourse, and in the relations of production. Call it 'woman' or 'oppressed classes of society,' it is the same struggle, and never the one without the other."

As this last quotation suggests, Kristeva's feminism opens out into a wider liberationist critique that may be accommodated to class, ethnic, and Third World struggles. For her, semiotic analysis discovers a "general social law" in "the symbolic dimension which is given in language" and reveals "that every social practice offers a specific expression of that law." Kristeva's own critical practice, however, which has gradually shed an early Marxist orientation, is open to the charge of romantic libertarianism. Moi notes Kristeva's "grossly exaggerated confidence in the political importance of the avant-garde," and Gayatri Spivak points out, with reference to a Kristeva passage about dissolving sexual identities, that "even if one knows how to undo identities, one does not necessarily escape the historical determinations of sexism."

Yet, Spivak goes on to assert, "there is in Kristeva's text an implicit double program for woman which we encounter in the best of French feminism: against sexism, where women unite as a biologically oppressed caste; and for feminism, where human beings train to prepare for a transformation of consciousness." For increasing numbers of recent feminist critics, the transformation of consciousness with which Spivak identifies feminism here specifically includes consciousness of class and race as well as gender and, thus, demands a coalition or interaction of feminism with other forms of ideological critique. Accordingly, a significant project of third phase feminism has been to define a feminist Marxist criticism which might overcome the historically "unhappy marriage," as Heidi Hartmann calls it, in which "like the marriage of husband and wife depicted in English common law [,] marxism and feminism are one, and that one is marxism." Many feminists have contributed to this project in ways that range from Catharine A. MacKinnon's documentation of the interlocking structures of "men's control over women's sexuality and capital's control over employees' work lives" (*Sexual Harassment of Working Women: A Case of Sex Discrimination*, 1979) to Gayle Rubin's influential feminist revision of Marxism, Freudianism, and Levi-Strauss's structural anthropology ("The Traffic in Women: Notes on the 'Political Economy' of Sex," 1975) to Nancy Fraser's synthesis of social theory and pragmatism (*Unruly Practices*, 1989) to Spivak's own interdisciplinary and internationalist criticism (*In Other Worlds: Essays in Cultural Politics*, 1988; *The Postcolonial Critic: Interviews, Strategies, Dialogues*, 1990).

The feminist criticism cited above strikingly differs in the objects of its attention from the criticism of Millett or Spacks; indeed, it has been many pages since we have mentioned literature or specifically literary analysis in this chapter. Our turn to discussions of linguistic, psychoanalytic, anthropological, and political theory in the chapter's latter pages is indicative of the fact that the work that most profoundly influences feminist literary criticism today is often not produced by literary scholars. This raises the question whether the "radical rethinking of the conceptual grounds of literary study" that Showalter takes to mark feminist literary criticism's third phase has produced, or is producing, a critical activity that is no longer grounded in nor aptly conceived as literary study. It is a question Robinson anticipated in a 1977 essay entitled "Working/Women/Writing," where she wrote:

It is a fundamental precept of bourgeois aesthetics that good art, although probably adhering and contributing to a tradition, is art that celebrates what is unique and even eccentric in human experience or human personality. . . . For both artist and audience, cultural expression serves as a refuge for one's uniqueness against the brutality, the uniformity, and the conformity of life under capitalism. But this retreat is not necessarily the place most conducive to revolutionary changes in our condition.

We must ask, then, Robinson continues, "whether the best role for the arts and for criticism is to celebrate that which is basic or that which is marginal, what is common or what is acceptable," and whether they should concern themselves with "the creation of myth at all" or, rather, with "the expression of fact."

Arguing along different lines than Robinson, Ellen Messer-Davidow explicitly concludes in "The Philosophical Bases of Feminist Literary Criticisms" (1987) that "the subject, subject matters, methods, and epistemology" of "traditional literary criticism" are unsuitable for feminist criticism, whose appropriate objects are not literary texts but "ideas about sex and gender that people express in literary and critical media." In the same year, however, the newsletter of the Modern Language Association was reporting that "among approaches to literary study, feminist criticism had had the greatest impact on curriculum," and the prominent critical theorist Peter Brooks was opining in the *New York Times Magazine* that "anyone worth his salt in literary criticism today has to become something of a feminist." This may have been an exaggeration, but some combination of feminism's moral force, its growing academic currency, and the antiessentialist theories of sexual identity and gender studies of its third phase has recently generated a substantial body of feminist criticism by men and much debate over the possibilities and limitations of "men in feminism." (See the collection under this title edited by Paul Smith and Alice Jardine [1987].) Undoubtedly, feminist criticism has had a powerful, multivalent, and abiding impact on literary studies over the course of more than two decades. But feminists might ask whether a situation in which it is felt that every critic "worth *his* salt" has to "become something of a feminist" is a measure of the achievement of their enterprise or a sign of its absorption and domestication. Is success for feminist critique a matter of being assimilated into mainstream literary studies or honing its oppositional edge on the margin? Of revising the canon or redefining the discipline? Of bringing to light women writers and artists or deconstructing the sign "woman"? Of eliminating sexism in the academy or transforming consciousness and revolutionizing social and economic relations in the world? Not all of these objectives, of course, are incompatible, but their often uneasy interrelations suggest that the playful question in the title of a 1984 talk by Robinson may have become more serious and more complex in the intervening years: "Feminist Criticism: How Do We Know When We've Won?"

5

❦

DECONSTRUCTION AND POSTSTRUCTURALISM

THOUGH DECONSTRUCTION, like feminism, is only secondarily a form of *literary* criticism, it too has posed a fundamental challenge to the institutionalization of academic literary criticism recounted in our second and third chapters. That process of institutionalization assumed that literature possessed unique qualities that distinguished it *as* literature from other forms of communication. It was this idea of "literariness" that justified the special disciplinary status of literary study as an academic department and field, whose objectivity and rigor were buttressed by frequent recourse to the language of scientific inquiry.

Whether one followed Northrop Frye, who claimed to uncover universal underlying archetypes of literary art and human imagination, or various New Critics who claimed to discover the defining structural principles of all poetry worthy of the name, the need for autonomous departments of literature seemed clear. The same need was indicated for different reasons, if one worked in literary history, by the presumably organic unity of national literary traditions such as that of the United States. Feminism, deconstruction, and the broader movement called poststructuralism, we suggested, all challenge these unitary images both of texts and of national literatures that have justified the disciplinary isolation of literary studies.

In each case, the identity in question (of integral literary work, national traditions, or academic departments) depends on a boundary distinction between an outside and an inside, which these new movements call into question. Just as feminism challenged the assumption that sexual power relations are outside literature (and therefore may be properly relegated to sociology departments), deconstruction has challenged the assumption that philosophical questions are properly outside literature – even as it has challenged the assumption of philosophy departments that the study of metaphor, rhetoric, and other literary concerns are outside, or merely tangential to, philosophy. These challenges themselves exemplify a key deconstructive tactic, which is to reveal how all ostensibly autonomous identities come into being through the violent differentiation of a valued "inside" from a devalued, and then excluded or repressed, "outside."

DECONSTRUCTION: CHARACTERIZATIONS
AND CARICATURES

Many have mistakenly understood deconstruction's challenge to the unity of texts, founding philosophical and political categories, and other identities as a denial of the meaningfulness or even the very existence of these entities. The popular assault on deconstruction (often accompanied by the proud assertion of the critic's inability to read deconstructive work) represents it as a random, arbitrary, perverse, nihilistic attempt to destroy meaning. The arguments of deconstruction's principal theorist and exponent, Jacques Derrida, about the "instability" and "undecidability" of meaning have been depicted as a species of irresponsible relativism, and deconstruction in the popular mind has come to be defined as the theory that there is no truth, or that reality is only words, or that texts can mean anything anyone wants them to mean.

Thus, Joseph Epstein claims that Derrida's message is that literature is "in need of destruction"; Dinesh D'Souza asserts that "deconstructionists hold that literature is simply empty of meaning"; and Jeffrey Hart dismisses deconstruction as a form of "imperial reading" that seeks to "capsize the author and his work in order to hand over semantic authority" to the narcissistic critic. In fairness to the caricaturists, these caricatures have been given credibility by some who call themselves deconstructionists or who praise deconstruction for abolishing all norms and standards. Yet, contrary to the popular caricatures, deconstruction is properly about not relativism but *relationality*, not meaning's absence but its unruly excesses, not referential anarchy but how terms mean through complex relations with other terms.

At the risk of perpetrating our own caricature, we here list what we take to be central postulates of deconstruction, which we will explain and examine in this chapter's subsequent discussion of deconstruction and poststructuralism.

1. Because language is a system whose symbols and concepts are comprehensible only by virtue of their relations to other symbols and concepts, the identity of any meaningful utterance is dependent upon what it is *not* – that is, it is defined by its difference. ("Tree" becomes meaningful for us only in relation to what it is not: to "bush" or to "tray" or "tee.") In other words, nothing simply *is itself*, independent of its relations.

2. An utterance's or a text's identity or meaning necessarily involves the exclusion or repression of those relations through which its meaning is produced, the differences upon which its identity depends. Thus, an utterance *says* something by *doing* something different; it grounds its meaning, establishes its identity, by repressing the "other(s)" that inform it.

3. The traces of whatever is excluded or repressed, however, inevitably

haunt the utterance. A deconstructive reading attempts to recover this repressed "other" by locating its traces in the utterance.

4. Because every text is haunted by others that it cannot assimilate, what a text says never coincides with what it does (these are really two forms of the same argument), and therefore every text is fundamentally unstable. Deconstruction overturns the law of identity that for Aristotle was fundamental to all logic and reasoning: A=A, or a thing cannot be both itself and something else at the same time and in the same relation. Derrida argues precisely that A can be itself only by being different from itself. This is not to say that identity and unity do not exist in the world or in texts, but rather that they are constituted by self-difference.

5. In a society or culture, discourses and explanatory narratives become dominant by repressing counterdiscourses, narratives, and voices that they cannot assimilate. Deconstructive readings attempt to elicit these unwanted "other" stories and show how they haunt the official discourse and thus undo its supposed coherence and inevitability. The political efficacy of deconstructive reading strategies (and their link to Marxism, feminism, and other directly sociopolitical forms of criticism) rests on a claim that these strategies can help shake dominant discourses by revealing their repressed contradictions.

6. To deconstruct a text, then, is not to *destroy* its meaning but to go back over how that meaning was constructed through exclusions and repressions. In this sense, deconstruction can be an instrument of historical analysis.

DECONSTRUCTION AND LINGUISTIC DIFFERENTIATION

Deconstruction derives in part from the work of the Swiss linguist, Ferdinand de Saussure (1857–1915), who argued in his *Course in General Linguistics* (1916) that meaning is generated by differential relations within the linguistic system rather than by any direct correspondence between words and things. One of Saussure's examples was "the 8:25 Geneva-to-Paris Express," a term whose meaning, he pointed out, is not impaired even if the train in fact arrives at eight-thirty or nine o'clock and even if it consists of a different engine and set of cars every night. "The 8:25 train" derives its meaning from its differential relation to the trains that precede and follow it in the railroad timetable system rather than by corresponding to a certain time or a certain physical object. For that matter, the concept of "train" itself derives its meaning through its difference from other forms of transportation – bicycles, cars, buses, trolleys, and so forth.

Does it follow, then, from Saussurean linguistics that there is something fallacious about the very idea that language can refer to a world outside language? This, according to many commentators, sympathetic as well as hostile, is the implication that Derrida and other poststructuralists have drawn from Saussure. Catherine Belsey, for example, writes that "if discourses articulate concepts through a system of signs which signify by means of their relationship to each other rather than to entities in the world, and if literature is a signifying practice, all it can reflect is the order inscribed in particular discourses, not the nature of the world."

Belsey's inference, however, is overstated and misleading. The argument that meaning is generated by the relationships of concepts "to each other" does not necessarily entail the position that language or literature can reflect or refer only to the order of discourse. What does follow, rather, is that our practices of reflecting or referring to the world themselves depend on our manipulation of linguistic differences. The difference is subtle but crucial: it is not that language is *cut off* from the possibility of referring to reality, as Belsey implies, but rather that reference to reality is inevitably mediated by language, or, as we have put it earlier, by interpretations and interpretive systems. The proper inference, in other words, is not that meaning is a matter of purely internal linguistic difference *instead of* reference, but rather that reference itself is made possible only by linguistic difference or relationality. The railroad timetable with its series of times (8:05 / 8:15 / 8:25, and so forth) gives the term "the 8:25 train" its meaning, but it does not follow that when we say, "I have to catch the 8:25 train tonight" we are somehow making reference only to words and not to any real train. Using the differential system is the way "referring to a real train" works.

What Derrida draws from Saussure, in ways that will become clearer as our chapter develops, is not that the external world is non-existent but that a principle of difference, division, and nonidentity is built into our acts of referring to the external world. This is another way of saying that the identities we describe in the world, indeed our own identities as speakers, depend upon a principle of nonidentity, the fact that meaning is generated through differences and relations among terms. As a consequence, the identities we describe and inhabit, and the concepts of "inside" and "outside," cannot be understood to be fixed and stable. Again, the point is not that there is no reality "out there" to be referred to, but that since reference to reality is always relational and contextual it is inevitably haunted by instabilities, a fact testified to at the common sense level by the extent to which our descriptions of reality are so frequently contested and debated.

One might object to our example, of course, that the "meaning" of something so quotidien as a train schedule is a trivial matter. According to Derrida (and Saussure), however, the meanings we ascribe to persons, texts, and nations are in principle as dependent on differential relations as is the meaning of "the 8:25 train." The concept of "Western culture," for instance, has meaning only in relation to cultures defined as non-Western. Moreover, as peoples who have been defined by "Westerners" as "non-Western" increasingly inhabit "the West," the instability of any unitary idea of "Western culture" becomes even more obvious, as does the fact that the unity posited by a term like "the West" is more a result of that term than something that neutrally preexists it. As the example illustrates, the argument that meaning is relational can carry significant stakes.

A usefully succinct "lay person's definition of deconstruction" is offered by the critic Barbara Johnson, who observes that, in most of our encounters with texts, readers are under pressure to answer the questions, "What does the text say?" or "What's the bottom line?" But, Johnson continues, "what deconstruction does is to teach you to ask, 'What does the construction of the bottom line leave out? What does it repress? What does it disregard? What does it consider unimportant? What does it put in the margins?'" One need not be a deconstructionist to recognize that any "bottom line" summary is selective, that it is a summary only insofar as it ignores or excludes some things. Accordingly, in her book *The Critical Difference* (1980), Johnson argues that

deconstruction is not synonymous with destruction. . . . It is in fact much closer to the original meaning of the word analysis, which etymologically means 'to undo' – a virtual synonym for 'to deconstruct.' The de-construction of a text does not proceed by random doubt or arbitrary subversion, but by the careful teasing out of warring forces of signification within the text itself.

Another commentator, Christopher Norris, replies to the frequently levelled charge that deconstruction obscures or refuses to articulate its ends when he asserts what is implicit in Johnson's definition: that deconstructive analysis should be imagined not as "some worked-out scheme of hierarchical ideas" but rather as a way of exploring particular instances of the processes of schematization by which texts organize themselves. "Deconstruction," Norris writes, "is therefore an activity of reading which remains closely tied to the texts it interrogates, and which can never set up independently as a self-enclosed system of operative concepts." For all of the narcissistic aggression sometimes ascribed to it, deconstructive analysis, more than any other mode of contemporary criticism, aims to linger as long as possible with and in the work that it addresses rather than reducing, abstracting, or supplanting the work by means of its own instruments of conceptual closure. Moreover, while deconstruction is commonly and rightly associated with the relationality (otherwise called constructivism, antiessentialism, or antifoundationalism) that some blame for the canon-busting, multiculturalist energies alleged to be destroying "Western culture," deconstructionists have tended to study the central philosophical and literary monuments of the West, often with meticulous care and stunning erudition.

In fact, Derrida himself pointedly questions the very possibility of the kind of apocalyptic break with the past and with traditional ways and categories of meaning that deconstruction is often thought to demand or to be. "I do not believe," he has stated, "in decisive ruptures; in an unequivocal 'epistemological break,' as it is called today. Breaks are always, and fatally, reinscribed in an old cloth that must continually, interminably, be undone." Far from proclaiming the death of past forms of thought, as its media image would have us believe, deconstruction thus maintains that past forms of thought inevitably reappear in the present. The return of the repressed past, the ghostly recurrence of what has been pronounced dead, is accordingly a major motif in deconstructive readings. For deconstruction, every break to some degree conserves what it ruptures, reinscribing it with a difference. A striking instance of this pattern of break and reinscription is seen in the way deconstruction both breaks with and reinscribes aspects of the New Criticism.

Deconstructive criticism certainly makes the same claim that Elaine Showalter has made for feminist criticism, in a remark that we quoted in our last chapter: that it has prompted a "radical rethinking of the conceptual grounds of literary study." But, it means something different by "radical rethinking." This is not simply to say that deconstruction and feminism often involve different objects and methods of analysis (although the phase of feminist criticism to which Showalter's remark refers owes much to deconstructive methods, and although Derrida himself draws suggestive connections between his central, yet traditionally marginalized, figure of "writing" and the traditional category of "women" that feminists were beginning to refigure as deconstruction emerged). Feminism has altered and expanded the terrain of literary study, insisting that academic criticism attend to issues, texts, experiences, and institutions previously held to be outside or beneath its scope. These new changes in literary study have required and generated new conceptualizations of the enterprise. But deconstruction's operation upon New Critical grounds may be viewed more literally as an act of rethinking – thinking through the New Criticism and thinking it again – that takes New Criticism's own identity, at its most radical, to lie in otherness, self-difference.

FROM NEW CRITICISM TO DECONSTRUCTION

In Chapter 3, we pointed out the suggestive metaphor of "the democratic state" that John Crowe Ransom used in *The New Criticism* (1941) to characterize poetic form, texture, and experience. The poem, Ransom argued, was democratic in that it was a "weakly regulatory" structure that restrained itself from "a really imperious degree of organization" and encouraged its constituent members (words, images) to "retain their personalities," to "display energy in unpredictable ways," and even to "[disrespect] whatever kind of logical content" the overall structure sought to enforce. Though Ransom's agrarian politics were reactionary, Ransom clearly associates poetry, here, with an energy of resistance – a view that was widely shared by modernist poets and critics across the political spectrum. What poetry, and more broadly literary experience and education, was thought to resist was variously defined. Sometimes, it was totalitarianism as a political system, democracy's antithesis. More often, as we will see, it was the cultural or aesthetic homogenization, degradation, and anaesthesis that many literary intellectuals, from the arch-conservative T. S. Eliot to the neo-Marxists of the German Frankfurt School, feared in the growth and spread of twentieth-century mass communications. For Ransom and his academic colleagues, however, poetry principally resisted the totalizing and objectivizing power of science and what Allen Tate called "the positivist attitude that has captured the modern world."

This conflict between science and poetry that marks much modernist art and criticism in fact replays an ancient controversy. The view that language is ideally a transparent medium of representation, a view that led twentieth century logical positivists to contrive a system of notation that admits the least possible distortion between linguistic description and observable reality, may be traced as far back as Plato's attacks on sophistic rhetoricians. Its early modern expression may be seen in the work of the scientific empiricists of the seventeenth century, who argued that language could be brought closer to the reality of natural phenomena by purifying it of metaphor and other figures of speech, which empiricists relegated to the supposedly useless and decorative art of poetry. In the reemergent conflict between advocates and opponents of "the positivist attitude" that mobilized the New Critics, a battle took shape between the claims of scientific and poetic language. The proper language of science was seen as austere, stripped of metaphor, connotation, and ambiguity, and designed to correspond to the objective world; the language of poetry, on the other hand, was extravagantly figurative, receptive to ambiguity, and concerned less with objectifiable data than with subjective emotions and states of mind or with experiential forms of knowledge that could not be scientifically verified.

As the New Critic Cleanth Brooks put it in a chapter entitled "The Language of Paradox" from *The Well Wrought Urn* (1947), "the tendency of science is necessarily to stabilize terms, to freeze them into strict denotations; the poet's tendency is by contrast disruptive. The terms are constantly modifying each other, and thus violating their dictionary definitions." Unlike the scientist, Brooks added, citing the theory of I. A. Richards, the poet "must work by contradiction and qualification" and "by analogies." The poet *must* work in these ways because the poet neither takes language to be passively reflective of reality nor takes reality itself to be simply or logically given. In other words, the New Critics argued, form and content were not static and separable entities, as least not in poetry. Rather than serving as a transparent medium through which a preexistent content or moral is conveyed, poetic language functions in a productive, transformative, or even "disruptive" way to effect a unique kind of meaning that is not reducible to prose paraphrase.

It is crucial to recognize that the New Critics, in defining their enterprise, their discourse, and their objects of attention against those of logical positivism or of science, unwittingly reinstated the positivist assumption of categorical differences between science and literature. This assumption, as we have seen, allowed the New Critics to argue that literature was a distinct form of expression that rewarded skilled interpretation, an object of investigation that demanded its own professional academic discipline. Like Ransom's "democratic state," however, the New Criticism is potentially destabilized and undone by the very values and insights that constitute it. In other words, there is a "disruptive" or "democratic" moment in the New Criticism itself that tends to undermine its own claims for literary unity and organic form. Following a deconstructive formula, one could argue that, in this disruptive moment, deconstruction is revealed to be the repressed other of the New Criticism.

In poems, the New Critics showed, language constructs and transforms rather than simply reflects the world. Poetry is rife with ambiguity, contradiction, paradox, unpredictability, and subversion rather than transparently understandable. Poetic meaning lies in the shifting, line-by-line process of its unfolding rather than in any paraphrasable message; in fact, it often presents an irreducible conflict between what it seems to say and what it performs. These are the qualities that define poetry as poetry and that distinguish poetic language from scientific language. Yet, if the tendency of poetry and of the discourse of the New Critics is to disrupt the definitions and distinctions that science seeks to stabilize, what exempts its own definitions and distinctions – including the distinction between the special case of poetic language and the normative case of scientific or nonliterary language – from the same destabilization? If language functions constructively, connotatively, contradictorily, performatively, ambivalently in the particular instance of literature, what reason is there to think it does not function the same way elsewhere?

On a deconstructive view, New Criticism represses its own latent disruptive impulse – blinds itself to its deepest, most radical insights – in order to establish the sovereign poetic object and to institute literary study as a discipline. By the terms of their own constitution, these entities cannot hold their centers or protect their borders; these constructs deconstruct themselves. Although New Critics stopped short of asserting that poetic instabilities were generalizable to language itself or that the disruptiveness of poetic language might effect social disruption, a shared insistence on the constructive and transformative powers of language links New Critical poetics to subsequent deconstructive and poststructuralist linguistic theory. Stanley Fish, a theorist most closely associated with a poststructuralist version of reader-response criticism (which we will discuss later in this chapter), lays heavy stress on New Criticism's anticipation of deconstruction when he writes that "deconstruction would have been literally unthinkable were it not already an article of faith that literary texts are characterized by a plurality of meanings and were it not already the established methodology of literary studies to produce for the supposedly 'great text' as many meanings as possible." Fish's remark helps explain the alacrity with which deconstruction was incorporated into academic literary study and adapted to the needs of its interpretation industry. But, while we too, thus far, have emphasized this connection, it must not be overstated. In fact, it now must be partly undone.

DERRIDA'S REREADING OF PLATO

As commentators such as Christopher Norris and Rudolph Gasché have warned, it is a mistake to understand deconstruction as a kind of literary criticism while ignoring its roots in philosophy, specifically in certain ancient philosophical problems and debates. Derrida has sometimes written about literature, but the late Paul de Man, along with such American followers as Barbara Johnson, J. Hillis Miller, and Joseph Riddel, have been the critics largely responsible for making deconstruction an "approach" to literature. Derrida's major work is concerned not with literature but philosophy, although the distinction between philosophy and literature is among the binary oppositions that he "deconstructs." To understand what this means, we have to look at Derrida's philosophical writings.

This is all the more necessary because what may look like mere irrationality or perversity in deconstruction appears in a different light when it is recognized that many of its concerns grow out of traditional philosophical discussions. A traditional and recurring theme in philosophy is the idea that the rigorous pursuit of reason to its strict logical conclusions leads to paradoxes and contradictions that reason cannot solve. Deconstruction has far more to do with the attempt to push reason to a greater awareness of its own limits and conditions than with the irresponsible irrationalism of which it has been accused. If deconstruction does call certain classical concepts of rationality into question, it claims to do so not in the name of simple unreason but of a philosophical rigor borrowed from classical rationality. In this respect, deconstruction can be seen as both an extension and a critique of the tradition of "transcendental" philosophy, which seeks to inquire into the "conditions of possibility" of reason itself, a project that for Derrida founders on the impossibility of achieving a detached perspective on the discourse in which one is necessarily implicated.

The immediate philosophical origins of deconstruction generally have been traced to the work of Nietzsche and Heidegger. Deconstructive concerns are anticipated, for example, in Nietzsche's reduction of reason to the will to power and in his demystified view of truth as "a mobile army of metaphors" whose merely metaphoric nature has been forgotten. They are also foreshadowed in Heidegger's analysis of the relational nature of all concepts and his later critique of the ruthless will to mastery in modern technocratic reason, a critique that underlay what Heidegger called his "destruktion" of Western metaphysics. Deconstruction also responds oppositionally to Heideggerian and Husserlian phenomenology and their extension in what came in the 1960s to be called the "criticism of consciousness," a school of critics centered in Geneva that included such figures as George Poulet, Jean Starobinski, and Maurice Blanchot, and that influenced the early work of J. Hillis Miller. As Sarah Lawall writes in *Critics of Consciousness* (1968), the school set out to study literature as a manifestation of "consciousness," or the so-called *cogito* of the author, rather than as a detached object. In *Poets of Reality* (1965), for example, Miller reconstructs the interior phenomenological worlds of such poets as T. S. Eliot, Wallace Stevens, and William Carlos Williams. But though such phenomenological criticism rejected the New Critical assumption of the organic integrity of individual literary works, it tended to relocate that organic integrity in the consciousness of the author, which is seen as unified and self-present. It is this totalized view of consciousness that deconstruction challenges.

Those who have sought to morally discredit deconstruction by pouncing on its links to Nietzsche and Heidegger (whose susceptibility to nihilistic and totalitarian thought, respectively, is well known) have ignored deconstruction's anti-totalizing character. As we have observed, Derrida rejects the apocalyptic strain of the work of these forerunners along with reductively totalitarian and anarchistic applications of the critique of reason. Thus the notorious deconstructionist concept of interpretive "undecidability" does not mean, as many have asserted, that any interpretation of a text is as good as any other or that interpretations are inarguable and not subject to rational dispute. Derrida argues, as we shall see, that complete license in interpretation is as illusory as complete infallibility.

Setting aside polemics for a moment, we propose to better elucidate deconstruction by tracing an important deconstructive analysis, Derrida's reading of Plato and particularly Plato's *Phaedrus* in the 1968 essay, "Plato's Pharmacy." This lengthy essay (which we can discuss only in part) provides a useful example for our purposes, illustrating as it does that, far from dismissively debunking canonical thinkers such as Plato, Derrida develops his own argument by taking them intensely seriously.

The key passage in the *Phaedrus* for Derrida is a discussion of the origins of writing that enforces a central theme of the dialogue: the superiority of philosophy to rhetoric as a means of seeking truth. Socrates recounts for Phaedrus the story of the Egyptian god Theuth, who is said by legend to be the inventor of writing. In the story, Theuth recommends writing to the Theban god Thamus or Ammon, boasting that it "will improve both the wisdom and the memory of the Egyptians." Ammon scornfully replies that Theuth has attributed to writing "quite the opposite" of its real effect. "Those who acquire it," says Ammon, "will cease to exercise their memory and become forgetful; they will rely on writing to bring things to their remembrance by external signs instead of on their own internal resources." And "as for wisdom, your pupils [those who rely on writing] will have the reputation for it without the reality."

Siding with Ammon's repudiation of writing, Socrates warns Phaedrus that it is foolish "to suppose that one can transmit or acquire a clear and certain knowledge of an art through the medium of writing, or that written words can do more than remind the reader of what he already knows on a given subject." The trouble with writing is its vulnerability to the vagaries of interpretation:

once a thing is committed to writing it circulates equally among those who understand the subject and those who have no business with it; a writing cannot distinguish between suitable and unsuitable readers. And if it is ill-treated or unfairly abused it always needs its parent to come to its rescue; it is quite incapable of defending or helping itself.

A written text is at the mercy of interpreters, since its author or "parent" is usually not present, the way an oral speaker is, to explain himself or correct misreadings. The fact that a written text goes on circulating and conveying meaning in the absence of its author, even after the author's death, makes writing peculiarly vulnerable to promiscuous appropriations. In its inability to speak for itself when questioned or misinterpreted, writing is curiously *mute* and *dumb*. Like paintings, says Socrates, written words "look like living beings, but if you ask them a question they maintain a solemn silence." Shockingly, written words *do not understand their own meanings*: "you might suppose that they understand what they are saying," says Socrates, "but if you ask them what they mean by anything they simply return the same answer over and over again" – that is, the reiterated words of the text itself. Even a text containing many layers of self-explanation cannot explain itself any further when questioned or misread.

Socrates' remarks on writing may seem merely naive and literal minded, yet they point up a profound paradox. One would think that, if a text "means what it says," then its meaning could be given by simply repeating the words of the text verbatim. Why is it, then, when we are asked what a text means, it is not considered a useful answer if we only reiterate the original words of the text? A verbatim repetition of a text is not considered to be an interpretation at all – in some contexts it can even be an act of plagiarism. (Students are sometimes honestly puzzled when accused of academic plagiarism: it does not make sense to them that repeating the words of a text does not count as a legitimate interpretation of it.) In other words, we do not count something as an interpretation of a text, much less a useful interpretation, unless it *changes* the words of the text. To be a legitimate interpretation it must "translate" the terms of the text into other terms, put them "in other words." On the other hand, neither do we count something as an interpretation unless it in some sense delivers "the same" meaning as the original text. Treating a text "on its own terms" seems to involve transforming it into different terms in order to replicate it. How can this be?

This is the paradox that troubles Socrates about writing, not just the fact that writing can be misread but that its exchange value in the world depends on change and difference. The meaning of a text evidently can only be explained by a second text, and one that will not be considered a valid interpretation of the "same" meaning as the original text unless it differs from it. Socrates reasons – and his view seems to accord with common sense – that if an utterance embodies the truth, which must be unitary, one, and indivisible, then it should naturally be self-interpreting and not dependent on something outside itself. Any form of expression that depends on a secondary act of interpretation – an "in other words" – must be corrupt, impure, and deceitful, a vehicle of *opinion* rather than *knowledge*.

For Socrates, then, writing contains a dangerous principle of otherness, exteriority, and self-division. It leads us away from pure wisdom and unity with ourselves and traps us in endless sectarian disputes between competing interpretations. It is a mere substitution for the truth, substituting a representation for true knowledge of the Logos or the Idea. Writing is infected with the same secondariness that Plato ascribes to poetry in the famous Book X of the *Republic*, where he banishes poets from the ideal state because they produce nothing better than an imitation of an imitation, a representation of a representation.

There is, however, a way out. Socrates maintains that the secondariness of writing can be overcome by sticking to face-to-face speech – as in the dialogues of the Platonic academy. In oral communication, after all, we feel ourselves so vividly in the immediate presence of our audience, our meaning, and our own voices that miscommunication seems impossible, and if any does occur we are right there on the spot to set things straight. Since spoken discourse (at least before the mechanical reproduction of sound) does not travel unpredictably from one place to the next unbeknownst to its author, it keeps us in control of ourselves and our meanings as written texts do not. Socrates argues that oral speech "is written on the soul of the hearer together with our understanding," that it knows how to defend itself and "can distinguish between those it should address and those in whose presence it should be silent." Oral utterances "can defend themselves viva voca," they "are not sterile," whereas written ones are at best "a kind of shadow" of "the living and animate speech of a man with knowledge." And just as speech is superior to writing, philosophical dialectic is superior to the arts of rhetoric and poetry, which allow a deceptive secondary layer of representation to intervene between us and knowledge of the Logos.

Far from debunking this example of Socratic wisdom, Derrida's argument boils down to the assertion *that Socrates was right*. Writing *is* dangerously vulnerable to a process of substitution and reduplication that estranges it from its own meaning. Writing is indeed out of control – once it leaves the author's hand and goes out into the world there is no telling what may happen to it. And this is not just because any text can be misread but because the very process of interpreting it correctly, of reproducing "the same" meaning, requires transforming the text into terms different from its own and thus risking misunderstanding and dispute. Or, as Derrida would put it, every reinscription of the same meaning is a reinscription with a difference, for difference is a precondition of producing sameness.

Writing, then, intrudes an unwelcome principle of difference, transformation, and becoming into Plato's world of unitary being. It is not simply that writing is promiscuously subject to the interpretation of anyone who chances to read it, whether that person is qualified or not. Writing, Socrates sees, contains within itself an *internal* principle of instability and disunity grounded in the fact that writing must interpret itself. Every text contains a self-reading or metacommentary, a fact we attest to every time we use an expression like "to put it another way," or "in conclusion, I am saying that . . . ," or "this is not to say," and so forth, anxious moments that betray our recognition that our words might be read differently from the way we intend them. The point is worth some emphasis, since it has been missed by critics of deconstructive assertions, like those of Paul de Man and J. Hillis Miller, of the "unreadability" of texts. As Miller writes, echoing de Man, "the unreadability of the text is to be defined as the text's inability to read itself, not as some failure on my part to read it." In other words, there is always a discrepancy between a text's meaning and its own attempt to formulate or summarize that meaning. This is de Man's point when he maintains that "sign and meaning can never coincide" in any utterance and that there is always a discrepancy between the logical and the rhetorical functions of a text. The "unreadability" of texts, then, is not mere meaninglessness but rather a division that opens between the text and its description of itself.

So Socrates is right when he says that written texts do not "understand what they are saying." As Derrida puts it, at once summarizing Plato and drawing out implications that Plato resists: "writing estranges itself immensely from the truth of the thing itself, from the truth of speech, from the truth that is open to speech." Or again: "writing appears to Plato" as a "process of redoubling," as "the supplement of a supplement, the signifier, the representative of a representative." Here and elsewhere, Derrida describes writing as a "dangerous supplement."

As for Socrates' exemption of oral speech from his strictures, Derrida suggests that these strictures are so powerful that they subvert the exemption. If Socrates were to maintain the rigor of his own reasoning, he would have to concede that oral discourse, despite the inward feeling of self-presence that may attend it, is no less dependent on interpretation than writing is, and no less vulnerable to the mediated and secondary nature of representations. Speech is as prone as writing to estrangement from its author, its object, and itself, an estrangement we experience when a tale, after circulating, comes back to us no longer resembling the one we originally told. Nor are speakers themselves privileged interpreters of their own speech — as we see on the many occasions when we think a person is blind to important implications of his or her words. In short, even when we seem to be speaking most spontaneously, we do not avoid having to "read" our own utterance in order to understand it. As Derrida would say, we are other than ourselves from the start.

Derrida makes this point by introducing a further complication into the argument. Socrates does not really attack all writing, he observes, but ends up distinguishing between a good and a bad kind. As Derrida puts it, "the conclusion of the *Phaedrus* is less a condemnation of writing in the name of present speech than a preference for one sort of writing over another." When

Socrates defines the truth of speech as a truth *"written* on the soul of the hearer," he is not contradicting himself, Derrida says, but is marking off a proper kind of writing that transparently imitates living speech, thereby purifying itself of the dangerous supplementarity of the bad kind of writing. Good writing is writing that does not interpose a representation between the knower and the truth of being.

But no such writing is possible. Again, Derrida argues, Socrates cannot escape the rigorous implications of his own earlier argument. For writing to become a transparent inscription of the living speech of the soul, it would have to cease to be writing, whose essence is doubleness, mediacy, nontransparency. What gives the game away for Derrida is that Socrates' good kind of writing can only be defined in terms of the bad kind, that is, in the metaphor of truth as a secondary "inscription" on the soul. Thus "good writing (natural, living, knowledgeable, intelligible, internal, speaking) is opposed to bad writing (a moribund, ignorant, external, mute artifice for the senses). And the good one can be designated only through the metaphor of the bad one." Philosophic truth thus proves to be dependent on the representation that compromises it, just as reason proves to be dependent on metaphor. As Derrida puts it, "is it not . . . remarkable here that the so-called living discourse should suddenly be described by a 'metaphor' [of inscription] borrowed from the order of the very thing one is trying to exclude from it?"

This following out of the self-subverting logic of Socrates' metaphors is a characteristic deconstructive gesture that runs throughout Derrida's essay. Socrates' praise of transparent writing, Derrida says, corresponds to certain patriarchal ethical and social investments, namely, Socrates' preference "for the fertile over the sterile trace, for a seed that engenders because it is planted inside over a seed scattered wastefully outside: at the risk of dissemination." The threat that writing poses to the self-presence of truth corresponds metaphorically to a threat to the stability of social hierarchy. It is significant for Derrida that Ammon, who rejects the gift of writing in Socrates' parable, is a king, and that Socrates compares the fallibility of writing to "the wayward, rebellious son," or the "son abandoned by his father."

Socrates' metaphors tell the story, as writing (in Derrida's words) "rolls (kulindeitai) this way and that like someone who has lost his way, who doesn't know where he is going, having strayed from the right path, the rule of rectitude, the norm; but also like someone who has lost his rights, an outlaw, a pervert, a bad seed, a vagrant, an adventurer, a bum." Derrida notes that the terms in which Socrates disparages writing are reminiscent of the terms in which Plato elsewhere disparages democracy. Derrida is not suggesting that there is something *inherently* subversive about writing, however, or that the doctrine of self-present truth is *always* necessarily complicitous with authority, though one can find reductive deconstructionists who make such claims. But he is suggesting that something like the hierarchical logic that operates in Socrates' discourse and in subsequent philosophy can be found in all discourses of legitimation. Indeed, Derrida's point is that a certain instability attends every act of legitimation.

Again, the implication of this argument is not that there is no truth, but that truth is structured and made possible by its other, by metaphor, representation, by all that Socrates associates with untruth. A similar argument underlies the controversial deconstructive concept of "undecidability," which, as we earlier implied, denotes not the impossibility of arriving at reasoned decisions on moral or interpretive choices (as critics of deconstruction have assumed), but rather a space of decision that makes choice and responsibility possible. "A decision," Derrida writes, "can only come into being in a space that exceeds the calculable program that would destroy all responsibility by transforming it into a programmable effect of determinate causes. There can be no moral or political responsibility without this trial and this passage by way of the undecidable."

According to Derrida, Plato's assumption of the necessity of self-presence as a foundation constitutes "a pattern that will dominate all of Western philosophy." In fact, Derrida sees Plato's exclusion of writing – the principle of difference, of representation, of secondariness – as the instituting gesture that founds the very discipline of philosophy, marking it off from rhetoric, history, and literature. Philosophy will henceforth constitute itself as a discipline (just as speech constitutes itself, in Socrates' argument, as full presence) by defining its arena as one of pure thought, whose truth value and meaning is independent of time, place, and the rhetorical and linguistic forms in which it may be expressed. And for Derrida, correspondingly, the return of writing or difference as a repressed "other" in Plato's text foreshadows a pattern that repeats itself in the history of philosophy down to the present.

Just as Plato cannot successfully repress writing, Derrida suggests that philosophy cannot establish itself as the pure theoretical science that thinkers from Plato to Descartes to Kant to Husserl have envisaged. Theoretical philosophy cannot escape its dependence on and contamination by rhetoric, history, politics, and literature – realms of immanent practice, rather than transcendent theory, which "problematize" philosophy's desire for purity. What is at stake in such an argument can be put less abstractly if we consider what implications it might have for the organization of departments in universities: how might academic curricula and research programs have to change if it were acknowledged that philosophy, literature, and politics are not autonomous but mutually codefining and dependent?

Deconstructive theories of instability and indeterminacy begin to seem less arbitrary when we understand that one of their targets is the assumed self-sufficiency and autonomy of disciplines like philosophy and literary study. Recent debates over these theories of indeterminacy and instability become less rarefied once we recognize that the questions they engage have to do with the validity of transgressing disciplinary boundaries – of asking political and historical questions about literature and philosophy, of asking linguistic and philosophical questions about political science or history, questions, in short, that force the disciplines to reflect on and justify the exclusions that have given them their identity. When literary texts are said to be indeterminate, what is often meant is that they are open to being read in different disciplinary contexts. In this sense, to say that a text is indeterminate is really to say that it is *over*determined.

POSTSTRUCTURALIST APPLICATIONS, IMPLICATIONS, AND ANXIETIES

Poststructuralism, which critic Louis Montrose rightly describes as a "multiplicity of unstable, variously conjoined and conflicting discourses," may be generally characterized as criticism that incorporates and develops these two closely related descriptions of textual meaning as indeterminate and overdetermined. Some have differentiated two faces of poststructuralism, one associated with the demonstration of the linguistic indeterminacy of meaning, the other associated with the specification and evaluation of meaning's extralinguistic (over)determinants. Howard Felperin, for instance, in his book *Beyond Deconstruction* (1985), labels these faces of poststructuralism "deconstructive textualism" and "political contextualism." While such labels may correspond to the divergent emphases of particular poststructuralist projects, the most radical implication of poststructuralism – and of Derridean deconstruction – is that "deconstructive textualism" and "political contextualism" are ultimately inseparable. As we have argued in our account of Derrida's critique of Plato, the exposure of Socrates' self-subverting argument for the immediacy of meaning in oral speech leads Derrida to a reading of the unspoken ethical and social investments that, he suggests, prompted Socrates' argument in the first place. Thus, as Michael Ryan puts it, "deconstruction describes the logical or structural necessity of turning such metaphysical principles as consciousness, ideal meaning, presence, and nature inside out and into a 'social text.' "

    Granting this necessity, poststructuralist criticism, as we observed above, asks political and historical questions about literature and philosophy. Incorporating knowledge and methods drawn from other disciplines such as sociology, anthropology, and psychoanalysis, poststructuralism explores the ways in which categories like "consciousness," "meaning," and "nature" are the variable products of cultural contexts, social situations, and racial, class, and gendered relations of power. But poststructuralist inquiry into what we may call the material conditions of textual or symbolic meanings cannot take the form of a simple displacement of determinate meaning from the language of the text itself to some fixed historical context or social reality that stands beyond or beneath the text. As Ryan's account of the poststructuralist move indicates, the social is also a "text," not a stable referent but a complex set of relations that people represent to themselves in various ways and know only through these representations. In other words, poststructuralism insists not only that symbolic practices are material but that social and material practices are also symbolic. Or, in Montrose's formulation, which is often cited as a shorthand definition of the form of poststructuralist criticism known as new historicism but may be more generally applied, poststructuralism is characterized by "a reciprocal concern with the historicity of texts and the textuality of history." Whether its object of attention is a literary text or an account of history, poststructuralist inquiry thus involves "the problematicization of those processes by which meaning is produced and grounded."

To problematize the processes by which meaning is produced and grounded is to challenge the assumption of autonomous textual – or disciplinary or personal – *identity*. This is the challenge exemplified by Derrida's critique of Western philosophy and addressed by subsequent poststructuralist critics to a range of different objects. In Derrida's deconstruction of Socrates' category of oral speech, an identity that is ostensibly fully possessed, naturally embodied, is revealed to be a self-identification, something conventionally produced, arbitrarily defined, in relation to some other, and thus existing only through and as (a part of) that relation. For Plato and many of the thinkers who followed him in establishing the discipline of philosophy in the West, philosophy's other is rhetoric. Classically, philosophy has distinguished itself from that other by claiming that its standard is the neutral, contextless, or absolute one of truth, while the standard of rhetoric is the interested, circumstantial one of appropriateness. Philosophical statements are supposedly true or false, while rhetorical ones are appropriate or inappropriate relative to the purpose, situation, and audience at hand. Derrida's characteristic method is to explode such dualisms and the hierarchies that they underwrite by showing that, as Fish puts it, "at every point the conditions that supposedly mark off the lesser or derivative case can be shown to be defining of the normative case as well."

An unexpected application of deconstruction to American materials is provided by Derrida himself in an essay entitled "Declarations of Independence" (a talk delivered at the Bicentennial celebration of 1976 in the

Thomas Jefferson rotunda at the University of Virginia). Derrida asks whether the reference to "we the people" of the United States in the Declaration is a *description* of a preexistent group or a *performative* utterance that produces "independence" by the act of declaring it. Is political legitimacy based on a prior and pregiven "law of nature and of nature's God," as the Declaration claims, or is it self-created out of its own rhetorical performance? Derrida suggests that the question is finally undecidable, as is the ultimate grounding of democratic political legitimacy.

Reflecting the influence of such deconstructive reading, American literature scholars such as Michael Warner and Jay Fliegelman develop further implications of this kind of instability respectively in *The Letters of the Republic* (1990) and *Declaring Independence* (1993). Sacvan Bercovitch had pioneered in the rhetorical reading of American self-legitimating texts in *The Puritan Origins of the American Self* (1975). Other notable applications to American literature of deconstructive or deconstructively influenced criticism include Joseph Riddell's *The Inverted Bell* (1974); Barbara Johnson's *The Critical Difference* (1980) and *A World of Difference* (1987); John Carlos Rowe's *The Theoretical Dimensions of Henry James* (1984); Evan Carton's *The Rhetoric of American Romance* (1985); Gregory Jay's *America the Scrivener: Deconstruction and the Subject of Literary History* (1990); and Eve Kosofsky Sedgwick's reading of James's "The Beast in the Jungle" in *Epistemology of the Closet* (1990).

The influence of deconstruction and other forms of recent theory has also had a transformative influence in areas such as textual editing and the new field of legal and literary interpretation. Reacting against the "romantic ideology" of the text as an autonomous product of original genius, Jerome McGann in *A Critique of Modern Textual Criticism* (1983) calls for a revisionist view of editing that understands both the text and the editing process itself as material and social practices. Though Hershel Parker in *Flawed Texts and Verbal Icons* (1984) rejects many of the readings encouraged by recent theory, he encourages a similarly theory-informed editing practice (a practice reflected in recent new scholarly editions of major American authors such as the edition of Herman Melville's works edited by Harrison Hayford, Parker, and others). New interest in the problematic and socially-constructed nature of interpretation has also led to a confluence of theorizing on legal and literary interpretation, including such works as Stanley Fish's *Doing What Comes Naturally* (1989) and the anthology *Interpreting Law and Literature* (1988), edited by Steven Mailloux and Sanford Levinson (see also Mailloux' *Rhetorical Power* on the relations between these developments and the recent turn toward rhetoric [1989]).

We shall soon discuss some important applications and implications of deconstructive insights in the critical projects that have come to be known, respectively, as speech act theory (which, as developed by English philosopher of language J. L. Austin, significantly anticipates Derridean deconstruction) and reader-response criticism. But, first, it will be illuminating to examine a brilliant and idiosyncratic instance of deconstruction's simultaneous incorporation and resistance in the work of one of the first influential American literary critics to seriously grapple with deconstruction, Yale romanticist Harold Bloom. For Bloom's theory of poetry, first fully elaborated in his 1973 book *The Anxiety of Influence*, indeed expresses – and seeks to contain – many of the characteristic anxieties that deconstruction's threat to traditional identities, dualisms, and hierarchies has produced, not only among journalistic observers and academic antagonists of recent critical theory but even among its leading practitioners.

Deconstructive critiques, as we have suggested, unsettle the boundaries by which ostensibly distinct and integral entities define themselves or are defined. Whether these entities are academic disciplines, discrete texts or events, human persons, or opposing concepts such as Plato's "speech" and "writing," their deconstruction reveals their "identities" or "selves" to be inhabited from the start by that which they try to exclude and from which they try to distinguish themselves. To recognize the always already deconstructed state of one's identity, its original inundation by that which it is not, is, one might say, to exist in a constant "anxiety of influence." And this state of anxiety figures to be most profound for those identities most heavily invested in the idea of their own distinction and originality: the post-Romantic identities, for instance, of the "poet," the "poem," "poetry" (and, perhaps, that appreciator and would-be producer of textual originality, the critic).

As our discussions of cultural studies and the new historicism in Chapter 7 will elaborate, romantic and modernist notions of the categorical distinctiveness and privileged status of literature have been notable casualties of poststructuralist criticism. But poets and poetry, and the critics who specialize in their analysis, are especially susceptible to the deconstructive argument that, as Stanley Fish puts it, the qualities of "the lesser or derivative case can be shown to be defining of the [superior, original, or] normative case as well." Indeed, romantic conceptions of poetry often distinguish it from prose precisely as Socrates distinguishes orality from writing in the Platonic dialogue that Derrida deconstructs. How does poetry survive the deconstruction of its distinction from any other sort of rhetoric? Is the poem still a poem if it is reconceived as a fragmentary site of a larger social text, or is its creator still a poet if, in the words of Wallace Stevens, "no one [is] ever simply himself but is always compounded of a lot of other people"? Bloom quotes this desperate assessment of poetic self-identity early in *The Anxiety of Influence*, and he acknowledges its desperation. A leading figure in the group of Yale professors (which also included J. Hillis Miller, Geoffrey Hartman, and Paul de Man) who were the earliest American importers of deconstruction into literary studies, Bloom accepts the Derridean implications of the "otherness" of self and text, the rhetoricity of poetry, and the infinite regress of originality. But, as the language of his book's opening paragraphs everywhere announces, Bloom also believes in "strong poets," "strong maker[s]," "figures of capable imagination." And, deconstructive principles notwithstanding, he later frankly confesses his "own addiction to a Romantic and prophetic humanism." How can Bloom possibly have it both ways?

The Anxiety of Influence begins with a one-page prologue, a prose poem whose first lines depict the self-division, secondariness, and loss of plenitude that, as Derrida argues, comprise writing's and the writer's inescapable condition: "After he knew that he had fallen, outwards and downwards, away from the Fullness, he tried to remember what the Fullness had been." To acknowledge this condition, as Bloom does, is to confront the same crisis of identity-as-difference that Derrida shows Socrates to confront. For Bloom, it is to recognize the nonidentity of the poet and the poem, their dependence on something outside themselves. With this recognition, "the impasse of Formalist criticism" appears absolute. The idea of a poem as a formal unity, a self-sustaining organic structure, is an exploded tautology (a problem that Geoffrey Hartman takes as his point of departure in *Beyond Formalism* [1970]). But the alternative, in Bloom's view, seems to be the reduction of poets and poems to mere transmitters of the data of semiological and sociological systems and the resignation of critics, as he contentiously puts it, to "the anti-humanistic plain dreariness of all those developments in European criticism that have yet to demonstrate that they can aid in reading any one poem by any poet whatsoever." Bloom's dialectical synthesis of these unacceptable alternatives is ingeniously simple. Against critical discussions of poetry that "vacillate between tautology – in which the poem is and means itself – and reduction – in which the poem means something that is not itself a poem," Bloom proposes an "antithetical practical criticism," which begins "by denying both tautology and reduction, a denial best delivered by the assertion that the meaning of a poem can only be a poem, but *another poem — a poem not itself*."

Sharing with deconstruction the Nietzschean insight that discourses of identity and truth are informed and divided by the struggle over an internalized otherness, Bloom introduces Freud's Oedipal theory to contain that struggle within the poetic family, to restrict the text's significatory inundation to a matter of "poetic influence." In this way, Bloom can ultimately reconstitute the "central poem" on the very ground of its decentering, its self-division: poetic identity is reconceived as "intra-poetic relationship."

Similarly, the poet's own belatedness and nonidentity (in the Freudian and Lacanian senses, discussed in Chapter 4) are not insurmountable obstacles to originality but the conditions under which originality is achieved. In short, by taking possession of the powerful alien influences that inhabit them, by thus turning necessity into virtuosity and otherness into identity, poems and poets of capable imagination become – in another Stevens phrase, at once "most truly and most strange" – themselves.

Bloom admits to a certain degree of arbitrariness in his proposal to avoid the "reduction" of the poem, "whether to images, ideas, given things, or phonemes," by insisting that "the meaning of a poem can only be another poem." "That even the strongest poets are subject to influences not poetical is obvious even to me," he writes, but goes on to reiterate that "my concern is only with *the poet in a poet*." This italicized phrase neatly encapsulates what Bloom himself might call his "strong misreading" of the deconstructive critique of essential identity. On the one hand, "the poet in a poet" exemplifies that critique, because in Bloom's context the phrase's customary or expected designation of some indwelling quality of genius in which the poet's own identity as poet resides is undone; the poet in a poet is not his essential self but, in fact, somebody else, some other poet. On the other hand, the phrase marks Bloom's "swerve" from deconstructive decentering, because it is through the appropriative incorporation of this other that the poet forges his own creative identity and thus redeems the sense of integral poetic selfhood in "the poet in a poet."

Bloom anatomizes a six-step revisionary process through which the strong poet passes from self-alienation, where poetic identity lies in the priority and exteriority of a precursor, to self-appropriation, where the precursor is incorporated and reproduced – with a difference – as the self. The notion of misreading – or "misprision," as Bloom terms it – is crucial to this process. For this principle of the noncorrespondence of any reading or interpretation with the text it reads, this recognition (so troubling, we recall, to Socrates) that representation is change, is what allows Bloom's poet to achieve originality through the reproduction of the other. In reading the precursor, then, the strong poet necessarily misreads him; in following, he necessarily "swerves," as Bloom puts it; and, thus, the reproducer of a source of influence attains creative priority. (For Bloom, this struggle for priority seems exclusively the business of fathers and sons; notable feminist "misprisions" of Bloom's model to the less agonistic relations between women writers, however, have been made by Sandra Gilbert and Susan Gubar in *The Madwoman in the Attic* [1979] and Joanne Feit Diehl in *Dickinson and the Romantic Imagination* [1981] and *Women Poets and the American Sublime* [1990].) Indeed, Bloom's theory of poetry explicitly extends to criticism as well, since "the anxiety of influence [is one] from which we all suffer, whether we are poets or not." And, insofar as deconstruction was a powerful emerging critical influence for Bloom as he wrote his book, *The Anxiety of Influence* may be considered, in one aspect, a strong misreading of Derrida. Against the grain of most post-structuralist theory, moreover, Bloom's book struggles to redirect some of the insights and methods that threatened to inundate literary study toward the preservation of its "literary" identity.

If Bloom may be seen as among the earliest literary heirs of and wrestlers with deconstruction, J. L. Austin certainly figures among deconstruction's modern philosophical influences. Austin's book *How To Do Things With Words* (1962), based on a series of lectures delivered at Harvard University in 1955, begins by observing that "it was for too long the assumption of philosophers that the business of a 'statement' can only be to 'describe' some state of affairs, or to 'state some fact,' which it must do either truly or falsely." This assumption obscures the function of language that most interests Austin. Language not only describes and states things, he points out, but actively does things, performs actions in the world. "Can saying make it so?" Austin asks in his first lecture, and then responds: "Such a doctrine sounds odd or even flippant at first, but with sufficient safeguards it may become not odd at all." For instance, he explains, to say "I do" in an appropriate circumstance (a marriage ceremony in which one is a principal) is not to *describe* what one is doing or to *state* that one is doing it: "it is to do it," to become married. Austin designates as "performatives" those utterances that constitute the actions to which they refer, and he distinguishes them from normative utterances, which he calls "constatives," that neutrally describe some state of affairs and may be judged true or false. Though Austin does not say so, this distinction reiterates the classic distinction between philosophy, with its criterion of truth, and rhetoric, with its criterion of appropriateness, that Derrida will deconstruct.

Can saying make it so? Austin wishes to answer in the affirmative, but only if "sufficient safeguards" can be maintained. Yet, as he explores the qualities of and relations between his two categories of utterances, these safeguards erode until, by the end of his book, he has *almost* performed a deconstructive analysis of himself. "Can we be sure," he wonders in his penultimate lecture,

that stating truly is a different *class* of assessment from arguing soundly, advising well, judging fairly, and blaming justifiably? . . . Is the constative, then, always true or false? When a constative is confronted with the facts, we in fact appraise it in ways involving the employment of a vast array of terms which overlap with those that we use in the appraisal of performatives.

Finally, just as Plato cannot keep writing from contaminating speech, Austin cannot prevent the "performative" and its standard of contextual appropriateness from overwhelming his careful safeguards and converging with the "constative" and its standard of truth. "What will not survive," he admits, "is the notion of the purity of performatives," which "was essentially based upon a belief in the dichotomy of performatives and constatives, which we see has to be abandoned." What follows from this is that "the familiar contrast of 'normative or evaluative' as opposed to the factual is in need, like so many dichotomies, of elimination." In other words, there are no longer any neutral constative truths that are independent of their contextual circumstances. As Austin puts it, " 'true' and 'false,' like 'free' and 'unfree,' [stand only] for a general dimension of being a right or proper thing to say as opposed to a wrong thing, in these circumstances, to this audience, for these purposes, and with these intentions."

Austin does not explore the potentially radical ramifications of these conclusions – that the distinction between saying and doing cannot be maintained, that saying is a form of doing, or what Austin calls illocutionary "force." If truth and falsity are as much actions as freedom and oppression, as he suggests in the passage just quoted, then Austin has implicitly anticipated the poststructuralist argument that discourse is inseparable from power. It is precisely this acknowledgement of performative force that is repressed, in Derrida's and de Man's view, when philosophic truth tries to distance itself from rhetorical power. For to acknowledge such force would be to ask the disturbing question: if language is force, what is the relation of such force to the rationality and logic for which philosophy claims to speak? Is philosophy mere violence, as Nietzsche thought?

Derrida does not give an unequivocal "yes" to this question, but he implies that the fact that it makes us uncomfortable is not a reason for avoiding it. Those who react with moralistic rage at the very suggestion that reason contains a dimension of violence only prevent critical thinking about the problems posed by the fact that ideas never exist in a pure neutral space but are always *instituted* somewhere. This fact is exemplified, most obviously, by the material consequences that may follow from the imputation of reason or lack of reason to an individual in our society. In certain circumstances, the determination that a person is irrational exerts tremendous force: it may warrant the appropriation of his possessions, the curtailment of his physical freedom, even the alienability of his control over whether he lives or dies. To perceive that reason is socially instituted, in other words, one need look no further than the long and not particularly ancient history of the violent institutionalization of those (most often and pervasively, as Carroll Smith-

Rosenberg and others have shown, "hysterical," or simply rebellious, women) who have been deemed devoid of it.

If philosophy has traditionally constituted itself by avoiding questions of force and social consequence, art and aesthetics similarly have constituted themselves in the modern period by divorcing themselves from rhetoric – that realm of practical usefulness with which Kant contrasted the aesthetic realm of "purposiveness with purpose." Yet, so the poststructuralist argument goes, if meaning involves performative force or rhetorical action in the world, then even language that understands itself to be purely engaged in the disinterested articulation of philosophic truth or aesthetic beauty (*especially* such language, some would claim) is neither pure nor disinterested. Contrary to Auden, then, poetry is not that which "makes nothing happen" but is itself an event in the world.

This emphasis on language as force indeed seems, at first blush, to vindicate the characterizations of poststructuralist theory as inherently nihilistic and potentially totalitarian. But one must recall here that the deconstructive critique of the unimplicated *neutrality* of a discipline or a text (or of their representatives or authors) is also a critique of its integral *identity*. What this means is that, while language exercises force, its speakers do not exercise complete control over its force. In the Heideggerian aphorism, in fact, the apparent power relationship between speaker and language is dramatically reversed: it is language that speaks man, not man who speaks language. This provocative statement, which has been widely echoed by deconstructionist and poststructuralist critics, does not endow language with some magically animistic life of its own, but rather insists that language comes to us already freighted with meanings through the history of its use. Language is a historical product (and a historical process) whose words and expressions become "sedimented" with meanings and conflicts over meanings through time. That is why, to take a familiar example, a man who refers to a woman as a "babe" cannot dismiss the charge of sexism by claiming, even if sincerely, that he did not *intend* the word to be degrading. "Babe" is freighted with a social history, which now includes the history of feminist challenges over the past thirty years to objectifying and trivializing characterizations of women, and that history shapes its meaning whether an individual speaker knows it or intends to activate it or not.

Heidegger believed, and in this deconstructionists follow him, that no user of language can ever be fully in control of all the meanings sedimented in his or her utterances. We control these meanings up to a point, but there is always a residue or surplus that exceeds our control – a fact that explains the vulnerability of our texts to conflicts of interpretation that hinge on whether a particular meaning is legitimately entailed by our use of words or not.

Perhaps even more to the point, Derrida would argue, is the fact that "we" ourselves are products of the sedimented meanings in our language, which is to say that "our" use of words and "our" control over them, even before they are given over to others to interpret, are never entirely "ours" to begin with. According to deconstructionists, as our sample deconstructive readings have shown, this openness of texts to a space of conflict – is such-and-such a meaning *in* the text or not? – is not an accidental feature that derives from careless writing or reading, but a structural condition of communication, something without which communication could not exist.

In this respect, the deconstructive argument converges with the influential "dialogical" theory of Mikhail Bakhtin, who argues that the language we use is already elaborately inhabited by the usages of other past and present speakers and writers. Thus, the voice of, say, a Dostoevsky novel contains (or is "dialogized" by) a myriad of previous voices and registers, including not only other literary languages but the languages of the law court, of criminology, and of different social classes. That language is inhabited by a vast number of others is a further source of its instability, but again such instability is not a disability but a source of language's creative power.

If we are never the sole owners of our "own" meanings, if our voice is inhabited by other unacknowledged voices, if our texts depend on repressed conflicts and meanings sedimented in their language, then there is a sense in which any individual, voice, or text is necessarily estranged from itself. The *Phaedrus*, in Derrida's analysis, is only a model instance of the anxiety that this self-estrangement produces, an anxiety that runs through the history of Western thought. Yet, Derrida argues, if this anxiety prompts self-deception, self-blinding, it also makes thought and expression possible. Indeed, it is only because of a certain anxiety that we think and communicate at all; it is our sense of a lack in our world that makes us feel the need to supplement that lack with language, endlessly describing, redescribing, interpreting, and reinterpreting. A world in which language could bring us to a terminal destination would be a world of death, certainly one that would provide no reason to speak or write. The desire for a completion that can never be reached is the condition of possibility for all expression, and it leaves traces in all expression that can be uncovered through a deconstructive reading.

In a variety of ways throughout this chapter, we have rehearsed deconstruction's challenge to the grounding philosophical assumption of identity, that A = A, which when translated into textual terms becomes the assumption that a text is self-identical or that, in order to exist and be intelligible, a text must be and remain itself. For E. D. Hirsch, the leading exponent of a foundationalist theory of interpretation, this principle of the text's self-identity is the necessary enabling condition of all interpretation. "If an interpreter did not conceive a text's meaning to be *there* as an occasion for contemplation or application, he would have nothing to think or talk about," Hirsch writes. "Its thereness, its self-identity from one moment to the next, allows it to be contemplated." In Hirsch's view, if a text were not itself, if it provided no inherent "safeguards" (to use Austin's term) against the prospect that it might change or be changed from one reading to the next, then stable meaning would be impossible and no interpretation could be more valid than any other. As we have seen, Derrida, while rejecting the notion of textual self-identity or self-presence, also rejects the identity/nonidentity dualism that is implicit in Hirsch's theory.

For deconstruction, again, the principle of nonidentity does not simply oppose or refute the principle of identity but informs and accounts for it. Texts are capable of being what they are only because they contain (both possess and repress) the potential to change and be something else; it is only the possibility of becoming something else that makes us what we are. This paradox is captured in Derrida's notion of "iterability," which he develops in a critique of Austin. In examining Austin's idea of the situation-specific "performative" utterance, Derrida argues that the power of such an utterance to retain its meaning when its immediate context is lost or altered (its "iterability") indicates not its immediate and complete possession of its meaning but the location of that meaning elsewhere. As Christopher Norris explains the point: "Austin's conditions of performative felicity require that the speaker 'mean what he says' in the sense of being presently involved in his utterance and faithfully *intending* its import. Yet . . . the 'iterability' of performatives means that they can be explained and located only within a larger system of non-self-present signification." Or, in Derrida's paradoxical phrase, "iterability always involves transformation."

As one might expect, this sort of elusive response – ingenious as it may be – fails to satisfy many of Derrida's critics, and indeed it does not fully respond to their objections. One significant and repeated objection is a subtler version of Hirsch's argument that stable meanings and valid interpretations could not be achieved if texts were understood to be nonidentical. This challenge is best stated as a question: since we *do* arrive at stable meanings and valid interpretations most of the time, how can texts be nonidentical? M. H. Abrams makes this point in a critique of Derrida when he observes that "in practice language often works, that it gets its job done. We live a life in which we have assurance that we are able to mean what we say and know what we mean." Yet arguably, Derrida and other deconstructionists do not deny that language "works." On the contrary, they are interested in the unnoticed and sometimes uncomfortable things that happen precisely when it does work. Nevertheless, deconstructionists have not directly responded to Abrams's demand for an explanation of how stable meanings are compatible with nonidentical texts. Certain "reader-response" critics who share deconstruction's "antifoundationalism" or "antiformalism," however, have addressed this issue.

In the introduction to *Reader-Response Criticism* (1980), a collection of landmark essays in the critical relocation of meaning from textual object to reading process, Jane Tompkins rightly cautions that "reader-response criticism is not a conceptually unified critical position." What links all versions, however, is some degree of challenge to the formalist assumption of the full *presence* of meaning *within* a stable text. Like deconstructive analysis, then, reader-response criticism tends to understand textual meaning to be produced rather than given, situational rather than absolute, interactive (and hence nonidentical) rather than self-present.

The reader-response theorist who has played out this position to its logical extreme, and whose version of anti-formalism or antifoundationalism most closely resembles Derridean deconstruction, is Stanley Fish. Like Derrida, Fish is interested in the "philosophical" (which he, too, refuses to differentiate from the "rhetorical") conditions of meaning, and, as Tompkins observes, Fish's early work, like Derrida's, seeks by meticulous analysis of the processes of reading to "[turn] the mind to an investigation of its own activities." Where Derrida deconstructs the opposition between the pure primacy of speech and the adulterated secondariness of writing, Fish performs a similar operation on the distinction between (a text's) meaning and (a reader's) interpretation. It is not a question of choosing, he argues, between meaning – imagined as what is "there" on the page – and interpretation; the choice is only "between an interpretation that is unacknowledged as such and an interpretation that is at least aware of itself." Interpretation, for Fish, moreover, entails something of the same dialectic that we have seen Derrida associate with "iterability." Echoing Derrida's statement that "iterability always involves transformation," Fish, in an essay entitled "Change" from his 1989 collection *Doing What Comes Naturally*, remarks: "explaining and changing cannot be opposed activities (although they may be the names of claims and counterclaims) because they are the same activities."

This assertion might appear to bespeak, and to license, the instability of interpretation, but in fact it offers a response to Abrams's challenge and an account of interpretive *stability* as well. The same passage from the essay "Change" goes on to insist that "interpretation is a structure of constraints, a structure which, because it is always and already in place, renders unavailable the independent or uninterpreted text and renders unimaginable the independent and freely interpreting reader." In *Is There a Text in This Class?* Fish advances his central theoretical claim, that there is no such entity as a text prior to interpretation, since what any text is seen to mean or to be is itself a product of interpretation. Thus it is deceptive to think, as we normally do, that interpretations can be supported or refuted by appealing to independent textual evidence, for according to Fish what looks to us like "independent evidence" will already have been tautologically predetermined by our interpretive assumptions. As Fish puts it, "The question of what is in the text cannot be settled by appealing to the evidence since the evidence will have become available only because some determination of what is in the text has already been made." It follows, then, for Fish that "all objects are made and not found, and . . . they are made by the interpretive strategies we set in motion." Whereas skilled reading is usually thought to be a matter of discerning what is "there," for Fish it is rather "a matter of knowing how to *produce* what can thereafter be said to be there." This argument does not lead to subjectivism or relativism, however, for the reader's "production" of meanings is not whimsical but is constrained by the conventions of his or her interpretive community.

A problem here is that Fish often seems to present an underdifferentiated model of interpretive constraint that does not adequately account for the *specificity* or *selectivity* of interpretation, the fact that readers activate only some of many potential strategies in their inventory, applying some strategies to some objects and not to others. Some of the consequences of such underdifferentiation will become apparent in our discussion of "new historicism" in Chapter 7. For the moment, however, it is useful to note that the lines of Fish's overall argument follow the Derridean analysis of textuality that this chapter has traced. The constraints upon the text's self-identity and control over meaning that Derrida exposes are the same constraints that, for Fish, operate upon – or, more accurately, produce – the reader. As Walter Benn Michaels puts it, invoking the American pragmatist philosopher C. S. Pierce to develop and buttress Fish's position, "the self, like the work, is a text" that is "already embedded in a context, the community of interpretation or system of signs," and it is this context that informs (at once generates and limits) both what the text is and what the reader does.

What Fish means by a community of interpretation is "not so much a group of individuals who [share] a point of view, but a point of view or a way of organizing experience that share[s] individuals." This formulation echoes the Heideggerian claim, cited earlier, that language speaks man, but a better way to understand it may be as an instance of the kind of argument about the productive and regulatory power of interpretive "paradigms" that Thomas Kuhn makes in his famous book, *The Structure of Scientific Revolutions* (1962). Like Kuhn's "paradigm" Fish's interpretive community is a historically contingent expression of a collective, disciplinary enterprise that informs and determines individual inquirers and their terms of inquiry. Such a community makes for interpretive stability, writes Fish, "because the observer is never individual in the sense of unique or private, but is always the product of the categories of understanding that are his by virtue of his membership." But the interpretive community also makes for change (when, for whatever historical reasons, disciplinary and institutional borders alter or become penetrable by those engaged in other sorts of collective enterprises) because "each of us is a member of not one but innumerable interpretive communities in relation to which different kinds of belief are operating with different weight and force." Thus, the work of interpretation – which is to say both the work that is interpreted and the interpretation that is worked – "is at the same time assimilative and self-transforming." Whether in any specific instance assimilation (stability) or transformation prevails, whether the paradigm holds or shifts, is for Fish not dependent on any objective fact of the matter outside interpretation, but is "a political question to which the answer will be different at different times."

So the conviction that meaning is produced and enacted in accordance with some "human structure of interests," rather than neutrally discovered and described, inevitably returns us to politics. As Tompkins writes of reader-response critics and of the trajectory of their work:

Relocating meaning first in the reader's self and then in the interpretive strategies that constitute it, they assert that meaning is a consequence of being in a particular situation in the world. The net result of this epistemological revolution is to repoliticize literature and literary criticism. When discourse is responsible for reality and not a mere reflection of it, then whose discourse prevails makes all the difference.

The "epistemological revolution" to which Tompkins refers predates both reader-response criticism and Derrida. Often described as a "linguistic turn" in twentieth-century thought, it has been advanced by theorists in many disciplines and derives in part from Immanuel Kant's self-declared "Copernican revolution" in philosophy at the end of the eighteenth century.

Kant argued that the human mind has no access to Things-in-Themselves, the world of "noumenal" reality, but only to things as they appear, as "phenomena" constituted by "categories" of the mind itself such as space, time, relation, and cause and effect. Neo-Kantians gave linguistic twist to this argument, suggesting that the categories that prestructure reality for us are those of language. This attentiveness to the shaping power of language was heightened by the rise of twentieth-century mass communications and by social analyses of the coercive and potentially demagogic force of advertising, popular culture, and mass politics. After both world wars, in particular, many shaken intellectuals devoted their energies to examining the seductive emotional appeals and uncritical clichés of the nationalistic rhetoric that had helped bring about the carnage. George Orwell's essay "Politics and the English Language" (1946) exposed the numerous euphemisms of modern political discourse, and his novel *Nineteen Eighty-Four* (1949) presented the ultimate horror of a world in which the systematic manipulation of language enabled tyrants to reduce entire populations to unquestioning slaves. In the dystopian world of Orwell's Oceania, the regime of Big Brother is in the process of replacing traditional English with "Newspeak," a language designed to eliminate the very ability to entertain such concepts as truth, honesty, freedom, and individuality.

As writers like Orwell were warning of governments' increasing political and technological capacities for totalitarian uses of language, linguists and anthropologists were examining the ways linguistic symbols affected how cultures experienced reality, with different cultures and historical epochs "constituting" reality in different ways. Benjamin Lee Whorf, for instance, argued on the basis of his study of an isolated Arizona tribe, the Hopi, that the tribe's concepts of time and space and its general world view were completely different from those of the dominant Western tradition. In its claim that different cultural languages are not rooted in any common objective referent, the so-called Whorfian hypothesis was a check against ethnocentric absolutism. But Whorf's cultural relativism also seemed to lead to the Orwellian nightmare – a world in which the truth differs so radically from culture to culture that "truth" becomes whatever the dominant discourse or dominant ruling class says it is.

Thus, a debate has taken shape – and still rages – on the moral and political implications and *uses* of two competing descriptions of the relation between language and the world we experience. For convenience, we will label these descriptions "constructivism" and "realism." The debate acquired urgency from the political situations within which it occurred: at first the clash of democracies and dictatorships before and after midcentury; later the cultural war over education of the 1980s and 1990s. Noteworthy in this debate is the fact that both constructivists and realists have tended to identify their own view with political enlightenment while casting the opposing view as a rationalization for totalitarianism.

Beginning with Kant himself, constructivists have often argued that once we acknowledge that our ideas of order and value derive from human consciousness, we take responsibility for our judgments and avoid the authoritarianism of claiming that these judgments are "truths" dictated by an impersonal, objective source. An anthropological version of constructivism, which was in part a reaction against the racist anti-Semitism of the Nazis, maintained that cultural relativism promoted tolerance of difference and resistance to the temptation to confuse local prejudice with universal truth and reason. Realists, on the other hand, have retorted that once we assume that language constructs our reality without accountability to anything external to itself, we are left with no basis from which to criticize totalitarian power and can only accede to the maxim that Whatever Is Is Right. Acknowledging that language *can* approximate to some external truth or reality is not the same, realists argue, as claiming that one's own language or culture has a monopoly on these things; it is merely to permit a standard against which various competing claims can be measured.

THE CASE OF PAUL DE MAN

Explosive fuel for the anticonstructivist engine was provided in 1988 by a Dutch graduate student named Ortwin de Graef who discovered a previously unknown fact about the late Yale critic, Paul de Man, the most celebrated deconstructive theorist in the American academy. De Man's criticism had tended to combine radical deconstructivism with an idealization of literature as a consciously self-deconstructing discourse that was "free from the fallacy of unmediated expression." Fiction, de Man wrote, "is not myth, for it knows and names itself as fiction"; the real mystifications, he continues, are perpetrated by critics who suppose that their discourses, "what they call anthropology, linguistics, psychoanalysis," are something other than "literature reappearing, like the Hydra's head, in the very spot where it had supposedly been suppressed." Literature originates in "the void that separates intent from reality," the revelation of "the inauthenticity of the existential project," the "reduction of the [authorial] self" that inhabits "the fallen temporality of everyday existence," the desire "to leap out of historical and everyday time." For these reasons, de Man insisted, "the critic has no need to linger over this preliminary stage. Considerations of the actual and historical experience of writers are a waste of time from a critical viewpoint. The regressive stages can only reveal an emptiness of which the writer himself is well aware when he begins to write." What de Graef disclosed about de Man's own actual and historical experience was that, between 1939 and 1943, he had written pro-Nazi and in several instances explicitly anti-Semitic articles for two Belgian collaborationist papers.

Given the twenty years that separate de Man's collaborationist journalism and his theoretical and critical writing, the extent and nature of any connection between the two is at least an open question. Yet, as de Graef's information circulated in the international press, many who had already decided that deconstruction was a threat to reason and decency took de Man's writings as conclusive proof of what they had been saying all along. The de Man case provided some with a clinching justification for not reading deconstructionist work and trying to assess it in dispassionate terms, for history itself seemed now to have delivered the final verdict. And, in fact, it is certainly possible in the wake of the de Man case to reinterpret de Man's later theorizing as an elaborate attempt to rationalize or excuse his collaborationist writings by denying the reliability of interpretations of texts as well as historical events, thus relieving writers and other agents of responsibility for their actions.

In the wake of the disclosures, certain passages in de Man's work that concern the impossibility of truly repentant expression do indeed become readable as coyly self-exculpatory references to his failure to reveal his actions in the "historical and everyday time" of his life before his emigration from Europe. De Man does return often in his later writing to the theme of the inauthentic nature of confession. He points out that in the *Confessions* of Rousseau, for example, the apparent humility of Jean-Jacques' confessions of sin and immorality is really a hypocritical tactic of self-aggrandizement, only making the ostensibly repentant sinner seem more admirable for his candor. It is an exemplary case of de Man's general argument that "sign and meaning" in language can never coincide, or that there is always discrepancy between what language says in its "constative" role and what it does as a performative action. Even as Jean-Jacques confesses his guilt, his act of confessing it subtly exonerates him of it. Read in the light of what we now know about his past, de Man seems to be implying that disclosing the facts about his collaborationist past would have been useless, since any such confession could only have been self-servingly equivocal in meaning.

This is a possible reading of one part of de Man's later work. It is also possible, however (and this is the tack taken by some of de Man's defenders), to reinterpret de Man's later theorizing as a repudiation of the "totalizing" concept of organic nationalism that had pervaded de Man's youthful praise of the German Reich. The powerful and persistent critique of romantic organicism in de Man's later work can now be read as a response to Nazism and its totalitarian version of romantic theories of culture and literature as a unified organic whole. That de Man connected the organic theory specifically to European totalitarian ideology in his analyses of Heidegger and Holderlin suggests that he himself thought of deconstruction as a critique of the totalitarian vision he had embraced in his youth.

De Man's later work has thus been adduced to support radically conflicting interpretations of its connection with de Man's past: for some it is a rationalization and for others a repudiation of that past. In this respect, de Man's career as a whole appears eerily to illustrate his later theory of interpretive undecidability, becoming itself a "text" that supports radically conflicting accounts of it. The story of a life, the story of history, is always divided, always several stories, except when condensed into simplifying narratives that reduce them to one. To take this view would be not to absolve de Man, for it allows one to hold that de Man's acts of collaboration were atrocious and inexcusable and that de Man to some extent both rationalized those acts and repudiated them in his later work.

Unwisely, however, some defenders of de Man, including Derrida himself, have attempted to minimize the extent of the anti-Semitism in de Man's collaborationist pieces, or have even questioned whether they should be called collaborationist, which does not seem in doubt. In this, these defenders have needlessly given credence to the charge that deconstruction is little more than a way to make texts mean whatever is convenient for the interpreter and to relativize moral distinctions out of existence. It simply strains credibility to assert, as Derrida and others have done, that a contemptuous reference by de Man to "vulgar antisemitism" could be a condemnation of anti-Semitism as such as vulgar. Nor does there seem to be a convincing way to minimize the obnoxiousness of the concluding passage of what has become de Man's most notorious wartime essay:

. . . one sees that a solution to the Jewish problem that would aim at the creation of a Jewish colony isolated from Europe would not entail, for the literary life of the West, deplorable consequences. The latter would lose, in all, a few personalities of mediocre value and would continue, as in the past, to develop according to its great evolutive laws.

As Robert Holub observes:

the contorted reasoning and exegetical maneuvering of de Man's early supporters served only to reinforce the view that they had something to hide. Instead of admitting in a candid and unequivocal fashion that de Man had acted reprehensibly for a short period during the war and then stating the obvious fact that people change and mature, and that his later work must be judged on its critical merits, they wound up damaging both deconstruction and their own credibility by composing such contrived defenses.

Holub goes on to note that some defenders of de Man have further weakened their case by arguing not simply that there is no inherent complicity between deconstructive theory and totalitarian politics, but that deconstruction is a uniquely privileged antidote to totalitarian thinking, as if we had to be deconstructionists in order to oppose totalitarianism. Such an argument should have been ruled out by deconstruction's own principle that there is no determinate or a priori relation, only a contextual one, between a philosophical argument and its political consequences.

In the ill will unleashed by the de Man case, it became difficult to judge deconstruction "on its critical merits." The scandal quickly became a skir-mish in the larger culture war over the study and teaching of the humanities, which began in the mid-1980s and continues today. When and if the heat of controversy diminishes, however, deconstructionists will be able to point to an influence on contemporary thought that goes well beyond the work done by members of the school itself. Far from having receded into memory, as some commentators have asserted, deconstruction has left its mark on a wide range of disciplines. And far from having been supplanted by new histori-cism and cultural and political criticism, deconstruction has shaped these movements in ways that our remaining chapters will explore.

6

❦

FROM TEXTUALITY TO MATERIALITY

A MONG THE POSTULATES of deconstruction that we presented in Chapter 5 was the following:

5. In a society or culture, discourses and explanatory narratives become dominant by repressing counterdiscourses, narratives, and voices that they cannot assimilate. Deconstructive readings attempt to elicit these unwanted "other" stories and show how they haunt the official discourse and thus undo its supposed coherence and inevitability.

We added that "the political efficacy of deconstructive reading strategies (and their link to Marxism, feminism, and other directly sociopolitical forms of criticism) rests on a claim that these strategies can help shake dominant discourses by revealing their repressed contradictions." Among the issues to which we now turn is the extent to which such claims of political efficacy can be justified.

If they think nothing else about it, media detractors of deconstruction believe that it is politically armed and dangerous. In the preceding chapter, we attempted to defuse some of the polemics and dispel some of the misapprehensions that have long surrounded deconstruction. We ended by agreeing, however, that the deconstructive argument that linguistic meaning is self-divided, performative, and interested "inevitably returns us to politics." Texts indeed become political, we suggested, when their meanings are understood not to be natural, stable, or simply "there," but instead determined, and thus "produced," by particular cultural interests and institutional circumstances, by the clash of social discourses and interpretive systems.

It must be noted, however, that there is a difference between the proposition that deconstruction logically renders meaning political and the claim that deconstructive critique actively promotes any specific political program or outcome. There is a difference, in other words, between making politics a general condition of discourse and intervening in particular discourses to advance specific social ends. Indeed, some have argued that, in bringing about a "general destabilization of all discourses of legitimation," deconstruction only paralyzes political action and critique. As outsiders to the academy attack deconstruction for obtruding politics where they have no place, many academic insiders attack it for having no real politics at all. If seeing the world as a "text" makes everything political, it may trivialize politics in the process.

The debates over the politics of textuality raise issues that will occupy most of this chapter and the next: What happens to the relationship between the aesthetic and the political when the world is viewed as a text? In what way and to what degree can literary criticism be politically significant? How do contemporary criticism's theories of textuality bear on its interests in material reality and aspirations to material consequence? Is literature (or criticism) a form of idealization or of demystification, or both? Can critics legitimately hope (as a contributor to a major collection of essays in cultural studies puts it) "not only to interpret, but to change things"?

POLITICS AND TEXTUALITY

Debates about the connection, or lack of connection, between theories or methods of textual interpretation and the achievement of political change have raged around and within all the recent sociopolitical criticisms. Stuart Hall, for example, a founder of the British cultural studies movement and a long-time director of its major institute, the Birmingham Centre for Contemporary Cultural Studies, argues in an essay entitled "Cultural Studies and its Theoretical Legacies" (1992) that cultural studies must live with the tension between "intellectual and theoretical work" and "political practice." While affirming that "culture will always work through its textualities," Hall admits to a "nagging doubt that this overwhelming textualization of cultural studies' own discourses somehow constitutes power and politics as exclusively matters of language and textuality itself."

Another set of doubts about the political efficacy of "theory" has come from American pragmatist critics associated with a certain form of new historicism. Howard Horwitz, for example, following Stanley Fish and Walter Benn Michaels, assails the complacent assumption of some left-wing poststructuralists that once a dominant belief has been shown to be "socially constructed" (rather than natural), its dominance has somehow been undermined and a blow has been struck for radical social change. Horwitz questions whether progressive political consequences follow from an "anti-objectivist vision of historical knowledge" or a constructivist theory of textual meaning. The problem, as Fish and Michaels argue elsewhere, is that the political consequences of a theory cannot be derived a priori from the theory itself, for a given theory can have opposing political effects in different situations. As

Horwitz puts it, "politics emerge in specific actions, not in the structure of cognition"; political critics not only "cannot ground oppositional politics in a model or theory of criticism," but the paradoxical result of attempting to do so is the "incapacity to contest competing interpretations." In other words, the notion that certain theories or textual practices are necessarily oppositional or hegemonic assumes uncritically that we can calculate their political effects without knowing the contexts in which they operate.

A similar point about certain claims of "subaltern" criticism is made by Gayatri Chakravorty Spivak, a founder of post-colonial criticism and translator of Derrida's *Of Grammatology* (1967, 1976). Spivak writes of the project of the Subaltern Studies collective of Indian postcolonial critics to retrieve the history and consciousness of the Indian underclasses (subalterns) under British colonialism. The Subaltern collective discerns the suppressed presence of a subaltern consciousness in "the texts of counter-insurgency of elite documentation." But, because it is derived only from the signs of its suppression, the subaltern consciousness that the collective "reads" in the writings of the colonial elite cannot be shown to exist apart from its critical construction in the act of reading. Moreover, if subaltern insurgency is by definition a feature of any text or any authoritative concept, as deconstructive theory suggests, then its effects become so predictable as to be trivial, and there is no particular need for Indian subaltern studies. When "what had seemed the historical predicament of the colonial subaltern can be made to become the allegory of the predicament of *all* thought, *all* deliberative consciousness," Spivak writes, the success of the collective's reading strategy marks the failure of the political purpose it was meant to serve.

Deconstruction, as we showed in Chapter 5, exposes the tensions that underlie (and underwrite) assumed totalities and unities. In Emily Dickinson's stunningly adaptable phrase, deconstruction discovers "internal difference / Where the Meanings, are." In Paul de Man's words: "a deconstruction always has for its target to reveal the existence of hidden articulations and fragmentations within assumed monadic totalities." According to critics like Hall, Horwitz, and Spivak, however, deconstruction can also result in totalizations more sweeping than those it opposes.

Does de Man's later deconstructive writing, for example, which dismisses all putative master narratives as "myth," repudiate the totalitarian cultural chauvinism of his collaborationist wartime essays, which celebrate Europe's "great evolutive laws"? Or does the later writing disavow de Man's earlier misdeeds through a fatalistic rationalization? As de Man concluded in an essay on Shelley's poem "The Triumph of Life," "nothing, whether deed, word, thought, or text, ever happens in relation, positive or negative, to anything that precedes, follows, or exists elsewhere, but only as a random event whose power, like the power of death, is due to the randomness of its occurrence." Does de Man's view that literature exposes "the fallacy of unmediated expression" help demythologize discourses of power that claim absolute historical facticity, or does it merely establish a new mythology of Literature, redefined as the one discourse that is true because it relinquishes any pretense of truthfulness?

Favoring the second interpretation, Edward Said, a leading contemporary cultural theorist and critic whose work we will discuss in chapter 7, sees de Man as a kind of decadent aesthete. In an essay published before the revelation of de Man's wartime affiliations, Said broadly censures the "ideology of refinement" and residual formalism of American "Left" Literary Criticism. De Man's "corrosive irony," according to Said, does not resist totalizing concepts or undo organized dogmas but leads only to de Man's endless reiteration of the "intellectual hobbles on the possibility of statement," the insupportability "of stating anything at all."

The literary work for [de Man] stands in a position of almost unconditional superiority over historical facticity not by virtue of its power but by virtue of its admitted powerlessness; its originality resides in the premise that it has disarmed itself 'from the start,' as if by having said in advance that it had no illusions about itself and its fictions it directly accedes to the realm of acceptable form. These ideas of course express a major tendency in all symbolist art, a tendency made considerably interesting by every variety of twentieth-century critical formalism.

When viewed in this way, Said goes on to suggest, the work of the leading American deconstructionist demythologizer of the 1970s and 1980s looks a lot like that of the leading structuralist mythographer of the 1950s and 1960s, Northrop Frye.

Indeed, critics such as Gerald Graff and Frank Lentricchia had already argued in the late 1970s and early 1980s that Frye's and de Man's seemingly antithetical notions of Literature ultimately ended in the same place. Both Frye's theory that literature expresses a visionary desire for complete coherence and de Man's theory that it constitutes an antivisionary confession of utter incoherence ultimately disengage literature from social referents. Frye's imaginative "world of total metaphor, in which everything is potentially identical with everything else" is one of mythic plenitude, while de Man's world of nonidentities displays (as we noted in Chapter 5) "the void that separates intent from reality." Whereas Frye distinguishes between "the world [man] sees and the world he constructs" and takes literature to embody the dream of living wholly in the constructed world, de Man collapses the distinction and takes literature to embody the nightmare of knowing that there is nowhere to live but in that constructed world.

Clearly, we are a long way from the postulate that we took up for examination at the outset of this chapter: that deconstruction returns us to politics. If Said is right, the corrosive irony of deconstruction leads not to politics and oppositional criticism but to aesthetic formalism. Interestingly, however, in the introduction to the book in which Said's essay on American "Left" Literary Criticism is collected, Said characterizes his own brand of "oppositional criticism" in terms that might describe the project of deconstruction:

> its identity is its difference from other cultural activities and from systems of thought or of method. In its suspicion of totalizing concepts, in its discontent with reified objects, in its impatience with guilds, special interests, imperialized fiefdoms, and orthodox habits of mind, criticism is most itself. . . . "Ironic" is not a bad word to use along with "oppositional."

Here, irony for Said is crucial to criticism's oppositionality and to its capacity to remain "life-enhancing" and "constitutively opposed to every form of tyranny."

Whatever the validity of the challenges to the political value of deconstructive theory, Said's example reveals how deconstruction has a way of leaving its traces in the work of political critics who claim to repudiate it. Deconstructive insights and methods have deeply shaped the politically engaged schools of academic criticism that have emerged over the last two decades. Cultural Studies, the New Historicism, Postcolonial Criticism, and theories of postmodernism and postmodernity differ from one another (and contain internal differences as well) in their origins, objects, attitudes, and interests. Yet these critical enterprises generally share what we called in Chapter 5 the "constructivist" or "antifoundationalist" account of the relation between language and the world upon which deconstruction and poststructuralism radically insist.

Moreover, to varying degrees, all of these recent critical projects make textual analysis – of literary works in particular and signifying practices in general – a vehicle of political response to dominant historical narratives and contemporary material conditions. All have been touched by the deconstructive model of the text, according to which textual meaning and identity are founded on the exclusion of an "other" that returns to haunt the text, leaving instabilities that can be mapped by a deconstructive reading. Whereas the unified text of the New Critics exemplified the organic society or nation, the deconstructive text that differs from itself becomes a model of how social legitimations gain authority by masking their vulnerabilities.

The question of whether deconstruction is "really" oppositional or escapist cannot finally be answered, then, for whether deconstruction entails either of these outcomes depends on how it is deployed and the contexts in which it operates. To reduce deconstruction to the claim that dominant discourses are inherently repressive, or that deconstructing these discourses is essentially subversive, is to miss the deconstructive point that ascribing a fixed, simple, predictable effect a priori to any text, theory, or linguistic practice ignores the instability of language and the contingency of meaning.

Politically speaking, Derrida observes in the volume *Limited Inc.*, "deconstruction is not 'inherently' anything at all that might be determined" a priori or in itself. Agreeing with pragmatist critics like Fish, Michaels, and Horwitz that to make politics a general condition of discourse is not to know in advance how any particular discourse furthers or subverts specific social ends, Derrida judges that deconstruction is "neither 'conservative' nor the contrary, [but] 'is' only what is done with it, there where it takes place."

ROLAND BARTHES AND THE POLITICIZATION OF "MYTH"

Nothing more vividly prefigured the move toward politics in the current critical generation than the contrasting uses of the word "myth" in two landmark works of critical theory published in the same year, 1957, on opposite sides of the Atlantic: Frye's *Anatomy of Criticism* and Roland Barthes' *Mythologies*. Although Frye does not neglect the social functions of myth, for him myths are most properly viewed as formal rather than substantive categories, structures of the imagination that are prior to and separate from questions of power relations. Myths, he writes, constitute a timeless repertoire of "abstract fictional designs," the "grammatical rudiments of literary expression," the set of "structural principles," "primitive formulas," or "archetypes" that inform ancient and modern literature alike.

This idea of the timelessness of myth underwrites Frye's project of a "total literary history" in which every literary work is part of a system of variations on "a relatively restricted and simple group of formulas that can be studied in primitive culture." Myth is therefore, as Frye suggests in his "Polemical Introduction," the proper object of the systematic critic, who is distinguished from the mere historian on the one hand and the book reviewer and dilettante on the other. Myth grounds the *wholeness* and *objectivity* of criticism – qualities unavailable to the partial and partisan projects of historical, sociological, and moral critics, who deal in "sheer sequence," "ideological perorations," or mere "value judgements" that "cannot help to build up a systematic structure of knowledge."

For Barthes, by contrast, "myth" is not a grammatical or imaginative structure but a social practice, "a type of speech." This difference turns out to have major consequences. Whereas for Frye myth is a transhistorical, transcontextual source of imaginative vision, for Barthes it is a socially and historically situated performance, a form of cultural and ideological work.

Mythic speech, Barthes argues, is not a privileged characteristic of literary expression but links literature to other signifying practices.

Accordingly, Barthes's analyses in *Mythologies* take up not only literary texts but also such sites of mythic speech as "The World of Wrestling," "Soappowders and Detergents," "The Face of Garbo," "The New Citroen," and "Photography and Electoral Appeal." Frye, too, sees myth as informing popular as well as high culture, but again as an eternally present set of patterns rather than as a socially strategic practice. For Barthes, myth is a modern communicative performance in the service of specific social purposes, not an eternal archetype that imparts visionary design to the whole of Literature.

Barthes defines myth as secondary not primary, partisan not objective, reductive not expansive. Myth is not apolitical or superpolitical speech, but "depoliticized speech," political speech that passes itself off as natural, performative action that passes itself off as uninvolved description:

What the world supplies to myth is an historical reality, defined, even if this goes back quite a while, by the way in which men have produced or used it; and what myth gives in return is a *natural* image of this reality. . . . The world enters language as a dialectical relation between activities, between human actions; it comes out of myth as a harmonious display of essences. A conjuring trick has taken place; it has turned reality inside out, it has emptied it of history and has filled it with nature.

Barthes and Frye agree that myth brings coherence out of complexity and multiplicity and displays "essences." But for Barthes the coherence and the essences that create it are merely rhetorical effects: myth's achievement is a "conjuring trick" that "abolishes the complexity of human acts, . . . does away with all dialectics, with any going beyond what is immediately visible, [and] organizes a world that is without contradictions because it is without depth."

Barthes's landmark essay "Myth Today" legitimates the contemporary critical project of demythologizing and repoliticizing cultural texts, exposing contradictions and resisting totalizations – often by recovering the suppressed voices and perspectives of those defined as "Other" by Euro-American dominance:

I am at the barber's, and a copy of *Paris-Match* is offered to me. On the cover, a young Negro in a French uniform is saluting, with his eyes uplifted, probably fixed on a fold of the tricolour. All this is the *meaning* of the picture. But, whether naively or not, I see very well what it signifies to me: that France is a great Empire, that all her sons, without any colour discrimination, faithfully serve under her flag, and that there is no better answer to the detractors of an alleged colonialism than the zeal shown by this Negro in serving his so-called oppressors.

The meaning of the image (the black soldier giving the French salute) that Barthes designates "the final term of the linguistic system" is also "the first term of the mythical system," a term, we might say, that produces "abstract fictional designs" very different from the ones Frye contemplates – in this case, the design of a strong, healthy, happy, egalitarian, multiracial French empire. As Barthes sees it, of course, the "fiction" that the image communicates is a dangerous lie that serves to naturalize and sanitize French colonialism, to promote aggressive nationalism, and to obscure the reality of racial discrimination in France.

Critics of Barthes such as Eugene Goodheart and Richard Levin have pointed out that the terms of his own analysis raise the question of whether there is any neutral standpoint from which to condemn the colonialist myth, or any other myth, as a "fiction" or lie. Since Barthes disparages the notion of an independent "reality" as itself a naturalizing myth of bourgeois realism and common sense, he would seem to leave no basis in the "real" for his demythologizing critique. We will return subsequently to this problem, which plagues all versions of poststructuralist theory.

To some degree at least, the differences between Frye's and Barthes's opposing notions of myth, literature, and criticism reflect the contrasting geopolitical histories and cultural experiences of America and Europe in 1957. In the United States, where political and cultural power seemed less centralized and where government had more often ignored or disdained art than deployed it, it was easier to see literature as an autonomous verbal system subject to structural definition and ethical celebration, a utopian alternative or even, as William Carlos Williams had called poetry, "a rival government." In Europe by contrast, as Philip Fisher remarks, a history of monarchic traditions and state socialisms of the right and left guaranteed that "by 1945 no European intellectual could any longer imagine what it might mean to live in a society without a state that owned, sponsored, and used for its own purposes all the media of cultural life."

The notoriously "politicized" turn of recent American criticism, then, may signal the transition from a provincial to a European and cosmopolitan orientation, in which literature is implicated in society rather than detached from it (although, as we explained in Chapter 4, indigenous influences such as the women's movement and the civil rights movement also propelled criticism in this direction). In assuming literature's embeddedness in networks of power, many contemporary critical approaches identify the ideology of capitalism, the West, bourgeois cultural hegemony, patriarchy, or instrumental reason – rather than the State – as the force of domination that produces and regulates literary expression along with other elements of social and cultural life. Though locating the exact nature of this force of domination has proved a problem, as we shall see, these approaches nonetheless all tend to deny literature the political and generic privilege that Frye grants it.

Accordingly, much contemporary criticism has heeded the call of British Marxist critic Terry Eagleton, among others, and taken "discursive practices" as its object of study rather than literature in the narrow sense. Yet, even in work that shares Eagleton's levelling assumptions and interests, the impulse to distinguish the literary does not simply disappear.

Two characterizations of literature by another prominent Marxist critic, author of *English in America* (1976) Richard Ohmann, may indicate the contested – perhaps even confused – current status of the literary in contemporary politically oriented criticism. On the one hand, Ohmann defines literature as a "piece of language which has been detached from any specific 'living' relationship and thus [is] subject to the 'reinscriptions' and reinterpretations of many different readers." On the other hand, Ohmann remarks: "Like all art, [literature] tends toward the rebellious and iconoclastic." The first statement initially seems to accord with Barthes' view of myth: detached from history (" 'living' relationship"), literature is a site of ideological mystification. Yet the statement goes on to suggest that its very lack of an immediate practical context and a fixed receiver makes literary speech peculiarly adaptable to interpretation, less limited than other language in its possible significances. The second statement accords more closely with Frye's ascription of a privileged freedom, even a revolutionary impulse, to the aesthetic object itself.

The tensions between these characterizations of literature pervade the contemporary critical scene and will be traced in our discussions of cultural studies, new historicism, postcolonial criticism, and theories of postmodernism and postmodernity in the following pages. Is literature a reservoir of imaginative possibility or a coercive social practice? Is it a site of private iconoclasm or of political liberation? Does it take its character from the conditions of its production, from its particular form, or from the varieties of its consumption? Does it have any character at all that sets it apart from other "discursive practices"? These remain pressing questions in the 1990s, but many of the ways in which they are currently addressed were formulated more than fifty years ago in the groundbreaking work of the group of cultural critics who first called their enterprise "Critical Theory": the expatriate European Jews of the "Frankfurt School." Any adequate comprehension of the principal critical directions of our own time must proceed through them.

THE FRANKFURT SCHOOL AND MARXIST
CULTURAL CRITICISM

Established by a group of socialist intellectuals in 1923, the Frankfurt Institute for Social Research, as described by its biographer Martin Jay, was "an

interdisciplinary institute dedicated to a radical dissection of bourgeois society." The founders included philosophers, literary critics, sociologists, psychologists, economists, and political scientists who combined the hope for
Marxist social transformation with the conviction that such transformation
could not be achieved in the modern world without a thoroughgoing revision
of Marxist social and cultural theory. The interdisciplinarity of the Frankfurt
School was itself a critique of the prevailing economistic Marxism, which
viewed social, cultural, and psychological life as merely secondary, "superstructural" expressions of the economic "base," dependent and determined
effects of capitalist relations of production. Economistic Marxism, the Frankfurt critics felt, had become mechanical and had neglected the important
elements of dialectical philosophy, critical self-reflection, and ideology critique in Marx's work. Accordingly, they rejected the deterministic theory
that the inherent economic contradictions of capitalism would inevitably
precipitate a spontaneous uprising of the masses leading to a socialist utopia.
This theory failed to reckon with the complex and powerful ideological
resources with which twentieth-century capitalism could deny, disguise, or
palliate the injuries it inflicted, and distract or disperse mass action against
it. These ideological resources included irrational systems such as nationalism, individualism, racism, and consumerism, and, above all, the power to
disseminate these systems through advertising, film, political propaganda,
and the other media of "the culture industry."

The members of the Frankfurt School, then, based their work on the
premise that the power of the modern industrial state was produced and
sustained not through sheer economic and physical domination, but through
the manipulation of images and ideas by various forms of social, cultural, and
psychological conditioning. Consequently, the chances of social transformation rested not on a fatalistic working out of economic laws but on an
interdisciplinary critique of ideology. These principles of the Frankfurt
School were shared by an Italian contemporary, the imprisoned communist
Antonio Gramsci, who supplied a key term – "hegemony" – for the means
by which systems and agents of authority came to seem legitimate and
voluntarily chosen in the minds of the ruled. Hegemony, in other words,
refers to a modern form of domination that is textual as well as material,
cultural as well as political, and that may be exercised by a liberal as well as a
fascist state. One cannot overstate the importance of these grounding principles of Critical Theory, not only for the projects of later Marxist theorists
such as Louis Althusser and Fredric Jameson, but for contemporary sociopolitical criticism in general. They underlie the claim for the political relevance of the literary intellectual and the work of cultural criticism.

Given the mission of Frankfurt School intellectuals to expose the ideological deceptions of the culture industry, their work necessarily assumed a negative cast. Herbert Marcuse, the Frankfurt School critic whose writings gained most influence in the United States (his best known colleagues include Walter Benjamin, Theodor Adorno, Max Horkheimer, and Erich Fromm), entitled one of his books *Negations* (1968) and began his essay, "A Note on Dialectic," by approvingly quoting Hegel's remark that: "thinking is, indeed, essentially the negation of that which is immediately before us." Dialectical or critical thought, Marcuse continued, "thus becomes negative in itself. Its function is to break down the self-assurance and self-contentment of common sense."

Negative critique may indeed be necessary, since "that which is immediately before us" often disguises or naturalizes a harmful and illegitimate status quo. But it also has inherent problems which many have observed in the work of the Frankfurt School and in subsequent socio-political criticism. One danger is inaccessibility, a problem that we discussed in Chapter 1. If the terms and ideas that are most apparent to "common sense" are themselves permeated or complicit with the dominant ideology, then, as Marcuse suggests, the oppositional critic who assails the self-assurance of these terms and ideas must presumably use language which seems alien, dissonant, and eccentric. In discussing French feminist theory, we have already seen the double bind posed by the idea that language is so permeated by patriarchy that it must be repudiated by feminists, a position that seemingly leads to silence, incoherence, and the self-isolation of radical critics from everyone else. The logic of similar ideas in the Frankfurt School suggests that a condition of articulating critique may be the loss of an audience.

A second related danger is elitism, the tendency of the intellectual who claims to see through the veil of appearances to disdain those who do not. The antagonism toward mass culture expressed by many of the Frankfurt School critics, who associated it with the fascist politics of mass manipulation that they witnessed in Germany in the early 1930s, has exposed them repeatedly to the charge of elitism, although this was a danger that they themselves recognized and addressed. Adorno distinguishes between "transcendent critique," in which the critic speaks from an imaginary point outside of culture, and his preferred "immanent critique," in which the critic rejects the stance of detachment and acknowledges his immersion in the object of his analysis; "wishing to wipe away the whole as with a sponge," Adorno cautions, transcendent critics "develop an affinity to barbarism."

A third problem of negative critique, especially when it addresses literary and cultural objects, is the absence of practical mechanisms and agents to translate critique into actual change. Once economic laws or the proletarian masses can no longer be counted upon to produce the revolution, then the means of radical social transformation become unclear. Art and literature thus risk becoming a sort of haven of oppositional consciousness for a left that can no longer appeal to traditional agents of revolution. Marcuse concedes that "whatever liberation [dialectical thought] may bring is a liberation in thought, in theory," but he adds that "the divorce of thought from action . . . is itself part of the unfree world" and that, while criticism alone cannot undo this divorce, it can "help to prepare the ground for their possible reunion." Marcuse's colleagues, Horkheimer and Adorno, argued that certain works of art functioned, in Russell A. Berman's characterization, as "place-holder[s] of a potential opposition to monopoly capitalism and the culture industry." As Adorno observes, such works only "point to a practice from which they abstain: the creation of a just life." The separation of thought from action, of progressive art from a just life, of aesthetic critique from material results, became increasingly burdensome for the Frankfurt School critics, leading to the pessimism marking their late work – a fourth inherent danger for the practitioner of negative critique. Introducing a recent collection of the major essays of the Frankfurt School, Paul Piccone charges that in its last years Critical Theory "checkmate[d]" its own former "hopes of social emancipation," refusing to "even attempt to prefigure the future by elaborating the mediations necessary to bring it about," and instead "retreated to defend particularity, autonomy and nonidentity [the ceaseless play of dialectic or negation] against an allegedly totally administered society."

Finally, there is the problem posed by this Marcusean idea of a "totally administered society," the sort of totalizing and accusatory concept that became a staple of the sixties counterculture and has been familiar in leftist polemics ever since. Recent versions of negative critique have sometimes attributed to cultural hegemony the very absolute existence and deterministic inevitability that the early work of the Frankfurt School denied to the privileged forces of classical Marxism, the "mode of production" and the "laws of History." Some new historicist criticism, for instance, as we will see in Chapter 7, has drawn from Michel Foucault's influential account of the dissemination of state power throughout the modern disciplinary society the lesson that oppositional critique itself may be impossible, since the identity and the discourse of the critic are inevitably produced, contained, and co-opted by the hegemonic culture that she or he would criticize. Theories that overstate the power of cultural hegemony, then, risk collapsing different kinds and degrees of coercive power into one pervasive and irresistible force of domination. Far from being unique to the Frankfurt School, the hazards of Critical Theory that we have enumerated identify some of the continuing problems of academic cultural criticism with which we will be concerned in this chapter.

If the Frankfurt School critics, as Piccone and others suggest, tended to overstate the undifferentiation and authoritarianism of modern administered society and mass culture, it must be remembered that their project developed in the context of the rise of European fascism. For Max Horkheimer, in his essay "The End of Reason" (1941), and for Horkheimer and Adorno in their book *Dialectic of Enlightenment* (1944), the fascist state was the ultimate expression of the fully rationalized technological society in which, as Adorno put it, "there are virtually no direct relationships between men, and in which each person has been reduced to a social atom, to a mere function of collectivity." Perceiving the incommensurability between his own power and that of the modern state or the modern economy, the individual experiences a sense of helplessness, Horkheimer explained, but "the veil of money" and "the veil of technology" make it "difficult for him to penetrate the human origin of his misery." Fascism, like any enthusiastic nationalism, offers such an individual compensation for his self-loss in the self-enlargement to be gained by identifying with the state. In such arguments, Frankfurt School critics regarded fascism as something more than an advanced system of domination, a modern social pathology, or the political consequence of a standardized mass culture. Rather, they viewed it, as the pun in Horkheimer's essay title wryly suggests, as the "*end* of reason" – at once the fulfillment, the culminating achievement, and the destruction or undoing of Enlightenment rationalism. As Horkheimer and Adorno saw what they called "the dialectic of enlightenment," the philosophical concept of reason, which had originally included the commitment to skepticism and self-critique, had eventually "extinguished any trace of its own self-consciousness" and become a mere "instrument oriented to expediency," to "the optimum adaptation of means to ends." This instrumentalist perversion of reason, moreover, its susceptibility to detachment from ethical and social ends, is reason's inherent tendency: "the age-old definition of reason in terms of self-preservation already implied the curtailment of reason itself." Thus, even as fascism traduces the Enlightenment reason from which "the ideas of freedom, justice and truth derived their justification," it epitomizes reason's practical equation of knowledge with power, the rationalist's quest "to learn from nature . . . how to use it in order wholly to dominate it and other men."

The assault on instrumental reason and the rationalized society that is central to Horkheimer's, Adorno's, and Marcuse's work drew on themes that had been developed by Max Weber and Georg Lukacs. For Weber, the prime instrument and effect of modern capitalism was "rationalization" – a process by which every sphere of social life was penetrated by the logic of the factory, a logic of efficiency, calculability, and quantifiability that atomized, objectified, and dehumanized the people it regulated. Lukacs' influential concept of

"reification" – literally, *thing*ification – combines Weber's sense of rationalization with Marx's notion of "commodity fetishism," summarized by Ann
Cvetkovich as "the illusion that value resides in objects rather than in the
social relations between individuals that produce commodities." Reification
is the process by which the rationalization of society comes to seem natural,
exploitative human relations are disguised as the way *things* (wages, prices,
employment conditions) are, and people come to accept and internalize their
own objectification.

As Weber and Lukacs were writing about rationalization and reification, a
number of artists were proclaiming that modernist avant-garde art was the
appropriate response – perhaps even the most effective vehicle of resistance –
to the fragmented, instrumentalist society the social theorists described. The
modernist work of art might express resistance to such a society in a number
of ways: through its sensuous immediacy; its anticonventionalism; its expressionism; its flaunting of instrumentalist criteria of value; its refusal, in its
conditions of production and consumption, to become a commodity. In its
reactionary version, this modernist aesthetics defined art as a mystical totality that overcame the devitalizing fragmentation and rationalism of democratic society. In its progressive version, modernist aesthetics took art to be
the bearer of an emancipatory heterogeneity and unpredictability that opposed the homogenizing administered society. In both versions, as Russell
Berman observes, modernism helped codify the now "commonly held assumption that innovative aesthetic activity is or ought to be a carrier of
antibureaucratic potential."

The avant-garde critique of instrumental reason continues to inform recent criticism on the left. Antibureaucratic potential and resistance to rationalist totalization are claimed as properties not only of innovative art but of
writing itself, of various social and cultural "others," and of the body. Such
claims, as we saw in Chapter 4, have been made by French feminists for
"écriture feminine" and by Lacanian critics for the subversive pressure of the
Imaginary, or the Kristevan "semiotic," on the patriarchal symbolic order.
In his influential arguments for the "heteroglossic" and "carnivalesque"
qualities of the novel and for the inherent dialogics of the linguistic sign,
the Russian theorist Mikhail Bakhtin takes narrative and language itself to
be sites of resistance to rationalization. Deconstruction, as we saw in Chapter 5 provides a method of eliciting writing's internal, destabilizing dialogics, or, in Terry Eagleton's phrase, of "show[ing] how texts come to
embarrass their own ruling systems of logic." The same antirationalist spirit
and hope prompts some critics to ascribe revolutionary potential to the
playful dissonances and dislocations of postmodernism. (The work on postmodernism of Ihab Hassan, Linda Hutcheon, Andreas Huyssen, and Marjo-

rie Perloff is important here.) And much of the ongoing cultural criticism that examines subcultures or popular culture, or the expression of those who by virtue of race, class, or sexual orientation are subordinated or marginalized by the "dominant culture," also shares in some measure the association of "otherness" with liberation – liberation not only from oppressive political and material conditions but from the constraints of Western or patriarchal or bourgeois reason itself.

Insofar as the Frankfurt School critique of instrumental reason continues in many different forms in subsequent cultural criticism, that criticism continues to be plagued by the same unanswered questions. In the absence of a revolutionary proletariat, by what agency does radical art or radical critical theory transform social life? And if Western reason has failed, what is supposed to take its place? If the Frankfurt School critics failed to resolve these questions, they nonetheless framed and debated approaches to them that contemporary critics still pursue. The critical intellectual, in their view, acted politically by mediating or defetishizing the objectifications – the supposedly self-evident and given "facts" – of the rationalized society. The critic's job, in other words, was to recognize and announce the glimpses of dystopian reality and utopian possibility that appeared through the cracks in the facade of reification. Marxist intellectuals of the 1920s and 1930s had long differed about whether it was the job of progressive art to present correct images of existing reality or to use the formal tools at its disposal to assault reification and what Marcuse called "the self-contentment of common sense." With some complications and qualifications, the Frankfurt School critics supported the latter position. Opposing "cultural conservatives who demand that a work of art should say something," Adorno holds that progressive potential resides in "a text whose language jolts signification and by its very distance from 'meaning' revolts in advance against positivist subordination of meaning." So formidable, for Adorno, is the power of the positivist administered society to coopt the directly "committed" or "tendentious" work of art that he insists that "the notion of a 'message' in art, even when politically radical, already contains an accommodation to the world." At the same time, Adorno acknowledges the critique of avant-garde antirationalism that Lukacs had earlier levelled against German expressionism and that, in our time, many have levelled against American postmodernism. In *The Jargon of Authenticity* (1973) he mounted a brilliant polemic against the totalitarian implications of Heidegger's irrationalism. And in an earlier essay on "Commitment (1962)," Adorno wrote of "the loss of tension evident in works . . . which have moved away from objective representation and intelligible or coherent meaning. Formal structures which challenge the lying positivism of meaning can easily slide into a different sort of vacuity, . . . empty juggling with elements . . .

and a bad positivism of meaninglessness." What Adorno never makes clear in all this is how one can tell whether an artistic refusal of meaning is a liberatory strike against positivism or a capitulation to incoherence.

While Adorno championed the individual art work that sought "autonomy" by means of formal innovation and resistance to statement, his older colleague, Walter Benjamin, conceived a somewhat more positive and communalizing function for progressive art. Like Adorno, Benjamin rejected the notion that the central value or identity of art lay in its tendentious content; but Benjamin based his preference for open, fragmentary, and public artistic genres not just on a fear of rationalization and cooptation, but on the belief that such art prompted the active and critical intervention of its collective audience. In his most famous and influential essay "The Work of Art in the Age of Mechanical Reproduction" (1936), Benjamin proposes that the cinema exemplifies the kind of art that can activate such revolutionary potential. By virtue of its modernity, its collective and technological production, its popular accessibility, and its use of avant-garde strategies of fragmentation and montage, cinema dissolves the mystifying "aura" that has traditionally surrounded works of art in bourgeois culture and induced silence, passivity, and submission on the part of art's audience. (In this respect Benjamin's ideas paralleled Bertold Brecht's attempt to "defamiliarize" conservative common sense by the use of "alienation effects.") For Benjamin, the cinema is a "postauratic" art form whose conditions of mechanical reproduction and mass reception give it an integral capacity to expose and critique these conditions, a view that reverses Adorno's negative estimation of mass culture and reclaims it for progressive uses. Benjamin himself, however, acknowledged subsequently that he had overestimated the progressive destiny of popular culture. For the prospects of radical critical response by a popular audience depended, as Adorno grimly insisted in a letter to Benjamin, on "the actual consciousness of actual workers who have absolutely no advantage over the bourgeois except their interest in the revolution, but otherwise bear all the marks of mutilation of the typical bourgeois character."

Adorno's remark points up the inevitable dependence of art's political potential on its possibility of realization in the consciousness of individuals and groups. If capitalist society coopts or "mutilates" the consciousness of its subjects, then how is the latent rebelliousness of avant-garde art to be recognized and mobilized? How, for that matter, does this rebelliousness come even to be felt and expressed in the first place? The Frankfurt School critics initiated a powerful case against the liberal vision of autonomous, even transcendent, selfhood, a case that subsequent criticism on the left has repeatedly taken up and struggled with. They viewed individualism, in Andrew Arato's summary, as "an ideological veil masking the new atomization and functionalization of concrete individuals." But, this view was not uniformly applied, either by the group as a whole or within the work of individual critics. For instance, Adorno's aesthetic claims, and his disparagement of the consciousness of the masses in the letter to Benjamin quoted above, show that he continued to grant to the artist and the critic a measure of personal exemption from ideological mystification. Benjamin perhaps most consistently argued that a genuine and satisfying personal identity depends upon membership in a cooperative social structure that gives meaning and communicability to individual lives. Yet, as Horkheimer pointed out, "the elimination of the conflict between individual and society" was, in the 1930s and 1940s, not just a utopian dream of socialism but an all too effective policy of fascism. However the Frankfurt School or later sociopolitical critics approached individuality and collectivity, this question persisted: if no modern form of social and cultural expression was free of the distorting effects of reification or "the marks of [ideological] mutilation," then how could conflict and resistance arise?

THE IDEOLOGY DILEMMA

Both for the revisionist Marxist criticism of the Frankfurt School that we have just looked at and the deconstructive and poststructuralist cultural criticism of our own time, no concept is more crucial than "ideology." Yet "ideology" is a term with many different meanings in the history of criticism and one that often shifts confusingly from one sense to another. In its first appearance in the late eighteenth century, "ideology" was used in a neutral way to denote any relatively systematic body of theory or doctrine, particularly in the realm of social thought. The term acquired a pejorative connotation in traditional Marxist theory, as in *The German Ideology*, where Marx and Engels define ideology as a realm of false consciousness, such as the distorted perceptions produced by capitalist class interest. Classic Marxism thus exempted *itself* from the critique it mounted of idealistic philosophies, distinguishing between the false consciousness that is the legacy of class societies and the undistorted consciousness of the emergent classless society for which Marxism presumably spoke. The assumption was that it is possible to stand outside the false consciousness of ideology and speak from an objective, scientific standpoint, that of "Marxist science" itself.

The Frankfurt School critics, as we have seen, questioned the availability of such a standpoint in their departure from what Adorno called Transcendent Critique. The repudiation of the "false consciousness" sense of ideology has been pushed even further by the most influential poststructuralist Marxist, Louis Althusser. Althusser starts by rejecting the classical Marxist theory of ideology as "positivist." In this formulation, as he puts it, "ideology is conceived as a pure illusion, a pure dream, i.e., as nothingness, . . . an imaginary assemblage, . . . empty and vain," set apart "from the only full and positive reality, that of the concrete history of concrete material individuals materially producing their existence." In Althusser's view, by contrast, ideology cannot be so easily emptied and distanced. In his revision, ideology ceases to be pejoratively equated with false consciousness and becomes the entire system of unconscious and unexamined representations that conditions the way any society sees the world.

Althusser redefines ideology as the "imaginary" set of representations by which individuals establish a relation to the "real relations in which they live." By such a definition, ideology becomes a necessary feature of any society and the term loses its pejorative connotation. As Catherine Belsey puts it, ideology thus understood is "the very condition of our experience of the world, unconscious precisely in that it is unquestioned, taken for granted." Ideology becomes those assumptions which seem so "obvious" to a culture that they appear natural rather than historically and socially produced – like the assumption, say, that everyone should work for a living or that bringing up children does not count as "work" or that "marriage" presupposes members of opposite sexes or that it is natural to regulate our behavior by the hours of the clock. One major way ideology functions, then, is in making "the way things are" seem a fact of nature rather than a product of human social relations and therefore something that might be changed by human action.

The concept of ideology and its counterpart notions undergo a similar expansion in other postmodern thinkers. Michel Foucault disavows the word "ideology," but his concept of "discourse" functions in some respects in the same way, as does Jacques Lacan's concept of the "symbolic order." Like Althusser, these thinkers assume that it is not possible for individuals (a word that itself becomes equivocal) to stand outside socially produced systems of representations – outside the ideological formations, the dominant discourses, the symbolic order of their society. For the individual is constituted as a subject by these systems. This view of ideology as an all-encompassing condition that virtually produces human subjectivities is reflected in the often noted (and deplored) tendency in recent criticism to speak of "subjects," "subject positions," or "positionalities" instead of "individuals, "selves," and "rational agents." Whereas "The soul" in the modern period gave way to "the self," the self in the postmodern era seems to be giving way in turn to "the subject."

With this redefinition of ideology has come a changed conception of the social function of literature and criticism. In classical Marxism, the progressive critic and artist shared a common critical responsibility, to strip away the myths and superstitions of ideology by representing the deeper objective truth of the historical process. Such a view saw the rise of realistic fiction as a historically progressive step, representing a heroic liberation from the idealism and romanticism of the received literary tradition. Georg Lukacs, the last Marxist critic in this classical line, praised the masters of nineteenth-century European realism for revealing, if often only unwittingly and against the class interest of the writer, the objective truth of social and historical development. As Lukacs argued, great "critical realist" novelists like Balzac and, in modern times, Thomas Mann accurately represented the real "typicality" of the historical process. By contrast, according to Lukacs, naturalists like Emile Zola and modernists like James Joyce and Franz Kafka had failed to capture this social typicality, Zola by presenting only vivid but unrelated details, Joyce and Kafka by succumbing to an alienated subjectivism. As such judgments suggest, the function of the critic for Lukacs was to measure the distance between literary representations and the truth of historical reality. New York Intellectuals like Trilling and Howe operated on a similar principle, as in Howe's attack on Susan Sontag and the "New Sensibility" of the 1960s and Trilling's attack on the modernist "adversary culture," both of which had elevated alienation into a universal principle and liquidated the distinction between fantasy and reality.

In the wake of Lukacs, and of Trilling and Howe's generation of American critics, literary realism has been not only stripped of its heroic role as the demystifier of ideology, but has come to be seen as the ultimate example of ideological mystification itself. Roland Barthes argues in *Writing Degree Zero* (1953) and subsequent works that the effect of realism is only to naturalize and normalize, making the way things are seem the way they must always be. Indeed, for Barthes the celebrated illusion of reality so powerfully conveyed by realist works is finally only a "reality-effect," a convention of rhetoric rather than a privileged transcription of reality itself. And because this reality-effect is achieved only by appealing to the audience's already existing sense of what is "obvious" and "real," realist works ultimately reassure their audiences rather than challenge their assumptions. By this logic, which echoes the Frankfurt School's defense of the avant-garde and continues in much modernist aesthetic theory, the claims formerly made for realism as the preeminently *subversive* aesthetic are transferred to such *anti*realist artistic conventions as surrealistic disruption, Brechtian "estrangement," and Russian formalist "defamiliarization." In Adorno's late essay "Commitment," for instance, Kafka appears not as the ineffectual subjectivist that he was for Lukacs but as the quintessential artistic revolutionary, "the inescapability of [whose] work compels the change of attitude which committed works merely demand."

The recent redefinition of ideology has brought with it a number of distinct gains for literary criticism. First of all, it does away with the vulgar-Marxist "reflection" theory of literature, in which literary works are reduced to second order, superstructural reflections of a first order economic base. Literature and art are granted a larger degree of autonomy from their material conditions, while more justice is accorded to their own determining influence on those conditions. Secondly, discarding the view that literary representations are essentially copies of a preexistent reality, we can now recognize the importance of literary and linguistic *convention* in shaping our sense of what is real. We can see that realistic novels, contrary to the claims of their advocates, do not necessarily match up more closely with reality than do romances or symbolist poems. Barthes seems right in arguing that realism is itself as much a set of literary conventions as romanticism.

Thirdly, the revised theory adds subtlety to ideological critiques by reconceiving ideology in terms of *presuppositions* rather than of doctrinaire *ideas*. Ideology becomes a function not of what is *said* in a text, or even of a deeper layer of meaning that can be extracted by a demystifying interpretation. It is sought instead in what is presupposed or taken for granted, in what "goes without saying" or is considered "too obvious" to need mention. This in turn shifts the attention of the critic from the content of a text to its mode of *address*, or what Althusser calls its way of "interpellating" or "hailing" subjects. To "interpellate" someone is to address the person in a manner that "places" her or him as a social subject.

What interests Althusser is the way in which power relations are subtly negotiated and confirmed through such modes of address, the process by which we are created as subjects by ideology. As he puts it, ideology interpellates us by "recruiting" us as certain kinds of subjects, subjects for example who understand themselves to be under the jurisdiction of the police. Therefore, when a policemen calls out, "Hey, you there!" the "hailed individual will turn round. By this mere one-hundred and eighty-degree physical conversion, he becomes a subject. Why? Because he has recognized that the hail was 'really' addressed to him, and that 'it was really him who was hailed and not someone else.' "

Althusser's point is not that we inhabit a police state, but that our sense of who we are is unconsciously produced by the linguistic conventions in which we are addressed. Other commonplace examples would be a teacher's announcement that "The class will come to order," which interpellates its hearers as "students," or a Master of Ceremonies' words "Ladies and gentlemen," which interpellates those being addressed as an audience, and one that is differentiated by gender. These seemingly innocuous modes of address, in short, reflect and reproduce assumptions about how the world is organized (there are two sexes; sexual difference is worth emphasizing) and which of us has the right to be in charge (it would not count if a student were to call the class to order). Again the point is not that these power – and authority – relations are necessarily evil, but that we come to accept them as "obvious," natural, and therefore nonnegotiable, when in fact they are social constructions that have not existed in all societies and that might be challenged and altered in our own. In general, then, the work of ideology is to make social hierarchies seem natural rather than constructed, and ideology does this work through a certain construction of the "real" and the "obvious" that is built into the presuppositions of language.

Productive as it has been, however, the newly expanded concept of ideology has encountered problems that many critics have pointed out. Perhaps the most persistent problem is the apparent double bind entailed by the view that all thought is unavoidably "ideological," a position that seemingly leaves no place for undistorted knowledge and thereby for political criticism itself. Althusser writes that "what really takes place in ideology" always seems to the subject of ideology "to take place outside it. That is why those who are in ideology believe themselves by definition outside ideology. . . . Ideology never says, 'I am ideological.' . . . As is well known, the accusation of being in ideology only applies to others, never to oneself." Althusser seems here to have fallen victim to a version of the philosopher's Liar's Paradox: if ideology by definition always denies itself, then how can we trust any critic who claims to expose the ideology of others? How can any of us fight free enough of ideology to criticize it convincingly? And if we cannot fight free enough of ideology to criticize it, what authorizes social critique or social change? This in effect is the quarrel Jurgen Habermas, a later representative of the Frankfurt School, has mounted against postmodern philosophies that cut their ties with the Enlightenment tradition of independent rationality. Althusser would seem to be simply contradicting himself when he says that ideologies "need only be 'interpreted' to discover the reality of the world behind their imaginary representation of that world." From what standpoint outside ideology can one possibly "interpret" ideologies as such?

This ideology dilemma has attracted more attention from the opponents of leftist sociopolitical critics than from these critics themselves. Richard Levin, one of those opponents who has tended to be dismissed rather than seriously refuted by his targets, maintains that when feminist and other recent politically oriented critics argue that all thought is necessarily ideological they trap themselves in a double bind: to say that all thought is ideological is to grant that your own social critique is ideological; but if your own critique is ideological have you not discredited it? The Liar's Paradox evidently blocks the door of the critic's den, leaving no way out of his self-declared prison house of ideology.

Levin points out that after declaring that everything is ideological and therefore that no appeal to an objective truth or reality is possible, these critics, when it suits their purposes, blithely go on to refer to social reality, as if such reference had not been problematized at all. Catherine Belsey, for example, after categorically denying that critical interpretations can possibly uncover "something there" in a text, goes on to speak of the play of ideological contradictions that "in reality constitutes the literary text." How can Belsey have it both ways? Similarly, Levin cites feminist Gayle Green's statement, in an essay entitled "The Myth of Neutrality Again" (1985), that "interpretations and judgments of literature really are determined by political ideology." Levin asks why one should prefer Greene's feminist interpretations and judgments if they are avowedly as "determined by political ideology" as any of the masculinist judgments she would contest. In its "strong" version (in philosopher of knowledge Mary Hesse's term), the ideology thesis seems to reduce all interpretation to an absurdist relativism or to an arbitrary Nietzchean will to power that would indeed undermine any rational basis for political critique.

This problem also arises for the various theorists of postmodernism who see the postmodern era as one in which "grand-metanarratives" are no longer possible, as Jean-Francois Lyotard suggests in *The Postmodern Condition* (1984), perhaps the most influential of the many discussions of postmodernism in our period. In contrast to earlier periods when human consciousness could be organized around grand unifying stories like those of Christianity, liberal progressivism, and Hegelian and Marxist dialectics, the postmodern age, according to Lyotard, is characterized by the collapse of such totalizing narratives and the consequent diffusion of social life into a plethora of contingent and shifting "language games," none of which can command a privileged position above the rest.

A corollary of Lyotard's argument is the fallaciousness of any idea of a universal subject of history (such as "the consciousness of the proletariat" traditionally invoked by Marxism) as well as appeals to universal concepts like "the common good." Entailed also is the consequent impossibility and arrogance of any attempt to "speak for the other," as intellectuals had since the Enlightenment when they claimed to speak for the conscience of humanity against inequality and exploitation. As Michel Foucault suggested in declaring and welcoming the death of "the universal intellectual," this attempt to speak for the interests of humanity not only failed to liberate the subjugated but was part of what was subjugating them. In Mary Louise Pratt's Foucauldian argument in *Imperial Eyes: Travel Writing and Transcultura-*

tion (1992), virtually any writing that claims to adopt a "view from above" – including even the anti-slavery reformers of the eighteenth and nineteenth centuries – is complicit with "totalizing forms of discursive authority" and consequently with imperialism.

Critics of this postmodern critique of totalization (like Martin Jay in *Downcast Eyes* [1993] and Bruce Robbins in *Secular Vocations* [1993]) raise the question of whether Lyotard, in declaring the death of grand metanarratives, had not merely substituted his own grand narrative, whether Foucault had not become the ultimate universal intellectual in declaring the end of such an intellectual. (Jacques Derrida had suggested as much in an early critique which observed that Foucault, in *Madness and Civilization* [1965], had not avoided "speaking for" madness even as he had written against doing so.) Elsewhere, responding to the Foucauldian arguments of Paul Bové, Robbins observes that, in effect, "the proposition that we should never speak for or to the people, just let them speak for themselves, becomes the claim that 'I speak for the people better than you do.' "

The problem all these critiques point to is the tendency of oppositional critics to overstate the uniformity of ideology – which is conceived as a coherent "system" of cultural assumptions that has but one determinate kind of political use – and thereby to reinstall presumably discredited concepts of false consciousness. That ideology within a single cultural system (or within a single academic discipline) is not monolithic is evidenced by the very fact, for example, that interpreters "produced" by the same society have advanced both classic masculinist and revisionary feminist readings of the same texts. And that interpretations are not entirely specific to any one ideology is evidenced by the fact that feminist rereadings have prompted critics who had not previously questioned the classic ones to change their minds, and by differences and changes among feminist critics themselves in response to challenges from other perspectives. The fact that disagreement, persuasion, and change do take place suggests that at any historical moment, and within any system of cultural assumptions, certain principles and propositions are subject to contestation while others (the large majority) comprise the rational and communicative grounds that make persuasion and contestation possible.

These grounding principles and propositions are themselves not eternally immune to challenge, but no one can coherently challenge them all at once. Thus, while all truth-claims may be ideological in the weak and non-pejorative sense that they emerge from and participate in historically and culturally situated assumptions and values, it does not follow that all truth claims are equally false, arbitrary, or unverifiable. Nor does it entail the belief that all arguments are equal, or equally immune to evaluation, with respect either to their evident merit or their social effects.

One can make these points another way with reference to the categories of *performative* and *constative* utterance that we discussed in Chapter 5. Although absolute separation of the contents of the two categories is rendered problematic by the performative (productive or practical) functions of most constative (definitional) utterances and by numerous instances – such as the ones Derrida identifies in Plato – in which ostensible statements of definition turn out to be disguised value judgments or enactments of power, nonetheless the categories themselves are not completely collapsible. Derrida himself, in fact, has cautioned that "the value of truth (and all of those values associated with it) is never contested or destroyed in my writing, but only reinscribed," removed from a particular location or context in which it was thought to reside and relocated, recontextualized. Indeed, Derridean or any other sort of critique requires, as Derrida goes on to say, "that there *are* and that there *should be* truth, reference, and stable contexts of interpretation," even though "this stability . . . is always provisional and finite."

The acknowledgement of the fact and the legitimacy of reference (which is to say, of a distinction between the constative and the performative) makes it possible, even within the general premises of the ideology thesis, to speak, as we do above, of "evidentiary merit" and of "social effects" as separable concerns. Accordingly, it is possible to maintain that certain statements (for instance, "the earth orbits the sun") may be both true and ideological – in the strong sense of conditioning the way human beings view ourselves and the world and entailing social effects – while others ("water cannot be frozen") may be false without necessarily being meaningfully ideological. It follows then that, while contemporary political criticism in some instances may challenge the truth or evidentiary merit of certain truth claims (such as the claim made by some that the course and practice of scientific inquiry is value-neutral), its proper target is not the viability of truth claims as such but how those claims *function* in particular social contexts.

These stipulations would allow critics of ideology to acknowledge the "ideological" nature of their own arguments without thereby undermining the claims of those arguments to truth. Similarly, they enable such a critic to show that a proposition can be perfectly truthful while functioning "ideologically" in various ways. The proposition, for example, that fifty percent of the members of social group X are unemployed may be true even as it serves an ideological function, either of rallying support for social group X or causing it to be blamed for its condition. For that matter, the very singling out of group X for notice may have ideological purposes and effects without involving any falsity or inaccuracy.

Increasingly, politically oriented critics may be recognizing that their projects cannot make sense in the absence of some arguable standard of validity. In a recent essay on the concept of ideology, for example, the Althusserian critic, James Kavanagh, writes that "the distinctive effect of ideology is not theoretical but pragmatic." Ideological discourses, writes Kavanagh, "will always contain and transmit some 'knowledges,' but are not vehicles for producing knowledge and should not be judged in those terms." From this perspective, Kavanagh adds, "the problem with specific ideological discourses and practices is not *that* they are ideological" – for it goes without saying that everything is ideological that has any significant social effect. The problem rather is "exactly *how*" these discourses and practices are ideological, what specific social effects do they have?

Note that by such an argument, judgments of the "subversive" or "complicitous" effect of any theory, art work, or representational practice become contextual or, in Marxist terms, "conjunctural." That is, any adequate political evaluation of a theory requires one to ask not simply about its truth but about the effect it has within a specific social context. The same theory may function progressively or subversively in one context and complicitously in another. Similarly, the same person may hold a number of different beliefs, which are variously activated and challenged by the different social contexts in which that person exists. All of these beliefs may be "ideological," but they do not always exercise the same function or force at the same time, and certain circumstances bring some of them into conflict with one another in ways that allow for reflection, reorientation, and the possibility of change. Thus it follows that statements about the inescapability of ideology or the subject's interpellation by ideology are empty without an empirical analysis of the specific historical conjuncture – the myriad contextual variables that shape "exactly *how*" ideologies and subjects "perform" themselves and each other at any given moment.

Shifting the discussion from *whether* discourses and practices are political to *how* they are political is essential to advancing current debates that have become clotted by confusion or emptied by abstraction. (Of course, this shift of focus will not persuade those who disapprove of raising either question about literature.) Such a tactic would enable us to resist the sweeping ideological generalizations that result from the tendency on both the right and the left to imagine ideology as an abstract totality. Thus we can question the generalization associated with poststructuralism that identifies objectivist and essentialist modes of thought with political conservatism. When Roland Barthes states that "the disease of thinking in essences is at the bottom of every bourgeois mythology of man," Barthes assumes that essentialist thinking inevitably reinforces the dominant social order, irrespective of the context in which it appears. Historically, however, essentialist thinking has as often been involved in opposing the dominant order as supporting it. A notable example is the American Civil Rights movement, where appeals to the essential humanity of black people have arguably had a profoundly oppositional effect, although it is possible to argue the converse in the context of more recent social debate, where the proposition that blacks and whites are just the same has been used as an excuse for not redressing continuing inequalities of racial opportunity. Barthes's own argument against essentialism is itself curiously "essentialist," assuming as it does that essentialism has some inherent – that is, essential – political effect. Indeed, as Diana Fuss has pointed out, much current social constructionist theory shares this blindness to its own essentializing positions.

The same point can be made against allegations of the inherent conservatism of literary realism – or of the inherently subversive quality of avant-garde disruptive techniques. Indeed, in a postindustrial consumer culture dominated by the revisionism of advertising images and of rapidly changing "life styles," the avant-garde "aesthetics of perpetual revolution" may become just another motif of capitalism (as Adorno and Marcuse feared), while the aesthetics of realism may acquire a new political valence. Precisely this point is made by Fredric Jameson:

In these circumstances, . . . there is some question whether the ultimate renewal of modernism, the final dialectical subversion of the now automatized conventions of an aesthetics of perpetual revolution, might not simply be . . . realism itself! For when modernism and its accompanying techniques of 'estrangement' have become the dominant style whereby the consumer is reconciled with capitalism, the habit of fragmentation itself needs to be 'estranged' and corrected by a more totalizing way of viewing phenomena.

Jameson concludes that "it may be Lukacs – wrong as he may have been in the 1930s – who has some provisional last word for us today." Again, Jameson's premise is that, taken in itself, the ideological function of the aesthetics of realism or antirealism is indeterminate. It becomes determinate only when viewed in specific contexts. Our last chapter examines some of the specific cultural, political, and historical contexts in which the principal forms of contemporary ideological criticism – cultural studies, new historicism, postcolonial criticism, and criticism of postmodernism and postmodernity – have sought to intervene.

7

CULTURAL AND HISTORICAL STUDIES

ETERMINING HOW CULTURAL PRACTICES work in specific social contexts has been a principal object of the recent critical projects known as "cultural studies" and "the new historicism." These terms now designate an exceptionally broad, often interlocking array of inquiries that make use of the critical theories and methods we have discussed in our last three chapters.

It may be debated whether cultural studies and new historicism should be seen as parallel, overlapping, or antithetical developments. To some critics, these terms designate two faces of the same oppositional impulse. To others, they represent diametrically opposed practices – with "cultural studies" being politically oppositional and materialist, and "new historicism" defusing or precluding oppositional politics by relentlessly textualizing history or implicating all cultural production in hegemonic power. In this contrastive usage, "cultural studies" and "new historicism" often boil down to code terms for Marx and Foucault, the one seeking the material transformation of society, the other seeing "power" as so pervasive and insidious that would-be resistance only reproduces it.

Generally, though, cultural studies and the new historicism can be neither simply identified nor neatly opposed. Instead of a polar opposition, these terms mark different emphases among a fluid range of theories and practices that so interact, overlap, and mingle that the taxonomy finally becomes of limited value. Nonetheless, the characteristic emphases of the two movements do differ in ways that reflect their diverse origins. Cultural studies began in England as a critique of postwar British society by neo-Marxist intellectuals and activists who were particularly concerned with class relations and material culture, who favored empirical analysis over theoretical abstraction, and who generally worked between or beyond traditional academic disciplines and outside the elite British universities. The new historicism, on the other hand, is a method of analysis developed by well-placed American literary critics – initially, by Renaissance scholar Stephen Greenblatt and such Berkeley colleagues as Catherine Gallagher and Walter Benn Michaels, who gathered around the journal *Representations*. In the wake of

1960s political activism and its subsequent pressure for socially engaged academic work, these scholars used the newly developing discourse theories to cross traditional boundaries between aesthetics and politics and between historical and contemporary studies. These different initial circumstances and motives suggest the subsequent directions, procedures, and problems of cultural studies and the new historicism, which we will now take up in turn.

CULTURAL STUDIES

Cultural studies first emerged in the 1960s out of the writings of a group of British Marxists whose working class identifications, interest in ethnography, everyday life, and the particularities of place, and orientation toward empirical research, put them out of sympathy with the abstraction and the elitism of many of their continental counterparts. One key figure, historian and social activist E. P. Thompson, articulated the general view of his early British colleagues when he assailed the "profoundly antidemocratic premises" of "Western Marxisms" that saw common people and their cultural practices as so many interchangeable products of capitalism. "Whether Frankfurt School or Althusser," Thompson charged in *The Poverty of Theory* (1978), "they are marked by their very heavy emphasis upon the ineluctable weight of ideological modes of domination – domination which destroys every space for the initiative or creativity of the mass of the people – a domination from which only the enlightened minority of intellectuals can struggle free."

Works such as Thompson's *The Making of the English Working Class* (1963) and Richard Hoggart's *The Uses of Literacy* (1958) helped define British cultural studies as a response to what Thompson called "the enormous condescension" toward the working class which united the privileged rulers of modern capitalist society and their elite intellectual critics. High French and German theory, like the high culture in which many of their practitioners were steeped, seemed too removed from the material conditions and symbolic practices of working class life to recognize its complexity, let alone to speak for it. Moreover, the founders of cultural studies argued, leftist theorists of "the ineluctable weight" of ideological domination tended to proceed from despairing national or global ("macropolitical") frames of reference; the view from the ground, by contrast, turned up many instances of creativity and "micropolitical" resistance in the local cultural forms and behaviors of the socalled masses.

Though some recent work in cultural studies retains this early hostility toward abstract theoretical discourse, both American and later British critics have increasingly drawn on the continental theory that Thompson and his colleagues rejected in their analyses of material culture. Still, cultural studies, as Cary Nelson, Paula A. Treichler, and Lawrence Grossberg describe it in their introduction to a recent compendium of essays (*Cultural Studies*, 1991), is "never merely a theoretical practice, even when that practice incorporates notions of politics, power, and context into its analysis." Rather cultural studies seeks to provide "a bridge between theory and material culture" and between "chronicle" and "intervention." This bridge is principally conceived and modelled in the early work of Raymond Williams, most notably *Culture and Society* (1958) and *The Long Revolution* (1961). Williams traced the historical and ideological processes by which "culture" – denoting, in the anthropological sense, the whole way of life of a people – came to be narrowed and restricted to the rarefied attainments of the "cultured" classes and to the supposedly nonutilitarian aesthetic products of uppercase High Culture.

Despite the efforts of elite minorities to appropriate and dematerialize it, however, Williams pointed out that "culture" had retained its broader sense as "a particular way of life, whether of a people, a period or a group," as well as its narrower sense as "works and practices of intellectual and especially artistic activity." Moreover, "culture" in the narrow sense depended for its forms and effects upon that broader "culture" or cultures that produced and consumed it, even as it informed and affected them. Over against the arbitrary separation or hierarchization of these two senses of "culture" Williams urged an inquiry into their interrelationships. His term for such an inquiry was "cultural materialism," defined as "the analysis of all forms of signification, including quite centrally writing, within the actual means and conditions of their production."

In order to account for complexity and change in cultural objects of signification, by reference not to rarefied notions of artistic genius or human spirit but to the "means and conditions of their production," Williams introduces three terms that have gained wide currency in subsequent cultural and historical criticism: *dominant, residual,* and *emergent.* These terms, which presuppose a Marxist concept of history as a direct (though not necessarily a teleological) process, enable us to locate and describe the dialectical interplay of moments or tendencies in a given text or cultural event. Thus, in analyzing the complex assumptions embedded in a given text, the cultural critic looks for those that are dominant in the culture at the moment of its production, those that are a residue of social conditions and ideas that are passing from the scene, and those that anticipate conditions and ideas that seem to be in process of formation but have not yet fully emerged. In many cases a single text embodies the layering and conflict of all three of these moments. Like any schematism, dominant/residual/emergent can be clumsily and reductively applied, but when flexibly used it provides an effective means of explaining contradiction, complexity, and change in literary texts and other cultural products without reducing them to mere reflections of material conditions.

Though Williams includes writing "quite centrally" among the symbolic productions that cultural studies must address, his vision of cultural studies tends to displace any hierarchy that would privilege literary writing over other kinds. Indeed, to reconceive literature as one of many "forms of signification" rather than as a uniquely valuable imaginative achievement, and to take as the object of criticism not individual texts or artists so much as the social conditions and effects of representational power, is to radically reconfigure the field of academic criticism. Following Williams, accordingly, cultural studies has challenged (though not necessarily eliminated) distinctions between high culture and low or popular culture; it has examined television, film, popular music, fan magazines, advertising, pornography, sports, and other institutions, industries, and media of cultural life; and it has explored the ways class, age, gender, region, ethnicity, and sexual orientation cut across both dominant cultures and subcultures. According to the editors of *Cultural Studies* , the "major categories of current work" in the field include: "gender and sexuality, nationhood and national identity, colonialism and post-colonialism, race and ethnicity, popular culture and its audiences, . . . pedagogy, the politics of aesthetics, cultural institutions, the politics of disciplinarity, . . . and global culture in a postmodern age."

OBJECTIONS

Not surprisingly, this movement to recenter academic criticism around social and cultural, as opposed to literary, study has met with numerous protests. One of the most common charges is that cultural studies abandons or actively disdains any standard of aesthetic value. It is true that the interests of cultural studies and the bases on which it selects objects for attention generally are not aesthetic, entailing no claims for the superior beauty, formal excellence, or transcendent truth of the cultural productions chosen for consideration. In fact, cultural studies assumes the legitimacy of feminist and deconstructive challenges (discussed in Chapters 4 and 5) to both the naturalness and the political neutrality of such categories as formal excellence and transcendent truth. Tony Bennett expresses a characteristic cultural studies view of value when he writes:

There neither is nor can be a science of value. Value is something that must be produced. A work is of value only if it is valued, and it can be valued only in relation to some particular set of valuational criteria, be they moral, political, or aesthetic. . . . [Value] is not an attribute of the text; it is rather something that is produced for the text.

Bennett's claim here is presumably not that a canonical novel like, say, Nabokov's *Lolita* does not possess textual attributes that allow it to fulfill traditional aesthetic criteria of value more successfully than, say, a typical Harlequin Romance. Rather, it is that the qualities that have caused Nabokov's novel to be assigned in college classes and discussed by critics (erudition, verbal playfulness, imagistic richness, and tonal and structural complexity) count as valuable only because a particular standard of judgment, an aesthetic one, has the authority to deem these the qualities to look for in the texts we study. Until recently, cultural critics argue, the dominance of this standard of value in literary study ensured that only certain privileged forms of cultural expression would merit critical attention and others would be ignored. Moreover, the dominance of aesthetic criteria foreclosed inquiry into the "actual means and conditions of [the] production" of the objects to which criticism attended. These criteria dictate *Lolita's* possession and the Harlequin's absence of critical interest and value. However, when criticism considers not only the textual qualities of novels but the economics of their production and the sociology of their reception, the significances and relations of *Lolita* and the Harlequin may change dramatically. And such critical reorientation arguably reveals something more – or at least something different – about gender and class relations, fantasy and desire, mass culture, freedom and constraint, and the institution of literature in modern America than is learned when we restrict our attention to Nabokov's artful treatment of these issues. We can learn from Lolita herself, in short, as well as from *Lolita*.

Yet even though Bennett may mean only to argue that standards of value are culturally determined, the claim that "[value] is not an attribute of the text" has also underwritten a stronger form of the constructivist position, one that in our view justifies some of the alarms. This more absolute constructivist theory seemingly asserts that texts are devoid not only of intrinsic value but of any intrinsic properties at all. Barbara Herrnstein Smith's *Contingencies of Value* (1988) is perhaps the most thoroughgoing defense of the "strong" version of value constructivism in recent criticism.

Smith is very effective in dismantling traditional aesthetic arguments that fail to acknowledge the social, historical, and contingent grounds of value. Noting the marginal status of evaluation in academic criticism in the wake of its dismissal by Northrop Frye, she properly brings evaluation back to the center of critical consideration. But Smith runs into problems of her own when she states that:

what may be spoken of as the "properties" of the work – its "structure," "features," "qualities," and, of course, its "meanings," – are not fixed, given, or inherent in the work "itself" but are at every point the variable products of some subject's [some person's or culture's] interaction with it."

Smith's claim that the work possesses no properties of its own prior to or independent of a reader's engagement with it is contradicted by Smith herself a few sentences after this passage. A work "will have an immediate survival advantage," she remarks, if it "performs certain desired/able functions particularly well at a given time for some community of subjects." She adds further that, for a given work, changes in taste may cause "a different set of properties and functions" to be valued than the ones that were valued by the work's contemporaries. In these latter formulations, the work recovers the very properties that Smith had just denied to it. Works of art now *do* possess "properties and functions," though, for contingent historical reasons, these may or may not be valued or recognized at a given moment by a given audience.

Like other forms of constructivism that we have discussed in Chapters 5 and 6, value constructivism in its recklessly strong form can lead not only to logical contradiction but to political disablement. In *Sensational Designs* (1985), an important American brief for cultural studies to which we referred in Chapter 2, Jane Tompkins sets forth a case for a new disciplinary selection and evaluation of texts "not as works of art [in the high cultural sense] embodying enduring themes in complex forms" but as performers of "cultural work." A traditionally subcanonical novel like *Uncle Tom's Cabin*, Tompkins argues, has a greater claim to inclusion in the American literary canon than Hawthorne's quintessentially canonical *The Scarlet Letter* when we judge it by the cultural work that was effected by its attempt "to redefine the social order."

In her account of Hawthorne's literary canonization, Tompkins shows that aesthetic standards and judgments are historically relative and thoroughly entangled with political and economic interests. But Tompkins is not content to challenge the aesthetic argument for elevating classics like *The Scarlet Letter*. Applying Stanley Fish's theory that texts and their meanings have no prior or independent existence in themselves, but are determined by the "interpretive communities" within which they are read, Tompkins claims: 1) that mid-nineteenth century American interpreters often did not perceive Hawthorne's works to be fundamentally different or better than those of his then-popular, now ignored, female contemporaries; 2) that Hawthorne's cultural evaluation and "survival advantage" has been a function of political and institutional power, not of any actual qualities of his writing; and 3) that, sustained as an object of attention only by the inertial fact of its institutionalization, a work like *The Scarlet Letter* does not "itself" endure over time but simply provides an occasion for each successive interpretive community to construct a new *Scarlet Letter* in its own image.

For Tompkins, recognition of the relativity of aesthetic standards, the politics of cultural judgment, and the necessity of interpretive change serve the radical revaluation of the work of women writers whom the shapers of the American canon dismissed as sentimental and propagandistic. But her strong version of value constructivism logically undermines her revisionist project. If revisionary readings create new texts rather than rediscover qualities that have been overlooked or undervalued in existing ones, then why should critics bother to recover any set of neglected writings? Indeed, how could they claim to be "recovering" them at all? Moreover, if interpretive communities produce the meanings of all texts according to the a priori expectations they bring to them, then how could one text, *Uncle Tom's Cabin*, be said to have done cultural work that its contemporary, *The Scarlet Letter*, did not? The very idea that texts do cultural work credits them with a causal force that is negated by the theory of their infinite rewritability by readers. Nor is it clear how cultural work in the form of resistance to a community's dominant principles is possible in the first place. And, even if it were possible, how could a critic operating within the interpretive framework of a later community claim to repossess the *Uncle Tom's Cabin* apprehended by the readers of the 1850s?

It would seem that to avoid such contradiction and paralysis, cultural criticism needs a weakened form of value constructivism. In *Making Sense of Literature* (1977), John Reichert develops an instrumental theory of value that acknowledges the social determination of value without dissolving the properties of works. Reichert argues that value terms like "good" are meaningful only when used with an implicit instrumental end: "good," that is, always means "good *for* something." This premise enables Reichert to claim that the statement that an art work is good (or bad) is not logically different from the statement that an automobile or a poultry knife is good. In both cases, "good" means "successful for fulfilling some specified functions."

Unlike cars and poultry knives, however, terms like "art" and "literature" have no predetermined singular functions. According to Reichert, who echoes E. D. Hirsch's argument that there are no privileged aesthetic criteria, a poultry knife is considered good if it cuts chickens efficiently, but there is no similarly agreed-upon and privileged function of a poem, despite the efforts of myriad critics and theorists to establish one. It does not follow, to revert to our earlier example, that one cannot say that *Lolita* is a good novel and a Harlequin is a bad one, because the former possesses a verbal inventiveness that the latter lacks. It does follow, however, that verbal inventiveness cannot simply be assumed to be an adequate or necessary basis for literary evaluation, that, rather, such a standard must be defended against the many possible competing standards that can be adduced. For Reichert, then, literary value lies in the combination of certain selected properties of literary works (such as

the inventiveness that *Lolita* possesses and the Harlequin lacks) with the
social judgment that these properties, and not some others, are what the
culture *should* value. In this view works retain their properties and some
properties serve certain functions better than others, but which functions are
the best ones to serve remains open to debate.

SUBCULTURAL CONSUMPTION AND PRODUCTION

While cultural critics have vigorously challenged the notion that aesthetic
value is a self-contained and immutable textual property, they have been less
self-critical of their own attributions of political value to texts. Logically, a
work's political effects are no less complex and contextual than its aesthetic
ones. Yet, as Rosalind Brunt points out, much early work in cultural criticism that was resolutely constructivist on the issue of value remained naively
essentialist in its account of the social meanings and effects of the cultural
objects it examined:

> The sheer productivity of textual analysis often rendered any reference to actual
> audiences redundant as the audience-text relationship became unproblematically
> inferred from a particular 'reading' of the by now extremely problematized text.
> Interpreted only as 'textual subjects,' audiences became primarily positioned
> [through], produced by, inscribed in, *the* text."

The reactions of actual audiences, Brunt argues, cannot be inferred from a
text itself or assumed in a critic's reading of it, especially once a text's
meaning has been held to be situational rather than absolute. Nor can a text's
cultural work be determined without empirical historical inquiry into the
ways that actual audiences have understood and used it.

Much recent work in cultural studies has in fact been devoted to such
inquiry – to issues of audience, reception, and appropriation. Work such as
Andrew Ross's *No Respect: Intellectuals and Popular Culture* (1989) has challenged the convenient assumption of an undifferentiated "mass audience"
passively manipulated by its ingestion of "mass culture." According to Ross
and others, the Frankfurt School vision of an administered society and culture
industry failed to see that "the masses" consist of communities and subcultures that differ not only in their consumption of cultural forms, but in their
ways of resisting, manipulating, and reinventing them.

Patrick Brantlinger writes that, for British cultural critics such as Dick
Hebdige and John Fiske (and, we would add, for Ross, Janice Radway, Diana
Fuss, and other American critics as well),

> the old . . . pessimism about mass culture is qualified and at times almost reversed.
> Fiske, for instance, defines "popular culture" as all of the interpretive practices

through which people make their own uncontrollable and "resistant" meanings from the uniform but nevertheless only imperfectly coercive "grid" of "mass culture." The mass media do not impose singular meanings on the multitude; instead, the multitude produce *their* meanings on the backs, as it were, of the mass media.

Enacting the project that Brantlinger describes, Hebdige's *Subculture: The Meaning of Style* (1979) exemplifies the effort of much work in British cultural studies to identify – and often celebrate – the forms of cultural resistance to capitalism, class privilege, and the bureaucratization of modern life that have been developed by marginalized or disempowered urban communities. Working class, youth, and especially "punk" subcultures, Hebdige suggests, cohere around the development of distinct styles of dress, speech, music, and social behavior that oppose the dominant bourgeois culture not only by rebelling against it but by subversively appropriating it.

American cultural critics also have argued that mass culture can be liberatory when reappropriated by subcultures. A growing body of theoretically sophisticated work on gay and lesbian culture, for instance, has examined how gays have at once stylistically defined and problematized their difference within a heterosexist society by parodically reproducing such cultural forms as fashion or mass market films and television shows. Thus Ross (following the lead of Susan Sontag in her 1964 "Notes on Camp") examines the ways gay and lesbian subcultures have appropriated for counterhegemonic purposes the seemingly "straight" sexuality exemplified by popular film actresses such as Bette Davis, Mae West, and Marlene Dietrich. And Diana Fuss explores the subversive implications of the fact that conventionally glamorous images of women in slick fashion magazines like *Mademoiselle* provide women a culturally legitimated opportunity to make other women the objects of their erotic gaze.

Fuss's argument implicitly dissents from that of critics like Teresa de Lauretis, who suggest that subverting "the standard frame of the hetero romance" requires resisting such conventions as "its seamless narrative space, its conventional casting and characterization," and the commercial techniques by which it is distributed. Fuss presumably would claim that dominant conventions of representation are not entirely "seamless." That even *Mademoiselle* cannot avoid being read as a repressed lesbian text reveals the potential "otherness" latent in the most powerful expressions of heterosexist culture. By appropriating such cultural forms (and developing others, such as "voguing," that combine original artistic expresson with parodic imitation and pastiche), gays can rewrite the texts of the dominant culture in ways that destabilize dominant models of gender identity, sexual orientation, and relations of power.

Recent criticism by African-Americanists illustrates still another version of the tactic of subcultural resistance by ironic appropriation of dominant discourses. This tactic has come to be known as "signifying," after the "signifying monkey," a prominent trickster figure in African American folk culture. As most influentially elaborated in the work of leading poststructuralist African-Americanist, Henry Louis Gates Jr., "signifying" is the act of strategic verbal indirection, veiled irony, or repetition with a difference by which an oppressed people sustains its creativity and energy of resistance when outlets for more formal creativity and more direct resistance are closed. For Gates, "signifying" constitutes the central distinguishing rhetorical device and stylistic feature of African American verbal culture. Answering the widely cited maxim of Audre Lorde that "the master's tools will never dismantle the master's house," Gates retorts that *only* the master's tools can dismantle the master's house.

In fact, as the mechanics of "signifying" themselves suggest, the cultural tools and edifice of the white master class in the United States have never been entirely separable from those of its black subculture. An explosion of multidisciplinary scholarship of the early 1990s has borne out Toni Morrison's claim in her 1989 essay, "Unspeakable Things Unspoken: The Afro-American Presence in American Literature," that mainstream American culture is profoundly and pervasively informed "by the four-hundred-year-old presence of, first, Africans and then African Americans in the United States." Compiled by Shelly Fisher Fishkin in her bibliographic essay, "Interrogating 'Whiteness,' Complicating 'Blackness': Remapping American Culture," this scholarship includes books by historians, such as David Roediger's *The Wages of Whiteness: Race and the Making of the American Working Class* (1991) and William Piersen's *Black Legacy: America's Hidden Heritage* (1993); by linguists, such as Joseph Holloway and Winnifred Vass's *The African Heritage of American English* (1993); by political theorists, such as Celeste Michelle Condit and John Lucas Lucaites' *Crafting Equality: America's Anglo-African Word* (1993); and by literary and cultural critics, such as Eric Sundquist's *To Wake the Nations: Race in the Making of American Literature* (1993) and Mel Watkins' *On the Real Side: Laughing, Lying, an' Signifying – the Underground Tradition of African American Humor that Transformed American Culture from Slavery to Richard Pryor* (1994). Insisting that American culture *is* African American, in the sense that virtually every facet of contemporary cultural life in the United States is the amalgamated product of the historical encounter of Africans and Europeans here, these and many other recent books and articles exhibit what Brantlinger identifies as the central conviction of cultural studies: that "in order to understand ourselves, the discourse of 'the Other' – of all the others – is that which we urgently need to hear." This deconstructive recognition that "the Other" is already present in the dominant further underwrites the attention paid to the consumption and production of culture by dominated or marginalized populations, whose experiences and forms of expression have traditionally had no place in university curricula and critical discussion.

Some have charged that this embrace of "the Other" by academic critics has resulted in more private moral self-congratulation than political force in a time of widespread conservative reaction against the cultural and political claims of minorities. Alan Liu, for example, argues forcefully in a 1990 essay, "Local Transcendence: Cultural Criticism, Postmodernism, and the Romanticism of Detail," that much cultural criticism today does not reflect genuine social commitment or advance practical political ends so much as it accommodates a new romanticism in which privileged, yet alienated or guilty, intellectual and economic elites identify with the struggles of the low or celebrate untutored speech, the solidarity of the folk, and the life of the body. Others, including prominent progressive critics, have more generally charged cultural criticism and other political criticisms with both critical and political reductiveness. Richard Poirier, for one, has argued eloquently in a number of books and essays that most of the profits of reading are not directly convertible into political currency and that criticism is more often than not impoverished by the demand that it engage with power "in an ideal, direct, glamorous, and potentially perilous transaction."

There are moments in cultural studies that warrant the skepticism about its sources and claims that Liu, Poirier, and others voice. But, whatever its ultimate political effects or potential may be, the best work in cultural studies has introduced into academic criticism a range of new issues, social groups and cultural practices, and new occasions for self-reflection. In challenging the entrenched hierarchies of high culture over low culture, "common culture" over subcultures, and Western culture over its "Others," this work has unsettled traditional assumptions, and stimulated fresh thinking, about personal and cultural identity and difference. As Brantlinger puts it, contemporary critics can no longer meaningfully engage with culture unless they are committed to " 'decolonizing' themselves . . . [by] abandoning the privileged status they have accorded to the western literary tradition" and learning about "other traditions, not equal, nor better or worse, higher or lower, but both human and different."

THE BEGINNINGS OF AMERICAN NEW HISTORICISM

The contemporary critical practices that tend to be grouped together as "the new historicism" share with work in cultural studies the rejection of the traditional separation of literature from other forms of signification and areas of social and cultural life. As a broad characterization, Brantlinger's description of cultural studies as an "exploration of the social production and circulation of meanings" seems equally applicable to new historicism. In fact, Stephen Greenblatt, whom many view as the founder of American new historicism, initially called his project "cultural poetics" and continues to prefer that term to the more commonly used label.

In his essay "Toward a Poetics of Culture," Greenblatt traces his adoption of the term "cultural poetics" to a moment of professional duress. During one of his lectures at Berkeley in the mid-1970s, he explains, a student stood up and angrily demanded that he make up his mind whether he was a formalist or a Marxist. Defining his project as "cultural poetics" in the aftermath of this encounter, Greenblatt implicitly rejects the student's either/or, challenging its assumed opposition between material culture and expressive form, between politics and aesthetics. Indeed, Greenblatt comes to argue that his particular area of specialization – the English Renaissance – has been misunderstood precisely because of the inability of conventional literary criticism to reconcile these oppositions.

As Louis Montrose explains, the established tradition of Renaissance studies had "selected out certain poetic and dramatic texts and canonized them as Renaissance Literature," valuing them "as enduring reflections of the subjectivities of their creators, or as exemplary instances of a distinctively aesthetic mode of perception; as compelling embodiments of timeless and universal truths; . . . [and as touchstones] of an apparently continuous tradition of religious, social, and aesthetic values shared by sixteenth-century poets and twentieth-century critics." Younger Renaissance scholars such as Greenblatt and Montrose himself mounted a simultaneously historical and textual assault on this "gentle/manly" view of the field. Through new historical researches, they sought to show their predecessors' representations to be "at variance with surviving documentary evidence of Elizabethan religious, economic, social and domestic violence, instability, and heterodoxy." Through textual analyses informed by poststructuralist theory, they discovered violence, instability, and heterodoxy in the very canonized texts that presumably exemplified Literature's serenity, transcendence, and truth. Thus these critics found the topical in the ostensible precincts of the timeless and the political in the midst of the aesthetic.

Going further, Renaissance new historicists argued that an adequate understanding of Renaissance culture precluded the arbitrary separations of a narrowly *literary* critical and historical practice, separations that themselves had grown up long after the Renaissance. This argument is, in one sense, an old one. Indeed, it echoes the complaint of historical scholars of the 1940s and 1950s such as Rosemund Tuve and J. V. Cunningham that the New Critics' formalist readings of Renaissance poetry presupposed a separation of poetic form from social context that would have puzzled Renaissance writers and audiences. But whereas these earlier scholars had seen the period's social history as part of the "background," however crucial, to the understanding of its literature, new historicists insisted that Renaissance politics and Renaissance poetics were mutually constitutive, that each was a form or enactment of the other. A primary example is the plays of Shakespeare, which have come to be seen as the essence of art but which in their own time functioned as a means by which royal power was displayed, ritualized, and reproduced. It is not that for new historicists Shakespeare ceases to be "art" and becomes part of "the circulation of social energy," but rather that this dualism itself is a product of a later time.

In their charge that the isolation and privileging of the literary in academic Renaissance Studies was ahistorical, new historicists argued for the interdependence not only of the poetic and the political but of the past and the present as well. The idealized, depoliticized view of the Renaissance, new historicists pointed out, had emerged out of twentieth-century historical pressures and desires, such as T. S. Eliot's search for a cultural counterweight to the modern condition of dissociated sensibility. To avoid self-deceptive presentism required a dialogical criticism, concerned not only with the objects of knowledge but with how knowledge is produced, interrogating both the historical past and its contemporary construction. As Montrose puts it: "the practice of a new historical criticism . . . necessitates efforts to historicize the present as well as the past, and to historicize as well the dialectic between them – those reciprocal historical pressures by which the past has shaped the present and the present reshapes the past."

The charge of "presentism" levelled by Renaissance new historicists against their predecessors is one that we have noted often in our account of recent criticism (for instance, in the feminist charge that classic constructions of American literature have taken their melodramatic form from the preoccupation of the field's founding fathers with their own "beset manhood"). This argument that critics have fashioned their objects in their own image often persuasively exposes blindness or bias in others but, as we observed in our discussion of ideology in Chapter 6 and of Tompkins's strong value constructivism above, the charge can readily be turned back upon the arguer. Like Reichert's instrumental constructivism, which both grants texts properties and acknowledges that they are relative to the social criteria of value that readers bring to them, Montrose's call for dialogism and critical self-reflectiveness presumes that the past has properties that both inform and resist its historical reconstruction in the present. This assumption of a dialectical relationship, not a complete identification, between past and present at

once theoretically enables new historicist criticism and practically moderates
it. But, as we will see, some new historicism has advanced a totalizing view
of history that, in its inability to imagine change and its projection of a
generalized "postmodern condition" upon the past, undoes any meaningful
historicism.

Greenblatt himself suggests the susceptibility of the new historicists to
the critique they aimed at their predecessors when he locates the origin of
Renaissance "cultural poetics" in the angry student's challenge to Greenblatt's own cultural politics. Just as the Renaissance of T. S. Eliot's midcentury humanism expressed Eliot's need to unify a dissociated sensibility, the
Renaissance of new historicism has expressed the contemporary need to
integrate art and politics. Stanley Fish has called this aspect of the new
historicism "the old high formalism writ political." Indeed, new historicism has both identified and, at times, exemplified what Jon Klancher
terms "the risk [of] making historical criticism a transhistorical echo of the
politics of the present."

The most intense debate about the new historicism, however, has focused
less on the problem of presentism in its reading of history than on the
particular political vision that informs much new historicist criticism. Like
other forms of recent criticism concerned with the entanglements of language, culture, and power, new historicism has assumed that a culture
defines and enacts itself through all the forms of expression or discourses that
it encompasses, including the discourses of art and criticism. The belief that
relations of power inform discourse is, on the one hand, necessary and enabling for anyone who wishes to claim that the study and critique of discourse may be a politically consequential activity. But, on the other hand,
this belief risks disabling the very political engagement that occasions it.
Indeed, for at least one strain of new historicism, art and criticism are so
thoroughly imbedded in structures of power that there remains no place from
which they can resist or criticize them.

This political vision or cultural "logic" links a number of prominent new
historicists with American antifoundationalist theorists like Fish and with
recent French theorists of postmodernity, notably Jean-Francois Lyotard and
Jean Baudrillard. It is a logic that proceeds from two different, though
closely related, inferences from the discursivity of modern power. The first,
as we have noted, is that power so thoroughly permeates discourse as to be
irresistible; the second is that power is so thoroughly discursive as to be
indefinable and unobjectifiable. This latter situation describes the "postmodern condition," in Lyotard's phrase, in which there remain no bases (except a
few local, marginal, and micropolitical ones) for reliably distinguishing
reality from the simulated "reality-effects" of a thoroughly mediated capital-

ist techno-culture and thus no persuasive grounds for oppositional thought or action.

Two essays by Baudrillard on the Gulf War comprise perhaps the most extreme recent assertion of the world's collapse into – or replacement by – an undecidable postmodern text. Responding to Western audiences' entranced televisual consumption of the aerial war on Iraq in 1991, Baudrillard suggests that we have reached a point at which only disembodied media simulacra and other structures of representation determine what counts as knowledge or truth. As subjects of this global network of textuality, he argues, we cannot confirm or deny its messages and thus cannot persuasively say that the Gulf War really happened. For many, such a suggestion epitomizes the epistemological and political irresponsibility to which the levelling postmodernist textualization of reality inevitably leads. Thus, in *Uncritical Theory: Postmodernism, Intellectuals, and the Gulf War* (1992), Christopher Norris assails the "conjunction of a vigorous expansionist mood among literary theorists – a desire to mount colonizing ventures into other disciplines like philosophy, law, and history – with an attitude of wholesale skepticism" that reduces these disciplines to "language-games" which can claim neither determinate knowledge nor real-world entailments.

As we have argued earlier in this chapter, constructivist or antifoundationalist theory need not delegitimate all claims to empirical knowledge or practical agency. Indeed, new historicist Renaissance scholars have generally not accepted (and Greenblatt has explicitly denounced) the view that powerlessness and undecidability logically follow from their positions on discourse and history. But the general destabilization of older models of personal, literary, and cognitive autonomy helps explain why new historicism has been attacked for what Klancher calls "this peculiar identification of a Renaissance moment, when politics and literature were still undifferentiated realms, with postmodern culture, when power is felt to saturate discourse of every kind." The problem for Klancher is that the identification "aligns a Renaissance culture saturated with power with a postmodern culture powerless to resist." To understand the rise and appeal of this vision of a postmodern culture at once saturated with power and powerless to resist, it is necessary to consider more fully the work of the most influential recent theorist of power, Michel Foucault.

FOUCAULT AND THE NEW HISTORICISM

One of the central ideas of the new historicism has been that societies exert control over their subjects not just by imposing constraints on them but by predetermining the very ways in which they try to resist these constraints.

Thus new historicism has tended to challenge an antithesis often assumed by both traditional and oppositional criticism as part of the legacy of romantic and postromantic aesthetics, the antithesis between rebellious works of art, visionary artists, or iconoclastic, truth-telling critics and the entrenched material conditions and ideological structures of their time. In new historicist analyses, these heretofore supposed agents of liberation are seen as products of the dominant social discourses that they claim to contest. To be sure, most new historicists acknowledge that any dominant social discourse contains openings or fissures in which some forms of contravention may take place, but these spaces of disruption are so local, delimited, and prone to "recuperation" or "containment" that they all but shrink to nothing.

In this respect, the new historicism shows the influence of Foucault, especially the later Foucault of works such as *Discipline and Punish* (1975) and *The Will to Know: History of Sexuality* 1 (1976), and the interviews in the collection, *Power/Knowledge* (1980). It is this later Foucault who rejects "the repressive hypothesis" that informed his earlier studies, in which deviant groups, such as those judged mad, were seen as repressed by the power of institutions like the modern insane asylum. Even in the earlier work, Foucault had hinted at a new understanding of power in speaking of the "production of madness" by the institutions of incarceration themselves. By the mid-1970s, he had fully articulated the theory of modern power as productive rather than repressive that would be documented by the wide-ranging historical and sociological analyses of the last decade of his life.

Though the workings of power as Foucault describes them never cease to look like domination and subjection, the shift away from the repressive model gives Foucault a formidable way of contesting the standard history of the Enlightenment, particularly the liberal humanist assumption that the transition from oligarchic social orders sustained by arbitrary force to democracies sustained by dispassionate law and consensual reason represents the progressive march of freedom. Arguing that rights that are customarily regarded as a legacy of progress have in fact operated as part of a network of social control, Foucault promotes a Nietzschean vision of history in which, as he puts it in an essay entitled "Nietzsche, Genealogy, History" (1971): "Humanity does not gradually progress from combat to combat until it arrives at universal reciprocity, where the rule of law finally replaces warfare; humanity installs each of its violences in a system of rules and thus proceeds from domination to domination." Thus, for the later Foucault, post-Enlightenment values are not more humane than pre-Enlightenment forms of domination; they are simply better at making domination seem like freedom and thereby getting subjects to internalize it. Post-Enlightenment forms of power overcome resistance not by stamping it out or negating it –

as did feudal forms of torture – but by organizing, channelling, and controlling it, assigning it rights and responsibilities that can then be efficiently policed.

Foucault's critique of the Enlightenment and of the rationalized "disciplinary" forms of coercion it effects in many respects parallels (and shares the central problems of) the Frankfurt School analysis of modern culture that we discussed in Chapter 6. In a 1983 interview, in fact, Foucault acknowledged these parallels, regretting that none of his teachers or early colleagues had ever mentioned the work of the Frankfurt School, with which he had been unfamiliar until late in his career – "a strange case of non-penetration between two very similar types of thinking." On the relation of subjectivity, individual identity, and knowledge to structures of domination, however, Foucault's position is more radical than that of the Frankfurt School.

For Foucault, the very emergence of the individual subject or self turns out to be a form of social control. The point is not simply that once we have identity cards and recorded identities we are more readily subject to governmental jurisdiction and commercial exploitation. More fundamentally, it is that the notion of individual identity itself is "already one of the prime effects of power" and "the individual which power has constituted is at the same time its vehicle." Modern bourgeois society, Foucault argues, is organized around "a whole series of subjected sovereignties," realms of ostensible autonomy which are really effects of the dominant discursive order that assigns these subjects their designated places. Such "subjected sovereignties" include "the soul (ruling the body, but subjected to God), consciousness (sovereign in a context of judgment, but subjected to the necessities of truth), the individual (a titular control of personal rights subjected to the laws of nature and society)." These categories are underwritten by the society's privileged discourses of truth and its disciplines of knowledge, with theology, philosophy, and law underwriting the categories of the soul, consciousness, and the individual and thereby making them seem natural.

It is the concept of discourse that enables social control to operate for Foucault without an identifiable controller. Just as in Orwell's *Nineteen Eighty-Four* we never see Big Brother or even find out if he exists, in Foucault's universe there seem to be no determinate agents who control other people, only massive discursive networks that control us all. Habituated as most of us still are to more traditional political analyses in which power is seen as concentrated in identifiable groups and institutions, this vision may appear far fetched, not to say paranoid. Yet, it gains persuasiveness as modern societies become so complex, bureaucratized, and image-driven that it is often indeed difficult to discover "who is in charge." The contemporary world economy, which proves so resistant to prediction, might be adduced as a plausible instance of action without clear agency, a vast network that no one group exactly controls even though it obviously works far more to the advantage of some than to others. This Foucauldian vision of a world of power without centralized or determinate agency has its counterpart in the world presented by postmodern fiction writers such as Thomas Pynchon and Don DeLillo.

One of Foucault's most notable illustrations of omnipresent discursive power is his analysis of how modern sexual identity is produced by discourses of sexuality. Modern societies control the unruly energies of human sexuality, Foucault argues, not by making sex the object of repressive taboos, as a post-Victorian culture has been led to suppose, but by generating a vast disciplinary discourse and knowledge about sex which defines, classifies, and reclassifies it. This process creates sexual subjects whose very assertion of their sexual identity participates in their own administrative control. The designation at the end of the nineteenth century of "the homosexual" as a distinct kind of person, for example, was not the neutral scientific taxonomy that it claimed to be, but the disciplinary production of a new identity category. Acts of same-sex relations, which had been practiced in all times and places, now became the basis for identifying a separate deviant class of persons, thereby also distinguishing "the heterosexual" as the normative type.

Foucault's historical analyses persuasively unveil diverse instances in which disciplinary knowledges rationalize and normalize social control. After Foucault, it is difficult to dispute that systems of knowledge participate in systems of power and that practitioners of intellectual disciplines must interrogate the uses and effects of their work. But, in its strongest articulation, Foucault's implication that all knowledge, like all power, tends toward domination encounters problems. In Foucault's Nietzschean formulas, "knowledge is not made for understanding; it is made for cutting," and "power is always exercised at the expense of the people." In other words, knowledge is part of the problem, never part of the solution. This attack on knowledge itself, and consequently on intellectuals, deepened in the wake of the failure of the intellectual left in 1968 to mobilize the masses to join the hemispherewide uprisings against the bourgeois capitalist system. "Intellectuals," Foucault pronounced, "are themselves agents of this system of power – the idea of their responsibility for 'consciousness' and discourse forms part of the system."

In such comments, as critics like Nancy Fraser and others have pointed out, Foucault's distrust of political and cognitive systems and his sweeping view of the workings of modern power subvert his own evident intellectual, political, and moral goals. Even as Foucault's historical, or "genealogical," researches unearth "subjugated knowledges" (the "popular," "local," and "low-ranking," "bodily," and "differential" modes of experience, suppressed and "disguised within the body of functionalist and systematizing theory"), these knowledges by definition could only unsettle the dominant scientific discourses and social norms, not modify or replace them. For "the particular elements of the knowledge that one seeks to disinter are no sooner accredited and put into circulation, than they run the risk of re-codification, recolonisation." Even as his social criticism assails the effects of the present system's power, Foucault must refrain from proposing any general social alternative. For since all power tends toward systematization and all systematization is domination, there can be no general alternative, but only the paradoxical certainty that "to imagine another system is to extend our participation in the present system." Only the most local, fragmentary, contingent, unconsolidated claims and resistances are thus legitimate and effective, although one cannot ultimately theorize either their legitimacy or their effects. In short, Foucault has embraced a logic in which only failure and marginality can remain politically virtuous.

A complete genealogy of Foucault's social thought would need to survey much of modern French, and more generally European, philosophical and political history. Foucault's often shocking pronouncements on the illegitimacy and incoherence of the bourgeois subject ("nothing in man – not even his body – is sufficiently stable to serve as the basis for self-recognition or for understanding other men") bears a resemblance to the efforts of other post-Sartrean French intellectuals to unburden themselves of the legacy of existential humanism. Foucault's extreme reaction to systematized power as such is also a reaction to the social and theoretical failures of economistic Marxism and the abuses of postwar totalitarianism on the left as well as the right. Any fair evaluation of Foucault's work as a social thinker and actor would also need to take into account the fact that, despite his mistrust of the liberatory possibilities of discourses of knowledge, Foucault's historical analyses of prisons, mental institutions, and the disciplines of penology, psychiatry, and sexology have affected practice in those institutions and disciplines. And despite his skepticism toward the power of oppositional personal agency, Foucault thoroughly engaged himself in a variety of social causes, supporting prison reform, factory workers' grievances, the claims of Vietnamese refugees to French aid, the struggles of Eastern European dissidents, and the campaigns of gay activists against heterosexism.

However Foucault's own intellectual and political life may be explained and judged, the fact remains that his thought has prompted and shaped intellectual work in fields and circumstances well beyond Foucault's own. Among contemporary movements in literary criticism, the new historicism has most enthusiastically embraced Foucault's concerns, assumptions, and methods. New historicist readings often juxtapose a literary text against one or several contemporaneous social discourses or practices (medicine, law, economic theory, fashion, theology, pornography, industrial management, advertising) that appear unrelated to it. Under the pressure of such juxtaposition, however, these different cultural expressions interpret one another, revealing surprising and even scandalous connections that unsettle assumed distinctions and hierarchies like those between the elite and the popular, the central and the marginal, the conservative and the subversive, the normative and the deviant, the real and the fictive. A variation on this Foucauldian strategy, also frequent in new historicist essays, is to begin with an anecdotal recovery of a seemingly trivial, anomalous, or random historical object, subject, or event and then, gradually, dramatically, to disclose its unimagined depths and breadth of significance.

New historicists have produced some dazzling and provocative cultural reinterpretations through their deployments of Foucauldian "genealogical" analysis. (Foucault defines "genealogy" as "history in the form of a concerted carnival," an "anti-Platonic" historical practice that "cultivate[s] the details and accidents that accompany every beginning" and attempts "to emancipate historical knowledges from . . . the coercion of a theoretical, unitary, formal, and scientific discourse.") But if, in the spirit of Foucauldian genealogy, new historicist researches and interpretations have sought to produce a more textured and less totalizing historical discourse, in which the cultural detail, the local or accidental event, and the life of the body are admitted in all their contingency and materiality, they have sometimes achieved just the opposite.

Critics of the new historicism have attacked the device of making local or eccentric anecdotes or details central to a broad historical revision and, similarly, have questioned the strategy of demonstrating the circulation of power within a cultural-historical moment through a juxtaposition of widely varied contemporaneous discourses. Alan Liu, for instance, has argued that new historicists and other cultural critics deploy rhetorical analysis as a "facsimile knowledge or pseudo-analytic" in which metaphorical associations and ingeniously contrived formal resemblances substitute for demonstrations of causal or material connection. Argument through suggestive juxtaposition, Liu continues, is less empirical than allegorical, entailing "an essential *et cetera* . . . far in excess of the margin-of-error requirements of normal science." Others have objected to what Carolyn Porter has called new historicism's "rhetorical personification" of power, whereby power "itself," undifferentiated in kind or degree, becomes both agent and agency, at once everywhere and nowhere, expressed by all and wielded by none.

What Frank Lentriccia assails as "a conception of power that is elusive and literally undefinable" is ideologically as well as methodologically vexed. As we have suggested, Foucault's multiplication of the sites and forms of power is one instance, perhaps the most extreme, of a contemporary revision of the classical Marxist view of power as concentrated in capitalist relations of production and bourgeois state apparatuses of enforcement. And, in one sense, as we observed above about the idea of the discursive nature of power, this revisionary view is enabling – even necessary – for oppositional critique. For, to the extent that power is seen to operate locally, culturally, discursively, and micropolitically, it may be critically engaged in all these arenas. But, decentering the Marxist view of power means abandoning Marx's vision of the theoretical necessity and perhaps even the practical possibility of a socialist or other alternative to dominant capitalism. As a result, resistance or subversion risks becoming precisely as pervasive and as unmeasurable as the power it opposes. That is, with the loss of socialism as the once privileged standpoint for measuring progress and regress, the evaluative criteria that critics bring to bear on cultural phenomena seem increasingly abstract, arbitrary, and inconsistent. A point is soon reached at which almost anything can be praised for its subversiveness or damned for its vulnerability to cooptation, for there is always some discursive frame of reference that will support either description.

In our view, current cultural criticism on the left is often caught in this predicament, in response to which the new historicism divides into radical and antiradical camps. Radical New Historicism takes advantage of contemporary theory's prolific production of opportunities and techniques for cultural subversion and its generous criteria of subversiveness. It assumes the subversiveness of any destabilization of determinate meaning or "rupture" of narrative closure, any decentering of the subject, any deconstruction of traditional cultural polarities. But, of course, such inflation of the currency of oppositional critique quickly diminishes its credibility and worth. As Bruce Robbins has wryly remarked, "with so much of this subversive quantity about, one would think the revolution was scheduled for next week at the latest."

Antiradical New Historicism not only shares this disillusionment with the often extravagant claims of "oppositional" criticism, but theorizes it along lines of argument taken, but by no means initiated, by Foucault. This is the argument, to which we referred earlier, that in modern rationalized societies the available discourses of resistance are themselves produced by power, so that what passes for transgression inevitably turns out to be yet another "ruse of power" by which power reproduces, redistributes, and further entrenches itself. This "logic" of cooptation has been a significant enough element of contemporary criticism to warrant a brief account of its history and a discussion of its deployment in one of the most celebrated and debated new historicist analyses of American literature and culture.

THE COOPTATION OF DISSENT

The Foucauldian tendency to totalize, rhetoricize, personify, and mystify power that Liu, Porter, and Lentricchia have questioned underwrites the claim, advanced by antiradical New Historicists and some theorists of post-modernism, that cooptation is not only prevalent but complete and unavoidable. Because all cultural objects and subjects are saturated by power, and because power always coopts, the very notion of an oppositional position is incoherent. Since there is no "outside" to power, the very question of alternatives to an established regime is foolish. Walter Benn Michaels's *The Gold Standard and the Logic of Naturalism* (1987) is widely acknowledged to be one of the most sophisticated and versatile new historicist expositions of this argument.

Michaels for example questions the very point of longstanding critical debates about whether Theodore Dreiser's novels glorify or criticize capitalism. For earlier socialist-influenced critics like Alfred Kazin and Irving Howe (as for Georg Lukacs), much of the power of realistic novels like *Sister Carrie* lay in their ostensible unmasking of the myths of capitalism. For later critics influenced by Barthes, Adorno, and French poststructuralism, the supposed realism of such texts is itself a myth that naturalizes the dominant "reality" of capitalism's historical moment. For Michaels, however, the whole debate is founded on a false premise.

Each of the opposing critical positions, in Michaels's view, depends on the fallacious notion that a subject of capitalist culture (the novelist or the critic, or both) can get sufficiently outside that culture and its discourses to evaluate it meaningfully. In fact, Michaels writes:

You don't like [your culture] or dislike it, you exist in it, and the things you like and dislike exist in it too. Even Bartleby-like refusals of the world remain inextricably linked to it – what could count as a more powerful exercise of the right to freedom of contract than Bartleby's successful refusal to enter into any contracts?

For Michaels, then, it is foolish to ask whether Dreiser "liked" or "disliked" capitalism, because in Dreiser's novels (and, equally, in the world of his critics) there is no standpoint outside the capitalist marketplace from which to make either judgment. It is the omnipresence of the market that, throughout *The Gold Standard*, the "logic of naturalism" demonstrates.

Michaels asserts that he is trying to "transform an argument about the affective relation of certain literary texts to American capitalism into an investigation of the position of those texts within a system of representation that, producing objects of approval and disapproval both, is more important than any attitude one might imagine oneself to have toward it." And indeed, his argument cuts very effectively against the sort of glib political criticism that proceeds by hunting down textual practices which have been predefined as liberatory or repressive and awarding ideological pluses and minuses accordingly. It also cuts effectively against a more traditional type of critical idealization which locates the defining characteristic of literature in its supposed independence of the realm of material circumstances, commodification, and practical utility. Michaels's readings demonstrate that literary naturalism is deeply implicated in the "system of representation" peculiar to the capitalist market. Commodification, Michaels suggests, merging Marx's analysis of the fetishism of commodities with deconstruction, produces a form of character systematically divided from itself and doomed perpetually to fail in its search for self-identity.

So far so good. But why should this argument about the implication of Dreiser and naturalist fiction in the capitalist market's system of representations invalidate questions about the ethical and political implications of that state of affairs, as Michaels maintains it does? The answer is that, for Michaels, "the market" and "the logic of naturalism," despite appearances to the contrary, are not temporally or situationally limited phenomena. They are no less than synecdoches for the abstract totality of "the culture," which is itself no more nor less than the disseminated expression and agent of an even more abstract and totalized "power." Not only the discourses of Dreiser and the naturalistic novel but also Michaels's own critical discourse, along with those of critics who think they oppose his views, find their origins – and thus, presumably, their destiny – in "consumer culture." It cannot be otherwise, Michaels argues: "transcending your origins in order to evaluate them" is logically unachievable, "not so much because you can't really transcend your culture but because, if you did, you wouldn't have any terms of evaluation left."

Michaels's book is perhaps the extreme expression of two key features of the new historicism: its insistence on the cultural situatedness of the contemporary subject as well as the historical object of criticism, and its commitment, in Montrose's words, to "substituting for the diachronic text of an autonomous literary history the synchronic text of a cultural system." But with its totalizing Foucauldian model of power and individual subjection, the new historicist's subject, text, and cultural system are all too easily flattened into a single monolithic identity. Thus, in *The Gold Standard and the Logic of Naturalism*, American consumer capitalism becomes a closed, complete, and unchanging "system of representations" that cannot be transcended or even meaningfully critiqued because anyone who might articulate such a critique and any possible terms or concepts of critique will always already have been produced and contained by the system.

A challenge to Michaels's position might begin by asking whether representation really does operate as a "system," as he assumes, or whether there really is such a thing as a single, unitary capitalist "system of representation." Though capitalist societies have doubtless generated characteristic forms of representation (such as the realist novel), these forms have been shown by critics like Lukacs and Bakhtin to be heterogeneous and internally contradictory, marked as they are by residues of precapitalist forms such as romance and epic. Moreover, the historical emergence of capitalism itself was and is characterized by unevenness, overlapping stages, continual transitions, and competing logics. In obscuring these complications, Michaels's argument subtly substitutes metaphysical entities for historical ones. As Brook Thomas points out, "Michaels operates as if, at some moment he does not designate, the country as a whole suddenly became transformed into a unified system of consumer capitalism." Consequently, his new historicist investigation of culture as

a structure of internal difference, results in a tendency to produce eternal sameness. . . . By conducting his analysis within an overriding logic of capitalism, the very critic who distrusts transcendental categories ends by adopting the Market as a transcendental category, much in the way that mechanical deconstructionists treat Writing, Play, and Differance.

The new historicist idea of culture as a set of "discursive practices," then, has provided an important arena for the critical exploration of relations between the literary text and the social text. In this sense, it has taken a significant step beyond the dualisms bequeathed to us by romanticism and postromantic New Criticism, which defined literature in such exceptionalist and separatist terms as to obscure its social and historical production and productiveness. The new concept of cultural discourse has incurred a new set of problems, however, when it has been wielded too rigidly and monolithically, ascribing the organic unity to discourses and cultures that had been rejected when ascribed to literary texts.

Once we recognize that a culture and its discourses are not pure and unified, but heterogeneous, contradictory, and inhabited by other cultures and discourses, it then becomes possible to see how a writer like Dreiser could indeed assume a critical perspective toward American consumer culture without laying claim (on his part or ours) to some transcendent perspective. For it then becomes possible to criticize some aspect of American culture (its greed or its fetishization of consumption) by pointing out its contradiction with some other aspect (its communitarian rhetoric or its egalitarian ideas). Arguably, it is the internal contradictions among our beliefs and practices that make it possible for us to change our minds, or to be persuaded by artists and critics who may appeal to beliefs we already hold and point out their discrepancy with our other beliefs and actions.

The impulse among some recent critics to rigidify concepts like culture, discourse, and ideology, however, may derive in part from the anxiety produced by the very fragmentation and contradictoriness of the current beliefs and cultural positions of U.S. intellectuals. The move back to "culture" as a central reference point of literary criticism has occurred at a moment when the question of what contemporary culture is and what role artists and critics play in it seems very much up for grabs. In this situation, oversimple appeals to discourse and ideology as absolute determinants of consciousness and events arguably substitute for the explanatory power of such grand narratives of society and history as classical Marxism. The successful challenges to New Critical humanism and literary formalism on one side and to Marxist economism and historical determinism on the other have opened up inquiry into the political capacities and effects of cultural productions and producers, while rendering these capacities and effects exceedingly difficult to measure or to agree upon in any given instance.

POSTCOLONIAL PROBLEMATICS

Informed by the methods and motives of the new cultural and historical criticism, postcolonial studies represents a kind of culmination of many of the changes in academic literary study over the last half-century that our narrative has traced. New courses and faculty positions in postcolonial literature and criticism attest to the expansion of the discipline's field of objects, beyond both Anglo-American masterworks and conventionally "literary" texts, and of its range of methods and interests in the direction of sociology, political theory, and material history. Indeed, this disciplinary trajectory is neatly plotted by the titles of the three chronological sections of postcolonialist Gayatri Chakravorty Spivak's collection of essays, *In Other Worlds* (1987): "Literature"; "Into the World"; "Entering the Third World."

Postcolonial studies may be the form of cultural studies that most obviously assumes the task of intellectual decolonization that Brantlinger calls for when, in a passage we quoted earlier, he challenges critics to "[abandon] the privileged status they have accorded to the western literary tradition" and learn about "other traditions . . . both human and different." In this regard, as Georg Gugelberger remarks, "postcolonial studies are what comparative literature always wanted or claimed to be but in reality never was, due to a deliberate and almost desperate clinging to Eurocentric values, canons, cultures, and languages." But, as conservative critics have pointed out, postcolonial and third world literatures are not categories that inclusively designate writings in non-European languages and traditions; nor has the enhancement of literary comparativism or academic pluralism been postcolonial studies' principal rationale or aim.

Contemporary critics commonly use both the terms "postcolonial" and "third world" to refer to non-European peoples, countries, and cultures marked by their exposure to European colonialism and imperialism and, perhaps, to more recent American neocolonial power. Thus, the terms themselves imply a leftist, often Marxist, critique of transnational capitalism. Accordingly, the reading and writing practices that postcolonial studies examines, and the texts labelled "third world," are exclusively modern and contemporary. Moreover, as is suggested by the title of an influential work in postcolonial studies, *The Empire Writes Back* (1989), these texts and practices are assumed not only to differ from "the Western literary tradition" but to oppose it.

Postcolonialists, then, share with feminists, African-Americanists, popular culture critics, and specialists in other marginalized cultures the project of recognizing neglected work, denaturalizing dominant formal and evaluative literary paradigms, and connecting politics with aesthetics. But the contents and uses of the postcolonial as a category are problematic and have been hotly debated within the field itself. Many of the problems proceed from the inevitably homogenizing effect of a term that, as Bill Ashcroft, Gareth Griffiths, and Helen Tiffin propose in *The Empire Writes Back* covers "all the culture affected by the imperial process from the moment of colonization to the present day." As many have objected, "the imperial process" has differed significantly in different parts of the world and at different historical moments, and the aftermaths of colonization have varied widely for formerly colonized peoples. The notions of "the Empire" and "the postcolonial" may efface the linguistic and historical differences between distant countries whose cultures more closely resemble those of their former colonizers than they do each other.

More troubling still is the charge that, in theorizing third world literature as a reaction to colonialism, postcolonial studies itself risks perpetrating a kind of reverse neocolonialism, which stereotypes and subordinates the cultures it would respect. Colonized societies, after all, have been not internally uniform but comprised of different classes, regions, and religious groups whose constituents have experienced colonization differently; nor did colonization simply cancel or replace the cultural forms, traditions, and experiences of these groups. Then, too, the theory of postcoloniality may implicitly devalue aspects of cultural life that were not produced by colonialism but predated, endured, and outlasted it or developed in response to other stimuli after colonial occupation had ceased. Thus, postcolonial studies has been charged, often by members of formerly colonized populations, with paradoxically dehistoricizing the history it seeks to recover and extending the Western cultural hegemony it hopes to undo.

Edward Said's *Orientalism* (1978), one of the founding texts of postcolonial studies, is a work that has been both widely admired and widely criticized for the reasons enumerated above. Orientalism, as Said defines it, is "a style of thought based upon an ontological and epistemological distinction made between 'the Orient' and 'the Occident,' " a distinction that has rationalized and helped effect Western imperial domination over "Oriental" peoples and lands. In other words, orientalism is an ideological system or, in the term that Said borrows from Foucault, a "discursive formation," that deploys false claims of disinterested knowledge in the service of illegitimate power. Displaying exceptional disciplinary, historical, and geographical range, Said shows how orientalism pervades the writings not only of English and French politicians and colonial administrators in India and the Middle East, but of European and American poets, novelists, essayists, historians, anthropologists, journalists, and policymakers up to the present day. Said, as Aijaz Ahmad remarks, is "our most vivacious narrator of the history of European humanism's complicity in the history of European colonialism." One might add that *Orientalism*, along with Foucault's work on post-Enlightenment disciplines of the body, most vividly illustrates the connections between modern systems of knowledge and power.

Orientalism has itself been criticized, however, for its Eurocentricity. As Ahmad puts it:

[*Orientalism*] examines the history of Western texts about the non-West quite in isolation from how these textualities might have been received, accepted, modified, challenged, overthrown, or reproduced by the intelligentsias of the colonized countries: . . . what is remarkable is that with the exception of Said's own voice, the only voices we encounter in the book are precisely those of the very Western canonicity which, Said complains, has always silenced the Orient.

Critics have noted, too, Said's ambiguity on the origins and causes of orientalism. While Said's political critique requires that orientalism be understood as a product of the political, economic, and intellectual histories and objectives of modern Western societies, Said sometimes represents it as a structural condition of the emergence of Western civilization that may be traced back to the Greeks, or even as an expression of the human mind's inherent categorizing impulse. Seeming to presume at times that all classification is violation, Said remarks that "the main intellectual issue raised by Orientalism" is whether "one [can] divide human reality, as indeed human reality seems to be genuinely divided, into clearly different cultures, histories, traditions, societies, even races, and survive the consequences humanly."

Insofar as knowledge and political action inescapably entail classification and differentiation, Said's mournful question here approaches the impasse that we have described in our accounts of the Frankfurt School, Foucault, and New Historicism. What prospects for a genuine knowledge, and what grounds for an antiimperialist politics, can there be if the very act of classification is inherently imperialist, if "all academic knowledge about India and Egypt is somehow tinged and impressed with, violated by, the gross political fact [of imperialism]," and if "it is finally Western ignorance which becomes more refined and complex, not some body of positive Western knowledge which increases in size and accuracy"? (The same question, as we noted in the previous chapter, may be addressed to Mary Louise Pratt's critique of any "view from above" in *Imperial Eyes*.) That Said does not himself assume the inevitability of scholarly inaccuracy or the incurability of Western cultural ignorance is evident in his having taken the trouble to write *Orientalism* for a Western academic audience. Said's most recent work, moreover, has begun to record and respond to non-Western voices and has sought to bring them to bear on Euro-American cultural conversations. Finally, Said's critical efforts to overcome ignorance and misrepresentation of Palestinian history and culture and his political activism toward the establishment of a Palestinian state demonstrate his belief that, as he observes elsewhere in *Orientalism*, "there are such things as positive history and positive geography."

Still, *Orientalism* exemplifies as it exposes some of the difficulties involved in claims to knowledge about other peoples and cultures, whether the claims are made by colonial apologists or postcolonial critics. However different their purposes, both groups share cultural categories that inevitably shape their representations; the interests of both, moreover, encourage representations of difference as antithesis and of others as "the Other," a figure that emerges in response to an image – whether complacent or dissatisfied, imperious or guilty – of oneself. The project of postcolonial criticism in the Western academy, then, often raises the same practical and theoretical problems of knowledge and representation around which debates about the so-called "postmodern condition" have revolved. The interesting connection between these problems of postcolonial criticism and the idea of postmodernity in contemporary cultural studies is illustrated by Fredric Jameson's "Third World Literature in the Era of Multinational Capitalism" (1986).

Two years before the appearance of this essay, Jameson had published an important analysis of postmodernism as the "dominant cultural logic or hegemonic norm" of our time ("Postmodernism, or the Cultural Logic of Late

Capitalism," 1984). In this earlier essay, Jameson assails postmodernism as "a culture of the image" in which "the emergence of a new kind of flatness or depthlessness" produces both "the waning of affect" and a society "bereft of all historicity." Discarding the "depth model" of understanding that traditionally allows for distinctions between appearance and reality or original and representation, Jameson argues, postmodernism creates a cognitive "hyperspace" in which it becomes almost impossible for individuals to map their relations to larger social structures. "For political groups which seek actively to intervene in history," Jameson observes, "there cannot but be much that is deplorable and reprehensible in a cultural form of image addiction which, by transforming the past [into] visual mirages, stereotypes, or texts, effectively abolishes any practical sense of the future and of the collective project." Out of this vision of contemporary Western culture, so bleak for Marxist intellectuals like Jameson, comes the antithetical and compensatory "cognitive aesthetics of third-world literature" that Jameson theorizes in "Third-World Literature in the Era of Multinational Capitalism."

Despite Jameson's descriptions of third world texts as "different," "neglected," and "resistant to our conventional western habits of reading," his very category of "third world literature" thoroughly depends upon his earlier representation of the "cultural logic" of the postmodern West. (Jameson in fact announces the later essay to be "a pendant to the essay on postmodernism.") The totalized abstraction that he names "third-world culture" is, in his terms, simply the "inversion" or "radical reversal" of "what obtains in the west," the antidote for the Western intellectual malaise of postmodern disorientation and paralysis. Specifically, Jameson argues that, while "we have been trained in a deep cultural conviction that the lived experience of our private existences is somehow incommensurable with the abstractions of economic science and political dynamics," third world literature denies this split and helps us overcome our debilitating cultural conditioning. Applying his idea of the political unconscious, Jameson writes that "all third world texts are necessarily . . . allegorical. . . . *the story of the private individual destiny is always an allegory of the embattled situation of the public third-world culture and society*" (Jameson's italics).

Jameson's categorical antithesis is contradicted by countless products of both Western and non-Western cultures, both colonizing and colonized societies. Indeed, current work in postcolonial studies has begun to break down what Homi Bhabha has called "those nationalist or 'nativist' pedagogies that set up the relation of Third World and First World in a binary structure of opposition." Bhabha has argued, for example, that the "unifying discourses of 'nation,' 'peoples,' or authentic folk tradition, those embedded myths of culture's particularity, cannot be readily referenced," and that the postcolo-

nial perspective must be one that explores "hybridity" and "resists the attempt at holistic forms of social explanation." The analysis of colonialism and
postcolonialism thus does not become a new master narrative but, in
Bhabha's view, returns us to "the problematics of signification and judgment
that have become current in contemporary theory – aporia, ambivalence,
indeterminacy, the question of discursive closure, the threat to agency, the
status of intentionality, the challenge to 'totalizing' concepts, to name a few."

Ironically, these are the very problematics of poststructuralist thought and
postmodern culture that Jameson imagines Third World literature has escaped or overcome. As Jameson himself remarks, conceding the objections to
his totalizing claims but contending that his argument had nonetheless been
worth making: "The essay was intended as an intervention into a 'first-world'
literary and critical situation, in which it seemed important to me to stress
the loss of certain literary functions and intellectual commitments in the
contemporary American scene." This remark returns us to a question that has
informed our history of modern criticism from the outset: What exactly are
the critic's "literary functions and intellectual commitments" and can they be
fulfilled in work addressed principally to readers who share the political
perspective or the professional situation of the critic? We conclude our history with a brief consideration of this question.

CONCLUSION:
ACADEMIC CRITICISM AND ITS
DISCONTENTS

I N THIS VOLUME we have told the story of the rise and development, between 1940 and the present, of a distinctly *academic* literary criticism. At the beginning of our period, as we observed, the very idea of a "criticism" rooted in the academy seemed inherently paradoxical. Criticism had been the purview of journalistic men (and in rare cases women) of letters. Literary academics, with the exception of the few cultural journalists who had infiltrated their ranks, were scholars and not critics, where "scholarship" often meant gathering philological and historical data addressed to other professionals and "criticism" often meant indulging in impressionistic or tendentious evaluation addressed to amateurs. With the expansion, modernization, and democratization of American higher education in the early decades of the twentieth century, however, the need arose for a study of literature that would be professional and disciplined but would serve broad cultural and educational functions beyond the scope of specialized research on language and scholarly accumulation of information. But it was only in the early 1940s that critical methods emerged that were capable of answering this need.

These were the methods of "the new academic criticism" that we discussed in our early chapters, methods that we now associate with "the New Criticism," though, as we point out, this name originally denoted a diverse group of approaches that were often in competition. The new academic criticism generated tremendous excitement, not least for its emphasis on the close reading or "explication" of particular literary texts. Literature, it now seemed, was finally being understood on its own terms – really being read in its aesthetic complexity and particularity, not merely "appreciated" in the subjective way of journalistic men of letters or inventoried for factual data in the bloodless fashion of academic research scholars. In their meticulous attention to literary technique and critical methodology, the new academic critics of the 1940s legitimated criticism as a properly academic endeavor, a discrete field of study susceptible to rational and even scientific principles of organization and analysis. But the successful efforts of these critics to establish the

445

disciplinary objectivity of literary study also served a deeper social and even missionary purpose.

For the most influential New Critics, the very qualities that made literary works intrinsically literary also made them repositories of complex humanistic values that opposed the dominant values – or valuelessness – of a rootless, materialistic modern age. This was an age, it was felt, in which spiritual meaning, individual ethical choice, and sustaining communal traditions were under siege and in danger of being replaced by instrumental rationality, vulgarized mass communication, and the wasteland culture of commerce. Apparently retreating into a purely aesthetic realm, the classics of modern literature actually constituted a profound indictment of this wasteland in their very aesthetic properties of structural tension, richness of texture, and ambiguity. Accordingly, the academic discipline that addressed itself to aesthetic properties also claimed a large public function and consequence.

Academic criticism's combined emphasis on the close reading of literature as a teachable verbal skill and as a defense of humanistic values suited American cultural and educational circumstances in several ways. A powerful strain of modernist thought, shared by such poets as W. B. Yeats and Wallace Stevens and notably recalling Matthew Arnold's argument in the late 19th century, held that poetry must compensate for the decline of religious faith by providing the spiritual meaning and order that many no longer derived from institutional religion. At the same time, the organized study of English in American colleges and universities promised to serve as a practical means of cultural and linguistic assimilation for a diverse student population substantially comprised of the children of immigrants. For some of its early advocates, English studies was a way to "Americanize" and thereby control the otherwise unruly energies of the uncultured masses. For other advocates, English studies was a means by which those masses could overcome traditional barriers of class, ethnicity, and social background. Either way – and literary study resulted both in social containment and social empowerment – English had acquired, by the beginning of our period, a far more prominent role in school and college education than it had had in the past. Then, as now, the fortunes of literary criticism had become intimately bound up with issues of pedagogy, curriculum, and – although this was less often explicitly charged or acknowledged – politics.

The cultural urgency that now attended academic literary studies led to a burst of theorizing and theoretical controversy over the nature of literature and criticism. Vigorous and important debates raged in the 1940s over such questions as "the problem of belief": did the truth or validity of the beliefs implicated in a literary work have any bearing on its aesthetic value? Did literary works embody beliefs at all? Another contested issue, as we discussed in Chapter 3, was the importance of literary nationality: did great literature express national identity, as an emergent postwar Americanist criticism argued, or did it transcend nationality, as some New Critics replied?

Though these questions energized the professional discourse of criticism, as that discourse became increasingly institutionalized and routinized its larger social and philosophical concerns tended to recede into the background. "Criticism," as presented to students, often was reduced to a set of context-less analytical exercises. One can see this tendency to reduction in the many introductory literature textbooks that appeared in the wake of Cleanth Brooks's and Robert Penn Warren's *Understanding Poetry* (1938), textbooks in which the New Criticism was condensed into a set of techniques for close reading with relatively little reference to the larger cultural and religious concerns that had animated Brooks, Warren, and other New Critics.

At the same time, as criticism became a legitimate alternative to historical scholarship as a form of "research" qualifying academics for tenure and promotion, the practice of explication often detached itself from purposeful cultural argument. Already in the 1950s, the excitement that critical explication had generated when it had been novel was beginning to give way to the feeling that explication had become the latest form of academic business as usual, not an antidote to instrumental rationality but its mirror-image. By the early 1960s there were increasingly persistent complaints – even from such authors of the movement as Brooks and Rene Wellek – that the New Criticism was merely churning out mechanical "explications" in a vacuum for no apparent purpose except professional advancement. By the mid-sixties, when feminists and New Left critics launched their assault on the mechanization of the literary academy, they were radicalizing a familiar critique that had been developed by founders of the academic establishment they assailed.

Once this history is recognized, it provides a useful model for understanding both what happened next in the academic humanities and what is happening now. Underscored by the social turmoil of the 1960s, the routinization and insularity of much textual criticism and traditional literary history prompted many literary academics to embrace the European-imported theories and critical methods that flooded into American humanities departments at the beginning of the seventies. David Richter, whose academic career began in that decade, recalls his tremendous excitement as "structuralism and semiotics, deconstruction, Lacanian psychology, Althusserian Marxism, Russian formalism, phenomenology, and reception theory" came successively into his awareness:

to me it felt like an enormously liberating experience. A profession that a few years before had been hacking out ninety-nine progressively less plausible ways of misreading *The Turn of the Screw* was now lit up with a rush of ideas, a dozen disparate systems with enormous reach and scope, many of them capable too of informing and channeling the social imperatives of women and minorities seeking a literary and critical manifestation of their need for greater freedom and power.

Looking back from today's vantage point, however, Richter admits to disappointment, to a feeling that the theory revolution has not fulfilled his and his generation's expectations of it, not delivered on its promises.

In the recent culture wars, the difficulties and disappointments of contemporary critical theory have been variously diagnosed, from the political right and the political left, and by theorists and anti-theorists. Some have argued that it was naive to begin with to believe that mere changes in academic literary criticism could effect significant political change, as if theoretical and social revolution were coextensive. Others have said that, even if it were possible for academic criticism to address the need of oppressed groups "for greater freedom and power," this is not a proper goal for the discipline of literary studies. Still others have cynically suggested that the theory movement itself boils down to the latest and fanciest form of academic careerism: an occasion for replacing the ninety-nine old-fashioned (and already published) ways of misreading *The Turn of the Screw* with ninety-nine new-fangled (thus, publishable) ways of misreading it – as a deconstructive map of misreading, for example, or a Foucauldian inscription of power-knowledge. Critical theory is itself inescapably insular, many journalists have jeered and academics lamented, because of its specialized language and esoteric concepts.

It is important to observe that such arguments are not new, that they do not simply represent a contemporary reaction against academic criticism but are an integral part of that criticism's history. Versions of these arguments have appeared throughout our pages and we have sought both to acknowledge their force where they seemed forceful and to caution against their oversimplifying and caricatural tendencies. We have suggested, for instance, that charges of theory's elitism or insularity need to be weighed against the broadly public contributions of academic criticism in our period: the recovery and reprinting of hundreds of authors and texts and the incorporation into our understanding of "culture" of literary forms and social constituencies that had previously been excluded; theory's impact on fields remote from literary criticism such as legal studies, which has been provoked into reexamining its understanding of how law works, what judges do, and how the processes of constitutional interpretation operate; the influence of far-reaching critiques of institutions, ideology, and disciplinary power that have been taken up by

AIDS activists and environmentalists, among others. Indeed, the academic discourses of feminist analysis, psychoanalytic theory, and multiculturalism have so permeated the larger nonacademic culture that their terms and concepts – in however loose or popularized form – have become part of the vocabulary of many who have never taken a course in criticism and might be surprised to learn that they were "talking theory." Thus, recent media attacks on the specialization and inaccessibility of academic criticism may be fueled by journalists' anxiety that the opposite is the case. For, having taken mass culture and politics into their province, academic critics now implicitly rival journalists for authority in the interpretation of contemporary cultural life.

In spite of these achievements, internal as well as external dissatisfaction with the principal directions of current academic criticism seems widespread as we complete this history in the spring of 1995. This dissatisfaction is not, of course, universal, but neither is it solely the property of those who disdain the vocabularies and concerns of theory or the interests and values of the cultural left. Academics such as Richter, who so eagerly welcomed the new methods and theories of the 1970s, and Jameson, the prominent Marxist critic whose lament of a contemporary "critical situation" marked by unfulfilled "literary functions and intellectual commitments" we noted at the close of our last chapter, plainly share this mood. Though the sources of internal discontent in intellectual disciplines are always various, Jameson's and Richter's conceptions of the functions and commitments of academic criticism themselves suggest the nature of much contemporary dissatisfaction with academic criticism.

While Richter's characterization of the theory revolution begins by celebrating the heterogeneity of "theory" ("a rush of ideas, a dozen disparate systems"), it quickly becomes clear that Richter also takes theory to promise the consolidation and mobilization of diverse intellectual energies toward large social ends. The "enormous reach and scope" of theoretical systems seems to render them capable not only of revitalizing a profession stalled in endless misreadings of *The Turn of the Screw*, but "capable too of informing and channeling . . . social imperatives." For Jameson as well, fulfillment of the "literary functions and intellectual commitments" of academic critics and criticism lies in the achievement of a social imperative: the reintegration of "the lived experience of our private existences" (the existences represented by individual characters in novels, for instance, or the private lived experience of reading them) with "the [real] abstractions of economic science and political dynamics." Criticism's social imperative, in other words, is to help restore to an alienated, divided, and disempowered contemporary citizenry a "practical sense of the future and of the collective project."

It is not the case, to be sure, that the critical object of every contemporary theorist or method is the eventual socialist transformation of "the era of multinational capitalism" that constitutes Jameson's frankly stated "collective project." But it is true that most of the influential discourses in recent academic criticism have approached particular acts and objects of cultural production, consumption, and interpretation in broadly social terms. These discourses, in other words, have tended to situate writers, readers, and cultural texts within large socio-historical narratives of ethnic, gender, class, and national struggle, or to assign them representative positions between such abstract conceptual and ideological poles as complicity and resistance, determinacy and indeterminacy, mystification and demystification, the symbolic and the semiotic, humanism and anti- or post-humanism. Thus, current models of disciplinary inquiry place enormous pressure on individual critics and works of criticism to define and defend themselves not merely as worthy respondents to specific textual or intellectual occasions but as contributors to one or another "collective project" of "enormous reach and scope" driven by clear "social imperatives."

Such disciplinary ambition has yielded mixed results. It has produced provocative cultural analyses and an unprecedented array of interpretive communities or sub-communities. But it has also denigrated more particularistic critical labor, encouraged critics to overstate the consequences and competency of their cultural "interventions," and prompted interpretive sub-communities to vigilantly police their borders and, at times, become discursive enclaves in which communicants preach to the converted. This danger of insularity or exclusion seems an unavoidable problem in criticism that intends democratic social reform yet fails to engage seriously with those both inside and outside the academy who do not already accept the legitimacy or priority of its political project. The problem becomes an ethical one as well when the project is enacted in the classroom – a communal space informed by power relations and social imperatives that are not identical to those that obtain in the society at large.

Though current radical pedagogical theorists call for a democratic curriculum, many of them presume a professorial commitment to social transformation, thereby narrowing the implied audience to those teachers who already share their politics and their vision of pedagogy as its appropriate instrument. Consider, for example, the following statements from an essay by Henry Giroux, a leading advocate of "critical pedagogy":

The notion of the liberal arts has to be reconstituted around a knowledge-power relationship in which the question of the curriculum is seen as a form of cultural and political production grounded in a radical conception of citizenship and public wisdom.

[Students need to take up] a language of critique and possibility, a language that cultivates a capacity for reasoned criticism, for undoing the misuses of power and the relations of domination, and for exploring and extending the utopian dimensions of human potentiality.

While Giroux claims to want a curriculum that embodies "public wisdom" and "human potentiality," he restricts these democratic capacities to their "radical conceptions[s]" and "utopian dimensions" alone. Critical thinking is equated with oppositional politics, implicitly shutting out those students and teachers for whom "a capacity for reasoned criticism" would not necessarily mean seeing "relations of domination" as the primary feature of American society, and for whom the goal of college humanities courses would not necessarily be "undoing the misuses of power."

Once academics in their teaching and writing address themselves to public affairs, they properly incur greater public obligations as well as the need for an effective public voice. Recent conservative attacks, however exaggerated and misleading, have shown that if socially engaged teachers and critics do not find ways to speak clearly for themselves to non-professional audiences, and to communicate responsively with the numerous constituencies outside the cultural left, it will be their detractors who will speak for them. Two related challenges that confront contemporary literary academics, then, are the challenge to define their public responsibility more flexibly and inclusively and the challenge to represent their work more effectively in the public sphere.

There are some encouraging signs that such an overdue clarifying mission may be underway. Not only have books such as Allan Bloom's *The Closing of the American Mind* and Camille Paglia's *Sexual Personae* (1990) provoked healthy self-examination and renewed attention to the need for public self-representation among progressive academic critics, but the very commercial success of these critiques has helped create a non-academic audience for counterstatements. In the early 1990s, literary academics have increasingly sought to engage that audience in books, essay anthologies, public symposia, and articles in general publications. Multi-authored collections such as *Debating PC: The Controversy over Political Correctness on College Campuses* (edited by Paul Berman, 1992) and *After Political Correctness: The Humanities and Society in the 1990s* (edited by Christopher Newfield and Ron Stickland, 1995), and books such as Michael Bérubé's *Public Access: Literary Theory and American Cultural Politics* (1994) and Henry Louis Gates's *Loose Canons: Notes on the Culture Wars* (1992) have addressed themselves to the prospects and problems for a new public intellectual criticism that will accommodate debate among voices across the cultural-political spectrum. Indeed, the establishment of a public intellectual criticism capable of bridging both academic and non academic audiences and issues has been an especially urgent concern for Gates and other prominent black intellectuals, who have advanced this project in such books as Toni Morrison's *Playing in the Dark: Whiteness and the Literary Imagination* (1992), Cornel West's *Race Matters* (1993), and Houston A. Baker's *Black Studies, Rap, and the Academy* (1993).

As Lauren Berlant and Michael Warner suggest in the most recent (May, 1995) issue of the official journal of the profession, *PMLA*, literary academics must "cultivate a rigorous and intellectually generous critical culture without narrowing its field" and must seek to produce "knowledge central to living." Berlant and Warner find such knowledge in criticism that combines political and personal engagement: specifically, gay and lesbian criticism ("queer commentary," in their preferred phrase), along with "feminist, African American, Latina/Latino, and other minority projects." While these kinds of knowledge are clearly crucial, the inclusive intellectual culture that we seek also depends on recognizing that they are not the only knowledges that are "central to living" or to the public and disciplinary responsibilities of literary academics. Indeed, what many both outside the academy and within it have reasonably resisted in recent academic criticism is its tendency to take political knowledge as the only worthwhile object of literary study. This assumption has not only implicitly disdained some of the legitimate interests and expectations of students and non-professionals, but it has also devalued the writing and teaching of academics whose primary professional commitment is to enhance discrete acts of reading and the interpretive powers and pleasures of individual readers. In fact, our own focus in this history on the partisans and opponents of the various collective critical projects of the last half century has led us to ignore many particularistic critics who have produced brilliant and enabling readings of specific writers, texts, and genres.

A publically and professionally responsive criticism, then, needs not only to avoid ideological insularity, but to include and engage the arguments of such broadly committed generalist critics as Richard Poirier and Harold Bloom, who have argued, in books such as Poirier's *The Renewal of Literature* (1987) and *Poetry and Pragmatism* (1992) and Bloom's *The Western Canon: The Books and School of the Ages* (1994), that what is central to criticism and to living are the powers and pleasures sustained in the local act of reading, rather than discharged through the application of finished readings to over-arching social or cultural ends. Ultimately, however, as Patricia Meyer Spacks suggested in her 1994 Presidential Address to the Modern Language Association, these are not categorical alternatives between which contemporary academic criticism must choose. Acknowledging the fact that there are other "careers that would more straightforwardly address the problems of a tumultuous and suffering world," Spacks recognizes too that

Examination of racial tensions in the writing of Joseph Conrad as well as Toni Morrison can fuel investigation of society and self. Instruction in the drawbacks of the passive voice may shed light on modes of political irresponsibility. . . . Contemporary education fits citizens for a contemporary democracy better than does the education of yesterday.

For all its political limitations, Spacks concludes, literary study retains significant political potential, including the potential to develop intellectual and affective resources that may "[help] people live their lives."

APPENDIX II
BIOGRAPHIES OF CRITICS

Our narrative is a history of the debates that shaped the field in our time, rather than a venture in canon-formation. Accordingly, the entries that follow are intended to help orient readers who may be unfamiliar with the general biographical circumstances, critical affiliations, and publications of the theorists who figure most significantly in our narrative – i.e., the nineteen critics whose work collectively represents the key moments and movements in criticism since 1940.

THEODOR ADORNO (1903–1969)

The writings of Theodor Adorno (discussed in Chapter 6) are among the most diverse and influential works of neo-Marxist critical theory. The term "critical theory" itself was coined by the interdisciplinary group of progressive European intellectuals who established the Institute for Social Research at the University of Frankfurt in 1923. Breaking with those principles of classical Marxism – economic and scientific determinism, and the doctrine of a vanguard revolutionary proletariat – that they found inapplicable to advanced, highly mediated, and complexly administered capitalist society, the Frankfurt School critics, as this group came to be called, sought to develop a more flexible social, philosophical, and cultural critique. Among their central concerns were the coercive or ideological force of putatively value-neutral instrumental reason, the psychological bases and effects of modern authoritarianism, the sociology of avant-garde and mass culture, the relationship between aesthetic and political criticism, and the role of cultural intellectuals in bringing about social change.

Adorno first became affiliated with the Institute in the late 1920s, having previously studied composing and music theory in Vienna, where he was influenced by the techniques and atonal music of Schoenberg. Along with his fellows at the Institute, most of whom were the sons of assimilated middle-class German Jews, Adorno fled Germany when Hitler came to power in 1933. Adorno and the Frankfurt School director, Max Horkheimer, with whom Adorno often worked collaboratively, continued their studies in London before moving to New York in 1936, where the Institute for Social Research relocated at Columbia University. Other notable critics associated with the Institute in the 1930s included Erich Fromm, Walter Benjamin, and Herbert Marcuse. In the early 1940s, Horkheimer and Adorno moved to Los Angeles, where they worked with Bruno Bettelheim and other social and psychological researchers affiliated with the Berkeley Public Opinion Study Group on a series of publications entitled *Studies in Prejudice*. Returning to Germany after the war, Adorno helped reestablish the Institute at the University of Frankfurt, becoming codirector in 1955 and working there until his death.

Adorno was the Frankfurt School's principal aesthetician, but his writings extend well beyond the philosophy of art into sociology, psychology, political history, media analysis, and music and literary criticism. In *The Dialectic of Enlightenment* (1947, trans. 1972), Adorno and coauthor Horkheimer argue that Enlightenment rationalism, though it at first opposed barbarism and superstition and served the ends of human freedom, always contained within itself the tendencies toward instrumentalism, technocratic absolutism, and domination that bureaucratic mass societies (of which fascist Germany is the extreme example) have elicited; the twentieth-century "end" (in both senses) of Reason, Adorno and Horkheimer grimly suggest, is barbarism. One chapter title from this early work, "The Culture Industry: Enlightenment as Mass Deception," indicates the profound distrust of mass and popular culture that – along with a related distrust of all positivistic, systematizing, or totalizing thought or expression – would pervade Adorno's later books and essays. Of these, the most important volumes are *Minima Moralia* (1951, trans. 1974); *Prisms: Cultural Criticism and Society* (1955; trans. 1967); *The Jargon of Authenticity* (1964, trans. 1973); *Negative Dialectics* (1966, trans. 1973); the unfinished *Aesthetic Theory* (1970, trans. 1984); and *Notes to Literature* (1974, trans. 1991–2). Favoring avant-garde modernist literature, atonal music, and other formal, defamiliarizing, and "aesthetic" works of art over the "committed" social realist works that earlier Marxist critics advocated, Adorno argues in these books that the greatest – and the only potentially liberating – art critiques administered society by negation, by unsettling its formulas, by denying the "petrified and alienated reality" of its reason.

ROLAND BARTHES (1915–1980)

Along with Jacques Derrida and Michel Foucault, Roland Barthes (discussed in Chapter 6) numbers among the postwar French intellectuals who have most profoundly influenced contemporary literary and cultural studies. Barthes explored a number of critical interests and experimented with various writing styles – from the analytic to the aphoristic to the poetic and autobiographical – over the course of his career, but the central and most far-reaching concerns of his work (roughly, in chronological order) were: the elements and conditions of linguistic meaning (structuralism); the logic of sign systems (semiology), especially the systems of signification that inform contemporary social, commercial, and cultural activities and institutions and produce the "mythologies" of everyday life; and the play of determinism and freedom, classicism and modernity, author and reader, hermeneutics and erotics, that comprises "textuality" and the experience of literature.

This last set of interests in the constraints, possibilities, and pleasures of writing and reading in fact connects Barthes's earliest with his latest work. The title of Barthes's first book, *Writing Degree Zero* (1953, trans. 1967), designates a literary modernity in which, as Jean-Michel Rabate summarizes it, "writers such as Albert Camus or the novelists of the *nouveau roman* . . . attempt to create a neutral literary style deprived of all traditional markers that heralds an encounter with language as such, while stressing the gap between language and the world." In Barthes's 1968 essay, "The Death of the Author" (trans. 1977, in *Image–Music–Text*), this gap comes to divide writers from the texts that linguistic and cultural codes, rather than they, originate. In *S/Z* (1970, trans. 1974), an analytic dismantling and ramification of Balzac's story "Sarrasine," Barthes dramatizes the "textuality" (the multiplicity of constitutive codes, possible meanings, and opportunities for readerly participation and pleasure) of even the most seemingly solid and authoritative realist work. And literary excess, transgression, and pleasure themselves are the central preoccupations of subsequent works such as *Sade, Fourier, Loyola* (1971, trans. 1976) and *The Pleasure of the Text* (1973, trans. 1975).

Other works by Barthes include *Criticism and Truth* (1966, trans. 1987), *Elements of Semiology* (1964, trans. 1967), *The Fashion System* (1967, trans. 1983), *Empire of Signs* (1970, trans. 1982), *Roland Barthes by Roland Barthes* (1975, trans. 1977), and *Camera Lucida* (1980, trans. 1981). In the early *Mythologies* (1957, trans. 1972, 1979), however, Barthes made perhaps his most influential contribution to contemporary criticism: his articulation of the concept of "myth" as the form of signification by which modern societies effect ideological pacification and the concealment of political power. Myth, for Barthes, is a secondary semiological system in which signs (which may refer, among many other things, to commercial products, social groups, fashions, or nations) are emptied of their specific, historical qualities and relations and abstracted, naturalized, universalized, and – in Barthes's term – "de-politicized" in ways designed to thwart historical understanding, social critique, and the prospect of change.

HAROLD BLOOM (1930–)

Harold Bloom's dozens of authored and edited books exhibit a literary and critical range that is aptly described by the title of his most recent volume, *The Western Canon: The Books and Schools of the Ages* (1994). Most characteristically, Bloom's work (discussed in Chapter 5) has extensively addressed itself to British and American writers in the romantic tradition; the relationship between poetics and criticism; religious tradition, mysticism, and Biblical interpretation; and the application of Freudian psychology and Derridean deconstruction to literary history and criticism. Bloom's abiding commitment, however, has been to the energy of the poetic imagination which, in his view, "strong" poetry and criticism is always an effort to arrogate, sustain, and renew.

Bloom received his B.A. from Cornell University in 1951 and his Ph.D. from Yale University, where he has taught since 1955. Trained as a specialist in British romanticism, Bloom sought in his early works to revalue the romantic poetry and poets that T. S. Eliot and the New Critics who presided over Bloom's disciplinary apprenticeship had disparaged. *Shelley's Mythmaking* (1959), *The Visionary Company: A Reading of English Romantic Poetry* (1961, revised 1971), and *Blake's Apocalypse: A Study in Poetic Argument* (1963) all celebrate the visionary power of the Blakean Imagination, by which natural phenomena and historical experience are converted into poetic images and ideas. In response to his readings of Nietzsche and Freud, Bloom subsequently revised his understanding of poetic imagination, placing particular stress on the will to power and on the intergenerational struggle (based on the Oedipal family romance) between the "belated" poet-son and his "precursor" poet-father for access to the muse-mother of poetic originality and plenitude.

Much of Bloom's work in the 1970s and early 1980s develops this psychopoetic or mythopoetic theory of literary influence and creativity and extends the theory to describe the relation between poet and critic as well: just as the poet necessarily "misreads" his precursor in order to establish the primacy and authority of his own poetic production (and the possessive pronouns here deliberately mark the patriarchal assumptions that inform Bloom's theory), so the activity of the strong critic, for Bloom, is necessarily one of misreading and supplantation, of literary competition and creativity. *The Anxiety of Influence: A Theory of Poetry* (1973), *Kabbalah and Criticism* (1975), *A Map of Misreading* (1975), *Figures of Capable Imagination* (1976), *Poetry and Repression: Revisionism from Blake to Stevens* (1976), *Agon: Toward a Theory of Revisionism* (1982), and *The Breaking of the Vessels* (1982) elaborate on these ideas.

Shared emphases on the mutability of textual meaning, its dependence on repression, and its implication in historical relations of power link Bloom's work to the deconstructive criticism of Jacques Derrida. Along with his Yale colleagues J. Hillis Miller, Geoffrey Hartman, and Paul de Man, Bloom contributed to the American academic establishment of deconstruction at Yale in the 1970s. In addition to *The Western Canon*, twenty-six essays on writers and works Bloom feels best reward the reader's attention, framed by opening and closing elegies on the demise of the "difficult pleasure" of reading, Bloom's most recent books are: *Ruin the Sacred Truths: Poetry and Belief from the Bible to the Present* (1989), *The Book of J* (1991), and *The American Religion: The Emergence of the Post-Christian Nation* (1992).

JUDITH BUTLER (1956–)

Trained as a philosopher, Judith Butler (discussed in Chapter 4) has taught in interdisciplinary programs at a number of universities, including George Washington University, Johns Hopkins, Wesleyan, Yale, and the University of California at Berkeley, and has recently emerged as an important critic of contemporary literature, rhetoric, and culture. Butler's 1990 book *Gender Trouble* which argued that gender roles were entirely performative, pointed out the lack of any logical or necessary correspondence between gender and anatomy, and explored the implications of the existence of multiple and nonbinary gendered subjectivities, quickly established her as a leading poststructuralist feminist theorist. This work, along with an influential article of the same year, "The Force of Fantasy: Mapplethorpe, Feminism, and the Discourse of Excess," and two subsequent books, *Bodies That Matter* (1993) and *Erotic Welfare: Sexual Theory and Politics in the Age of Epidemic* (1993), have also helped define the field of gay and lesbian criticism. Butler's sophisticated critiques of "the workings of heterosexual hegemony in the crafting of matters sexual and political" are among the most widely cited texts in current "queer theory." Butler's first book, *Subjects of Desire: Hegelian Reflections in Twentieth-Century France* (1987), is less well-known among literary and cultural critics.

PAUL DE MAN (1919–1983)

Born in Antwerp, Belgium, Paul de Man (discussed in Chapters 5 and 6) studied sciences and philosophy in Brussels and immigrated to the United States in 1948, first teaching French at Bard College. Between 1960 and his death in 1983, he taught comparative literatures and criticism at Cornell, Johns Hopkins, and Yale Universities. De Man's teaching and writing played a significant part in the dissemination and acceptance of European poststructuralist theory in the American academy during the 1960s and 1970s. The close affiliation between de Man's work and that of Jacques Derrida, in particular, has prompted many to consider de Man the principal American deconstructionist.

De Man's most influential essay, "The Rhetoric of Temporality" (1969), argued that the privileging of symbolism over allegory in romantic aesthetics is based on a mystification of the relationship between language and the world, and of romantic literature itself. Symbolism aspires to – and assumes the possibility of – an organic and continuous relationship between life and form, referent and sign, a "unity between the representative and semantic function of language," while "allegory designates primarily a distance in relation to its own origin, and, renouncing the nostalgia and the desire to coincide, establishes its language in the void of this temporal difference." Allegory, in this sense, functions for de Man as a figure for literature itself, which de Man celebrates as a uniquely demystified form of signification by virtue of its consciousness of its own fictiveness, its formal discontinuity with life, and its accommodation of the destabilizing rhetoric and figurative play of language.

De Man's critical readings, in *Blindness and Insight: Essays in the Rhetoric of Contemporary Criticism* (1971) and *Allegories of Reading: Figural Language in Rousseau, Nietzsche, Rilke, and Proust* (1979), typically reveal disparity or contradiction between a text's assertions and its performance, its representations and its tropes. Moreover, as the titles of both of these volumes suggest, no act of reading can resolve or totalize textual meaning; in the terms of de Man's early major essay, reading is itself an allegorical rather than a symbolic practice, one whose every insight is grounded in a necessary blindness. De Man's later essays and papers have been collected in several posthumous volumes, which include *The Rhetoric of Romanticism* (1984), *The Resistance to Theory* (1986), *Aesthetic Ideology* (1992), and *Romanticism and Contemporary Criticism: The Gauss Seminars and Other Papers* (1992).

After his death as well, it was discovered that in his early twenties de Man had been a wartime journalist who contributed a number of essays to two collaborationist Belgian newspapers, including one article, "Les Juifs dans la littérature actuelle," that betrayed anti-Semitic sentiments and approved notions of European cultural organicism and unity. This 1987 revelation prompted a series of attacks, counterstatements, and reevaluations that continued throughout the late 1980s and addressed themselves not only to de Man's life and work but to the philosophical and political implications of deconstruction and poststructuralist theory themselves.

JACQUES DERRIDA (1930–)

Jacques Derrida (discussed in Chapter 5) is a French philosopher whose intricate undoings or "deconstructions" of the central texts and assumptions of the Western philosophical tradition have profoundly influenced contemporary thinking throughout the humanities and social sciences about knowledge, identity, and the conditions of meaningful utterance. Following the structural linguist Ferdinand de Saussure, Derrida understands language to be a differential system in which words derive their meanings not by correspondence with things in the world but through their systematic and differential relations to other words within the language. Derrida has largely devoted himself to interrogating the history of Western metaphysics in light of this theory of language, drawing as well on the ontological and epistemological inquiries of such predecessors as Hegel, Husserl, Nietzsche, and Heidegger, and conversing with the anthropological, psychological, sociological, and semiotic researches of such French contemporaries as Barthes, Foucault, Lacan and Lévi-Strauss.

In Derrida's analysis, Western metaphysical thought has required the concept of a "transcendental signified," a meaning or truth immediately present to consciousness. The philosophical tradition has sought to produce and protect such a concept through its construction of various hierarchical distinctions: philosophy over rhetoric, internal essence over external appearance, the self-presence of speech over the displacement and derivativeness of writing. Deconstruction, the method of philosophical and rhetorical critique with which Derrida's name has become virtually synonymous, reveals the impossibility and self-contradictoriness of this demand for full presence by showing how – in any text or act of signification, including the central philosophical arguments for the hierarchical distinctions listed above – the identity of the privileged term in each of these hierarchies not only collapses into the devalued "secondary" term but, in fact, depends on it. Identities are "grounded" only in differences, selves forged out of otherness, significations fixed by the arbitrary suppression (or repressive denial) of the ongoing play of signifiers – the mutiplicity, instability, and constructedness of meaning in language.

Derrida teaches at the Collège de Philosophie in Paris and has had occasional visiting appointments at several American universities, including Yale, Johns Hopkins, and the University of California at Irvine. The literary, political, and ethical implications and applications of his philosophical readings, and of his theories of textuality and the history and production of meaning, continue to be explored and contested in many intellectual disciplines. Derrida's principal writings include the following works: *Speech and*

Phenomenon: Introduction to the Problem of Signs in Husserl's Phenomenology (1967, trans. 1978), *Of Grammatology* (1967, trans. 1976), *Writing and Difference* (1967, trans. 1978), *Dissemination* (1972, trans. 1981), *Positions* (1972, trans. 1981), *Margins of Philosophy* (1972, trans. 1983), *Spurs: Nietzsche's Styles.* (1976, trans. 1981). *Of Spirit: Heidegger and the Question* (1987, trans. 1989), *Limited Inc.* (trans. 1988), *The Other Heading: Reflections on Today's Europe* (1990, trans. 1992), and *Acts of Literature* (trans. 1992).

STANLEY FISH (1938–)

Stanley Fish (discussed in Chapters 5 and 7) has long been the leading American exponent of the reader-response method of literary criticism. His most recent work has more generally and influentially advanced antifoundationalist and neo-pragmatist approaches to literary and legal interpretation and to questions of disciplinary and political definition. He has taught in the English Departments at the University of California at Berkeley and Johns Hopkins University, and is currently Professor of English and of Law at Duke University and Director of Duke University Press.

Beginning his career as a scholar of seventeenth-century English literature, Fish gained notoriety beyond his field of specialization with the 1967 publication of *Surprised by Sin: The Reader in "Paradise Lost."* Milton's epic, Fish argued, relied on the temporality of the reading process (in which meaning is not revealed all at once but constructed, revised, and reconceived in the ongoing experience of the reader) to replicate Adam and Eve's fall in the reader's interpretive temptations, confusions, and errors. Over the next decade, Fish converted this textual reading into a sweeping theory of the relationship between textual meaning and readerly experience, developing his argument in *Self-Consuming Artifacts: The Experience of Seventeenth-Century Literature* (1972) and fully articulating it during the 1970s in a number of important essays collected in *Is There a Text in This Class?* (1980). Fish's radical contention was that the fundamental New Critical (and apparently commonsensical) injunction against the "affective fallacy" – the fallacy of equating a reader's response to a work with the meaning of the work itself – was self-deceiving and empty because textual meaning is simply a function of reader response: texts only mean by virtue of, and in the terms of, someone's reading of them; readers and readings, then, are not produced by texts but produce them.

Like deconstruction and other poststructuralist critical positions, Fish's reader-response criticism takes meaning to be relational and historical, rather than absolute, and at least potentially unstable and multiplicitous. In his more recent work, Fish has developed the idea that individual interpretive acts and actors are at once authorized and regulated by the "interpretive communities" to which they belong; the shared assumptions and commitments of such communities account for commonality and stability of interpretation, while the possibility of an interpreter's affiliation with more than one community, and of shifts of purpose and self-definition within particular communities, accounts for interpretive divergence and change. Fish's theory of meaning's production according to the values and practical needs of competing communities has led him to argue "against theory" (where "theory" is defined as an abstract and objective guide to critical and social judgment) and, in his latest essays, collected in *Doing What Comes Naturally: Change, Rhetoric, and the Practice of Theory in Legal Studies* (1989) and *There's No Such Thing as Free Speech, and It's a Good Thing, Too* (1994), to explore some of the practical implications of this argument for contemporary legal, literary and social practices.

MICHEL FOUCAULT (1926–1984)

In the early 1950s, Michel Foucault (discussed in Chapter 7) took academic degrees in both philosophy and psychology, but he gained international renown, beginning in the 1970s, for his historical and political analyses of modern institutions, technologies, and "discourses" of social control and for his theory of power in post-Enlightenment societies as a diffuse and immanent force that insidiously produces its subjects' consciousnesses of themselves and the world rather than overtly and externally assaulting or constraining their bodies. Foucault's understanding of power's dissemination through cultural discourses, his interest in the social and historical construction of individual subjects, and his emphasis on the implication of disciplines and institutions of knowledge in systems of political domination have deeply engaged and influenced contemporary cultural critics and literary and social historians.

Before he began his teaching career (he taught first in Sweden and Poland, took positions at several French universities after his return in the early 1960s, gave several visiting courses and lectures at Berkeley in the 1970s, and held a chair in the History of Systems of Thought at the Collège de France in Paris from 1970 until his death), Foucault spent several years observing patients at, and researching the history of, French mental hospitals. His early books, *Madness and Civilization: A History of Insanity in the Age of Reason* (1961, trans. 1965) and *The Birth of the Clinic: An Archaeology of Medical Perception* (1963, revised 1972, trans. 1975), drew on that experience and research to construct a critique of psychology and medical practices and institutions in general. In subsequent work, Foucault extended this critique, arguing that other ostensibly "humane" social institutions and disciplines of knowledge in fact functioned as "technologies of power" that monitored, categorized, and normalized modern populations, pervasively conditioning individuals' experiences of their "own" identities. Foucault's best known and most important investigations into the history and problematics of the modern subject and its relations to discourses of power and knowledge include *The Order of Things: An Archaeology of the Human Sciences* (1966, trans. 1970), *The Archaeology of Knowledge and the Discourse on Language* (1969), trans. 1972), *Discipline and Punish: The Birth of the Prison* (1975, trans. 1977), *The History of Sexuality* (vol. 1, 1976, trans. 1978; and vols. 2 and 3, 1984, trans. 1986), and the essays collected in *Language, Counter-Memory, Practice: Selected Essays and Interviews* (1977) and *Power/Knowledge: Selected Interviews and Other Writings, 1972–1977* (1980).

NORTHROP FRYE (1912–1991)

The Canadian critic Northrop Frye (discussed in Chapters 3 and 6), studied English, philosophy, and theology in Toronto, was ordained a minister in the United Church of Canada in 1936, and subsequently took his graduate degree in English at Oxford. Frye's academic career was spent principally in Canada, where he held professorships first at Victoria University and then at the University of Toronto. His *Anatomy of Criticism: Four Essays* (1957), which remains one of the most influential works of literary criticism ever written, established a vocabulary, a method, and a precedent for the systematic analysis of imaginative structures, genres, and archetypes and for the theorization of Literature itself. This work also played a central role in the consolidation of literary study's claim to be an autonomous profession with a distinctive and empirically describable disciplinary object.

Frye's earliest literary interest and abiding inspirational figure was William Blake, from whom he once claimed he had learned everything he knew. In particular, Frye's work draws on Blake's topological interpretations of the Bible and adaptation of the Biblical myth of creation, fall, redemption, and apocalypse to the projects and products of secular imagination. For Frye, as Richard Stingle puts it, "the coherence of criticism and literature [are a function of] the mythology at the center of every society." Frye's criticism elaborately charts what he takes to be the central *mythoi* of Western culture as they inform its literary and religious history, linguistic modes, and structures of thought and desire. In addition to *Anatomy of Criticism*, Frye's major works include *Fearful Symmetry: A Study of William Blake* (1947), *The Educated Imagination* (1963), *Fables of Identity: Studies in Poetic Mythology* (1963), *The Critical Path:: An Essay on the Social Context of Literary Criticism* (1971), *Spiritus*

Mundi: Essays on Literature, Myth, and Society (1976), *The Secular Scripture: A Study of the Structure of Romance* (1976), *The Great Code: The Bible and Literature* (1981), *Words with Power: Being a Second Study of the Bible and Literature* (1990), and *The Double Vision: Language and Meaning in Religion* (1991).

HENRY LOUIS GATES, JR. (1950–)

Henry Louis Gates, Jr. (discussed in Chapter 7) is the most prominent contemporary academic critic of African American literature and culture. Educated at Yale and Cambridge Universities, Gates has taught English and African American Studies at Yale, Cornell, Duke, and Harvard. Gates's important books, *Figures in Black: Words, Signs, and the "Racial" Self* (1987) and *The Signifying Monkey* (1988), and the influential special issue of the journal *Critical Inquiry*, entitled *"Race," Writing, and Difference*, that he edited in 1986, met the challenge for the field of black literary criticism that Gates himself had set in an early essay, "Criticism in the Jungle" (1984): "to derive principles of literary criticism from the black tradition itself, as defined in the idiom of critical theory but also in the idiom which constitutes the 'language of blackness,' the signifyin(g) difference which makes the black tradition our very own." Bringing the "language of blackness" and the "idiom of critical theory" into dialectical relation, Gates's work helped establish black literary criticism as at once a distinctive social and cultural practice and a centrally disciplinary one, at once authentically "black" and authoritatively "literary critical."

Gates's labors as an editor, publicist, lecturer, and mentor have also been prodigious and synthetic. He has participated in the recovery and republication of numerous slave narratives and other little known or out-of-print works of African American literature; he has served as series editor of *The Schomburg Library of Nineteenth Century Black Women Writers* and has edited dozens of collections of critical essays on African American writers who, until recently, had been under-studied. Increasingly, too, Gates's work has addressed public issues and constituencies and sought to bring them into productive dialogue with literary and academic ones. His most recent books are *Colored People: A Memoir* (1994), *Loose Canons: Notes on the Culture Wars* (1992), and the edited collection *Reading Black, Reading Feminist* (1990).

STEPHEN GREENBLATT (1943–)

Stephen Greenblatt (discussed in Chapter 7) is a critic of English Renaissance literature who is best known as the developer and principal theorist–practitioner of the New Historicism, a politically and poststructurally conscious form of cultural history that first established itself around Greenblatt at Berkeley in the early 1980s. Greenblatt's own preferred term for his critical project, "cultural poetics," suggests a key premise of the New Historicism (which it shares with other recent critical theories and movements): that, at any historical moment, poetic practices form part of a network of social and cultural institutions, discourses, and beliefs and must be understood in relation to the other constitutive parts of the cultural network. New Historicism thus rejects formalist notions of literary autonomy but rejects as well the objectification of material history by older Marxist and positivist historicisms as either the determinative ground of literature, on the one hand, or its neutral referential background, on the other. Instead, New Historicists tend to see material and textual practices, politics and poetics, as reciprocally constitutive.

Early New Historicist readings of these dialectical relations focused principally on the Elizabethan and Jacobean periods, but in the last decade they have proliferated among Romanticists and Americanists as well. While Greenblatt has proclaimed and advocated its theoretical heterogeneity, the New Historicist project is significantly indebted to the cultural anthropology of Clifford Geertz and to Michel Foucault's theories of power and the discursive construction of the modern subject. For characterizations of New Historicism, see Greenblatt's introduction to the special issue of *Genre* on *The Forms of Power and the Power of Forms* (1982) and his 1989 essay "Towards a Poetics of Culture." Greenblatt's books include *Renaissance Self-Fashioning* (1980), *Shakespearean Negotiations: The Circulation of Social Energy in Renaissance England* (1988), *Learning to Curse: Essays in Early Modern Culture* (1990), and *Marvellous Possessions: The Wonder of the New World* (1991).

FREDRIC JAMESON (1934–)

Fredric Jameson is perhaps the foremost and certainly among the most prolific and wide-ranging American Marxist critics. His work in the 1980s and 1990s has been particularly important to literary and film studies, to studies of cultural imperialism, to debates over the meanings and effects of postmodernism, and to analyses of the symbolic and material forms of postindustrial multinational capitalism. While Jameson has flexibly responded to and incorporated a range of contemporary critical discourses, his abiding commitment to Marxist critical methodology and historical explanation has typically prompted him to suspect poststructuralist and postmodernist enthusiasm for fragmentation, disorientation, and linguistic play, and to disparage representations of language as funhouse or prison-house that are not historicized by the consideration of modes of production.

Jameson's most influential works of cultural and social theory include *Marxism and Form: Twentieth-Century Dialectical Theories of Literature* (1971), *The Prison-House of Language: A Critical Account of Structuralism and Russian Formalism* (1972), *Fables of Aggression: Wyndham Lewis, the Modernist as Fascist* (1979), *The Political Unconscious: Narrative as a Socially Symbolic Act* (1981), *Postmodernism, or the Cultural Logic of Late Capitalism* (1991), and *The Geopolitical Aesthetic: Cinema and Space in the World System* (1992). Jameson currently teaches at Duke University.

JULIA KRISTEVA (1941–)

Among French feminist critics, Julia Kristeva (discussed in Chapter 4) has most significantly influenced the study of language, gender, and culture in the American literary academy. A Bulgarian by birth, Kristeva moved to Paris in 1966 to finish a dissertation in French literature, studied structural linguistics, became a research assistant at Claude Lévi-Strauss's Laboratory of Social Anthropology, and, in the late 1970s, completed her training in psychoanalysis. As a professor of linguistics and social theory at the University of Paris VII and a practicing psychoanalyst, Kristeva shares with other prominent contemporary French intellectuals a resistance to disciplinary classification. Indeed, like Foucault and others, she has devoted significant critical energies to challenging the totalizing, normalizing, and rationalizing powers of the very discourses and disciplines within which she works.

Kristeva draws on the psychoanalytic theory of Jacques Lacan (whose revisionist reading of Freud understands the Oedipal resolution to be the child's acceptance of and entry into the patriarchal order of language) to link the excluded, marginalized, or suppressed "others" (poetry, the semiotic, the body, woman) of the orders of symbolic language, consciousness, and patriarchy. These others, however, in Kristeva's view, are not stable oppositional entities (*"woman as such* does not exist," she asserts) but disruptive positionalities beneath or at the edges of oppressive discourses of identity and, thus, potential vehicles of liberation. Kristeva explores these positions and potentialities in books such as *Revolution in Poetic Language* (1974, trans. 1984), *About Chinese Women* (1974, trans. 1977), *Desire in Language: A Semiotic Approach to Literature and Art* (1977, trans. 1980), *Powers of Horror: An Essay on Abjection* (1980, trans. 1982), *Language: the Unknown: An Initiation to Linguistics* (1981, trans. 1989), *In the Beginning Was Love: Psychoanalysis and Faith* (1985, trans. 1987), and *Strangers to Ourselves* (1989, trans. 1991), and the widely read essay "Women's Time" (1979, trans. 1981).

F. O. MATTHIESSEN (1902–1950)

F. O. Matthiessen (discussed in Chapter 3) is known principally as the author of the monumental *American Renaissance: Art and Expression in the Age of Emerson and Whitman* (1941), the book that established the modern canon of classical American writers and the principles of American literary canonicity that would inform American literary historiography until the feminist challenges of the 1970s. At once a committed 1930s socialist and an admirer of T. S. Eliot's formalist criticism, Matthiessen sought in *American Renaissance* to integrate sociopolitical and literary values (and argued that his five representative American writers pursued a similar synthesis). Though many later critics would argue that Matthiessen ultimately subordinated politics to aesthetics, Matthiessen's explicit insistence that the literary work of the American writer and critic advance democracy nonetheless defined a central and abiding problematic for his successors. Matthiessen's pedagogical influence, as professor of American history and literature at Harvard, was also enormous. His students included many of the important critics and theorists of American literature of the 1950s and 1960s: Leo Marx, Henry Nash Smith, R. W. B. Lewis, Quentin Anderson, Kenneth Lynn, Laurence Holland. Moreover, the lesbian feminist poet and activist Adrienne Rich recalled that Matthiessen's lectures "affected my life as a poet more than anything else that happened to me in college" and remembered Matthiessen as that "rare teacher of literature at Harvard who referred to a world beyond the text."

In addition to *American Renaissance*, Matthiessen's books include *The Achievement of T. S. Eliot: An Essay on the Nature of Poetry* (1935), *Henry James: The Major Phase* (1944), *From the Heart of Europe* (1948), and *Theodore Dreiser* (1951).

JOHN CROWE RANSOM (1888–1974)

John Crowe Ransom (discussed in Chapters 2 and 3) was a distinguished poet and literary critic who helped establish American academic criticism and both named and led its first dominant – and still, arguably, its most successful – movement: the New Criticism. Ransom was a Southerner who, in the 1930s, joined other conservative intellectuals in calling for the revival of agrarian and religious values to arrest the progress of industrialism and soulless instrumentalism in modern society and thought. With the failure of the Agrarian Revival movement, Ransom turned to literature and literary education as sites of resistance to the "devouring" abstraction and positivism that he associated with science and the rise of a technological and technocratic culture. Poetry, for Ransom, sustained the values of emotion, texture, and materiality – what Ransom called, in the title of his important 1938 collection of essays, "the world's body." And poetry required what he termed, in his 1941 book *The New Criticism*, an "ontological criticism." This criticism, an intimate exploration of the poem's distinctive and constitutive poetic properties and character, came to be known as "the New Criticism" and defined American literary study and literary pedagogy for more than a quarter century. Along with Allen Tate, Cleanth Brooks, Robert Penn Warren, R. P. Blackmur, and Rene Wellek, several of whom taught with Ransom at the University of the South, Vanderbilt University, or Kenyon College, or served with him on the advisory boards of such journals as the *Southern Review*, the *Sewanee Reivew*, and the *Kenyon Review*, Ransom shaped the early course of academic criticism and mass literary education in America.

Ransom's major critical works are *The World's Body* (1938), *The New Criticism* (1941), and *Selected Essays* (1984).

LILLIAN ROBINSON (1941–)

Lillian Robinson (discussed in Chapter 4), one of the foremothers of American feminist criticism, anticipated in her early essays many of the later critical issues and directions of academic feminist studies. A graduate student at Columbia in the late 1960s, Robinson became a civil rights and antiwar activist whose subsequent critical labors remained informed by a commitment to practical social change. Robinson's work linked feminist with Marxist critique, explored intersections of gender and class, rejected formalist, modernist, and Frankfurt School elevations of "autonomous" high art over popular and mass culture, and questioned the adequacy of an academic and literary feminist criticism to the larger social objectives and constituency of the women's movement well before these affiliations and concerns became prominent in feminist studies.

Robinson's influential early essays are collected in *Sex, Class, and Culture* (1978). She coauthored an examination of the interdisciplinary situation and possibilities of feminist criticism entitled *Feminist Scholarship: Kindling in the Groves of Academe* (1985). Significant recent essays include "Treason our Text: Feminist Challenges to the Literary Canon" (1984), "Canon Father and Myth Universe" (1987), "Feminist Criticism: How Do We Know When We've Won?" (1988), and "What Culture Should Mean" (1989). Robinson has taught at a number of universities, including the University of Hawaii, the University of Texas at Austin, and, currently, Virginia Polytechnic Institute.

EDWARD SAID (1935–)

Edward Said (discussed in Chapters 6 and 7) is one of the most prominent contemporary cultural critics and one of the few "public intellectuals" whose work and life successfully reconciles academic and textual studies with practical social and political action and influence. The title of Said's important collection of essays, *The World, The Text, and the Critic* (1983) implicitly privileges its first term and suggests a point that Said's work makes repeatedly: that "texts [and critics] . . . are in the world, and hence [must be] worldly." Said's sophisticated and eclectic criticism has made use of many contemporary discourses and methods but it has typically insisted on remaining "secular," in Said's term, skeptical of any single dogma or identity, and positioned in loose "affiliation" with various theories and constituencies rather than "filially" identifying with one.

The problem of sustaining the dialectic of personal, intellectual, and political involvement and detachment upon which, Said argues, a simultaneously worldly and oppositional criticism depends is central to Said's work. This dialectic, moreover, informs Said's personal history. A Palestinian Arab, Said studied in Jerusalem and Cairo before completing his education in (Western) humanities and comparative literature at Princeton and Harvard and, in 1963, becoming a professor at Columbia, where he still teaches. His first book, *Joseph Conrad and the Fiction of Autobiography* (1966), examines questions of identity, agency, and responsibility in the work of fellow non-native Anglophone and exile Joseph Conrad, questions to which his second book *Beginnings: Intention and Method* (1975) more systematically and panoramically returns. Between these two works, however, Israel had occupied and begun to settle Palestinian territories captured in the 1967 war, and Said had become involved as a critic, a public spokesperson, and a political actor in the Palestinian cause.

This involvement produced *The Question of Palestine* (1979) and *Covering Islam: How the Media and the Experts Determine How We See the Rest of the World* (1981) along with Said's many essays, lectures, and public dialogues on the history, politics, and cultures of the Middle East and their representations in the West. It also gave rise to *Orientalism* (1978), a brilliant, controversial, and ambitiously "worldly" synthesis of historical narrative, ideology critique, literary and cultural interpretation, and Foucauldian analysis of institutional and discursive power, and a book that marks a decisive – if not the inaugural – moment in the development of postcolonial criticism in the U.S. academy. More recently, Said has elaborated his thinking on "the general relationship between culture and empire" in *Culture and Imperialism* (1993). Said also remains a music critic for *The Nation* and is the author of the collection *Musical Elaborations* (1991).

GAYATRI CHAKRAVORTY SPIVAK (1942–)

Gayatri Chakravorty Spivak (discussed in Chapters 4, 6, and 7) is, along with Edward Said, one the foremost "postcolonial" critics and intercultural intellectuals in the American literary academy. A Bengali, born in Calcutta, Spivak received a degree in English from Presidency College in Calcutta before coming to the United States in 1962 to study comparative literature at Cornell. She has taught literature and cultural studies at a number of universities, including Emory, the University of Texas at Austin, and the University of Pittsburgh.

Spivak's unique contribution to academic criticism and theory proceeds from her ability and conscious effort to bring a number of critical discourses, "subject positions," and national languages, literatures, and cultures into reciprocally interrogative and illuminative relation. Self-consciously occupying the position, as Sarah Harasym describes it, of "highly commodified so-called Third World Marxist-feminist-deconstructionist critic working in the United States," Spivak cultivates a critical idiom and practice that explores the connections and contradictions among these elements of her own professional and political identity and material situation. Accordingly, her work has prompted and modelled critical engagements between gender and ethnic theory, between deconstruction and Marxism, between French, Anglo-American, and Indian analytical frames and cultural contexts, and between the institutional and ideological postionalities contained within United States academic postcolonial criticism.

Spivak's works include *Myself, I Must Remake: The Life and Poetry of W. B. Yeats* (1974), her introduction and English translation of Jacques Derrida's *Of Grammatology* (1976), and the essays on the politics of interpretation, Indian Subaltern Studies, French feminism, and deconstructive, postcolonial and Third World criticism collected in *In Other Worlds: Essays in Cultural Politics* (1989), *The Post-Colonial Critic: Interviews, Strategies, Dialogues* (1990), and *Outside In the Teaching Machine* (1992).

RAYMOND WILLIAMS (1921–1988)

Raymond Williams (discussed in Chapter 7) pioneered, exemplified, and helped institutionalize within British universities the interdisciplinary, materialist criticism that has come to be known as Cultural Studies. The son of a working-class Welsh family, Williams brought passionate political convictions and a commitment to practical social activism to bear on his literary studies at Cambridge. After teaching literature in Oxford University's extension program (the Department of External Studies) for fifteen years, Williams returned to Cambridge in 1961. Throughout the 1960s, he provided key intellectual and political support for the Centre for Contemporary Cultural Studies, established by Richard Hoggart in 1964 at the University of Birmingham, and was active in labor politics and the Campaign for Nuclear Disarmament, among other movements.

While Williams held the title of Professor of Drama at Cambridge, his prolific career as a critic and writer was breathtakingly interdisciplinary. His more than 650 publications include novels, plays, pamphlets, journalism, television criticism, and twenty seven academic books on social and economic history, criticism, fiction, drama, and communications theory. Most broadly, Williams's work may be said to have elaborated the socio-historical development of forms of communication and the contemporary relations of these forms to social institutions and political economies. His major works include *Culture and Society* (1958), *The Long Revolution: An Analysis of the Democratic, Industrial, and Cultural Changes Transforming Our Society* (1961, 1966), *Communications* (1962, 1976), *The Country and the City* (1973), *Television: Technology and Cultural Form* (1974), *Keywords: A Vocabulary of Culture and Society* (1976, 1983), *Marxism and Literature* (1977), *Politics and Letters: Interview with "New Left Review"* (1979), *Problems in Materialism and Culture: Selected Essays* (1980), *Culture* (1981), and *Towards* 2000 (1983).

CHRONOLOGY
1940–1995

Mary Anne Stewart Boelcskevy

CHRONOLOGY, 1940–1995

This chronology follows the narrative lines set out in this volume. In effect it brings together three different kinds of narrative: American Poetry, Americanist literary criticism, and literary criticism in America. The selection of texts was made entirely under the guidance of Evan Carton, Gerald Graff, and Robert von Hallberg, and I am grateful to them for their help at every stage. Under American Events and Other Events, the chronology traces matters of cultural significance, from both politics and the arts, as well as scientific developments and technological changes (e.g. in the fields of space and communications). For their assistance with the manuscript, I would like to acknowledge Stephanie Hawkins, Cyrus Patell, and Margaret Reid. For his continued generosity, Sacvan Bercovitch has my special gratitude. And finally, for their love and support: András Boelcskevy and our children, Anna and Steve.

Mary Anne Stewart Boelcskevy

	Texts	American Events	Other Events
1940	Hayden, Robert (1913–80), *Heart-Shape in the Dust* (poetry) McGrath, Thomas (1916–90), *First Manifesto* (poetry) Winters, [Arthur] Yvor (1900–68), *Poems*	Congress enacts law requiring registration of alien residents; five million aliens in U.S. Selective Service and Training Act signed, first peacetime military draft. Giant cyclotron at U. of Calif., production of mesotrons from atomic nuclei. Piet Mondrian arrives in New York. European composers move to U.S. (Schönberg, Stravinsky, Bartók, Hindemith, Krenek, Milhaud, Martinu, Weill, Toch, Kálmán, Benatzky, Abraham, Stolz, and Oskar Straus). Thirty million U.S. homes have radios. U.S. population, approx. 132 million.	World War II continues: German invasion of Denmark and Norway, Holland, Belgium, and Luxembourg; Churchill becomes British Prime Minister. Italy declares war on Great Britain and France; Marshal Pétain concludes armistice with Germany. Battle of Britain. British North Africa offensive. Trotsky assassinated in Mexico on Stalin's orders.
1941	Brooks, Van Wyck (1886–1963), *On Literature Today* (criticism) Burke, Kenneth (1897–1986), *The Philosophy of Literary Form: Studies in Symbolic Action* (criticism) Mathiessen, F[rancis] O[tto] (1902–50), *American Renaissance* (criticism)	President Roosevelt begins his third term. Lend-Lease Act signed, aid to Allies.	World War II continues: German U-boat warfare intensifes; German invasion of Russia. Roosevelt and Churchill draft Atlantic Charter. Pan-American Conference in Havana.

Ransom, John Crowe (1888–1974), *The New Criticism* (criticism)

Roethke, Theodore (1908–63), *Open House* (poetry)

Williams, William Carlos (1883–1963), *The Broken Span* (poetry)

Wilson, Edmund (1895–1972), *The Wound and the Bow: Seven Studies in Literature* (criticism)

1942 Berryman, John (1914–), *Poems*

Burnham, James (1905–87), *The Managerial Revolution* (nonfiction)

Cunningham, J[ames] V[incent] (1911–85), *The Helmsman* (poetry)

Kazin, Alfred (1915–), *On Native Grounds: An Interpretation of Modern American Prose Literature* (criticism)

Stevens, Wallace (1879–1955), *Notes Towards a Supreme Fiction; Parts of a World* (poetry)

Unlimited state of national emergency, Roosevelt orders freezing of all German and Italian U.S. assets and seizure of their vessels in American ports, closes German consulates.

U.S. Savings Bonds and Stamps go on sale.

Manhattan Project begins intensive atomic research.

Art of This Century, gallery of abstract and Surrealist art opens in New York.

National Gallery of Art opens in Washington, D.C.

Rationing of food, clothing, gasoline; rent freeze; air raid sirens installed; periodic blackout drills begun.

Congress votes conscription of males age eighteen years or older.

Japanese-Americans relocated to inland camps.

Enrico Fermi splits the atom.

Magnetic recording tape invented.

Joseph E. Widener collection of painting and sculpture presented to newly opened National Gallery of Art.

Pearl Harbor, the Philippines, Wake and Guam islands attacked by Japanese (Dec. 7).

U.S. and Britain declare war on Japan; Japan allies Germany and Italy declare war on U.S.; U.S. declares war on Germany and Italy.

World War II continues:

Quisling becomes Premier of Norway.

Japanese capture Singapore, Java, and Rangoon; British bomb Lübeck and Cologne.

Bataan Death March.

U.S. defeats Japanese at Midway.

Germans reach Stalingrad; battle of El Alamein.

British and Indian troops in Burma.

Murder of Jews in Nazi gas chambers begins.

Texts	American Events	Other Events
1943 **Abel, Darrel** (1911–), "Intellectual Criticism" **Eliot, T[homas] S[tearns]** (1888–1965), *Four Quartets* (poetry) **Winters, [Arthur] Yvor** (1900–68), *The Giant Weapon* (poetry); The Anatomy of Nonsense (criticism)	FBI captures eight Nazi spies and saboteurs landed in New York and Florida. Rationing of shoes, meat, cheese, fats, and all canned foods; wage, salary, and prices frozen to avert inflation. Race riots in Detroit and New York. Pentagon, world's largest office building, opens. Lessing J. Rosenwald collection of prints and drawings presented to National Gallery of Art. Epidemic of infantile polio. Zoot suit popular; lindy hop replaces jitterbugging as popular dance.	Gandhi demands independence for India. World War II continues: Roosevelt and Churchill at Casablanca Conference agree on goal of unconditional surrender; General Paulus surrenders at Stalingrad. RAF attack on Berlin. Massacre in Warsaw ghetto; German army surrenders in Tunisia. Allies land in Sicily, occupy Palermo; Mussolini dismissed; Marshal Badoglio takes over in Italy. Allies invade Italy; Italy's unconditional surrender Sept. 8; Italy declares war on Germany. U.S. forces regain Pacific islands. Teheran Conference, Churchill, Stalin, and Roosevelt. Allies begin round-the-clock bombing of Germany.
1944 **Lowell, Robert [Traill Spence, Jr.]** (1917–77), *Land of Unlikeness* (poetry) **Shapiro, Karl [Jay]** (1913–), *V-Letter and Other Poems* (Pulitzer)	Congress approves appointment of first five-star generals (Arnold, Eisenhower, MacArthur, Marshall) and admirals (King, Leahy, Nimitz).	World War II continues: bombing of Berlin. D-Day. U.S. captures Guam. UN established at Dumbarton Oaks.

| | | De Gaulle enters Paris; Brussels liberated. |

Williams, William Carlos (1883–1963), *The Wedge* (poetry)

1945 Burke, Kenneth (1897–1986), *A Grammar of Motives* (criticism)
Shapiro, Karl [Jay] (1913–), *Essay on Rime* (criticism)
Ebony founded by John Johnson.

Servicemen's Readjustment Act (G.I. Bill of Rights).
Uranium pile built at Clinton, Tenn.
New cyclotron completed at Washington.
Aaron Copeland's ballet *Appalachian Spring* performed by Martha Graham and her dancers in Washington, D.C.

President Roosevelt begins fourth term, dies April 12 in Warm Springs, Georgia; Harry S Truman inaugurated as thirty-third President.
Rationing of meat, butter, and other commodities ends.
First atomic bomb detonated July 16 near Alamogordo, New Mexico.
Point-contact transistor invented at Bell Telephone Laboratories.
Round-the-world airplane service begins.
Ezra Pound committed.
Igor Stravinsky becomes U.S. citizen.

De Gaulle enters Paris; Brussels liberated.
First V-1 (June) and V-2 (Sept.) launched against Britain.
Vietnam declares her independence from France under Ho Chi Minh.
World Bank (1946–) set up.

World War II continues: invasion of Germany.
Roosevelt, Churchill, Stalin at Yalta.
Incendiary bombing of Dresden, Tokyo, and other cities.
V-E Day, May 8, surrender signed in Berlin.
Fifty nations sign UN charter in San Francisco.
Truman, Attlee, and Stalin at Potsdam divide Germany and Berlin into four zones.
U.S. drops atomic bomb on Hiroshima and on Nagasaki; V-J Day, September 1.

American Events

Charlie Parker's bebop form of jazz becomes popular.

War dead estimated at forty-five million (including ten million in Nazi death camps).

Nuremberg trials of Nazi war criminals begin.

1946 **Bishop, Elizabeth** (1911–79), *North & South* (poetry)

Lowell, Robert [Traill Spence, Jr.] (1917–77), *Lord Weary's Castle* (Pulitzer for poetry)

Williams, William Carlos (1883–1963), *Paterson* (poetry, five volumes, 1946–58)

Atomic Energy Commission created.

John D. Rockefeller, Jr. donates $8.5 million for UN headquarters site in New York City.

Lea Act allows radio stations to continue use of recorded music rather than live musicians.

War Department announces "Eniac," first electronic computer.

Xerography process invented by Chester Carlson.

Telephone service installed on railroad trains.

League of Nations disbanded; assets assigned to UN.

International Court of Justice of the United Nations holds first session in The Hague.

Winston Churchill gives "Iron Curtain" speech at Fulton, Missouri.

Tribunal at Nuremberg delivers verdicts.

Albania and Transjordan, independent states; Hungary establishes republic.

Philippine independence from U.S.: The Republic of the Philippines.

Juan Péron elected President of Argentina.

War against French control of Indochina (1946–54).

1947 **Brooks, Cleanth** (1906–), *The Well Wrought Urn* (criticism)

Post of Secretary of Defense created, James Forrestal appointed.

Treaty of Rio, inter-American mutual defense.

Cunningham, J[ames] V[incent] (1911–85), *The Judge is Fury* (poetry)

Duncan, Robert [Edward] (1919–88), *Heavenly City, Earthly City* (poetry); "The Homosexual in Society" (essay)

Stevens, Wallace (1879–1955), *Transport to Summer* (poetry)

Wilbur, Richard [Purdy] (1921–), *The Beautiful Changes* (poetry)

Winters, [Arthur] Yvor (1900–68), *In Defense of Reason* (criticism)

1948 Auden, W[ystan] H[ugh] (1907–73), *Age of Anxiety: A Baroque Eclogue* (poetry)

Berryman, John (1914–), *The Dispossessed* (poetry)

Hofstadter, Richard (1916–70), *American Political Tradition and the Men Who Made It* (history).

Hyman, Stanley Edgar (1919–70), *The Armed Vision: A Study in the Methods of Modern Literary Criticism* (criticism)

Pound, Ezra [Weston Loomis] (1885–1972), *Pisan Cantos* (poetry)

Roethke, Theodore (1908–63), *The Lost Son* (poetry)

Spiller, Robert (1896–1988), ed., *The Literary History of the United States*

Committee on Un-American Activities investigates government employees and Hollywood creative community.

Taft–Hartley Labor Act, restricting power of organized labor, passed over Truman's veto.

Bell Telephone Laboratories invent junction transistor.

Polaroid Land camera introduced.

Jackie Robinson becomes first African American to play in a major league (Brooklyn Dodgers).

Marshall Plan (Economic Co-Operation Administration) authorizes $5.3 billion in relief for Europe.

General Motors–United Auto Workers contract contains first escalator clause tying wage increases to cost-of-living.

Federal rent control bill passed.

52,000 World War I veterans march down Fifth Avenue in New York as part of the annual American Legion Convention.

Selective Service Act continues military draft (until 1973).

British establish atomic reactor at Harwell.

Palestine partitioned; Jewish state of Israel established (1947–8).

India, Pakistan, Burma, and Ceylon (Sri Lanka) gain independence from Britain.

Indo-Pakistan Wars (1947–9).

Greek Civil War (1947–9).

Republic established in Bulgaria.

Pablo Casals vows not to play in public while Franco remains in power.

Organization of American States.

Hague Congress for European Unity.

World Council of Churches organized.

World Jewish Congress in Montreux.

First World Health Assembly, in Geneva.

Gandhi assassinated.

Communist coup in Czechoslovakia.

U.S.S.R. blockade of Berlin (1948–9).

Arab–Israeli War.

Chiang Kai-shek reelected President of China.

Texts	American Events	Other Events
Tate, J[ohn Orley] Allen (1899–1979), *On the Limits of Poetry* (criticism) Bollingen Prize in Poetry established.	Peter Goldmark invents long-playing record. First telecasts of opera (NBC) and major symphony orchestras (CBS; NBC).	Communist Party seizes control in Hungary.
1949 Eliot, T[homas] S[tearns] (1888–1965), *Notes Towards the Definition of Culture* (criticism) McGrath, Thomas (1916–90), *Longshot O'Leary's Garland of Practical Poesie* (poetry) Rahv, Philip (1908–73), *Image and Idea: Essays on Literary Themes* (criticism) Warren, Austin (1899–1986), **and Rene Wellek** (1903–89), *Theory of Literature* (criticism) Bollingen Prize to Ezra Pound	Truman begins second term as President; first televised inaugurals. Airlift to Berlin. Eleven U.S. Communist Party leaders convicted of conspiracy. Wesley Brown first African American graduate of Annapolis. U.S. test launch of guided missile achieves altitude of 250 miles. Vaudeville returns to New York's Palace Theater. First televised charity fund raiser, *The Damon Runyon Memorial Fund.* Samba becomes fashionable.	U.S.S.R. tests its first atomic bomb, ending U.S. nuclear monopoly. German Federal Republic established, Bonn as capital. Republic of Eire proclaimed in Dublin. NATO and Warsaw Pact established. Apartheid begins in South Africa. People's Republic proclaimed in Hungary. Israel admitted to UN. Vietnam state established at Saigon. Dutch grant independence to Indonesia. Communist Party led by Mao Tse-tung takes control in China; Communist People's Republic proclaimed with Chou En-Lai as Premier.

1950 **Brooks, Cleanth** (1906–), **and Robert Penn Warren** (1905–1989), *Understanding Poetry* (textbook, orig. 1938)

Burke, Kenneth (1897–1986), *A Rhetoric of Motives* (criticism)

Duncan, Robert [Edward] (1919–88), *Medieval Scenes* (poetry)

Smith, Henry Nash (1906–86), *Virgin Land: The American West as Symbol and Myth* (criticism)

Trilling, Lionel (1905–75), *Liberal Imagination* (criticism)

Wilbur, Richard [Purdy] (1921–), *Ceremony* (poetry)

National Book Awards founded.

Bollingen Prize to Wallace Stevens.

Internal Security Act passed over presidential veto.

Alger Hiss sentenced for perjury.

Senate Kefauver Committee investigates organized interstate crime.

Assassination attempt on Truman by two Puerto Rican nationalists.

Julius and Ethel Rosenberg arrested.

UN Building in New York completed.

National Council of the Churches of Christ organized.

Bebop experiments develop cool jazz, hard bop, and soul jazz.

Abstract Expressionism develops split: action painting and chromatic abstraction.

Credit cards, in use in U.S. since 1930s, come into widespread use in 1950s.

Miltown in wide use as tranquilizer.

1.5 million TV sets in U.S.

U.S. population 150,697,999.

Oder-Neisse line declared border of Poland and East Germany.

Korean War (1950–3) begins: UN sends troops and support to South Korea; U.S. proclaims state of emergency.

Indonesia admitted to UN.

Communist China recognized by Britain.

Vietnam recognized by U.S.

European Broadcasting Union formed.

Antiapartheid riots in Johannesburg, South Africa.

Israel recognized by Britain.

Pope Pius XII proclaims dogma of bodily assumption of Virgin Mary.

1951 **Lowell, Robert [Traill Spence, Jr.]** (1917–77), *The Mills of the Kavanaughs* (poetry)

Merrill, James [Ingram] (1926–), *First Poems*

Rich, Adrienne [Cecile] (1931–), *A Change of World* (poetry)

Signing of peace treaty with Japan.

Mutual defense pact with Australia and New Zealand.

Twenty-second Amendment limits President to two terms.

Korean War continues; American truce efforts at Panmunjom fail.

Coalition government formed in Israel after Ben-Gurion's government is dissolved.

	Texts	American Events	Other Events
	Roethke, Theodore (1908–63), *Praise to the End!* (poetry)	Truman relieves MacArthur of Far East command.	King Abdullah of Jordan assassinated in Jerusalem.
	Bollingen Prize to John Crowe Ransom.	Electric power produced from atomic energy, Arcon, Idaho.	Purge of Communist Party in Czechoslovakia.
		Lake Shore Drive Apartments, designed by Ludwig Mies van der Rohe.	Juan Péron reelected President of Argentina.
		Approx. 15 million TV sets in U.S. CBS airs first commercial color television broadcast.	Foundation stone laid for British National Theatre in London.
		Live TV coverage of Kefauver Crime Commission hearings, Truman's Japan Peace Treaty speech.	
1952	**Blackmur, R[ichard] P.** (1904–65), *Language as Gesture: Essays in Poetry* (criticism)	U.S. H-bomb tests in Pacific.	U.S., Britain, and France sign peace treaty with West Germany.
	Creeley, Robert [White] (1926–), *Le Fou* (poetry)	Richard Nixon gives "Checkers" speech.	Puerto Rico becomes first U.S. commonwealth.
	Davie, Donald (1922–), *Purity of Diction in English Verse* (criticism)	First telecasts of national conventions.	British have atomic bomb.
	Mathiessen, F[rancis] O[tto] (1902–50), *Responsibilities of the Critic* (criticism)	Declaration of Independence and Constitution moved to National Archives.	Anti-British riots in Egypt; Gen. Mohammed Naguib forms government; 1923 constitution abolished.
	O'Hara, Frank (1926–66), *A City Winter* (poetry)	Supreme Court rules radio broadcasts on public buses not an invasion of privacy.	Prince Hussein Ibn Talal proclaimed King of Jordan.
	Revised Standard Version of Bible.	G.I. Bill extended to Korean War veterans.	West Germany becomes member of World Bank.
	Bollingen Prize to Marianne Moore.		

482

King George VI of England dies; Elizabeth II succeeds to throne.

Cinerama, originally the Waller Flexible Gunnery Trainer in WWII, brought to movie theaters.

Lever House, New York City, completed.

Korean armistice at Panmunjom.

U.S.S.R. explodes H-bomb.

Stalin dies (born 1879).

Republic proclaimed in Egypt.

Yugoslavia proclaims new constitution; Marshal Tito elected President.

Eisenhower inaugurated as thirty-fourth President.

Earl Warren appointed to Supreme Court as Chief Justice (1953–69).

Congress creates new post, Secretary of Health, Education, and Welfare.

Vietnamese rebels attack Laos.

First global census by UN: 2.4 billion.

Ex-President Truman rejects attempt by the House Un-American Activities Committee to subpoena him as invasion of Presidential powers.

New Zealander Edmund Hillary and Sherpa guide Tensing Norkay scale Mount Everest.

Eisenhower issues executive order barring homosexuals from all federal jobs.

American James Dewey Watson and British Frances H. C. Crick find structure of DNA.

RCA "compatible" color television prevails when CBS withdraws its process.

1953 **Abrams, M. H.** (1912–), *The Mirror and the Lamp: Romantic Theory and the Critical Tradition* (criticism)

Ashbery, John [Lawrence] (1927–), *Turandot and Other Poems* (poetry)

Creeley, Robert [White] (1926–), *The Kind of Act of; The Immoral Proposition* (poetry)

De Beauvoir, Simone (1908–), *The Second Sex* (orig. 1949; trans. H. M. Parshley)

Feidelson, Charles (?–), *Symbolism and American Literature* (criticism)

Jarrell, Randall (1914–65), *Poetry and The Age* (criticism)

Miller, Perry (1905–63), *The New England Mind, From Colony to Province* (criticism)

Olson, Charles (1910–70), *In Cold Hell, in Thicket; The Maximus Poems 1–10* (poetry)

Roethke, Theodore (1908–63), *The Waking* (Pulitzer for poetry)

Bollingen Prize to Archibald MacLeish and William Carlos Williams.

	Texts	American Events	Other Events
1954	**Gunn, Thom** (1929–), *Fighting Terms: Poems* (poetry) **Hecht, Anthony [Evan]** (1923–), *A Summoning of Stones* (poetry) **Stevens, Wallace** (1879–1955), *Collected Poems* **Williams, William Carlos** (1883–1963), *The Desert Music* (poetry); *Selected Essays* Robert Creeley, editor (1954–7) of *The Black Mountain Review* Bollingen Prize to W. H. Auden.	Brown v. Topeka Board of Education overturns Plessy v. Ferguson. Five Congressmen wounded by Puerto Rican Nationalists firing from gallery in House of Representatives. Communist Control Act. U.S. offers Japan $800,000 indemnity for nationals harmed during thermonuclear testing at Pacific Proving Grounds. Live TV coverage of Army–McCarthy hearings; in Dec., Senate censures Senator McCarthy. *Nautilus*, first atom-powered submarine. Salk anti-polio vaccine. The words "under God" are added to the Pledge of Allegiance. First annual Newport Jazz Festival. Perez Prado's mambo gains popularity. Twenty-nine million U.S. homes have TV sets.	Berlin meeting of British, French, U.S., and U.S.S.R. foreign ministers; Russians reject German reunification. Civil War in Algeria (1954–62) leads to French withdrawal. In Egypt, Colonel Nasser becomes premier and head of state. Indochina armistice; Communists occupy Hanoi. SEATO established. Burma–Japan treaty. U.S.–Japan defense agreement. Eurovision network formed.
1955	**Davie, Donald** (1922–), *Brides of Reason* (poetry); *Articulate Energy: An Inquiry into The Syntax of English Poetry* (criticism)	U.S. Air Force Academy opens. AFL and CIO merge under George Meany.	Perón resigns as President of Argentina.

Fiedler, Leslie (1917–), *An End to Innocence: Essays on Culture and Politics* (criticism)

Lewis, R[ichard] W[arrington] B[aldwin] (1917–), *The American Adam Innocence, Tragedy, and Tradition in the Nineteenth Century* (criticism)

Rich, Adrienne [Cecile] (1931–), *The Diamond Cutters and Other Poems* (poetry)

Bollingen Prize to Leonie Adams and Louise Bogan.

Emmett Till lynched while visiting Mississippi.

Boycott of Montgomery, Alabama segregated bus lines follows arrest of Rosa Parks for refusing to give up her seat to a white man.

"The New Decade" New York Exhibition of Modern Art.

Charlie "Bird" Parker dies (born 1920).

Anthony Eden elected British prime minister.

Germany joins NATO.

Gronchi elected President of Italy.

Vienna Treaty restores Austria's independence.

Universal Copyright Convention takes effect.

UN draws up international principles and standards of criminal justice.

1956   Ashbery, John [Lawrence] (1927–), *Some Trees* (poetry)

Berryman, John (1914–), *Homage To Mistress Bradstreet* (ode)

Bowers, Edgar (1924–), *The Form of Loss* (poetry)

Ginsberg, Allen (1926–), *Howl and Other Poems* (poetry)

Krieger, Murray (1923–), *The New Apologists for Poetry* (criticism)

Miller, Perry (1905–63), *Errand Into the Wilderness* (criticism)

Olson, Charles (1910–70), *The Maximus Poems*

11–23

Senate rejects proposal to change electoral system to nationwide popular elections.

July strike of steelworkers affects ninety percent of country's steel output.

AAUP censures eight institutions of higher learning for violation of academic freedom over loyalty oath.

New York Coliseum opens.

Transatlantic cable telephone service.

Neutrino produced at Los Alamos Labs.

Sabin oral polio vaccine.

Ampex Corporation markets first video recorder.

Nasser elected President of Egypt.

Egyptian takeover of Suez Canal leads to Israeli invasion and British–French occupation of Canal.

Khrushchev denounces Stalin.

Soviets march into Hungary after widespread demonstrations; U.S.S.R. censured by UN General Assembly.

Japan admitted to UN.

Pakistan becomes Islamic Republic.

Sudan proclaimed independent democratic republic.

American Events   Other Events

Wilbur, Richard [Purdy] (1921–), *Things of This World* (poetry)

Bollingen Prize to Conrad Aiken.

1957   **Chase, Richard** (1904–88), *The American Novel and Its Tradition* (criticism)

Cunningham, J[ames] V[incent] (1911–85), *Trivial, Vulgar and Exalted: Epigrams* (poetry)

Eliot, T[homas] S[tearns] (1888–1965), *On Poetry and Poets* (criticism)

Frye, Northrop (1912–), *Anatomy of Criticism* (criticism)

Gunn, Thom (1929–), *The Sense of Movement* (poetry)

Hall, Donald (1928–), **Robert Pack** (1929–), **Louis Simpson** (1923–), eds., *New Poets of England and America* (anthology)

Howe, Irving (1920–), *Politics and the Novel* (criticism)

Winters, [Arthur] Yvor (1900–68), *The Function of Criticism: Problems and Exercises* (criticism)

Bollingen Prize to Allen Tate.

1958   **Artaud, Antonin** (1896–1948), *The Theatre and Its Double* (orig. 1938; trans. Mary Caroline Richards)

Hoggart, Richard (1918–), *The Uses of Literacy* (criticism)

American Events (1957):

Eisenhower begins second term.

Southern Christian Leadership Conference organized by Dr. Martin Luther King, Jr.

Harry S Truman Library in Independence, Mo. dedicated and presented to federal government.

Eisenhower Doctrine, protection of Middle East from Communist aggression.

Federal troops sent into Little Rock after Arkansas Governor Orval Faubus calls out National Guard to oppose desegregation.

New words: "beat," "beatnik," and "angry young man."

American Events (1958):

Vice President Nixon on South American goodwill tour.

Congress passes National Defense Education Act.

Other Events (1957):

Treaty of Rome establishes European Economic Community (EEC/Common Market).

International Atomic Energy Agency.

U.S.S.R. launches *Sputnik I*, first satellite in orbit around earth.

Eden succeeded by Macmillan as Prime Minister of Great Britain.

British explode thermonuclear bomb.

Castro leads Cuba uprising against Batista.

Israel withdraws from Sinai Peninsula; UN reopens Suez Canal.

Ghana receives its independence from Britain.

Vietnam War (1957–73).

Other Events (1958):

In Cuba, Fidel Castro begins total war against Batista government.

West Indies federation.

Hollander, John (1929–), A Crackling of Thorns (poetry)

Roethke, Theodore (1908–63), Words for the Wind (poetry, Bollingen)

Bollingen Prize to e e cummings.

1959 de Saussure, Ferdinand (1857–1913), Course in General Linguistics (orig. 1916; trans. Wade Baskin)

Jung, Carl (1875–1961), Archetypes and the Collective Unconscious (trans. R. F. C. Hull)

Lowell, Robert [Traill Spence, Jr.] (1917–77), Life Studies (poetry)

Merrill, James [Ingram] (1926–), The Country of a Thousand Years of Peace (poetry)

Rosenberg, Harold (1906–78), The Tradition of the New (criticism)

Snodgrass, W[illiam] D[ewitt] (1926–), Heart's Needle (poetry)

Bollingen Prize to Theodore Roethke.

Unemployment reaches almost 5.2 million.

U.S. launches Explorer I.

National Aeronautics and Space Administration (NASA) established.

Seagram Building, New York.

Guggenheim Museum, designed by Frank Lloyd Wright, opens.

"New American Painting" exhibition tours Europe (1958–9).

Quiz shows scandal.

Cha Cha Cha popular dance.

St. Lawrence Seaway opens.

Eisenhower invokes Taft–Hartley Act to end steelworkers' and longshoremen's strikes.

Alaska becomes forty-ninth state, Hawaii fiftieth.

Eisenhower visits nine European, Middle East, and African countries (Dec. 3–22).

Castro on goodwill tour of U.S.

Khrushchev on U.S. visit.

U.S.–Soviet cultural exchange, New York Coliseum and Moscow Sokolniki Park exhibitions.

Khrushchev elected USSR Premier; visits Peking.

In France, De Gaulle elected President of new government.

United Arab Republic formed by Egypt and Syria under President Nasser.

Ayub Khan becomes Prime Minister of Pakistan.

Imre Nagy executed in Hungary after secret trial.

Cuban president Batista flees to Dominican Republic; Fidel Castro becomes Premier of Cuba, expropriates U.S.-owned sugar mills.

Western Summit Conference in Paris.

Anti-U.S. demonstrations in Panama.

Hutu revolt topples Tutsi monarchy in Rwanda; 150,000 in exile in Uganda.

UN adopts Declaration of the Rights of the Child.

Texts	American Events	Other Events
	First U.S. nuclear-powered merchant vessel, *Savannah*, launched; *George Washington*, first ballistic-missile submarine; *Long Beach*, first nuclear-powered surface vessel. Modal jazz debuts in *Kind of Blue* with Miles Davis, John Coltrane, Bill Evans.	Breshnev becomes President of U.S.S.R. Neo-Nazi political groups banned in West Germany. French African colonies become independent. Iran, Iraq, Kuwait, Libya, Saudi Arabia, and Venezuela form OPEC; Arab nations form OAPEC. Belgian Congo granted full independence. Anti-U.S. demonstrations in Japan. China shells Quemoy and Formosa. Cyprus becomes independent republic; Archbishop Makarios president.
1960 Allen, Donald Merriam (1912–), *The New American Poetry: 1945–1960* (anthology) Bell, Daniel (1919–) *The End of Ideology* (sociology) Cunningham, J[ames] V[incent] (1911–85), *Tradition and Poetic Structure* (criticism) Duncan, Robert [Edward] (1919–88), *The Opening of the Field* (poetry) Fiedler, Leslie (1917–), *Love and Death in the American Novel* (criticism) Olson, Charles (1910–70), *The Maximus Poems 1–23*; *The Distances* (poetry) Plath, Sylvia (1932–63), *The Colossus* (poetry) Williams, Raymond (1921–88), *Culture and Society, 1780–1950* (criticism) Bollingen Prize to Delmore Schwartz.	U.S. protests Cuban expropriations. Eisenhower visits Puerto Rico, Brazil, Argentina, Chile, Uruguay, South Korea, the Philippines, Formosa, and Okinawa. Downing of U-2 airplane of Gary Powers over U.S.S.R. makes public U.S. Aerial reconnaissance flights. First sit-ins staged by students of North Carolina A&T University. Nixon and Kennedy debates telecast. U.S. Post Office ban on *Lady Chatterley's Lover* declared unconstitutional. Pop art and "post-painterly abstraction" emerge as new art movements.	

Paul de Man at Cornell (1960–7).

Hughes Aircraft announces first laser.

FDA approves marketing of birth control pill.

TV sets number 85 million.

Population: 179,323,000.

U.S. breaks off diplomatic relations with Cuba and Dominican Republic.

In farewell address, Eisenhower warns of "military-industrial complex".

John F. Kennedy inaugurated as thirty-fifty President.

Bay of Pigs invasion attempt fails.

Freedom Riders on interstate buses into Deep South; U.S. marshals ordered in to curb violence.

Four American airliners are hijacked.

Rafael Trujillo, dictator of Dominican Republic, assassinated; U.S. show of force supports Balaguer over Trujillo family.

UN General Assembly condemns apartheid.

Qatar joins OPEC.

Berlin Wall constructed.

Yuri Gagarin (U.S.S.R.) becomes first man to orbit the earth (April 13).

U.S.S.R. resumes nuclear testing.

Escaped Nazi Eichmann found guilty of war crimes in Jerusalem trial.

Museum of Chinese Revolution opened in Peking.

Republic of South Africa declared after Union of South Africa withdraws from British Commonwealth.

1961   **Aaron, Daniel** (1912–), *Writers on the Left: Episodes in American Literary Communism* (criticism)

Booth, Wayne C[layson] (1921–), *The Rhetoric of Fiction* (criticism)

Dugan, Alan (1923–), *Poems* (poetry)

Hollander, John (1929–), *The Untuning of the Sky: Ideas of Music in English Poetry, 1500–1700* (criticism)

Jones, LeRoi [Imamu Amiri Baraka] (1934–), *Preface to a Twenty Volume Suicide Note* (poetry)

Lowell, Robert [Traill Spence, Jr.] (1917–77), *Imitations* (translations)

Roethke, Theodore (1908–63), *I Am! Says the Lamb* (poetry)

Wilbur, Richard [Purdy] (1921–), *Advice to a Prophet* (poetry)

Williams, Raymond (1921–88), *The Long Revolution* (criticism)

Bollingen Prize to Ivor Winters.

Texts	American Events	Other Events
1962 Ashbery, John [Lawrence] (1927–), *The Tennis Court Oath* (poetry)	Cuban missile crisis, October 22–28.	OAS lifts sanctions against Dominican Republic; Baraguer resigns; Bonnelly interim president; Juan Bosch elected in Dec.
Austin, J. L. (1911–60), *How to Do Things With Words* (philosophy)	Federal troops ordered James Meredith as he enters the University of Mississippi.	Assassination attempt on DeGaulle.
Bly, Robert [Elwood] (1926–), *Silence in the Snowy Fields* (poetry)	U-2 pilot Powers traded for Soviet spy Abel.	Uganda and Tanganyika become independent.
Creeley, Robert [White] (1926–), *For Love* (poetry)	AT&T's Telstar communications satellite.	U.S. military command in South Vietnam.
Hall, Donald (1928–), ed., *Contemporary American Poetry* (anthology)	John Glenn's first orbital space flight telecast.	Indonesia joins OPEC.
Hayden, Robert (1913–80), *A Ballad of Remembrance* (poetry)	Thalidomide causes birth defects.	Eichmann hanged.
Hollander, John (1929–), *Movie-Going* (poetry)	*Mariner II*, Venus probe. *Titan II*.	Pope John XXIII opens the Twenty-first Ecumenical Council in Rome.
Kuhn, Thomas (1922–), *The Structure of Scientific Revolution* (history of science)	*Minute Man I*; *Polaris I*, first SLBM.	Border clashes on Indian–Chinese border.
Merrill, James [Ingram] (1926–), *Water Street* (poetry)		
Oppen, George (1908–84), *The Materials* (poetry)		
Walcott, Derek Alton (1930–), *In a Green Night: Poems 1948–1960* (poetry)		
Bollingen Prize to John Hall Wheelock and Richard Eberhart.		
1963 Bowers, Edgar (1924–), *The Astronomers* (poetry)	Kennedy calls out 3,000 troops to protect civil rights demonstraters in Birmingham, Alabama.	Nuclear test ban treaty signed by U.S., Great Britain, and U.S.S.R.
Friedan, Betty (1921–), *The Feminine Mystique* (nonfiction)		

Jones, LeRoi [Imamu Amiri Baraka] (1934–), *Blues People: Negro Music in White America* (criticism)

Levine, Philip (1928–), *On the Edge* (orig. limited 1961; poetry)

Lukács, Gyorgy (1885–1971), *The Meaning of Contemporary Realism* (trans. John and Necke Mander)

Merwin, W[illiam] S[tanley] (1927–), *The Moving Target* (poetry)

Plath, Sylvia (1932–63), *The Bell Jar*

Rich, Adrienne [Cecile] (1931–), *Snapshots of a Daughter-in-Law* (poetry)

New York Review of Books founded during printers' strike against New York newspapers.

Bollingen Prize to Robert Frost.

1964 Berryman, John (1914–), *77 Dream Songs* (poetry)

Davie, Donald (1922–), *Events and Wisdoms: Poems 1957–1963* (poetry)

Duncan, Robert [Edward] (1919–88), *Roots and Branches* (poetry)

Jones, LeRoi [Imamu Amiri Baraka] (1934–), *The Dead Lecturer* (poetry)

John F. Kennedy assassinated in Dallas, Texas.

Lyndon B. Johnson sworn in as President.

During live news telecast: alleged assassin Lee Harvey Oswald shot and killed by Jack Ruby.

Medgar Evers assassinated.

Martin Luther King gives his "I Have a Dream" speech to more than 250,000 at March on Washington.

Bomb explodes in Birmingham church killing four African American children.

Equal Pay Act.

King wins Nobel Prize for Peace.

Civil Rights Act of 1964 passed.

Race riots in many U.S. cities against enforcement of civil rights laws.

Twenty-fourth Amendment, bans poll tax.

Warren Commission report concludes Oswald acted alone.

Britain rejected by EEC/Common Market.

Military coup deposes President Bosch of Dominican Republic.

The Organization of African Unity (OAU) founded.

Iraq and Yemen join United Arab Republic.

South Vietnamese President Ngo Dinh Diem killed in military coup.

Second Vatican Council, changes include move from Latin to vernacular in Roman Catholic Mass.

Pope John XXIII dies; succeeded by Pope Paul VI.

Kosygin replaces Khrushchev as Prime Minister; Breshnev becomes Party Secretary.

African National Congress leader Nelson Mandela imprisoned for sabotage.

Walcott, Derek Alton (1930–), *The Castaway, and Other Poems* (poetry)

Bollingen Prize to Horace Gregory.

1966 Ashbery, John [Lawrence] (1927–), *Rivers and Mountains* (poetry)

Cassity, Turner (1929–), *Watchboy, What of the Night?* (poetry)

Dorn, Ed[ward] Merton] (1929–), *Geography* (poetry)

Duncan, Robert [Edward] (1919–88), *The Years as Catches* (poetry)

Heimert, Alan (1928–), *Religion and The American Mind, From the Great Awakening to the Revolution* (criticism)

Jones, LeRoi [Imamu Amiri Baraka] (1934–), *Home: Social Essays*

Merrill, James [Ingram] (1926–), *Nights and Days* (poetry)

Plath, Sylvia (1932–63), *Ariel* (poetry)

Poirier, Richard (1925–), *A World Elsewhere: The Place of Style in American Literature* (criticism)

Rich, Adrienne [Cecile] (1931–), *Necessities of Life* (poetry)

Snyder, Gary [Sherman] (1930–), *A Range of Poems* (poetry)

Sontag, Susan (1933–), *Against Interpretation* (criticism)

Miranda vs. Arizona, suspects must be informed of Constitutional rights against self-incrimination.

U.S. B-52 crashes near coast of Spain, drops four unarmed H-bombs.

Rioting in Chicago and Cleveland (July).

Black Panther Party founded in Oakland, California by Huey Newton and Bobby Seale.

Maulana Karenga founds U.S. human rights organization.

NOW (National Organization of Women) formed.

Surveyor I makes soft landing on moon; Aldrin on spacewalk from *Gemini 12*.

Minute Man II.

Abstention from meat on Fridays, except during Lent, lifted for U.S. Catholics.

Cultural Revolution in China under Mao Tse-tung (1966–69).

U.S.S.R. *Luna I* makes landing on moon.

Vorster named Prime Minister of South Africa.

Indira Gandhi becomes Prime Minister of India.

Kiesinger elected West German Chancellor.

British Guiana becomes independent nation of Guyana.

Israeli–Jordanian clash over Hebron.

	Texts	American Events	Other Events
1967	Bly, Robert [Elwood] (1926–), *The Light Around the Body* (poetry) Creeley, Robert [White] (1926–), *Words* (poetry) Dorn, Ed[ward Merton] (1929–), *North Atlantic Turbine* (poetry) Hecht, Anthony [Evan] (1923–), *The Hard Hours* (Pulitzer for poetry) Hirsch, E. D. (1928–), *Validity in Interpretation* (criticism) Johnson, Ronald (1935–), *Book of the Green Man* (poetry) Kermode, Frank (1919–), *The Sense of an Ending: Studies in the Theory of Fiction* (criticism) Lowell, Robert [Traill Spence, Jr.] (1917–77), *Near the Ocean* (poems and translations) Merwin, W[illiam] S[tanley] (1927–), *The Lice* (poetry) Bollingen Prize to Robert Penn Warren.	Thurgood Marshall appointed to Supreme Court, first African American. Twenty-fifth Amendment ratified, provides for appointment of vice president and acting president. Executive Order 11375, prohibits discrimination in federal contracts. Black Power conference, Newark, N.J. Close to 500,000 protest war at Lincoln Memorial. Anti-Vietnam War marches in New York and San Francisco. Race riots in Cleveland, Newark, Detroit. Synthetic DNA produced at Stanford. U.S. manned space flights suspended after astronauts Grissom, White, and Chaffee are killed in launching pad fire. CBS and NBC cover Super Bowl I.	Nguyen Van Thieu and Nguyen Cao Ky elected President and Vice President of South Vietnam. Che Guevara captured and killed by Bolivian army. Tanker *Torrey Canyon* runs aground, spills oil, polluting coast of SW Britain and Normandy. Six Day Arab–Israeli War; Israel gains control of the Sinai Peninsula. PLO organized under leadership of Yasser Arafat. People's Republic of China explodes its first H-bomb. Abu Dhabi and the United Arab Emirates join OPEC.
1968	Benjamin, Walter (1892–1940), *Illuminations* (orig. 1955; trans. Harry Zohn)	My Lai massacre (March 16). Martin Luther King, Jr. assassinated.	Great Britain restricts immigration from India, Pakistan, and the West Indies.

494

Dubcek becomes First Secretary of Czechoslovak Communist Party; issues "Action Program".

Student rioting in France, West Germany, Poland, Czechoslovakia, and Japan.

Israelis and UAR agree to exchange prisoners of war.

Saddam Hussein comes to power in Iraq.

Mauritius becomes independent state within Commonwealth.

Tet offensive, Communist air strikes.

Russian troops invade Czechoslovakia.

Czech refugees enter Austria.

Aswan Dam in Egypt completed.

Separatist Parti Québecois formed.

Robert Kennedy assassinated.

Widespread demonstrations; students occupy Columbia University buildings.

SAC B-52 crashes in Greenland, four unexploded hydrogen bombs spread radioactive material over wide area.

USS *Pueblo* seized in Jan. in Sea of Japan; eighty-three man crew released in Dec.

Violence inside Democratic Convention and on streets of Chicago.

Shirley Chisholm elected to House of Representatives, first African American female to hold that office.

WEAL (Women's Equality Action League) founded.

U.S. underground test of H-bomb.

New communications satellite, *Intelstat 3A* launched.

Three-man crew in *Apollo 8* orbits moon.

Yale announces it will admit women.

Pope Paul's *Humanae Vitae* proscribes artificial contraception.

Duncan, Robert [Edward] (1919–88), *Bending the Bow* (poetry); *The Truth and Life of Myth: an Essay in Essential Autobiography* (criticism)

Ellmann, Mary (1921–89), *Thinking About Women* (criticism)

Ginsberg, Allen (1926–), *Planet News* (poetry)

Glück, Louise (1943–), *Firstborn* (poetry)

Hollander, John (1929–), *Types of Shape* (poetry)

Kinnell, Galway (1927–), *Body Rags* (poetry)

Levine, Philip (1928–), *Not This Pig* (poetry)

Marcuse, Herbert (1898–1979), *Negations* (trans. Jeremy J. Shapiro)

Olson, Charles (1910–70), *Maximus IV, V, VI* (poetry)

Oppen, George (1908–84), *Of Being Numerous* (poetry)

Pinsky, Robert (1940–), *Landor's Poetry* (criticism)

Snodgrass, W[illiam] D[ewitt] (1926–), *After Experience* (poetry)

Snyder, Gary [Sherman] (1930–), *The Back Country* (poetry)

Williams, C[harles] K[enneth] (1936–), *A Day for Anne Frank* (poetry)

	Texts	American Events	Other Events
1969	Creeley, Robert [White] (1926–), *Pieces* (poetry) Lowell, Robert [Traill Spence, Jr.] (1917–77), *Notebook, 1967–68* Merrill, James [Ingram] (1926–), *The Fire Screen* (poetry) Rich, Adrienne [Cecile] (1931–), *Leaflets* (poetry) Snyder, Gary [Sherman] (1930–), *Earth House Hold* (essays); *Riprap & Cold Mountain Poems* Trilling, Lionel (1905–75), *Sincerity and Authenticity* (1969–70 Norton lectures) Wilbur, Richard [Purdy] (1921–), *Walking to Sleep* (poetry) Williams, C[harles] K[enneth] (1936–), *Lies* (poetry) *Journal of Black Studies* founded by Molefi Asante and Robert Singleton at UCLA. Bollingen Prize to John Berryman and Karl Shapiro.	Warren Burger appointed to Supreme Court as Chief Justice (1969–87). Agnew's media as "effete intellectual snobs" speech. Students seize Cornell student center to protest racism on campus. Millions observe Moratorium Day to protest war in Vietnam. Stonewall Riots, Gay Power. Plane hijacking incidents. Woodstock. Gallup Poll shows 70% feel religion's influence is waning in U.S. General Motors recalls almost five million defective cars. Use of DDT banned. Live TV coverage of lunar landing; walk on the moon by Armstrong and Aldrin (*Apollo 11*). Sony introduces video cassette. Fusion jazz debuts in *Bitches Brew*.	Solzhenitsyn expelled from Soviet Writers' Union. Inflation worldwide problem. First troop withdrawals from Vietnam. Ho Chi Minh dies (born ?1892). Thirty-nine nation conference in Rome on sea pollution. Algeria joins OPEC. Protestant–Roman Catholic violence in Northern Ireland; British send troops into Belfast. De Gaulle resigns; Pompidou elected President of France. Willy Brandt elected West German Chancellor. Yasser Arafat elected Chairman of PLO. Golda Meir elected Prime Minister of Israel. Dubcek fired; new Party guidelines in Czechoslovakia. *Concorde* makes its first test flight. Price of gold on free market falls.
1970	Ashbery, John [Lawrence] (1927–), *The Double Dream of Spring* (poetry)	Recession. Federal grand jury acquits "Chicago 7."	

U.S. troops sent into Cambodia on April 30; last troops withdrawn June 29.

U.S. troops in Vietnam below 400,000.

Helicopter attempt to rescue U.S. POWs near Hanoi fails.

U.S.–Soviet accord to standardize spacecraft docking systems.

Gambia proclaimed republic within British Commonwealth.

Salvador Allende elected President of Chile.

Heath succeeds Wilson as British Prime Minister.

Israel–U.A.R. 90-day truce along Suez.

UN Commission on Human Rights establishes grievance procedure.

Large-scale U.S. bombing against North Vietnam; bombing of Ho Chi Minh Trail in Laos.

Church of England and Roman Catholic Church end 400-year dispute over meaning of Eucharist.

First major postal workers' strike.

Colleges and universities closed or on strike to protest Cambodian invasion; four students killed at Kent State University by Ohio National Guard.

Postal Reorganization Act.

National Air Quality Control Act (Dec. 31).

Office of Management and Budget created.

First Earth Day, April 22.

Environmental Education Act passed.

Environmental Protection Agency established.

First complete synthesis of gene (University of Wisconsin).

Minute Man III, MIRV.

U.S. population, 203,302,031.

Omnibus Crime Control Act, federal aid to state, local law enforcement.

Lieutenant William L. Calley, Jr. convicted in My Lai massacre.

Twenty-sixth Amendment lowers voting age.

Foucault, Michel (1926–84), *The Order of Things: An Archaeology of the Human Sciences* (orig. 1966)

Freire, Paulo (1921–), *The Pedagogy of the Oppressed* (trans. Myra Bergman Ramos)

Hartman, Geoffrey (1929–), *Beyond Formalism: Literary Essays* (criticism)

Howe, Irving (1920–), *Decline of the New* (criticism)

McGrath, Thomas (1916–90), *Letter to An Imaginary Friend, Parts I & II* 1970

Millett, Kate (1934–), *Sexual Politics* (criticism)

Snyder, Gary [Sherman] (1930–), *Regarding Wave* (poetry)

1971 Bly, Robert [Elwood] (1926–), *The Teeth Mother Naked at Last* (poetry)

de Man, Paul (1919–83), *Blindness and Insight: Essays in the Rhetoric of Contemporary Criticism* (rev. 1983, criticism)

Gunn, Thom (1929–), *Moly* (poetry)

	Texts	American Events	Other Events
	Hollander, John (1929–), *The Night Mirror* (poetry) Kinnell, Galway (1927–), *The Book of Nightmares* (poetry) Levine, Philip (1928–), *Red Dust* (poetry) Plath, Sylvia (1932–63), *Crossing the Water* (poetry) Rich, Adrienne [Cecile] (1931–), *The Will to Change* (poetry) Wright, Jay (1935–), *The Homecoming Singer* (poetry) Bollingen Prize to Richard Wilbur and Mona Van Duyn.	Portions of *Pentagon Papers* published. Amtrak begins service. Ninety-day wage, price, and rent freeze. Five-day uprising at Attica State Prison ends in forty-two deaths. U.S. devalues dollar. Supreme Court rules unconstitutional federal and state aid to parochial schools. Federal Election Campaign Act passed. NASDAQ founded. Kennedy Center for the Performing Arts in Washington, D.C. opens. *Apollo 14* and *Apollo 15* to moon; *Mariner 9*, first to orbit another planet (Mars).	Canada–China diplomatic relations; U.S. table tennis team visits China; Nixon lifts U.S. trade embargo on China; Mainland China joins UN. Violence increases in Northern Ireland. U.S.-U.S.S.R. ban on ocean floor nuclear weapons. Algeria seizes French oil and gas interests. Nigeria joins OPEC.
1972	Adorno, Theodor (1903–69), and Max Horkheimer (1895–1973), *The Dialectic of Enlightenment* (orig. 1969; trans. John Cumming) Ashbery, John [Lawrence] (1927–), *Three Poems* (poetry) Barthes, Roland (1915–80), *Mythologies* (orig. 1957; trans. Annette Lavers)	Nixon approves Space Shuttle development. Screening of U.S. airline passengers and luggage to combat hijacking. Five arrested in break-in at Democratic National Headquarters in Watergate Hotel.	U.S. returns Okinawa to Japan. Nixon orders mining of Haiphong Harbor. At year's end, U.S. troops in Vietnam fewer than 24,000; heavy B-52 bombing of North Vietnam resumes.

Levine, Philip (1928–), *They Feed They Lion* (poetry)

McGrath, Thomas (1916–90), *The Movie at the End of the World: Collected Poems* (poetry)

Merrill, James [Ingram] (1926–), *Braving the Elements* (poetry)

Palmer, Michael (1943–), *Blake's Newton* (poetry)

Williams, C[harles] K[enneth] (1936–), *I am the Bitter Name; The Sensuous President* (poetry)

Feminist Press, founded by Florence Howe, begins reprinting works of women's literature. *Feminist Studies* journal.

Alabama Gov. George Wallace shot.

Equal Rights Amendment passed.

Angela Davis acquitted.

National Black Political Convention in Gary, Indiana.

Shirley Chisholm presidential candidate.

Sally Priesand ordained, first female rabbi.

Senate approves SALT (Strategic Arms Limitation Treaty).

Water Pollution Control Act passed over Nixon veto.

All-volunteer armed forces phased in. Phase II wage, price, and profit controls.

U.S. petroleum product shortage.

Apollo 16 and *Apollo 17* crews explore moon surface; *Pioneer 10* to Mars and Jupiter launched.

Lon Nol takes control of government of Cambodia.

Britain imposes direct rule on Northern Ireland.

Nixon visits China and Russia.

Arab terrorists kill Israeli athletes taken hostage at Munich Summer Olympics.

Philippine President Ferdinand Marcos declares martial law.

Allende continues to nationalize Chile's large industries.

R. Leakey and G. Isaac discover 2.5 million-year-old human skull in Kenya.

1973   Bidart, Frank (1939–), *Golden State* (poetry)

Bloom, Harold (1930–), *The Anxiety of Influence: A Theory of Poetry* (criticism)

Bly, Robert [Elwood] (1926–), *Sleepers Joining Hands* (poetry)

Richard Nixon begins second term as President; Vice President Spiro Agnew resigns; Gerald Ford named Vice president.

Paris Peace Accords.

U.S. withdrawal of troops from Vietnam.

Breshnev visits U.S.

Texts	American Events	Other Events
Bowers, Edgar (1924–), *Living Together* (poetry)	Watergate scandal: Attorney General Richard G. Kleindienst and Nixon aides H. R. Haldeman, John D. Ehrlichman, and John W. Dean resign; Senate hearings begin; Archibald Cox named Special Prosecutor (May); existence of White House taping system revealed (July); Cox and Deputy Attorney General William D. Ruckelshaus fired; Attorney General Eliot Richardson resigns (Oct.); William B. Saxbe named Attorney General and Leon Jaworski Special Prosecutor.	United Kingdom, Ireland, and Denmark join the EEC/Common Market.
Cassity, Turner (1929–), *Steeplejacks in Babel* (poetry)		Violence continues in Northern Ireland.
Hass, Robert (1941–), *Field Guide* (poetry)		East and West Germany establish diplomatic relations.
Kenner, (William) Hugh (1923–), *The Pound Era* (criticism)		Yom Kippur Arab–Israeli War.
Lowell, Robert [Traill Spence, Jr.] (1917–77), *For Lizzie and Harriet; History; The Dolphin* (Pulitzer) (poetry)		Spanish Premier Blanco assassinated.
Oppen, George (1908–84), *Seascape* (poetry)		Arab oil embargo in retaliation for U.S., western Europe, and Japan's support of Israel leads to world-wide energy crisis.
Palmer, Michael (1943–), *C's Songs* (poetry)	Energy crisis: cutbacks in fuel-consuming services and industries; unemployment up.	Britain grants Bahamas independence.
Rich, Adrienne [Cecile] (1931–), *Diving into the Wreck* (poetry)	Nixon ends most wage–price controls.	Premier Papadopolous ousted in Greece; General Phaedon Gizikis, President.
Slotkin, Richard (1942–), *Regeneration Through Violence: The Mythology of the American Frontier* (criticism)	*Roe v. Wade.*	Destabilization and fall of Allende government in Chile.
Walcott, Derek Alton (1930–), *Another Life* (poetry)	Nixon signs Alaska Pipeline Act.	Juan Perón and his wife elected President and Vice President of Argentina.
Bollingen Prize to James Merrill.	Seventy-day occupation of Wounded Knee.	
	National Black Feminist Organization founded.	

1974 **Booth, Wayne C[layson]** (1921–), *The Rhetoric of Irony* (criticism)

Levine, Philip (1928–), *1933* (poetry)

Mitchell, Juliet (1940–), *Psychoanalysis and Feminism* (criticism)

Palmer, Michael (1943–), *The Circular Gates* (poetry)

Snyder, Gary [Sherman] (1930–), *Turtle Island* (poetry and prose, Pulitzer)

National Book Critics Circle founded.

MELUS journal started.

Critical Inquiry journal started.

National Gay and Lesbian Task Force founded in New York City.

Skylab I, II, and *III.*

All price and wage controls ended.

President Nixon visits Egypt, Saudi Arabia, Syria, Israel, U.S.S.R.

Watergate: House impeachment inquiry against Nixon begins May 9; House Judiciary Committee votes three articles of impeachment July 27 and July 30.

President Nixon resigns on August 8; Gerald Ford sworn in as thirty-eighth President; Nelson D. Rockefeller, Vice President.

Ford pardons Nixon; grants limited amnesty to Vietnam War dodgers and deserters.

Freedom of Information Act passed.

American Psychiatric Assn. removes homosexuality from list of mental disorders.

Gasoline shortages.

Mariner 10 transmits pictures of Venus and Mercury.

Former Nixon aides convicted in Watergate scandal.

Ecuador joins OPEC.

Worldwide inflation.

Syria–Israel cease-fire on Golan Heights.

Schmidt succeeds Brandt as West German Chancellor.

Wilson succeeds Heath as British Prime Minister.

In Argentina, President Perón dies; succeeded by his wife, Maria Estela.

Military government in Greece resigns; Constantine Caramanlis, Premier.

Portuguese Guinea granted independence as Guinea-Bissau.

Grenada declares independence.

India explodes nuclear device; nuclear testing by Great Britain, France and China.

1975 **Ashbery, John [Lawrence]** (1927–), *Self-Portrait in a Convex Mirror* (poetry)

Saigon falls.

Texts	American Events	Other Events
Baudrillard, Jean (1929–), *The Mirror of Production* (orig. 1973; trans. Mark Poster)	Unemployment 8.2 percent.	Cambodian Khmer Rouge oust Lon Nol.
Barthes, Roland (1915–80), *The Pleasure of the Text* (orig. 1973; trans. Richard Miller)	Marianas Islands, U.S. Commonwealth.	Pathet Lao in control of Laos.
Bercovitch, Sacvan (1933–), *The Puritan Origins of the American Self* (criticism)	Two assassination attempts on President Ford.	Suez Canal reopened.
Bloom, Harold (1930–), *A Map of Misreading* (criticism)	Civil Service Commission eliminates ban on federal employment of homosexuals.	Christian–Moslem civil war in Lebanon.
Cassity, Turner (1929–), *Yellow for Peril, Black for Beautiful* (poetry)	Jacques Derrida at Yale, begins yearly seminars at U.S. universities.	Gabon joins OPEC.
Dorn, Ed[ward Merton] (1929–), *Gunslinger* (poetry)	Spring 1975, first of Michel Foucault's visiting appointments at University of California at Berkeley.	Portugal declares all its African colonies independent.
Glück, Louise (1943–), *The House on Marshland* (poetry)	Video cameras come into use; Sony introduces Betamax format VCR, Matsushita introduces VHS format; video games introduced.	Papua New Guinea receives its independence from Australia.
Hartman, Geoffrey H. (1929–), *The Fate of Reading and Other Essays* (criticism)		President Ford meets with Mao Tsetung in China; visits Indonesia, Philippines.
Hollander, John (1929–), *Tales Told of the Father* (poetry); *Vision and Resonance: Two Senses of Poetic Form* (criticism)		Spain's right-wing dictator Franco dies; King Juan Carlos I comes to power.
Kermode, Frank (1919–), *Classic Literary Images of Permanence and Change* (criticism)		OPEC raises oil prices ten percent.
Kolodny, Annette (1941–), *Lay of the Land: Metaphor as Experience and History in American Literature* (criticism)		Helsinki Accords, human rights.

Pinsky, Robert (1940–), *Sadness and Happiness* (poetry)

Spacks, Patricia Ann Meyer (1929–), *The Female Imagination* (criticism)

Signs journal.

Bollingen Prize to A. R. Ammons.

1976 **Bishop, Elizabeth** (1911–79), *Geography III* (poetry)

Creeley, Robert [White] (1926–), *Away* (poetry)

Derrida, Jacques (1930–), *Of Grammatology* (orig. 1967; trans. Gayatari Chakravorty Spivak)

Eagleton, Terry (1943–), *Criticism and Ideology: A Study in Marxist Literary Theory* (criticism)

Gunn, Thom (1929–), *Jack Straw's Castle and Other Poems* (poetry)

Hirsch, E[ric] D[onald] (1928–), *Aims of Interpretation* (criticism)

Hollander, John (1929–), *Reflections on Espionage* (poetic commentary)

Levine, Philip (1928–), *The Names Of the Lost* (poetry)

Merrill, James [Ingram] (1926–), *Divine Comedies* (Pulitzer for poetry)

Moers, Ellen (1928–), *Literary Women* (criticism)

Bicentennial celebrations include Operation Sail, tall ships from thirty-one nations.

Televised Ford–Carter debates; first Vice Presidential debates (Dole–Mondale).

EPA bans mercury-based pesticides.

Air Force Academy all-male tradition ends with admission of 155 women.

Reverend Moon's Unification Church.

Outbreak of "Legionnaires' Disease" at Philadelphia convention.

Gases from spray cans found harmful to ozone.

Federally funded Conrail corporation takes over management of six failed Northeast railroads.

Viking I lands on Mars.

Last U.S. forces leave Thailand.

U.S. and Soviet Union agree to limit nuclear testing and mutual inspection of test sites.

North and South Vietnam reunited as Socialist Republic of Vietnam, with Hanoi as capital; Saigon renamed Ho Chi Minh City.

Khieu Samphan Chairman of the State Presidium of Cambodia; Pol Pot, Premier.

Coup in Thailand.

Soweto rioting against apartheid.

Israeli commandos rescue hostages at Entebbe Airport in Uganda.

Premier Chou En-Lai, People's Republic of China, dies (born 1898).

Perón government in Argentina ousted by military junta.

Texts	American Events	Other Events
Ohmann, Richard (1931–), *English in America: A Radical View of the Profession* (criticism)		Mao Tse-tung dies; Hua Kuo-fent appointed Premier and Chairman of Chinese Communist Party; Gang of Four.
Rich, Adrienne [Cecile] (1931–), *Of Woman Born: Motherhood as Experience and Institution* (criticism)		Civil war in Angola.
Wilbur, Richard [Purdy] (1921–), *The Mind-Reader* (poetry)		
Wright, Jay (1935–), *Dimensions of History* (poetry)		
1977 Althusser, Louis (1918–90), *Reading "Capital"* (orig. 1965; trans. Ben Brewster)	Jimmy Carter inaugurated as thirty-ninth President.	Czech Human Rights Manifesto.
Ashbery, John [Lawrence] (1927–), *Houseboat Days* (poetry)	Aid to Argentina, Uruguay, and Ethiopia cut off for human rights violations.	Angolan forces invade Shaba Province, Zaire.
Bidart, Frank (1939–), *The Book of the Body* (poetry)	Department of Energy created.	Indira Gandhi resigns; Morarji R. Desai becomes Prime Minister of India.
Davie, Donald (1922–), *In the Stopping Train* (poetry)	Richard Helms (1966–73 head of CIA) given fine and suspended sentence for false testimony in Senate hearings on CIA operations in Chile.	Menahem Begin succeeds Rabin as Iraeli Prime Minister.
Douglas, Ann (1940–), *The Feminization of American Culture* (criticism)		Martial law declared in Pakistan.
Foucault, Michel (1926–84), *Discipline and Punish: The Birth of the Prison* (orig. 1975; trans. Alan Sheridan)	Jacqueline Means, first female Episcopal priest in U.S.	Leonid Breshnev elected President of the Soviet Union.
Hecht, Anthony [Evan] (1923–), *Millions of Strange Shadows* (poetry)	U.S. Justice Dept. investigates South Korean lobbying.	Panama Canal treaties signed. Egyptian President Anwar Sadat visits Israel.
Lacan, Jacques (1901–81), *Ecrits: A Selection* (orig. 1966; trans. Alan Sheridan)	U.S. establishes 200-mile fishing zone.	Military junta takes control in Thailand.

Lowell, Robert [Traill Spence, Jr.] (1917–77), *Day by Day* (poems)

Palmer, Michael (1943–), *Without Music* (poetry)

Pinsky, Robert (1940–), *The Situation of Poetry* (criticism)

Showalter, Elaine (1941–), *A Literature of Their Own: British Women Novelists from Brontë to Lessing* (criticism)

Smith, Barbara (1946–), "Toward a Black Feminist Criticism" (criticism)

Snodgrass, W[illiam] D[ewitt] (1926–), *The Führer Bunker* (poetry)

Williams, C[harles] K[enneth] (1936–), *With Ignorance* (poetry)

Bollingen Prize to David Ignatow.

1978 Baym, Nina (1936–), *Woman's Fiction: A Guide to Novels by and about Women in America, 1820–1870* (criticism)

Bercovitch, Sacvan (1933–), *The American Jeremiad* (criticism)

Chodorow, Nancy (1944–), *The Reproduction of Mothering: Psychoanalysis and The Sociology of Gender* (psychology)

New company markets the first personal computer, Apple II.

Roots draws largest TV audience in history.

Massive blackout in New York City.

Alaska Pipeline opens.

U.S. tests neutron bomb.

Space shuttle *Enterprise* on first manned flight; *Viking II* lands on Mars; *Voyager I* and *II* launched to explore outer solar systems.

Rhodesian Prime Minister Ian Smith ready for political settlement with black majority.

Steven Biko, South African black leader, dies.

Longest coal strike in U.S. history.

Age of mandatory retirement raised from 65 to 70.

Ex-FBI director Patrick L. Gray and two others indicted on conspiracy charges.

Airline industry deregulated.

In Guyana, over 900 members of People Temple commit suicide.

Violent campaign by Nicaraguan Sandinista guerrillas to overthrow Somoza government begins.

Military junta seizes power in Afghanistan.

Texts	American Events	Other Events
Creeley, Robert [White] (1926–), *Later* (poetry) **Derrida, Jacques** (1930–), *Writing and Difference* (orig. 1967; trans. Alan Bass) **Foucault, Michel** (1926–84), *The History of Sexuality 1* (orig. 1976; trans. Robert Hurley) **Hollander, John** (1929–), *Spectral Emanations* (poetry) **Rich, Adrienne [Cecile]** (1931–), *The Dream of a Common Language* (poetry) **Riffaterre, Michael** (1924–), *Semiotics of Poetry* (criticism) **Said, Edward** (1935–), *Orientalism* (criticism) **Williams, C[harles] K[enneth]** (1936–), *Sophocles's Women of Trachis* (translation) 1979 **Ashbery, John [Lawrence]** (1927–), *As We Know* (poetry) **Duncan, Robert [Edward]** (1919–88), *Fictive Certainties* (essays)	National Energy Act sets natural gas prices and fuel standards. Love Canal declared federal disaster area. U.S. ratifies Panama Canal Treaties. Congress extends ratification of Equal Rights Amendment to June, 1982. Bakke decision, Supreme Court rules on reverse discrimination. Brig. General Margaret A. Brewer first female general in U.S. Marine Corps. U.S. dollar plunges to record low against Japanese yen, West German mark and Swiss franc. Compact Disc introduced by Philips. *Pioneer 1* and *2* probe Venus. Discovery of moon orbiting Pluto. *Chicago Daily News* ceases publication (1875–1978) Energy Crisis: gas shortage, soaring gas prices, demand for more efficient cars; three hundred thousand autoworkers lose jobs; federal loans of $1.5 billion save Chrysler from bankruptcy.	Solomon Islands, Tuvalu (Ellice Islands), and Dominica become independent nations. Military junta seizes control in Honduras. Bilateral peace treaty negotiations between Israel and Egypt in Washington, D.C. Martial rule in Iran; strikers shut down oil industry; self-exiled Ayatollah Khomeini calls for removal of Shah. Army ousts Bolivia's President. Pope John Paul I elected, dies after 34 days; Pope John Paul II (Pole) becomes first non-Italian elected Pope in 456 years. Lesley Brown, first "test-tube baby". Supertanker *Amoco Cadiz* breaks up off France's Brittany coast, polluting 110 miles of coastline. Control of Panama Canal Zone passes to Panama. Sandinista guerrillas campaign to overthrow government of President Anastasio Somoza in Nicaragua.

Margaret Thatcher elected British Prime Minister.

Collapse of Pol Pot regime in Cambodia.

Peace Treaty between Egypt and Israel.

Popular revolution in Iran deposes Shah; Ayatollah Khomeini, leader of Iran.

Islamic students take staff of U.S. embassy in Iran hostage, demand return of Shah from New York hospital in exchange.

Attacks on U.S. embassies in Pakistan and Libya.

Soviets invade Afghanistan.

OPEC doubles oil prices from fourteen to twenty-eight dollars a barrel.

U.S. establishes full diplomatic relations with China.

House votes to allow live TV coverage.

Department of Education created.

Andrew Young resigns as U.S. Ambassador to UN after unauthorized contacts with PLO revealed.

General Accounting Office reports U.S. troops in Vietnam sprayed with Agent Orange.

Three Mile Island nuclear power plant accident.

President Carter authorizes development of MX strategic missile.

Voyager 1 in closest approach to Jupiter.

Pioneer 2 discovers new rings and an eleventh moon around Saturn.

Gilbert, Sandra (1936–), **and Susan Gubar** (1944–), *The Madwoman in the Attic: The Woman Writer and the Nineteenth-Century Literary Imagination* (criticism)

Harari, Josué (1944–), ed., *Textual Strategies: Perspectives in Poststructuralist Criticism* (criticism)

Hass, Robert (1941–), *Praise* (poetry)

Hecht, Anthony [Evan] (1923–), *The Venetian Vespers* (poetry)

Levine, Philip (1928–), *Seven Years From Somewhere; Ashes* (poetry)

MacKinnon, Catherine A. (1946–), *Sexual Harassment of Working Women: A Case of Sex Discrimination* (law)

Pinsky, Robert (1940–), *An Explanation of America* (poetry)

Rich, Adrienne [Cecile] (1931–), *On Lies, Secrets and Silence* (criticism)

Steele, Timothy (1948–), *Uncertainties and Rest* (poetry)

Bollingen Prize to W. S. Merwin.

1980 **Belsey, Catherine** (1940–), *Critical Practice* (criticism)

Ousted Nicaraguan ruler Anastasio Somoza Debayle assassinated in Paraguay.

U.S. boycott of Summer Olympics in Moscow.

Texts	American Events	Other Events
Christian, Barbara (1943–), *Black Women Novelists: The Development of a Tradition, 1892–1976* (criticism)	FBI Operation Abscam.	Striking Polish shipyard workers, led by Lech Walesa, in Gdansk win right to have independent trade unions, form Solidarity.
Dove, Rita (1952–), *The Yellow House on the Corner* (poetry)	Banking industry deregulated; limit for FDIC accounts raised to $100,000.	Iran–Iraq War (1980–8).
Fish, Stanley (1938–), *Is There a Text in This Class?: The Authority of Interpretive Communities* (criticism)	U.S. breaks off diplomatic relations with Iran; eight killed and five injured in failed military mission to rescue hostages.	Mohammed Reza Pahlavi, deposed Shah of Iran, dies.
Glück, Louise (1943–), *Descending Figure* (poetry)	Beginning of savings and loan crisis (1980–8).	Zimbabwe, last British colony in Africa to receive independence.
Greenblatt, Stephen (1943–), *Renaissance Self-Fashioning from More to Shakespeare* (criticism)	Race riots in Miami following acquittal of four white policeman charged in beating death of African American man.	
Kinnell, Galway (1927–), *Mortal Acts, Mortal Words* (poetry)	Mt. St. Helens erupts.	
Kristeva, Julia (1941–), *Desire in Language* (orig. 1968, 1977; trans. Thomas Gora, Alice Jardine, and Leon S. Roudiez)	First female graduates from West Point.	
Lentricchia, Frank (1940–), *After the New Criticism* (criticism)	Carter authorizes government land in Washington, D.C. to be set aside for memorial to veterans who died in Southeast Asia.	
Marks, Elaine (1930–), **and Isabelle de Courtivron** (1946–), eds., *New French Feminisms: An Anthology* (criticism)	*Trident IV*.	
Olds, Sharon (1942–), *Satan Says* (poetry)	U.S. population, 226,545,805.	
Palmer, Michael (1943–), *Alogon* (poetry)		

Wright, Jay (1935–), *The Double Invention of Komo* (poetry)

L=A=N=G=U=A=G=E founded (1980–4)

1981 Ashbery, John [Lawrence] (1927–), *Shadow Train* (poetry)

Bahktin, Mikhail (1895–1975), *The Dialogic Imagination* (orig. 1975; trans. Caryl Emerson and Michael Holquist)

Derrida, Jacques (1930–), *Dissemination* (orig. 1972; trans. Barbara Johnson)

Greenblatt, Stephen (1943–) ed., *Allegory and Representation* (criticism)

Jameson, Fredric, (1934–) *The Political Unconscious: Narrative as a Socially Symbolic Act* (criticism)

Johnson, Barbara (1947–), *The Critical Difference: Essays in the Contemporary Rhetoric of Reading* (criticism)

Levine, Philip (1928–), *One for the Rose* (poetry)

Palmer, Michael (1943–), *Notes for Echo Lake* (poetry)

Rich, Adrienne [Cecile] (1931–), *A Wild Patience Has Taken Me This Far* (poetry)

Shapiro, Alan (1952–), *After the Digging* (poetry)

Bollingen Prize to Howard Nemerov and May Swenson.

Ronald Reagan inaugurated as fortieth President.

Fifty-two U.S. hostages returned after 444 days in Iran.

Sandra Day O'Connor appointed to the Supreme Court, first woman.

President Reagan and three others shot by John W. Hinckley, Jr.

Federal air traffic controllers begin strike; government dismisses strikers eight days later.

Two Navy F-14 fighters shoot down two Libyan fighters off Libyan coast.

Maya Y. Lin designs Vietnam Veterans Memorial.

IBM markets its first personal computer.

MTV Networks begin broadcasts.

NASA launches *Columbia*, first Space Shuttle.

Martial law imposed in Poland.

Egypt's President Anwar Sadat assassinated.

Assassination attempt on Pope John Paul II.

Israel bombs Iraqi nuclear reactor site, attacks possible PLO headquarters in Beirut.

Protests in Western European countries against planned deployment of U.S. tactical nuclear weapons.

U.S.–Soviet talks in Geneva on arms reduction.

Greece joins European Economic Community (Common Market).

	Texts	American Events	Other Events
1982	**Creeley, Robert [White]** (1926–), *Echoes* (poetry)	Unemployment rate 10.2 percent.	British battle Argentina over Falkland Islands.
	Gilligan, Carol (1936–), *In a Different Voice: Psychological Theory and Women's Development* (psychology)	In settlement of 1974 anti-trust suit, AT&T divests itself of twenty-two Bell System companies.	Lebanese Christian Phalangists kill hundreds in Palestinian refugee camps in West Beirut.
	Gunn, Thom (1929–), *The Passages of Joy* (poetry)	U.S. imposes economic sanctions against Libya for international terrorism role.	Egypt regains Sinai.
	Howe, Susan (1937–), *Pythagorean Silence* (poetry)		Leonid Breshnev dies; Yuri Andropov succeeds him.
	Hull, Gloria T. (1944–), **Patricia Bell Scott** (1950–), **Barbara Smith** (1946–), eds., *All the Women are White, All the Blacks are Men, But Some of Us are Brave* (criticism)	Equal Rights Amendment fails to achieve ratification.	
	Jay, Karla (1947–), *Out of the Closets: Voices of Gay Liberation* (criticism)	U.S. Marines ordered into Beirut as part of multinational peacekeeping force.	
	Lacan, Jacques (1901–81), *Feminine Sexuality* (orig. ?; trans. Jacqueline Rose)	President Reagan announces record $110 billion deficit.	
	Leithauser, Brad (1953–), *Hundreds of Fireflies* (poetry)	Reintroduced Compact Disc replaces LP and cassette as preferred recording medium.	
	Merrill, James [Ingram] (1926–), *The Changing Light of Sandover* (poetry)		
	Rorty, Richard (1931–), *Consequences of Pragmatism* (philosophy)		
	Trachtenberg, Alan (1932–), *The Incorporation of America* (criticism)		
	Tulsa Studies in Women's Literature journal.		

1983		
Bidart, Frank (1939–), *The Sacrifice* (poetry) Dove, Rita (1952–), *Museum* (poetry) Eagleton, Terry (1943–), *Literary Theory: An Introduction* (criticism) Ferry, David (1957–), *Strangers: A Book of Poems* (poetry) Howe, Susan (1937–), *Defenestration of Prague* (poetry) Jones, LeRoi [Imamu Amiri Baraka] (1934–), *Confirmation: An Anthology of African American Women* (criticism) Lentricchia, Frank (1940–), *Criticism and Social Change* (criticism) McGrath, Thomas (1916–90), *Echoes Inside the Labyrinth* (poetry) Palmer, Michael (1943–), *Code of Signals* (criticism) Said, Edward (1935–), *The World, The Text, and The Critic* (criticism) Shapiro, Alan (1952–), *The Courtesy* (poetry) Williams, C[harles] K[enneth] (1936–), *Tar* (poetry) *Representations* journal started. Bollingen Prize to Anthony Hecht and John Hollander.	President Reagan declares Times Beach, Missouri a federal disaster area due to release of dioxin. Unemployment reaches twelve million. U.S. admits shielding Nazi Gestapo chief Klaus Barbie. GM–Toyota agree on joint venture to produce subcompact cars for U.S. Reagan challenges scientists to develop a "Star Wars" defense system. *Challenger* space shuttle with four aboard on five-day mission; Sally Ride, first woman to travel in space. Camcorder, streamlined video camera, simplifies personal video recording; home video games very popular. Scientists Sagan and Ehrlich warn of "nuclear winter" as aftermath of detonation of only portion of U.S. and Soviet arsenal.	Nicaragua charges that Contra rebels backed by U.S. have invaded from Honduras. U.S. embassy in Beirut damaged by car bomb; forty-seven killed (April). Soviets shoot down Korean Air Lines passenger flight, killing 269. Mass demonstrations in Western Europe protest deployment of U.S. missiles. U.S. and Caribbean forces invade Grenada. Benigno Aquino slain in Manila. Car bomb attack on U.S. Marine headquarters in Beirut kills 241 servicemen. Egyptian President Hosni Mubarak meets in Cairo with PLO Chairman Yasser Arafat. Disarmament talks between U.S. and U.S.S.R. suspended.

Texts	American Events	Other Events
1984		

Texts	American Events	Other Events
Andrews, Bruce (1948–), **and Charles Bernstein** (1950–), eds., *The L=A=N=G=U=A=G=E Book* (criticism)	Unemployment and inflation down; U.S. dollar up on international markets.	José Napoleón Duarte elected President of El Salvador.
Ashbery, John [Lawrence] (1927–), *A Wave* (poetry)	Jesse Jackson bids for Democratic nomination for President.	Indira Gandhi assassinated.
Baker, Houston A., Jr. (1943–), *Blues Ideology and Afro-American Literature: A Vernacular Theory* (criticism)	Geraldine Ferraro, first female vice-presidential candidate of major party.	U.S. and Vatican exchange diplomats for first time in 116 years.
Bennett, William J. (1943–), *To Reclaim a Legacy: A Report on the Humanities in Higher Education* (NEH Report)	President Reagan rebuked by Congress for use of federal funds to mine Nicaraguan harbors.	U.S. Marines ordered out of Beirut.
Creeley, Robert [White] (1926–), *Memories* (poetry)	Kathryn Sullivan, first woman to walk in space.	U.S.S.R. leader Andropov dies; Konstantin Chernenko named successor.
Hass, Robert (1941–), *Twentieth Century Pleasures: Prose on Poetry* (criticism)		Toxic gas leaks from Union Carbide plant in Bhopal, India kills 2,000, injures 150,000.
Johnson, Ronald (1935–), *Ark 50* (poetry)		
Kristeva, Julia, (1941–), *Revolution in Poetic Language* (orig. 1974; trans. Margaret Waller)		
Lyotard, Jean François (1924–), *The Postmodern Condition: A Report on Knowledge* (orig. 1979; trans. Geoff Bennington and Brian Massumi)		
Milosz, Czeslaw (1911–), *The Separate Notebooks* (translation, poetry)		
Olds, Sharon (1942–), *The Dead and the Living* (poetry)		

Palmer, Michael (1943–), *First Figure* (poetry) **Pinsky, Robert** (1940–), *History of My Heart* (poetry) **Snyder, Gary [Sherman]** (1930–), *Axehandles* (poetry)	President Reagan inaugurated for second term.	Mikhail Gorbachev becomes U.S.S.R. leader, new policies of *glasnost* and *perestroika*.
1985 **Fisher, Philip** (1941–), *Hard Facts: Setting and Form in the American Novel* (criticism)	Reagan draws criticism for visit to Bitburg Cemetery in West Germany, burial site of many SS officers.	South Pacific Forum draws up the South Pacific Nuclear Free Zone Treaty.
Gilbert, Sandra (1936–), **and Susan Gubar** (1944–), *The Norton Anthology of Literature by Women: The Tradition in English* (criticism)	Thirty-nine remaining hostages freed in Beirut.	Reagan–Gorbachev summit on arms reductions and cultural exchange.
Glück, Louise (1943–), *The Triumph of Achilles* (poetry)	Walkers, father and son, sentenced in Navy espionage case.	Nineteen killed in terrorist attacks at Rome and Vienna airports.
Irigaray, Luce (1939–), *This Sex Which Is Not One* (orig. 1977; trans. Catherine Porter and Carolyn Burke)	Reagan signs Gramm–Rudman Act, requiring Congress to balance budget.	
Moi, Toril (1953–), *Sexual/Textual Politics: Feminist Literary Theory* (criticism)		
Showalter, Elaine (1941–), ed., *Feminist Criticism: Essays on Women, Literature and Theory* (criticism)		
Tompkins, Jane (1940–), *Sensational Designs* (criticism)		
Bollingen Prize to John Ashbery and Fred Chappell.		
1986 **Bercovitch, Sacvan** (1933–), **and Myra Jehlen** (1940–), eds., *Ideology and Classic American Literature* (criticism)	Explosion of Challenger space shuttle kills seven-member crew. Martin Luther King, Jr.'s birthday becomes national holiday.	Intervention of U.S. and Western Fleets in the Persian Gulf. Spain and Portugal join EEC (Common Market).

Texts	American Events	Other Events
Buell, Lawrence (1939–), *New England Literary Culture From Revolution Through Renaissance* (criticism)	President Reagan imposes economic sanctions against Libya after terrorist attacks in Rome and Vienna.	Haiti's President Jean-Claude Duvalier flees to France.
Cassity, Turner (1929–), *Hurricane Lamp* (poetry)	U.S. House rejects $100 million aid bill for Nicaraguan rebels.	President Marcos flees Philippines.
Cixous, Hélène (1937–), *The Newly Born Woman* (orig. 1975; trans. Betsey Wing)	Secret initiative to send arms to Iran and diversion of funds from arms sales to Nicaraguan Contras revealed: Iran–Contra affair.	Sweden's Prime Minister Olaf Palme assassinated.
De Lauretis, Teresa (1938–), ed., *Feminist Studies/Critical Studies* (criticism)	Union Carbide settles Bhopal gas leak suit.	U.S. planes attack Libya terrorist centers.
de Man, Paul (1919–83), *Resistance to Theory* (criticism)	AIDS virus reported.	Desmond Tutu elected Archbishop in South Africa.
Dove, Rita (1952–), *Thomas and Beulah* (poetry)	*Voyager 2* explores Uranus.	Chernobyl nuclear power plant disaster.
Leithauser, Brad (1953–), *Cats of the Temple* (poetry)	Robert Penn Warren named first U.S. poet laureate.	
Milosz, Czeslaw (1911–), *Unattainable Earth* (translation, poetry)		
Snyder, Gary [Sherman] (1930–), *Left Out in the Rain* (poetry)		
Steele, Timothy (1948–), *Sapphics Against Anger and Other Poems* (poetry)		
1987 Ashbery, John [Lawrence] (1927–), *April Galleons* (poetry)	President Reagan submits first trillion-dollar budget in U.S. history.	Three American Beirut University faculty captured by Muslim terrorists.
Bloom, Allan, (1930–92) *The Closing of the American Mind: How Higher Education Has Failed Democracy and Impoverished the Souls of Today's Students* (nonfiction)	William H. Rehnquist appointed Chief Justice of Supreme Court.	President Reagan and Canadian Prime Minister Brian Mulroney sign free trade agreement.

Carby, Hazel (1948–), *Reconstructing Womanhood: The Emergence of the Afro-American Woman Novelist* (criticism)

Graff, Gerald (1937–), *Professing Literature* (criticism)

Howe, Susan (1937–), *Articulation of Sound Forms in Time* (poetry)

Leithauser, Brad (1953–), *Between Leaps* (poetry)

Messerli, Douglas (1947–), *"Language Poetries: An Anthology"* (poetry)

Michaels, Walter Benn (1948–), *The Gold Standard and The Logic of Naturalism* (criticism)

Olds, Sharon (1942–), *The Gold Cell; The Matter of This World* (poetry)

Poirier, Richard (1925–), *The Renewal of Literature* (criticism)

Shapiro, Alan (1952–), *Happy Hour* (poetry)

Williams, C[harles] K[enneth] (1936–), *Flesh and Blood* (poetry)

Bollingen Prize to Stanley Kunitz.

1988 Cheney, Lynne V., (1941–) *Humanities in America: A Report to the President, the Congress, and the American People* (NEH Report)

Tower Commission concludes top Reagan advisors responsible for Iran–Contra affair and President out of touch with actions of his National Security Council.

Televised hearings on Iran–Contra affair.

Drug AZT approved to treat AIDS.

Austrian President Kurt Waldheim banned from entering U.S. because of his activities with German army during World War II.

Wall Street suffers worst day in history (Oct. 19); Dow Jones falls 22.6 percent.

Secretary of Defense Caspar Weinberger resigns; Frank Carlucci named successor.

Ivan Boesky fined $100 million for illegal insider trading activities.

U.S. Poet Laureate, Richard Wilbur.

Civil Rights Restoration Act passed over Presidential veto.

U.S. lists trade sanctions against Poland after release of political prisoners.

U.S. and Soviet Union INF treaty to dismantle all medium- and short-range missiles based in Europe.

Iraqi missiles attack U.S. frigate in Persian Gulf, killing thirty-seven; Iraqi apology.

Thatcher wins third term as British Prime Minister.

Klaus Barbie, Lyons Gestapo chief in World War II, sentenced to life by French court for war crimes.

Pan American flight 103 explodes over Lockerbie, Scotland.

Texts	American Events	Other Events
Davie, Donald (1922–), *To Scorch or Freeze: Poems about the Sacred* (poetry) **Gates, Henry Louis, Jr.** (1950–), *The Signifying Monkey: A Theory of Afro-American Criticism* (criticism) **Milosz, Czeslaw** (1911–), *Collected Poems, 1931–1987* (translation, poetry) **Pinsky, Robert** (1940–), *Poetry and the World* (criticism) **Spivak, Gayatri Chakravorty** (1942–), *In Other Worlds: Essays in Cultural Politics* (criticism) **Stimpson, Catharine R.** (1936–), *Where the Meanings Are* (criticism)	Former National Security Advisor Robert MacFarlane pleads guilty in Iran–Contra. Resolution Trust Corporation to dispose of insolvent assets in savings and loan crisis. First Ph.D. program in African American studies (Temple). Harvard University awarded first patent for a higher life form (genetically altered mouse). Almost 1.4 million illegal aliens apply for amnesty before government May 4 deadline. Barbara Harris, first American female Anglican bishop. U.S. Poet Laureate, Howard Nemerov.	U.S. Navy cruiser *Vincennes* in Persian Gulf shoots down an Iranian airliner, killing 290 passengers and crew. Soviets begin withdrawal of troops from Afghanistan. Plane explosion kills Pakistani President Mohammad Zia ul-Haq; Benazir Bhutto, first Islamic woman Prime Minister, chosen as successor.
1989 **Alter, Robert** (1935–), *The Pleasures of Reading in an Ideological Age* (criticism) **Bowers, Edgar** (1924–), *For Louis Pasteur* (poetry) **Cavell, Stanley** (1926–), *This New Yet Unapproachable America: Lectures After Emerson After Wittgenstein* (philosophy) **Dove, Rita** (1952–), *Grace Notes* (poetry)	George Bush inaugurated as forty-first President. Unemployment rate 5.1 percent. Oliver North convicted of three of twelve charges against him in Iran–Contra trial. Congress renews forty million dollar aid for Nicaraguan Contra rebels.	U.S. invades Panama, removes President Manual Noriega, and installs Guillermo Endara to head new government. Popular prodemocracy uprisings throughout Eastern Europe. Open elections in Namibia, southwest Africa.

Fish, Stanley (1938–), *Doing What Comes Naturally* (criticism)

Fuss, Diana (1960–), *Essentially Speaking: Feminism, Nature & Difference* (criticism)

Hass, Robert (1941–), *Human Wishes* (poetry)

Howe, Susan (1937–), *A Bibliography of the King's Book: Or, Eikon Basilike* (poetry)

Ross, Andrew (1956–), *No Respect: Intellectuals and Popular Culture* (criticism)

Sollors, Werner (1943–), *The Invention of Ethnicity* (criticism)

Veeser, H[arold] Aram (1950–), ed., *The New Historicism* (criticism)

American Literary History journal started.

Bollingen Prize to Edgar Bowers.

1990 Alexander, Elizabeth (1962–), *The Venus Hottentot* (poetry)

Bhabha, Homi K. (1949–), *Nation and Narration* (criticism)

Bidart, Frank (1939–), *In The Western Night, Collected Poems 1965–90* (poetry)

Butler, Judith (1956–), *Gender Trouble* (criticism)

Gates, Henry Louis, Jr. (1950–), ed., *Reading Black, Reading Feminist: A Critical Anthology* (criticism)

Supreme Court places new restrictions on women's right to abortion.

Earthquake in Northern California, Oct. 17.

Pictures of Neptune transmitted back to earth by *Voyager 2*.

Spaces Services, Inc. of Texas, first private commercial space launch. *Voyager 2* explores Neptune and its moons.

Exxon Valdez spills 11 million gallons of crude oil in Alaska's Prince William Sound.

U.S. Poet Laureate, Howard Nemerov.

Michael Milken assessed $600 million in fines and restitution and ten years for violating federal tax and securities laws.

U.S. Court of Appeals overturns North conviction.

Supreme Court rules burning American flag to be protected free speech.

Flaw found in Hubble telescope shortly after launch.

F. W. de Klerk elected President of South Africa.

Iran's Ayatollah Khomeini dies.

Berlin Wall opened.

Democracy rally in Tiananmen Square in Beijing; Chinese government kills thousands, severely represses activists.

Communist government in Romania toppled; President Ceausescu executed.

Hngary's Imre Nagy reburied as national hero of 1956 uprising.

General Noriega surrenders in Panama.

Violeta Barrios de Chamorro inaugurated as President of Nicaragua.

East and West Germany reunited.

Lech Walesa elected President of Poland.

John Major succeeds Thatcher as British Prime Minister.

| |

Texts	American Events	Other Events
Glück, Louise (1943–), *Ararat* (poetry) Greenblatt, Stephen (1943–), *Learning to Curse: Essays in Early Modern Culture* (criticism) Howe, Susan (1937–), *Singularities; The Europe of Trusts* (poetry) Lauter, Paul (1932–), ed., *The Heath Anthology of American Literature* Leithauser, Brad (1953–), *Mail From Anywhere* (poetry) Palmer, Michael (1943–), *Sun* (poetry) Pinsky, Robert (1940–), *The Want Bone* (poetry) Sedgwick, Eve Kosofsky (1950–), *Epistemology of the Closet* (criticism) Spivak, Gayatri Chakravorty (1942–), *The Postcolonial Critic: Interviews, Strategies, Dialogues* (criticism) Steele, Timothy (1948–), *Missing Measures: Modern Poetry and the Revolt Against Meter* (criticism)	U.S. Poet Laureate, Mark Strand. U.S. population, 248,709,873.	Gulf War begins when Iraq invades Kuwait; U.S. sends 527,000 forces to Saudi Arabia in Operation Desert Shield. Ban against political opposition groups in South Africa lifted; Nelson Mandela of the African National Congress and other political prisoners released. Tutsi forces enter Rwanda from Uganda. Gorbachev assumes emergency powers.
1991 Ashbery, John [Lawrence] (1927–), *Flow Chart* (poetry) Cassity, Turner (1929–), *Between The Chains* (poetry) Hahn, Susan (1941–), *Harriet Rubin's Mother's Wooden Hand* (poetry)	Unemployment rate 6.5 percent. Justice Thurgood Marshall announces retirement from Supreme Court; Clarence Thomas nominated as successor.	War in El Salvador ends. Operation Desert Storm (Jan. 17–Feb. 27). President Jean-Bertrand Aristide of Haiti deposed by military coup.

Jameson, Frederic (1934–), *Postmodernism, or, The Cultural Logic of Late Capitalism* (criticism)

Levine, Philip (1928–), *What Work Is* (poetry)

Milosz, Czeslaw (1911–), *Provinces* (translation, poetry)

Olds, Sharon (1942–), *The Sign of Saturn* (poetry)

Shapiro, Alan (1952–), *Covenant* (poetry)

Spillers, Hortense J. (1942–), ed., *Comparative American Identities: Race, Sex, and Nationality in the Modern Text* (criticism)

Warhol, Robyn R. (1955–), **and Diane Price Herndl** (1959–), eds., *Feminisms: An Anthology of Literary Theory and Criticism* (criticism)

Wright, Jay (1935–), *Boleros* (poetry)

Bollingen Prize to Laura Riding Jackson and Donald Justin.

Thomas–Hill hearings on sexual harassment charges before Senate Judiciary Committee; Clarence Thomas confirmed.

Charles Keating convicted of fraud in savings and loan crisis.

U.S. regulators seize BCCI (Bank of Credit and Commerce International) on charges of worldwide fraud and money laundering.

Last American hostages held in Lebanon are released.

Popular debate about political correctness and canon revision reaches height.

Basketball star Earvin "Magic" Johnson announces retirement due to testing HIV positive.

U.S. Poet Laureate, Joseph Brodsky.

South Africa's President de Klerk repeals Land Acts of 1913 and 1936, Group Areas Act, and Population Registration Act (the legal foundation for apartheid).

Republic of Croatia declares independence from Yugoslavia; Republics of Slovenia and Macedonia declare independence from Yugoslavia.

Berlin again becomes Germany's capital.

Warsaw Pact dissolved.

Gorbachev resigns; Commonwealth of Independent States formed; Boris Yeltsin President of Russian Republic; Lithuania, Estonia, and Latvia win independence.

European Community imposes sanctions on Yugoslavia for invasion of Croatia.

Maastricht Treaty (takes effect 1994). China accepts nuclear nonproliferation treaty.

U.S. signs START II nuclear arms treaty with Russia.

1992   **Ashbery, John [Lawrence]** (1927–), *Hotel Lautréamont* (poetry)

Americans with Disabilities Act takes effect.

Texts	American Events	Other Events
Ferry, David (1957–), *Gilgamesh: A New Rendering in English Verse* (poetry)	Riots in Los Angeles follow the acquittal of four white Los Angeles police officers in the beating of Rodney King.	Bush and Yeltsin announce formal end to Cold War.
Gallop, Jane (1952–), *The Daughter's Seduction: Feminism and Psychoanalysis* (criticism)	Senate approves Strategic Arms Limitation Treaty.	Aid to Russia from seven industrial nations.
Garber, Marjorie B. (1944–), *Vested Interests: Cross-Dressing & Cultural Anxiety* (criticism)	Twenty-seventh Amendment, barring Congress from voting itself pay raises until election of Representatives.	U.S. depart Subic Bay Naval Base, ending military presence in Philippines.
Gates, Henry Louis, Jr. (1950–), *Loose Canons: Notes on the Culture Wars* (criticism)	U.S. lifts trade sanctions against China.	Operation Restore Hope: U.S. Marines and Navy SEALS land in Mogadishu, Somalia.
Glück, Louise (1943–), *The Wild Iris* (poetry)	U.S. only nation at first Earth Summit not to sign biodiversity treaty.	Referendum in South Africa supports new constitution; violence between Xhosas and Zulus.
Grossberg, Lawrence (1947?–), and Paula Treichler (1943–), eds., *Cultural Studies* (criticism)	H. Ross Perot enters Presidential race.	Republic of Bosnia and Herzegovina secede from Yugoslavia; Yugoslav Federation breaks up; new, smaller Republic of Yugoslavia formed.
Gunn, Thom (1929–), *Man with Night Sweat* (poetry)	Senate overrides Presidential veto on removal of "gag rule" at federally financed family planning clinics.	U.S. and UN vote sanctions against Belgrade.
Olds, Sharon (1942–), *The Father* (poetry)	President Bush pardons six Reagan Administration officials charged in Iran–Contra affair.	
Williams, C[harles] K[enneth] (1936–), *A Dream of Mind* (poetry)	R. H. Macy and TWA file for bankruptcy.	
	U.S. Poet Laureate, Mona Van Duyn.	

1993 **Ferry, David** (1957–), *Dwelling Places: Poems and Translations* (poetry)

Hahn, Susan (1941–), *Incontinence* (poetry)

Howe, Susan (1937–), *The Birth-mark: Unsettling the Wilderness in American Literary History* (criticism); *The Nonconformist's Memorial* (poetry)

Robbins, Bruce (–), *Secular Vocations: Intellectuals, Professionalism, Culture* (nonfiction)

Shapiro, Alan (1952–), *In Praise of the Impure: Poetry and the Ethical Imagination* (criticism)

Sundquist, Eric (1952–), *To Wake the Nations: Race in the Making of American Literature* (criticism)

West, Cornel (1953–), *Race Matters* (criticism)

William J. Clinton inaugurated as forty-second President.

World Trade Center bombing (Feb. 26).

North American Free Trade Agreement enacted.

Branch Davidian compound in Waco, Texas attacked; eighty killed.

"Don't Ask; Don't Tell" policy on gays and lesbians in the military.

Brady Bill passes.

Two of four Los Angeles police officers found guilty of violating Rodney King's civil rights.

Supreme Court sets new definition of sexual harassment in workplace.

Space shuttle astronauts fix Hubble telescope.

U.S. radiation tests in 1940s and 1950s on humans revealed.

Walter H. Annenberg announces $500 million gift to educational reform groups.

Sears Catalog ceases publication.

U.S. Poet Laureate, Rita Dove.

NAFTA takes effect.

U.S., French, and British aircraft attack Iraqi missile sites.

Withdrawal of U.S. troops from Somalia; UN takes over Somalia relief.

U.S. exerts pressure on Haiti's ruling military junta; Haitian refugees continue to arrive.

All political parties in South Africa except Inkatha Freedom Party approve new constitution.

Vaclav Havel elected Czech President.

U.S. airdrop of supplies to Bosnia.

Clinton–Yeltsin summit, U.S. aid to Russia.

Israel and PLO recognize each other's right to exist.

China conducts nuclear test.

CIA reports North Korea has atomic bomb.

U.S.–U.S.S.R. agreement bans production, stockpiling, and use of all chemical weapons.

Secret contacts between British and IRA.

Maastricht Treaty, European Union (EU) takes effect.

1994 **Ashbery, John [Lawrence]** (1927–), *And The Stars Were Shining* (poetry)

Texts	American Events	Other Events
bell hooks (1952–), *Teaching to Transgress: Education as The Practice of Freedom* (criticism) Bloom, Harold (1930–), *Western Canon: The Books and School of Ages* (criticism) Glück, Louise (1943–), *Proofs and Theorems* (criticism) Levine, Philip (1928–), *The Simple Truth* (poetry) Pinsky, Robert (1940–), *The Inferno of Dante* (poetry, translation)	Crime bill passes, funding for new police, more prisons, ban on assault weapons. Family Leave bill passes, time off without pay for child/parent care. Supreme Court rules antiracketeering laws can be used to sue violent antiabortion protestors. U.S. lifts telecommunication equipment and small computer export restrictions on sales to China, Russia and eastern Europe. Los Angeles earthquake. Nineteen-year trade embargo on Vietnam lifted. Over ninety-four million U.S. homes own TV sets.	U.S. stops interception and return of Haitian refugees; negotiates with junta; leaders granted amnesty; Aristide returned to power. Continuing violence in Rwanda. Ernesto Zedillo Ponce de Léon elected President of Mexico. Mandela elected President of South Africa. Hebron mosque attack by Baruch Goldstein. Muslim–Croat alliance against Serbs establishing Federation signed in Vienna. First war actions in NATO history (against Serb militia). IRA declares ceasefire in N. Ireland.
1995 Creeley, Robert [White] (1926–), *Loops* (poetry) Dove, Rita (1952–), *Mother Love* (poetry) Leithauser, Brad (1953–), *Penchants and Places* (criticism) Milosz, Czeslaw (1911–), *Facing the River* (translation, poetry) Rich, Adrienne [Cecile] (1931–), *Dark Fields of the Republic: Poems 1991–1995*	Bombing of Federal Office Building in Oklahoma City kills over 160, injures more than 400, leads to calls for greater investigative powers for FBI. Celebrations mark fifty-year anniversary of end of World War II.	EU membership expanded to sixteen (includes Austria, Finland, Norway, and Sweden). UN convenes first War Crimes Tribunal since Nuremburg and Tokyo, to hear evidence on alleged Serbian atrocities; for first time, rape is considered a war crime.

BIBLIOGRAPHY

This selected bibliography is drawn from lists provided by the contributors to this volume. It represents works that they have found to be especially influential or significant. The bibliography does not include dissertations, articles, or studies of individual authors. We have also excluded primary sources, with the exception of certain collections that present materials that have been generally unknown or inaccessible to students and scholars.

Abelove, Henry, Michele Aina Barale, and David M. Halperin, eds. *The Lesbian and Gay Studies Reader.* New York: Routledge, 1993.

Abrams, M. H. *The Mirror and the Lamp: Romantic Theory and the Critical Tradition.* New York: Oxford University Press, 1953.

Adams, Hazard, and Leroy Searle, eds. *Critical Theory Since 1965.* Tallahassee: Florida State University Press, 1986.

Adorno, Theodor. *Negative Dialects.* Translated by E. B. Ashton. New York: Seabury Press, 1973.

Adorno, Theodor, and Max Horkheimer. *Dialect of Enlightenment.* Translated by John Cumming. London: Verso, 1979.

Ahmad, Aijaz. *In Theory: Classes, Nations, Literatures.* London: Verso, 1992.

Althusser, Louis. *Lenin and Philosophy, and Other Essays.* Translated by Ben Brewster. New York: Monthly Review Press, 1972.

Altieri, Charles. Enlarging the Temple: New Directions in American Poetry during the 1960s. Lewisburg, Pa.: Bucknell University Press, 1979.

   Self and Sensibility in Contemporary American Poetry. Cambridge University Press, 1984.

Arato, Andrew, and Elke Gebhardt, eds. *The Essential Frankfurt School Reader.* New York: Continuum, 1982.

Ashbery, John. *Reported Sightings: Art Chronicles, 1957–1987,* ed. David Bergman. Cambridge, Mass.: Harvard University Press, 1991.

Austin, J. L. *How to Do Things With Words.* Cambridge, Mass.: Harvard University Press, 1962.

Baker, Peter. *Obdurate Brilliance: Exteriority and the Modern Long Poem.* Gainesville: University of Florida Press, 1991.

Bakhtin, Mikhail. *The Dialogic Imagination: Four Essays,* ed. Michael Holquist. Translated by Caryl Emerson and Michael Holquist. Austin: University of Texas Press, 1981.

Barthes, Roland. *Mythologies.* Selected and translated by Annette Lavers. New York: Hill & Wang, 1972.

   Writing Degree Zero. Translated by Annette Lavers and Colin Smith. New York: Hill & Wang, 1968.

Bartlett, Lee. *Talking Poetry: Conversations in the Workshop with Contemporary Poets.* Albuquerque: University of New Mexico Press, 1986.

Bawer, Bruce. *The Middle Generation: The Lives and Poetry of Delmore Schwartz, Randall Jarrell, John Berryman, and Robert Lowell.* Hamden, Conn.: Archon Books, 1986.

Beach, Christopher. *ABC of Influence: Ezra Pound and the Remaking of American Poetic Tradition.* Berkeley and Los Angeles: University of California Press, 1992.

Belsey, Catherine. *Critical Practice.* London: Methuen, 1980.

Benjamin, Walter. *Illuminations,* ed. Hannah Arendt. Translated by Harry Zohn. New York: Schocken Books, 1969.

Bennett, Tony. *Formalism and Marxism.* London: Methuen, 1979.

Bercovitch, Sacvan. *The American Jeremiad.* Madison: University of Wisconsin Press, 1978.

   The Rites of Assent: Transformations in the Symbolic Construction of America. New York: Routledge, 1993.

Bernstein, Charles. Content's Dream: Essays, 1975–1984. Los Angeles: Sun and Moon Press, 1986.

   A Poetics. Cambridge, Mass.: Harvard University Press, 1992.

Berryman, John. *The Freedom of the Poet.* New York: Farrar, Straus, & Giroux, 1976.

Bhabha, Homi. *The Location of Culture.* London: Routledge, 1994.

Birkerts, Sven. *The Electric Life: Essays on Modern Poetry.* New York: William Morrow, 1989.

Bloom, Harold. *The Anxiety of Influence: A Theory of Poetry.* New York: Oxford University Press, 1973.

   A Map of Misreading. New York: Oxford University Press, 1975.

Bly, Robert. *American Poetry: Wildness and Domesticity.* New York: Harper & Row, 1990.

   Talking All Morning. Ann Arbor: University of Michigan Press, 1980.

Booth, Wayne C. *Critical Understanding: The Powers and Limits of Pluralism.* Chicago: University of Chicago Press, 1979.

   The Rhetoric of Fiction. Chicago: University of Chicago Press, 1961.

Boyers, Robert, ed. *Contemporary Poetry in America: Essays and Interviews.* New York: Schocken Books, 1974.

Breslin, James E. B. *From Modern to Contemporary: American Poetry, 1945–1965.* Chicago: University of Chicago Press, 1984.

Breslin, Paul. *The Psycho-political Muse: American Poetry Since the Fifties.* Chicago: University of Chicago Press, 1987.

Brooks, Cleanth. *The Well Wrought Urn.* New York: Reynal & Hitchcock, 1947.

Brooks, Cleanth, and Robert Penn Warren. *Understanding Poetry: An Anthology for College Students.* New York: Henry Holt & Company, 1938.

Burke, Kenneth. *A Rhetoric of Motives.* New York: Prentice-Hall, 1950.

    The Philosophy of Literary Form: Studies in Symbolic Action. New York: Vintage Books, 1957.

Butler, Judith. *Gender Trouble: Feminism and the Subversion of Identity.* New York: Routledge, 1990.

Byers, Thomas B. *What I Cannot Say: Self, Word, and World in Whitman, Stevens, and Merwin.* Urbana: University of Illinois Press, 1989.

Carby, Hazel V. *Reconstructing Womanhood: The Emergence of the Afro-American Woman Novelist.* New York: Oxford University Press, 1987.

Chawla, Louise. *In the First Country of Places: Nature, Poetry, and Childhood Memory.* Albany, N.Y.: SUNY Press, 1994.

Clark, Tom. *The Poetry Beat: Reviewing the Eighties.* Ann Arbor: University of Michigan Press, 1990.

Conte, Joseph M. *Unending Design: The Forms of Postmodern Poetry.* Ithaca, N.Y.: Cornell University Press, 1991.

Creeley, Robert. *The Collected Essays.* Berkeley and Los Angeles: University of California Press, 1989.

Culler, Jonathan. *Structuralist Poetics: Structuralism, Linguistics, and the Study of Literature.* Ithaca, N.Y.: Cornell University Press, 1975.

Damon, Maria. *The Dark End of the Street: Margins in American Vanguard Poetry.* Minneapolis: University of Minnesota Press, 1993.

Davidson, Michael. *The San Francisco Renaissance: Poetics and Community at Mid-Century.* Cambridge University Press, 1989.

Davison, Peter. *One of the Dangerous Trades: Essays on the Work and Workings of Poetry.* Ann Arbor: University of Michigan Press, 1991.

De Lauretis, Teresa, ed. *Feminist Studies, Critical Studies.* Bloomington: Indiana University Press, 1986.

de Man, Paul. *Allegories of Reading: Figural Language in Rousseau, Nietzsche, Rilke, and Proust.* New Haven, Conn.: Yale University Press, 1979.

    Blindness and Insight: Essays in the Rhetoric of Contemporary Criticism. Minneapolis: University of Minnesota Press, 1983.

de Saussure, Ferdinand. *Courses in General Linguistics,* ed. Charles Bally and Albert Sechehaye in collaboration with Albert Reidlinger. Translated by Wade Baskin. New York: McGraw-Hill, 1959.

Derrida, Jacques. *Dissemination.* Translated by Barbara Johnson. Chicago: University of Chicago Press, 1981.

    Of Grammatology. Translated by Gayatri Chakravorty Spivak. Baltimore: Johns Hopkins University Press, 1976.

    Spurs: Nietzsche's Styles. Translated by Barbara Harlow. Chicago: University of Chicago Press, 1979.

    Writing and Difference. Translated by Alan Bass. Chicago: University of Chicago Press, 1978.

Dickey, James. *Babel to Byzantium: Poets and Poetry Now.* New York: Farrar, Straus, & Giroux, 1968.

Diehl, Joanne Feit. *Women Poets and the American Sublime.* Bloomington: Indiana University Press, 1990.

Dodd, Wayne. *Toward the End of the Century: Essays into Poetry.* Iowa City: University of Iowa Press, 1992.

Douglas, Ann. *The Feminization of American Culture.* New York: Knopf, 1977.

Duncan, Robert. *Fictive Certainties: Essays.* New York: New Directions, 1985.

Eagleton, Terry. *Literary Theory: An Introduction.* London: Basil Blackwell, 1983.

Elder, John. *Imagining the Earth: Poetry and the Vision of Nature.* Urbana: University of Illinois Press, 1985.

Faas, Ekbert, ed. *Towards a New American Poetics: Essays and Interviews.* Santa Barbara, Calif.: Black Sparrow, 1978.

Feidelson, Charles. *Symbolism and American Literature.* Chicago: University of Chicago Press, 1953.

Felperin, Howard. *Beyond Deconstruction: The Uses and Abuses of Literary Theory.* New York: Oxford University Press, 1985.

Fetterley, Judith. *The Resisting Reader.* Bloomington: Indiana University Press, 1978.

Fiedler, Leslie. *An End to Innocence: Essays on Culture and Politics.* Boston: Beacon Press, 1955.

Love and Death in the American Novel. New York: Stein & Day, 1960.

Finkelstein, Norman. *The Utopian Moment in Contemporary American Poetry.* Lewisburg, Pa.: Bucknell University Press, 1993.

Fish, Stanley. *Doing What Comes Naturally.* Durham, N.C.: Duke University Press, 1989.

Is There a Text in This Class?: The Authority of Interpretive Communities. Cambridge, Mass.: Harvard University Press, 1980.

Foucault, Michel. *Discipline and Punish: The Birth of the Prison.* Translated by Alan Sheridan. New York: Pantheon, 1977.

The History of Sexuality, vol. 1. Translated by Robert Hurley. New York: Pantheon, 1978.

Power/Knowledge: Selected Interviews and Other Writings, 1972–1977. Edited and translated by Colin Gordon. New York: Pantheon Books, 1980.

Fraser, Nancy. *Unruly Practices: Power, Discourse, and Gender in Contemporary Theory.* Minneapolis: University of Minnesota Press, 1989.

Fredman, Stephen. *Poet's Prose: The Crisis in American Verse.* Cambridge University Press, 1983.

Frye, Northrop. *Anatomy of Criticism: Four Essays.* Princeton, N.J.: Princeton University Press, 1957.

Fables of Identity: Studies in Poetic Mythology. New York: Harcourt, Brace & World, 1963.

Fuss, Diana. *Essentially Speaking: Feminism, Nature and Difference.* New York: Routledge, 1989.

Gates, Henry Louis, Jr. *The Signifying Monkey: A Theory of African-American Literary Criticism.* New York: Oxford University Press, 1989.

ed. *Reading Black, Reading Feminist: A Critical Anthology.* New York: Meridian, 1990.

Gilbert, Roger. *Walks in the World: Representation and Experience in Modern American Poetry.* Princeton, N.J.: Princeton University Press, 1991.

Gilbert, Sandra, and Susan Gubar. *The Madwoman in the Attic.* New Haven, Conn.: Yale University Press, 1979.

Gotera, Vince. *Radical Visions: Poetry by Vietnam Veterans.* Athens: University of Georgia Press, 1994.

Greenblatt, Stephen. *Learning to Curse: Essays in Early Modern Culture.* New York: Routledge, 1990.

Renaissance Self-Fashioning: From More to Shakespeare. Chicago: University of Chicago Press, 1980.

Greenblatt, Stephen, and Giles Gunn, eds. *Redrawing the Boundaries: The Transformation of English and American Literary Studies.* New York: Modern Language Association, 1992.

Groden, Michael, and Martin Kreiswirth, eds. *The Johns Hopkins Guide to Literary Theory and Criticism.* Baltimore: Johns Hopkins University Press, 1994.

Grossberg, Lawrence, Cary Nelson, and Paula Treichler, eds. *Cultural Studies.* New York: Routledge, 1992.

Grossman, Allen, with Mark Halliday. *The Sighted Singer: Two Works on Poetry for Readers and Writers.* Baltimore: Johns Hopkins University Press, 1992.

Gunn, Thom. *The Occasions of Poetry: Essays in Criticism and Autobiography,* ed. Clive Wilmer. San Francisco: North Point, 1985.

Shelf Life: Essays, Memoirs, and an Interview. Ann Arbor: University of Michigan Press, 1993.

Hall, Donald. *Goatfoot, Milktongue, Twinbird: Interviews, Essays, and Notes on Poetry, 1970–1976.* Ann Arbor: University of Michigan Press, 1978.

Poetry and Ambition: Essays, 1982–1988. Ann Arbor: University of Michigan Press, 1988.

Remembering Poets: Reminiscences and Opinions. New York: Harper & Row, 1978.

Harari, Josue V., ed. *Textual Strategies: Perspectives in Post-Structuralist Criticism.* Ithaca, N.Y.: Cornell University Press, 1979.

Hartley, George. *Textual Politics and the Language Poets.* Bloomington: Indiana University Press, 1989.

Hartman, Geoffrey. *Beyond Formalism: Literary Essays.* New Haven, Conn.: Yale University Press, 1970.

Hass, Robert. *Twentieth Century Pleasures: Prose on Poetry.* New York: Ecco, 1984.

Heaney, Seamus. *The Government of the Tongue: Selected Prose, 1978–1987.* New York: Farrar, Straus, & Giroux, 1988.

Hebdige, Dick. *Subculture: The Meaning of Style.* London: Methuen, 1979.

Hecht, Anthony. *Obbligati: Essays in Criticism.* New York: Atheneum, 1986.

Hirsch, E. D. *The Aims of Interpretation.* Chicago: University of Chicago Press, 1976.

Validity in Interpretation. New Haven, Conn.: Yale University Press, 1967.

Holden, Jonathan. *Style and Authenticity in Postmodern Poetry.* Columbia: University of Missouri Press, 1986.

Hollander, John. *Vision and Resonance: Two Senses of Poetic Form.* New York: Oxford University Press, 1975.

Howard, Richard. *Alone with America: Essays on the Art of Poetry in the United States Since 1950.* New York: Atheneum, 1971.

Howe, Irving. *Celebrations and Attacks: Thirty Years of Literary and Cultural Commentary.* New York: Horizon Press, 1979.

Decline of the New. New York: Harcourt, Brace & World, 1970.

Hull, Gloria T., Patricia Bell Scott, and Barbara Smith, eds. *All the Women are White, All the Blacks are Men, But Some of Us are Brave.* Old Westbury, N.Y.: The Feminist Press, 1982.

Huyssen, Andreas. *After the Great Divide: Modernism, Mass Culture, Postmodernism.* Bloomington: Indiana University Press, 1986.

Hyman, Stanley Edgar. *The Armed Vision: A Study in the Methods of Modern Literary Criticism.* New York: Knopf, 1948.

Irigaray, Luce. *This Sex Which is Not One.* Translated by Catherine Porter with Carolyn Burke. Ithaca, N.Y.: Cornell University Press, 1985.

Iser, Wolfgang. *The Act of Reading: A Theory of Aesthetic Response.* Baltimore: Johns Hopkins University Press, 1978.

Jackson, Richard. *The Dismantling of Time in Contemporary Poetry.* Tuscaloosa: University of Alabama Press, 1988.

Jameson, Fredric. *The Political Unconscious: Narrative as a Socially Symbolic Act.* Ithaca, N.Y.: Cornell University Press, 1981.

Postmodernism, or the Cultural Logic of Late Capitalism. Durham, N.C.: Duke University Press, 1991.

Jardine, Alice, and Paul Smith, eds. *Men in Feminism.* New York: Methuen, 1987.

Jarrell, Randall. *Poetry and the Age.* New York: Knopf, 1953.

A Sad Heart at the Supermarket: Essays and Fables. New York: Atheneum, 1962.

The Third Book of Criticism. New York: Farrar, Straus, & Giroux, 1969.

Johnson, Barbara. *The Critical Difference: Essays in the Contemporary Rhetoric of Reading.* Baltimore: Johns Hopkins University Press, 1985.

Kalaidjian, Walter. *Languages of Liberation: The Social Text in Contemporary American Poetry.* New York: Columbia University Press, 1989.

Kazin, Alfred. *On Native Grounds: An Interpretation of Modern American Prose Literature.* New York: Reynal & Hitchcock, 1942.

Keller, Lynn. *Re-Making It New: Contemporary American Poetry and the Modernist Tradition.* Cambridge University Press, 1987.

Kenner, Hugh. *The Pound Era.* Berkeley and Los Angeles: University of California Press, 1973.

Kermode, Frank. *The Genesis of Secrecy: On the Interpretation of Narrative.* Cambridge, Mass.: Harvard University Press, 1979.

The Sense of an Ending: Studies in the Theory of Fiction. New York: Oxford University Press, 1967.

Kinnell, Galway. *Walking Down the Stairs: Selections from Interviews.* Ann Arbor: University of Michigan Press, 1978.

Kizer, Carolyn. *Proses: On Poems and Poets.* Port Townsend, Wash.: Copper Canyon, 1993.

Krieger, Murray. *The New Apologists for Poetry.* Minneapolis: University of Minnesota Press, 1956.

Kristeva, Julia. *Desire in Language: A Semiotic Approach to Literature and Art,* ed. Leon S. Roudiez. Translated by Thomas Gora, Alice Jardine, and Leon S. Roudiez. New York: Columbia University Press, 1980.

Kumin, Maxine. *To Make a Prairie: Essays on Poets, Poetry, and Country Living.* Ann Arbor: University of Michigan Press, 1979.

Kutzinski, Vera M. *Against the American Grain: Myth and History in William Carlos Williams, Jay Wright, and Nicolás Guillén.* Baltimore: John Hopkins University Press, 1987.

Lacan, Jacques. *Ecrits: A Selection.* Translated by Alan Sheridan. New York: Norton, 1977.

Lane, Michael, ed. *Structuralism: A Reader.* New York: Basic Books, 1970.

Lauter, Paul, and Louis Kampf, eds. *The Politics of Literature: Dissenting Essays on the Teaching of English.* New York: Pantheon Books, 1972.

Lawall, Sarah N. *Critics of Consciousness: The Existential Structures of Literature.* Cambridge, Mass.: Harvard University Press, 1968.

Lensing, George, and Ronald Moran. *Four Poets and the Emotive Imagination: Robert Bly, James Wright, Louis Simpson, and William Stafford.* Baton Rouge: Louisiana State University Press, 1976.

Lentricchia, Frank. *After the New Criticism.* Chicago: University of Chicago Press, 1980.

Criticism and Social Change. Chicago: University of Chicago Press, 1983.

Levine, Philip. *Don't Ask.* Ann Arbor: University of Michigan Press, 1981.

Levinson, Sanford, and Steven Maillous, eds. *Interpreting Law and Literature.* Evanston, Ill.: Northwestern University Press, 1988.

Lewis, R. W. B. *The American Adam: Innocence, Tragedy, and Tradition in the Nineteenth Century.* Chicago: University of Chicago Press, 1955.

Libby, Anthony. *Mythologies of Nothing: Mystical Death in American Poetry, 1940–1970.* Urbana: University of Illinois Press, 1984.

Lieberman, Laurence. *Unassigned Frequencies: American Poetry in Review, 1964–1977.* Urbana: University of Illinois Press, 1977.

Lowell, Robert. *Collected Prose,* ed. Robert Giroux. New York: Farrar, Straus, & Giroux, 1987.

Lukács, Gyorgy. *The Meaning of Contemporary Realism.* Translated by John and Necke Mander. London: Merlin Press, 1963.

Lyotard, Jean-François. *The Post Modern Condition: A Report on Knowledge.* Translated by Geoff Bennington and Brian Massumi. Minneapolis: University of Minnesota Press, 1984.

Mackey, Nathaniel. *Discrepant Engagement: Dissonance, Cross-Culturality, and Experimental Writing.* Cambridge University Press, 1993.

Mariani, Paul. *A Usable Past: Essays on Modern and Contemporary Poetry.* Amherst: University of Massachusetts Press, 1984.

Marx, Leo. *The Machine in the Garden: Technology and the Pastoral Ideal in America.* New York: Oxford University Press, 1964.

Matthiessen, F. O. *American Renaissance.* New York: Oxford University Press, 1941.

McClatchy, J. D. *White Paper: On Contemporary American Poetry.* New York: Columbia University Press, 1989.

McCorkle, James. *The Still Performance: Writing, Self, and Interconnection in Five Postmodern American Poets.* Charlottesville: University of Virginia Press, 1989.

McDowell, Robert, ed. *Poetry after Modernism.* Brownsville, Ore.: Story Line Press, 1991.

McGann, Jerome J. *A Critique of Modern Textual Criticism.* Chicago: University of Chicago Press, 1983.

McHugh, Heather. *Broken English: Poetry and Partiality.* Hanover, N.H.: Wesleyan University Press, 1993.

Merrill, James. *Recitative: Prose,* ed. J. D. McClatchy. San Francisco: North Point, 1986.

Mersmann, James F. *Out of the Vietnam Vortex: A Study of Poets and Poetry against the War.* Lawrence: University of Kansas Press, 1974.

Michaels, Walter Benn. *The Gold Standard and the Logic of Naturalism.* Berkeley and Los Angeles: University of California Press, 1987.

Miller, J. Hillis. *Poets of Reality: Six Twentieth Century Writers.* Cambridge, Mass.: Belknap Press of Harvard University Press, 1965.

Millet, Kate. *Sexual Politics.* New York: Avon, 1970.

Mills, Ralph J., Jr. *Cry of the Human: Essays on Contemporary American Poetry.* Urbana: University of Illinois, 1975.

Mitchell, Juliet. *Psychoanalysis and Feminism.* New York: Vintage, 1974.

Moi, Toril. *Sexual/Textual Politics: Feminist Literary Theory.* London: Methuen, 1985.

Molesworth, Charles. *The Fierce Embrace: A Study of Contemporary American Poetry.* Columbia: University of Missouri Press, 1979.

Montefiore, Jan. *Feminism and Poetry: Language, Experience, Identity in Women's Writing.* London: Pandora, 1987.

Nelson, Cary. *Our Last First Poets: Vision and History in Contemporary American Poetry.* Urbana: University of Illinois Press, 1981.

Nemerov, Howard. *Figures of Thought: Speculations on the Meaning of Poetry and Other Essays.* Boston: David R. Godine, 1978.

New and Selected Essays. Carbondale: Southern Illinois University Press, 1985.

ed. *Poets on Poetry.* New York: Basic Books, 1966.

Norris, Christopher. *Deconstruction: Theory and Practice.* London: Methuen, 1982.

Ohmann, Richard. *English in America: A Radical View of the Profession.* New York: Oxford University Press, 1976.

Olson, Charles. *Human Universe and Other Essays,* ed. Donald Allen. San Francisco: Auerhahn Society, 1965.

Ostroff, Anthony, ed. *The Contemporary Poet as Artist and Critic: Eight Symposia.* Boston: Little, Brown, 1964.

Parker, Hershel. *Flawed Texts and Verbal Icons: Literary Authority in American Fiction.* Evanston, Ill.: Northwestern University Press, 1984.

Parkinson, Thomas. *Poets, Poems, Movements.* Ann Arbor: UMI Research Press, 1987.

Paul, Sherman. *Hewing to Experience: Essays and Reviews on Recent American Poetry and Poetics, Nature and Culture.* Iowa City: University of Iowa Press, 1989.

   The Lost America of Love: Rereading Robert Creeley, Edward Dorn, and Robert Duncan. Baton Rouge: Louisiana State University Press, 1981.

Perloff, Marjorie. *The Dance of the Intellect: Studies in the Poetry of the Pound Tradition.* Cambridge University Press, 1985.

   The Poetics of Indeterminacy: Rimbaud to Cage. Princeton, N.J.: Princeton University Press, 1981.

   Radical Artifice: Writing Poetry in the Age of Media. Chicago: University of Chicago Press, 1991.

Pinsky, Robert. *Poetry and the World.* New York: Ecco, 1988.

   The Situation of Poetry: Contemporary Poetry and Its Traditions. Princeton, N.J.: Princeton University Press, 1976.

Poirier, Richard. *Poetry and Pragmatism.* Cambridge, Mass.: Harvard University Press, 1992.

   The Renewal of Literature: Emersonian Reflections. New Haven, Conn.: Yale University Press, 1987.

Pratt, Mary Louise. *Imperial Eyes: Travel Writing and Transculturation.* New York: Routledge, 1992.

Rahv, Philip. *The Myth and the Powerhouse.* New York: Farrar, Straus, & Giroux, 1965.

Ransom, John Crowe. *The New Criticism.* Norfolk, Conn.: New Directions, 1941.

Reichert, John. *Making Sense of Literature.* Chicago: University of Chicago Press, 1977.

Reinfeld, Linda. *Language Poetry: Writing as Rescue.* Baton Rouge: Louisiana State University Press, 1992.

Reising, Russell. *The Unusable Past: Theory and the Study of American Literature.* New York: Methuen, 1986.

Rexroth, Kenneth. *American Poetry in the Twentieth Century.* New York: Herder and Herder, 1971.

   Assays. Norfolk, Conn.: New Directions, 1961.

   Bird in the Bush: Obvious Essays. New York: New Directions, 1959.

Rich, Adrienne. *Blood, Bread and Poetry: Selected Prose, 1979–1985.* New York: Norton, 1986.

   On Lies, Secrets, and Silence: Selected Prose, 1966–1978. New York: Norton, 1979.

   What Is Found There: Notebooks on Poetry and Politics. New York: Norton, 1993.

Ricoeur, Paul. *The Conflict of Interpretations: Essays in Hermeneutics,* ed. Don Ihde. Evanston, Ill.: Northwestern University Press, 1974.

Riffaterre, Michael. *Semiotics of Poetry.* Bloomington: Indiana University Press, 1978.

Robinson, Lillian. *Sex, Class, and Culture.* Bloomington: Indiana University Press, 1978.

Roethke, Theodore. *On the Poet and His Craft: Selected Prose,* ed. Ralph J. Mills, Jr. Seattle: University of Washington Press, 1965.

Rorty, Richard. *Consequences of Pragmatism.* Minneapolis: University of Minnesota Press, 1982.

Rosenberg, Harold. *The Tradition of the New.* New York: Horizon Press, 1959.

Rosenthal, M. L. *The New Poets: American and British Poetry since World War II.* New York: Oxford University Press, 1967.

Rosenthal, M. L., and Sally M. Gall. *The Modern Poetic Sequence: The Genius of Modern Poetry.* New York: Oxford University Press, 1983.

Ross, Andrew. *No Respect: Intellectuals and Popular Culture.* New York: Routledge, 1989.

Rothenberg, Jerome. *Pre-Faces and Other Writings.* New York: New Directions, 1981.

Sacks, Sheldon. *Fiction and the Shape of Belief.* Berkeley and Los Angeles: University of California Press, 1964.

Said, Edward W. *Orientalism.* New York: Pantheon, 1978.

   The World, the Text, and the Critic. Cambridge, Mass.: Harvard University Press, 1983.

Schwartz, Delmore. *Selected Essays,* ed. Donald A. Dike and David H. Zucker. Chicago: University of Chicago Press, 1970.

Schweik, Susan. *A Gulf So Deeply Cut: American Women Poets and the Second World War.* Madison: University of Wisconsin Press, 1991.

Sedgwick, Eve Kosofsky. *Epistemology of the Closet.* Berkeley and Los Angeles: University of California Press, 1990.

Shapiro, Alan. *In Praise of the Impure: Poetry and the Ethical Imagination.* Evanston, Ill.: Northwestern University Press, 1993.

Shaw, Robert B. *American Poetry Since 1960 – Some Critical Perspectives.* Cheshire, England: Carcanet, 1973.

Showalter, Elaine, ed. *Feminist Criticism: Essays on Women, Literature, and Theory.* New York: Pantheon, 1985.

Shumway, David R. *Creating American Civilization: A Genealogy of American Literature as An Academic Discipline.* Minneapolis: University of Minnesota Press, 1994.

Silliman, Ron. *The New Sentence.* New York: Roof, 1987.

Simpson, Eileen. *Poets in Their Youth: A Memoir.* New York: Random House, 1982.

Smith, Barbara Herrnstein. *Contingencies of Value: Alternative Perspectives for Critical Theory.* Cambridge, Mass.: Harvard University Press, 1988.

Smith, Dave. *Local Assays: On Contemporary American Poetry.* Urbana: University of Illinois Press, 1985.

Smith, Henry Nash. *Virgin Land: The American West as Symbol and Myth.* Cambridge, Mass.: Harvard University Press, 1950.

Snodgrass, W. D. *In Radical Pursuit: Critical Essays and Lectures.* New York: Harper & Row, 1975.

Snyder, Gary. *The Real Work: Interviews and Talks, 1964–1979,* ed. William Scott McLean. New York: New Directions, 1980.

Spacks, Patricia Myer. *The Female Imagination.* New York: Knopf, 1975.

Spiegelman, Willard. *The Didactic Muse: Scenes of Instruction in Contemporary American Poetry.* Princeton, N.J.: Princeton University Press, 1989.

Spiller, Robert, et al., eds. *Literary History of the United States.* New York: Macmillan, 1948.

Spivak, Gayatri Chakravorty. *In Other Worlds: Essays in Cultural Politics.* New York: Methuen, 1987.

The *Post-Colonial Critic: Interviews, Strategies, Dialogues,* ed. Sarah Harasym. New York: Routledge, 1990.

Stafford, William. *Writing the Australian Crawl: Views on the Writer's Vocation.* Ann Arbor: University of Michigan Press, 1978.

Steele, Timothy. *Missing Measures: Modern Poetry and the Revolt against Meter.* Fayetteville: University of Arkansas Press, 1990.

Stepanchev, Stephen. *American Poetry since 1945: A Critical Survey.* New York: Harper & Row, 1965.

Stitt, Peter. *The World's Hieroglyphic Beauty: Five American Poets.* Athens: University of Georgia Press, 1985.

Thurley, Geoffrey. *The American Moment: American Poetry in the Mid-Century.* New York: St. Martin's Press, 1977.

Tompkins, Jane. *Sensational Designs: The Cultural Work of American Fiction, 1790–1860.* New York: Oxford University Press, 1985.

ed. *Reader Response Criticism: From Formalism to Post-Structuralism.* Baltimore: Johns Hopkins University Press, 1981.

Trilling, Lionel. *Beyond Culture: Essays on Literature and Learning.* New York: Viking Press, 1968.

The *Liberal Imagination: Essays on Literature and Society.* Garden City, New York: Doubleday, 1953.

Turner, Frederick. *Natural Supernaturalism: Essays on Literature and Science.* New York: Paragon House, 1985.

Veeser, H. Aram, ed. *The New Historicism.* New York: Routledge, 1989.

Vendler, Helen. *The Music of What Happens: Poems, Poetics, Critics.* Cambridge, Mass.: Harvard University Press, 1988.

Part of Nature, Part of Us: Modern American Poets. Cambridge, Mass.: Harvard University Press, 1980.

Soul Says: Recent Poetry. Cambridge, Mass.: Belknap Press, 1995.

von Hallberg, Robert. *American Poetry and Culture, 1945–1980.* Cambridge, Mass.: Harvard University Press, 1985.

Waldman, Anne, and Marilyn Webb, eds. *Talking Poetics from Naropa Institute: Annals of the Jack Kerouac School of Disembodied Poetics.* Two volumes. Boulder, Colo.: Shambhala, 1978.

Warren, Austin, and Rene Wellek. *Theory of Literature.* New York: Harcourt & Brace, 1949.

Warren, Robert Penn. *Democracy and Poetry.* Cambridge, Mass.: Harvard University Press, 1975.

Wilbur, Richard. *Responses: Prose Pieces, 1953–1976.* New York: Harcourt Brace Jovanovich, 1976.

Williams, Raymond. *Culture and Society, 1780–1950.* New York: Doubleday, 1960. *The Long Revolution.* New York: Columbia University Press, 1961.

Williamson, Alan. *Introspection and Contemporary Poetry.* Cambridge, Mass.: Harvard University Press, 1984.

Wilson, Edmund. *Axel's Castle: A Study in the Imaginative Literature of 1870–1930.* New York: Charles Scribner's Sons, 1931.

Winters, Yvor. *In Defense of Reason.* New York: Swallow Press & W. Morrow, 1947.

Yorke, Liz. *Impertinent Voices: Subversive Strategies in Contemporary Women's Poetry.* London: Routledge, 1991.

INDEX